V!VA TRAVEL GUIDES

Nicaragua

1st Edition
April 2010

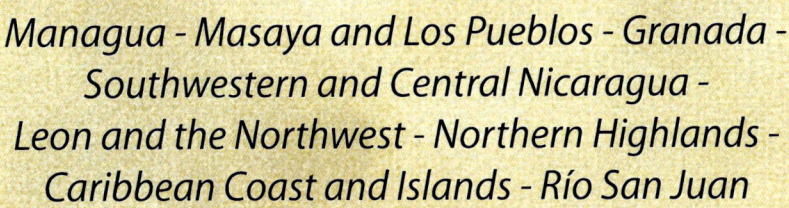

Managua - Masaya and Los Pueblos - Granada - Southwestern and Central Nicaragua - Leon and the Northwest - Northern Highlands - Caribbean Coast and Islands - Río San Juan

ELEVATION
1525 - 3050m
610 - 1525m
305 - 610m
0 - 305m
Honduras
El Salvador
San Miguel
Nacaome
Los Manos
NUEVA SEGOVIA
Ocotal
Somoto
MADRIZ
Condega
ESTELI
Estelí
Miraflor Nature Reserve
Jinotega
Selva Negra
Matagalpa
Guasaule
Potosi
CHINANDEGA
LEON
Sebáco
Chinandega
Cerro Negro
Leon
Boaco
Lago de Managua
Puerto Sandino
Managua
Masaya
Granada
Laguna de Apoyo
MANAGUA
Masachapa
Pacific Ocean
Isla de Ometepe
Las Salinas
RIVAS
Rivas
San Juan del Sur
Peñas Blancas
La Cruz
LEGEND
Primary Road
Secondary Road
Highlights
REGIONS
Cities and towns
N
25 km
50 km
25 mi
Scale

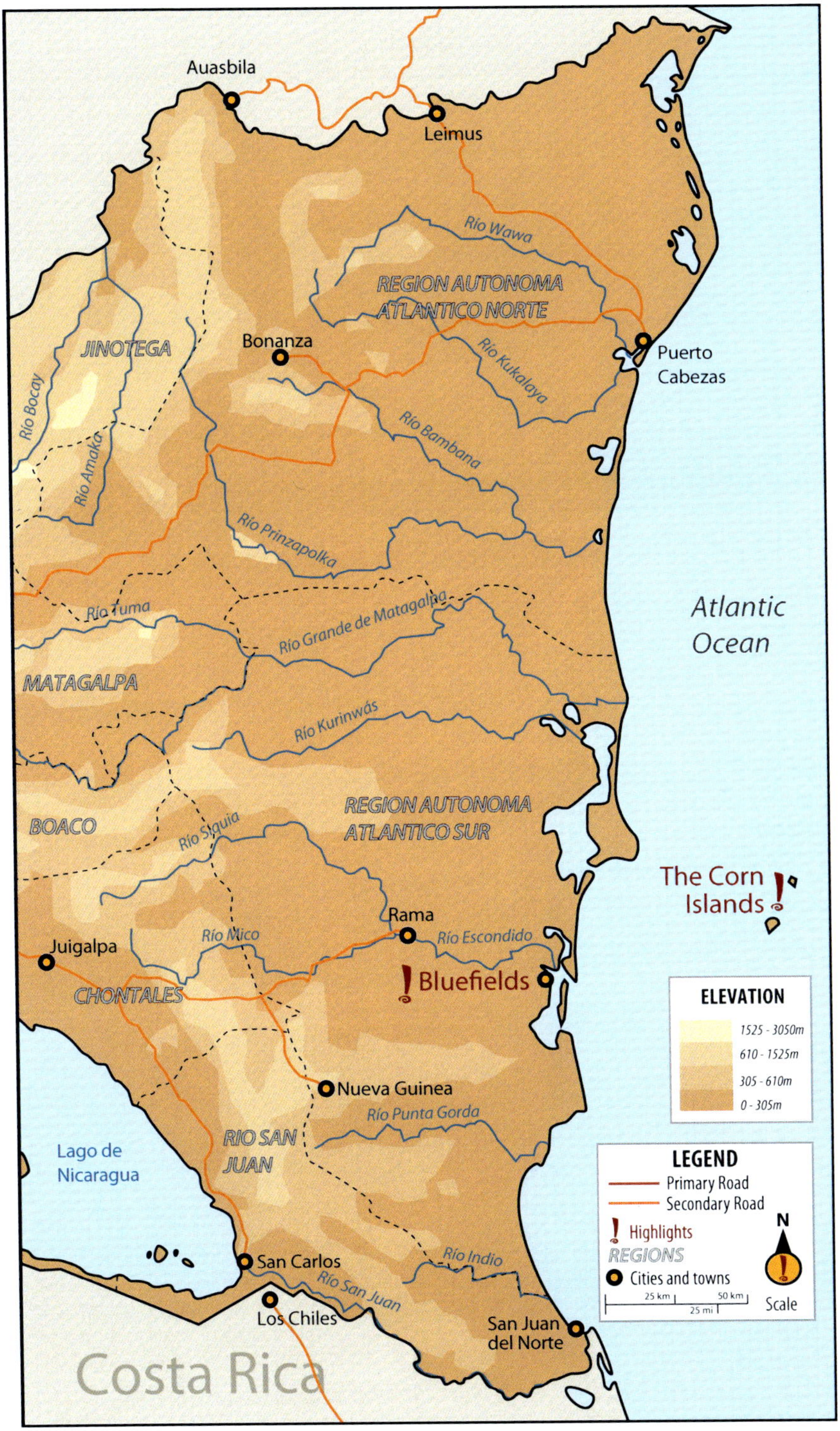

Auasbila
Leimus
Río Wawa
REGION AUTONOMA ATLANTICO NORTE
Bonanza
Puerto Cabezas
JINOTEGA
Río Bocay
Río Kukalaya
Río Bambana
Río Amaka
Río Prinzapolka
Río Tuma
Río Grande de Matagalpa
Atlantic Ocean
MATAGALPA
Río Kurinwás
REGION AUTONOMA ATLANTICO SUR
BOACO
Río Siquia
The Corn Islands
Rama
Juigalpa
Río Mico
Río Escondido
Bluefields
CHONTALES
ELEVATION
1525 - 3050m
610 - 1525m
305 - 610m
0 - 305m
Nueva Guinea
Río Punta Gorda
Lago de Nicaragua
RIO SAN JUAN
LEGEND
Primary Road
Secondary Road
Highlights
REGIONS
Cities and towns
N
25 km
50 km
25 mi
Scale
Río Indio
San Carlos
Río San Juan
Los Chiles
San Juan del Norte
Costa Rica

NICARAGUA Highlights

▲ Isla de Ometepe

Formed by two volcanoes emerging from the depths of Lake Nicaragua, Isla de Ometepe is the outdoor sports capital of Nicaragua. If it's kayaking, trekking, mountain biking or horseback riding that appeals to you, Ometepe is the place to be. Don't forget to bring your hiking boots and your sense of adventure.

▲ The Corn Islands

Big and Little Corn Islands sparkle off the country's eastern shore, giving travelers to Nicaragua a taste of the Caribbean. Should you tire of lounging on the islands' white-sand beaches, wading into their turquoise waters or reading under their rustling palm trees, you can charter a boat and explore Nicaragua's best snorkeling and diving sites.

▲ San Juan del Sur

The center of Nicaragua's burgeoning beach scene, San Juan del Sur is one of the hottest destinatio in the country. It has an intoxicating mix of locals, travelers and expats, as well as quaint seaside hot and restaurants unmatched anywhere in the country. Some of Nicaragua's best surfing and swimm beaches line the coast north and south of town, making it a great place to relax and spend some tim

▲ Granada

A charming city built on the shores of Lake Nicaragua, Granada is many travelers' favorite destin tion in the country. The city's colonial churches and nineteenth-century mansions are th best-preserved in the country, and a number of stylish restaurants, appealing art galleries ar boutique hotels have popped up in its historic core. Travelers to the town can also take daytri to the mangrove islands in the lake or the towering Volcán Mombacho.

NICARAGUA Highlights

▲ Flor de Caña rum

Nicaragua's highest-profile export and national drink is one of the world's finest rums. You can pick up a bottle pretty much anywhere in the country, from the dustiest corner shop to the fanciest Managua club, but it hails from Chichigalpa, near Leon. Ask for *servicio completo* and you'll get a bottle of rum with limes, ice and cola— all you need to make a first-class Nica Libre.

▼ Attend a baseball game

While most of Latin America is crazy for fútbol, Nicaraguans are baseball fans— serious, serious baseball fans. Even if you aren't a fan yourself, do not pass up the opportunity to enjoy a game. You don't need to know what a pinch hitter is in order to enjoy sitting in the grandstand with the shouting crowd and the brass band, watching the cheerleaders and downing rum shots.

▲ Beaches on the Northern Pacific Coast

While San Juan del Sur is the most visited surfing spot in Nicaragua, Playa Maderas is just a 20 minute drive north and known to locals as one of top surfing beaches in the country. Good snorkling can be found at Playa Marsella and the hidden Bahia Majagual (once a get-a-way for high ranking Sandinista officers) is one of the most beautiful beaches in Nicaragua.

▼ Volcano boarding on Cerro Negro

If you're bored of snowboarding, you might want to consider the emerging sport of volcano boarding— and the gravely slopes of the active Cerro Negro volcano are among the few spots in the world where you can give it a whirl. Try to enjoy the panoramic views of the northern Nicaraguan countryside as you slide towards it at speeds reaching 50 kilometers (30 mi.) per hour.

▲ Explore the cloudforest at Miraflor

Covering 254 square kilometers (98 mi.^{2}) rolling farmland and cloud forest near Este the Miraflor Nature Reserve protects some the most important ecosystems and striki landscapes in northern Nicaragua. Visitors c bike, hike and ride horses on the reserve trails, hunt for orchids with a local guide, a stay with a campesino family overnight.

▲ Palo de Mayo festival in Bluefields

The unique culture of the Atlantic Coast comes alive during the Palo de Mayo festival in early M Melding Brish, African and indigenous traditions, the festival is dominated by infectious music a dancing. While you are in Bluefields, make sure to try the delicious and unique local cuisine, wh features seafood and coconut.

NICARAGUA Highlights

▼ Leon

Nicaragua's second city and intellectual hub is a charismatic place, with a long and fascinating history— including a leading role in the Sandinista movement. Travelers should devote at least a day to exploring its crumbling colonial architecture, evocative political murals and engaging museums. Nearby attractions include the beach at Poneloya and the Cerro Negro and Momotombo volcanoes.

▲ Laguna de Apoyo

With dazzlingly clear waters set in the crater of the dormant Volcán Apoyo, Laguna de Apoyo is a favorite spot for relaxation and recreation. A number of low-key hotels and resorts line the enchanting lake, where visitors can try their hand at kayaking or paragliding and dip into the cool water. The surrounding forest is protected as a national park and echoes with birdsong and howler monkey calls.

▲ Volcan Mombacho

Towering 1300 meters (4000 feet) over Lake Nicaragua, Mombacho dominates the Granada skyline and gives visitors an excellent introduction to Nicaragua's tropical and cloud forests. Visit the butterfly farm, the coffee plantation, and take the canopy tour on the volcano's slopes. From the informative visitor's center near the top, take a hike on the reserve's well-maintained trails as the chatter of monkeys and birds fills the forest.

▼ Shopping at Masaya

If you want to return home with a souvenir two from Nicaragua, make sure to stop Masaya. The expansive handicrafts market has endless supply of textiles, pottery, hammoc and paintings. Prepare to bargain hard. If you a dragging along someone shopping-averse, t steaming and hissing craters of Volcán Masa are located just outside town.

▲ The coffee plantations near Matagalpa and Esteli- Selva Neg

The area around Matagalpa produces some of the world's tastiest arabica coffee, much of it from Selva Negra, a large organic farm. The farm has been opened to visitors and provides a great way travelers to learn about how coffee goes from the seed to the mug. If you get tired of hearing abc harvesting and roasting, you can hike the numerous trails that lead out into the pristine cloud fo

RECOMMENDED ITINERARIES

Classic Nicaragua

In two weeks:

Days 1-2: Arrive in Managua and take in the capital's handful of sites.

Days 3-4: Move north to Leon, where you can visit the city's churches and museums, climb Momotombo or Cerro Negro, tour the ruins of Leon Viejo, and relax on the beach at Poneloya.

Days 5-6: Double back and go south of Managua to the colonial town of Granada. Enjoy the city's graceful, historic core, take a boat ride through the islands and party at one of the discos on the lakeshore.

Days 7-10: Head to the village of San Jorge, near Rivas, where you can catch the ferry to Isla Ometepe. Spend the next few days hiking, biking or horseback riding around Ometepe's extraordinary landscapes. Return to Rivas.

Days 11-12: Head to the coastal resort of San Juan del Sur, where you can relax on the beach, soak up the backpacker vibe and try your hand at surfing.

Day 13: Head back to Rivas, then north to Masaya to stock up on souvenirs and visit the active volcano outside of town.

Day 14: Return to Managua to catch your flight or onward bus.

Granada Skyline

Boating on Río San Juan

Natural Thrills
In two weeks:

Day 1: Arrive in Managua.

Days 2-4: Head north to Leon and explore Nicaragua's second largest city, and kayak among the mangroves of the nearby Isla Juan de Venado.

Day 5: Travel to the highland city of Estelí, and then make arrangements to travel to Reserva Natural Miraflor.

Day 6: Hike the cloud forest at Miraflor.

Day 7: Take a travel day to get from Matagalpa to the village of San Jorge, via Managua and Rivas.

Days 8-10: Take the ferry over to Isla Ometepe and explore the island's volcanoes, forests and hiking trails, or try kayaking on the island's rivers.

Days 11-13: Catch the long boat ride to San Carlos, where you can explore the exotic Río San Juan and try fishing on Lake Nicaragua.

Day 14: Take the long, bumpy bus ride back to Managua.

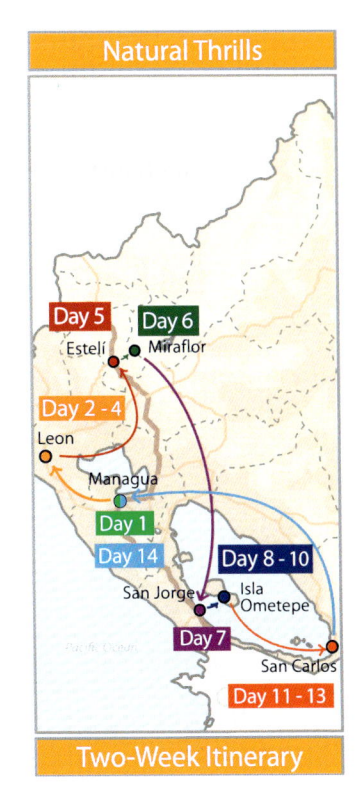

Two-Week Itinerary

Nica History

In one week:

Day 1: Arrive in Managua and walk around the Plaza de la Revolución to check out the last remaining bits of pre-earthquake Managua, and then head to the Huellas de Acahualinca to see the oldest evidence of human settlement in Nicaragua.

Days 2-3: Move on to Granada, a jewel of a city and home to a number of important colonial-era buildings and churches. Stop off at nearby Masaya, which has several landmarks related to its role in the revolution.

Days 4-5: Double back to Leon, which has colonial churches and a number of museums that tell of the city's long history. Nearby, Leon Viejo, preserves the ruins of Nicaragua's first capital.

Day 6: Head northeast to Estelí, which was an important city during both the Sandinista revolution and the Contra War that followed. The city has the museums (and bullet holes) to prove it.

Day 7: Hop a bus back to Managua, following the route taken by the Sandinista revolutionaries during their march on the city.

History Mural in Managua

Volcanoes

In one week:

Day 1: Arrive in Managua and catch a bus to the colonial city of Granada.

Days 2-3: Explore the placid Volcán Mombacho, which towers over Granada, and the steaming, trembling craters at Volcán Masaya.

Days 4-6: Head to Leon, where you can climb Momotombo and surf (or slide) down gravelly Cerro Negro.

Day 7: Return to Managua.

Volcán Momotombo on a clear day

Surfing Safari

Days 1-2: Arrive in Managua and head straight to Masachapa, the nearest surf beach.

Days 3-4: Bus back to Managua, then down to San Juan del Sur. Though the town itself backs up on a placid bay, this is a quintessential gringo surfing town. Good breaks can be found north and south of town, especially at Playa Maderas.

Days 5-6: Head to Popoyo, northwest of Rivas. This is the most famous break in Nicaragua, and it rarely disappoints.

Day 7: Catch the bus from Rivas back to Managua.

Surfing at Playa Maderas

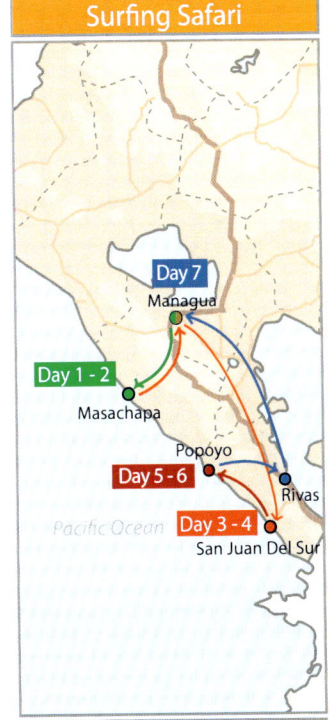

Caribbean Coast

In one week:

Days 1-2: Fly from Managua to Bluefields, on the Atlantic. Soak up the unique culture, sample the fresh seafood, and take a day trip to Pearl Lagoon or Rama Key.

Days 3-4: Take the ferry over to Big Corn Island and park yourself at a nice beach hotel, a good reward after the difficult crossing.

Days 5-6: Take the ferry to tiny, wild Little Corn Island for some top-notch snorkeling or diving.

Day 7: Catch a flight back from Big Corn to Managua.

Northern beach on Little Corn Island

Market pottery

Artesanías and Shopping

In one week:

Day 1: Arrive in Managua and catch a bus to Masaya, home to the country's best crafts market.

Day 2-3: Finish up your shopping at Masaya and wind your way through the Pueblos Blancos, where many of the crafts are produced.

Day 4: Head to Camoapa, near Boaco. It is the center of Nicaragua's straw-working industry and a great place to pick up traditional hats and baskets.

Day 5-6: Move north to Estelí. The traditional, agricultural town has a reputation for producing fine leather goods, soapstone carvings and pottery. It's also the place to tour cigar factories and pick up some bargains.

Day 7: Catch a bus to Managua and finish up your shopping at the expansive Huembes Market.

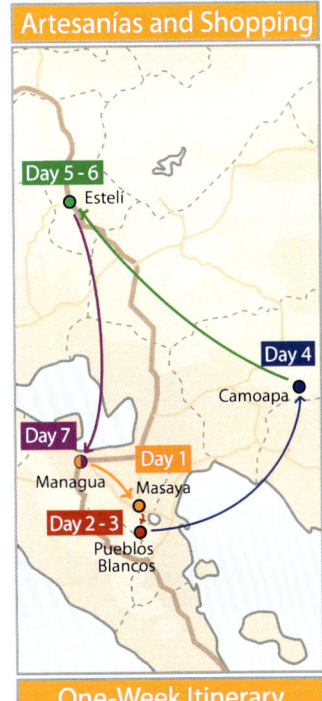

V!VA TRAVEL GUIDES

Nicaragua

About this Book

At V!VA, we believe that you shouldn't have to settle for an outdated guidebook. You can rest assured that in your hands is the most up-to-date guidebook available on Nicaragua because:

-- The final research for this book was completed on March 1, 2010.
-- Each entry is "time stamped" with the date it was last updated
-- V!VA's hyper-efficient web-to-book publishing process brings books to press in days or weeks, not months or years like our competitors
-- V!VA's country guides are updated at least once per year.

When you buy a V!VA Guide, here's what you're getting:

-- The expertise of professional travel writers, local experts and real travelers in-country bringing you first-hand, unbiased recommendations to make the most out of your trip
-- The wisdom of editors who actually live in Latin America, not New York, Melbourne, or London like other guidebook companies
-- Advice on how to escape the overly-trodden gringo trail, meet locals and understand the culture
-- The knowledge you'll need to travel responsibly while getting more for your money

V!VA Boot Camps

Contributors to this book were students at V!VA's Granada, Nicaragua Boot Camp. Join V!VA at an upcoming Travel Writers Boot Camp and learn all you need to become a guidebook writer.

Santiago, Chile bootcamp

Buenos Aires, Argentina bootcamp

Cuernavaca, Mexico bootcamp

Antigua, Guatemala bootcamp

Join us at the next Boot Camp:
Costa Rica September 27 - October 1, 2010
find out more at www.vivatravelguides.com/bootcamp/

V!VA Travel Guides Nicaragua.

ISBN-10: 0-9791264-8-7

ISBN-13: 978-0-9791264-8-2

Copyright © 2010, Viva Publishing Network.

Voice: USA (831) 824-4395

Website: www.vivatravelguides.com

Information: info@vivatravelguides.com

www.vivatravelguides.com

Copyright 2010, Viva Publishing Network.

All rights reserved. No part of this book may be reproduced, stored in a retrieval system, or transmitted in any form or by any means, electronic, mechanical, photocopying, recording in any format, including video and audiotape or otherwise, without the prior written consent of the publisher.

Travel is inherently dangerous. While we use a superior process for updating guidebooks and have made every effort to ensure accuracy of facts in this book, Viva Publishing Network, its owners, members, employees, contributors and the authors cannot be held liable for events outside their control and we make no guarantee as to the accuracy of published information. V!VA encourages travelers to keep abreast of the news in order to know the safety situation of the country. Please travel safely, be alert and let us know how your vacation went!

The following photos are licensed under the Creative Commons license (see http://creativecommons.org/licenses/by/2.0/ and http://creativecommons.org/licenses/by/3.0/ for details):

"Le volcan Momotombo (Nicaragua)," by Dalbera, http://www.flickr.com/photos/dalbera, 2009; "Volcán Concepción," by Matt Honan, http://www.flickr.com/photos/honan, 2008; "North Coast of Little Corn," by H Dragon, http://www.flickr.com/photos/hllewellyn, 2006; "Sunset in San Juan del Sur," by Thombo2, http://www.flickr.com/photos/brucethomson, 2007; "Park Central, Granada," by Matt Honan, http://www.flickr.com/photos/honan, 2008; "Baseball_9261," by JorgeMejia, http://www.flickr.com/photos/mejiaperalta, 2008; "Karen Leavitt, Surfing, Buena Vista Surf Club, Playa Maderas, Nicaragua, December 22 2009," by Over_Kind_Man, http://www.flickr.com/photos/over_kind_man, 2009; "Untitled [Extreme Sandboarding]," by H Dragon,http://www.flickr.com/photos/hllewellyn, 2006; "Descending from the Sky [Repelling Down a Waterfall]," by Scarleth White, http://www.flickr.com/photos/iloveblue, 2008; "IMG_1088tepe_nov, [Nicaraguan Dancers]," Jorgemejia, http://www.flickr.com/photos/mejiaperalta, 2009; "Nicaragua_Leon Catedral," by Javier Losa, http://www.flickr.com/photos/javier_losa, 2009; "View of Laguna de Apoyo from Catarina," by Vitimin C9000, http://www.flickr.com/photos/celestemarie, 2007; "Zip Lining Around Mombacho," by Tarariffic7, http://www.flickr.com/photos/22830626@N06, 2009; "Untitled [Nicaragua Masks]," by Ruben i, http://www.flickr.com/photos/djrue, 2008; "Fair Trade Coffee Beans," by William Neuheisel, http://www.flickr.com/photos/wneuheisel, 2007; "Frente Interno_8240 [History Mural in Managua]," by Jorgemeijia, http://www.flickr.com/photos/mejiaperalta, 2009; "Managua_5607av [Volcan Momotombo]," by Jorgemeijia, http://www.flickr.com/photos/mejiaperalta, 2009; "Karen Leavitt Surfing at Playa Maderas, Nicaragua, December 23 2009," by Over-kind-Man, http://www.flickr.com/photos/over_kind_man, 2009; "Little Corn Northside," by Matt Honan, http://www.flickr.com/photos/honan, 2008; "IMG_6838altereco, [Market Handicrafts]," by Jorgemejia, http://www.flickr.com/photos/mejiaperalta, 2009.

INTRO & INFO

CONTENTS
Geography	12
Flora	12
Fauna	13
Climate	13
History	14
Today's Politics and Government	17
Economy	18
Population	19
Language	20
Religion	20
Culture	21
Holidays and Fiestas	26
Social and Environmental Issues	27
Nicaragua By Numbers	28
Embassies and Consulates	30
Visa Information	32
Getting To and Away from Nicaragua	33
Border Crossings	34
Getting Around	35
Tours	39
Sports and Recreation	41
Hiking and Trekking	42
Mountain Biking and Cycling	43
Horseback Riding	44
Kayaking and Rafting	44
Diving and Snorkling	44
Surfing	45
Fishing	46
Birdwatching	46
Wildlife Watching	47
Studying Spanish	47
Volunteering	47
Working	48
Living	48
Lodging	49
Food and Drink	51
Shopping	53
Health and Safety	55
The Media	58
Mail and Packages	58
Internet Access	59
Money and Costs	59
Etiquette and Dress	62
Business and Officialdom	62
Responsible Tourism	62
Photography	63
Travel Tips	63
Suggested Reading	67

Managua and Around — 68
History	68
Highlights	69
Economy	69
When to Go	69
Getting To and Away	70
Getting Around	71
Safety	71
Things to See and Do	73

Join VIVA on Facebook. Fan "VIVA Travel Guides Nicaragua."

Tours	78
Lodging	79
Restaurants	79
Nightlife	80
Barrio Martha Quezada	81
Barrio Boloñia	84
Centro Commercial and Carretera Masaya	87
Around Managua	92
Chocoyero – El Brujo Nature Reserve	93
Pochomil and Masachapa	95
Lago de Nicaragua	96
Puerto Diaz	96

Masaya and The Pueblos — 98

Highlights	99
History	99
When to Go	99
Safety	100
Things to See and Do	100
Tours	100
Lodging	100
Restaurants	100
Masaya	100
Parque Nacional Volcán Masaya	107
Nindirí	108
Reserva Nacional Laguna de Apoyo	109
Los Pueblos Blancos	112
Diriomo	114
Niquinohomo	114
Masatepe	115
San Marcos	116
Diriamba	117
Jinotepe	119
La Máquina	121
La Boquita	121

Granada and Around — 124

History	124
Things to See and Do	125
Granada	125
Around Granada	143
Las Isletas	143
Reserva Natural Volcán Mombacho	143
Parque Nacional Archipiélago Zapatera	144

Southwestern Nicaragua — 146

History	147
When to Go	147
Safety	147
Tours	147
Lodging	147
Highlights	148
Rivas	148
Tola	151
Playa Pie de Gigante	152
Las Salinas y Playa Guasacate	153
El Astillero	154

Find the best price on a flight to Nicaragua: vivatravelguides.com/flights/

San Jorge	155
Isla de Ometepe	156
Merida	159
San Juan del Sur	167
Around San Juan del Sur	

Leon and the Northwest — 180

History	181
Highlights	181
When to Go	181
Safety	182
Things to See and Do	182
Tours	182
Lodging	182
León	182
Barrio Sutiava	197
Poneloya	198
Las Peñitas	199
Puerto Sandino	199
El Transito	200
San Jacinto	201
Volcán Telica and Volcán San Cristobal	201
El Sauce	201
Nagarote	203
La Paz Centro	204
Chinandega	204
El Viejo	208
Chichigalpa	209
Corinto	210
Reserva Natural Padre Ramos	212
Potosi	213

The Northern Highlands — 216

History	217
Highlights	218
When to Go	218
Safety	218
Things to See and Do	218
Tours	219
Lodging	220
Restaurants	220
Estelí	220
Reserva Natural Miraflor	228
Reserva Natural Meseta Tisey-Estanzuela	229
Condega	231
Ocotal	232
Around Ocotal	235
Jalapa	237
Somoto	239
Matagalpa	242
Around Matagalpa	253
Reserva Natural Cerro Musun	254
Sebaco	256
Ciudad Darío	256
Jinotega	256
Bosawas Biosphere Reserve	263
Siuna	263
Bonanza	264

Join VIVA on Facebook. Fan "VIVA Travel Guides Nicaragua."

Central Nicaragua — 266
- Highlights — 267
- History — 267
- When to Go — 267
- Things to See and Do — 267
- Safety — 267
- Tours — 267
- Lodging — 267
- Restaurants — 267

- Boaco — 268
- San Jose de Los Remates — 270
- Camoapa — 272
- Comalapa — 273
- Juigalpa — 273
- Santo Domingo — 278
- Nueva Guinea — 279

Caribbean Coast and the Islands — 280
- History — 281
- When to Go — 283
- Safety — 283
- Things to See and Do — 283
- Tours — 283
- Lodging — 283
- Puerto Cabezas — 283
- Waspam and Río Coco — 287
- El Rama — 289
- Bluefields — 291
- Laguna de Perlas — 295
- The Corn Islands — 298
- Big Corn Island — 299
- Little Corn Island — 305

Río San Juan — 312
- History — 312
- When to Go — 313
- Safety — 313
- Highlights — 314
- Things to See and Do — 314
- Tours — 314
- San Carlos — 315
- Refugio Los Guatuzos — 320
- Reserva Esperanza Verde — 320
- Islas Solentiname — 321
- The Other Islands of Islas Solentiname — 326
- Boca de Sábalos — 327
- El Castillo — 329
- San Juan de Nicaragua — 333
- Costa Rica Border Crossings — 333

Index — 336
- Traveler Advice — 344
- Packing Lists — 347
- Useful Contacts — 349
- Useful Spanish Phrases — 351

ABOUT THE WRITERS

A member of the V!VA staff between 2008-2009, **Rachael Hanley** is a journalist, editor and blogger with an eye for detail. She received a BA from Smith College, an MA in Communications from Stanford University, and an MPhil in English Renaissance Literature from the University of Cambridge. A one-time Third Culture Kid, Rachael has lived in Nicaragua, Guatemala, Spain, England and Ecuador. She currently resides in Vermont and works as a web writer for the Massachusetts-based boarding school Northfield Mount Hermon.

A staff writer for V!VA in 2007-2008, then a contributing author for this guidebook, **Nili Larish** can't get enough of Latin America. While on assignment in less-visited Northern Nicaragua, talking to medicine men, entrepreneurs, activists, peace corps volunteers, altar boys and expats was all part of her job description. Nili is currently pursuing a master's degree in public health at Columbia University. She occasionally gets a hankering for gallo pinto.

Despite being a New York City girl, **Sara Levavi** loves camping, farming, riding the chicken bus, and sleeping at less-than-four-star hostels. Although she suffered a number of animal-related mishaps (including getting thrown from a horse, bit by a dog, and having feces thrown at her by an angry gorilla) writing about Nicaragua was one of the greatest adventures of her life. In 2007 Sara graduated with a degree in Archaeology from the George Washington University and is currently planning on moving to Israel to pursue a Masters.

Andrea Davoust joined V!VA after over two years of working and living out of a suitcase in Eastern Europe and various African countries. Before that, she studied political science and international relations in Paris, and earned a degree in journalism in Scotland. As VIVA's resident Frenchwoman, Andrea brings her expertise of France, Europe and the African continent.

OUR CONTRIBUTORS:

Dyani Makous contributed San Jan del Sur, Rivas and Big Corn Island content; **Mike Karanicolas** did a first sweep of Granada, Bluefields, Little Corn Island and Leon. **Karina Zobolotny** hit up the beaches to find us the country's top surfing spots. Additionally, Dr. Crit Minster, John Howison, Rick Segreda, Tammy Portnoy, Tom Ravenscroft, Margaret Rode and Will Gray contributed reviews.

◊ Cover Design: Jason Halberstadt, 2010 ◊
◊ Cover Photo: Elicia Bolton, "Through the Door," 2009 ◊
◊ Cover Photo: Adam Baker, "Caballo y Telica," www.flickr.com/photos/atbaker/ 2008 ◊
◊ Back Cover Photo: Jamesu24, "Granada," 2009 ◊
◊ Color Insert Photos: "Flor de Cana Rum," Jason Halberstadt, 2010; "Classic Nicaragua," Andrea Davoust, 2009; "Natural Thrills," Andrea Davoust, 2009 ◊

MANY THANKS TO:

Jena Davison, and **Melanie DePaulis**—VIVA's intern superheroes; **Jesua Silva** (map-maker extraordinaire); Thanks also to **Rigoberto Pinto** and **Cristian Avila**, the programming masterminds who keep www.vivatravelguides.com running smoothly and are always willing to lend a hand to the not-so-computer-savvy staff; and to the whole **Metamorf** team for their support.

Additional thanks to **Walter Pineda Martinez** who painstakingly helped us to get our Managua maps spot on. Also, Chilo and Patrick Werner, Nicaraguan expert extraordinaire, Barbara and Benjamin Abaunza, Heather Rankin and Carrol Barrick.

Join VIVA on Facebook. Fan "VIVA Travel Guides Nicaragua."

ABOUT THE EDITORS

Paula Newton is VIVA's operations expert. With an MBA and a background in New Media, Paula is the Editor-in-Chief and the organizing force behind the team. With an insatiable thirst for off-the-beaten-track travel, Paula has traveled extensively, especially in Latin America, Europe and Asia, and has explored more than 30 countries. She currently lives in Quito.

Nick Rosen is a staff-writer and editor for VIVA. He holds a BA in International Development from Montreal's McGill University and has worked on public health projects in Kenya and Ghana. He maintains that nothing compares to the sublime beauty of his native New Jersey.

Mark Samcoe is a staff writer/editor at VIVA. Hailing from western Canada, Mark has degrees in Writing and English Literature from the University of Victoria. His travels include stints in Europe, South America and Asia, where he lived for several years in South Korea. He currently resides in Quito.

Emma Mueller is a graduate of Kenyon College, where she received a bachelors degree in English literature and Spanish Area Studies. After spending four years in middle-of-nowhere Ohio, she couldn't wait to join the V!VA team down in Quito, Ecuador. Her most notable travel experiences include studying shamanism in the Peruvian jungle and conversing in Quechua with highland potato farmers.

Michelle Lillie is a staff editor/writer at V!VA. She holds a BA and MA in International Relations from Loyola University Chicago, and brings to VIVA some substantial globe-trotting experience. Michelle has not only traversed Europe, Asia, North Africa, Central and South America, but has also lived in Italy, Thailand and China. Michelle currently resides in Quito, Ecuador.

Karen Nagy is a staff editor/writer at VIVA. She studied travel writing and learned the joys of Mediterranean island-hopping in Greece, and went on to receive BA degrees in Journalism and International Studies from the University of Oregon. After living in Argentina in 2007, she was eager to make a South American base-camp for herself once again in Quito.

Rachel Anderson is currently a staff editor/writer at V!VA. Midwestern born and bred, she earned a BA in Psychology and a minor in Eastern Religion from Gustavus Adolphus College. Her life's varied landscape includes studying psychiatry in Fiji and unleashing her inner Inca as a volunteer in Cusco, Peru. Before V!VA, Rachel studied copywriting at an advertising school in Minneapolis, Minnesota.

Find the best price on a flight to Nicaragua: vivatravelguides.com/flights/

About VIVA Travel Guides

We began VIVA Travel Guides back in 2007 because we simply wanted a better travel guide to our home country of Ecuador. All the guidebooks at the time were years out of date and weren't nearly as helpful as they should have been to real travelers. We knew we could do better.

We asked the question: "What would the travel guidebook look like if it was invented today from the ground up in the era of Google, Facebook, Wikipedia and nearly ubiquitous Internet connectivity?"

We concluded that the key to creating a superior guide is a knowledgeable community of travelers, on-the-ground professional travel writers, local experts and street-smart editors, all collaborating together on the web and working toward the goal of creating the most helpful, up-to-date guide available anywhere.

Continuously Updated
Traveler reports come in daily via the web and we take advantage of highly efficient 'web to book' technology and modern digital printing to speed the latest travel intelligence to the printed page in record time. We update our books at least once per year–more often than any other major publisher. We even print the date that each piece of information in the book was last updated so that you can make informed decisions about every detail of your trip.

A Better Way to Build a Guidebook
We're convinced we make a better guidebook. It's a more costly, painstaking way to make a guidebook, but we think it's worth it, because you're be able to get more out of your trip to Nicaragua. There are many ways that you can get involved in making VIVA Travel Guides even better.

Help other travelers by writing a review
Did you love a place? Will you never return? Every destination in this guidebook is listed on our website with space for user ratings and reviews. Share your experiences, help out other travelers and let the world know what you think.

Make corrections and suggestions
Prices rise, good places go bad, and bad places go out of business. If you find something that needs to be updated or improved in this book, please let us know. Report any inaccuracies at www.vivatravelguides.com/corrections and we'll incorporate them into our information within a few days. As a small token of our thanks for correcting an error or submitting a suggestion we'll send you a coupon for 50 percent off any of our E-books or 20 percent off any of our printed books.

Make your reservations at www.vivatravelguides.com
You can support VIVA's mission by reserving your hotels and flights at www.vivatravelguides.com. When you buy from our website, we get a commission, which we reinvest in making our guides a better resource for travelers. Find the best price on flights at www.vivatravelguides.com/flights and efficiently reserve your hotels and hostels at www.vivatravelguides.com/hotels.

We sincerely hope you enjoy this book, and your trip to Nicaragua even more.

Happy Trails,

Jason Halberstadt
Founder, VIVA Travel Guides

Join VIVA on Facebook. Fan "VIVA Travel Guides Nicaragua."

Travelers' discussions. User reviews. Feedback. Photo contests. Book updates. Travel news. Apps. Writing contests. Give-aways.

VIVA TRAVEL GUIDES

Follow us online
www.facebook.com/vivatravelguides
www.twitter.com/vivatravelguide
www.vivatravelguides.com

REGIONAL SUMMARIES

Managua and Around (p.68)
Nicaragua's sweaty, sprawling capital city is essentially a historical monument in and of itself. Managua has been shaken by numerous natural disasters and political uprisals in the past, but today it still stands—though only as little more than a scattered collection of concrete buildings, restaurants and historical sites. Without any real city center, and with few tourist attractions, it is not one of Nicaragua's biggest draws by any means, but with a happening nightlife, some higher-quality services and a reputation as a transportation hub, most people do stop in Managua even if only for a short stay.

Masaya and Los Pueblos (p.98)
Masaya and its neighboring towns are a hotbed of culture and creativity. Indigenous influence is strong here, and craftsmen from this region produce some of Nicaragua's most widely sought after handicrafts and artisan products. Markets and shops showcase and sell these impressive locally made ceramics, leather goods, furniture and hammocks. Outside of Masaya rest Laguna Apoyo and Nicaragua's oldest national park, Parque Nacional Volcán Masaya, which houses the still-active Volcán Masaya. Whether you hike through one of the park's numerous craters or just witness the volcano's spewing lava from a distance, this is a must-see if you are in the area.

Granada and Around (p.124)
Granada is one of those places where people plan on coming for a few nights, but end up staying for a few weeks or months instead. Whether it's the chilled-out tropical vibe, the aesthetic colonial architecture or the successful tourism infrastructure, there are many alluring aspects to this most-popular Nicaraguan destination. With great eats and well-equipped accommodations, Granada attracts volunteers, travelers and those seeking to study Spanish from all over the world, making it a surprisingly international city as well. Better yet, it is also a convenient base for exploring the surrounding region, as Pueblos Blancas, Mombacho, Masaya and hundreds of *isletas* are all within close reach.

Southwestern Nicaragua (p.146)
This sliver of land between the Pacific Ocean and Lago de Nicaragua is a both a surfers' paradise and a geologists' dream come true. Fringed with long, sandy beaches, southwestern Nicaragua is perfect for those looking to escape the tourist-crowded beaches of nearby Costa Rica and the Caribbean coast without having to sacrifice the beauty and excellent surf. San Juan del Sur is a popular spot due to its fishing-village vibe and its easy accessibility to traveler services and tons of other enticing beaches closeby. The Southwest also includes the Isla Ometepe, where Nicaragua's famous twin volcanoes, the active Volcán Concepción and the dormant Volcán Maderas, reside and offer fantastic hiking opportunities.

Leon and the Northwest (p.180)
Home to the country's highest volcano, the oldest Spanish ruins and the colonial city of León, the northwest corner of Nicaragua is a standout region. Considered to be the country's intellectual capital, León is brimming with university students, colonial churches—including the largest cathedral in Central America—and some historical monuments and museums. From León, it is relatively easy to explore the surrounding forts, prisons, beaches and volcanic peaks of the Northwest. From kayaking through mangrove swamps to summiting the mighty Volcán Cosigüina to sampling the best of Nicaraguan food, the Northwest is full of contrast and adventure.

The Northern Highlands (p. 216)
The lush Northern Highlands is the prime coffee-growing region of Nicaragua. Here, the countryside is freckled with numerous plantations, where you can taste a cup of locally

---

Join VIVA on Facebook. Fan "VIVA Travel Guides Nicaragua."

grown and produced coffee or take a tour of the grounds. With cooler temperatures and mountainous terrain, the Northern Highlands is both rugged and undeveloped. Matagalpa and Jinotega are two cities in this region that are worth a visit, and they are both steeped in political and military history. Also occupying this area are some exceptional ecological reserves tucked into gorgeous expanses of cloud forest where toucans and howler monkeys can be spotted.

Central Nicaragua (p.266)
Central Nicaragua is characterized by rolling hills, grazing cattle and cowboys galore. This rural central region, which include the departments of Boaco and Chontales, is Nicaragua's biggest producer of beef and dairy. Rodeos and bullfights seem to be a cultural by-product here and can best be experienced in Juigalpa, the most developed city in the area. Excellent hiking and horseback riding in the Amerrisque mountains come as an added bonus, with numerous peaks to choose from like Mombacho, La Cebadilla and Quizaltepe. Though Central Nicaragua sees few tourists and is a bit difficult to get to, spending some time here will certainly harbor an alternative perspective on the country.

Caribbean Coast and the Islands (p. 280)
The Caribbean coast is the most ethnically and geographically diverse region in Nicaragua. Co-inhabited by wild jungle, swampy mangroves, coastal rainforests and several wildlife reserves, this region goes way beyond any vision of just a Caribbean beach getaway. However, you most certainly can get that here as well, especially with a visit to the tropical Big Corn and Little Corn Islands, located about 80 kilometers (50 mi) off the coast in the Caribbean Sea. Without electricity or phones, these island escapes come with plentiful amounts of palm trees, crystal-clear water and vibrant coral reefs. From the largest southern city of Bluefields, you can also visit the exquisite Laguna de Perlas, or "Pearl Lagoon," and the 18 islands offshore known as the Pearl Cays. The Caribbean Coast is also a hybrid of different cultures, as Moshiko Indians, English-speaking Creoles, members of African tribes and Caribbean folk all reside here and heavily influence this area.

Río San Juan (p. 312)
Extremely remote and exceptionally charming, Río San Juan is perhaps the best off-the-beaten track destination in Nicaragua. The region's southeastern seclusion means that it is much less visited than other areas of the country and that it is much more difficult to travel to, requiring more patience, flexibility and spending money. However, the rewards are bountiful and come in many forms: from the tranquil, artsy Solentiname Islands to the historically significant abandoned forts to the extensive wildlife reserves and rainforest that all pepper the area surrounding the river.

Find the best price on a flight to Nicaragua: vivatravelguides.com/flights/

Introduction

Long neglected by travelers, Nicaragua is an ideal location for nature lovers, outdoor aficionados, history buffs and adventure travelers.

Due to years of political instability, economic problems and social turmoil, the tourism infrastructure in Nicaragua is just starting to flourish—making the country one of Central America´s best kept secrets and the newest hot spot for surfing, diving and hiking. Neighboring Costa Rica has become crowded with tourists and costs have gone up, encouraging travelers looking for extreme sporting opportunities and more authentic experiences to head to Nicaragua.

Currently, Nicaragua has the reputation for being the cheapest country to travel through in Central America. Be sure to take advantage of this up and coming destination before it becomes part of the beaten path. Updated: Mar 09, 2009.

Geography

At 129,494 square kilometers, Nicaragua is the largest country in Central America and the least densely populated. Slightly smaller than New York state, Nicaragua is sandwiched between Honduras to the north, and Costa Rica to the south, while the Pacific Ocean and Caribbean Sea lap against the 565 miles (910 km) of shoreline that flank Nicaragua to the east and west. The country boasts 25 volcanoes, which form a spine running down the west side of the country. Over 40 percent of its land is covered with jungle. The land is divided into three major geographic areas, west to east: the Pacific lowlands, the central highlands and the Caribbean lowlands.

The Pacific coastal region is a low plain made fertile by ash from the dozens of volcanoes. It also contains Lake Nicaragua, the largest freshwater body in Central America, and Lake Managua, which has the country's capital city on its shore.

Springing from the low mountains in the north and Nicaragua's flat belly are a mix of rainforest, cloud forest, mixed pine and oak forest. The country also has a sprinkling of the rarest of sectors: the tropical dry forest.

The Caribbean lowlands consist mainly of wet, hot and humid plains, with pine savannahs to the north and a large expanse of rainforest toward the south, marked by mangroves and numerous rivers that drain from the central mountains. Updated: May 07, 2009.

Flora

Nicaragua has 5.5 million hectares of forest that is divided into Caribbean rainforest, Pacific dry forest, upland pine forest and mountainous broad leaf forest. Along with the large number of trees, there are also more than 9,000 species of vascular plants in Nicaragua's forests. Many of these plants are used for medicinal purposes.

However, Nicaragua has a major problem with deforestation. Many of its valuable hardwood trees are being cut down for commercial purposes.

The country's problems with deforestation have gained worldwide attention, and now many groups are working to protect Nicaragua's flora and fauna. Nicaragua now has 76 protected areas, ranging from national parks to nature reserves, wildlife refuges and more. All of these different types of

Fast Facts

Before the construction of the Panama Canal, early plans called for a canal to be constructed across Nicaragua.

Nicaragua is the largest country in Central America.

Nicaragua is named after an Indian chief, Nicarao, who ruled the region at the end of the fifteenth century.

The United States maintained troops in Nicaragua from 1912 to 1933.

After Haiti, Nicaragua is the poorest nation in the western hemisphere.

In 1998, Hurricane Mitch killed 9,000 people and did $10 billion in damage in Nicaragua.

In 2002, former Nicaraguan president Arnoldo Alemán was sentenced to 20 years in prison for fraud and corruption.

Lake Nicaragua is home to species of sharks and tuna which have adapted to its fresh water. Updated: Apr 06, 2009.

Join VIVA on Facebook. Fan "VIVA Travel Guides Nicaragua."

reserves work to protect and preserve the plant and animal species of Nicaragua. Updated: Sep 02, 2009.

Fauna

One of Nicaragua's biggest attractions is its wide variety of wildlife species. Its huge ecosystem is home to over 700 bird species, 176 species of mammals, more than 1,000 species of fish, 172 species of reptiles and countless insects. While those numbers alone are impressive, it's suspected that many species of fauna remain undiscovered, hidden in the mountains, volcanoes, lakes, forests, and oceans of this small country.

Nicaragua's most famous creature is the sea turtle, and the country is home to five endangered species of this majestic animal. Each year between July and January, both the Loggerhead and Olive Ridley sea turtles emerge from the sea to lay their eggs on Nicaragua's Pacific beaches. A few months later, thousands of tiny sea turtles emerge from the sand and make their way into the sea. La Flor Wildlife Reserve (located 22 kilometers south of San Juan del Sur) is one of the few places in the world that allows visitors to view the hatching of the sea turtles. Sadly, the sea turtles are dying off due to illegal poaching for the turtles' meat and eggs.

Another well known Nicaraguan marine species is the bull shark, found in Lake Nicaragua, the only known freshwater shark in the world, though unfortunately, numbers of the species in Lake Nicaragua are dwindling after profitable shark fin plants killed most of the population during the 1970s.

More than forty different fish species can be identified in the lakes region of Nicaragua. Other notable creatures include the three-toed sloth, Tamandua anteater, armadillo, jaguar, iguana, chocoyos green parrot and Guardabarranco, Nicaragua's national bird.

Nicaragua also boasts an impressive 250,000 species of insects. With many areas of the rainforest still undiscovered, new species of insects are frequently being added to the already numerous, known species of butterflies, moths, spiders and ants that live within the country. Updated: Jun 09, 2009.

Climate

Nicaragua is a land of either burning sun or torrential rains—the type of weather that you end up with is largely determined by the timing of your visit. The two seasons—one dry and one rainy—are clearly marked in Nicaragua. During the wet season (May through October), the majority of the country is hit with storms at least once a day. Unlike more temperate climes, where a rainy forecast means a day of clouds and cold, Nicaragua often produces weather and skies as fiercely beautiful and powerful as an eruption from the volcanoes below.

Photo by Kim Pickering

The curtains of rain can be heavy enough to force cars off the roads, flood deep culverts in the city and cause mudslides in the countryside. While the most severe thunderstorms may produce flash flooding and severe lighting, they are short-lived, coming to an abrupt end after anywhere between a few minutes to a couple of hours.

The Caribbean lowlands receive such heavy rainfalls that they are frequently flooded. The Pacific area is somewhat sheltered by the mountain range, but may also be hit by hurricanes. In the plains, temperatures hover around 30 degrees Celsius (86 F), 20 at night (68 F). The highlands are milder, with daily averages of 24 to 27 degrees (75-81 F) and cooler nights of 15 to 20 degrees Celsius (59-68 F).

In the dry season (November to April), the Nicaraguan land becomes dusty and cracked.

Find the best price on a flight to Nicaragua: vivatravelguides.com/flights/

Streams disappear and rivers dwindle to muddy trickles. Although you may find the temperatures uncomfortably hot, the dry season is the best time to visit Nicaragua if you plan to go further off the beaten path. In the most remote areas you may find that Nicaraguans use the dry riverbeds as impromptu roads. Updated: Mar 09, 2009.

History

PRE-HISPANIC

The area of present-day Nicaragua has been inhabited for centuries, since long before the arrival of the Spanish in the early sixteenth century. The indigenous peoples of Nicaragua were diverse, and there were different cultures on either coast and in the central highlands. Some of the cultures had language and trade ties to the Maya of the north, but the Maya Empire collapsed before fully integrating the region.

When the Spanish first arrived, it is estimated that there were about one million people living in present-day Nicaragua. The most powerful cultures at the time were those of the Niquirano people, led by Chief Nicarao (who would give his name to "Nicaragua") and the Chorotega who lived in the center of the country. Both were decimated by Spanish attacks and disease, and today there is little to remind us of these original cultures.

THE SPANISH CONQUEST

The region was first "conquered" by Gil González Dávila in 1522-1523, but his mission was essentially one of plunder and enslavement and he left no settlements behind. The first settlements, León and Granada, were established in 1525 by Francisco Hernández de Córdoba. The first years of the colony were marked by wars and violence as the conquistadors enslaved and wiped out native populations even while warring among themselves. One of the casualties of the civil wars among the conquistadors was Córdoba himself, beheaded in 1526.

The remote region was made part of the Viceroyalty of New Spain (Mexico) and was later included in the jurisdiction of the Captaincy-General of Guatemala. León, then the capital, was destroyed by a volcanic eruption in 1610 and moved to its present location.

In 1655, the Mosquito Coast, which was home to one of the last independent indigenous groups in Central America, was claimed by Great Britain as a protectorate, as a British trading company had set up friendly commerce with the Miskito Indians. Although the claim was disputed by Spain, nothing much ever came of it from either the Spanish or the British, and the region was returned to Nicaragua in 1860, although it remained autonomous until the José Santos Zelaya administration (1893-1909).

INDEPENDENCE

Nicaragua joined the rest of Central America in declaring independence from Spain on September 15, 1821. For two years Central America was part of Mexico, but in 1823 they established an independent republic known as the Federal Republic of Central America. The republic was doomed, however, and was quickly done in by bitter fighting between liberals and conservatives. By 1838 it had disintegrated, leaving the member states to make their own nations. The fighting between opposing political parties continued in Nicaragua, where the liberal city of León frequently clashed with conservative Granada over just about everything.

US INTERVENTION

Historically, the United States has been very involved with Nicaragua and its internal politics. In 1856, American filibuster William Walker took over the nation with a small squad of American mercenaries, though he was driven out the following year. Responding to chaos, the US sent marines to Nicaragua in 1912; they remained until 1933 (with a nine month hiatus in 1925). During this time they supported the conservative government in its fight against liberal leader Juan Batista Sacasa. The US brokered the 1929 Espino Negro Accord, which disarmed both sides, kept the conservative goverment in power, and created the National Guard.

THE SOMOZA DYNASTY

When the US left Nicaragua in 1933, they left behind a coalition government led by rebel General Augusto Sandino, head of the National Guard Anastasio Somoza Garcia, and President Juan Bautista Sacasa. Within a year, Somoza had ordered the assassination of Sandino, and by 1936 he was able to muscle out Sacasa, leaving himself solely in charge of the nation. Thus began the Somoza Dynasty, which would last through Anastasio Somoza García and two of his sons until 1979.

For forty three years, Nicaragua was little more than a feudal kingdom absolutely ruled by the Somozas. They nationalized valuable

History

industries and then sold them off to family members for a fraction of their worth. They controlled the railroads and transportation and used state money and resources to move their goods. Projects were awarded to Somoza cronies, and state funds paid for them even if they were never completed. The looting was brazen and had a devastating effect on Nicaragua's economic development.

THE SANDINISTAS

The Sandinista movement began in 1961 by Nicaraguans fed up with the Somoza government. For years, they fought the dictatorship but could make little headway. In 1972, Anastasio Somoza Debayle, the last of the Somoza line of dictators, made a crucial mistake. An earthquake devastated Managua, leaving half of the city homeless. Humanitarian aid

Pirates

The 17th century was the hey-day of pirates and many of the most famous ones made their way to Nicaragua by becoming privateers to fight the Spanish (state-sponsored piracy was a form of warfare popular with the British, French and Dutch).

While under British occupation, the Corn Islands served as a safe haven for pirates who were avoiding the wrath of the Spanish navy. Historically, pirates are often remembered for their negative roles—plundering local towns and villages—and not for the positive, such as the fact that pirates (or privateers) founded the cities of Pueblo Viejo, Bilwi (Puerto Cabezas) and Bluefields.

The Dutch pirate Abraham Blauvelt explored the coasts of Honduras and Nicaragua in the 1630s and, while raiding the Spanish, discovered land on which he wanted to build an English settlement. After proposing this idea to the Queen of England, he created what is now known as Bluefields. Both the Bluefield River and town are named after their founder.

The 192 kilometer San Juan River is the route pirates and English privateers used in the 17th century to get from the Caribbean Sea to Lake Nicaragua where they could easily reach and attack the Spanish city of Granada. The route through San Juan River is also the same one used by Francisco Hernández de Córdoba when he founded Granada in 1524.

The convenience of the San Juan River was a mixed blessing; while it made the landlocked city a wealthy port, the news of Granada's prosperity meant that the area fell prey to multiple pirate attacks. An armed fort called El Castillo de La Immaculate Concepción, (The Castle of the Immaculate Conception) was built on San Juan River as a response to Granada being attacked by the pirate Gallardillo in 1670. Even with the fort fully constructed, British pirate Frances Dampier still managed to sail through the San Juan River, ravage Granada, and set it on fire in 1685.

The "king of all pirates," Henry Morgan, was reputed to be one of the most cruel and violent of all pirates. Morgan managed to find a loophole in his privateering contract with the British monarchy where he wouldn't have to split his spoils with the government if he attacked on land. Morgan spent the next few years in Central America making land raids on cities.

In 1663, he convinced David Marteen, John Morris, as well as Captains Jackman and Freeman to take part in a joint mission to attack the Spanish settlements of Villahermosa in Mexico, Trujillo in Honduras and Granada in Nicaragua. By the time the successful bout of pillaging was over, and the men had regrouped in Port Royal, Jamaica, they were all very rich.

The French, British and Dutch privateering was so legendary, and persisted for so long, that a legacy of fabulous pirate legends remains. Ask Nicaraguans about the pirates and you'll hear amazing tales of sunken ships, waterlogged treasure chests and hidden gold. No matter where you're heading in the country, you'll find that tales of pirates—the violent raids, nautical battles and the riches lost at sea—make for a mysterious and facinating chapter in Nicaraguan history. Updated: Mar 09, 2009.

Augusto Sandino

Some called him an outlaw and others a hero, but whatever his label, Augusto Nicolás Calderón Sandino was indisputably a pivotal figure in Nicaraguan history.

Born May 18, 1895, the son of a wealthy Sandino and a family servant, Augusto Sandino was forced to flee the country after he shot a man at age 26. Eventually landing in Mexico, Sandino studied that country's revolution and became involved with various spiritual groups, while working the oil fields.

Sandino came back to Nicaragua just in time for the war between President Juan Bautista Sacasa's supporters and the conservative government. Sandino, who had found a job in a gold mine, rallied his fellow miners and led an attack on a conservative garrison in El Jácaro. Although his forces were defeated, liberal commanders eventually gave him their nod of approval. Sandino returned to the Segovia mountains to lead attacks on government troops, and his successes included the rescue of a column of liberal soldiers as they advanced on Managua.

Sandino considered the 1927 Espino Negro Accord, which ended the war, a betrayal of the fatherland, and continued to fight. He named his group "The Army in Defense of the National Sovereignty of Nicaragua" and adopted the image of a peasant beheading a Marine. He also started calling himself Augusto "Cesar" Sandino. Employing guerilla tactics, Sandino led his forces in raids around Matagalpa, Jinotega and the eastern coast.

Though Sandino's political interests were originally confined to demanding fresh and fair elections and the withdrawal of US troops, Sandino's philosophy evolved and he began to call for all Latin American countries to unite in order to resist US imperialism.

When the liberal's Espino Negro signatory, General Moncada, won rigged national elections, Sandino declared the appointment unconstitutional and that his peasant army was the only legitimate body. He would eventually pronounce his troops an instrument of divine punishment against the US and, as his paranoia grew and outside aid dwindled, that he was God on earth and that his wife was the reincarnation of the Virgin Mary.

In 1931, an earthquake destroyed the center of Managua and killed over 2,000 people. Sandino, taking the earthquake as a sign in his favor, continued to lead his army on raids in the south and west.

Following Nicaraguan presidential elections in 1932, the US Marines began to pull out of Nicaragua. In 1933, president Sacasa granted Sandino's soldiers amnesty and allowed them to settle on 36,000-square kilometers in the Rio Coco basin. In return, Sandino pledged his loyalty to the president and had his forces surrender their weapons, but was allowed to retain a small force of 100 armed men.

The following year, under commander Anastasio Somoza García, the National Guard ambushed Sandino, executed him in Managua and massacred those living in the Sandinista cooperatives. Updated: Mar 09, 2009.

came flowing in, but the Somozas and their crooked cronies stole most of it. This gross indifference to the plight of common Nicaraguans fed the rebellion.

As popular opposition to the Somoza regime grew, so did political repression. The National Guard bombed cities where Sandinista guerrillas had taken cover. Nicaraguan intelligence assassinated opposition figures, most notably La Prensa editor Pedro Chamorro in 1978. The draconian actions of the government only served to galvanize support for the Sandinistas, however.

In 1979, the Sandinistas marched into Managua and installed a new government which came to be run by Daniel Ortega. Somoza went into exile in Paraguay, where he was assassinated by a team of Argentine rebels.

Join VIVA on Facebook. Fan "VIVA Travel Guides Nicaragua."

Ronald Reagan took office in 1981 and began undermining the communist Sandinista Regime, imposing a trade embargo and authorizing the CIA to do what it could to topple the government. The remnants of the Somoza era and National Guard organized a counter-revolutionary force, which eventually became known as the Contras. The Reagan administration would be embarrassed by their support for the Contras when it was revealed first that arms sold to Iran were financing the rebels and subsequently that the Contras were linked to sales of narcotics in the United States.

The Sandinista government limped along until 1990, when a coalition of opposition parties elected Violeta Barrios de Chamorro as president, displacing Sandinista leader Daniel Ortega. There was little that Chamorro, or her successor in 1996 Arnoldo Alemán, could do with an economy in tatters after forty years of dictatorship followed by ten years of communism, war and embargo. Alemán was later convicted of corruption and sentenced to 20 years prison.

Nicaragua continues to suffer from topsy-turvy politics, but the dust is finally beginning to settle after years of hardship. Although corruption is as bad as ever, at least the wars are over, and some key industries—including tourism—are making a comeback. Updated: Mar 09, 2009.

Today's Politics and Government

Nicaragua is a democratic republic, where the president is both the chief of state and head of government. Daniel Ortega began serving his latest presidental term on January 10, 2007. He belongs to the Sandinista National Liberation Front or FSLN, the Socialist Nicaraguan political party currently in power.

The Nicaraguan government is divided into four branches, the aforementioned executive, legislative, judiciary and electoral. Legislative power is found in the 92 seats of the unicameral National Assembly and judiciary power lies with the 16 judges on the Supreme Court; judges are elected to

Daniel Ortega

The man who would twice serve as Nicaragua's elected president was born in 1945 in La Libertad. José Daniel Ortega Saavedra was raised by staunch opponents to the Anastasio Somoza García dictatorship and grew up idolizing the revolutionary leader Augusto C. Sandino.

As an 18-year old law student, Ortega joined the Frente Sandinista de Liberación Nacional (Sandinista National Liberation Front) or FSLN. He was imprisoned in 1967 after a bank robbery, but was released as part of a prisoner exchange seven years later. Ortega was also briefly exiled to Cuba, where he learned guerrilla fighting; upon his return, Ortega applied this knowledge in the fight against the Somoza regime.

After Somoza fled the country in 1979, a so-called Junta of National Reconstruction took over the government. Ortega became the de facto leader after the two other most-influential leaders resigned. Ortega's term was opposed by Contra rebels, who had funding from the Ronald Regan administration. The conflict between Sandinistas and Contras lasted from roughly 1979 to 1990 and is reported to have killed tens of thousands of Nicaraguans.

Ortega called for national elections in 1984 and won re-election on the Sandinista platform. In 1990, however, he was defeated by Violeta Chamorra. Ortega ran as the FSLN's presidential candidate in 1996 and 2001, but dogged by rumors of corruption and a sex scandal, he lost both times. In 2006, however, due in part to a strategic alliance formed with the Liberal Conservative Party, Ortega won a plurality of the presidential vote and took office.

His second stint as president has been almost as controversial as the first was. He has drawn the ire of the west by befriending leaders like Mahmoud Ahmadinejad and Hugo Chavez, and foreign aid was cut to the country when the FSLN was accused of rigging local elections. Domestically, his opponents have argued that Ortega has been curbing press freedoms in an effort to tighten his grip on the country. Updated: Jun 16, 2009.

Find the best price on a flight to Nicaragua: vivatravelguides.com/flights/

five-year terms by the National Assembly. The electoral branch includes the Supreme Electoral Council which is responsible for organizing and holding elections.

Nicaragua's 1987 constitution has been updated three times—in 1995, 2000 and 2005 —to guarantee freedom of speech, peaceful assembly and association, religion, and movement within the country. However, these rights have decreased and political tension has increased since the November 2008 municipal elections. According to other political parties, Ortega's government has limited free and open discussion in the media and academia, and has curtailed the ability for Nicaraguans to peacefully assemble. Many international observers such as Freedom House have accused Ortega and his government of authoritarianism and intolerance.

One frustration for Nicaraguan civil society and democracy advocates has been the so-called "Pacto" (Pact) between Ortega and former President Arnoldo Alemán. Alemán, a conservative and natural opponent to Ortega's Sandinista government, has thrown his political support, and accompanying voting bloc, behind constitutional changes that benefited Ortega and which were instrumental in the Sandinistas' return to power. Many allege this was part of an agreement in which Ortega has reciprocated by throwing out Alemán's conviction on corruption charges. Updated: Mar 09, 2009.

Economy

Many Central American economies have been adversely affected by colonialism, political instability, civil war, foreign intervention and natural disasters. Nicaragua is no exception.

Nicaragua went from a well-developed agrarian society, to a thriving, but exploited, coffee and "banana republic" industry, to 1960's industrialization. The country was hit hard by a five-year blockade by the United States and the civil war between Sandinistas and Contras, which left most of the fragile infrastructure in ruins. Nicaragua remains, in the wake of Hurricane Mitch in 1998, a struggling economy.

Despite exports of $1.978 billion, the country relies on an estimated $471 million in economic aid. In 2005, under the Heavily Indebted Poor Countries (HIPC) initiative, finance ministers of the leading eight industrialized nations (G8) agreed to pardon some of Nicaragua's foreign debt. Recently, in March 2007, Poland and Nicaragua signed an agreement to write off $30.6 million, which had been borrowed by the Nicaraguan government in the 1980s.

PAST

It is difficult to pinpoint where things went wrong. Colonialism, a history of foreign exploits and intervention caused the people of Nicaragua to develop a distrust of foreign investors—although the government has a differing opinion. Nicaragua, due to its abundance of natural resources and geographical location, is an anomaly. It should have a thriving Central American economy, but only few have been able to take advantage of the country's wealth.

Nicaragua's economic history is diverse. From the coffee boom (1840s to 1940s), to diversification and growth (1945 to 1977), to the Sandinista Era (1979 to 1990), to Chamorra's "Plan of 100 Days," to Aleman's fall due to corruption, and then the return of Daniel Ortega, Nicaragua's economy has been a roller coaster. And let's not forget the legendary Somoza family, who ruled the country as dictators.

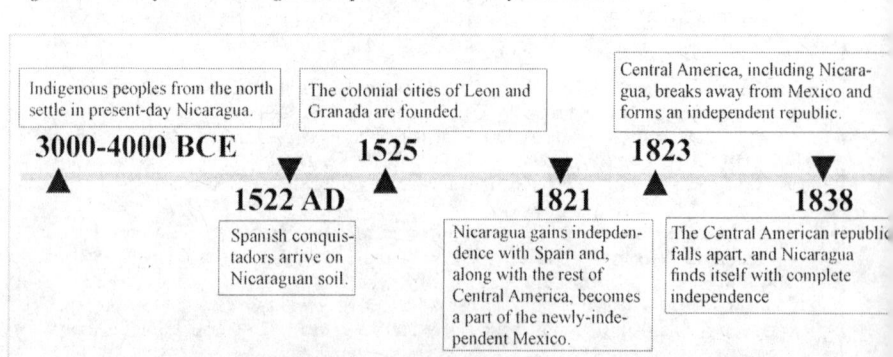

3000-4000 BCE	1525	1823
Indigenous peoples from the north settle in present-day Nicaragua.	The colonial cities of Leon and Granada are founded.	Central America, including Nicaragua, breaks away from Mexico and forms an independent republic.
1522 AD	1821	1838
Spanish conquistadors arrive on Nicaraguan soil.	Nicaragua gains independence with Spain and, along with the rest of Central America, becomes a part of the newly-independent Mexico.	The Central American republic falls apart, and Nicaragua finds itself with complete independence

Join VIVA on Facebook. Fan "VIVA Travel Guides Nicaragua."

Some analysts estimate that by the mid-1970s, the Somoza family owned or controlled 60 percent of the nation's economic interests and owned a third of the land. They had dealings in the food processing industry, and controlled import-export licenses. They also either owned outright or partially controlled transportation, the country's main seaports and the national airline. Profit from these projects was reinvested in real estate throughout the United States and parts of Latin America.

When the Somozas fled Nicaragua in 1979, the family's worth was estimated to be between $500 million and $1.5 billion in US currency. In comparison, the average Nicaraguan earns $280 per month (2007 est.). For the majority of Nicaraguans, the Samozas ran away with an unimaginable amount of money.

PRESENT

With a civil war, heavy foreign intervention, several natural disasters and the Somoza family behind it, Nicaragua needs to look internally for stability. Tourism is once again on the rise and is estimated to be the nation's second largest industry, affecting the agricultural, commercial, finance industries, as well as the construction industry.

In July 2007, Daniel Ortega's government negotiated a new IMF agreement, which required free-market policies and included interests associated with energy, pensions, municipal-led improvement projects, and spending on poverty. Nevertheless, Nicaragua is still the second poorest country in Latin America after Haiti. Although economic efforts have reduced the scope and severity of poverty, 48 percent (2007 est.) of the population lives below the poverty line.

In 2007, experts estimated that 700,000 Nicaraguans live in the U.S and 1.5 million live abroad. The emigrant labor force accounts for $990 million in remittances sent home (2007 est.) Subsequently, labor force is Nicaragua's real main export.

UNEMPLOYMENT: over 3.6 percent (2007 est.)

UNDEREMPLOYMENT: 46.5 percent (2007 est.)

GDP PER CAPITA: $2,600 (2007 est.)

DEBT: 63 percent of GDP (2007 est.)

AGRICULTURAL EXPORTS: bananas, chemicals, coffee, cotton, gold, meat, shellfish, sugar.

EXPORT COMMODITIES: coffee, shrimp, tobacco, sugar, gold, peanuts, copper.

MAIN INDUSTRIES: food processing, chemicals, metal products, textiles, clothing, petroleum refining and distribution, beverages, footwear.

Nicaragua Today

Nicaraguan history has been pitted with crises which have left the country to deal with an inflated economy and a landscape scarred with landmines. Yet, for a history so marred in brutality and foreign military intervention, Nicaraguan hospitality has managed to remain relatively unscathed. Nicaraguans welcome American tourists and have voted left-winged Daniel Ortega, leader of the Sandinista party, back into the presidency. Updated: Mar 09, 2009.

Population

The population in Nicaragua is 7.8 million (2009 est.) It has a growth rate of 1.825 percent (2008 est.) Nicaragua's capital city

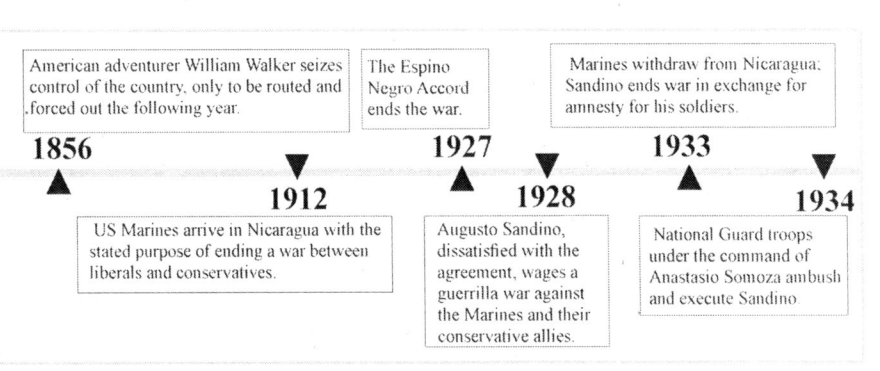

1856 — American adventurer William Walker seizes control of the country, only to be routed and forced out the following year.

1912 — US Marines arrive in Nicaragua with the stated purpose of ending a war between liberals and conservatives.

1927 — The Espino Negro Accord ends the war.

1928 — Augusto Sandino, dissatisfied with the agreement, wages a guerrilla war against the Marines and their conservative allies.

1933 — Marines withdraw from Nicaragua; Sandino ends war in exchange for amnesty for his soldiers.

1934 — National Guard troops under the command of Anastasio Somoza ambush and execute Sandino.

Find the best price on a flight to Nicaragua: vivatravelguides.com/flights/

is Managua. Its population of 1.5 million is rapidly growing, prompting a construction boom in the late 1990s.

The population is 69 percent Mestizo (mixed Amerindian and white), 17 percent white, 9 percent black, and 5 percent Amerindian. The Mestizo population is concentrated in the Pacific coastal region and the northern highlands, where the Spanish settled before independence. Most Mestizos have retained that Spanish legacy through their language and Roman Catholicism.

The black and indigenous populations hail mostly from the country's eastern coast. In this area, ruled by Britain during the colonial era, Caribbean-inflected English and native languages predominate, and Protestant churches draw most congregants.

With its weak economy and internal strife, Nicaragua has attracted relatively few immigrants over the past half-century. However, there are small Chinese and Lebanese communities in a few of the larger cities.

Although Nicaragua is the largest nation in the region, it is also the least densely populated because approximately 1 million people were in exile during the 1980s, but today many are returning. Updated: Sep 23, 2009.

Language

Spanish is the official language in Nicaragua, but you'll find that a mix of English and native languages are also spoken in the country, particularly closer to the Carribean coast. There have been nine native languages identified along the coast, but only seven are considered "living languages," and the Rama language is nearing extinction.

Only an estimated 1,500 people still speak Garifuna along the Caribbean coast, where the ethnic population is a blend of West African and Carib Indian. About 200,000 Nicaraguans still speak Miskito and roughly 6,700 speak Sumo-Mayangna, both Misumalpan languages. About 30,000 people speak Nicaraguan Creole English, also called Miskito Coast Creole. Nicaraguan Creole English speakers, who are usually the descendants of Africans, Europeans or Amerindians, live mainly around Bluefields.

As with South American countries like Argentina or Colombia, you may hear Spanish-speaking Nicaraguans referring to you as "vos." The voseo form, a second person sigular pronoun, is used in place of "tú." Although it's still much more common to hear the voseo form in conversation, you may also notice it in advertisements or newspaper articles.

Particularly in the rural areas, Nicaraguans tend to drop the ends of their words or slur their consonants. This regional habit has made them the butt of jokes in neighboring countries, where Nicaraguans are either teased as being so poor they can't afford an "s" or as mucos, a bull with no horns. Still, although Nicaraguan Spanish is more fluid and changeable than in other countries, those who already speak the language should have little trouble being understood. Updated: Mar 09, 2009.

Religion

Ever since the Spanish conquest of Nicaragua in the 16th century, its population has been predominantly Roman Catholic. Before the Spanish arrived in the region that came to be known as Nicaragua, the peoples of the region honored both Aztec and Mayan deities, as they were situated in Mesoamerica along Aztec and Mayan trade routes.

There were a few minor exceptions to the Catholic dominance throughout most of Nicaragua's colonial history. Tribal communities

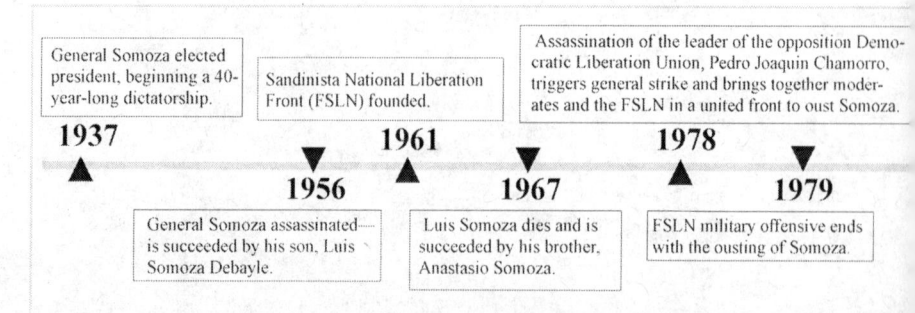

General Somoza elected president, beginning a 40-year-long dictatorship.	Sandinista National Liberation Front (FSLN) founded.	Assassination of the leader of the opposition Democratic Liberation Union, Pedro Joaquin Chamorro, triggers general strike and brings together moderates and the FSLN in a united front to oust Somoza.
1937 ▲	**1961** ▼	**1978** ▲
▼ **1956**	▲ **1967**	▼ **1979**
General Somoza assassinated—is succeeded by his son, Luis Somoza Debayle.	Luis Somoza dies and is succeeded by his brother, Anastasio Somoza.	FSLN military offensive ends with the ousting of Somoza.

Join VIVA on Facebook. Fan "VIVA Travel Guides Nicaragua."

Nicaraguan Sign Language

Imagine what it would be like to witness, first hand, the formation of a new language. Then imagine that language becoming the way in which thousands of deaf school children function in their society. Now imagine it was the deaf children themselves who created, out of necessity, a new language that became known as Nicaraguan Sign Language (known to experts as I.S.N., for Idioma de Signos Nicaragense).

The first wide-ranging effort to educate deaf children came after the 1979 Sandinista revolution, which saw the inauguration of a new government. Hundreds of students were enrolled in two Managua schools, one in the neighborhood of San Judas and the other, later, in Villa Libertad. These children were raised in Managua city neighborhoods.

However, they were not able to access more than 200 other known sign languages and their teachers were unable to help them. Managua's deaf children in these two communities started from scratch. They had no Spanish language acquisition, no grammar, no sentence structure; they just had each other and a series of rudimentary gestures otherwise known as *mimincas* in Spanish that they had developed within their families.

What came into being was a new sign language, distinctive to their needs and formed by them to function as a means of communication and learning. Later, as linguists began to study and analyze this new language phenomenon, they noticed the children themselves began to add verb agreements and other grammar conventions. The development of I.S.N has given scholars an opportunity to study the formation of languages. It has been widely reported on, argued about, and in general, has caused quite a ruckus in the linguistics community. Updated: Mar 09, 2009.

as the Ramas and the Mayangas were able to retain much of their culture. These populations, small to begin with, have radically diminished in recent times, mostly through assimilation, and are likely to disappear in the near future if economic and social factors continue as they are.

Of course, Nicaragua's own Roman Catholic culture was never monolithic, but rather divided politically throughout much of the 20th century. Factions were divided between those who supported the Somoza dictatorship, in the name of anti-communism, and those critical of the corruption and human rights abuses of the same regime. The most famous, or infamous (depending on one's politics) religious figure during this time was the priest Ernesto Cardenal, a proponent of liberation theology who supported the Sandinista revolution and was appointed minister of culture during the 1980s.

However, a serious challenge to Roman Catholic hegemony in the last 30 years has been the arrival of Protestant evangelical missionary churches, such as the Seventh Day Adventists and the Latter Day Saints, who have successfully proselytized many of the poorest segments of the Nicaraguan populace. Updated: Mar 09, 2009.

Art

No matter the size or shape, color or medium, artistic expression in Nicaragua is ever-present. There are formal displays of fine arts,

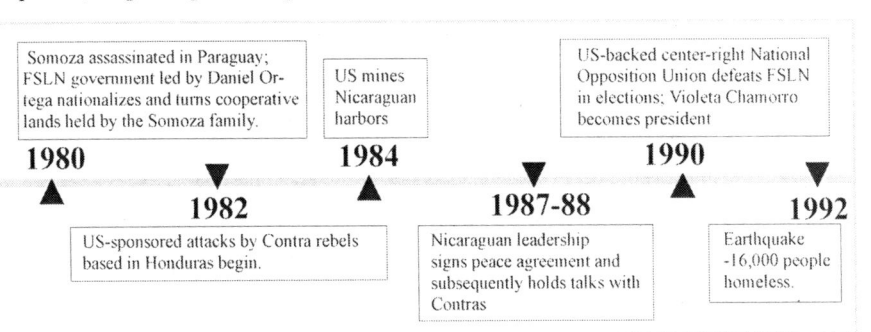

1980 — Somoza assassinated in Paraguay; FSLN government led by Daniel Ortega nationalizes and turns cooperative lands held by the Somoza family.

1982 — US-sponsored attacks by Contra rebels based in Honduras begin.

1984 — US mines Nicaraguan harbors

1987-88 — Nicaraguan leadership signs peace agreement and subsequently holds talks with Contras

1990 — US-backed center-right National Opposition Union defeats FSLN in elections; Violeta Chamorro becomes president

1992 — Earthquake -16,000 people homeless.

such as Managua's art gallery district, which is home to museums offering both domestic and international art, but artistic expression is not limited to canvases and galleries; it can be found on practically every corner.

Masaya and its surrounding villages have long been a center for artesanal production, churning out beautiful hammocks, ceramics and other folk art. Beautiful traditional handicrafts are produced elsewhere around the country as well, and make great souvenirs (see Shopping on p. 53).

Just as important as the artesan scene in Nicaragua, the "primitivist" style art from Solentiname, (an archipelago consisting of four large and some 32 smaller islands in southern Lake Nicaragua), is essentially emblematic of the country's creative contributions. Founded in 1965 by priest and poet Ernesto Cardinal, Solentiname was, and still is, a spiritual artist community for native Nicaraguans. Two years after it had been destroyed during the country's revolution, Cardinal sought to restore this lush land. What developed out of his desire for justice and community was a space for the poor and oppressed to experiment with a creative and imaginative folk art.

With the help of renowned painter Roger Perez de la Rocha of Managua, impoverished individuals learned new painting techniques and styles, and were encouraged to think freely, expressing the hopes and dreams that sprang out of the hardship that was the reality of their daily lives. Starting with poor campesinos, or farmers, the community eventually grew to more than 50 painters, each contributing intricate, colorful, and symbolic works with themes like religion, nature, and daily life. Although much of the original art from Cardinal's community was destroyed by the Somoza dictatorship, the Sandinista National Liberation Front eventually brought the expressive community back out into the open after years of censorship. Today, there is a small art gallery on the island, which features works by local craftsmen, woodworkers, muralists, and painters. Updated: Mar 09, 2009.

Music and Dance

Music and dance are key parts of life in Nicaragua, as you are likely to notice the minute you step out on the street. Tunes flow from homes, cars and restaurants. Various rhythms provide the background to traditional festivals, performances and family gatherings. Music and the accompanying dances tell the Nicaraguan story from their indigenous origins to colonialism to the birth of a developing nation—a developing nation with an exceptionally bumping nightlife. Music is now influenced equally by present-day hip hop as it is by indigenous customs.

THE MUSIC OF THE WESTERN COAST

Traditionally, the Pacific region of Nicaragua offers a mix of indigenous and European sounds. Most notably is the contribution of the marimba, a unique xylophone-type instrument made of carved hardwood slabs set over metal or bamboo tubes. To play, the instrument is set on the performers knees and struck with mallets to create different sounds from each key. The marimba is most often accompanied by the guitar, fiddle and guitarilla.

The dances that accompany this traditional Mestizo music also reflect both a Spanish and indigenous heritage. Dances like "El Güegüense o Macho Ratón," "El Toro Huaco," "El Viejo y La Vieja," "Aquella Indita," "Los Diabilitos," and "Las Negras," mock the Spanish conquest, poke fun at old

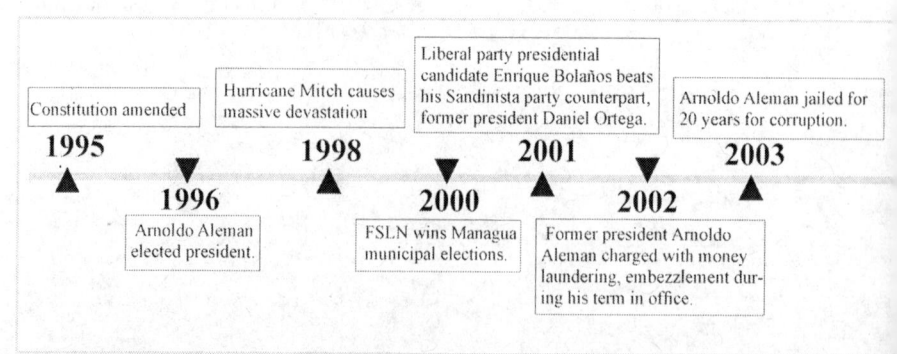

1995 — Constitution amended
1996 — Arnoldo Aleman elected president.
1998 — Hurricane Mitch causes massive devastation
2000 — FSLN wins Managua municipal elections.
2001 — Liberal party presidential candidate Enrique Bolaños beats his Sandinista party counterpart, former president Daniel Ortega.
2002 — Former president Arnoldo Aleman charged with money laundering, embezzlement during his term in office.
2003 — Arnoldo Aleman jailed for 20 years for corruption.

Join VIVA on Facebook. Fan "VIVA Travel Guides Nicaragua."

age, and playfully embrace sexuality. They encourage community and celebration.

In the northern highlands, German settlers brought an appreciation for Polka music which continues to this day. Local celebrations in the area also feature the Mazurka, another music and dance style from Central Europe.

FROM THE CARIBBEAN

More modern and noticeably more sensual, Nicaragua shares soca, reggaeton and reggae with its Caribbean neighbors. Soca, from Trinidad and Tobago, is a calypso and procession-based beat, so popular that it now even has sub-groups, (chutney soca and ragga soca). Panama's reggaeton can be heard all over Nicaragua and unquestionably provides a soundtrack for lively city nightlife in Managua and other parts of the country. The beat is distinctly Latino, with hip-hop influences from the States. It carries a repetitive tone and demands dancing, unlike Jamaican-based reggae, a more laid back tune that often explores themes of peace, protest, love, sexuality, poverty, and injustice.

BLUEFIELDS

For the whole month of May, the sultry southeastern seaport of Bluefields hosts the Palo de Mayo Festival, also known as ¡Mayo Ya!, providing one of Nicaragua's most distinct musical contributions. This Afro-Caribbean music and dance performance is lively and seductive, celebrating culture, telling stories of sensuality, and creating a beat unique to this Caribbean coastal town. The music and dance draw from African rain and fertility ceremonies, Germanic paganism, and British customs, like dancing 'round the May Pole. Resounding through Bluefields, the music accompanies parades, costumes, feasting, and dancing. Updated: Mar 09, 2009.

Museums

While Nicaragua doesn't boast a Louvre or a Guggenheim to show off its history, a number of the country's 50+ museums are worth a visit.

The museums, spread out throughout the country, focus on Nicaragua's favorite sons and daughters, its history, its art, and its archaeological heritage. The museums document the narrative of Nicaragua and undoubtedly provide a starting point for understanding the culture which is present today.

However, Nicaragua's museums do tend to lack the spit-and-polish of museums in wealthier societies. Though the displays may be a bit dusty, they are frequently brought to life by the docents and curators, who provide a lively (and often firsthand) explanation of the exhibits. Indeed, it is these earnest explanations that are the highlight of most trips to a Nicaraguan museum. Some of the museums do charge entry, though this is usually $2 or less. Others are free (donations appreciated), so this leaves you no excuse to miss out. Updated: Mar 09, 2009.

Film

Whatever Nicaragua had in terms of a film industry, or even film culture, perished during the Sandinista revolution (from 1979 to 1990). Before the revolution, there had been a small, publicly-funded production outfit, Producine, dedicated entirely to promulgating propaganda for the corrupt and draconian Somoza dynasty in the form of opinionated news films, usually shown before an imported commercial feature film. Otherwise, Nicaragua's extreme poverty made filmmaking nearly impossible. Nicaraguans usually had to be content with imported commercial fare from Hollywood, Mexico, and Argentina.

2004 — Russia writes-off Nicaragua's multi-billion-dollar Soviet-era debt.

2004 — World Bank wipes 80% of Nicaragua's debt to the institution.

2005 — Political crisis eases as Congress agrees to delay constitutional reforms, which will weaken the powers of the president Bolaños; he leaves office in 2007.

2006 — Free trade deal with the US comes into effect. Nicaragua's Congress approves the Central American Free Trade Agreement (CAFTA)

2006 — Ex-president Daniel Ortega is returned to power in elections

2007 — Poland and Nicaragua sign an agreement to write off 30.6 million dollars of debt

---

Find the best price on a flight to Nicaragua: vivatravelguides.com/flights/

Free Trade

Most Free Trade Zones (known as *maquilas*) are located in developing or economically depressed countries; Nicaragua is no exception to that unofficial rule. The Nicaraguan government currently allows 112 factories—most of them owned by American or Taiwanese multinational companies—to operate within the country's 12 maquilas.

International companies receive incentives and benefits from the Nicaraguan government when they import raw materials, assemble goods or export products. The free trade zone rules encourage corporations such as Chentex, which makes jeans for companies like Bugle Boy, Cherokee and Gloria Vanderbilt, to set up shop in the country, and then export the completed products.

In Chentex's case, the products are sold at stores like Target, K-Mart, JC Penney and Kohl's. International companies find Nicaraguan Free Trade Zones very attractive due to the existence of cheap labor and the country's relative political stability. The government makes no tax revenue off these factories; the main benefit for Nicaragua is the creation of thousands of desperately needed jobs for its citizens.

In August 2004, the Nicaraguan government signed the DR-CAFTA (Central American-Dominican Republic Free Trade Agreement). The agreement came into effect on April 2006, eliminating 80 percent of trade barriers for United States' exports into Nicaragua and increasing the amount of sugar and beef that Nicaragua could ship to North America. The regional trade agreement was created with a similar format and ambition as NAFTA, but included the countries of Costa Rica, the Dominican Republic, El Salvador, Guatemala, Honduras, Nicaragua, and the United States.

As well as increasing Nicaraguan exports to the United States, DR-CAFTA has created thousands of jobs for workers (90 percent are single uneducated mothers who would otherwise have no means of support). However, the wages are so low that workers remain poverty stricken. On the world stage, the agreement remains very controversial. DR-CAFTA supporters argue that the new jobs are better than nothing, particularly in a country that has the second lowest per capita income in the Western Hemisphere. Opponents of the agreement claim the working conditions permitted under DR-CAFTA are inhumane and the fact that the workers are not allowed to unionize is a violation of human rights. Updated: Mar 09, 2009.

After the Sandinistas overthrew Anastazio Somoza, they reinvented a national cinema. The Sandinista government had both funding and technical support from Cuba. Modeling the Soviet approach to pictures as populist pedagogy, the new government established the Instituto Nacional de Cine Nicaraguanse, or INCINE. The Instituto Nacional promulgating propaganda for the Sandinista cause in the form of biased news films, called noticieros. A typical noticiero would highlight a new public works project, the building of a school, or the bravery of female Sandinista soldiers. Strangely enough, such films were shown in movie houses, rather than on television, which had long since become the predominant mass medium for social evolution. The theater presentation of the noticieros was a result of a rivalry between the state-run television network and INCINE.

After two years, INCINE decided to move beyond the non-fiction format, which though inexpensive, was limited in its impact, and thus ventured into full-length fictional feature films. As was the standard for all cinema made under Marxist auspices at the time, feature films made by INCINE all conveyed the Sandinista party line.

However inhibiting this might have been for genuine artistry, INCINE scored a surprise success with their very first film, Alsino y el Condor (1982). INCINE employed Miguel Littin, who had been exiled from Chile, and adapted a traditional folk story of a boy longing to fly like a condor, only in the film his daydreams were set against the backdrop of the Sandinista-Somoza war. The movie featured American actor Dean Stockwell as a sinister U.S. adviser. The film was praised for muting its political message through obliquely poetic poignancy, and was nominated for an Oscar for Best Foreign Film.

Nothing that INCINE would later do matched the success of Alsino y el Condor either in prestige or popularity. Its last film, 1988's The Specter of War, about an aspiring dancer who overcomes his reluctance to sacrifice his career for the sake of military service, broke INCINE's budget. Two years later, the anti-Sandinista candidate, Violeta Chamorro, won the presidency and INCINE became merely another chapter in Nicaragua's cinematic history.

Since the demise of INCINE, filmmaking in Nicaragua has been sporadic, consisting mainly of short socially-conscious documentaries responding to the aftermath of decades of war, poverty, and instability. In post-civil war Nicaragua, the Asociación Nicaragüense de Cinematografía (ANCI) has also emerged to unify the country's new generation of filmmakers. Updated: Mar 09, 2009.

Literature

Nicaraguan literature not only holds its own in the Latin American art world, but has made an unparalleled imprint on the history of literature as a whole. With a compact series of literary movements and only a handful of well-known writers, it's somewhat surprising that the country has produced a body of writing that has proven itself to be so aesthetically and politically powerful. What's most important to realize is that literature in this country is celebrated like almost no where else; poets are respected, revered and recited.

The first significant work produced in Nicaragua was the esteemed satirical drama El Güegüense, a witty and ironic song and dance performance written in the 17th century. While the author remains anonymous, this post-Columbian composition has played a considerable role in Nicaraguan culture, so much so that it was named a UNESCO Master Play of the Oral and Immaterial Patrimony of Humanity. El Güegüense is still performed in Nicaragua each year towards the end of January, during the feast of San Sebastian.

The modernismo movement that sprang from Nicaragua in the late 19th and early 20th centuries is held in high regard among Nicaraguans and the literary public. This is due largely in part to the "father of modernism," Nicaragua's own Rubén Darío. A blend of European symbolism, romanticism, and parnassism, modernismo expresses passion and rhythm, the idea of art solely for art's sake, and rich verbal harmonies. While the literature was mainly socially neutral, the political climate in Nicaragua at the time demanded that some works speak of social order and the innate struggle of Latin America's indigenous people.

This politically charged literature seems to have been picked up by the poetry that came after Modernismo and the later Vanguardia movement. Both brought forth strong and radical writers, most prominently Ernesto Cardenal—the Nicaraguan Catholic priest who promoted liberation theology, the arts, and the Sandinista regime—and José Coronel Urtecho, who began Vanguardia in Granada in the late 1920's.

These movements confronted once untouchable themes such as religion, politics, and sexuality, and they dared to suggest new novel forms. The Sandinista government at the time promoted literature and the arts in Nicaragua, and from that came immense support and contribution from a political angle. Many who were imprisoned for political involvement against the Somoza regime used their prison sentences as an opportunity to create poetry.

Major literary contributors, aside from those already mentioned, include: Gioconda Belli, who is radical and sexual and considered one of the 100 most important poets in the 20th century; Sergio Ramirez Mercado—head of the "Group 12," intellectuals who publicly supported the Frente Sandinista de Liberation Nacional (FSLN); Tomás Borge—former Nicaraguan Head of State Security; and Daniel Ortega—current president of Nicaragua.

For more on literature from and about Nicaragua, see Suggested Reading on p. 67. Updated: Mar 16, 2009.

Rubén Darío

The 19th-century Nicaraguan poet Rubén Darío led a poetic revolution so profound that it resounded throughout the literary and Hispanic worlds.

Rubén Darío is considered the father of modernism (modernismo). This poetic movement was heavily influenced by the French symbolists and parnassians, who relied on exact workmanship of the language, while also striving for the emotional and aesthetic ideal of romanticism. While Darío's masterpiece "Azul" evokes a magical world of fairies

Find the best price on a flight to Nicaragua: vivatravelguides.com/flights/

and artists in search of beauty, his actual life reads more like a tragicomedy.

The poet was born Feliz Rubén Garcá Sarmiento in 1867 in Metapa, Nicaragua, the town now known as Ciudad Darío. After his parents separated, he was raised by an aunt in the intellectually active town of León. A child prodigy, he learned to read at age 3, and at 13, had his first poem, an elegy, published in a local newspaper. Gaining fame as "El Niño Poeta" (the Child Poet), the young Darío started contributing to a literary magazine in León.

In 1881, at the age of 14, he moved to Managua to further his education and began collaborating with national newspapers. While living in Managua, Darío fell in love with Rosario Murillo, the woman with whom he pursued an on-off love affair most of his life. Initially, he was so smitten that he wanted to marry her, though she was a mere girl of 11. Darío's friends prevented this marital haste by encouraging him to go to El Salvador in 1882.

There, he was taken under the wing of Salvadorian poet Francisco Gavidia, who had a crucial influence on the young man's writing by introducing him to French poetry. Darío continued to experiment with verse upon his return to Managua one year later, where he picked up his romance with Murillo.

But, by 1886, he had grown restless and decided to spread his wings by moving to Chile to work as a journalist. While in the port of Valparaiso, at the age of 21, Darío published his seminal work "Azul," a collection of poems and prose. Although some critics responded to the book with derogatory comments about Darío's Indian background, the powerful Spanish critic Juan Valera endorsed the author and hailed Darío for his talent. Riding on the back of his new fame, Darío traveled back to Central America and became director of a new Salvadorian publication.

In 1890, while in San Salvador, Darío married; the day after the wedding, his bride was tragically killed in a coup. Darío promptly remarried, but his luck with a second marriage proved no happier, ending after just three years with the second wife falling terminally ill.

The poet then embarked on a second career as a diplomat in Argentina. Around that time, he rekindled his affair with Murillo, whom he married under pressure from her family. Once in his new consular position in Buenos Aires, Darío led a libertine lifestyle and drank heavily. He also moved in intellectual circles and published two essential books: "Los Raros," a collection of articles, and "Prosas Profanas y Otros Poemas," the anthology that helped establish the modernismo form.

In 1898, as correspondent for Argentina's La Nacion, Darío moved to Spain, where he met yet another woman. Francisca Perez del Pozo, while she was an illiterate peasant, became his companion in his later life, much to the dismay of his wife, Murillo.

Darío also traveled throughout Europe and Latin America, flitting from careers in journalism, diplomacy, and poetry as his alcoholism worsened.

At the outbreak of World War I, Darío left Europe for good, leaving behind Perez del Pozo and two sons. He eventually found his way back to Nicaragua, where he died of cirrhosis in 1916. He is buried in the cathedral of León. Updated: Jul 27, 2009.

Holidays and Fiestas

January 1: Año Nuevo, or New Year's Day—Celebrated beach-side by most Nicaraguans.

End of March/Early April: Semana Santa, or Holy Week—Includes Holy Thursday, Good Friday, and Easter. Semana Santa is the most celebrated holiday in Nicaragua, filled with religious and cultural celebrations.

Month	Event
May 1	Día de los Trabajadores, or Labor Day.
May 30	Mother's Day.
June 19	National Liberation Day—Commemorates the day that the National Liberation Army defeated the oppressive Anastasio Somoza García dictatorship.
June 23	Father's Day.
July 25	Fiesta de Santiago—Celebrated in Boaco, Somoto, and Managua.
July 26	Fiesta de Santa Ana—Celebrated in Nandaime, Niquinohomo, Moyogalpa, and Ometepe.

Join VIVA on Facebook. Fan "VIVA Travel Guides Nicaragua."

August 1	Fiesta de San Domingo—Celebrating the patron saint in Managua; incorporates over two weeks of festivities, beginning in late July. Festivities include joyous processions, solemn masses, and horse parades on the 1st and 10th.
September 14	Battle of San Jacinto—A commemoration of the final battle that ultimately freed Central America from Spain's domination.
September 15	Independence Day—A joyous, month-long celebration of the 1821 freedom of Central America from Spain.
November 2	Día de los Muertos—To honor loved ones who have died, families head to local cemetaries to both clean and decorate the graves. Family members set up candles, wreath the tombs with flowers, and even sleep in the cemetery in loving memory of los difuntos (the deceased).
December 7, 8	La Purísima—An extremely important holy day in Nicaragua, La Purisma honors Mary's Immaculate Conception of Christ. La Gritería is the cheerful execution of fireworks, house-to-house caroling, treats, prayers and praise offered to la Virgen.
December 25	Navidad, or Christmas

Updated: Mar 09, 2009.

Social and Environmental Issues

The social and environmental issues in Nicaragua are heavily intertwined with the continued economic problems in the country. The economic crisis of the 1980s, coupled with the Contra War, has worsened the greatest social problems Nicaragua has faced in the past few decades, namely unemployment, underemployment, and poverty. Rampant poverty and unemployment have lead to housing shortages, malnutrition, and rising crime and illiteracy. An estimated 48 percent of Nicaraguans live in poverty; the statistics for unemployment and underemployment are just as high, reaching 50 percent of the population.

In the big cities such as Managua, the urban poor live in slums made of cardboard and sleep on dirt floors; many people do not have access to safe drinking water or sanitary plumbing systems. The cramped living conditions of the slums allow for the rapid spread of diseases such as pneumonia, gastroenteritis and diarrhea—easily curable ailments in most developed countries that have proven to be fatal to Nicaraguans, due to the inaccessibility of affordable and adequate health care. Although the urban areas of Nicaragua may have inadequate social services, the rural areas are where services such as health, water, education and sanitation are nearly nonexistent.

Education in Nicaragua is technically free, but there are always hidden costs for uniforms and books that many people cannot afford to pay. Numerous families living in the countryside do not send their children to school. Instead, the young ones are put to work to help support their families.

There were some improvements in health care and education made during the Sandinista regime, particularly in the rural areas. Any ground gained was slowly lost again as what little money the government had was diverted from social programs into funding the war with the Contras.

The economic crisis of the 1980s left the country in dire conditions. After years of hyperinflation, salaries became nonexistent. Many Nicaraguans were forced to supplement their so-called salaries by working in the black market or as street vendors and taxi cab drivers.

Rising unemployment and underemployment led directly to the rise in crime, gangs, and violence in the 1990s as people used any means necessary to get what they needed to survive.

The economic situation in Nicaragua has been improving. The country has been following an International Monetary Fund program, with the goal of creating more jobs, decreasing poverty, and opening the economy to foreign trade.

Many international organizations have also stepped up to help. In 2005, the United Nations classified Nicaragua as a Heavily Indebted Poor Country, and forgave some of the country's foreign debt. Around the same time, Nicaragua also signed the DR-CAFTA (Central American-Dominican Republic Free

Trade Agreement). The agreement has arguably created thousands of jobs for those previously unemployed; 90 percent of the workers are single, uneducated mothers with no other means of support. However, critics point out that the wages are so low that many women remain poverty stricken.

Due to the immensity of problems with poverty and unemployment, the environmental degradation of Nicaragua's lakes and forests went largely unnoticed before the 1980s. Nicaragua's enormous foreign debt has also contributed to the destruction of natural resources; Nicaragua lost 21 percent of its forest cover between 1990 and 2005.

The biggest environmental problems facing Nicaragua are all due to human causes: deforestation, pollution caused by agricultural production, water pollution, over-fishing and poor land management. Deforestation in Nicaragua occurs at a rampant rate; the country's forest cover is at 4 million hectares or half of the estimated 8 million hectares that Nicaragua had in the 1950s.

Nicaragua's tropical forests are disappearing ten times as fast as the Amazon rain forest in Brazil. If the rate were to continue at the same speed, scientists estimate that Nicaragua's rain forest will disappear between 2010 and 2021.

Urgent steps need to be taken to save the tropical forests or Nicaragua may face the same fate as its neighbor El Salvador, where only three percent of the original forest cover remains. Approximately 75 percent of Nicaraguan forests have already been turned into crop and pasture land. The use of pesticides such as DDT (dichloro-diphenyl-trichloroethane) increased dramatically during the Sandinista regime, resulting in widespread environmental contamination in Nicaragua. The Sandinistas used DDT to control malaria and sold pesticides to farmers for little to nothing. While pesticides meant farmers could grow more, their use also resulted in environmental damage from toxic runoff.

During the Somoza dictatorship, industrial plants were allowed to dump toxic waste into Lake Managua. As a result, many of Nicaragua's lakes and rivers were severely contaminated. The combination of sewage and chemical waste means Lake Managua is unsuitable for swimming, fishing, or providing drinking water.

The combination of pollution and over-fishing has destroyed a once-thriving fishing industry in lakes such as Managua. Endangered or extinct marine species in Nicaragua include the American crocodile, a form of freshwater shark, and all of the green sea, hawkbill, leatherback and olive ridley turtles.

In an effort to correct the poor usage of natural resources, Nicaragua created the Nicaraguan Institute for Natural Resources and Environment (IRENA) in the 1980s. The institute has established both the Bosawas Natural Resources Reserve and Indio-Maiz Biological Reserve. The two parks form the largest forest reserves in Central America and protect many species such as jaguars, tapirs, howler monkeys, frogs, rare birds, and orchids. Nicaragua is also home to 74 other protected land areas.

However, even with these efforts, Nicaraguan is still facing numerous hurdles when it comes to protecting the country's rain forests and revitalizing both damaged lands and waters. Updated: Mar 10, 2009.

Nicaragua by Numbers

Country Name: República de Nicaragua

Capital: Managua.

Independence Day: September 15, 1821 (from Spain).

President: President Daniel Ortega Saavedra (since January 10, 2007).

Currency: Gold Cordoba (NIO)

Exchange Rate: One US dollar = 20.63 cordobas (October 2009).

Population: 5.8 (July 2009 est.).

Nationality: Nicaraguan(s).

Ethnic Groups: mestizo (mixed Amerindian and white) 69 percent; white 17 percent; black 9 percent; Amerindian 5 percent.

Religions: Roman Catholic 58.5 percent; Evangelical 21.6 percent; Moravian 1.6 percent; Jehovah's Witness 0.9 percent; other 1.7 percent; none 15.7 percent (2005 census).

Languages: Spanish 97.5 percent (official), Miskito 1.7 percent, other 0.8 percent (1995 census); English and indigenous languages are spoken on the Atlantic coast.

Join VIVA on Facebook. Fan "VIVA Travel Guides Nicaragua."

Literacy: 67.5 percent (age 15 and over can read and write).

Coastline: 910 km (565 mi)

Highest Point: Mogoton at 2,438 m (8,000 ft).

Natural Resources: gold, silver, copper, tungsten, lead, zinc, timber, fish.

Natural hazards: destructive earthquakes, volcanoes, landslides; extremely susceptible to hurricanes.

Environmental Issues: deforestation, soil erosion, water pollution.

GDP Per Capita: $2,800 (2007 est.).

Population Below the Poverty Line: 48 percent (2005).

Unemployment Rate: 5.6 percent, plus underemployment of 46.5 percent (2008 est.)

Agriculture Products: coffee, bananas, sugarcane, cotton, rice, corn, tobacco, sesame, soya, beans; beef, veal, pork, poultry, dairy products; shrimp, lobsters.

Industries: food processing, chemicals, machinery and metal products, textiles, clothing, petroleum refining and distribution, beverages, footwear, wood.

Export Commodities: coffee, beef, shrimp and lobster, tobacco, sugar, gold, peanuts.

Export Partners: US, El Salvador, Honduras.

Updated: Sep 23, 2009.

pdated: May 07, 2009.

Travel Insurance

Taking out a travel insurance policy is an essential precaution for all tourists who plan on traveling to Nicaragua, or anywhere in Central America for that matter. As there are a great deal of different insurers offering a wide variety of products, it is worth spending some time to research the policy that is most suitable for your trip. Before you do this, check to see if you already have coverage, as some credit and bank cards provide basic travel insurance.

Travel insurance policies cover a wide range of potential problems, including cancellation of transportation, delays, hijacking, the loss or theft of valuables, and legal expenses. The most important part of any policy is the medical provision. The costs of medical treatment for serious injuries can quickly mount up. Find out how much your insurance will pay for necessary emergency expenses and if your policy includes helicopter rescue and emergency evacuation, should you need to return home, or be flown to the US for serious medical attention. Most policies (and hospitals in Nicaragua) will demand that you pay for your medical treatment up front (usually in cash). If you have to pay cash at a hospital, make sure that you get receipts for any medical care you receive, as you will need to provide copies when making your claim.

Before you leave for your trip, make sure that the policy you choose covers all the activities that you intend on doing, or think that you might try; activities such as climbing, scuba diving and even trekking may be considered adventurous activities and thus not covered under a basic policy.

Although medical coverage is extremely important, most travel insurance claims relate to lost or stolen items. If you intend on taking expensive belongings such as cameras, laptops or iPods to Nicaragua, there is a chance that they could be stolen or damaged. Purchase a policy that offers an appropriate level of protection to cover all the items you intend to take on your trip, or consider leaving any extremely expensive items at home. If you are robbed while in Nicaragua, report the incident to the police within 24 hours. Make sure to obtain a copy of the report, as your insurance company may demand this (along with the item's receipt) when you make your claim.

Basic travel insurance policies may not include any provision for the loss or theft of valuables and, in general, the more money you are willing to spend, the greater the level of protection you will have. If you purchase a more comprehensive policy, the deductibles will be smaller; single item limits will be higher; there may be coverage for cash and the cost of re-issuing passports. Check the details very closely to make sure that you are happy with the level of coverage your policy provides.

Note: Be sure to bring your insurer's 24-hour emergency contact number and a copy of your policy number with you. It is also a

---

Find the best price on a flight to Nicaragua: vivatravelguides.com/flights/

Embassies and Consulates

Argentina
Calle Prado Ecuestre 235 B, Managua
Tel: (505) 2-55-0062 / 55-0089 / 76-0116
Fax: (505) 2-76-2654
E-mail: embargentina@alfanumeric.com.ni
Hours: Monday to Friday, 8 a.m. to 12 p.m.

Brazil
Km. 7 3/4 Carretera Sur, Quinta Los Pinos, Managua
Tel: (505) 2-65-1729 / 0035 / 1681
Fax: (505) 2-65-2206
E-mail: ebrasil@ibw.com.ni
Hours: Monday to Friday, 8 a.m. to 3 p.m.

Canada
Costado Oriental de la Casa Nazareth, Calle El Nogal, #25, Managua
Tel: (505) 2-68-0433 / 2-68-3323
Fax: (505) 2-68-0437
E-mail: mngua@international.gc.ca
Hours: Monday to Thursday, 7:30 a.m. to 4:30 p.m.; Friday, 7:30 a.m. to 1:00 p.m.

Chile
Rpto. Los Robles, Semáforos Hotel Milton Princess, 1c. abajo, 1c. sur y ½c. abajo, Managua
Tel: (505) 2-78-0619 / 2-70-1130 / 2-78-7015
Fax: (505) 2-70-4073
E-mail: echileni@cablenet.com.ni
Hours: Monday to Friday, 8:30 a.m. to 12:30 p.m.

China
Óptica Matamoros 2c. abajo ½c. al lago, Carretera a Masaya, Planes de Altamira, Managua
Tel: (505) 2-77-1333, 2-77-1334, 2-70-0421, Fax: (505) 2-67-4025
E-mail: nic@mofa.gov.tw, embchina@ibw.com.ni
Hours: Monday to Friday, 8:30 a.m. to 12:30 p.m. and 1:30 p.m. to 5:30 p.m.

Colombia
2da. Entrada Las Colinas, 1 cuadra arriba, 1/2 cuadra al lago, Casa No. 97, Managua
Tel: (505) 2-76-2149 / 0864
Fax: (505) 2-76-0644
E-mail: emanagua@cancilleria.gov.co
Hours: Monday to Friday, 8 a.m. to 1 p.m.

Costa Rica
Repto las Colinas, Calle Prado Ecuestre, No. 304 primera etapa, Managua
Tel: (505) 2-76-1352 / 0115
Fax: (505) 2-76-0115
E-mail: infembcr@cablenet.com.ni
Hours: Monday to Friday, 8 a.m. to 4 p.m.

Cuba
3ra entrada Las Colinas 400 metros arriba y 75 metros al sur, Managua
Tel: (505) 2-76-0742 / 2307 / 0326/ 2299
Fax: (505) 2-76-0166
E-mail: embacuba@embacuba.net.ni
Hours: Monday to Friday, 8 a.m. to 12 p.m. and 2:30 to 4:30 p.m.

Dominican Republic
Las Colinas, Prado Ecuestre No. 100, Managua
Tel: (505) 2-76-2029 / 1607
Fax: (505) 2-76-0654
E-mail, embdom@cablenet.com.ni
Hours: Monday to Friday, 8 a.m. to 2 p.m.

Ecuador
Barrio Bolonia, Sede Central Los Pipitos 1½ c. Oeste, Managua
Tel: (505) 2-68-1098
Fax: (505) 2-66-8081
E-mail: ecuador@ibw.com.ni
Hours: Monday to Friday, 8 a.m. to 2 p.m.

El Salvador
Las Colinas, Av del Campo y Pasaje, Los Cerros No. 142, Managua
Tel: (505) 2-76-0712 / 0160
Fax: (505) 2-76-0711
E-mail: embelsa@cablenet.com.ni
Hours: 8 a.m. to 12 p.m. and 1 p.m. to 4 p.m.

European Union
Carretera Masaya del Colelgio Teresiano 1c. al Este, frente a la Clínica Tiscapa, Managua
Tel: (505) 2-70-4499
Fax: (505) 2-70-4484
E-mail: delegation-nicaragua@cec.eu.int
Hours: Monday to Thursday, 8 a.m. to 12:30 p.m. and 2 p.m. to 5:30 p.m.; Friday, 8 a.m. to 1 p.m.

Finland
Edificio el Centro, 2do piso. Avenida de las Naciones Unidas, Managua
Tel: (505) 2-78-1216 / 1218
Fax: (505) 2-66-3416
E-mail: sanomat.mgu@formin.fi
Hours: Monday, 1 p.m. to 3 p.m.; Tuesday to Thursday, 9 a.m. to 3 p.m.; Friday, 9 a.m. to 12 p.m.

Join VIVA on Facebook. Fan "VIVA Travel Guides Nicaragua."

Embassies and Consulates

France
Reparto El Carmen Iglesia 1 1/2c. abajo, Bolonia, Managua
Tel: (505) 2-22-6210 / 6615
Fax: (505) 2-68-5630 / 5475
E-mail, info@ambafrance.ni.org
Hours: 7:30 a.m to 12:30 p.m, 1:30 p.m a 4:30 p.m

Germany
De la Rotonda El Güegüense 1 1/2 c. al lago, contiguo Optica Nicaragüense, Managua
Tel: (505) 2-66-3917 / 3918 / 7500 / 7944
Fax: (505) 2-66-7667
E-mail: alemania@cablenet.com.ni
Hours: Monday to Friday, 9 a.m. to 12 p.m., Wednesday closed to the public.

Guatemala
Km. 11 y 1/2 Carretera a Masaya, Managua
Tel: (505) 2-79-9834 / 9609
Fax: (505) 2-79-9610
E-mail: embanic@minex.gob.gt
Hours: Monday to Friday, 9 a.m. to 1 p.m.

Honduras
Reparto Las Colinas, Paseo Ecuestre, No. 298, Managua
Tel: (505) 2-76-2406
Fax: (505) 2-76-1998 / 2524
E-mail: miespino@yahoo.com/embahonduras@yahoo.es
Hours: Monday to Friday, 8 a.m. to 2 p.m.

Italy
Reparto Bolonia, De la Rotonda "El Güegüense" 1c. al Lago 10 vrs. A bajo., Managua
Tel: (505) 2-66-6486 / 2961 / 2918 / 4319
Fax: (505) 2-66-3987
E-mail: ambasciata.managua@esteri.it
Hours: Monday, Tuesday, Thursday and Friday, 7:45 a.m. to 2:30 p.m.

Japan
Rotonda el Güegüense 1c. abajo, 1c. al lago, Residencial Bolonia, Managua
Tel: (505) 2-66-8668 ex. 71
Fax: (505) 2-66-8566
E-mail: embjpnic@ibw.com.ni
Hours: Monday to Friday, 8 a.m. to 12 p.m. and 2 p.m. to 5 p.m.

Mexico
Km. 4 1/2 Carretera a Masaya, 25 varas Arriba, Altamira, Managua
Tel: (505) 2-78-4919 ext. 21
Fax: (505) 2-78-2886 / 9578
E-mail: embamex@turbonett.com.ni
Hours: Monday to Friday, 8 a.m. to 1 p.m. and 2:30 p.m. to 5 p.m.

Netherlands
Km. 5 carretera Masaya. Del Colegio Teresiano 1 cuadra sur, 1 cuadra oeste, Managua
Tel: (505) 2-76-8630 / 2-76-8643 / 2-70-4482
Fax: (505) 2-70-0399
E-mail: mng@minbuza.nl
Hours: Monday to Thursday, 8 a.m. to 4:30 p.m.; Friday, 8 a.m. to 2 p.m.

Panama
Reparto Mántica, del Cuartel General de Bomberos 1 cuadra abajo, Casa No. 93, Managua
Tel: (505) 2-66-8633
Fax: (505) 2-66-8633
E-mail: embdpma@yahoo.com
Hours: Monday to Friday, 8:30 a.m. to 1:30 p.m.

Peru
Las Cumbres, casa no. D-13, Managua
Tel: (505) 2-66-8678 / 8677
Fax: (505) 2-66-1408
E-mail: eccarrillo42@hotmail.com
Hours: Monday to Friday, 9 a.m. to 2 p.m.

Russia
Las Colinas, calle Vista Alegre, casa N° 214, Managua
Tel: (505) 2-76-0462 / 0131 / 0374 / 0131
Fax: (505) 2-76-0179
E-mail: rossia@cablenet.com.ni
Hours: Monday to Thursday, 8 a.m. to 12:30 p.m. and 2:30 p.m. to 6:30 p.m.; Friday, 8 a.m. to 2 p.m.

Sweden
Rotonda El Güegüense, 1 cuadra al lago, 2 1/2 cuadras abajo, Managua
Tel: (505) 2-55-8400
Fax: (505) 2-66-6778
E-mail: ambassaden.managua@sida.se
Hours: Monday to Thursday, 8 a.m. to 12:30 p.m. and 1:30 p.m. to 5 p.m.; Friday, 8 a.m. to 1 p.m.

Switzerland
BANPRO Las Palmas 1 cuadra al lago, casa esquinera a mano izquierda, Managua
Tel: (505) 2-66-3010 / 7328
Fax: (505) 2-66-6697
E-mail: managua@sdc.net,
Hours: Monday to Friday, 8 a.m. to 4:30 p.m.

Find the best price on a flight to Nicaragua: vivatravelguides.com/flights/

Spain

Avenida Central #13 - Las Colinas, Managua Tel: (505) 2-76-0966 / 0967
Fax: (505) 2-76-0937
E-mail: embespni@correo.mae.es
Hours: Monday to Friday, 8 a.m. to 1:30 p.m.

United Kingdom

The British Embassy in Managua closed in 2004; the British Embassy in Costa Rica now covers Nicaragua as well. The United Kingdom maintains an honorary consul in Managua:

Dr. José Evenor Taboada, Taboada & Asociados, Avenida Bolivar # 1947, del hospital Militar 1 cuadra al Lago
Tel: (505) 2-54-5454 /3839
Fax: (505) 2-54-5295
E-mail: jetaboada@consortiumlegal.com.

United States of America

Km. 5 ½ Carretera Sur, Frente al Parque de "las Piedrecitas," Managua
Tel: (505) 2-52-7100 / 7317 / 7515
Fax: (505) 2-52-7300
E-mail: EmbassyInfo@state.gov
Hours: Monday to Friday, 7:30 a.m. and 4:15 p.m.

good idea to keep your insurance details in an email account so you can access them wherever you are, even if someone steals your bags. Updated: Mar 11, 2009.

Visa Information

If you plan to travel in Nicaragua, make sure your passport is valid for six months after the date you plan to arrive in country. When you arrive, Nicaraguan border authorities will ask you to present a valid passport, a return ticket to the country of origin or residence, and perhaps, depending on how long you plan to stay, a visa inside your passport.

Even if you are not required to have a visa, you ought to get a Nicaraguan tourist card for $5. These cards can usually be purchased for 30-90 days; be sure to request the appropriate amount of time when you make your purchase.

While traveling in Nicaragua it is important to carry valid proof of your identity on you at all times. Such documentation might include: a permanent residency card, a temporary residency card, a valid passport or travel documents with entry stamps.

Note that Nicaragua takes part in the Central American Border Control Agreement (CA-4). Under the agreement, tourists are allowed to travel between participating countries (El Salvador, Guatemala, Honduras, and Nicaragua) for up to 90 days, without completing entry or exit forms at border checkpoints. Travelers who exceed the 90-day limit will be fined. However, it is possible for you to get a 30-day extension if you apply before your 90-day limit expires. Updated: Mar 09, 2009.

Tourist Visas

Nicaragua has recently thrown open its doors, and now citizens from any country in the world can travel in Nicaragua for 90 days without a tourist visa. Granted, if you are a citizen of a North American or European country, you did not need a tourist visa before, but now your Nepalese and Eritrean friends can tag along without a visa, as well.

If you would like to spend more than 90 days in the country, you have several options for prolonging your stay. First, you can apply for some sort of visa that grants temporary residency. Your second option is to renew your visitor's pass at the Immigration Office in Managua; technically the officers there can deny you an extension, but usually they will grant you up to 90 additional days in 30 day increments.

The third option, and one which is quite popular with long-term visitors, is to simply leave the country for a few days and then re-enter to receive a fresh 90-day stamp in your passport. In the past, you could do this at either border, but now that Nicaragua and Honduras are treated as a single entity for visa purposes, your only option is to cross the border into Costa Rica. The law states that you must be out of the country for 72 hours, though it's possible that you will be let back into Nicaragua on the same day that you exit. You can continue doing this indefinitely to prolong your time in the country. It's important to note that immigration regulations do change frequently, so it's worth checking with a Nicaraguan consulate before you finalize your plans. Updated: Jun 11, 2009.

Student and Volunteer Visas

Students and volunteer workers are usually eligible for temporary resident visas, which are typically granted in one-year increments.

The requirements for such a visa change frequently and vary greatly depending on which immigration official reviews your file. As a general rule, however, you will need a medical certificate, a police background check, proof of financial self-sufficiency, and a letter from the organization you'll be working with or school you'll be attending. All of these will have to be translated into Spanish, notarized, and stamped with an apostille. Assembling these documents and getting them modified to the immigration office's liking is best done before you leave home, even if you plan to make the actual visa application in Managua. Before starting on the process, however, it is essential to get in touch with a Nicaraguan consulate or embassy to get the most up-to-date information. Updated: Jun 10, 2009.

Work Visas

Work visas are difficult to come by in Nicaragua. With the country's stratospheric unemployment rate, it is very hard for foreigners to find work here, and even harder to find work that isn't under the table. To qualify for a work visa, you have to prove that you provide some service that a Nicaraguan can not. Very few gringos in Nicaragua, even the longtime residents, have such visas; many run their own businesses and have permanent resident visas, or they have retired and stay on with a pensioner visa. Those lucky people who do get work visas are usually employed by international aid organizations or multinational corporations, and their employers typically handle most of the practicalities. Updated: Jun 15, 2009.

Getting To and Away From Nicaragua

There are three possible ways to enter and leave Nicaragua: by plane, by road from Costa Rica or Honduras, and by boat from Costa Rica and El Salvador. Although there are plans to build a railway through the length of Central America, currently there are no rail connections between Nicaragua and the neighboring countries. Updated: Mar 11, 2009.

BY AIR

Nicaragua has two international airports, though in all likelihood you will be flying into (or out of) the Augusto C. Sandino International Airport in Managua. There is a small airstrip in Granada and from here light aircrafts occasionally fly to San Jose in Costa Rica, technically making the location an international airport.

The airline TACA offers flights between Nicaragua and all the other countries in Central America. Outside of the local area there are very few international flight routes that serve Nicaragua.

There are a couple of direct flights a day from various cities within the USA. If you are flying from any other destination in Europe, Australia, or New Zealand, you will have to change at a North or Central American hub, most likely in Miami or Houston, as there are no direct flights.

Since there is not a great deal of demand, flights into Nicaragua are generally expensive. Nicaragua also charges a $5 entry tax, payable on arrival, and a $32 exit tax that is payable at check-in. Updated: Mar 09, 2009.

BY LAND

Getting into Nicaragua over land is usually an easy process. On foot, you will be granted entry into the country as long as you have an up-to-date passport and $7. You'll have a short wait in a queue, unless you happen to arrive at the same time as an international bus when the queues become much longer. Crossing the border on an international bus is also an easy process as the driver will help you with any problems you may have.

If you intend on taking a motor vehicle across the border, this is a longer process; you shouldn't have any problems as long as you have proof of ownership and $20 (keep the receipt as you will need it when you leave the country).

Of the three possible border crossings between Nicaragua and Costa Rica it is possible to drive across only one, as the other two involve river trips. The only road crossing is at Peñas Blancas.

There are three major road crossings into Honduras. See the Border Crossings section on p. 34 for more information. Updated: Mar 09, 2009.

BY BUS

Due to the high prices of international flights, many visitors choose to cross the Nicaraguan border by bus. Two companies—Ticabus (www.ticabus.com) and Transnica (www.transnica.com)—operate fast, reliable, and reasonably priced international buses that service Nicaragua.

From Managua there are regular bus routes to Tegucigalpa, Choluteca, and San Pedro Sula in

---

Find the best price on a flight to Nicaragua: vivatravelguides.com/flights/

Honduras; San Salvador in El Salvador; San Jose in Costa Rica; Panama City in Panama; Guatemala City in Guatemala; and as far as Tapachula in Mexico. The buses that operate on these routes are modern, complete with air-conditioning, toilets, TVs, and they make regular stops for food. Buses are a great way to travel quickly to and from Nicaragua without spending a fortune—as such, they are very popular and should be booked in advance.

If you have more time, then a cheaper and possibly more fun option is to ride a local bus to the border, walk across, and then continue your journey again by bus. Although they are undoubtedly less expensive, local buses can take considerably longer, be much less comfortable and mean that you must cross the border without assistance (which the international bus drivers provide). Updated: Mar 09, 2009.

BY BOAT

Although there are several posible ways to enter and leave Nicaragua by boat, only one is truly feasable for the average traveler—taking the ferry which runs several times daily along the Río Frío between San Carlos and Los Chiles in Costa Rica. The Border Crossings section has details about this trip.

The two other ways of entering Nicaragua by boat are rather unrealistic for all but the most adventurous and wealthy travelers since the trips are complicated and expensive. The first is in the far southeast of the country where some of the higher-priced fishing lodges can organize river trips between San Juan de Nicaragua (formerly known as San Juan del Norte and, before that, Greytown) in Nicaragua and Barra in Costa Rica. The second is in the far northwest of the country, where you can hire a small boat to make the four hour, sometimes treacherous, journey across the Gulf of Fonseca, between Potosí and La Union in El Salvador. Updated: Apr 14, 2009.

Entry and Departure Taxes

Nicaragua charges a fee for all tourists entering and leaving the country.

BY AIR

Foreigners flying into Nicaragua have to pay a $5 tax on arrival. There is also a hefty $32 departure tax which is payable when you check in. Although some airlines include this tax in their ticket prices, most do not, so don't be surprised if you are asked to pay the fee at the airline counter.

BY LAND

Entry and departure taxes for foreigners who visit Nicaragua by land are also steep compared to other Central American countries: foreigners have to pay a $7 entry tax and a $2 departure tax. Among the neighboring countries, Costa Rica does not levy either an entry or exit tax and Honduras allows visitors to exit for free but charges a $3 entry tax. Updated: Mar 09, 2009.

Border Crossings

COSTA RICA

The main border crossing between Nicaragua and Costa Rica is at Peñas Blancas, southeast of Rivas and San Juan del Sur. The crossing is the busiest in Nicaragua, and is open 6 a.m.-8 p.m. every day. The procedure is basically the same on both sides of the border; you have to fill out a form and pay a fee to receive your exit stamp, then you cross the border and pay for an entry stamp. Although this process sounds straightforward, there are hassles going in both directions. Entering Nicaragua, immigration and custom officials are particularly eager to stop narcotics smuggling, so you can expect lots of drug-sniffing dogs and bag searches. Costa Rican officials, meanwhile, work very hard to stem the flow of undocumented immigrants and migrant workers from Nicaragua, erecting roadblocks on the Pan-American and searching every vehicle that passes through. Usually the border crossing can be done in an hour, but around holidays, when thousands of Nicaraguans move across the border, it can take the better part of a day.

If all of this still sounds too efficient for your taste, you can also cross the border at Los Chiles. Leaving Nicaragua, your first stop will be the immigration office in San Carlos. You will have to wait for a few hours to get your exit stamp, and then go to the dock to get one of the two ferries that leaves every day. The trip takes about an hour and costs $10. When you arrive in Los Chiles, you must go to the Costa Rican immigration office to get your passport stamped. Going in the other direction, you need to get a stamp at the immigration office in Los Chiles and then board the boat. Upon arrival at San Carlos, you must stop at the immigration office to pay your entrance fee and get stamped again. Updated: May 04, 2009.

Join VIVA on Facebook. Fan "VIVA Travel Guides Nicaragua."

HONDURAS

There are three main border crossings between Nicaragua and Honduras. The procedure is roughly the same at all of them: you must stop by the immigration office of the country you are leaving and pay to get an exit stamp, then walk across the border, fill out a form, pay a fee, and receive your entry stamp. The busiest crossing is at Guasaule, north of Chinandega on the Pan-American. This crossing is open 24 hours, but it can be quite slow-going due to the heavy truck traffic and ongoing roadwork on the Nicaraguan side. Still, this is the best crossing if you are traveling along the Pacific coast, and there is frequent public transportation between the border and Chinandega.

Travelers making their way between Tegucigalpa and Managua will be better off using the crossing at Los Manos. The border is open from 6 a.m. to 6 p.m., but public transportation stops running after about 4 p.m. The crossing can be reached from Danlí in Honduras and Ocotal in Nicaragua. Nearby, there is a little-used crossing at El Espino, which is also open from 6 a.m. to 6 p.m. The crossing is reached from San Marcos or Choluteca on the Honduran side and Somoto on the Nicaraguan side. As at Los Manos, public transportation stops at around 4 p.m.

There is, at least theoretically, an additional border crossing on the Río Coco near Leimus, but it is hardly ever used by travelers. There is no public transportation, and the nearest towns on both sides of the border are hours away. If you do cross at Leimus, you will need to get your passport stamped in Puerto Lempira (Honduras) and Puerto Cabezas (Nicaragua). Updated: May 05, 2009.

Getting Around

Getting around Nicaragua is generally not a difficult prospect. Although the country is the largest in Central America, most of the main tourist destinations are concentrated in a relatively small strip of land along the Pacific Coast. The distances in this region are not overwhelming and all the major places of interest are connected by a network of relatively good roads—by Central American standards—including the Pan-American Highway, which runs the entire length of the country.

Nicaragua has an extensive local bus service that takes advantage of the good roads; you can also rent a car, or even bicycle around the Pacific region with relative ease.

On the Caribbean side of the country the situation is very different; getting around by car or bus can be extremely difficult, especially during the rainy season. The only serious way to get to or around this region is by plane or by boat, along Nicaragua's many rivers and lakes. Updated: Mar 11, 2009.

BY BICYCLE

Road cycling can be a rewarding way to travel in Nicaragua, but it is imperative that cyclists take precautions, as the few paved roads tend to be the main arteries between cities and can have dangerous amounts of traffic. All cyclists are required by law to wear a helmet, and would be wise to avoid cycling at night. If you are going to ride along roads, it is advised to attach a mirror so that you can see the traffic overtaking you.

If you intend on bringing your own bike to Nicaragua it is sensible to have proof of ownership with you to ease the customs process. This can be complex depending on the officer; if you are charged, ask to speak to a superior and find out exactly what you are paying for. You should also bring all spares for any repairs that you may have to do, as imported parts are extremely hard to find. Most towns will have a bike shop where basic repairs can be covered, however, it is often best to do everything you can do yourself. The best way to secure your bike at night is to take it into your hotel room with you, something that many places will let you do.

Renting a bike is a great, cheap way to explore Nicaragua's countryside and keep fit at the same time. Bikes are widely available for hire in all tourist hot spots from rental stores, as well as many hotels and hostels. As with all rented bikes, the equipment may be old and not in the best condition; check your bike thoroughly, and if you are not satisfied, find another. Updated: Mar 11, 2009.

BY AIR

Although there are not many domestic airline routes in Nicaragua, flying can dramatically reduce your travel time, especially if you intend on heading to the Corn Islands or anywhere on the Caribbean Coast. Air travel is a convenient and affordable way to access these areas of tropical beauty, which normally would take over a day and a half to get to overland.

Find the best price on a flight to Nicaragua: vivatravelguides.com/flights/

Getting Around

La Costeña operates internal flights within Nicaragua. Most of these domestic routes originate or terminate at Managua International Airport, where the domestic airline is housed in offices just to the west of the international terminal.

As the planes used on these domestic routes are very small, it is always worth booking as early as possible. Some flights fill up quickly, and showing up early to confirm is always a good idea, since there is a chance you may find that your seat has been given away. It is also advisable to keep all vital items on your person, as weight restrictions may require some baggage to be left behind.

Note that Nicaragua has a domestic departure tax of $2. This fee is payable at the airport in either dollars or córdobas.

As of February 2008 these are the daily flight routes, times and prices for both of Nicaragua's domestic airlines. Although these details are accurate at time of writing, flight frequency and prices will undoubtedly change as demand fluctuates.

NOTE: While Atlantic Airlines used to provide domestic air service, as of September 2009, they have indefinitely ceased operations.

La Costeña:
Tel: 263 2142
URL: www.lacostena.com.ni

FROM MANAGUA:

Bluefields (1 hr): One-Way: $82.46 / Round Trip: $126.86. Daily at 6:00 a.m. & 10:00 a.m., Monday – Saturday at 6:30 a.m. & 2:30 p.m.

Corn Islands (1 hr 30 mins via Bluefields): One-Way: $106.74 / Round Trip: $164.21. Daily at 6:30 a.m. & 2:00 p.m.

San Carlos (45 mins): One-Way: $75.53 / Round Trip: $116.19. Monday – Saturday at 8:30 a.m. Sunday – Friday at 1:30 p.m.

Las Minas - Siuna, Bonanza, Rosita (55 mins): One-Way: $96.33 / Round Trip: $148.21. Daily at 9:00 a.m. Check ahead as limited demand on this route can lead to cancelations.

Bilwi (Puerto Cabezas) (1 hr 30 mins): One-Way: $96.72 / Round Trip: $148.80. Daily at 6:30 a.m. & 10:00 a.m. Monday – Saturday at 2.30 p.m., Monday, Wednesday & Friday at 10:30 a.m. (2 hr 10 mins, via Bluefields).

Waspám (1 hr 30 mins): One-Way: $103.66 / Round Trip: $159.47. Tuesday, Thursday & Saturday at 10:00 a.m.

FROM BLUEFIELDS:

Managua (50 mins): One-Way: $82.46 / Round Trip: $126.86. Daily at 8:40 a.m. & 4:10 p.m. Tuesday, Thursday & Saturday at 11:10 a.m., Monday, Wednesday & Friday at 1:10 p.m., Monday – Saturday at 7:10 a.m.

Corn Island (20 mins): One-Way: $64.16 / Round Trip: $98.71. Daily at 7:40 a.m. and 3:10 p.m.

Bilwi (Puerto Cabezas) (1 hr): One-Way: $96.33 / Round Trip: $148.21. Monday, Wednesday & Friday at 11:00 a.m.

FROM CORN ISLAND:

Managua via Bluefields (1 hr 20 mins): One-Way: $106.74 / Round Trip: $164.21. Daily at 8:10 a.m. & 3:40 p.m.

Bluefields (20 mins): One-Way: $64.16 / Round Trip: $98.71. Daily at 8:10 a.m. & 3:40 p.m.

FROM BILWI (PUERTO CABEZAS):

Managua (1 hr 20 mins): One-Way: $96.72 / Round Trip: $148.80. Daily at 8:20 a.m., 12:20 p.m. & 4:10 p.m., Monday, Wednesday & Friday at 12:10 p.m. (2 hrs, via Bluefields).

Bluefields (50 mins): One-Way: $96.33 / Round Trip: $148.21. Monday, Wednesday & Friday at 12:10 p.m.

FROM SAN CARLOS:

Managua (40 mins): One-Way: $75.53 / Round Trip: $116.19. Monday – Saturday at 9:25 a.m., Sunday – Friday at 2:25 p.m.

FROM LAS MINAS - SIUNA, BONANZA, ROSÍTA:

Managua (1 hr): One-Way: $82.46 / Round Trip: $126.86. Daily at 10:30 a.m. Check ahead as limited demand on this route can lead to cancelations.

FROM WAPSÁM:

Managua (1hr 30 mins): One-Way: $103.66 / Round Trip: $159.47. Tuesday, Thursday & Saturday at 11:40 a.m. Updated: Apr 17, 2009.

BY BUS

Public buses are the main means of getting around Nicaragua and, if you are traveling independently, you will undoubtedly find yourself crammed into an ex-US school bus at

---

Join VIVA on Facebook. Fan "VIVA Travel Guides Nicaragua."

Getting Around

some point while in the country. The so-called "chicken bus" is usually a cheap and efficient way to get between towns; city buses themselves are often dangerous and it is always recommended that you take a taxi instead.

On domestic routes, it is impossible to reserve seats or buy a ticket before getting on the bus, and seating is allocated on a first-come-first-served basis. Buses will often cruise around town before leaving in an effort to try to find more passengers. However, it is always worth finding the "bus station," usually a large and busy lot next to a market, as embarking at a main stop will greatly increase your chance of finding an available seat. On the Pacific side of the country, regular buses run between most major towns, stopping frequently whenever anyone wants to get on or off.

The chicken buses are cheap and you should expect to pay around $1 an hour on local buses. Although you may get a paper ticket on longer journeys (which you should hang on to), don't be surprised if you are not issued one. Buses advertised as direct or express will take less time and make less stops, but will cost a little more.

As Nicaraguan buses have no luggage space underneath and get very busy, baggage has to go on the roof, or behind the back seats. Try to sit at the rear of the bus to keep an eye on your belongings. Make sure the bags which go on the roof have no valuables in them.

MINIBUSES

If you do not fancy using the extensive chicken bus network, another option is to travel by minibus. These 10- to 15-seater vans operate on many of the country's major routes, leave when they are full, and are a fast and safe way to get between towns. The only disadvantages of this form of transportation is the cost (around 25 percent higher then regular buses) and the often cramped conditions as drivers will pack in as many people as possible.

Transportation aimed solely for the tourist market is slowly appearing in Nicaragua and takes the form of shuttles operating between major points of interest. These luxury minibuses are a very convenient way to get around, but are substantially more expensive than using local transport. Updated: Mar 11, 2009.

BY TRAIN

Nicaragua's first train tracks were laid in 1878 and by 1940, the rail system had grown to over 380 kilometers (236 mi) of track. Throughout the second half of the 20th century, both passenger numbers and freight transportation declined. As falling demand met skyrocketing costs—natural disasters such as earthquakes and floods caused constant (and expensive) damage to the tracks —the national rail company, Ferrocarril del Pacifico, became increasingly reliant on government subsidies in order to survive.

In 1993, the Nicaraguan government made the decision to close most lines and sell the track for scrap. Since 2001 no trains have operated in Nicaragua. There are no domestic rail services in Nicaragua and no international train services into the country. Updated: Mar 09, 2009.

BY TAXI

Taxis in Nicaragua are an inexpensive way to travel. In towns and cities, cabs are often not only the the most convenient, but in many cases, the cheapest and safest way to get around. If you are in a group, taxis also offer a reasonably priced, hassle-free way to travel between cities. If you take a longer trip in a cab, make sure to pick a taxi which is in good condition. Agree on a price before you start the journey; a good rule of thumb is to plan on paying around $10 for every 20 kilometers (12 mi). None of Nicaragua's taxis have meters, which means you should negotiate a fee before you get in. Unless you can pass as Nicaraguan, avoiding paying a vastly inflated price will be difficult, as in all likelihood the driver will try to overcharge you (although doubling the price may only cost you an extra dollar). Price inflation becomes more of a problem in areas where taxi drivers are regularly in contact with tourists, such as Managua, Leon, Granada, and at international border crossings. It is always a good idea to find out from a local how much your fare should be (in many towns there are set rates), and remember that in Nicaraguan cities, taxis are abundant. If one taxi is too expensive, try another.

Most taxis that you can hire on the street operate as collectives, which means they may stop to pick up other people heading to the same, or nearby locations. If you don't want to share your taxi, you will be charged extra. Taxi fees are usually paid per person, not per taxi, so when negotiating the price for a group of people, make sure that the price you agree on is for everyone, not a fee for each person. Having the exact money to pay your fare avoids problems, as taxi drivers don't

---

Find the best price on a flight to Nicaragua: vivatravelguides.com/flights/

carry much change and may "confuse" larger payments with tips. Updated: Mar 09, 2009.

BY HITCHHIKING

As there are not many privately-owned vehicles in Nicaragua, many people use hitchhiking as a means of getting around, especially in the countryside. Hitchhiking anywhere in the world involves certain risks and, although the practice is common and relatively safe in Nicaragua, use common sense and take all possible precautions: travel in a group (single females are advised not to hitch) and ride in the back of pick-ups, rather than inside vehicles.

Although most Nicaraguans are too polite to pose the question, you may occasionally be asked to contribute a small amount of money towards gas (which is expensive). If you are not asked, then the polite thing to do is to offer $1 or so per person, especially if the trip is a long one. This money will usually be refused, although the gesture will be appreciated. Updated: Mar 11, 2009.

BY CAR

Nicaragua has one of the best road networks in Central America. That said, the country's road network is not in anything like what most Westerners would consider to be good condition.

The only paved roads in the country run between large towns in the Pacific and Central regions. Away from these major routes, and in the Caribbean region, the quality of roads deteriorates quickly and public transport is recommended.

Driving in Nicaragua can be dangerous, especially if you are not accustomed to the unique driving style of Latin Americans. If you do choose to rent a car, make sure you stay constantly alert to avoid potholes, random objects blocking the road, and especially the other, sometimes erratic, drivers. It is not a good idea to drive at night when the lack of visibility and occasional drunk driver makes the roads exponentially more hazardous. In larger cities, driving only during the day is especially important as criminals often target cars at night.

Extensive driving through Managua, Estelí, and León are probably best avoided day or night, as complicated one-way systems can act as traps for policemen looking for bribes.

It is easy to rent a car in most major cities and airports (rentals at Managua airport cost around 15 percent more than elsewhere): all that is required is that you be over age 25, have a credit card, and a driver's license. Rentals are relatively cheap and cost as little as $20 per day, including all taxes and mandatory insurance—however, if you intend on heading off major roads, or are driving in the rainy season, you will need a 4X4. Such vehicles cost between $35 and $120 per day.

Before you drive away, check you have all your paperwork and that the car is in good condition. Updated: Mar 11, 2009.

BY BOAT

With so much of Nicaragua covered by lakes and rivers, it is no surprise that in many areas of the country, boats are the best way to get around.

Regular public ferry services operate on Lago de Nicaragua and throughout the Caribbean region. These boats provide a cheap, reliable, interesting, and often beautiful way to get to some of the country's more remote areas.

On the lakes, along the Pacific Coast and throughout the Caribbean region, small motor boats called pangas are often available for private hire. These pangas will give you a lot of freedom but are much more expensive than public transport.

Lago de Nicaragua has been an important navigable body of water for a long time, and traveling by boat is the only way to get to the popular tourist destinations of Isla de Ometepe and the Solentiname Islands. Along with the hundreds of pangas that are available for private hire, there are currently several cheap ferry services that operate the following regular services on the lake:

Granada to San Carlos via Isla de Ometepe:

This service runs twice a week in each direction (weather permitting). The journey takes 13 hours in total (four hours between Granada and Ometepe and nine hours between Ometepe and San Carlos). The ferry is old and doesn't provide a particularly pleasant ride.

San Jorge to Moyogalpa (on Isla de Ometepe): This is the quickest and most convenient way to get to the Isla de Ometepe. Regular services throughout the day make the hour-long crossing using either ferries (capable of taking cars) or smaller boats (lanchas). If the weather is good, then this is a very scenic cruise. However, if the lake is rough, it can be very unpleasant in a lancha and you might want to wait for the larger, more stable ferry.

Join VIVA on Facebook. Fan "VIVA Travel Guides Nicaragua."

San Carlos to the Archipelago de Solentiname: These boats run in a loop from San Carlos to the island of San Fernando, then on to Mancarrón and back to San Carlos on Tuesdays and Fridays. From San Carlos there are also regular services along the Río Frío to Los Chiles in Costa Rica and down the Río San Juan to El Castillo and San Juan del Norte.

Caribbean Region

On the east side of the country, as the roads that exist are poor and often impassable, river transport is the most reliable way to get around. Bluefields is the transport hub. From there, daily services run to El Rama and Tasbapauni, and twice weekly services go to the Caribbean island of Big Corn.

The best way to explore this region is in a small motor boat. These are readily available for private hire in the towns of Waspám, Bilwi, and Bluefields, and can be found in many other smaller settlements. Privately hired pangas are much more expensive than public transport but give you complete freedom and allow you to explore areas that would otherwise be impossible to get to. Updated: Mar 11, 2009.

Tours

With its culturally-rich colonial cities and a wide variety of scenery, from spectacular volcanoes to beautiful beaches, Nicaragua has a great deal to offer tourists. The diverse country can be explored independently, on an inclusive tour, or through a combination of solo traveling and taking advantage of well-chosen, short excursions.

The main advantage of taking a tour is the ease and security with which you can enjoy some of what this country has to offer. Itineraries organized by local experts allow you to experience a great deal in a relatively short space of time, while eliminating the hassle of doing the organizing yourself. This is even more useful if you don't speak much Spanish. In some cases, particularly on the Caribbean side of the country, organized tours can provide access to places that would be almost impossible to get to independently.

It can also be scary waiting until you arrive in the country to make travel arrangements. To take off some of the pressure of planning, many tour operators offer all inclusive packages where everything from the breakfast time to daily activities is pre-arranged for you. These trips can usually be booked before you leave home and can accommodate independent and group travelers

These comforts and advantages come at a price—an organized tour will undoubtedly cost more than arranging all the elements of your trip independently. Also, booking any tour from outside the country will always be more expensive than arranging things in Nicaragua through one of the many tour agencies that operate in all the major cities. As a general rule, the closer you are to the place you want to see, or the activity you want to take part in, the cheaper the trip will be.

Nicaragua has a great variety of tours on offer that attempt to cover all aspects of this varied country. It is worth spending some time to figure out which tour best suits your individual requirements. Tours range in length from one-day excursions to several-week organized itineraries that include all accommodation, food, drinks and transport.

Before paying for any tour, try to find out the exact details of the trip. Ascertain exactly what you are paying for. Does the tour include food? Refreshments? All your transport? An English-speaking guide? Entrance fees to any museums or national parks you may be visiting? Also find out how many people will be joining you on your tour. In general, the larger the party, the cheaper the tour will be. However, a big group may decrease the quality of your trip. Updated: Aug 12, 2009.

DAY TOURS

You can arrange day trips covering a vast range of activities in all major Nicaraguan cities and tourist hot-spots. Popular day trips include cultural city tours and visits to the more impressive volcanoes. Day tours are also useful ways to take part in activities that would be hard, or impossible, without guides and specialist equipment, such as volcano boarding or zip-lining.

CANOPY TOURS

Ready, set, jet—Nicaragua boasts numerous zip-line courses, allowing travelers to take flight and soak in the scenery while zinging across cable lines strapped to trees. A popular canopy tour is in Cutirre, the beautiful privately-owned coffee planation situated on the eastern slopes of the Mombacho volcano, about nine miles south of Granada. Zip-liners swing between 17 platforms, engulfed by the massive trees below. The canopy offers impressive views of Volcán Concepción and Isla de la Zapatera, located within

Find the best price on a flight to Nicaragua: vivatravelguides.com/flights/

the freshwater Lake Nicaragua—the largest lake in Central America.

Not afraid of water? Lob yourself over the Tiscapa Lagoon, located in Managua. Travelers fly 70 meters from the top down to the shore along three long cables, giving you plenty of time to take in the beautiful views of the lagoon and city below.

Explore sea to sky in the Pacific surfer town of San Juan del Sur. Perched in the foothills behind the city, Da Flying Frog canopy line is the country's longest at 2.5 kilometers (1.55 mi). Its 16 cables allow fliers to zig-zag their way down the bird and monkey-filled hills, offering gorgeous views of the town's crescent bay. Updated: Aug 14, 2009.

CITY TOURS

Cultural and historical day tours usually run seven days a week around the three most visited cities: Managua, León, and Granada. Organized tours are a safe and easy way to get a good overview, visit the major attractions, and find out a great deal about Nicaragua's most important cities. If you are not going to spend much time in these places, then a tour is a good way to see a lot, quickly; if you have more time then the tours can serve as useful introductions.

There is no shortage of agencies offering city tours with prices and quality that can vary greatly, so shop around to find a guide who speaks your native language and can offer the service you're looking for.

VOLCANO TOURS

Since volcanoes are a highlight of Nicaragua's natural wonders, tours to see them are very popular. Getting to many of the country's spectacular volcanoes is impossible without a guide or your own transportation—a tour can be an easy way to gain access to them. The Mombacho and Masaya Volcanoes are both very easily accessible from either Granada and Managua and make great day trips.

Mombacho is also one of the many places in Nicaragua where you can go on exhilarating zip-lining canopy tours. Another popular alternative way to visit a volcano is by taking part in the strange, but fun, adventure sport of volcano boarding. Updated: Mar 09, 2009.

MULTI-DAY TOURS

Many international and Nicaraguan-based agencies offer multi-day (mostly inclusive) tours that allow you to get a great taste of this country. The most popular tours are the overview, "best of" tours that can last between five and fourteen days and take you around the highlights of the country. These trips usually include visits to the colonial cities of León and Granada, the market town of Masaya, several volcanoes, and possibly one of the country's beaches. Longer tours allow you to see the country in more depth and may include visits to the island of Ometepe and the less accessible Caribbean region.

As well as general overview tours there are a great deal of specialist tours that focus on individual aspects of this varied country. You can find multi-day trips throughout Nicaragua that are based around bird-watching, walking, volcano hiking, archaeology and anthropology, political history, art, jungle, river tours, coffee plantations, kayaking, mountain biking and sailing. Taking part in a specialist tour not only allows you to concentrate your time on what interests you, but also has the advantage of grouping you with like-minded travelers. However, these tours can cost more than doing similar itineraries on your own. Updated: Mar 09, 2009.

Alternative Tourism

Tourism has grown rapidly in Nicaragua and is now its second largest industry. As an alternative to traditional tourism, such as cultural or beach resort tourism, there are now plenty of other options which allow you to see a different side of the country you're visiting, get you closer to the local community and offer you the chance to give something back in the process.

Nicaragua's rich biodiversity attracts many thousands of tourists every year. Eco-tourism has flourished in recent years.

Social and community-based tourism projects are often run by not-for-profit organizations or faith groups and provide short and long term volunteer opportunities for travelers. There are countless opportunities to suit all interests, from TEFL teaching to health education, building community shelters, environmental conservation, and fundraising. URL: www.idealist.org is a good source of info for current projects.

Agro-tourism put visitors in touch with local farmers. This allows farmers to reach out to new potential markets at the same time as

Ecotourism

Soon to surpass Costa Rica as the number one destination for ecotourism, Nicaragua is home to an impressive twenty-five volcanoes, holds 7 percent of the world's biodiversity, boasts the largest rainforest and fresh water lake in Central America, as well as white sand beaches on both the Atlantic and Pacific Oceans.

After years of political instability, Nicaragua is still recovering from its bad reputation, and the numbers of tourists today remain quite low. As a result, the country is an ideal destination to explore uninterrupted: enjoy the outdoors as well as unusual animal and plant species.

Home to 76 protected land areas, eco-tours in Nicaragua can take you to a number of different and unique natural areas. There are numerous packages available at a variety of prices to meet every traveler's needs. Please remember to thoroughly research your tour operators and ask questions before buying to make sure you are getting an eco-tour that takes real steaps to minimize its impact on the environment. All tour operators should follow the International Ecotourism Society's definition of eco-tourism: responsible travel to natural areas that conserves the environment and sustains the well-being of local people. Organized eco-tours are likely to visit the Los Guatuzos Wildlife Refuge, Solentiname Archipelago, Montibelli Wildlife Reserve, El Chocoyero Nature Reserve, Masaya Volcano National Park or the Indo-Maíz Biological Reserve. The low tourist demand drives down the prices for many tours in Nicaragua, making this both a beautiful and inexpensive way to enjoy what this Central American country has to offer. Updated: Mar 16, 2009.

diversifying their income. At CECOCAFEN, a fair trade coffee co-operative in northern Nicaragua, you can have a tour of the farm, learn about coffee harvesting, cook a traditional meal, and even stay overnight. E-mail: turismo@cecocafen.com.

See also V!VA's info on Responsible Tourism in Nicaragua on p. 62. Updated: Jun 11, 2009.

Resort Holidays

In contrast to its southern neighbor, Nicaragua has relatively few resort hotels lining its two coastlines. The only major resort destination in the country is the Montelimar, a massive all-inclusive complex near Pochomil. Most of the country's other beach resorts are located near San Juan del Sur or on the Corn Islands. In general, these places are much lower-key than Montelimar, or indeed, most beach resorts around the world.

Prices at Nicaraguan resorts can fluctuate greatly between low season and high season. An economical alternative to splurging at a resort hotel is to stay at one of the retirement-and-vacation home communities that have sprung up along the Pacific coast. They offer many of the amenities of traditional resorts, such as golf courses, multiple swimming pools and organized activities. Condos in these communities are frequently available to rent, usually by the week. Updated: May 25, 2009.

Sports and Recreation

Unlike most Latin American countries, fútbol (soccer to North Americans) is not Nicaragua's most prominent national sport; you do not need to spend much time in this country to realize that baseball holds the honor. As you travel around the country it is impossible not to notice how important and popular baseball is to Nicaraguans; every town has a baseball diamond or stadium, the largest of which is the 30,000-seater Dennis Martinez National Stadium in Managua. Named after the first Nicaraguan to play in Major League baseball, the stadium is a great place to catch a baseball game and hosts about five per week.

Although fútbol has stayed in baseball's shadow, the sport is gaining popularity in Nicaragua and is widely played. Nicaragua has one of Central America's weakest national teams; they have never qualified for a major tournament. Although the government is making an effort to improve the quality of the national league, FIFA ranks the Nicaraguan team 182nd (in 2008). FC Diriamba is the most popular and successful club team, having won the Primera División de

Nicaragua 26 times. In recent years though, they have developed a fierce rivalry with Real Esteli, and over the last eight years the two teams have shared the title.

It is worth noting that boxing is also a popular sport in Nicaragua; the country has produced several world champions. Most prominent them is Alexis Argüello who was world champion on three occasions. Due in part to his fame as a boxer, Aruello was elected mayor of Managua in November 2008 for a four-year term, before comitting suicide in 2009.

Nicaragua has an extremely varied geography and thus is the perfect setting for a wide variety of outdoor sports. The mountains and volcanoes are great for hiking and biking; while the coastal areas are perfect for swimming, sailing, and surfing. Nicaragua is also becoming popular with golf enthusiasts, and the country has several courses that meet international standards. One of the top spots is the Nejapa Golf and Country Club, located in Managua. Updated: Jul 01, 2009.

Adventure Travel

If swimming inside a smoking volcano, sailing into a hidden coastal bay once inhabited by pirates, or hiking through the rainforest sound like your kind of activities, then look no further than Nicaragua. The wide array of beaches, volcanoes, rainforests, and tropical climate make Nicaragua an ideal location for adventure travel. With nearly a fifth of Nicaragua covered by forest reserves, the country is quickly becoming the hot spot for adventurers. There are a growing number of travel agencies offering various week- to ten-day-long guided tours involving jungle trekking, hiking, surfing, diving, snorkeling, swimming, rafting, kayaking, mountain biking, and horseback riding.

Hiking and Trekking

Nicaragua's abundance of volcanoes and natural reserves makes for numerous hiking opportunities. Trek through cloud and rainforest; enjoy city and ocean panoramas from the slopes; peer into craters; visit coffee plantations; and spot ocelots, macaws, and butterflies. The Pacific lowlands and Central highlands have the largest and best selection of hikes, and there are trails for every skill level throughout the country. Hiring a guide is mandatory in order to access many volcano trails.

PACIFIC LOWLANDS

Here, a chain of volcanoes—dormant and active—runs parallel to the ocean, stretching from north to south. Several are suitable for hikes, including Volcán Telíca. Reach its crater and you may catch a glimpse of boiling lava over 30 meters (100 ft) below. The massive San Cristóbal, (El Viejo to the locals) spews smoke and ash, and provides a challenging climb with outstanding scenery. The squat Volcán Cosigüina, sitting on a peninsula in the far northwest, is a less difficult ascent. From its crater edge you can see the Gulf of Fonseca, Honduras, and El Salvador. Wetland hikes in the area are also rewarding, with swathes of mangrove trees and, if you time it right, flocks of migratory birds. Just half an hour from Managua, you can hike to the smoking Santiago crater in Parque Nacional Volcán Masaya. For a demanding trek, test the steep, rocky trails of Volcán Momotombo. Near Granada, Volcán Mombacho has a wealth of wildlife, including howler and white face monkeys, deer, and endemic salamander. After hiking the barren slopes of young Cerro Negro, run (or ski) down a scree slope to the bottom in several minutes. Guided hikes are offered in the Reserva Silvestre Privada Domitil, a dry tropical rainforest brimming with plants and wildlife. The volcanic cones of Maderas and Concepción that form Isla Ometepe in Lake Cocibolca are popular trekking destinations. Hike dormant, forest-covered Maderas or smoking, dominant Concepción—from banana plantations, up through dense forest—for views of the island, lake and mainland. The top of Chico Largo, a small hill on Ometepe, is a great place to watch the sunset.

CENTRAL HIGHLANDS

Central Nicaragua is home to the country's highest mountain range, the Cordillera Isabella. Hike an extensive set of trails through cloud forest and coffee farms. In the north you'll also find Nicaragua's biggest biosphere reserve, Bosawás. Nearly two million acres in size, this largely uncharted, densely forested area has a host of trails of varying difficulty. The Peñas Blancas Massif, which forms part of the reserve, makes for great sightseeing. It is home to tapirs and pumas. The town of Matagalpa is a good base from which to explore Cerros Apante and El Toro. Cerro El Arenal, located in a natural reserve, has excellent paths and diverse flora and fauna. Near Jinotega, Cerro La Cruz gets plenty of visitors to the cross on its summit. If you hike in the Reserva Natural Miraflor, you can overnight in one of five communities in three different microclimates. Views of neighboring Honduras and El Salvador can be had

Baseball

For over a hundred years, baseball has been the most popular sport in Nicaragua. The country's love for this sport was started by a US retailer named Albert Addlesberg.

Albert had noticed that Caribbean coast residents, then under British occupation, were playing a confusing game, also known in the UK as "cricket." He convinced two local cricket teams to convert to baseball and the country never looked back.

In 1887, Bluefields locals formed two teams called "Southern" and "Four Roses." The first official game was played the following year. While the original teams no longer exist, Nicaraguans founded a team in 1904 that continues to remain popular. Following a strange tradition to name sporting teams after ongoing conflicts, the team was dubbed "Bóer" (the British had just finished fighting the Second Bóer War with residents of South Africa). Later that year the "Japan" and "Russia" teams were also formed, named after the Russo-Japanese War in Manchuria which would eventually lead to the Russian Revolution of 1905.

The arrival of US marines in 1912, during disputes over the building of a Nicaraguan Canal, had a large impact on baseball in the country. The marines brought both their knowledge of and enthusiasm for the sport, kicking off an influx of both foreign players and visiting professional teams. Local interest in the sport increased proportionally, culminating in the creation of La Liga Nicaragüense de Beisbol Profesional (LNBP) in 1956. Unfortunately, the league was disbanded in 1967 due to a lack of funding during the Anastasio Somoza García dictatorship.

The professional league was re-established in 2004. Currently four teams—Indios del Bóer, Tigres del Chinandega, Leones de León and Fieras del San Fernando—compete for the yearly championship.

Over the years, Nicaragua has produced many Major Leaguers, including most notably Dennis Martínez after whom the national stadium is named, and its national team has been amongst the strongest in the world. Updated: Mar 09, 2009.

from Meseta Tisey-Estanzuela, and there's a 36-meter high waterfall and swimming hole at popular Salta Estanzuela. Follow the Río Coco through a more-than-a-kilometer-long canyon at Somoto, where cliff walls stretch as high as 200 meters.

CARIBBEAN LOWLANDS

Hike around the 2.9 square kilometer Little Corn Island. Sections of it are unsettled, and highlights include walking up to a lighthouse, and climbing an area known as El Bluff. Updated: Aug 12, 2009.

Mountain Biking and Cycling

Crisscrossed by thousands of miles of unpaved roads, tracks and trails, Nicaragua is a wonderful destination for mountain biking. The dearth of paved roads which makes mountain biking so easy, however, presents problems for road cyclists, and visitors who would like to experience the country on two wheels should plan to do so on a sturdy mountain bike.

The two centers of mountain biking in the country are Isla Ometepe and San Juan del Sur. It is hard to think of more inviting terrain for mountain bikers than Ometepe's, with the island's two volcanoes, dry and wet forests, and interesting diversions like petroglyph sites. Bikes are also relatively easy to find on the island, as most hotels have a Huffy or two lying about to rent to visitors. San Juan del Sur also boasts a number of trails winding through the hills above town, where riders are rewarded with views down to the Pacific. Again, bicycles are easy to track down around town.

There are some opportunities off the beaten bike path, too. The mountains around Estelí are steep, cool, and covered in dirt paths. The hills around Managua also have a number of trails for riders to enjoy. Particularly adventurous riders can tackle the barren, gravelly slopes of Cerro Negro, a volcano near León. Finding a decent bike to rent in these locations is tough, but buses

Find the best price on a flight to Nicaragua: vivatravelguides.com/flights/

and taxis will usually carry bicycles for you. Your best bet for ensuring you have a good bike is to bring yours from home, but bikes can also be purchased at the modern big-box stores near Managua, as well as outside Roberto Huembes Market. Another option, if you don't have your own bike, is to take one of the mountain biking trips offered by many tour operators. For more information on road cycling, please see the Getting Around section on p. 35.

Horseback Riding

One of the best ways to enjoy the natural beauty of Nicaragua is by riding a horse along some of the country's numerous beaches, islands, volcanoes and jungles. Horseback riding solo, or with a group, will allow you to get closer to the flora and fauna of Nicaragua than you would in a vehicle (which means good wildlife watching). Many resorts, hotels, and tour companies rent horses, with or without guides, per hour or half day. Listed below are a few popular horseback riding locations:

Playa Pochomil is a wide, sparsely populated stretch of sand that offers horseback riders unparalleled views of the ocean and the setting sun.

Home to some of the most visited beaches on the country's Pacific Coast, San Juan del Sur has plenty of places to ride. Horseback riding is offered at the major hotels in the area; Playa Marsella has miles of untouched beach.

For those with a little more time and money, there are a variety of islands where horseback riding is one of the major activities. With two volcanoes and the white sand Playa Santa Domingo, Isla de Ometepe is a great place to see some of Nicaragua's varied landscape. The island has numerous horseback riding opportunities.

Many of the finest forests and volcanoes in the country are accessible by horse, but some of the 76 protected lands forbid horses. Double check on the accessibility of the area where you're heading before you try to saddle up.

Kayaking and Rafting

Nicaragua should be a natural destination for kayakers and rafters, as its mountains and rivers combine to create some truly world-class rapids. The whitewater is difficult to access in Nicaragua, however, and most paddling opportunities involve calm waters.

The most popular kayaking trip involves setting off from Granada for a passage though Las Isletas on Lake Nicaragua. It's usually a great way to spend a day; the lake is calm, the birds are abundant, and the sharks are rarely around. Birdwatchers will also be interested in kayaking down the Río Istián on La Isla de Ometepe. Another popular trip is around Isla Juan Venado, off the coast from Las Peñitas. The island is designated as an ecological reserve, which protects Juan Venado's mangroves and dry forests, as well as its population of birds and crocodiles.

Very few people have completed the rafting trip along the full length of the Río Coco, from its headwaters in the northern coffee country to its outlet into the Caribbean at Cabo Gracias a Dios. The trip can be like something out of Joseph Conrad's Heart of Darkness, as the river traverses some of the most remote, undeveloped territory in the country. That said, the river has good Class III and IV rapids, and those who take the time to explore it will gain a unique perspective into the lives of the Miskito villagers who live along the Coco's banks. It should be noted that there are several parts of the river that must be portaged, and it can be difficult to get a kayak or raft up to any of the launching points.

Waspám is a good place to start if you want to explore a portion of the river. However you choose to approach the river, it is essential to hire an experienced guide, not only for the trip itself but also for sorting out the logistics before departure.

Nearly as adventurous is the trip down the historic Río San Juan, where paddlers can battle the heat, the crocodiles, and the Costa Rican border patrols. Technically, you could travel the whole course from San Carlos to San Juan del Norte, but you would run the very real risk of being stranded in the latter once you arrive. The easiest portion to tackle, in terms of organizing return transportation, is between San Carlos and the old Spanish fort at El Castillo. The river is relatively placid for most of its course, but there are good rapids at El Castillo. Again, it is highly recommended that you talk to a guide before you set off; San Carlos is the best place to find rafts, kayaks, and guides.

Diving and Snorkeling

Nicaragua is not usually considered a premier destination for divers, but it does have some

Join VIVA on Facebook. Fan "VIVA Travel Guides Nicaragua."

good scuba and snorkeling opportunities. Diving in Nicaragua will particularly appeal to those who seek their adventures away from the usual Cozumel-Cayman Islands scuba circuit.

The scuba industry is still in its infancy in Nicaragua, but there are some reputable dive operators in the country. The two heavy-hitters are Dive Nautilus (www.divebigcorn.com/index.html) on Big Corn and Dive Little Corn (www.divelittlecorn.com) on Little Corn Island. Both have been in operation for a while, are well-regarded, and offer a variety of dives around the reef that protects the Corn Islands. The reef near Little Corn is in slightly better shape, but the area around both islands has abundant marine life, including sharks and rays, and good visibility. The water around the reef is relatively shallow in most places, and is probably best suited for novice divers; both of the dive shops run training and certification courses for newbies. More experienced divers can go farther off-shore and explore the Blowing Rock, a volcanic formation that rises 32 meters (100 ft) from the ocean floor to the surface of the Caribbean. It teems with life, especially sharks, and also has some beautiful coral formations attached to it.

Diving on the Pacific side of the country is not as established as it is on the Corn Islands. The ocean around San Juan del Sur has abundant marine life, as well as a ship wreck and underwater caves to explore, but the water is colder and murkier than on the Caribbean side. There are also no reputable scuba companies working on the Pacific coast right now, as several San Juan del Sur dive shops have ceased operations in the past few years. If another dive operator opens in San Juan del Sur, or if you make arrangements for a diving trip with an outside tour company, the best time to explore the Pacific is between December and April. Outside of those months, the sediment dumped into the ocean by Nicaragua's rivers tends to significantly reduce visibility. One other option for those in the area is to try some fresh water diving in the Laguna de Apoyo, which fills a volcanic crater near Masaya. The biological research station there (www.gaianicaragua.org/station.html) runs trips for certified divers, who have the opportunity to aid the station's research into the lake's marine life. Open-water diving certification courses are also available on the site.

Snorkeling is largely confined to the Corn Islands. The Pacific is too cold and too murky to appeal to many snorkelers, especially because much of its marine life lives far below the surface. With warm, calm waters, the Caribbean makes for a much more pleasant snorkeling experience, and the Corn Islands host many tropical fish that live in the shallow waters near the reef. The two dive shops on the Corn Islands both run snorkeling trips, and the Paraiso Beach Hotel (www.paraisoclub.com/activities.htm) on Big Corn rents out snorkeling gear, in addition to offering its own snorkeling trip.

Surfing

Nicaragua is blessed with two coastlines, beautiful weather and arguably the best surf breaks in Central America. Without question, the most surf-friendly beaches are located on the Pacific side of the country, not far from Managua, the capital city.

Some of the biggest surf spots include San Juan del Sur, Playa Gigante, Popoyo, Masachapa and Quizala. San Juan del Sur is the gateway to some of Nicaragua's best beaches, including the popular Playa Madera (also called Maderas, Playones or Punta Quilla) where both beginners and experts can find great waves. Most surfers use San Juan del Sur as a jumping off point for nearby surf breaks that can only be accessed by boat.

Find the best price on a flight to Nicaragua: vivatravelguides.com/flights/

North of San Juan del Sur is the isolated Playa Gigante where the best waves are also accessible by boat. Be careful of where you're going as nearby land owners have been known to escort surfers off their property with armed guards.

Considered by many to be the best surf spot in Central America, Popoyo (also called Popollo or Las Salinas) is a classic Nicaraguan surf break, but is for experts only—beginners should avoid Popoyo's dangerous, rocky sea floor.

The best break in Masachapa is found just south of the city on a piece of wide and uncrowded beach. Surfers need to be at least at an intermediate level before challenging the surf of Quizala; trying to learn to surf here is not a good idea.

While Nicaragua has great waves all year round, the best months for attempting any of the Pacific coast surf breaks are from March to September, during the rainy season. If you can stand an hour or two of downpours in the afternoon, the rest of the day is usually warm and sunny.

The heaviest of the rainy season occurs in October when the country endures tropical storms and substantial amounts of rain. The water temperature averages between 75 and 82 degrees Fahrenheit, with the lower temperature occurring during the Nicaraguan dry season from December to April. During the dry season, you should wear a wetsuit to stay warm in the chilly water.

Unless you are staying at one of the numerous surf lodges that line the beaches on the Pacific coast, you will need water transportation or a vehicle with a guide to get around. Most beaches are unmarked and not all breaks are accessible by car.

Also, not all beaches offer surf board rentals, (the more touristy beaches will rent them anywhere from $10-30 a day) so consider buying a board and selling it when you leave if you plan on heading to the more distant breaks. Make sure to bring your own wax, sunscreen, rash guard, and first aid kit just in case.

For beginner surfers, or those who would like a bit more structure, there are multiple surf tour companies that, for a set weekly price (most hover around the $1200 mark), will provide transportation to the various breaks as well as surf lessons, room and board. There is also a plethora of surf schools offering lessons at hourly rates ($10-30). You can find the schools clustered around the more touristy areas such as San Juan del Sur.

Fishing

As sport fishing has only recently caught on in Nicaragua, the waters are known as "virgin territory." They are exotic and plentiful, a wonderful place to find a variety of fish and other wildlife, good for sport and scenery. Travelers looking to fish in Nicaragua will be pleasantly surprised at how accessible, and also unique, the experience will be. As you have both oceans available, as well as numerous lakes, rivers and preserved reserves, there is no lack for location.

Depending on where (and also when) you go, you will yield all kinds of different rewards. On some of the rivers you will find snapper, grouper, rainbow bass, and even 30-pound roosterfish. It is also said that Nicaragua's Rio San Juan is the best place in the world to catch giant tarpon. Other species available in the waters of Nicaragua are marlin, snook, machacas, dorado, small yellowfin tuna and sailfish, which are most abundant during the most fruitful fishing months of May through October. Note however, that September and October bring about Nicaragua's rainiest seasons, and fishing can become near impossible in the tropical downpours of some of the beach towns.

You can bring your own equipment, though an easier option would be to rent or go with a tour agency that provides it (consider Super Fly Sport Fishing, Tel: 443-451-4300, URL: www.superflynica.com, or check out the surfing/fishing tour combo companies). Some companies promise to bring you to a spot which has never been fished before, so signing up with someone might not be such a bad idea. If setting out on your own, bring a map and proper provisions. Updated: Jun 18, 2009.

Birdwatching

Nicaragua boasts an impressive 703 identified species of birds, including: pelicans, quetzals, vultures, trogons, finches, hummingbirds, kingfishers, and gulls. Scientists expect the list to grow to over 800 species in the next few years as new birds are found.

As part of the recent development in ecotourism, birdwatching is becoming an increasingly popular past time for tourists in Nicaragua. The country is home to 19 of the 21 endemic bird species found in Central

Join VIVA on Facebook. Fan "VIVA Travel Guides Nicaragua."

America; these species represent the huge amount of biodiversity and variation in the eco-systems of Nicaragua.

The tropical dry forest is located on the Pacific side of Nicaragua, where during the dry season, long tailed manakins, white throated magpie-jays, Hoffman's woodpeckers, lesser ground cuckoos and Pacific parakeets can be found.

The rainforest in Nicaragua is situated on the northeastern and southeastern sides of the country encompassing the Bosawás Biosphere Reserve and the Indio Maíz Biological Reserve where the great green macaw, quetzals, guacamayas, harpy eagles (the largest eagle in the Americas) can be seen.

The Nicaraguan cloud forest is also near the Bosawás region where the Mombacho and Maderas Volcanoes are located; this area is inhabited by slaty-tailed trogons, three-wattled bellbirds and world famous resplendent quetzals.

Many of the bird species in Nicaragua are migratory birds that go north during the spring and summer months, making the best time to bird watch between September and April. There is also a large number of bird species that can be seen year round in Nicaragua, generally in the more forested areas of the country.

Although the country is considered off the beaten track for birdwatching, the wide variety of bird species, coupled with the accessibility of many great birding locations, makes Nicaragua an ideal location to see rare and exotic birds.

Wildlife Watching

Did the description of Nicaragua's fauna earlier in this chapter capture your imagination? You are not alone; it might not be the Serengeti, but a growing number of visitors to Nicaragua are seeking out the country's wildlife.

If you're making your own itinerary for a wildlife watching trip, note popular reserves (like The Bosawás Biosphere Reserve or Montibelli Private Wildlife Reserve) and plan to camp or stay at ecolodges in the area. Here you can talk with guides, set up walks or longer treks, or just bring your binoculars and hope for the best! The alternative option is to pre-plan a tour. Nicaragua's tourism infrastructure is pretty developed, and booking beforehand, or finding one while you are on the road, should be simple enough. Check out tours that meet your wildlife wants, whether its birding or volcanoing, luxury or budget; you shouldn't have to compromise since it's all out there. As for any means of travel, remember to be responsible and respect the land you are traveling on and the people it supports.

For before-you-go resources, check out www.nicaragua.com/wildlife, as well as the Rainforest Alliance and Eco-Index. Updated: Jun 18, 2009.

Studying Spanish

The majority of Spanish schools are clustered in the major cities of Nicaragua, namely Managua, León, Granada, and San Juan del Sur. The average price for one week of classes (20 hours of classroom teaching), homestay (with a local Nicaraguan family including 3 meals and afternoon activities)—ranges from $140-200 with prices going down with each extra week due to long-stay discounts. If you elect not to stay with a host family, the price goes down by about $60 a week. Rates also vary by the number of students in the class; one on one lessons are more expensive than group lessons (group discounts can usually be arranged.)

Beware as many schools require an additional registration fee ($30-75) as well as a 50 percent deposit of the total program fee upfront.

Most Spanish schools also offer "total immersion programs" which combine Nicaraguan culture classes and tours, and are usually much more intensive than regular classes. Volunteer opportunities, internships, and discount tours can also be arranged through many of the schools.

Nicaraguans have a distinct way of speaking which is very different from the slow, clear Spanish of neighboring Costa Rica or the Andean dialect to the south. Nicaraguans speak Spanish very rapidly and have a habit of chopping the "s" off the end of their words. The speach patterns can make understanding the Spanish difficult at first. With a bit of time and patience, though, studying Spanish in-country is an inexpensive way to learn the language and about Nicaraguan culture. Updated: Jun 18, 2009.

Volunteering

The need for assistance in Nicaragua is tremendous. With a population of 5.2 million and nearly half the country living below the poverty

---

Find the best price on a flight to Nicaragua: vivatravelguides.com/flights/

line, Nicaragua is one of the poorest countries in the Western Hemisphere. Burdened with large debts and few resources, the government provides little assistance to the country's poor. International and local non-governmental organizations have had to fill the gap, and many of these organizations rely on the aid of foreign and Nicaraguan volunteers.

When visiting a country like Nicaragua, even for a short term, volunteering is a valuable experience and can make a trip that much more rewarding. There are many volunteer opportunities available, particularly in and around Managua. To choose a suitable one, think about what your interests are and help out by doing something you enjoy. Whether it's working with children, the environment, sports, building and construction, or writing, there should be work to match your skills and interests.

Contact one of these organizations for volunteer opportunities:

Agua Para La Vida
They work to provide water to rural communities and volunteers can help in the Managua office. They seek volunteers to help with the sanitation programs or people with backgrounds as civil engineers, social educators and health educators to assist with the planning and integration of projects. All fees and accommodations are arranged by the volunteer, therefore no application fees are required. Volunteers here are of best service if staying in the area for an extended period of time. URL: www.aplv.org.

If you're looking for the sort of position that requires payment, but provides accommodation, transportation, and meals try:

Seeds of Learning
Volunteers help build classrooms and schools, but for those who want less physical work, they can also teach children. Work missions are eleven days and cost $1200 plus airfare. URL: www.seedsoflearning.org.

Witness for Peace
Supports justice, peace, and sustainable economies in Nicaragua and other Latin American countries. Week-long delegations involve learning about organizing grassroots movements, peacemaking, advocacy, and cultural sensitivity. Cost is $850 plus airfare. URL: www.witnessforpeace.org.

A useful website with more information on volunteering in Nicaragua is: www.volunteerabroad.com/Nicaragua.cfm. Updated: Mar 09, 2009.

Working

Unemployment and immigration laws are two of the obstacles that stand in the way of foreigners getting paid work in Nicaragua. It's difficult, though not impossible, to get a job here. Nicaragua has a 3.6 percent unemployment rate and a 46.5 percent underemployment rate which means when trying to find work in this country, foreigners will be facing the same dismal statistics as the citizens of Nicaragua. Also, due to immigration laws, foreigners will have to prove that their job could not have been given to a Nicaraguan citizen.

There are a few colleges and English language institutes located in the major cities which hire English-speaking natives and pay anywhere between three and ten dollars an hour. Nicaragua's status as a "Highly Indebted Poor Country" means that many non-profits and international organizations also work in the country and hire foreigners with engineering, medical, agricultural, economic, and development experience. The best source of updated information for Nicaraguan work permits is still through the United States Embassy of Nicaragua at http://nicaragua.usembassy.gov/immigration_laws.html. Updated: Mar 09, 2009.

Living in Nicaragua

Nicaragua is a stable and peaceful place to live, but it is also a developing country that is still recovering both politically and economically from a long civil war as well as the devastation of Hurricane Mitch. As the second poorest country in the western hemisphere, Nicaragua has the lowest cost of living in Central America, and the US dollar goes a long way. Foreigners living in Nicaragua will enjoy a rather high standard of living as the price of living is estimated to be 20 to 60 percent lower than in the United States.

Many expats head to Nicaragua for the beautiful weather, beaches and landscape, but stay in the country because of the kindness and generosity of the people. The effects of the civil war still linger after 16 years, but as far as security, Nicaragua now has a crime rate lower than the United States.

With low property taxes, cheap beach-front real estate and inexpensive health care,

Nicaragua has become a major destination for retirees and foreigners looking to move to a warmer climate.

Foreigners planning on living in Nicaragua for longer than 90 days must obtain a residency permit through the Nicaraguan government. It is also recommended to hire a Nicaraguan lawyer to help guide you through the paper work. There are many subtypes of permit residency including: immigrant resident, investors, resident leasing or renting property or goods, retired or pensioned resident and resident through family extension.

As well as qualifying for one of the above categories, foreigners must also provide the following information to the immigration office: a residency request form, passport (valid for at least an additional six months), photocopy of every used page of your passport, two Nicaraguan passport-size photographs, a background check, health certificate, birth certificate, as well as paying the fees, ranging from approximately $12 for the residence card to $30 for the residency fee.

Check with the United States Embassy of Nicaragua for more information. Updated: Mar 09, 2009.

Lodging

Lodging options in Nicaragua can be a little limited by western standards, even in comparison to other Central American countries. However, tourism is becoming an increasingly important industry and the range and coverage of quality accommodation is increasing rapidly.

Luxury hotels and quality accommodations are available in all the major cities and tourist hot-spots, but if you stray from these popular areas, finding high-end lodging becomes more of a challenge.

At the other end of the scale, Nicaragua has a wide range of budget options with many small bed and breakfasts, guest houses, and a growing network of hostels. Although it is often easy to find extremely cheap accommodation, there is a great variety in the quality—so shop around and make sure you ask to see your room before you commit.

Note that often paying as little as a dollar extra can have a huge effect on the quality of your lodgings. Such a small amount might mean the difference between a sweltering room and an air conditioned one, for example.

Outside of the cities, ecotourism is slowly developing and the countryside now is dotted with jungle lodges and excellent hacienda-style accommodations, many of which are based around coffee plantations or fincas. For the more adventurous, camping is also an option.

No matter where you decide to lay your head, make sure to keep a close watch on any valuables. Don't leave any expensive items in an unlocked room or unsecure space and make sure you think twice about leaving cash or personal items with the staff of any establishment.

Also be aware of any place that advertises itself as a "motel" or as "open 24 hours," in many cases these establishments may be love hotels that charge by the hour. Updated: Feb 03, 2009.

Hotels

Good, quality, clean hotels to suit all budgets can be found in most towns across the country. Hotels in Nicaragua come in many forms —from small, family run establishments to large internationally owned chains—and the diversity of accommodations means that you should be able to find a room that fits your needs. Of course, areas that attract the most visitors, such as León, Granada, Managua, and places along the Nicaraguan coast, have the greatest depth of accommodation, and it is only in these locations where top-end luxury hotels can be found. As the tourism industry continues to grow and evolve, so too does the range of hotels available; colonial mansions are being converted and purpose-built hotels are continually springing up in locations all across the country. Nicaragua's portfolio of hotels is expanding quickly so it's well worth taking the time to investigate each area you visit to see what new offerings are available. Updated: Mar 11, 2009.

Hostels

As Nicaragua is fast becoming "the" backpacker destination of Central America, the country's network of hostels is having to expand quickly to support the rising demand for cheap and sociable accommodation. Nicaragua has an increasing number of hostels that offer good options for people on limited budgets, those who need not only a cheap bed for the night but also want to meet other like-minded and independent travelers. All of the backpacker hot spots now contain several hostels of varying quality that can offer accommodation for as little as $3 a night in a dormitory. It can be more difficult finding a hostel outside of the main touristy areas.

Find the best price on a flight to Nicaragua: vivatravelguides.com/flights/

However, coverage in the country's more remote, less-visited destinations is also growing and Nicaragua can now offer hostel accommodation in most locations that tourists visit. Updated: Mar 11, 2009.

Apartments

If you plan on staying in one location for an extended period of time, renting an apartment is an option worth considering. Currently there are not a great deal of apartments to rent in Nicaragua (although the number is slowly increasing), so finding one to suit your needs will require doing some serious research, for which you may be richly rewarded. Staying in an apartment will provide you with more independence and privacy than a hotel and may also be the most economical choice if you're traveling in a group. Apartments can cost as little as $20 a night, but make sure to check exactly where the property is, the quality of the accommodation, and that the person advertising the apartment has the right to rent the space to you. Updated: Mar 11, 2009.

Eco-lodges

The variety of Nicaragua's geography and wide range of ecological habitats make it the ideal destination for the environmentally minded. Even after the 1990 move to democracy, many remote areas have remained dangerous for foreigners (due to banditry, old ammunition stockpiles, and landmines). However, over the last decade these areas have been cleaned up and are now considered increasingly safe.

In fact, the wilderness that was once off limits to all but Sandinistas or, later, Contra guerrillas, has been recognized for its value by both the Nicaraguan people and their government. Nicaragua now has 76 nationally protected areas. With such beauty and diversity, and the recent rise in safety, it is no wonder that Nicaragua is becoming a popular destination for birdwatchers, biologists, nature lovers and hikers.

Across the country an increasingly large network of eco-lodges is providing accommodation for those who want to do as little damage to the environment as possible. As the tourism infrastructure is still not fully developed in Nicaragua, eco-lodges are reasonably priced compared to neighboring Costa Rica, and in all likelihood you will have a more rustic, authentic experience.

When choosing an eco-lodge it is worth doing a little research to make sure that the place you stay has actually been built and run in an environmentally friendly manner. Nicaraguan hotel owners, like all entrepreneurs, recognize that "eco" is a buzzword that drives the tourism industry. Beware of the hotels and lodges that have "eco-lodge" in the name just as a gimmick to gain more business. Updated: Mar 11, 2009.

Fincas

Fincas are large farms, often coffee plantations, that can be found dotting the Nicaraguan countryside. Many of these fincas now provide lodgings, ranging from luxury to budget, in anything from hammocks and dormitories to private rooms or cabañas (cabins). Staying at these farms is a relaxing way to enjoy some of the country's more remote locations, places where other accommodation

Gallo Pinto

Chief among Nicaragua's many culinary treats is gallo pinto. The rust-red-tinged dish of beans and rice can be found in all regions of the country and is a flavor unique to Nicaragua. Granted, other nations have traditional dishes of beans and rice, but nothing can compare to some home-cooked gallo pinto.

The dish is prepared by frying white rice and red beans separately and then frying them together. The result is a super-fried, red medley that derives its name as a result of sharing the same color as the comb of a rooster. gallo pinto is consumed in the campo as well as in the city, and is generally eaten for breakfast, lunch and dinner. It can be accompanied with cheese, chili, meat, or bread, but is so tasty as to be enjoyed alone. The pinto is tastiest when it is fresh off the fryer, but refried versions add a bit of crunchiness. Great pride is taken in the making of the pinto, so if a plate is exceptionally tasty, or the texture just right, then a compliment to the cook is in order.

Many visitors to Nicaragua develop a taste for gallo pinto, but trying to replicate it without the wood fire, the massive amounts of oil, or the rich flavor of a fryer seasoned by generations of use and the country itself is nearly impossible. Updated: Mar 09, 2009.

Join VIVA on Facebook. Fan "VIVA Travel Guides Nicaragua."

options are usually limited. Due to the requirements of coffee growing, former fincas normally occupy fertile, scenic land, often near, or even on, the slopes of volcanoes. Staying at a finca is one of the easiest ways to access and enjoy the beautiful, more remote landscapes that Nicaragua has to offer. As many fincas are still working plantations, there may be opportunities to visit the coffee fields or even volunteer and work on the farm. It is also often possible to purchase coffee from where you are staying, which can make for a great souvenir. Updated: Mar 11, 2009.

Camping

Outside of Nicaragua's urban areas, especially along the coast, camping is a good option for the budget traveler. "Camping" will in all likelihood not involve a tent, as many Westerners would expect, but will have you swinging in a hammock, hopefully covered by a mosquito net. If you intend on doing a lot of camping then consider buying the essential three: a net, a hammock, and a tarpaulin.

There are few official campsites, but most of the camping options are available through hostels and fincas, which offer accommodation in hammocks under covered areas at cheaper rates than you would pay for a room. In most of these cases you will have the option of either hanging your own hammock or using one provided by the hostels.

Purchasing your own equipment allows you to be much more adventurous, as there are places to be found to sling a hammock all over the country; if you're wandering through the countryside and want to set up camp, just remember to ask permission first, if possible. Updated: Mar 11, 2009.

Food and Drink

Nicaraguan food is unlikely to ever replace French or Italian cuisine among the world's favorites, but it is hearty, filling fare. Like the cuisine of its Central American neighbors, it derives its flavors from the mixing of ingredients and techniques from Europe and the New World. The sharp regional divides in the country are also reflected in the cuisine, with the foods of the Pacific and Caribbean coasts baring little resemblance to one another and plenty of local dishes popping up on menus.

BASICS

The staple around which many meals are built is gallo pinto, a dish of lightly-spiced fried rice and red beans. Many Nicaraguans eat it for breakfast, lunch and dinner, and after some time in the country, you might feel that you do, too. For lunch and dinner, the gallo pinto usually serves as an accompaniment to a large serving of chicken, beef, or pork.

At some restaurants, especially on the coast and on the lake shores, you can get a whole fish, fried and smothered in a tomato-based sauce. You can sometimes also find lobster, which divers catch by hand off the Caribbean coast. While most of Nicaragua's haul of shrimp and crab ends up on North American plates, some portion of it does make its way to Nicaraguan restaurants. The best places to look for good seafood, reasonably enough, are the coastal resort restaurants and the small fishing villages.

LOCAL SPECIALTIES

For such a small country, Nicaragua does offer a great deal of regional variation in food. Around Bluefields, the cooking uses a lot of coconut milk and chili peppers, reflecting a strong Caribbean influence. The signature dish of the region is ron don, a starchy, vegetable-and-meat stew, and even a simple dish like rice and beans tastes different along the Caribbean, as it is cooked in coconut oil and sometimes simmered in coconut milk. The region around León offers up quesillo, a snack featuring soft, local cheese and onions, doused in cream and vinegar and then wrapped up in a tortilla. Granada's specialty is vigorón, a dish of yucca, pork rind, cabbage and tomato, all served atop a plantain leaf. The northern region of Matagalpa produces sweet corn tortillas called güirilas. Around Masaya, you'll find many menus listing tripe soup.

Every weekend, nacatamales are consumed in the thousands, or maybe millions, across the country. Similar to the Mexican tamale, the Nicaraguan version usually has meat, onions, and peppers encased in corn dough. The whole concoction is then wrapped in a plantain leaf and boiled for hours. Nacatamales are easiest to find on Sunday mornings, when they are sold on many street corners.

VEGETARIAN OPTIONS

Vegetarians can certainly survive in Nicaragua, but they will not have a wide range of choices. Gallo pinto is everywhere and is a good source of protein. It can be supplemented by fruits and nuts, which are widely available. In the bigger cities and spots on the tourist trail, you will find restaurants that cater reasonably well to vegetarians' dietary needs.

DESSERT

Nicaragua is not a bad destination for those with a sweet tooth. In addition to all the fresh, exotic fruit produced in the country, there are a number of baked treats on offer. Perhaps the most famous is tres leches, a cake soaked in three kinds of milk which is popular throughout Latin America. A Nicaraguan specialty is cajeta de coco, a candy made with coconut and yucca. On a hot day, raspados, made of shaved ice and fruit juice and topped with a dash of condensed milk, can be delicious and refreshing.

PLACES TO EAT

Managua, Granada, León, and the coastal resorts all have proper restaurants serving Nicaraguan and international dishes. Many locals, however, eat at street-side carts, stalls and stands, or at little diners called comedores. In smaller towns, you will not have any choice but to eat at such places; fortunately, the vast majority of them churn out safe, tasty meals for a pittance. Comedores often serve a multi-course, set meal called a comida corriente.

ALCOHOLIC DRINKS

Nicaragua's gift to the world of drink is Flor de Caña rum. Considered to be among the world's finest, Flor de Caña is available virtually everywhere and at an incredibly cheap price, especially given the quality. More often than not, rum is consumed as a Nica libre, mixed with Coke, ice, and lime. In a bar, if you ask for servicio completo, you'll be handed a half-liter bottle of Flor de Caña, accompanied by the mixers needed to construct your own cocktails to taste. If the $5-7 price tag scares you off, you can switch to Flor de Caña's cheaper cousin, Ron de Plata. Homemade liquor, widely available throughout the country in gallon-sized jugs and small plastic bags, is probably best reserved for those travelers who feel no strong attachment to their livers.

If you choose to drink beer instead, the two national brands are Toña and Victoria. They are largely indistinguishable lagers, though Nicaraguans are sometimes zealous advocates of one or the other. Although neither is a world-class beer, both are cheap and refreshing enough after a hot day under the Central American sun. Upstarts Búfalo and Brahva have carved out niches in the beer market, as well, and some imported beers are available in the bigger towns and cities.

Culinary Vocabulary

Corn is one of the staples in the Nicaraguan diet, but many locally grown fruits and vegetables like jacote, mango, papaya, tamarind, pipian, bananas and avocados are added to make the country's cuisine both varied and delicious. As the Nicaraguan culture frowns upon wastefulness, typically the entire pig, cow or chicken will be used in a dish (including the stomach, hoofs and tail).

The following is an overview of some of the most famous Nicaraguan dishes and drinks:

Gallo Pinto: eaten as a daily staple, this is mixture of fried rice with onion, sweet pepper and red beans boiled with garlic. On the coast coconut is added to the dish. (See p. 25.)

Indio Viejo: this is a soup made with tortillas, long strips of meat, onions, garlic, sweet pepper and tomato.

Nacatamal: dough made from ground corn is filled with pieces of pork or chicken, rice, potatoes, tomatoes, onion and sweet pepper and then packed into plantain tree leaves (which are not eaten) and cooked.

Quesillo: a piece of cheese called quesillo is placed inside a tortilla, which is then wrapped up in a plastic bag. Onions, vinegar, fresh cream and a bit of salt are added.

Arroz-con-piña: pineapple and rice is boiled then cooled and blended with a little vanilla, strawberry and sugar to make a sweet drink.

Rosquillas: dough made from corn is combined with cheese, egg, butter, lard and then cut into circles and baked until crisp.

Tres Leches: prepared with milk, condensed milk and cream, this dairy-filled cake is then topped with meringue. Updated: Mar 11, 2009.

Join VIVA on Facebook. Fan "VIVA Travel Guides Nicaragua."

NON-ALCOHOLIC DRINKS

Teetotalers are well looked-after in Nicaragua, too. Refrescos are cold drinks, usually made by mixing grains or seeds with water, milk, and sweet seasoning. Common varieties are chicha de maíz, made with corn; arroz con piña, a drink made with rice and pineapple that tastes better than it sounds; semilla de jicaro, made from calabash seeds; and Nicaragua's favorite refresco, pinolillo, made from corn and chocolate. There is an almost endless variety of refrescos based on Nicaragua's many fruit species, as well. Travelers who are new to the country might want to allow their stomachs time to adjust before knocking back these refreshing drinks, however, because they are rarely made with purified water.

There are also the more mundane carbonated beverages, referred to as gaseosas, which are available everywhere. Just remember that Nicaragua is recycling-mad, and taking a glass bottle out of a shop is an expensive proposition unless you return one at the same time. One alternative is to have the shop owner pour your gaseosa into a plastic bag (yes—a bag, not a cup) for you. For a country that produces some great coffee beans, it is surprisingly difficult to find a good cup of café in many parts of the country. All too often, you will receive a large mug of hot milk, a jar of instant coffee, and sugar. Updated: Apr 27, 2009.

Shopping

Archeologists have named Nicaragua's earliest inhabitants Los Concheros, or "the Shell Collectors." The country is still attracting collectors, of one type or another, to this day. A wide range of interesting goods are available for purchase across Nicaragua, from artesanía (handicrafts) and clothing to premium tobacco. Best of all, discerning shoppers can get great value for their money. Indeed, for less than $40, you can buy a bottle of some of the world's best rum and the hand-woven hammock you'll pass out in when you've polished it off.

WHERE AND HOW TO SHOP

Most travelers do their serious shopping in two places: the Mercado de Artesanía in Masaya and Mercado Roberto Huembes in Managua. In both, vendors sell handicrafts from across the country (and beyond), and good-natured bargaining is required to arrive at a price. Of the two, the market in Masaya is definitely easier to get around and more pleasant. Most large towns and cities also have shops selling handicrafts, often at (relatively high) fixed prices. Granada has a particularly large concentration of artesanía shops. Another appealing option, if you have time to explore, is to buy directly from the craftspeople who make the goods; prices are generally lower, and you will get a better glimpse into Nicaraguan life. All manner of consumer goods from North America, Europe, and Asia can be found at Managua's two modern shopping malls.

ARTESANÍA

Most of the things travelers bring home fall under the category of handicrafts. Among the most popular items are hammocks. Beautiful, comfortable, and usually priced at less than $30, they are well worth the slight hassle of carrying them home. You can buy hammocks in Managua, but most are produced in Masaya, and the market and one-room factories there are the best places to buy them. Pottery is another commonly-purchased item. In Nicaragua, most pottery comes in earth tones, and it can range from the rough and crude to the intricate and refined. Near to Masaya is San Juan de Oriente, a town that has quality pottery and other clay ceramics. Art from here is unique and inventive, as local workers use kick-wheels to form their ceramics, consistently changing the design and luring shoppers from all over the globe. In San Juan there are small family-run shops set up alongside the road, and behind them, workshops where local artists may invite you in to explore.

Soapstone sculpture from around Estelí is also popular and available at the craft markets. Woodcarving is another traditional art form, and wooden sculptures of different sizes abound in tourist shops and markets. The woodcarvers around Masaya are famous for the beautiful furniture they produce, and it is simple enough to have a rocking chair disassembled to carry home. Even easier to carry home are the baskets made from straw and reeds, which are also attractive and practical.

PAINTING

Nicaragua has a strong artistic tradition. Starting in the 1960s, with Ernesto Cardenal's community in the Islas Solentiname, primitivist painting has been one of Nicaragua's most famous cultural outputs. Not surprisingly, the artesanía markets are flooded

Nicaraguan Coffee

Coffee not only powers office workers around the world through their 9 a.m. meetings, but it also provides employment for a large segment of Nicaragua's population.

German immigrants brought Coffea arabica seeds with them 150 years ago and quickly began cultivating the crop in the cool, moist hills around Matagalpa and Estelí. The conditions in the Northern Highlands and the Carazo proved perfect for coffee. Sales of the crop were driving the country's economic growth by the turn of the century, and the circle of wealthy coffee planters and exporters developed into a powerful political force in León and Managua.

Political instability, the American military occupation, and banditry conspired to reduce production in the following decades, but by the eve of the Second World War, coffee exports had rebounded to account for half of the country's export earnings. Later, Anastasio Somoza used the pretense of the war to expropriate coffee farms belonging to the descendants of German immigrants, which enable him to amass huge personal holdings.

Following the Sandinista revolution, the new government turned many of the large coffee estates, especially those owned by the Somozas and their allies, into collective coffee farms. The government promoted the formation of cooperatives, and smallholders became an important force in the coffee industry. However, a US embargo on Nicaraguan coffee imports and the Contra War, fought mostly in the northern coffee-growing areas, stymied production and discouraged investment. Nicaragua's coffee industry fell far behind those of its neighbors.

In 1990, with the election of Violeta Chamorro, the American ban on Nicaraguan coffee was lifted, and the industry started to rebuild itself. Many of the cooperatives that had been formed by the Sandinistas continued to produce and market coffee collectively, and they brought in a good living for the country's small coffee farmers.

By the late 1990s, however, coffee production in countries like Brazil and Vietnam surged, which flooded the market with cheap beans and caused the world price to plummet more than 60 percent. This triggered a humanitarian crisis in the Northern Highlands, and relief agencies poured into the region to distribute food aid to small holding farmers and coffee pickers unable to earn a living wage.

The coffee industry has had to rebuild itself yet again. Rather than trying to compete with the cheap Robusta beans grown in Brazil and Vietnam, Nicaraguan coffee farmers have attempted to brand their product as a high-end luxury item. There is also a growing effort to market Nicaraguan beans as fair trade, which means that the producers and pickers are paid a good, living wage for their backbreaking effort.

Today, coffee accounts for almost 15 percent of Nicaragua's export earnings. The area around Matagalpa and Estelí is the still the center of the industry, and many farms and cooperatives in the region, including the famous coffee estate at Selva Negra, are open to visitors. Even if you can't fit a farm visit into your schedule, you should seek out a bag or two of premium Nicaraguan coffee, since the country's beans are considered some of the finest in the world. They are all Arabica, and most are grown in the shade and at high altitudes. If you're looking for something unique, search out Pacamara Peaberry, a large bean with a strong, fruity flavor.

with paintings of varying size and quality. Many portray village scenes, and almost all make use of bright, vibrant colors. Paintings done on canvas will naturally be easier to carry than those painted on wood, but they need to be wrapped up carefully.

CLOTHING

Many travelers also choose to buy the traditional clothing of Nicaraguan campesinos. You can find finely-embroidered, lightweight shirts and blouses in many markets and tailor shops. Leather goods, particularly belts and cowboy boots, are a specialty of the Estelí area and can be purchased at several stores there. Comoapa, near Boaco, is famous for producing the straw hats that are sold in the Managua and Masaya markets.

TOBACCO AND RUM

Nicaragua can take care of your minor vices, as well. Many Cuban cigar makers relocated to Nicaragua after the Cuban revolution, and they have established a thriving cigar industry centered around Estelí. The largest, most famous manufacturers in the country operate under free-trade laws that forbid them from selling their products domestically, but smaller producers are under no such restrictions. These smaller producers range from the mid-sized factories around Estelí to small mom-and-pop shops in Granada that roll their own stogies at a back table. The quality and value are very high almost everywhere you go.

Flor de Caña rum has been judged among the best in the world, and it can be purchased in Nicaragua for a fraction of the price it fetches abroad. It also makes a good souvenir for those who hate shopping, since it is available at corner stores almost everywhere in the country. The normal light and dark rums are quite good, but those with a particularly discerning palate might want to spring for Flor's Centenario label, which is aged for 12 years. Updated: Apr 23, 2009.

MAPS

The best map currently available for Nicaragua is ITMB's (International Travel Maps and Books) Nicaragua travel reference map (ISBN: 9781553413486).

Now in its forth edition this 1:755,000 scale map shows all the major urban areas and roads; the reference also highlights the roads that are only passable during dry weather, which is very important in Nicaragua. There is also a small insert showing a central plan of Managua and the legend is in both English and Spanish.

Although ITMB only has one retail outlet, they ship worldwide from their website: shop.itmp.ca, and their products are available from specialist map shops and major bookshops (like Borders) that have large travel sections.

If you are traveling to other countries in the region then ITMP also publishes a 1:1,100,000 scale map that covers the whole of Central America (ISBN: 1553410521), and the publisher, Reise Know-How, publishes a 1:650,000 scale map that covers Honduras, Nicaragua, and El Salvador (ISBN: 3831771758). Updated: Mar 09, 2009.

Health and Safety

Be aware of your surroundings and keep expensive jewelry and clothing to a minimum as petty theft and robbery do occur. Before entering Nicaragua the following vaccines are recommended: yellow fever, hepatitis A and B, rabies and typhoid. Malaria pills are also suggested if you plan on traveling outside the urban areas, but, as always, consult your doctor before visiting the country. Updated: Mar 11, 2009.

Major Health Problems

While traveling, especially in developing countries, there is always the possibility of developing or catching a major health problem, especially in rural or remote areas. While relatively uncommon, the list below is of possible illnesses which can be contracted while traveling throughout Nicaragua. Heed your doctor's advice above all and come prepared.

DENGUE FEVER

In recent years there have been growing reports of dengue fever in Nicaragua. While it is not a great threat, mosquito-borne diseases are a possibility, and it is recommended to dress in full coverage and wear proper repellent to dramatically reduce the risk.

DYSENTERY

This digestive illness is the far more serious version of traveler's diarrhea. It involves mucus and blood in one's feces, and is contracted most often from drinking, or eating foods washed with untreated and unsanitary water. This water carries micro-organisms, or parasites, which destroy the intestinal lining and cause bacterial infections in the system. Symptoms of dysentery include excessive bowel movements and vomiting. The best way to remedy dysentery is by oral rehydration therapy given in proper medical facilities.

HEPATITIS A

Hepatitis A is a severe and infectious disease of the liver, caused by the ingestion of fecal matter, even microscopic amounts. Hepatitis A causes jaundice and liver inflammation, and while the disease usually lasts for a couple of weeks, it does not lead

Minor Health Problems

to chronic infection. If you are planning to visit Nicaragua, you are required to get a vaccination against hepatitis.

MALARIA

While most of Nicaragua is not at risk for malaria, the disease cannot be ruled out and proper precautions should be taken when traveling here. Rural areas and the outskirts of Managua show reports of the mosquito-borne disease. Symptoms are flu-like, followed by exhaustion, fever, and at severe stages, a coma. Chloroquine is recommended as an antimalaria drug, however, consult your doctor before leaving for any risk areas.

RABIES

There are stray dogs throughout Nicaragua that are, for the most part, harmless. However, many home-owners train guard dogs to attack trespassers, and other feral dogs can be dangerous. On long hikes in rural areas, always carry a walking stick to defend yourself if a dog starts to attack, and in the city don't feed or antagonize strays. It is recommended to be pre-vaccinated for rabies, however in the case that you are attacked by a dog, and you were not vaccinated before your trip, rabies vaccinations should be available in Managua. Be sure to see a doctor immediately if you believe you were infected, whether or not you have had the vaccine.

TYPHOID

The typhoid vaccination is among one of Nicaragua's required three. This disease is caused by ingesting contaminated food and water, and symptoms include dangerously high fever, profuse sweating, and severe, but non-bloody, diarrhea. Wash your hands as frequently as possible, and try your best to eat food from restaurants with good reputations. Oral or injectable vaccinations are recommended by the World Health Organization, and should be taken before travel if you are planning to be in Central America for an extended period of time (six months or more). The injection needs boosting every three years.

YELLOW FEVER

This mosquito-borne disease is endemic to many parts of Central and South America, however not to Nicaragua. If you plan to visit any of the endemic areas (mostly tropical places) within a year before traveling to Nicaragua, you will most likely need to show proof of vaccination at some point; carry your vaccine certification along with your passport. Updated: Mar 06, 2009.

Minor Health Problems

While traveling, especially in developing countries, there is always the possibility of developing or catching a minor health problem, especially in rural or remote areas. While relatively uncommon, the list below is of possible illnesses which can be contracted while traveling throughout Nicaragua.

CHAGAS DISEASE

Chagas is most common in northern Nicaragua, as well as rural areas of the country. It is an illness carried by parasitic insects that pass infection through bites and defecation on exposed skin. The severity of the disease varies, as most symptoms show local swelling and possible fever or tiredness. If chagas goes untreated, there is the possibility of swelling in lymph glands, spleen, and liver. If you suspect you have been infected, see a doctor immediately.

SUNBURN/HEAT EXHAUSTION

It's from 10 a.m. to 4 p.m. that the sun in Nicaragua is hottest and most harmful. If you're looking for a tan, it is safest to sit outside early mornings or late afternoons, however travelers should take proper precautions to protect themselves from ultraviolet radiation. Note that you will burn faster here than in Europe or the US. For prevention, apply sunscreen with at least an SPF of 30 every few hours you are outside. If you get severe sunburn, treat it with a cream and stay out of the sun for a while. To avoid overheating, wear a hat and sunglasses and drink lots of water. Overweight people are more susceptible to sun stroke. The symptoms of heat exhaustion are profuse sweating, weakness, exhaustion, muscle cramps, rapid pulse, and vomiting. If you experience heat stroke, go to a cool, shaded area until your body temperature normalizes and drink lots of water. If the symptoms continue, consult a doctor.

MOTION SICKNESS

Even the hardiest of travelers can be hit by motion sickness on the bumpy buses in Nicaragua. Sit near the front of the bus or stay above deck on any boats you may take, and focus on the horizon. If you are prone to motion sickness, eat light, non-greasy food before traveling and avoid drinking too much, particularly alcohol. Over-the-counter medications such as Dramamine can prevent it.

Join VIVA on Facebook. Fan "VIVA Travel Guides Nicaragua."

While in all Spanish-speaking areas, go to a pharmacy and ask for Mareol, a liquid medicine similar to Dramamine. If you know that you commonly suffer from severe motion sickness, you may want to get a prescription for something stronger for your travels, such as a medicinal patch.

TRAVELER'S DIARRHEA

This is probably the most common disease for travelers. There is no vaccine to protect you from traveler's diarrhea; it is avoided by eating sensibly. Contrary to popular belief, it is usually transmitted by food, not contaminated water. To best prevent traveler's diarrhea, eat only steaming hot foods that have been cooked all the way through in clean establishments. Avoid raw lettuce and fruit that cannot be peeled, like strawberries. Vegetables are usually safer than meat. An inexpensive vegetable wash can be purchased at large supermarkets and is a good way to ensure clean fruit and vegetables if you are cooking your own meals.

Make sure any milk you drink has been boiled. In many areas outside of Managua, milk is unpasteurized, and therefore powered or tinned is advised. Water in the capital city has been tested and is clear to drink, however bottled water is still always recommended. Also, avoid ice cubes.

If you do get diarrhea, the best way to remedy it is to let it run its course while staying hydrated with clear soups, lemon tea, Gatorade, and soda that has gone flat. Bananas are also a good source of potassium and help stop diarrhea. If you need to travel and can't afford to let the illness run its course, any pharmacy will give you something that will make you comfortable enough for a bus trip. If the diarrhea persists for more than 5 days, see a doctor. Updated: Mar 06, 2009.

Safety

Although most trips to this Central American country will be trouble-free, travelers must still be aware of potential risks they could encounter.

As the second poorest country in the western hemisphere, Nicaragua has problems with theft and gang activity. When traveling in large cities such as Managua or Granada, take the same precautions as you would take in any other large metropolis. There have been few violent crimes against gringos, but foreigners are far more susceptible to pick-pocketing and personal item theft. (Keep a particularly close eye on cameras, laptops, iPods, purses, backpacks, and rental cars).

To have a trouble free trip, please use common sense by keeping track of your belongings, traveling without expensive jewelry or other flashy items, and not drawing obvious attention to yourself. If, however, you are subject to theft, be sure to report it to the local police and your nearest embassy or consulate.

If you are driving in Nicaragua, there is a likely chance that the police will pull you over for an arbitrary or minor offense. Getting pulled over means that you will have to pay a substantial amount of money as a bribe. Due to the growing rate of highway robberies where criminals dressed as police men pull over unsuspecting drivers, the United States Embassy of Nicaragua has issued a warning for travelers to avoid the Tipitapa-Masaya Highway at night as well as exercising caution when driving from the Managua International Airport in the dark.

Nicaragua has a vast number of natural wonders, yet such splendors also come with a few hidden dangers. Be careful when you are swimming or surfing along the Pacific Coast. The Pacific Ocean has a strong undertow with equally powerful currents and waves. So strong is the pull of the sea that unwary visitors have both broken bones and drowned in its pull.

When hiking and climbing around the Nicaraguan jungles and volcanoes, make sure you have the proper footwear and are adequately protected from the elements. If you plan to hike in an especially isolated area, please hire a local guide. There have been cases of hikers getting lost and injured along some of the more remote paths. Updated: Mar 09, 2009.

Hospitals

Most modern hospitals in Nicaragua are located in Managua. Further away from the city, medical care becomes limited. Few medical professionals speak English and the majority of both hospitals and doctors require payment up front (usually only in cash).

Hospital Metropolitano Vivian Pellas opened in 2004 and is currently the most modern medical facility in Nicaragua. Metropolitano Vivian Pellas employs over 300 medical specialists, has a modern emergency room, maternity ward, pharmacy, and laboratory. The

---

Find the best price on a flight to Nicaragua: vivatravelguides.com/flights/

hospital is open 24 hours and has a higher proportion of English-speaking doctors than most other facilities.

Hospital Privado Salud Integral offers many of the same services as Hospital Metropolitano Vivian Pellas but at a lower price.

Hospital Bautista is one of the best hospitals in Managua and the favorite for travelers.

Medical care is significantly cheaper in Nicaragua then in more developed countries, but it can still strain a traveler's budget. The best source for information on physicians and hospitals in Nicaragua is the United States Embassy website: http://managua.usembassy.gov/medical_resources_in_managua.html. Updated: Mar-10, 2009.

Doctors

Modern medical services are located mainly in Nicaragua's capital city of Managua. Most doctors speak only Spanish and expect cash payment upfront for checkups, hospital stays and other procedures. Adequate medical services and English speaking doctors are more difficult to come by the further you venture from the urban dwellings. The Nicaraguan government also runs health clinics in most cities that are free to both locals and travelers. The clinics usually have long lines, overworked doctors, and outdated medical equipment. Updated: Mar 09, 2009

Pharmacies

In the urban areas of Nicaragua you'll find numerous pharmacies selling cheap generic drugs imported from Mexico or El Salvador. Most of the same over-the-counter drugs as in the United States, as well as those that require a prescription, are available cheaply and without a doctor's note in Nicaragua. Be sure to know the scientific name of your brand name prescription as most pharmacists will only know the drug by the former identification. Nicaragua has arguably the cheapest medications in Central America and prescription drugs cost between $10-20. Updated: Mar 10, 2009.

The Media

The current Nicaraguan Constitution provides for freedoms of both speech and press, which can be seen in the various pro-and anti-government positions taken by the print media.

There are three major daily newspapers in Nicaragua: La Prensa, Barricada and El Nuevo Diario. La Prensa is conservative and anti-Sandinista; Barricada was originally a Sandinista National Liberation Front (FLSN) newspaper but changed positions after publishing news of a FSLN inter-party disagreement; El Nuevo Diario is loyal to the FSLN party.

Most citizens do not read the newspaper, relying instead on either one of the country's 10 television stations or 100 radio stations for news. (The Voice of Nicaragua is the name of the government radio station).

The media depends on government advertising for monetary support. International critics have accused the media of falling prey to government propaganda.

A few very powerful Nicaraguan families maintain control over most of the media outlets. The Chamorro family runs the privately owned newspapers, while the Sacasa family controls the majority of the television industry. Updated: Mar 10, 2009.

Mail and Packages

The national postal system is called Correos de Nicaragua. Correos (post offices) can be found in almost every city and are usually reliable and safe. The regular mail service averages about two days to reach destinations throughout Nicaragua but becomes slower as points get further away. Postcards and standard letters can usually be sent to North America and Europe for less than $1. Correos are open during standard business hours, closed for the traditional two hour Latin American lunch, and are not open on Sundays.

Mail can be received at the central correo in any town with a valid ID; however, be prepared to pay a small fee (think roughly fifteen cents) per letter. All the standard international courier services (DHL, UPS, FedEx) are available as well.

When picking up a package that needs customs clearance, you must fill out a postal police form and list the items in the package as well as their monetary value. Before leaving the correo you must pay the duty. Taxes on most items are surprisingly low, at 15 percent, and there are no duties on books, CDs and DVDs. The duty will be higher on more expensive items such as electronics. Updated: Apr 29, 2009.

Join VIVA on Facebook. Fan "VIVA Travel Guides Nicaragua."

Telephones and Calling Cards

Nicaragua's state telephone company, TELCOR, was privatized in 2003 and has been rebranded as ENITEL. It has offices in nearly every town across Nicaragua, and the procedure for making a call from their offices is relatively simple. If you'd rather not make a call from the office, or if you want to call outside of normal business hours, you can use one of the card-operated ENITEL or Publitel pay phones. You can purchase the calling cards from corner stores around the phone booths. Updated: Apr 29, 2009.

Local Calls

As of April 2009, all phone numbers switched from 7 digits to 8 digits. Now, a 2 is placed in front of all old land line numbers, and an 8 in front of all cell phone numbers. Calls to a landline in another municipality or to any cell phone require you to dial a zero before the phone number. If you are using a cell phone, rates are much cheaper if you call someone who uses the same carrier as you. Updated: October 20, 2009.

Calling Abroad

To call abroad, you must dial 00, then the country code (for instance, in the case of Canada and the U.S., it is 1), then the phone number. Rates tend to be expensive, though one good option is to make your long-distance calls from a cyber café. Most cyber cafés with high-speed connections have telephone booths that function in much the same way as those at the ENITEL office, except that the call is carried on the café's internet connection, rather than the local phone lines, and the rates tend to be half those of a regular pay phone. When you finish making your call, the staff member at the internet café will tell you how much you owe. For making calls to Nicaragua, you must use the country code, 505. Updated: Apr 30, 2009.

Cell Phones

Nicaragua's cell networks use the 850 and 1900 MHz frequency bands, which are the same ones used in the United States and Canada. As a result, some travelers from those countries are able to use their cell phones from home; however, if you choose to do this, you will probably incur exorbitant international roaming charges from your carrier. If you are going to be spending a significant amount of time in Nicaragua, it works out cheaper to buy a Nicaraguan cell phone and pre-paid minutes. The two local cell carriers, Movistar and Claro, have networks that stretch across the country, and it is easy to re-load credit onto your phone. Most expats suggest Claro because of its superior coverage. Updated: Apr 30, 2009.

GSM Technology

All cell phones in Nicaragua work on the Global System for Mobile Communication (GSM), as do cell phones in most parts of the world. However, phones from Europe and Asia, which run on different frequencies, will not work unless they are tri-band or quad-band. Only a few major North American carriers (AT&T Wireless, T-Mobile and Fido, at the time of writing) use GSM, but those that do are on the same frequencies as Nicaragua. If you want to take advantage of local rates, you will need to buy a SIM card from a Nicaraguan carrier (Movistar or Claro), which will give you a Nicaraguan phone number. If you bring an unlocked GSM 850/1900 MHz phone from home, it should work with a Nicaraguan chip. Updated: Apr 30, 2009.

Internet Access

With so many of Nicaragua's citizens living abroad, and the growth of the country's tourism industry, internet access has expanded dramatically in the past decade. There are internet cafés in all of the large cities, and they are especially easy to find in Managua, Granada, and León. Most places charge around $1 per hour, and connection speeds range from fast to frustratingly slow. Internet cafés with fast connections often have facilities for making cheap international calls over the internet; this almost always works out cheaper than any other way of phoning home. WiFi is rare, and most small towns are not connected to the web at all, though the introduction of satellite and GPS technology means that a few very rural spots have internet access. Some higher-end hotels include internet access in the room rate, while others levy additional fees for its use. Updated: Apr 27, 2009.

Money and Costs

Prices of hotels and restaurants have been creeping up over the last few years as Nicaragua has become increasingly well-known as a tourist destination; the country is still one of the cheapest to travel in, however. Westerners will find that their money goes a long way, especially in comparison to neighboring Costa Rica, where tourism is already a very well-established industry.

Find the best price on a flight to Nicaragua: vivatravelguides.com/flights/

By staying in shared dormitories, eating at cheap restaurants, and traveling on local buses, budget travelers will be able to get by spending as little as $10-20 a day. If you have a larger budget, then an extra $10 a day will allow you to live much more comfortably. Of course it is also possible to spend a lot more, as Nicaragua has both luxury hotels and expensive restaurants.

US dollars are accepted in many places, as well as Nicaragua's currency, which is the córdoba; the current rate of just over 20 to the dollar makes conversion quite easy. A combination of withdrawing money from ATMs and using credit cards is the best way to pay for things. Traveler´s checks are hard to use in the country, so don't bother to bring them. Updated: Mar 09, 2009.

Nicaraguan Currency

Nicaragua's currency is called the córdoba (denoted as C$) which is dived into 100 centavos (¢). Introduced in 1912, the currency was named in honor of conquistador Francisco Hernandez de Córdoba, the founder of both the Spanish colony of Nicaragua, and the historical cities of León and Granada; his picture can be seen on the rarely used centavo bills.

Unless otherwise indicated, all prices in this book are given in US dollars. At the time of writing in October 2009, $1 USD = C$20.63.

Córdoba bills, which are often also referred to as pesos, are available in the following denominations: C$500 (red), C$100 (blue), C$50 (purple), C$20 (orange), C$10 (green).

Coins are minted with the values C$5, C$1, 50¢, 25¢, 10¢, and 5¢. Unusually, Nicaragua also has small Monopoly-like bills with the values of 25¢, 10¢, 5¢, and 1¢. The one centavo note has a value of roughly 1/2000th of a dollar and has little use, even in Nicaragua. Along with córdobas, US dollars ($) in reasonably good condition are also widely accepted. You will always, however, get your change back in córdobas.

If you intend on bringing money into the country, then dollars are the only choice, as other major currencies including the euro (€) and pound (£) will be practically impossible to use or exchange. Costa Rican colónes (¢) and Honduran limpiras (L) are also very difficult to exchange away from their respective borders. Although it is possible to use the dollar in most places, carrying córdobas is a good idea since dollars are not excepted as payment on buses, for example. Many small shops and restaurants may also round the exchange rate up.

Large denomination notes of both currencies ($20, $50, $100, $500 and C$100) can be extremely hard to use or exchange, especially outside of Managua. Vendors of all stripes are reluctant to except large bills due to the fear of counterfeiting, or simply because they don't have enough change.

For current exchange rates visit: http://www.xe.com/. Updated: Mar 09, 2009.

Banks

Normal banking hours in Nicaragua are 8 a.m. to 4 p.m. Monday to Friday and 8.30 a.m. to midday on Saturdays (closed Sundays). If you want to exchange money, bring your passport and be prepared for a long wait as banking can be a very slow process. Queues are longest on the 15th and last day of the month, as this is when most Nicaraguans get paid. Lines are usually shortest in the early afternoon.

If there isn't a bank available, a much less safe option is to exchange money with individuals know as coyotes. If you are going to use these money changers, be sure to know both the exchange rate, and the amount of córdobas you should be receiving, before the exchange, and count your money carefully after the transaction. Although many coyotes are honest, others will see a foreigner as an opportunity to make a quick buck. Updated: Mar 09, 2009.

ATMs

Cajeros automáticos, or ATMs, can be found at both local banks or petrol stations in most of Nicaragua's major tourist destinations, with the exceptions of the Isla de Ometepe and the Corn Islands.

The majority of ATMs will dispense córdobas, although occasionally you will have the option of withdrawing dollars. If you withdraw dollars, though, be aware that cash machines generally have very unfavorable rates. Most machines will also charge you up to $2 per transaction, on top of whatever your bank charges you for withdrawals abroad.

ATMs can attract dodgy characters, so it is best to go with a friend during daylight

---

Join VIVA on Facebook. Fan "VIVA Travel Guides Nicaragua."

hours. The safest machines are those located off the street, inside banks, and shopping centers. Avoid, if at all possible, counting your money in public where theives might be watching you.

Communication problems, which are not uncommon in Nicaragua, can stop ATMs from getting confirmation; if you have a problem with a machine, try returning a bit later or look for a different one.

The following towns and cities have ATMs that accept MasterCard (for their exact addresses check the ATM finder at: www.mastercard.com/cac/en/atmlocations/index.html):

Chinandega - 1 ATM
Granada - 1 ATM
León - 1 ATM
Managua - 33 ATMs
Masaya - 1 ATM
Matagalpa - 1 ATM
Rivas - 1 ATM

The following towns and cities have ATMs that accept VISA (for their exact addresses check the ATM finder at: http://visa.via.infonow.net/locator/lac/jsp/SearchPage.jsp):

Chinandega - 1 ATM
Esteli - 1 ATM
Granada - 2 ATMs
Juigalpa Chontales - 2 ATMs
León - 2 ATMs
Managua - 23 ATMs (Including one at the airport)
Masaya - 1 ATM
Matagalpa - 1 ATM
Rivas - 1 ATM
Updated: Mar 09, 2009.

Using Credit Cards

The use of credit cards is becoming increasingly common in Nicaragua; most mid-range to high-end restaurants and shops in major tourist areas will accept some form of plastic payment.

If you're traveling to Nicaragua, though, you should in no way rely on credit cards to provide for all your needs, especially if you intend on leaving the major cities. Many places will only accept cash. The power also cuts out frequently, especially in the Caribbean, and will render your cards useless, since the card scanners will no longer work. The general rule is: the smaller and more remote the establishment, the less likely they are to accept payment by card.

Visa and MasterCard are the most widely accepted cards and carrying both is a good idea as many places will either accept one or the other. (American Express and Diners Club are also sometimes accepted, but not as frequently as Visa and MasterCard.)

NOTE: Before you leave home, make sure to inform your bank of your travel plans to ensure that your card is not blocked while you are abroad. As a precaution, take photocopies of your cards (leave a copy with a trusted friend at home and keep a copy with you, but separate from the actual card) and keep the number of your credit card company handy, so that you can easily call up and cancel your cards if they are lost or stolen. A good idea is to scan a copy of your card and keep it in your e-mail, so it's accessible anywhere. Updated: Mar 09, 2009.

Traveler's Checks

Traveler's checks (also known as cheques) are almost impossible to exchange anywhere in Nicaragua, making credit cards a much more reliable source of money. If you do decide to bring traveler's checks, do not rely on them as your first source of money; you will be lucky to find anywhere to exchange them.

Banco de America Central (Bancentral) is a good place to try if you have to exchange a traveler´s check. If they do accept it, you are unlikely to get a favorable rate and will be charged at least a 3 percent commission.

American Express traveler's checks in dollars are the most likely to be exchanged, although the American Express website (www.aetclocator.com) doesn't list any locations in Nicaragua where they are guaranteed to be accepted.

When using traveler's checks anywhere in the world, make sure that you have a record of the serial numbers kept separate from your travelers check's, possibly in an e-mail account, as you will be asked to provide these if your checks are lost or stolen. Updated: Mar 09, 2009.

Wiring Money to Nicaragua

Wiring money to Nicaragua is a relatively easy process since Western Union has agents located in almost all mid-sized and large population centers across the country.

Find the best price on a flight to Nicaragua: vivatravelguides.com/flights/

Due to their very high rates, however, you should only consider transferring money to Nicaragua as a last resort.

To find the exact locations of Western Union agents, check online at: www.westernunion.com/info/agentLocator.asp?country=NI. Updated: Mar 09, 2009.

Etiquette and Dress

Except in the central highlands, the climate in Nicaragua is hot and humid, even during the May to December rainy season. If you're traveling to the country during the wet season, make sure to take a light, breathable rain jacket and waterproof shoes. During the dry season, lightweight, tropical clothing will be your best bet.

The Nicaraguan clothing style is rather conservative; rarely do either men or women wear shorts unless they are at the beach. However, most Nicaraguans are used to seeing tourists in shorts and liberally cut clothing. You usually don't need to worry about offending local sensibilities, but make sure not to bring clothes that are too see-through or skimpy.

As a tourist, keep in mind that you're already the center of attention. Wearing too little is not advisable, as is going to the other extreme. Overdressing, or wearing expensive items such as jewelry and watches, can make you a target for theives and other undesirables. Khakis, jeans, T-shirts and polo shirts are the norm for Niaraguan men. The same is true for women—with the addition of modestly cut dresses and skirts. Nicaraguan women usually have their hair pulled back in a ponytail or bun.

Even when they are dressing casually, Nicaraguans prefer to maintain a well-kept appearance and are very conscious that their clothes are clean and wrinkle free. Nicaraguans are generally friendly, open people who will engage travelers in pleasant conversation while still keeping a polite distance. Greetings between friends and acquaintances are very important in Nicaraguan society; each exchange includes some kind of physical touch like a handshake or kiss on the cheek. Handshakes often turn into hugs among well acquainted colleagues and women usually kiss each other on the cheek when greeting and departing one another. Updated: Mar 09, 2009.

Business and Officialdom

Policy instability, corruption and access to financing are the greatest threats facing foreign companies doing business in Nicaragua. In the general atmosphere of corruption, bribery is commonplace, especially when business owners try to deal with registries, permit services, and public utilities such as electricity, water, and telephone companies.

Complicated bureaucratic procedures, which can normally take months to complete, promote the buying off of officials in order to get the necessary documents in a decent amount of time. As the Nicaraguan government lacks transparency, there are not any overall agencies or watchdog groups to whom business owners can report incidents of corruption. Nepotism and powerful political interests make the legal system of Nicaragua one of the weakest in Latin America.

The legal environment is regulated, in theory, but severely unregulated in practice, and resolving legal disputes can take years before a judge will make a ruling—making investing in Nicaragua a risky endeavor, at best. Foreign investors are often at a disadvantage in disputes against Nicaraguans, who may have political or personal ties to court officials.

Formal dress attire is normally not worn when conducting business and showing up to an initial meeting overly dressed would be in poor taste.

Impromptu meetings generally do not occur; most meetings will be pre-arranged. It is acceptable to arrive up to 30 minutes late to a meeting, after that the tardiness is considered rude and you should prepare a very good excuse. Do not hurry through a meeting or schedule another meeting right after, as it is a sign of disrespect to rush off and leave the meeting unfinished. A fair amount of caution and restraint should always be exercised when dealing with Nicaraguan businesses and official government agencies. Updated: Mar 09, 2009.

Responsible Tourism

Phrases like ecotourism, green tourism, and sustainable tourism are often used by tour operators and travel agencies to advertise certain services. Responsible tourism is the newest global trend that aims to help travelers have a smaller negative effect on the environment and a greater positive impact on the local people and infrastructure. Responsible tourism creates better places for people to live in, and better places

Join VIVA on Facebook. Fan "VIVA Travel Guides Nicaragua."

to visit, as defined by the 2002 Cape Town Declaration on Responsible Tourism.

The first step is to learn about the country and its culture. Be aware of the social and religious norms of the local people and be respectful of their wishes for privacy by asking permission before taking photos. The second step is to minimize your environmental impact by putting trash and recyclable items in their proper place and reusing water bottles and bags as much as possible.

The next step is to support the regional economy as much as possible by buying locally made goods, eating locally grown food and staying in locally owned accommodations. The final step is to be conscious of your status as a guest in the country and always remember the golden rule of treating others how you would like to be treated. Make sure that when you travel both you and the people around you are left with the feeling that the visit has been a positive experience. Updated: Mar 13, 2009.

Photography

Most Nicaraguans do not own cameras, so the availability of most photographic, film, or video equipment is very limited and expensive. Make sure you stock up on film, memory cards, batteries, and other necessities before entering Nicaragua. If you are using a digital camera, bring your own memory card reader, as most internet cafes will not have one.

Be cautious when taking pictures in Nicaragua. Avoid photographing military sites and personnel, police and police stations, mines and airports, as the authorities in Nicaragua consider these people and locations to be off limits. Travelers have had their film and cameras confiscated for taking pictures of places the Nicaraguan government considers important for national security. As always it's good to avoid attending and taking photos of protests and other civil demonstrations in foreign countries, especially in Nicaragua, since such pictures are prohibited.

Many small towns have a local photographer who goes to all the local weddings, birthday parties and baptisms and takes photos for the whole town. The locals then go to the photographer's house and, although not obligated, can purchase pictures of these events. Some of the wealthier people in town will hire the photographer to take pictures or make a video of an important family event, but most just rely on the traditional method of purchasing photos after the event.

The majority of Nicaraguans will happily let you take their picture; however, many will ask for either a copy of the photo or a small amount of money. It's not considered rude or offensive to take photos of daily life such as a funeral procession or birthday party, but a certain measure of respect is expected from the photographer. When in doubt about whether you can take a picture, ask first. Updated: Mar 16, 2009.

Travel Tips

WHEN TO GO

Most tourists go to Nicaragua during the dry season from November to April. The climate in April and May warms up and many student travelers choose to visit Nicaragua during their school breaks of July and August. The rainy season lasts from June to October, with the end months being the wettest.

BEFORE YOUR TRIP

Make sure to register with your country's embassy as well as submit your itinerary. As a precaution, the embassy will send E-mails informing travelers of various dangers and annoyances that occur in the country. It's recommended to see your health care provider about 4 to 6 weeks before your trip in order to have enough time for the proper vaccines to take effect. Typhoid, rabies, hepatitis A and B are suggested for travel to Nicaragua as well as being up to date on routine shots like polio, MMR (measles, mumps, rubella) and DPT (diphtheria, pertussis, tetanus) vaccines.

DRINKING WATER

Even if the water is safe to drink in various regions of Nicaragua, it will still be different from the water your body is used to drinking. It's good to stick to drinking only bottled or carbonated drinks in cans or bottles. Avoid tap water, fountain drinks, and ice cubes. If you purchase fresh fruits and vegetables, wash them with bottled water before eating.

BUSINESS HOURS

Banks are open from 8:30 a.m. until 4:30 p.m. and do not close for lunch. Nicaraguans get paid bi-monthly, so avoid the large lines at the bank around the 15th and 30th of the month. Government offices are open from 8 a.m. until 4 p.m. Stores and other businesses in shopping centers and malls are open from 10 a.m. until 8 p.m. Most restaurants open from 11 a.m. to 11 p.m. Updated: Mar 25, 2009.

Women Travelers

Besides the usual catcalls and whistles by men on the streets, women traveling alone (provided they take the usual safety precautions) should not have any more trouble in Nicaragua then in any other part of Central America. Nicaraguan women are subjected to the same air-blown kisses and hisses; they seem to take the attention in stride and generally ignore it. Don't be alarmed by the words of love whispered by Nicaraguan men—that should be as far as it goes since touching unknown women, foreign or local, is frowned upon.

As always, dress for the amount of attention you want. Women traveling alone, or even in a small group, should dress modestly (leave the mini skirt and spaghetti strap tank tops at home). Nude or topless sunbathing is not socially acceptable.

Nicaragua has its fair share of petty thefts and robberies (especially in some of the poorer Managua neighborhoods) but the number of physical assaults, murders, and rapes is very low, although the United States Embassy does warn that violent crimes are on the rise in Managua.

Avoid walking late at night, drinking at bars alone and carrying either large sums of money or important documents (although be sure to have a photocopy of your passport on you at all times). Above all else, trust your instincts when deciding if a situation is dangerous. If you are cautious and careful, traveling through Nicaragua as a single woman can prove to be both a rewarding and empowering experience. Updated: Mar 09, 2009.

Gay and Lesbian Travelers

The leftist overthrow of the conservative Somoza dictatorship in 1979 inspired hope for many homosexual Nicaraguan men and women that their new progressive government would provide an opportunity for a gay civil rights movement. Even after the regime change, though, a deep-seated cultural prejudice against homosexuality remained and progress was slow. It was not until 1989 that Nicaragua saw its first gay community center, located in Managua. When the American embargo was lifted, foreign NGOs geared toward assisting the nascent gay activist movement arrived, and 1991 saw the country's very first gay pride parade.

However, the following year saw a major setback for gay civil rights in Nicaragua, and by extension, all of Latin America. The Social Christian party drafted legislation that not only criminalized homosexuality, but imposed a three-year jail sentence for those who even advocated gay civil liberties. Despite widespread international condemnation, the bill was passed by congress and signed by president Violeta Chamorro. It was later upheld by Nicaragua's Supreme Court. Gay life continued in Nicaragua, albeit with a high degree of discretion; it was not until March of 2008 that legislators revised the penal code and decriminalized homosexuality.

There are now a number of openly gay businesses throughout the country, in Managua, particularly, but also in tourist towns such as Granada and San Juan del Sur. The website, www.gaynicaragua.net (not suitable for work, by the way) lists a variety of gay, or gay-friendly bars, discos, restaurants, and hotels. A Belgian couple runs the Club Alegria, a gated gay community, and the Hotel Joluva, both in Granada. The club and hotel are particularly ambitious operations that cater to a clientele of mostly homosexual men.

While Nicaraguan gay men are increasingly open about their sexuality, their lesbian counterparts have been burdened by not only homophobia but sexism, and their socializing is still limited to mainly informal gatherings. Updated: Mar 09, 2009.

Senior Travelers

Nicaragua is rapidly emerging as a destination for snowbirds and retirees, so senior travelers will be in good company. Older travelers are, in ever-increasing numbers, drawn in by Nicaragua's fine beaches, beautiful landscapes, vibrant artistic traditions and relaxed pace of life. In most of Latin America, including Nicaragua, older people are held in high regard, and seniors should expect to be treated with respect in the country.

Nicaragua, however, is not well set-up for organized touring, so older travelers uncomfortable with driving or using public transportation will have limited mobility or will be faced with expensive inter-city taxi fares. Seniors with major, pre-existing health conditions might want to think twice about visiting, as well; prescription drugs are cheap and easily available over the counter, but medical facilities outside Managua are generally overcrowded, under-staffed, and under-equipped. Those seniors who do make the trip should invest in good travel medical insurance, since very few regular health insurance plans cover medical expenses

Join VIVA on Facebook. Fan "VIVA Travel Guides Nicaragua."

in Nicaragua. None of this should deter the adventurous older traveler, however, as most seniors return from Nicaragua raving about their experiences. Updated: Apr 28, 2009.

Disabled Travelers

Travel in Nicaragua will prove challenging for many travelers with disabilities. Nicaragua has many disabled citizens, due largely to the wars of the 1970s and 1980s and the continued presence of landmines, but very little is done to accommodate them in this resource-poor country. The government has been criticized recently for failing to protect the equal rights of citizens with mobility issues and other disabilities, like blindness and deafness. Disabled travelers will encounter difficulties in Nicaragua, as well. Public transportation is one obvious problem, as are the uneven sidewalks found in many cities. Relatively few hotels have low beds or roll-in showers, and elevators are usually found only in the more expensive hotels in major cities. That said, with patience and perseverance, many disabled travelers have been able to get around the country.

One possible solution is to take an organized tour, and Accessible Nicaragua (www.accessiblenicaragua.com) runs tours specifically designed for travelers with disabilities. It could still be rough going—there is only so much a tour operator can do to shelter clients from the difficulties of travel here—but Accessible Nicaragua does have experience in helping visitors with a range of disabilities to enjoy the country. Craig Grimes, who runs Accessible Nicaragua, also writes a column about living and traveling with disabilities in Nicaragua for the Nica News (http://www.craiggrimes.com/category/nicability/). Updated: May 05, 2009.

Traveling with Kids

Traveling with your children in Nicaragua is perfectly feasible and may very well enhance your enjoyment of the country. Family is central to Nicaraguan life, and children are particularly adored. As a result, your kids are likely to attract a good deal of friendly attention and may help break down the barriers between you and the Nicaraguans you meet. On the other hand, the combination of oppressive heat, long, uncomfortable bus journeys and strange food can induce whining from even the best-behaved children.

For the sake of both parent and child, it is wise to break up long journeys into multiple segments. Whenever possible, try to book a hotel with a pool, so that the kids have a fun way to beat the heat. While vigorón might not be on every kid's must-eat list, there are plenty of places to appease your children with pizza or ice cream, and Managua offers most of the foods from home that they'll miss. It is also relatively easy to fit child-friendly activities, like going to the beach, checking out volcanoes or boating on Lake Nicaragua, into your itinerary.

The practical issues involved in taking your children to Nicaragua are not dramatically different from those surrounding domestic travel with kids. The Nicaraguan sun is particularly strong, so make sure your child's skin is well-protected. Diapers are available in some of the larger cities, but they are expensive, and it may be better to bring some from home if you'll only be traveling for a short time. Most other items your baby would need, from pacifiers to bottles, are readily available across the country. As a general rule, if a child can travel on your lap, he or she will not be charged for a bus ticket. Hotels are often flexible about rates for families, as well, so it never hurts to ask. Single parents should, whenever possible, carry a letter from the other parent giving permission to take the child into Nicaragua. Updated: May 08, 2009.

Tips For Budget Travelers

Alongside Guatemala and Honduras, Nicaragua is one of the least expensive destinations in Central America. Budget travelers will be happy to see their money go a long way here, as it's possible to get by on about $20-30 a day, depending on your travel style and preferences. Your main expenditures will undoubtedly be food, accommodations, and travel, all of which can be done on a shoestring in Nicaragua.

For food, try ordering cheap set menus, common lunches called almuerzos, and checking out the local fare at markets. You will usually find some of the freshest fruit and most interesting options at these mercados. Be brave, but smart, and make sure you're only eating food your stomach can handle! Not as fresh, but just as tasty, you can also try street food sold by venders, either on the street, informal barbeques (fritangas), or on local and long distance buses. This is often a not-so-sanitary option, but some budget travelers (and all the locals) really love the experience—as well as the low price.

Accommodations in Nicaragua run from the very basic to the very complete, all depending on where you are, and also how much you are willing to spend. For travelers on a budget, try some of the youth hostels or hospedajes. These will likely have just a bed with

Find the best price on a flight to Nicaragua: vivatravelguides.com/flights/

sheets and not much more, but they get the job done at around $4-6 per person. For even less, check out places on the beach, as some charge just a few bucks to hang your hammocks on hooks outside their hostel. Also, consider carrying a light weight tent, as there are tons of camping opportunities throughout the country, either in private reserves or less-developed beaches. A good tip: Some of the less expensive hostels will let you pitch it in the back for a cheaper charge.

Transit in Nicaragua is definitely where backpackers can save a buck. Public transportation like buses and minibuses are extremely reasonable, just try to make sure you know where you are going, and that you are paying the same as locals! Taxis should also be fairly inexpensive, though note that you will likely pay per person (usually under $1), and you might get picked up by an already full cab (called collectivos). For budget travelers, buses are the best option for traveling from city to city, but within a short distance, cabs can serve more conveniently. Hitchhiking, while inherently dangerous, is also a possible way to get around Nicaragua. Updated: Jun 18, 2009.

Tips For Mid-Range Travelers

Mid-range travelers are the luckiest of the bunch, as paying a little gets you a long way in Nicaragua. Budget travelers will get by fine roughing it, and luxury vacationers will be happy with their high-end resources, but mid-range spenders should enjoy the best of both worlds. Good (and sanitary) food, clean and comfortable accommodations, as well as tours and transportation should all be up to par at this level of spending. As a mid-range traveler, however, you will have to be flexible. For example, some small towns may only offer a grungy hospedaje or high-end hotel, and you will have to decide which way your budget will swing.

Travelers in this mid-range category should plan to spend about $30-50 a day, though cutting costs here and there, or splurging once in a while may change that number. If you set a planned budget and wish to stick to it, mid-range travelers have it easy, in that there is liberty to cut costs relating to transportation (try mini-busing around town instead of taking a taxi), food (grab breakfast at a local market), or housing (a night or two in a dorm will save a bunch). By giving and taking from some of these areas, you make it financially feasible to adventure out and take that scuba-diving class you wanted or a guided tour of the volcanic lowlands.

As Nicaragua's tourism is quite structured and developed, it is easy for mid-range travelers to book all their plans online, either at home or from Internet cafés once in transit. Often it is the mid- to higher-end establishments (tours, hotels, etc.) that have resources on the web, so be sure to take advantage of this planning possibility. Updated: Jun 18, 2009.

Tips for Luxury Travelers

Luxury, all-inclusive, full service resorts are the norm in Central American countries like Mexico, Panama, and Costa Rica. Nicaragua, however, has a very basic tourism infrastructure compared to other touristy destinations and lacks many of the extravagances that luxury travelers desire. What Nicaragua may lack in luxury, it makes up for in charm, natural beauty and price. As Nicaragua is an up-and-coming tourist destination, 4- and 5-star hotels often go for as low as $100 a night. Many resorts are located on white sand beaches or in prime city center locations; they offer fine dining restaurants and unique housing accommodations.

Most resorts and high end hotels are located in major cities and tourist destinations which make them convenient driving distances to airports like Bluefields, León, Managua International, Montelimar or Punta Huete. Aero Caribbean, La Costena, Copa, and NICA are all airlines that service Nicaragua and many offer first class, non-stop flights from major domestic and international cities. La Gran Francia and Hotel Darío are upscale hotels located in Granada which share a bit of Nicaraguan history.

La Gran Francia was built in the 1500s, making it one of the oldest buildings in the Americas. Built in the neoclassical style, Hotel Darío became a private residence for the Granada elite in the early 1900s. Both hotels offer elegance and a location that's difficult to beat. In Managua, Hotel Intercontinental Real Metrocentro is the best business class hotel in the area, boasting to be centrally located in a city that claims to have no center. Hotel Los Robles is a sanctuary located in Managua's best neighborhood that offers a complimentary cell phone for each guest.

For the luxury traveler looking to avoid big cities, try the resorts on the beaches of Montelimar or San Juan del Sur. Located on the Pacific Ocean, Montelimar Beach is home to white sandy beaches and the secluded tropical getaway, Barcelo Hotel and Resort.

Join VIVA on Facebook. Fan "VIVA Travel Guides Nicaragua."

A more active vacation can be found in San Juan del Sur, another beach located on the Pacific Ocean known for its great surfing and relaxing beaches. Piedras y Olas Hotel and Resort is one of the most exclusive resorts in Nicaragua. More expensive than other Nicaraguan resorts, part of the profits go towards the Fundación A. Jean Brugger, a non-profit organization devoted to the education and welfare of the local community. What Nicaraguan resorts lack in glamour and luxury, they more then make up for in natural beauty and personal service. Updated: Mar 11, 2009.

Suggested Reading

Nicaraguan literature reflects a country with a long history of occupation, war, revolution, and oppressive dictatorships. Most literature has a revolutionary theme and many are personal accounts of the author's interaction with either the Sandinista or Somoza regimes. (For more on the country's authors see Literature in Nicaragua on p. 25).

Below is a list of Nicaraguan authors and their most notable work, written during the tumultuous 20th century:

Violeta Barrios de Chamorro (1930-) —anti-Somoza leader and newspaper magnate, her autobiography, Dreams of the Heart, Simon and Schuster, 1996, shows Chamorro's transition from housewife to first president of Nicaragua.

Gioconda Belli (1948-)—radical, sexual, and an active participant in the Sandinista struggle, both a novelist and poet, Belli is considered one of the 100 most important poets of the 20th century. The Country Under My Skin: A Memoir of Love and War, Anchor Books, 2003, is Belli's autobiography about her time as a Sandinista.

Omar Cabezas (1950-)—a revolutionary author whose guerrilla memoir, Fire From the Mountain, Jonathan Cape, 1985, is the best-selling book in Nicaraguan history. The book is famous for being a Nicaraguan vernacular account of fighting against the Somoza dynasty.

Ernesto Cardenal (1925-)—a Nicaraguan Catholic priest who was very politically and literary prominent during the Sandinista regime, published El Evangelio de Solentiname (The Gospel of Solentiname), Orbis Books, 1982, and became famous for beginning the Liberation Theology movement.

There are many other political and social commentaries written by non-Nicaraguan authors which also provide some insight into revolutionary Nicaragua. Here are some of the more well known authors and their books:

Steven Kinzer (1951-)—New York Times journalist and foreign correspondent, wrote an eye-witness account to the triumphs and defeats of the Sandinistas in Blood of Brothers: Life and War in Nicaragua, Harvard University Press, 2007.

Margaret Randall (1936-)—a feminist poet, writer, photographer, and social activist who wrote extensively about social movements in Latin America published a series of interviews with Nicaraguan writers who were involved with the Sandinistas: Risking a Somersault in the Air: Conversations with Nicaraguan Writers, Curbstone Press, 1995. Randall is a prolific writer and one of her largest topics is the struggle of women. Sandino's Daughters: Testimonies of Nicaraguan Women in Struggle, Rutgers University Press, 1995, discusses the role of women in the Sandinista movement.

Salman Rushdie (1947-)—on a break from writing his controversial novel, Satanic Verses, Rushdie wrote The Jaguar Smile: A Nicaraguan Journey, Random House, 2008. Originally published in 1987 after Rushdie took a trip to Nicaragua by invitation of the Sandinista Association of Cultural Workers, this book is his account of the people and politics of Nicaragua in 1986.

Holly Sklar (1955-)—a syndicated columnist and policy analyst, her book Washington's War on Nicaragua, South End Press, 1999, (originally published in 1988) is a critique of the United States' foreign policy towards Nicaragua during the Reagan administration.

Matilde Zimmermann (1943-)—both a professor, author and active socialist, Zimmermann's 2001 book, Sandinista: Carlos Fonseca and the Nicaraguan Revolution, Duke University Press, is a biography of the founder of the Sandinista National Liberation Front (FSLN). Updated: Mar 16, 2009

!!!!!

Find the best price on a flight to Nicaragua: vivatravelguides.com/flights/

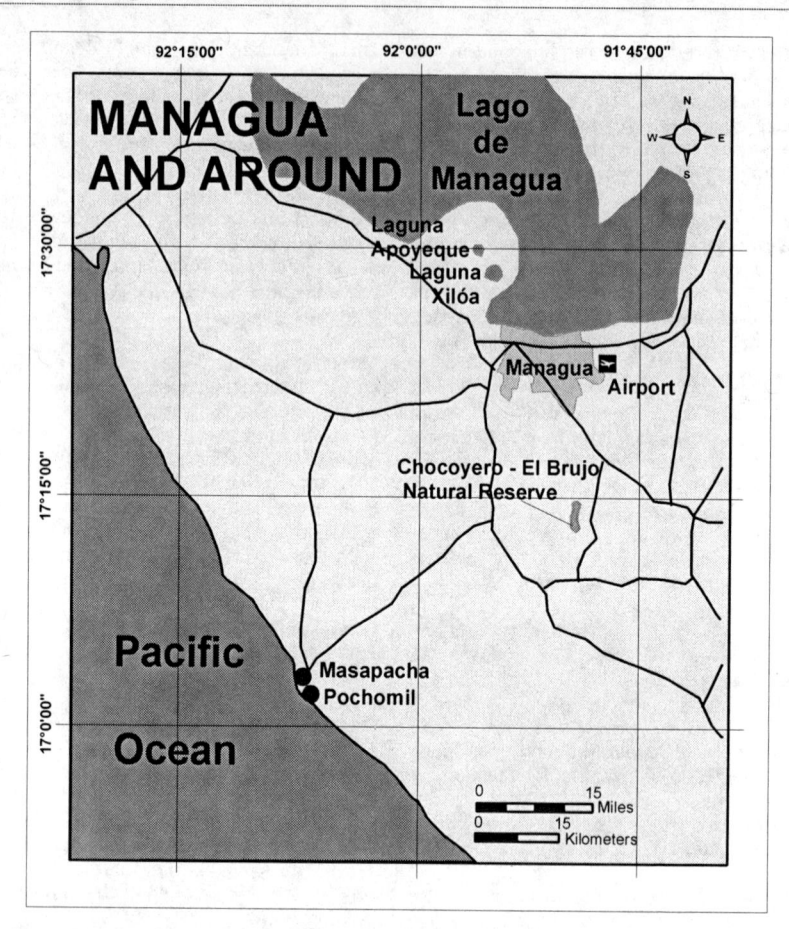

Managua and Around

59 m | **1,800,000** | **24**

Managua, like Nicaragua, is a survivor of a brutal past that has left significant bruises. Natural disasters like earthquakes in 1931 and 1972, damage from the 1978 – 1979 revolution, and flooding from Hurricane Mitch in 1998 have almost rendered this lakeside capital void of the colonial buildings and historic monuments that are scattered among neighboring Central America capitals. All that remains are low-rise, spread-out concrete structures, which are perfect for a city near the intersection of three continental plates, but perhaps not ideal for a strolling tourist.

Upon first (and probably second) glance, Managua seems to offer few tourist attractions. In fact, Managua appears less of a city and more of a pueblo with no real downtown center: buildings, restaurants, and historical sites are scattered throughout the town. However, for those who don't mind digging away at the surface can uncover some interesting finds in Managua. Updated: Dec 16, 2008.

History

Managua, the capital and largest city in Nicaragua, contains a third of the country's population, with roughly 1.4 million residents. The city is at an altitude of 50 meters (165 feet) above sea level, and stretches 338 miles along the shores of Lake Managua (Lago Xolotlán). At least 6,000 years ago, Paleo-Indians inhabited the site; their fossilized footprints, called the *Footprints of Acahualinca*, have been discovered along the lakeshore.

Become a travel writer! See how at vivatravelguides.com/bootcamp/

Highlights

- One of the few structures that didn't get destroyed in the earthquake of 1972, the **Teatro Ruben Dario (p.78)** is Nicaragua's center for the arts. Opened in 1969 to commemorate its namesake (the famous Nicaraguan poet) its interior contains an elegance that is seldom seen in buildings elsewhere in Central America.

- Visiting the **Laguna Tiscapa** in the center of the city is a great way to spend an afternoon. There are a few restaurants that provide views of the foliage and water below, or if you're more adventurous, take a **canopy tour (p.75)**.

- Comprised of classical structures that offer a glimpse into Nicaragua's history, the **Plaza de la Revolución (p.76)** is a worthwhile place to wander and take in some national culture.

- Behind **La Galería (p.73)** shopping center is a promenade of bars and restaurants that fills up with diners in the warm evenings. Take a seat in one of the many outdoor patios and enjoy a meal from the variety of restaurants.

Originally established as a fishing village, Managua was named Nicaragua's capital city in 1852 to settle the feud between Granada and Leon, as both cities had been competing for the title. Natural and political disasters have done a number on the city throughout the years, with large fires decimating Managua in 1931 (after an earthquake) and 1936. In 1972, another earthquake destroyed 90 percent of the city and killed over 10,000 people. Rather than rebuild the old city center, the Managua of today was built up in a circle around the disaster zone. Updated: Nov 26, 2008.

Economy

Many multinational corporation offices and factories are located in Managua, and foreign investment has allowed for newer buildings to be constructed throughout the city. However, it's the city's *mercados* (markets) that see the most commercial action. Hundreds of thousands of merchants sell food and wares here, the most extensive market being the **Mercado Oriental**—the largest in Central America. Unfortunately, the Mercado Oriental suffered some damage in 2008 when a fire ripped through the market and destroyed over twelve acres of stall space; vendors have slowly been rebuilding since then. Updated: Nov 26, 2008.

When to Go

Managua's concrete jungle is always scorching, though slightly more bearable between the end

Street Smarts

As you make your way around Managua, don't be surprised to receive directions along the lines of *de donde fue el Cine, 50 meters abajo y uno cuadro a la montaña* (from where the theater was, 50 meters down and one block toward the mountain). Other than the largest roads, such as **Carretera Sur** and **Carretera Masaya**, Managua has no street names, numbers or other regular addresses.

The whole system of identifying locations is based on the old city, before that beloved place was destroyed in the 1972 earthquake. Back then, South was *a la montaña* (to the mountains), North was *hacia al lago* (towards the lake), East was *arriba* (up, based on a now obscured hill) and West was *abajo* (down, same hill). Although the city has changed dramatically—outgrowing the old up and down boundaries, spreading out chaotically—the old directions have remained, as have references to landmarks that no longer exist.

That theater you're looking for? It's now a fried chicken restaurant. Luckily, Nicaraguans are patient and helpful. They may not know where Av. Bolivar or the Zona Monumental are, but they're sure to point you in the right direction if you explain that you're looking for the old cathedral (take a right at the chicken restaurant and keep on walking). Updated: Mar 21, 2009.

of the rainy season and start of the dry season (September to January). The capital celebrates two major festivals during the height of the dry season: the first two weeks of August are dedicated to *Santo Domingo de Guzman*, the city's patron saint, while the *Dia de la Revolucción* is celebrated on July 19 in Managua's historic center. Bring plenty of water if you plan to attend either event. Residents also honor the Virgin Mary on December 7. Updated: Jun 23, 2009.

Getting To and Away From Managua

BY TAXI

Just outside of the airport, you will likely be approached by one of the red-clad airport taxi drivers. These men typically charge at least $10 to take you to a city location, but often times ask for much more. You might agree to a price and then spend a few minutes waiting for your assigned driver to make a circuit around the airport before driving up. The official taxi drivers have also been known to take passengers right back to the airport if they don't like the destination or the price that's been agreed upon by their managers.

On the highway just outside the airport, taxi prices drop dramatically (and, like everything, can be negotiated). If you feel uncomfortable picking a driver, have one of the airport guards suggest a reliable cab. Taxis are also shared (think of small buses), so if you want to ride alone, ask the driver beforehand. Updated: Apr 15, 2009.

BY BUS

There are three main bus terminals in Managua, each serving routes to different parts of the country. On the most-traveled routes, the first departures are usually before dawn and the last buses pull out of the station around dusk. One notable exception is transportation to San Juan del Sur, which does not get going until mid-morning. Minibuses also leave from the bus terminals, as well as from the Universidad Centroamericana.

TO THE NORTH OR EAST

The bus terminal is located at Mercado El Mayoreo, on the southeast side of the city, and provides service to the north and east, including hourly express buses to the northern cities of Estelí, Matagalpa, Jinotega and Ocotal. There are also departures every half hour to Boaco. There are less-frequent departures to Somoto (six daily) and Río Blanco (five daily) in the North, and San Carlos (seven daily), Siuna (five daily), Esquipulas (six daily), Nueva Guinea (five daily) and El Rama (three daily) in the east. There are two departures each day to San Jose de los Remantes (6:15 a.m. and 12:15 p.m.), Santa Lucia (10:45 a.m. and 1:10 p.m.) and Valle San Juan (2:05 p.m. and 3:05 p.m.). There is one bus every day to each of the following: Comalapa (2:45 p.m.), San Miguelito (6:30 a.m.), El Cacao (11:40 a.m.) and Puerto Cabezas (9:15 a.m.).

TO THE WEST

The bus terminal at Mercado Israel Lewites is the hub for transport in the Pacific

Become a travel writer! See how at vivatravelguides.com/bootcamp/

regions west and north of Managua. There are departures every half hour to León, La Paz Centro, Nagarote, Chinandega and Diriomo, with more frequent departures to Monte Tabor, Pochomil, Villa El Carmen, Carazo and Mateare. There are hourly express buses to León, as well. Less frequent services include two departures to El Sauce (7:45 a.m. and 2:45 p.m.) and three to Cuajachillo (7:30 a.m., 12:30 p.m. and 5:30 p.m.). Minibuses also leave frequently from Israel Lewites for Masatepe, Chinandega and Chichigalpa. Minibuses bound for León leave from a spot one block south of the bus terminal.

TO THE SOUTH
The bus terminal at Managua's main market, Mercado Roberto Huembes, is the departure point for most buses headed to the south of the country. Buses for Nandaime, San Juan del Sur and the Costa Rican border leave every half-hour, while there are departures every 20 minutes for Masaya, Granada and Rivas. More frequent buses run to Masatepe, Ticuantepe, Veracruz, Santo Domingo and Tipitapa. Frequent minibuses also run to Granada, Rivas, Masatepe, Nandaime and San Marcos.

MINIBUSES
The terminal at the Universidad Centroamericana has frequent minibus service to Masaya, Granada, Jinotepe and León. Updated: May 04, 2009.

Getting Around
BY BUS
Buses work on a confusing system of numbered routes (don't look for a route map—it doesn't exist) with set, but not very well defined, bus stops. The best way to get around by bus is to repeatedly ask locals for directions. City officials may not understand the bus system (none of the local agencies claim responsibility for it), but locals know basic routes and market vendors are particularly well informed. Buses operate between 5 a.m. and 10 p.m., pass by their stops regularly, and cost $0.12.

Good routes to know include: **164**, from Reparto Shick to the Malecón; **110**, which passes the American Embassy on the way from Mayoreo to Batahola Sur; **111**, from Via Fraternidad to Mercado Oriental; and **109**, which passes Plaza Intur.

BY TAXI
Taxis are a much easier (though more expensive) way to navigate the city. Regular fees are $1.45 for destinations within the urban center and $1.94 – $2.43 for points on the outskirts of the city. Trips to the airport regularly cost $10 – $15. Agree on the price beforehand and keep in mind that taxi drivers regularly quote foreigners $0.50 – $1 more than the price for locals.

Make sure you have as close to the fee as possible, since drivers rarely have change. Taxi scams range from doubling the price at the end of the ride to kidnapping express where gun-wielding robbers jump into the taxi at a stoplight and make the helpless passenger withdraw money from all the local ATMs until their account is exhausted.

ON FOOT
Managua was not designed as a walking city; major monuments (with the exception of the historic center) are spread apart and the heat is enough to deter most from wandering. If you do head off on foot, stick to populated areas such as Zona Hippa, and take a cab at night. Updated: Jun 23, 2009.

Safety
The best way to protect yourself in Managua, or any big city, is to follow the advice of the locals. Residents will tell you what areas to avoid and why (parts of Barrio Martha Quezada are known to be hangouts for drug dealers and alcoholics, for example). In the city, sections such as the Mercado Oriental are not safe to visit on your own. As the city has expanded, Managua has become increasingly dangerous, particularly for foreigners. Thieves target visitors, who are more likely to be carrying cash, passports and electronics, so be on alert for pickpockets and avoid putting yourself in a dangerous situation, such as walking along the streets at night. As always, keep your valuables as inconspicuous as possible, and travel with copies of all of your important documents. Updated: Jun 23, 2009.

Services
TOURISM
The tourism office, **INTUR**, offers brochures, cultural information and detailed maps of the city. You can buy videos or music there and the office will provide you with lists of hotels and restaurants, including phone numbers and directions. If your Spanish is

rocky, ask for one of their English-speaking staff. Open Monday – Friday, 8 a.m. – 5 p.m. From the Hotel Crowne Plaza one block to the south, one to the west. Tel: 505-2-254-5191 ext. 237. Updated: Nov 26, 2008.

MONEY

As Nicaragua's capital city, Managua has dozens of bank and ATM locations, including **HSBC, Citi, Bancentro, Banco ProCredit** and **BDF**. Most 24-hour cajeros accept Visa exclusively; BAC machines accept all credit cards and can be found at: **Grupo Pellas**, Km 4 ½ Carr. Masaya; Km 5 ½ Carr. Norte; **Plaza España**; **Las Brisas**, Carr. A Refineria; **Ciudad Jardin** in front of Tip-Top; **Camino al Oriental** in front of the national lottery; Km. 9, Carr. Sur; and one block north of Clinica Las Palmas.

BAC (505-2-274-4444, www.bac.net) also has ATMs in major shopping centers: Centro Commercial Managua, Galerias Santo Domingo, Plaza Las Américas and Metrocentro. BAC, which stands for Banco de America Central, is also one of the few banks countrywide where you can cash traveler's checks.

KEEPING IN TOUCH

Correos de Nicaragua (Tel: 505-2-549-2552) is located half a block south of Enitel Central. Make sure the only things you write on your package are the to and from addresses (anything else is prohibited as an illegal message), and remember to leave one flap open so the contents can be inspected.

Managua has dozens of cyber cafés where you can find high speed Internet as well as booths for national and international calls.

MEDICAL

Managua has many hospitals and private clinics, but visitors are most often directed to **Hospital Alemán-Nicaragüense** in Barrio Carlos Marx (505-2-249-3368), **Hospital Bautista** in Barrio Largespada (505-2-249-7070), **Hospital Metropolitanio** Vivian Pellas at Km. 9.8 Carr. Masaya (505-2-255-6900) and **Hospital Militar Escuela** at Lomas de Tiscapa (505-2-222-2763). The city also has dozens of pharmacies where you can refill your prescriptions (but make sure you know the generic name). Updated: Jun 23, 2009.

LAUNDRY

Most hotels and hostels offer some sort of laundry service. In Barrio Martha Quezada you can also find **First Class Dry Cleaning** (Tel: 505-2-222-7937), a block west and a half a block north of the old Cabrera cinema (which doesn't actually exist any more). You cold also try **DryClean USA**, which has locations across the city, but most conveniently at Km. 3 1/2, Carr. Masaya, next to Panadería Baguette and in Barrio Bolonia, 1 ½ block east of Optica Nicaragüense.

SHOPPING

With three sprawling outdoor markets and just as many commercial malls, Nicaragua's capital city hardly lacks for shopping opportunities. Take a walk through one of the city's many markets and you could come away with a nifty souvenir—or find that your purse and pockets have been turned inside out by pickpockets—so be careful!

Managua also has a range of small galleries and boutique shops. **Mama Delfina**, on Camino a las Nubes (just north of Av. Jerusalem), has one of the loveliest selections of higher end Nicaraguan arts and antiques. Open Monday – Friday, 9:30 a.m. – 6:30 p.m.; Saturday, 10 a.m. – 2 p.m. Tel: 505-2-267-8288, E-mail: titulacayo@hotmail.com. Updated: Jun 23, 2009.

El Huembes

El Huembes, as it's known locally, is the second largest market in Nicaragua and is generally considered safer than Managua's Mercado Oriental. Although **Mercado de Artesanias de Masaya** is more upscale and tourist-oriented, El Huembes offers a greater variety of products and prices. Since the asking price of any one item can vary from stall to stall, make sure to fully investigate the market's offerings before deciding how much you want to spend. Woven hammocks, for example, can range from $5 to $30 depending on their size, quality and construction. Market vendors are used to haggling and will quickly lower their initial asking price if you appear to lose interest. Don't be afraid to poke through multiple stalls to see who is willing to give you the best deal.

Besides hammocks, items to be found at the market include traditional wooden rocking chairs, wicker furniture, baskets, hand-tooled leather bags, paintings and finely embroidered clothing. Those with limited room in their suitcases can also pick up souvenirs like funny Tshirts, CDs of traditional Nicaraguan music, wooden toys, and small ceramics.

Become a travel writer! See how at vivatravelguides.com/bootcamp/

If all that shopping makes you hungry, head to the section of El Huembes filled with food stalls. Amid this variety of fresh fruits and vegetables, you'll be able to find local goodies like milk and fruit *cajetas* (a gelatin desert) or *quesillos* (a type of flan). There are also indigenous drinks like *cacao* and *tiste*, both chocolate drinks, or *semilla de jicaro*, a drink made from rice, spices and ground jicaro seeds.

The market itself is easily accessible by taxi (just ask for El Huembes—all local drivers know it) and is roughly a 10-minute drive east of the Centroamérica rotunda. Once you pass the rotunda, you should find the market on your right.

Mercado Oriental

As the largest, busiest and most dangerous open market in Nicaragua, Mercado Oriental is not the place to wander without a local guide. If you plan to enter this labyrinth of stalls, leave your valuables behind, tuck your money in your shoes and be aware that anyone bumping by you may be trying to rob you. A safer way to catch a glimpse of the market is by way of the buses between Centro Commercial to Plaza Intur, which pass through Oriental's furniture corner, where armoires and child-sized chairs are piled on top of bed frames.

Plaza Inter

Plaza Inter mall has clothing stores, ATMs, a movie theater and a food court with all the fast food classics: Subway, McDonalds, Pizza Hut, American Donuts, Pollo Estrella and Tiptop, among others. The food court is also where Plaza Inter hosts a range of evening events, from karaoke and dice games to Chinese writing classes. The mall is open daily 10 a.m. – 10 p.m. **Cinemas Inter** is open Monday – Friday, 1:30 – 9 p.m., and Saturdays and Sundays from 12:30 – 9:30 p.m. Av. Bolivar and Calle Colon, north of Hotel Crown Plaza. The following buses pass the mall: 118, 116, 154, 101, 107, 109, Mini Ruta 4. Tel: 505-2-222-2611 ex. 13, URL: www.plazintermall.com.ni. Updated: Mar 22, 2009.

MetroCentro

MetroCentro may have been knocked off the top shopping spot by Galleria, but the often referenced city landmark is still a buzzing commercial center. A short distance from the UCA bus stop, MetroCentro has an airy atrium, more than 50 shops, a small food court and Cinemark theater. There is no shortage of places to buy department store clothing or get a cheap haircut, but if you're looking for higher end items or local crafts, there are better places to shop.

Centro Comercial Galerias Santo Domingo

With the prow of a cruise liner and the interior of an airplane hanger, Centro Comercial Galerias Santo Domingo has become Managua's premier place to see and be seen (preferably with shopping bags, of course). The city's newest mall is filled with top brands, art galleries and a Cinemark. Leather couches, fountains and a flock of paper birds fill the mall's large interior. Along the cobbled lanes of the food court are 14 of the city's finest restaurants serving everything from sushi and tapas to buffalo wings. Galereias Santo Domingo also hosts events such as runway shows and demonstrations most weekends. Tel: 505-2-276-5080, Fax: 505-2-276-5086, URL: www.galerias.com.ni. Updated: Jun 23, 2009.

BOOKSTORES

English bookstores in Managua are few and far between, and most cater exclusively to Spanish speakers. **Libreria Jeremias 33.3** sells a jumble of new and used books near the Roberto Huembes bus stop. Comb through the selection and you might luck out with a dog-eared paperback in English; the libreria is also one of the few places with a selection of English-Spanish dictionaries. Open daily 8 a.m. – 6 p.m. Tel: 505-2-255-2305.

Located along el Camino a Las Nubes, **Frontera Books** is one of the few Managua bookstores offering books in both English and Spanish. The selection makes the trek up from Zona Hippas worthwhile, plus you can shop in Mama Delfina or grab a bite at Pane E Vino on your way. Tel: 505-2-270-2345, Fax: 505-2-270-2346, E-mail: fronterabooks@ibw.com.ni. Updated: Jun 12, 2009.

Things to See and Do

MUSEUMS

Las Huellas de Acahualinca
If you're passing by this way, you might want to check out the ancient footprints that were found near the shore of Lake Xolotlán and that are now displayed in a local museum. After they were discovered in 1874, experts identified these impressions in the volcanic soil as created by humans some 6,000 years

ago. The museum is small and can be visited in under ten minutes. Open Monday – Saturday, 8 a.m. – 5 p.m. From La Bodega de Cadala Maria, 1 block towards the lake. Tel: 505-2-266-5774. Updated: Dec 02, 2008.

Palacio Nacional de la Cultura
(ENTRANCE: $4) With the Casa Presidential and Catedral Vieja off limits, the only building along the Plaza de la Revoluccíon that you can really explore inside and out is the Palacio Nacional de la Cultura, an imposing building whose Greco-Roman columns are partially obscured by giant pink Sandinista posters.

Turn right when you enter the building to buy tickets to the **Museo Nacional de Nicaragua Dióclesiano Chaves** (open from Tuesday – Sunday, 9 a.m. – 4 p.m.). The museum's entrance fee (taking pictures or video costs an additional $1 and $2.42 extra, respectively), which includes a guided tour in either Spanish or English. The guides will take you on a quick jaunt back outside to learn a bit about the history of the plaza, and then walk you through exhibits on Nicaragua's geological, archeological, political and cultural history. The museum's collection includes stone statues from Ometepe, a mural by Mexican artist Arnold Belkin, and one of the Acahualinca footprints; a small area is devoted to photographs of Managua, before and after the December, 1972 earthquake.

The exhibits are not as extensive as you might expect for a national museum, but they are well labeled and manage to cover a lot of ground (check out the wooly mammoth teeth!), which makes the Museo Nacional a good place to whet your appetite for further Nicaragua explorations. Updated: Jun 23, 2009.

CHURCHES
La Catedral Nueva
Pass by La Catedral Nueva (or, more officially, *La Catedral Metropolitana de la Purísima Concepción de María*) and you might think that the huge Catholic monument is either a mosque or modern art museum. Completed in 1993, the cathedral was designed by architect Ricardo Legorreta and topped by a series of supposedly tremor-resistant concrete half-shells.

Officially, the domes represent Nicaragua's 63 major Catholic churches, although few would be able to figure this out on their own.

The inside of the cathedral is just as modern; the main vestibule is cool and airy, with skylights in the domes, while the walls are painted bright yellow, pink and blue. Large wooden partitions can be opened outward during services to let in the breeze. Masses are at 12 p.m. and 6 p.m. from Tuesday to Saturday and at 8 a.m., 11 a.m. and 6 p.m. on Sunday. Updated: May 04, 2009.

La Catedral Vieja
La Catedral Vieja is arguably the most vivid and poignant reminder of the devastation wrecked on Nicaragua's capital in 1972. The church, once known as La Iglesia Catedral Santiago de Los Caballeros, survived a massive 6.8 earthquake in 1931, only to succumb 41 years later to a quake that measured 7.9 on the Richter scale. Much of the interior collapsed and, during the subsequent years of war and turmoil, the cathedral was never restored. By the early 1990s, the grand old church had been replaced by the modern Catedral Nueva. In 2009, experts were in the process of reinforcing the Catedral Vieja's delicate adobe structure with concrete, but there were no plans to open the interior to the public. The cathedral's neoclassic frame is impressive (even if you can only stand outside it), serving as a stark monument to the crumbled glory of Managua's former center. Updated: Jun 12, 2009.

PARKS
Arboretum Nacional
The Arboretum Nacional may have a caring staff, but the tiny, fenced-in park along Av. Bolivar is a poor representative of Nicaragua's diversity. The 250 species, labeled with wooden signs, are supposedly divided according to the regions they represent, but it's hard to tell. The half dead national tree was particularly sad. The Arboretum appears to be devoted primarily to cultivating seedlings for other areas and, although someone will appear to collect your entrance fee, guided tours are not as forthcoming. Tel: 505-2-222-2558. Updated: Jun 12, 2009.

Parque Historical Nacional "Loma de Tiscapa"
(ENTRY: $1) Set high upon a hill and crowned with the famous silhouette of Augusto C. Sandino, Parque Historical Nacional "Loma de Tiscapa" is a spot known for its panoramic views, impressive historical artifacts and canopy tour. Once home to the

Become a travel writer! See how at vivatravelguides.com/bootcamp/

presidential palace, the hilltop location was where Augusto C. Sandino signed a peace treaty ending his guerilla war against the Liberals. In 1934, he was executed on the palace grounds by Anastasio Somoza Garcia, who decided that the palace could be put to better use as a prison. (You can see what remains of the infamous torture cells on the lake side of the park.)

But it was the Sandinistas who would have the final say. After ousting the Samozas in 1979, victorious rebels hauled their booty to the top of the hill: a National Guard tank captured during a battle for León and named after fallen comrade Aracely Perez; a second tank said to have been given to Somoza by Benito Mussolini; and, as a mark of irrepressible Nicaraguan humor, the bronze backside of a horse, which is all that remains of the dictator's mounted statue. The park also hosts temporary exhibits, such as a politically charged display called "Sandino Vive," in what remains of the palace.

On the other side of the park, **Canopy Tour Tiscapa** ($15 foreigners, $10 nationals; 505-8-886-2836/ 805-6213/ 872-2555; canopytiscapa@hotmail.com, open from Tuesday – Sunday, 9 a.m. – 5 p.m.) offers the chance to go zipping over the lagoon. From a thatched platform you fling across the first of three lines (480, 250 and 520 meters long), either in a seated position, facing forward or hanging up-side-down. At the end of the ride, Canopy Tour picks you up and drives you back to the starting point. To get there, take the road behind the Crowne Plaza Hotel up the hill. Updated: Jun 23, 2009.

Parque De La Paz

Parque de la Paz is an expansive stretch of concrete monuments built in 1990 by President Violeta Barrios de Chamorro to commemorate the end of the Contra conflict. The park might have once been beautiful, but the location has suffered from obvious neglect. Weeds and debris choke the reflection pool and the odd, concrete lighthouse in the middle was ravaged in February 2009. Would-be thieves smashed all of the glass in the walkway around the lighthouse, broke open a lock and were attempting to steal the fixtures inside when they were scared away by park guards. Officials have since twisted heavy wire around the tower door, effectively sealing it off.

A wall of cement-encased weapons has been similarly attacked. The part of the wall not already choked with weeds has been ripped apart by vandals. Even a carved monument, honoring residents of Hiroshima and Nagasaki (as a 1998 symbol of peace and amnesty between Nicaragua and Japan) bears marker scribblings.

All in all, the Peace Park is a fairly depressing side note off a busy highway. If you plan to go, do so in daylight, before the park is taken over by the homeless. The guards on duty are also happy to walk you around the grounds, although they can provide little in the way of explanation. Along Dupla Norte, towards Carr. Norte. Updated: Mar 24, 2009.

Puerto Salvador Allende

Lago de Managua, or Xolotlán, may be one of the most polluted lakes in Central America, but that didn't stop Empresa Portuaria Nacional de Nicaragua (the country's port authority) from opening a new port on the lake shore.

Puerto Salvador Allende (named for the Chilean president deposed during a military coup) is a clean and pleasant, if not yet booming, tourist attraction. Since the port is located on the western edge of the Malecón, just beyond a dilapidated amusement park, it's not the kind of place you tend to stumble upon by mistake. Still, with a small park, picnic tables and historical displays, Puerto Allende is one of the nicest spots along the shore.

The star of the port is the **"Novia del Xolotlán,"** a ferry offering daily tours around la Isla de Amor (general admission $3.40, upper level seating $4.85, reservations 505-2-222-2745) and weekend trips to see Managua at night (Friday to Sunday, 6:30 p.m.).

EPN is currently working on plans to extend the ferry services north, to a new Puerto Carlos Fonseca at San Francisco Libre, and west, to the proposed Puerto Patricio Argüello Ryan at León Viejo. Check back to see if these planned routes are in service. Tel: 505-2-222-2059, Fax: 505-2-266-7973, URL: www.epn.com.ni.

Puerto Allende has not done much to help neighboring **Puerto Touristico Ruben Dario** or the existing ferry line, **Empresa de Transporte Turística Milton Arcia** 505-2-278-8190 / 278-8180, gerencia@

transportelacustre.com, www.transportelacustre.com). Like La Novia, Milton Arciaoffers tours on the weekends around Isla de Amor, Península Chiltepe and to León Viejo. The trips costs $2.42 per hour. The company, owned by Milton Arcia Marin, also runs a ferry service between San Jorge and Isla de Ometepe. Updated: Jun 23, 2009.

PLAZAS

Plaza de la Cultura de Guatemala

Plaza de la Cultura de Guatemala might have once been a nice little park, as it's located right across from Managua's historic center, but the intervening years have not been kind; the plaza has long since been abandoned to vandals and the homeless. The grounds are filled with broken bottles and trash, the benches are wrecked, the trees overgrown and the monuments defaced. If you're walking back from the Malecón, Plaza de la Cultura is not where you should linger. Speed up your pace or take a detour through the nicer Plaza de la República, across the street. Updated: Jun 23, 2009.

Plaza de la República

Directly across from the Catedral Vieja is the Plaza de la República, also known as José Dolores Estrada Park. The shady square has a massive gazebo (the dragon head fountains are impressive, even if the water has dried up), but the greatest emphasis is reserved for a memorial to Sandinista commander Carlos Fonseca Amador. "Nicaragua entera te dice presente" declares the inscription, which is surrounded by an empty pool, banners in both national and Sandinista colors and a (somewhat surprisingly) still burning eternal flame. The park is where hopeful vendors wait for tourists, so don't be surprised if a couple of children approach you with their palm frond masterpieces. Updated: Jun 12, 2009.

La Plaza de la Revolución

La Plaza de la Revolucción was once Managua's central square before the devastating earthquakes of 1972 destroyed the heart of the city; it is now the hub of the historical district. The plaza was named in honor of the Sandinista-led revolution against Anastasio Somoza Debayle, son of Nicaraguan dictator General Anastasio Somoza García. The Sandinistas marched to victory in 1979, Somoza fled the country and, in November, thousands of Nicaraguans filled the plaza to celebrate. A mounted statue of the dictator, which had stood in the plaza, was pulled down during those initial days of victory. You can see photos of the statue's demise at the Museo Nacional and find pieces of the bronze horse at the Parque Historicó Nacional Loma de Tiscapa. Updated: Jun 12, 2009.

Plaza de la Fé Juan Pablo II

At Plaza de la Fé Juan Pablo II, the pope gives his blessing from a white obelisk in the middle of an empty concrete lot. In 1996, on his second trip to the country (he had also visited in 1983), Pope John Paul II stood in the same plaza and addressed the Nicaraguan people. You can find more monuments commemorating his visit at Catholic churches around the countryside, particularly in Jinotepe and Niquinohomo. Plaza de la Fé Juan Pablo II is now mainly used as a parking area when infrequent events are held at the Concha Acustica. During the day, the empty plaza is also patrolled by a couple of friendly guards. Across from the Malecòn. Updated: May 04, 2009.

MONUMENTS

Estatua al Soldado

As you head into the Zona Monumental, look for huge Estatua al Soldado (Nameless Guerilla Soldier), a bare-chested figure. The soldier, who looks like he's in the middle of a war cry, holds a pick ax and a flag-draped rifle. At his feet is the politically inspired inscription: *solo los obreros y campesinos irán hasta el fin* (only the workers and peasants will go to the end). Those campesinos are represented across the highway in a bronze monument to the Nicaraguan Worker, where a tired looking couple are bent to their work. Updated: Jun 23, 2009.

La Concha Acustica

Just four years old, La Concha Acustica Taiwan has started to succumb to the same lack of maintenance that seems to plague all of the Managua monuments. Artist Glen Howard would no doubt be dismayed to see the cracks and stains that have started to appear on his work, erected in 2004.

The Acoustic Shell, which looks like a huge white wave surging up from Lake Managua to crash on shore, is still used as a staging area for concerts and cultural events—at least according to locals, who couldn't remember the last time one took place. The stark white beauty of the shell is also slightly overshadowed by the mammoth pink FSLN

Become a travel writer! See how at vivatravelguides.com/bootcamp/

Activities

1 Arboretum Nacional A2
2 Casa Presidencial B1
3 Canopy Tour Tiscapa A2
4 Catedral Vieja B2
5 Centro Cultural Managua B2
6 Estatua Soldado A2
7 La Concha Acustica A1
8 Palacio de la Cultura B2
9 Parque de la Paz B2
10 Plaza de la Cultura de Guatemala A2
11 Plaza de la Fé A1
12 Plaza de la Revolución B2
13 Teatro Nacional Rubén Darío A1

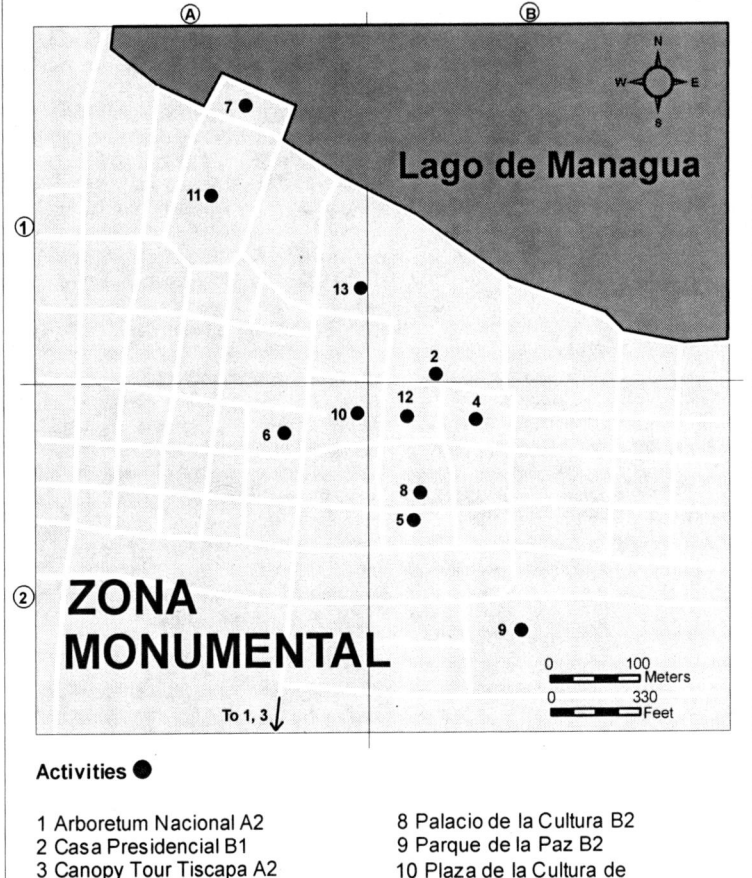

billboards, which have sprouted nearby, along with a sea of national and political flags. For a night of culture, Managua-style, a better bet is to head to the grand Teatro Nacional Rubén Darío, located just to the south. Updated: May 04, 2009.

Casa Presidential

On the north side of La Plaza de la Revolución is the Casa Presidential. Once a social club for the Nicaraguan elite, the building was destroyed (along with the rest of the city center) in 1972. Rebuilt by Nicaraguan President Arnoldo Alemán during his tenure in the late 1990s, the brightly painted brick building is now a presidential office space. (No one actually lives there.) After winning the 2006 elections, President Daniel Ortega changed the name of the building to "Casa de los Pueblos," a rather futile gesture since the grounds are still off limits to the general public. Outside, a bronze Sandino stands with his coat over his arm as though he, too, is waiting to go inside. Updated: Jun 23, 2009.

Fuente Audiovisual

The Fuente Audiovisual, which used to offer a spectacular nightly show with dancing fountains and music, was removed from the Plaza de la Revolución shortly after President Daniel Ortega took power. The official reason for the fountain's disappearance was an attempt to restore the historically important plaza to its original state. However, since the fountain was constructed by Ortega's rival, Liberal party ex-President Arnoldo Alemán, politics likely had something to do with the decision. At the time the fountain was removed, officials promised to reconstruct it elsewhere in the city, but Managua residents aren't holding their breath. Updated: Jun 24, 2009.

ARTS & ENTERTAINMENT

Teatro Nacional Rubén Darío

It's hard to think of a better way to celebrate the life of Nicaragua's most famous and beloved poet than with a national theater. For the past 40 years, Teatro Nacional Rubén Darío has been the place to see the best of the best of Nicaragua's cultural events, such as readings of *El Gúegúense o Mucho Ratón*, the earliest known poem in the country. The theater's program is eclectic, from evenings with the national orchestra or Nicaragua's folklore ballet company to spectaculars with Las Vegas musicians. In 2009, the theater hosted the Miss Nicaragua competition. The Rubén Darío is a beautiful theater, with a pillared entrance and chandeliers, and is the perfect place to head for an upscale evening.

You can check ahead on the theater's website for dates and times of the performances. Since most events take place at night when the historic district is deserted, plan on either driving to the theater or taking a taxi. *Note: The theater is closed to visitors if a performance is planned for the same evening.* Open Monday – Friday, 9 a.m. – 5 p.m.; Saturday and Sunday, 10 a.m. – 3 p.m. Tel: 505-2-222-7426, URL: www.tnrubendario.gob.ni. Updated: May 04, 2009.

El Centro Cultural Managua

El Centro Cultural Managua, located between Dupla Norte and the Palacio Nacional de la Cultura, is home to the national art and music schools, as well as scattered galleries and shops. The building was once Managua's Grand Hotel and, in early 2009, the center closed down for much-needed renovations to the old building. El Centro Cultural was expected to reopen in the spring of 2009 with a new slate of art exhibits, concerts and craft fairs. Tel: 505-2-222-5291. Updated: Jun 12, 2009.

Centro Nicaragüense de Escritores

The Centro Nicaragüense de Escritores has one of the most extensive collections of modern Nicaraguan literature in the country. The center has over 140 titles (in Spanish), including cookbooks and children's literature. Once a month the center holds cultural events such as author readings. There are also a limited number of Nicaraguan paintings and large, stone sculptures available for sale. Open daily 8:30 – 5 p.m. Reparto Los Robles, 2 blocks south of Hotel Seminole. Tel: 505-2-267-0304/ 505-8-843-4770, Fax: 505-2-278-5781, E-mail: escritor@ibw.com.ni, magallymiller@yahoo.com. Updated: Jun 24, 2009.

Tours

INTUR Central, one block west and one south of Crowne Plaza, can provide a list of Managua-based tour operators, as well as maps, brochures and other information. The INTUR list of 24 tour operators cover every sort of excursion, from Nicaraguan safaris to lake tours and trips around the country's volcanoes. Tel: 505-2-222-3333, E-mail: www.intur.gob.ni.

If you'd rather explore on your own, a good first stop is the distant **Marena Central** (Ministry of the Environment & Natural Resources, Tel: 505-2-263-2830, URL: www.marena.gob.ni). The officials there are extremely helpful and generous with both their time and maps of Nicaragua's protected areas (possibly because no one ever makes the journey out to their office). If you'd like to get copies of all of their maps, bring a memory card with you. Updated: Jun 23, 2009.

El Porvenir

El Porvenir is an organization based in Denver that relies on donations from companies and individuals to help build water projects for communities in Nicaragua. Created as a branch of Habitat for Humanity, El Porvenir, meaning *the future*, was established in the 1980s with the mission to "improve the standard of living of poor people in Nicaragua

El Centro Cultural Managua

through sustainable self-help water, sanitation and reforestation projects."

Communities that request a water or sanitation project come to one of the El Porvenir offices located in small villages throughout Nicaragua and apply for assistance. El Porvenir sponsors the projects and oversees the planning, construction and follow-up, while the community members do the labor and the maintenance. The projects are sustainable because they are not only actively sought out and manned by the villagers, but they are also projects in which the entire community can take pride.

With the brigades and educational tours, a fee is charged that covers all the costs, but if you are interested in coming on your own and paying your own expenses, there are always ways for you to help. U.S. Address: 1420 Ogden Street #204, Denver, CO 80218. Tel: 1-303-861-1499, E-mail for work trip and tour inquiries: Jo Buesher tours@elporvenir.org, E-mail for executive director in Nicaragua: Rob Bell nicaragua@elporvenir.org, Tel: 505-2-268-5781, E-mail: info@elporvenir.org, URL: www.elporvenir.org. Updated: Jan 20, 2009.

Lodging

As is only to be expected from a capital city, Managua has a full range of accommodation options, from the most basic of bedrooms with padlocks on the doors and shared outhouses, to the most plush suites with beds like clouds, staff at your beck and call, and bathtubs big enough to swim in.

For the most part, what you're willing to pay will determine where in the city you should look for a room. **Barrio Martha Quezada** has a range of backpacker hostels and hospedajes (of both the sordid and spotless varieties); the **Centro Commercial** has cornered the market when it comes to grand, higher end hotels (the exception being the Crown Plaza on Martha Quezada outer edge); and both **Barrio Boloñia** and **Los Robles** claim a number of boutique and business-oriented hotels.

Weekends are the best time to stay in the centro, since the expensive hotels lower their prices. You're unlikely to ever be stuck without a room in Managua, but if you have your heart set on a particular hotel, make sure to call ahead and have them reserve a space. Updated: Jun 22, 2009.

BUDGET

Nicaragua Guest House - Bello Horizonte

(ROOMS: $16 – 35) Nicaraguan Guest House (also known to taxi drivers as *Backpacker's*) is one of the few hotels in Managua that you can book online. The hotel has clean, though perhaps austere, rooms with large bathrooms and is within walking distance of Centro Comercial Las Americas, a mall with a food court and movie theater. Each room has a fan, TV and air conditioning (although the latter costs $35 to use).

While the guest house is secure and has a friendly staff, the owners have oddly strict rules. Bello Horizonte's bars might be just down the road, but the hotel is only open between the hours of 4:30 a.m. and 11 p.m.— the latter being both a guest curfew and the time at which the electricity is shut off in the hotel (but not in the rooms). Signs over the toilets note that sexual tourism is prohibited and sets of guest rules are taped to almost every wall. Combine the curfew with a 10 a.m. checkout time, a bowl of fruit and cracker packet for breakfast, and a location that airport taxis don't want to go to, and Nicaragua Guest House becomes the place to book if you want a secure night before moving on to a *better* location. Bello Horizonte Vi Etapa 217 Rotonda Larreynaga 2 C. South 2 1/2 blocks. Tel: 505-2-249-8963, E-mail: oscar3701@yahoo.com, URL: www.3dp.ch/nicaragua. Updated: Mar 23, 2009.

HIGH-END

Best Western Hotel Las Mercedes

(ROOMS: $76 – 90) For weary travelers, finding the Best Western Hotel Las Mercedes across from the airport is a bit like being greeted at the arrival gate by a friend. The sprawling complex includes 196 rooms, spa, beauty salon, two pools, three private parking lots, five conference rooms and a gym. It is a typical Best Western, but with tropical twists such as birds of paradise in the lobby. The hotel is currently undergoing a slow, but extensive, renovation to the older rooms and corridors. All the rooms have air conditioning and cable TV. Km 9.5, across from the airport. Tel: 505-2-255-9900 ext. 5 (for reservations), Fax: 505-2-263-1083. Updated: Apr 21, 2009.

Restaurants

Managua has no shortage of restaurants serving typical Nicaraguan dishes; it also has plenty of alternatives to tickle your taste buds. There are fine restaurants of all price ranges spread throughout the city, with clusters of fine dining options along Zona Hippo's in Los Robles and at the food court of Galerias Santo Domingo. For fast food options, check out the Carr. Masaya, Metrocentro or Plaza Inter. Updated: Jun 22, 2009.

Casa Mexico

Casa Mexico offers authentic Mexican food in a warm and fun setting, with a large selection of dishes freshly prepared as you order, as well as variety of of Tequila drinks. Near La laguna de Tiscapa by the bust of Jose Marti 1/2 block up on the left. Tel: 505-2-222-5944. Updated: Jul 13, 2007.

Intermezzo del Bosque

(ENTREES: $6 – 18) Intermezzo del Bosque is a fine dining option situated just outside downtown Managua. The tables are on an outdoor terrance that has a beautiful view of the city and, surprisingly, of nearby woods. Their extensive and varied menu offers salads, seafood, fondue, shrimp and steaks. This place is a great pick if you want a gourmet meal in a quiet (and romantic) setting, and are looking to escape the hustle and bustle of Managua without venturing too far outside the city. Colegio Interaméricano 5 km south. Tel: 505-2-883-0071, Fax: 505-2-884-0996, E-mail: intermezzodelbosque@gmail.com, URL: www.intermezzodelbosque.com. Updated: Nov 20, 2008.

> **V!VA ONLINE REVIEW**
> INTERMEZZO DEL BOSQUE
>
> "They have the BEST food, drinks, music, staff service, all wrapped up in one awsome place on top of a mountain, surrounded by trees and a cool breeze..."
>
> USA, November 08, 2008

Restaurante Lakun Payaska

(ENTREES: $6 – 14) For beer and a bite to eat at a place with a view, Restaurant Lakun Payaska at Puerto Salvador Allende is one of your best bets. The restaurant is clean and reasonably priced, with a covered patio overlooking the water. If you don't want to eat outside, the restaurant has a spacious interior that's decorated with fish and an enormous mirror. The menu includes chicken, beef, pork, soups and rice dishes, with a nice list of liquors; however, the specialty is the seafood, imported daily from Puerto Cabeza. Puerto Salvador Allende de la Concha Acustica, 75 varas down. Tel: 505-2-222-3586/ 909-0425. Updated: Apr 20, 2009.

Bar y Restaurant El Muellecito

(ENTREES: $8 – 9) All along the Malecon, you'll find a series of ramshackle bars and eateries, all serving local food and drinks. The loudest and largest of all of the lake side establishments is Bar y Restaurant El Muellecito, a brightly colored building where waiters will fight to get you to sit in their sections during slow days. The bar—open from 10 a.m. to 5 a.m.—is a better bet at night, when the dance floor starts to heat up. During the day, the Malecon is a crowded warehouse of empty tables where the smell of sewage-tainted water rises through the barred windows. There is no set menu; the restaurant serves various forms of *comida* typical Nicargauan fare. Updated: Mar 22, 2009.

Nightlife

Chaman

(COVER: $1.45 – 8.75) Just beyond Lake Tiscapa is a small Mayan temple, but forget ancient gods—*this* pyramid was built as a temple for salsa, merengue, rock and techno. Since January 2009, the temple has housed the nightclub Chaman. The club—open Wednesday through Saturday from 8 p.m. to 5 a.m.—features black block furniture, a raised dance floor, a suspended DJ booth and a rotating schedule of events. Chaman is known as one of the few places where the Managua elite go to party; the cover charge ranges from $1.45 general admission on Wednesdays to $3.88 for women and $8.75 for men most Saturdays. From the Restaurant El Tiscapa, Chaman is located 200 m south and 40 m west. Tel: 505-2-274-1872, E-mail: chamanbar@cablenet.com.ni, URL: www.chamanbar.com. Updated: Mar 22, 2009.

Fussion Chill-Out Bar Concert and Gallery

Very few bars can boast that their drink servers are also Nicaraguan art-world royalty. Fussion Chill-Out Bar Concert and Gallery is Atahuallpa and Dirhiangém Mejia's latest entrepreneurial and artistic endeavour. The duo are second generation members of one of Nicaragua's most legendary musical families.

Become a travel writer! See how at vivatravelguides.com/bootcamp/

Fussion is a laid-back, eclectic lounge with odd gallery pieces set among comfortable seating. Among the stranger decorations are the lamps taken out of pastiche cinema, sawed-off oil barrels, ironing boards that serve as coffee tables, old doors hanging by wires from the ceiling, and antique sewing machines. The bar also plays a mix of world music, electronica and local favorites.

During the week, Fussion is a low-key place to unwind; weekend concerts usually attract a crowd of local Nicaraguans who prefer the bar's art feel to that of the discotheques. Updated: Nov 20, 2008.

El Caramanchel

The name *El Caramanchel* is Nicaraguan for "shack", but this bar has adopted the word with a sly wink. Located in Managua's historic downtown, the bar was formerly home to the popular clubs Café Amatl and Jarro. The new owners have tried to revive the mix of salsa, dance hall and electronic music present during the earlier years. They have also added bar food with a range of flavors, including Colombian empanadas, Mexican quesadillas and burritos, Nicaraguan tortas, and a variety of hamburgers. You might also want to sample El Caramanchel's *micheladas*, a drink that includes tomato juice and a little Tabasco sauce; the Cuban mojitos are also a good choice.

There is seating under a roof or under the trees with Chinese-style lamps, but don't sit for long; dancing is a must! El Caramanchel is located three blocks south and ½ a block east from from Plaza Inter. Open Wednesdays to Saturdays. Updated: Nov 21, 2008.

Barrio Martha Quezada

Barrio Martha Quezada has a well-earned reputation as the go-to place for cheap rooms in Managua. Located to the west of the Crowne Plaza Hotel (a great, white pyramid also known as the old Intercontinental Hotel) and just south of the Denis Martínez National Baseball Stadium, the neighborhood has retained a largely residential feel, even with a growing number of backpackers and the hotels that cater to them. Of course, the influx of tourists has brought an accompanying rise in crime. Barrio Martha Quezada is not the place to wander the streets at night; locals will also warn you to stay away from streets known to be inhabited by drug dealers and alcoholics. The barrio is centered around Tica Bus terminals, and is also convenient to the Zona Monumental. Updated: Jun 21, 2009.

Lodging

The streets around Tica Bus are known as the best place in Managua to find backpacker friendly budget accommodations. Not all rooms are created equal, though. More than in other parts of the city, there is a drastic difference between the cheapest of the cheap and the next step up. You can always find a $5 place to rest your head, but don't expect spotless facilities (or even fresh sheets). Another $3 will buy you a much better—and cleaner—space to rest (and in some hostels, a private bathroom as well). Shop around before settling on a room; you may even find yourself accompanied by a local "guide"—homeless men whom hostel owners pay to bring in clients. Updated: Jun 21, 2009.

BUDGET
Hospedaje Mesa

(ROOMS: $5 and up) If you only have $5 left in your pocket when you get to Barrio Martha Quezada, you can try visiting Hospedaje Mesa. The hostel is one of the cheapest accomodations around, but for good reason: Despite a layer of colorful paint, the 24 rooms are dim and dirty-looking. They have what could be called "private bathrooms"— if you think a spigot sticking out from a three-walled corner is private. While the sheets on the beds appear relatively clean, the rooms are not secure, so you shouldn't leave valuables there. There are fans, but no air conditioning or other amenities. From the Tica bus, one block north and half a block east. Tel: 505-2-222-2046/493-3410. Updated: Mar 21, 2009.

Santos

(ROOMS: $6 and up) A rustic, older hostel located across the street from Los Cisneros, Santos provides cheap, private rooms and a spacious balcony. Rooms are slightly dingy, though, and the private bathrooms are rather run-down. A snack bar is located on the main floor. From the Tica Bus, one block to the lake, 1 1/2 blocks down. Tel: 505-2-222-3713. Updated: Nov 26, 2008.

Casa Vanegas

(ROOMS: $8 – 15) Given that Casa Vanegas is on a prominent corner near the Tica bus station, you might be led there by one of the persistently helpful street folk. The rooms are

BOLONIA AND MARTHA QUEZADA

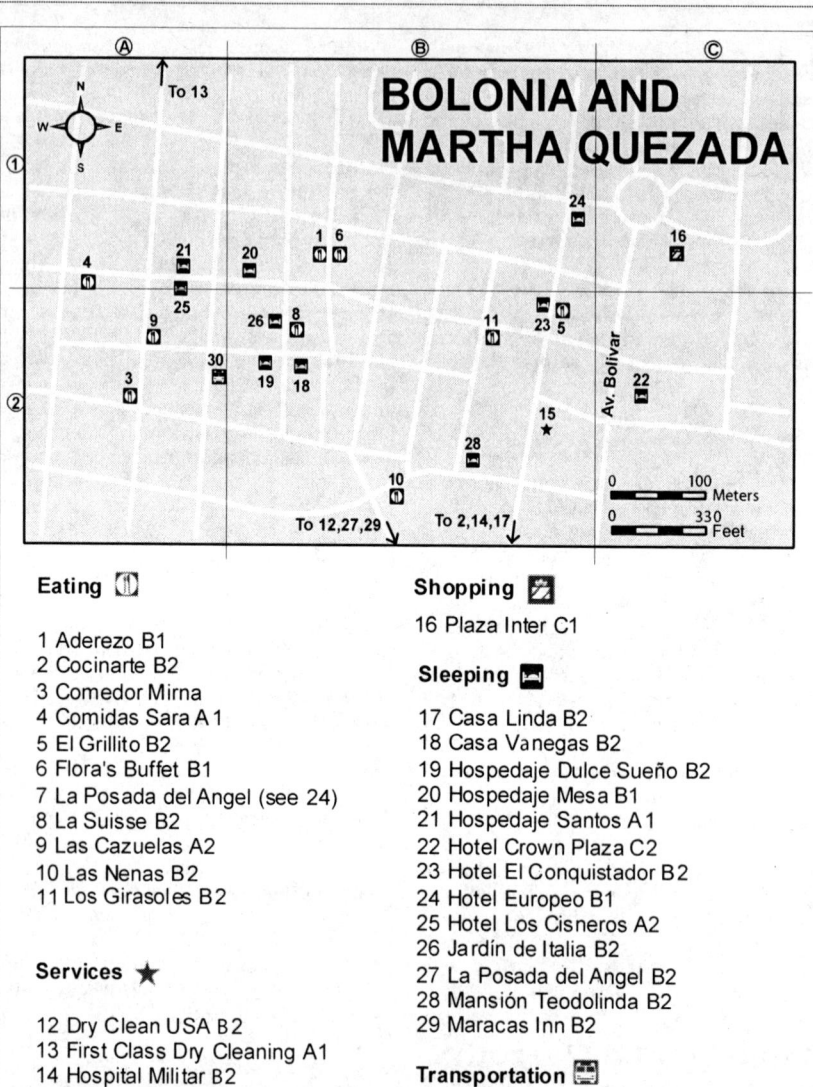

Eating
1 Aderezo B1
2 Cocinarte B2
3 Comedor Mirna
4 Comidas Sara A1
5 El Grillito B2
6 Flora's Buffet B1
7 La Posada del Angel (see 24)
8 La Suisse B2
9 Las Cazuelas A2
10 Las Nenas B2
11 Los Girasoles B2

Services
12 Dry Clean USA B2
13 First Class Dry Cleaning A1
14 Hospital Militar B2
15 INTUR B2

Shopping
16 Plaza Inter C1

Sleeping
17 Casa Linda B2
18 Casa Vanegas B2
19 Hospedaje Dulce Sueño B2
20 Hospedaje Mesa B1
21 Hospedaje Santos A1
22 Hotel Crown Plaza C2
23 Hotel El Conquistador B2
24 Hotel Europeo B1
25 Hotel Los Cisneros A2
26 Jardín de Italia B2
27 La Posada del Angel B2
28 Mansión Teodolinda B2
29 Maracas Inn B2

Transportation
30 Tica Bus A2

stark white and clean, with matrimonial beds, but the well-trafficked hospedaje has started to feel a little worn (especially compared to newer places in the area). The fact that the walls don't quite meet the ceilings in the shared bathroom can also make a toilet run feel a bit too outdoorsy. Still, Vanegas is quiet, safe (the outer doors are locked at 10 p.m.) and has a friendly, helpful staff. There is also Internet for $1/hour. From Tica bus 100 varas east. Tel: 505-2-222-4043, E-mail: casavanegas@cablenet.com.ni. Updated: Jun 21, 2009.

Hospedaje Dulce Sueño
(ROOMS: $10 and up) Just steps away from the Tica Bus station, Hospedaje Dulce Sueño is a new hostel that has clean, comfortable rooms and private bathrooms. A good budget option, this lodging has two levels and a spacious common area. The staff is friendly. Breakfast is available at an extra cost. From the Tica Bus, 75 yards up. Tel: 505-2-228-4125 / 424-0272, E-mail: Hospedaje_dulcesueno@yahoo.com. Updated: Nov 26, 2008.

Become a travel writer! See how at vivatravelguides.com/bootcamp/

MID-RANGE

Jardín de Italia

(ROOMS: $15) While the name suggests a garden, the reality is more of a concrete courtyard with some plants. That said, Jardín de Italia is secure and has clean rooms with private bathrooms. There is a computer with Internet that can be used for $0.50 an hour, and a kitchen where one can buy breakfast and snacks. The rooms have TV and air conditioning, and the price is comparable to other hostels in the area. From the Tica Bus, one block up, 1/2 a block to the lake. Tel: 505-2-222-7967, E-mail: info@jardindeitalia.com, URL: www.jardindeitalia.com. Updated: Nov 26, 2008.

Hotel Los Cisneros

(ROOMS: $20 – 45) Los Cisneros is one of the more expensive hotels in the area, but it also has the most services, making it reasonably priced. If you are looking for a place to stay long term, this hotel might be a good option: Los Cisneros has rooms available with a fridge and a mini kitchen. Altogether there are 14 rooms ranging from singles to triples. All rooms have either overhead fans or air conditioning. The hotel also has an inner garden space with hammocks and a small outdoor café. Tours can also be arranged through the hotel. From the Tica Bus, one block north, 1 1/2 blocks to the west #555. Tel: 505-2-222-3535 / 222-7273, E-mail: loscisneros@hotmail.com, URL: www.hotelloscisneros.com. Updated: Nov 26, 2008.

HIGH-END

Crowne Plaza

(ROOMS: $135 – 650) The great, white homage to a Mayan pyramid that is Crowne Plaza has been a Managua landmark for over 35 years. The hotel was one of the few buildings that the devastating 1972 earthquake failed to knock down and has been used by the foreign press and the Sandisista government.

Crowne Plaza's 140 executive rooms are elegant in every detail (such as a CD with relaxation suggestions), and the glittering downstairs includes a fitness center, casino, club lounge, swimming pool, business center, two in-house restaurants and an area for renting cars, getting your hair done, shopping or arranging a tour. Once you check in, you may never want to leave. Octava calle S.O. No. 101. Tel: 505-2-228-3530, Fax: 505-2-228-3087, E-mail: managua@ichotelsgroup.com, URL: www.crowneplaza.com/cpmanagua. Updated: Mar 26, 2009.

Restaurants

There are plenty of cheap, local eateries where you can get a bite to eat in Barrio Martha Quezada. This neighborhood is where you'll find the best street food, particularly greasy fritangas, large buffets and tiny, family-run eateries where the only indication that you can get food there is a set of plastic tables and chairs in the front yard. Martha Quezada is not the place for haute cuisine, but is the perfect spot to try Nicaraguan comida corriente and typical Nicaragua fare. Updated: Jun 21, 2009.

Cafe Mirna

(ENTREES: $0.72 – 1.95) Cafe Mirna, located just a block and a half away from the Tica Bus station, is a little gem with all the charm of a neighborhood diner. Mirna serves cheap and tasty breakfasts and buffets, which make the establishment a local favorite in Barrio Martha Quezada (and you might soon find yourself falling in love with it, too).

The cafe is decorated with panoramas of the world (along with a Human Rights poster and an Obama campaign shirt). There is a small seating area in a blue-tiled courtyard and more seating just inside. The breakfast menu, in both English and Spanish, includes omlettes, pancakes and fruit, while the lunch menu varies from day to day. If you're hungry and waiting for a bus, Cafe Mirna is the perfect place to recharge. Open: 7 a.m. – 2 p.m., with buffet served from noon – 2 p.m. From where Cine Dorado was, one block south, one block east. Tel: 505-2-222-7913. Updated: Mar 22, 2009.

Comida's Sara

(ENTREES: $3 – 3.50) Spot Comida's Sara from the street (bare bulbs, unpainted front, plastic furniture along the sidewalk, neon yellow posters) and you might be tempted to keep on walking. However, all the Barrio Martha Quezada residents know that Comida's Sara serves some of the tastiest curry around. The salsas also come in wonderful variety—pineapple, sweet, beer and cheese, to name a few—and can top beef, pork, chicken, fish, pasta or vegetable plates. The comedor is also reasonably priced, with all entrees set at $3.50, except for vegetable dishes, which are $3. Open daily 4 p.m. – 10 p.m. 2 blocks south of Casa del Obrero, and 1 block up. Tel: 505-2-918-3223. Updated: Mar 26, 2009.

Flora's Buffet
(ENTREES: $5 – 6) One of the heartiest budget options in Barrio Martha Quezada is Flora's Buffet. The restaurant may appear to be housed in a garage, but the interior is spacious, clean and cool, with comfortable wooden furniture and a bathroom. Flora's, like similar establishments, serves a wide, and constantly changing, array of *comida typica*. On any given day, you might find the rice and bean combination, gallo pinto, fried plantains and empanadas, as well as a selection of meat stews and salads. Buffets are a good option for vegetarians, since they usually have a wide variety of salads and non-meat side dishes. Flora's also has sodas, juice and water, but no beer. The restaurant is open from 7:45 a.m. – 9:30 p.m., Monday – Saturday, and is closed Sunday. From the corner of the old cine, 2 blocks down and 1/2 block to the South. Updated: Mar 22, 2009.

Las Cazuelas
Las Cazuelas is one of your safer bets for getting a tasty meal or a light snack at a good value in Barrio Martha Quezada. It's also within the two-block radius of the Tica Bus. There's a street front patio with a few tables, so you can dine *al fresco* (outside). The menu has a wide range of choices like chicken entrees and spaghetti, as well as soups and pizza. There are many seafood options as well, but you'll be able to get fresher fish elsewhere. From the Tica bus, 1 block down, right hand side. Tel: 505-2-228-6090. Updated: Nov 26, 2008.

Aderezo: Comida Casera
Open during lunchtime, Aderezo serves *comida casera* (home-style food) in a clean and charming atmosphere. The restaurant is probably the nicest in Barrio Martha and has good food for relatively cheap. At least four types of meat are served every day, along with the traditional sides of rice, beans, and vegetables. You can choose what you want from the buffet and pay according to the size of the heap on your plate. From the Tica Bus, 2 blocks up, 1/2 a block to the south. Open daily 11 a.m. – 2:30 p.m. Tel: 505-2-254-5317 / 251-4927. Updated: Nov 26, 2008.

La Suisse
For a light meal or snack, La Suisse has a couple tables where you can sit and enjoy a coffee and a pastry. The breads are fresh, and the place is clean and welcoming. Everything here will cost you under a dollar. From the Tica Bus, 100m to the east, 15 m to the north. Tel: 505-2-222-2717 Updated: Nov 26, 2008.

Barrio Boloñia
Barrio Boloñia is Martha Quezada's quietly upscale (and slightly safer) residential neighbor. Boloñia, within walking distance to Plaza Inter and the Zona Monumental, is the happy medium between the pricey downtown hotels and the cheap backpacker hostels. More than other neighborhoods, Barrio Boloñia has managed to resist the influx of tourist fever. The neighborhood, sprinkled with TV stations and residences, is a good place to escape from the busy city. However, it offers relatively few dining options, so you might find yourself heading in the evening to the restaurant-packed Centro Commercial. Updated: Jun 21, 2009.

Lodging
The Barrio Boloñia accommodation scene is largely made up of boutique hotels, with all the varieties on that theme. Want business boutique with a refrigerator, kitchenette and microwave in your room? Boloñia's got that. How about a hotel filled with antique furniture and wrought iron beds? Boloñia's has that, too. Or perhaps you seek a commercial hotel with conference facilities that won't break the company account? The neighborhood has you covered. The area's shady streets are a nice alternative to the traffic snarls downtown, and although they offer plenty of amenities, most are still quite affordable. Updated: Jun 21, 2009.

MID-RANGE

Casa Linda
(ROOMS: $30 – 60) Despite the name, Casa Linda is not particularly beautiful, but the house part rings true: walk in and you might find baby toys on the floor of what is obviously the owner's living room. Despite an interior that can feel a bit crowded, Casa Linda offers all the regular amenities, with breakfast included, air conditioning, private bathrooms with hot water, cable TV, Internet and laundry service. It is also one of the more reasonably priced locations in this barrio (the establishment is one of the few that won't charge double if you're one person in a room with two beds).

Casa Linda styles itself as a B&B, making it the place to go if you're tired of hotels and are looking for a room with the feel of a

---
Become a travel writer! See how at vivatravelguides.com/bootcamp/

homestay. Casa Linda does not accept walk-ins before 11 a.m., so if you plan to arrive earlier, make sure you have a reservation. 2 blocks north, 170 meters west from Hospital Militar, Boloñia. Tel: 505-2-266-8575, Fax: 505-2-266-8575, E-mail: casalindamanagua@yahoo.com. Updated: Mar 23, 2009.

Hotel Europeo
(ROOMS: $47 – 67) Hotel Europeo is a cheaper alternative to the other hotels located within the main business and commerce area of Managua. It's a great value, though, as it offers many of the same services and amenities without skimping on room quality and atmosphere. Hotel Europeo has 35 rooms and, as a smaller establishment, creates a more intimate feel. Many of the rooms also back onto a palm tree-surrounded pool. If you want to rent a car, Hotel Europeo has an agreement with Budget and can offer deals with special rates. From Canal 2, 75 varas below, Residencial Boloñia. Tel: 505-2-268-2130 / 31 Fax: 505-2-268-4930, E-mail: europeo@ibw.com.ni, URL: www.hoteleuropeo.com.ni. Updated: Nov 20, 2008.

La Posada del Angel
(ROOMS: $50 – 75) La Posada del Angel offers rooms at about the same price range as other hotels in the Barrio Bolognia, but the interior—decorated with afghan rugs, dark wood furniture, paintings and gilt sculptures—can only be described as sumptuous. Throw in wrought iron beds, a garden pool and fountains, and La Posada makes the perfect getaway. With Iglesia San Francisco across the street, you'll also be able to enjoy plenty of tranquility. If you plan to stay for awhile, La Posada also has eight apartments with kitchens for $900 per month, which includes daily breakfast at the hotel.

All the hotel rooms have air conditioning and cable TV. They also offer airport transportation (via taxi) for $20 or $30 for two people. Reservations are required. From the Military Hospital, 1 block north, 3 blocks west, 20 meters north, in front of San Francisco Church. Tel: 505-2-268-7228 ext. 31, Fax: 505-2-266-1347, E-mail: pdelangel@cablenet.com.ni / posada_d_angel@yahoo.com, URL: www.hotelposadadelangel.com.ni. Updated: Mar 25, 2009.

Maracas Inn
(ROOMS: $50 – 90) This is not the place to go if your idea of a hotel involves the words "stylish" or "elegant." The heavy coat of yellow paint, some lovely vases of flowers and nooks filled with El Gueguense masks and figures cannot overcome the sense that the Maracas Inn is the Nicaraguan version of a Holiday Inn. Still, the hotel has found a niche and fills it well. Maracas is the perfect place to go if you need a comfortable bed, all the regular amenities (including a rather green-looking pool that was scheduled to undergo a renovation in March 2009) and a conference facility. Maracas has four meeting rooms with air conditioning, audiovisual equipment and white boards. There are also discounts for groups and for longer stays. Airport transportation ($15 per person), lunch ($9 – 12) and dinners ($7) can all be arranged. From Hospital Militar, 1 block north, 1 ½ blocks west. Tel: 505-2-264-2610/ 266-8464/ 266-8612, Fax: 505-2-266-8982, E-mail: maracasi@ibw.com.ni, URL: www.maracasinn.com. Prices do not include tax. Updated: Mar 26, 2009.

El Conquistador Hotel and Suite
(ROOMS: $55 – 75) Murals around El Conquistador's spacious reception area, bar and lounge make the hotel feel more like an oasis than you might assume, considering the hotel's location (a block away from Plaza Inter mall and 27 de Mayo). The 19 rooms are decorated with Nicaraguan art and there is a nook with a pool table on the first floor. The location is convenient, right off Carr. Norte. There is a private parking area and small cafe (open from noon to 10 p.m.). El Conquistador attracts its fair share of business travelers and tourists. The rooms have both WiFi and cable TV. 1 block south and 1 block west of Plaza Inter. Tel: 505-2-222-4789, Fax: 505-2-222-3657, E-mail: info@hotelelconquistador.com / ventas@hotelelconquistador.com, URL: www.hotelelconquistador.com. Updated: Mar 27, 2009.

HIGH-END
Hotel Mansion Teodolinda
(ROOMS: $70 – 95) Hotel Mansion Teodolinda is on the higher end of Barrio Bolonia accommodations. The rooms are fairly standard, but offer more amenities than most. There are fully equipped kitchenettes in all 48 rooms (except for nine on the third floor). The kitchenettes have microwaves, refrigerators, sinks, electric stoves, dishes, cutting boards, toasters—and even blenders. There are four conference rooms with a capacity of up to 100 people each. The owners have recently started construction on

a new building, which will have 30 rooms and 10 suites. The new facility, which will use solar heated water, is scheduled to be complete at the end of 2009.

Note: prices increase by $5 during the high season (1 June – 30 Nov.) and decrease by $5 during the holiday season (1 Dec. – 14 Jan. and Semana Santa).

1 block south and 1 block west of Plaza Intur, Boloñia. Tel: 505-2-228-1060, Fax: 505-2-222-4908, E-mail: hotel@teodolinda.com.ni, URL: www.teodolinda.com.ni. Updated: Mar 26, 2009.

Restaurants

Many of the Barrio Boloñia hotels have attached restaurants (often destinations in their own right), which is a good thing since the neighborhood has a rather small number of dining options. The establishments that are there may be a bit harder on your wallet, but in exchange offer the escape of a garden oasis, the succulent flavor of Spanish cuisine, or smooth fruity drinks. For a more economical meal, the neighboring Barrio Martha Quezada has plenty of fritangas and buffets, just follow the smells of frying foods. Updated: Jun 21, 2009.

Las Nenas

(SIDES: $0.50 – $0.66, LUNCH: $2.04) Las Nenas is a charming little two-table establishment hidden among Bolognia's residences. The eatery is open from 7:30 a.m. – 2 p.m., but only serves enchiladas, fruit juice and tortillas in the morning hours. There is no set menu and the daily lunch special varies (from chicken in wine sauce to fried pork or stuffed peppers) but always includes a juice, rice and salad. The eatery has a rather depressing view of an empty lot, but the motherly and delightful owners make up for the lack of scenery. From the Channel 10 station, 1/2 a block west. Tel: 505-472-5751. Updated: Mar 23, 2009.

El Grillito

(ENTREES: $2.02 – 7.10, BEER: $0.69 and up, CIGARETTES: $ 2.02, TEQUILA: $25.50) Bar and Restaurante "El Grillito" is the perfect place to get a beer and fried food, as long as you don't mind tables that are a bit sticky and grimy. Despite the gaudily painted mural outside, El Grillito is more of a neighborhood drinking space than a place to take a date. A side window serves *fritangas* starting at noon. The main patio area is open daily 6 p.m. - 6 a.m. North of Plaza Inter, Boloñia. Tel: 505-2-266-8567. Updated: Mar 24, 2009.

Pollo Estrella

(ENTREES: $2.60 – $14.50 for a family 12 piece combo) Pollo Estrella, a chain of fast food chicken restaurants, has locations all over Nicaragua, including this one in Barrio Boloñia. Identifiable by the logo—a bright yellow star with a happy chicken face—Pollo Estrella restaurants are best if you want a quick meal and are willing to pay a little more than you would at a local eatery. Like other fast food joints in Managua, you may find that Pollo Estrella is out of multiple items on the menu, but combos (with chicken, a roll, French fries and a soda) are perpetual staples that run between $3 and $4.50. Pollo Estrella also has hamburgers, a lighter menu, a kids menu and larger combos for groups. Tel: 505-2-254-5336/ 254-5341, URL: www.polloestrella.com.ni. Updated: Mar 22, 2009.

Restaurant Girasoles

(ENTREES: $6 – 12) Restaurant Girasoles, part of Hotel Mansion Teodolinda, is a good stop in Barrio Bolonia for a upscale lunch or early dinner. The menu's range is the usual fare of pork, chicken, fish, shrimp and pasta; if you call ahead, Girasoles can also prepare vegetarian meals. Unlike most hotel restaurants, Girasoles has a separate entrance. The windows overlook Teodolinda's outdoor pool and courtyard. Open daily 6 a.m. – 6 p.m. From Plaza Intur, 1 block south, 1 block west, Boloñia. Tel: 505-2-228-1060, E-mail: hotel@teodolinda.com.ni, URL: www.teodolinda.com.ni. Updated: Mar 26, 2009.

La Posada del Angel Restaurant

(ENTREES: $7 – 15) La Posada del Angel Restaurant, in the gorgeous hotel of the same name, offers a select menu of higher end dishes including pastas, fish, salads, soups and the house specialty, a 10 ounce black pepper and cognac tenderloin. The restaurant is open from 6 – 10 p.m. La Posada also serves lunch if you make reservations ahead of time. From the Hospital Militar, 1 block towards the lake, 3 blocks down, 20 vrs. towards the lake; across from la Iglesia San Francisco, Boloñia. Tel: 505-2-268-7228 ext. 31, E-mail: posada_d_angel@yahoo.com, URL: www.hotelposadadelangel.com.ni. Updated: Mar 26, 2009.

Los Ranchos

A popular restaurant for lunch and dinner, Los Ranchos serves large portions and has

---

Become a travel writer! See how at vivatravelguides.com/bootcamp/

great grilled meats. The garden patio interior with surrounding foliage and a mini-waterfall provides an oasis from the city streets of Managua. There service here is top-notch, and the food is very reasonably priced. Los Ranchos is highly recommended if you're looking to fill your belly and enjoy some quality Nicaraguan beef. Carretera Sur km 3 1/2. Tel: 505-2-266-0526. Updated: Nov 26, 2008.

Cocinarte

Platos tipicos such as Indio Viejo, as well as vegetarian dishes, smoothies and fruits drinks are all available in Managua's Cocinarte. Colorful murals line the outside walls, and the seating under the restaurant's thatched roof is airy and spacious. From Intur, 1 block south. Updated: Nov 26, 2008.

Rincón Español

A small, Spanish restaurant, Rincón Español has a menu that includes paella, torta Española, Manchego cheese, and of course, sangria. The service is attentive and the food is tasty, but the interior looks as though it hasn't been updated in the last 20 years. This is a higher-end restaurant that is unpresuming but well established in the city. From the national stadium and the fire station, 1 block down. Tel: 505-2-266-3843. Updated: Nov 27, 2008.

Centro Commercial and Carretera Masaya

If the Zona Monumental was the heart of the old city, then the new Managua is slowly growing a new heart in the busy, chaotic, commercial downtown. The Centro Commercial is where you'll find the Catedral Nueva, Metrocentro Mall (a local landmark), the UCA bus terminal and all the top hotels and restaurants. To the east is the upscale Los Robles, a tree-lined residential area where family homes are increasingly giving way to galleries, upscale restaurants (check out Zona Hippa for the best in eating) and the area's mid-range hotels.

To the south is the Carretera Masaya, a formerly sleepy highway that is now the go-to area for the city's most glittery casinos and clubs. Centro Commercial may be busy, but it's also one of the safest neighborhoods. Updated: Jun 21, 2009.

Lodging

Centro Commercial is where businessmen and upscale travelers spend their weeks couched in luxury. The biggest and brightest of the lot are Hotel Princess, Seminole Plaza Hotel, Holiday Inn and, the grand dame, Real Intercontinental Metrocentro. Along the side streets, particularly in Los Robles, are the smaller boutique options and what pass for budget rooms in the commercial center. No matter where you sleep, you'll be within walking distance of discos and a slew of restaurants. Updated: Jun 21, 2009.

BUDGET
Hotel San Luis

(ROOMS: $20 – 30) This hotel is located south of the new center of Managua, with a lot of local services available within a seven-minute radius. Here guests can relax in a friendly atmosphere filled with comfort and high-quality service. Internet and international calls are free. Prices remain the same throughout the year. Colonia Centroamérica B-163. From Farmacia Vida 1 block south, 1\2 a block to the west. Tel: 505-2-278-0935, E-mail: hotel.sanluis@hotmail.com, URL: www.hotelsanluis.com.ni. Updated: Jun 10, 2009.

> **V!VA ONLINE REVIEW**
> HOTEL SAN LUIS
>
> *This is a smaller hotel, but the rooms are quite comfortable, and very clean as well. Breakfast is included, and they also have free WiFi.*
>
> The Netherlands, December 01, 2008

MID-RANGE
Hotel Sol y Luna

(ROOMS: $50 – 90) Hotel Sol y Luna offers pleasant, if not particularly extraordinary, accommodations down one of Los Robles' shaded streets, behind Rest. La Marsellaise. The rooms (single, $50; matrimonial $60; double $70; triple $90; breakfast included, tax is not) have WiFi, trundle beds and private bathrooms, as well as air conditioning and cable TV. The hotel itself is a cheery yellow with a sunken couch in the middle of the lobby and a few breakfast tables behind the front desk. Sol y Luna provides airport transfers between $20 and $25 (depending on the time of day). Behind Rest. La Marsellaise, Los Robles. Tel: 505-2-277-1009/505-2-278-6006, E-mail: solyluna@cablenet.com.ni. Updated: Jun 23, 2009.

Hotel Colon

(ROOMS: $60 – 72) Hotel Colon is a solid mid-range option in Los Robles, although the

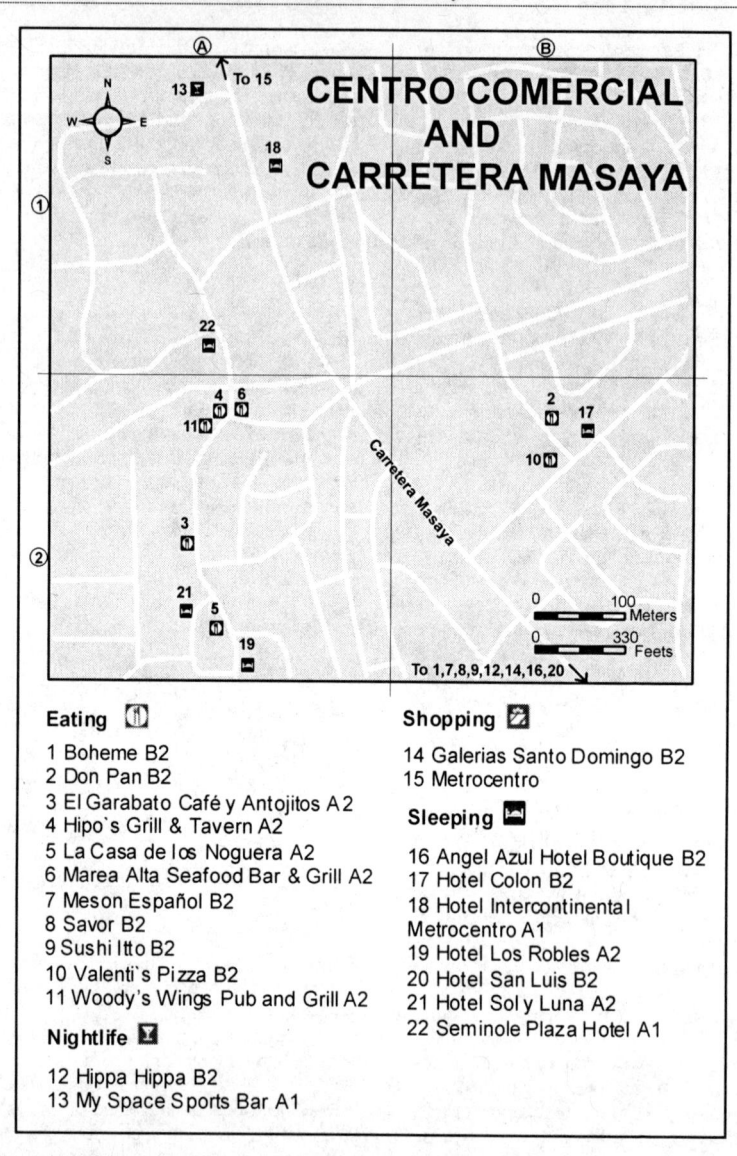

Centro Comercial and Carretera Masaya

CENTRO COMERCIAL AND CARRETERA MASAYA

Eating
1 Boheme B2
2 Don Pan B2
3 El Garabato Café y Antojitos A2
4 Hipo's Grill & Tavern A2
5 La Casa de los Noguera A2
6 Marea Alta Seafood Bar & Grill A2
7 Meson Español B2
8 Savor B2
9 Sushi Itto B2
10 Valenti's Pizza B2
11 Woody's Wings Pub and Grill A2

Nightlife
12 Hippa Hippa B2
13 My Space Sports Bar A1

Shopping
14 Galerias Santo Domingo B2
15 Metrocentro

Sleeping
16 Angel Azul Hotel Boutique B2
17 Hotel Colon B2
18 Hotel Intercontinental Metrocentro A1
19 Hotel Los Robles A2
20 Hotel San Luis B2
21 Hotel Sol y Luna A2
22 Seminole Plaza Hotel A1

location has started to appear a bit down in the heel. The shrieking lime-colored rooms don't help, either; Colon has gone a bit overboard on the faux-colonial pastel theme. Still, the hotel is fairly close to Metrocentro and there are a handful of bars and restaurants right around the corner. Like most options in the same price range, Colon offers air conditioning, cable TV, telephones and WiFi in all rooms. There is also a complimentary breakfast in the morning. Km. 4 ½ Carr. a Masaya, From BAC, 2 blocks up, Colonial Los Robles. Tel: 505-2-278-2490/ Cell:505-8-886-4578/US:239-449-8537/239-963-8293, Fax: 505-2-267-0191, E-mail: hcolon@ibw.com.ni, URL: www.hcolon.net. Updated: Mar 26, 2009.

Angel Azul Hotel Boutique

(ROOMS: $75 – 90) Angel Azul Boutique Hotel is housed in a family home surrounded by gardens and a beautiful pool. The hotel is located in the most central and safe residential area in Managua and is within a few meters of Carretera a Masaya and the exclusive

Become a travel writer! See how at vivatravelguides.com/bootcamp/

shopping center Galerias Santo Domingo (one of the biggest in the country). Prices may vary according to season. Villa Fontana No.17, 1 block to the east, and 75 meters North of Club Terraza. Tel: 505-2-278-2368, E-mail: reservas@angelazulhotel.com, URL: www.angelazulhotel.com. Updated: Jan 16, 2009.

Hotel Los Robles

(Room: $75 – 90) Hotel Los Robles is a charming hotel in the residential area of Managua. This converted colonial house has only 14 rooms and prides itself on being able to offer individual attention to guests. The rooms have antique, wooden furniture complete with iron bed frames. Each room has a unique layout and style, which helps Los Robles avoid the cookie-cutter feeling of some hotels. All rooms come with international TV. One unique feature (which other hotels might do well to emulate) is that guests are all provided with a cell phone to use for the duration of their stay. Near La Marseillaise Restaurant, 30 m south, Los Robles. Tel: 505-2-267-3008, Fax: 505-2-270-1074, E-mail: info@hotellosrobles.com, URL: www.hotellosrobles.com. Updated: Nov 20, 2008.

HIGH-END
Seminole Plaza Hotel

(ROOMS: $119 – 139) Seminole Plaza Hotel's faux baroque accents and flawless service put it in the top tier of Managua hotels. Located at the north end of Zona Hippos, in the middle of the commercial district, Seminole is an oft-cited local landmark. Think you've heard the name before? The hotel was built by the Seminole Tribe of Florida, who filled the building with afghan rugs, gilded birdcages and fleur de lis. Along with a pool, gym and sauna, Seminole also has an exclusive business center, where secretaries are available to help guests. From Bancentro Carretera a Masaya, 1 block west, 1 block south. Tel: 505-2-270-6496, Fax: 505-2-270-5694 / 270-5695, E-mail: res@seminoleplaza.com, URL: www.seminoleplaza.com. Updated: Jun 12, 2009.

Hotel Intercontinental Metrocentro

(ROOMS: $200 – 800) Hotel Intercontinental is an established chain of luxury accommodations that offer a wide range of services and amenities, but which are mainly geared toward business travelers and those willing to pay the pricey rates. The Managua hotel is conveniently located right next to the Metrocentro shopping mall and is within walking distance to many restaurants and shops. Both a lounge and restaurant are located on the main floor of the hotel; there is also a pool and sundeck. South of the Metrocentro shopping center, Carretera Masaya. Tel: 505-2-278-8989, URL: www.ichotelsgroup.com/intercontinental/en/gb/locations/managua. Updated: Nov 27, 2008.

Restaurants

The Centro Commercial has a wide variety of restaurants—arguably the best range in the city—with everything from fast food joints to fine dining. Outside of Galeria Santo Domingo's cobbled (and extensive) food court, the best place to go to grab a nice meal in the city is the Zona Hippo's section of Los Robles, a strip of eateries that include student bars, family-friendly seafood eateries and romantic, candlelit bistros. If you're nostalgic for some United States fast food, Carretera Masaya is where you'll be able to get your fix, with a Papa John's among the highway offerings. Updated: Jun 21, 2009.

BUDGET
Casa de Cafe

(ENTREES: $0.50 – $5.90) Casa de Cafe gives off a familiar vibe, as though you've stumbled into the Starbucks of Managua. The Nicaraguan coffeehouse offers all of the drink varieties you would expect, as well as a tasty selection of pastries. There are also breakfast and lunch options such as croissants, sandwiches, hamburgers and salads. In Los Robles, the two-level location has muraled columns and overlooks a brand new park. Residents and visitors alike head there for a cup o' joe (hot or iced) and to take advantage of the cafe's WiFi. Open Monday to Friday, 7 a.m – 9 p.m.; Saturday, 8 a.m. – 9 p.m.; and Sunday, 8 a.m. – 4 p.m. From Lacmiel, 1 block up, 1 1/2 south.

Casa de Cafe also has locations in Altamira, Galerias mall, Metrocentro mall, Multicentro Las Americas mall and the airport. Tel: 505-2-278-2081 / 278-0605. Updated: Mar 27, 2009.

Tortas Locas

(ENTREES: $2.50 – 6.30, up to $200 for 16 people) Tortas Locas Hipocampo is a loud Mexican restaurant with a bright blue and yellow theme that features a mural of frog musicians. Part of a chain that includes branches in Mexico, Honduras and Puerto Rico, Tortas Locas serves all of the typical dishes—burritos, enchiladas, even a plate called "gringos" that has tacos—that you might expect from a commercial Mexican restaurant. The tortas are the specialty and range in price from $3.40 – $6.30. Tortas also has a decent drink menu and a fiesta buffet special that can feed 16 people. From Lacmiel, 120 varas. up. Tel: 505-2-270-9992, E-mail: restaurants@tortaslocas.com, URL: www.tortaslocas.com. Updated: Apr 21, 2009.

El Garabato Cafe y Antojitos
(ENTREES: $2.25 for tapas, $12 for dinner) Traditional enough to have waitresses in Nicaraguan garb and local art displayed around the walls (but skirting around this side of camp), El Garabato is the chic place to grab a dish of local cuisine. The café is vegetarian friendly, but with a menu of seafood, beef, chicken and pork dishes, meat lovers need not despair. When you're done with your meal, be sure to grab a pen and sign the restaurant's extensive wall of signatures. In an ongoing effort to support local artists, El Garabato hosts regular cultural events. From Hotel Seminole 2 1/2 blocks South. Main Street of Los Robles. Managua. Tel: 505-2-278-2944, E-mail: elgarabatocafe@gmail.com. Updated: Jun 22, 2009.

Don Pan
(ENTREES: $3.48 – $8.95) Don Pan, a series of bakery delis, features cases of delicious goodies and shelves of breads. The lunch specialty is a rather pricey salad ($8.95), although Don Pan also has paninis, sandwiches, hamburgers and, of course, pastries for dessert. If you're not feeling that peckish, try cooling off with a thickly mixed fruit shake. Don Pan also serves breakfast, including pancakes. The Los Robles location is open from 7 a.m. to 8 p.m., Monday to Saturday. From Monte Olivos, 200 varas. south, Los Robles. Tel: 505-2-278-4091/ 505-2-278-2247, URL: www.donpan.com.ni.

Don Pan also has locations in: Carr. Norte (Tel: 505-2-250-6385); Carr. Sur (Tel: 505-2-254-3687); and Carr. Masaya in Plaza Gourmet (Tel: 505-2-276-0593). Updated: Mar 26, 2009.

Marea Alta Seafood Bar and Grill
(ENTREES: $3.45 – 24.75) Marea Alta Seafood Bar and Grill is one of the best places in the city to grab a plate of seafood; don't let the almost cartoon-like nautical theme (with waiters in sailor garb) put you off. The extremely varied menu ranges from oyster cocktails and octopus ceviche to seafood spaghetti in wine sauce and surf n' turf. The restaurant even offers escargot. Sick of the sea? Try one of Marea Alta's tasty USDA Choice ribeyes. The family-friendly restaurant has been a Managua favorite for decades and currently has three locations. (Marea Alta also delivers.) The Los Robles location is open Monday to Wednesday, 12 p.m. – 10:30 p.m.; Thursday to Saturday, 12 p.m. – 12 p.m.; Sunday, 12 p.m. – 10 p.m.

The locations are as follows: **Marea Alta Los Robles**: Tel: 505-2-278-2459 / 270-7959, E-mail: marealta@ibw.com.ni. **Hotel Seminole**: 1 c. al sur, Zona Hippo's, Los Robles Marea Alta Santo Domingo (Zona Viva). Tel: 505-2-276-5290, E-mail: maltagsd@ibw.com.ni. **Marea Alta Metrocentro Food Court**: Modulo FC-16. Tel: 505-2-271-9158. Updated: Apr 21, 2009.

Valenti's Pizza
(ENTREES: $3.70 – 13.40) Managuans all know that Valenti's Pizza is where to head when they want to satisfy their deep dish pizza craving. The Los Robles branch is housed in a two-floor, mock colonial building next to BAC. The atmosphere is jovial and family-friendly, the wait staff are attentive and, best of all, the menu features all of the cannelloni, lasagnas ($3.70) and pizzas ($5 – 13.40) your Italian-lovin' heart could desire. From Lacmiel, 1 block up, Los Robles. Tel: **Los Robles**: 505-2-278-7474; **Salvadorita**: 505-2-249-8597; **Las Americas**: 505-2-278-7474; **Linda Vista**: 505-2-268-2121; **Carr. Sur**: 505-2-265-0179 Updated: Apr 21, 2009.

MID-RANGE
Hippo's Grill and Tavern
(ENTREES: $5 – 12) Hamburgers are the specialty at Hippo's Grill and Tavern where students from the nearby university come to hang out over the Blue Cheese patties and frozen cocktails (2-for-1 Happy Hour is from 4 – 7 p.m.). Hippo's serves both USDA and Nicaraguan beef, as well as a few vegetarian options and lighter dishes. Hippo's has become so popular that the stretch of restaurants to either side of the trademark wooden hippopotamus statues

is known locally as "Zona Hippo's." Open daily 11:30 a.m. – 1:30 a.m. Tel: 505-2-267-1346, URL: www.zonahippos.com. Updated: Jun 21, 2009.

Woody's Pizza Pub and Grill
(ENTREES: $5 – 13) A pizza joint that evokes the spirit of TGIFriday's (although the red uniforms don't have as much flair), Woody's offers a good range of sandwiches, seafood and Mexican-style comfort food. Of course, there are pizzas too, including a massive pie called Woody's Ultimate. During the 4 – 7 p.m. Happy Hour, beer and national rum is 2-for-1. Woody's is open from midday to 1 a.m. daily. Updated: Jun 21, 2009.

Woody's Wings, Pub and Grill
(ENTREES: $5 – 14) A grown-up version of Woody's Pizza. Pub and Grill, Woody's Wings is the classic dark wood bar with tall seats, sports on the TV and walls decked with familiar rockers and starlet photos. The blue, yellow and red stripes around the room can feel like you've stumbled onto a favorite college joint. The menu is right in line with the atmosphere: wings, sandwiches, fajitas, quesadillas, salads and a healthy selection of cocktails. Woody's is one of the more popular spots along Zona Hippo's to grab a frozen drink, a shot of tequila and a beer while you relax with the local crowd. Open daily 11 a.m. – 2 a.m. The pub is located 2.5 blocks south of Hotel Seminole. All credit cards are accepted. Updated: Jun 26, 2009.

Scampi
(ENTREES: $3.50 – 25) Featuring a black interior, with metal bamboo and neon yellow table cloths, Scampi is part club, part restaurant and all seafood. The menu ranges from fried fish to international cuisine such as tempura, teriyaki and sushi rolls. The tilapia is so fresh that you can see your dinner swimming around in the ponds at the front of the restaurant. Multi-layered Scampi has a disco with a dance floor upstairs, a long bar on the back terrace and traditional Japanese rooms. Open 11 a.m. – 3 a.m. weekdays and until 4 a.m. on weekends. Tel: 505-2-270-6013 / 505-2-270-6019. Updated: Jun 21, 2009.

Savor
One of the restaurants in La Galeria's promenade, Savor has Mediterranean and Italian dishes, like antipasto plates and ricotta ravioli. There are vegetarian options and a good selection of appetizers and panini. Quality food is provided at reasonable prices. The restaurant also has an extensive wine and drink list. Galerias Santo Domingo, Zona Viva. Tel: 505-2-276-5382. Updated: Nov 27, 2008.

Sushi Itto
When you want raw fish in Managua your best bet (and *only option*) is one of the two locations of Sushi Itto. In Galerias Santo Domingo, the Sushi Itto location is a sleek, modern building on the corner of the Zona Viva. The décor tries a little too hard to evoke the orient, with boxy shelves and a predominant use of glossy black, and the 1980s music is a bit disconcerting (although "Hungry Eyes" was strangely appropriate). The fish in the sushi and sashimi offerings could also stand to be fresher (this is a Japanese restaurant after all), but the hibachi and hot sake are right on. Delivery service includes a 10 percent additional charge. Galerias Santo Domingo Zona Viva Modulo 2-A; Plaza Caracol, Costado Oeste Rotonda Periodista. Tel: 505-2-270-3230/ 505-2-270-3120 / 505-2-278-4886. URL: www.sushi-itto.com. Updated: May 04, 2009.

HIGH-END
Bistro Sebastian
Bistro Sebastian is the new kid on the Zona Hippo's block, a modern cube full of international wine and culinary delights. The fusion dishes mix Asian, French, Italian and American fare (shrimp and sea bass with a ginger and sesame oil sauce, for example), while the bistro's wine bar is similarly high-end and eclectic, with Chilean house wines and a solid list of Italian, Argentine, French and Spanish labels (for between $10.20 and $45). The bistro is open from midday to 2 a.m., Monday to Saturday, and is closed on Sunday. *Note: As of April 2009, the owners were planning to expand into the lunch hour.* Tel: 505-2-277-3476. Updated: Jun 26, 2009.

Meson Español
(ENTREES: $6.70 – 20.50) A long-time Barrio Boloñia staple, Meson Español made the leap across the city to Galerias Santo Domingo when the mall opened. The restaurant's forte isn't hard to figure out: tapas, paellas and sangria. The house specials are piglet prepared Segovia-style and Australian lamb chops.

Loved it? Loathed it? Write a review and help other travelers.

Open daily 12 p.m. – 3 p.m. and 6 p.m. – 11 p.m. or until 8 p.m. Sunday. Galerias Santo Domingo food court. Updated: Jun 21, 2009.

Boheme

(ENTREES: $17 – 30) Boheme specializes in mixing Mediterranean dishes with Nicaraguan salsas. The paella marinera "La Boheme" is the house specialty, but a close second in terms of menu favorites is the lamb, imported from New Zealand and grilled. The wine list isn't too shabby either. Boheme aims for romantic faux colonial: the interior is filled with dark woods, there are polished horns on the walls, and plenty of candles light up the place. The restaurant is open from noon – 3 p.m. and from 6 p.m. – midnight daily. Galerias Santo Domingo food court. Updated: Jun 21, 2009.

La Casa de Los Nogueras

Set in a converted house and garden, La Casa de Las Nogueras is a quiet, classy restaurant that provides fine service in a handsome atmosphere. The outdoor patio is lined with candles, and the surrounding mango trees provide cover and privacy. Main dishes incorporate fresh, local ingredients with an international menu. Prices are in the higher range, but are still reasonable. Los Robles, from Restaurant La Marseillaise ½ a block to the north R-17. Tel: 505-2-278-2506. Updated: Nov 27, 2008.

> **V!VA ONLINE REVIEW**
> LA CASA DE LOS NOGUERAS
>
> Great food cooked to perfection. The pescado de la casa was delicious, and the patio is gorgeous..
>
> Vancouver, November 06, 2008

Nightlife

Hippa Hippa

(COVER: $2.50 – $4.85) Hippa Hippa is a popular club for the young and hip, with DJs spinning reggeaton and electronica through the night around an oddly placed plastic palm tree. The club is open from Wednesday (Ladies' Night) to Saturday 9 p.m. – 3 a.m., with varying entry fees. The club's website is under construction, but will eventually include event postings. Plaza Familiar (past Galerias Santo Domingo). Tel: 505-2-473-1947 to reserve a table, URL: www.hippahippa.com.ni. Updated: Jun 24, 2009.

Marcelo's Sports Bar

Marcelo's Sports Bar is a open-air establishment whose precarious perch on a heavily trafficked corner makes you wonder about staggering customers and oncoming cars. The bar food includes hamburgers, sandwiches and salads, while the more extensive drinks menu offers popular liquors by both the glass and bottle (a bottle of tequila can run from $29 – 64.50). The bar has an open seating area. When you start longing to shoot a little pool, head across the road to Marcelo's sister bar, **Henry's Pool Place**. Both Marcelo's and Henry's are open from Monday to Saturday, noon – 2 a.m.; Sunday, noon – 5 p.m. The bars accept all credit cards. From Lacmiel, 1 block up, ½ a block south, Carr. Masaya. URL: www.marcelossportbar.com. Updated: Apr 21, 2009.

My Space Sports Bar

Catering to the collegiate crowd from the neighboring UCA, My Space Sports Bar has a large, open seating area and a friendly atmosphere. The menu features a decent selection of bocas, with an emphasis on student favorites such as nachos and wings. The drink list is not extensive, but the beer ($0.60 – 1.75) is cold and cheap. In the evenings, My Space is apt to play anything from reggae and merengue to electronica, with the two floors getting livelier as the night wears on. My Space is open from Monday to Saturday, 1 p.m. – 2 a.m.(or earlier if there are no customers); closed on Sunday. From Metrocentro, 100 m. south. Tel: 505-2-278-5689 Updated: Apr 21, 2009.

AROUND MANAGUA

Nicaragua's capital city may have evolved as a modern metropolis—and developed all the pitfalls of a concrete jungle with urban sprawl, dodgy markets and snarling, roaring traffic—but Managua's growth spurt has managed to leave behind some hidden pockets of wild jungles, tranquil lakes and sandy beaches.

Bird watchers (or lovers of any stripe) should plan to make special trips to **Chocoyero-El Brujo Nature Reserve** (172 bird species) and the private **Montibelli Reserve** (105 species of birds). Both reserves require

---

Become a travel writer! See how at vivatravelguides.com/bootcamp a special effort to get to—they are well off main roads and Montibelli guests need to schedule a visit ahead of time—but are noteworthy for their preservation of jungle in areas otherwise given over to farmland and residences. The private Montibelli reserve has been so successful in turning coffee plantations into reclaimed forest that investigators recently discovered a new species of dragonfly there. Make advance reservations to experience the diversity, and the BBQ, for yourself.

Only 20 kilometers from the city, and much easier to access, are the lagoons of **Xiloa** and **Apoyeque**. The public park at Xiloa has walkways and rough-hewn eateries with beer. You might have to wade through mud and plants, but the water is clear and carpeted with tiny, fossilized shells along the bottom. Xiloa was devastated by the 1998 Hurricane Mitch, but is slowly starting to reclaim its former status as a family friendly place to spend the afternoon in a bathing suit and a beer in your hand. Make sure not to take photos of the Nicaraguan military on maneuvers. Apoyeque is a day's hike away; the deep crater lake is a fisherman's dream (just watch out for the resident crocodiles).

The beaches of **Pochomil** and **Masachapa** aren't too shabby either, with surfing spots, restaurants and cheap accommodations. Plus, the long stretches of beach will make you forget that you were ever sweating away on the hot Managua streets. Updated: Sep 28, 2009.

CHOCOYERO - EL BRUJO NATURE RESERVE

Hard to reach, but still popular, the Chocoyero-El Brujo Nature Reserve ($2.50 foreigners, $1.20 nationals, $4.85 guided tour) is well worth your time if you're looking for an escape from Managua and have a day to spare. The reserve covers 184-hectares of jungle, which are tucked away beyond banana groves, pitahaya fields and coffee farms.

The narrow valley (originally set aside as an aquifer) is home to 172 species of birds, 52 of mammals, 33 of reptiles and 150 species of plants. Of course, you probably won't spot all of that flora and fauna, but the reserve's three trails through the jungle are still a treat —well-marked, well-cared-for and very easy going. A trail of about 1,200 meters (3,937 ft) will take you to the reserve's main attractions: the **El Brujo waterfall** and **El Chocoyero** (Place of the Parakeets).

Five species of parakeets reside in the park, with the chalky cliffs being their favorite nesting spot. The best times to see them are from May to June (when the birds are laying eggs) and in September (when the fledglings are taking to the air). Visit in the late afternoon to see the parakeets returning to their nests after a day of foraging.

The Chocoyero-El Brujo visitor's center is rather bare, with informational posters and tables of skulls and pickled snakes. If you like the reserve and want to stay, there are two cabanas ($7.28 per person with bathroom but no water), tents and campgrounds ($2.42 – $3.88). Check ahead, since there is no camping in the rainy season. A new butterfly and orchid house was expected to open in late 2009 behind the visitor's center.

To get to the reserve, it's best to either use a 4x4 vehicle or hire a mototaxi from Ticuantepe. If you're driving from Managua, take the Masaya highway to the Ticuantepe-La Concepcion turnoff. The road to the reserve is at km 21.5 of Ticuantepe-La Concepcion and the visitor's center is a 40-minute drive from there.

The reserve has an interactive website with cartoon parakeets and birdsong at www.chocoyero.com. The visitor's center is open daily 7:30 a.m. – 5 p.m. Tel: 505-2-2276-7810. Updated: Sep 28, 2009.

MONTIBELLI RESERVE

Montibelli is a large, private reserve whose 165.5 hectares are made up of three former coffee plantations. The owners still grow a bit of coffee—plus lemons, bananas, pineapples and pitahaya—but the majority of the land is devoted to reforestation. A former farmhouse has been converted into a visitor's center and dining area (be sure to try the BBQ). There is also a basic camping area (the owners are planning to build a more formal shelter) with bathrooms and guided tours along the reserve's three trails: 700 meters (2,296 ft) to a lookout point called "El Mirador," a 2.5 kilometer

(1.55 mi) loop known as "Los Balcones", and "El Pochote," a 3 kilometer (1.86 mi) loop where you can see many butterflies and the occasional howler monkey.

Located in the Sierras de Managua, Montibelli has roughly 115 species of trees, 105 species of birds and 32 mammal species. The reserve protects a variety of endangered species, including the Pacific parakeet, Congo monkey, agouti and six types of hummingbirds. If that's not enough for you, Montibelli also has 55 species of butterflies.

The reserve is not the easiest place to reach; you have to get to kilometer 19 of the Ticuantepe-La Concepcion highway and then go another 2.5 kilometers (1.55 mi) after the turn off—but mototaxis can take you there from the Ticuantepe bus stop (if you're willing to pay). The reserve also asks that you make a reservation in advance for your visit. The reserve is open from Tuesday to Sunday. Tel: 505-2-270-4287, Fax: 505-2-270-4289, E-mail: info@montibelli.com. Updated: Sep 28, 2009.

LAGO XILOÁ

The large, placid expanse of Xiloa, just 20 kilometers (13 miles) northwest of Managua, was once a favorite getaway for families who wanted to beat the city heat, but knew better than to chance the polluted waters of Lago de Managua (or other area lagoons). The 180 mph winds of Hurricane Mitch in 1998 wiped the Peninsula de Chiltepe clean, taking out Xiloa's thatched umbrellas, eateries and houses. The lake, which didn't have an ample shore in the first place, lost slim beaches beneath mud and muck. It would be another decade before visitors returned to Xiloa in any significant numbers. In the meantime, private landowners moved in and claimed much of what had been public lakeshore. (Where the blame rests for the loss of public land depends on who you ask.)

Xiloa is just starting to rebuild its family-friendly reputation, with a much reduced park, new restaurants and the familiar thatched umbrellas. The park is open Monday to Saturday, 7 a.m. – 7 p.m., and until 8 p.m. on Sundays. The entry fee is $0.25 per person, $0.50 per motorcycle, $1.20 per automobile, $1.70 per truck and $9.70 per bus.

The rustic and slightly scummy **Licroria-Disco Bar El Primo** serves plates of pork, beef, shrimp, fish and fried chicken on the lake shore (ENTREES: $2.90 to $8.75; open daily 10 a.m. – 8 p.m.). The park has crude bathrooms and changing rooms, which are locked more often than not. A new, unnamed Xiloa bar was scheduled to open in late 2009, with a range of alcoholic drinks and mains (including controversial turtle eggs).

To get to Xiloa, take a $0.20 bus to Cuidad Sandino on the Managua-Leon highway and then catch a $0.50 taxi to the lagoon. Updated: Sep 28, 2009.

LAGO APOYEQUE

Xiloa's sister crater is a wild Shangri-La, about as far off the beaten tourist trail as you can get this close to Managua. The steep jungle shore is populated with monkeys, parrots, iguanas and crocodiles. Apoyeque is a favorite fishing spot for local farmers (who reportedly catch the lagoon's large, passive fish by throwing in unbaited lines), but only attracts a handful of visitors each year—mainly because the lagoon is so difficult to reach. Forget about an easy walking trail from Xiloa (the Nicaraguan military carries out maneuvers in the area): the only way to get to Apoyeque is to hike from the tiny village of Conmarka Alfonzo Gonzales.

Locals are slowly cutting a swath to this gorgeous and isolated lake with the hopes of eventually building a road to the lookout. Until conditions drastically improve, though, you should not attempt the trip without a guide. The unmarked path has dangers like poisonous snakes, crumbling footholds and the very real possibility of heat stroke. Although you're more likely to get caught on thorns or twist an ankle, it's not unheard of for hikers to be robbed while in the countryside.

At Conmarka Alfonzo Gonzales, you can hire a local guide for about C200 (US $10). **Elias and Jorge Calderon** are reliable, friendly and knowledgeable about the area (Tel: 505-368-2855). Bring plenty of water, a hat and sensible hiking shoes. The one-way hike up to the crater lip takes between 40 minutes and 1.5 hours, depending on your physical condition. The trail is very steep and there is little shade. The trek from the crater lip to the shore is roughly two hours each way. You can camp along the lake shore, but there are no services. Updated: Sep 28, 2009.

POCHOMIL AND MASACHAPA

Managua's closest beaches, Masachapa and Pochomil, are easily accessible by car or bus. Their long stretches of sand are lined with hotels and restaurants, making the beaches a good place to visit for a weekend or a day trip. Fresh fish can be bought from the local fisherman or ordered from one of the various establishments. Local eateries also serve cold beer and provide great views of the Pacific ocean. Updated: Sep 28, 2009.

Lodging

MID-RANGE

Hotel Vista al Mar

(ROOMS: $40 and up) Hotel Vista al Mar is located on the beach in Masachapa and is a small hotel with simple rooms and a tiny swimming pool. The hotel's restaurant has two levels, both of which look out to the ocean, and the menu features typical Nicaraguan dishes and seafood plates. The hotel and restaurant each have mid-range prices and are of average quality. At the parking lot in Masachapa it is 100 yards towards the ocean. Tel: 505-2-269-0115. Updated: Jan 30, 2009.

Hotel Summer

(ROOMS: $40 - 50) Hotel Summer, one of the biggest and most popular hotels in Masachapa, has comfortable rooms suitable for families with children. The hotel's restaurant overlooks the ocean and has a large deck that fills up with diners from both Managua and local areas on the weekends. Service is friendly and dishes incorporate traditional Nicaraguan seafood specialties. Prices for meals are slightly higher than surrounding establishments, but the food is fresh and well worth it. From the Park, 100 varas towards the water, Masachapa. Tel: 505-2-269-0115. Updated: Jan 29, 2009.

HIGH-END

Los Cardones

(ROOMS: $65 - 99) An eco/surf lodge in front of the beach, Los Cardones provides a tranquil setting in a beautifully natural atmosphere. The resort promotes sustainable tourism by having a minimal environmental impact and also by helping with local community projects. You can stay in one of the six bungalows with thatched roofs and private patios. Los Cardones also has a spacious beachfront restaurant where you can dine or relax. Food is fresh, creative and includes Italian style pizza. Room rates include three daily meals. Carretera Masachapa km 49, 15 km al mar, Rotulos Los Cardones. Follow the Los Cardones signs. Tel: 505-2-618-7314, E-mail: infoloscardones@yahoo.com, URL: www.loscardones.com. Updated: Jan 30, 2009.

Gran Pacifica

(ROOMS: $150 - 250) An hour drive from Managua and on a beautiful expanse of beachfront land, Gran Pacifica is one of Nicaragua's growing seaside communities. At Gran Pacifica, you can either stay for a vacation or, if you become enchanted with the area, buy yourself a piece of property. Fully equipped condos and homes are available for both short and long-term stays.

Located on 2,500 acres of land, and containing 3.5 miles of beach, Gran Pacifica is a resort with ample space for surfing. The owners are also constructing an 18-hole golf course that is expected to be ready in late 2009.

If you only want to visit for a day of surfing, you can pay a $5 fee (per person) at the entrance, which can be applied to your restaurant/bar tab. Spending the afternoon at the oceanside restaurant is an option as well. A concierge service (**La Vida Nica**) is available to help arrange activities and tours. At km 49 on carretera Masachapa, it is 12 km to the west. Tel: 505-2-270-3856 / 1-800-959-NICA, Fax: 505-270-3862, E-mail: info@granpacifica.com, URL: www.granpacifica.com. Updated: Jan 30, 2009.

Hotel Vistamar

(**ROOMS: $138 and up**) Hotel Vistamar is a beachfront resort and conference center located in Pochomil. The hotel features 17 exotic bungalows, holding up to four people per room. Each room has its own bathroom, ceiling fan, air conditioning, cable TV, beach chairs, hammocks, and private terrace. The hotel offers an all-inclusive package or room-only services. The resort also features a spa, pool, restaurant and bar. Petronic

Gas Station, 300 meters South, 600 meters West Pochomil, Nicaragua. Tel: 505-2-265-8099, E-mail: reservaciones@vistamarhotel.com, URL: www.vistamarhotel.com. Updated: Nov 20, 2008.

LAGO DE NICARAGUA

Mar Dulce, or, "Sweet Sea," seems an odd nickname for Lake Nicaragua when you realize that it's the only lake in the world to sport freshwater sharks. In the 17th century pirates also braved the lake waters not one, but three times to sack the port city of Granada. The lake, also known as Lago Granada, Lake Cocibolca, Gran Lago, Gran Lago Dulce or Lake Granada, is approximately 99 miles (160 km) long, 45 miles (72 km) wide and 84 feet (26 m) deep.

Lake Nicaragua is the largest lake in Central America and the second largest in Latin America (after Lake Titicaca). It is connected to Lake Managua by the Tipitapa River and to the Caribbean Sea by the San Juan River. Historically speaking, such connections made Granada an Atlantic port, even though the city is closer to the Pacific. Under a 1884 treaty between the United States of America and Nicaragua, plans were made to build a canal linking the Caribbean Sea and the Pacific Ocean. However, due to political unrest, construction was halted in 1893 and the once planned Nicaragua Canal was moved to Panama.

As well as being home to freshwater sharks, the lake waters contain other fish that are usually only found in the salty ocean, such as swordfish, tarpon and tuna. One of the current theories is that their ancestors were trapped in Lake Nicaragua by lava flow that blocked access to the Pacific Ocean. (However, the lava didn't stop Henry Morgan in his pirate days from canoeing in from the Río San Juan and sacking Granada in 1665 and two more times before 1670.)

Lake Nicaragua has hundreds of islands, including an archipelago of over 350 tiny islets near Granada, all with lush plant and wildlife. People living on these islands fish and farm crops such as bananas, coffee, tobacco, wheat and sesame. On the island of **Zapatera** pre-Columbian statues were found and are now exhibited in the museum of the Convent of Saint Francis of Granada. Further south you'll be able to find the lake's largest island, **Ometepe**, which was formed by the lava flow of two volcanoes: **Concepción**, which is still active, and the now-dormant **Maderas**. Both volcanoes can be climbed, although Volcán Concepción is more physically demanding. Visitors can stay in Moyogalpa or Altagracia and get there by ferry from Granada or San Jorge. Updated: Jan 26, 2009.

PUERTO DIAZ

On your way to the little fishing village on the eastern shores of Lake Nicaragua, panoramic views of Volcán Mombacho and Ometepe Island frame the open pasture and fresh-water marsh. Along the road, people are out and about doing any number of daily tasks: collecting firewood, preparing for a cross-community trip, or searching for the rogue cow on horseback. Wide-eyed children stare unabashedly at foreigners before cheerfully returning a friendly wave.

The town itself exists like an island: a few dozen humble homes occupy a rock outcropping that separates them both geographically and culturally from the rest of the region. Most of the Chontales region, and much of the east side of the lake, is based on a cattle economy, while Puerto Díaz and other small fishing towns that dot the shores earn a living on the water.

Making the trek to this side of the lake is a grand opportunity to meander off the beaten trail. Leaving the highway in Juigalpa and bouncing the 20 kilometers down the dirt road towards the port town is like entering a separate plane of existence.

Puerto Díaz is proud of its fish and the town's two main restaurants happily offer heaping portions of greasy, fried lake fish served with icy drinks. While there is little in the way of tourist infrastructure (according to some, that's the best part of Puerto Díaz), a boat trip along the shores and into some of the nearby creeks can be arranged, and is a great opportunity to explore the unexplored. Visitors should realize that anyone giving you a ride on the water is most likely giving up their work time, and should be compensated accordingly.

If time does not allow for exploration by boat, there are a number of paths and trails that criss-cross away from town, up gentle hills and into hidden mango groves. The inhabitants are extremely knowledgeable

---
Become a travel writer! See how at vivatravelguides.com/bootcamp/

about the local natural history, and, if prompted politely, are more than willing to impart their wisdom. Whether you decide to trail-tromp or spend some time chatting with the locals, Puerto Díaz is rife with adventure for the intrepid traveler. Updated: Dec 15, 2008.

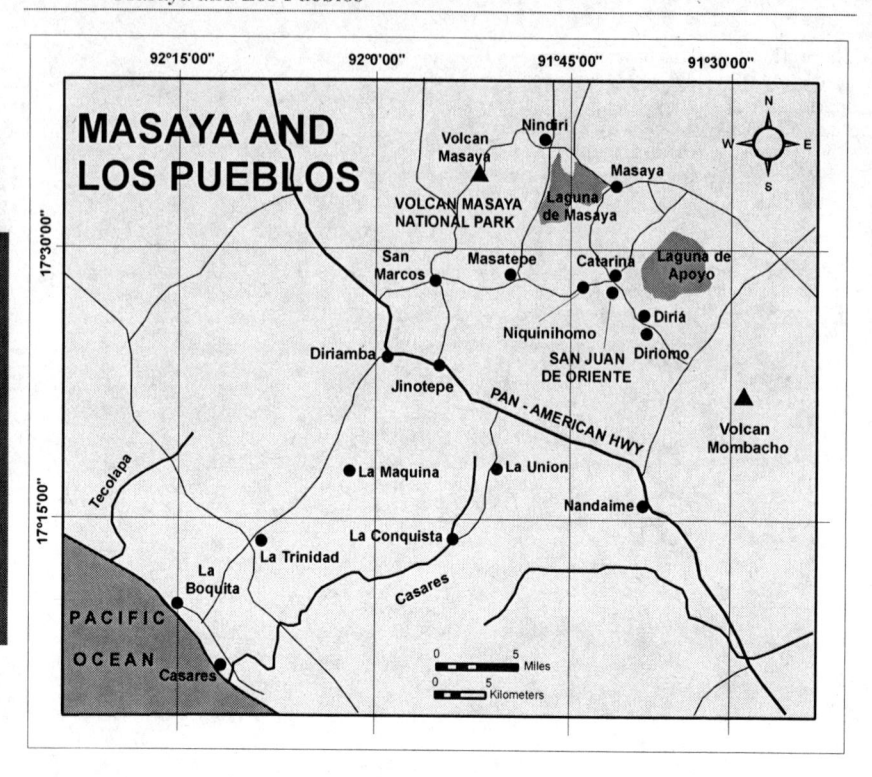

Masaya and Los Pueblos

Masaya and its neighboring towns have become known as the place to go for the best of Nicaraguan art and handicrafts. Ceramics of all shapes and sizes—some painted, some with fluted edges or incised with patterns of stars and flowers—are all made in small workshops around the city and imported to the famous Mercado de Artesanías. Craftsmen in the area also produce furniture, hammocks and tooled leather items. There is no end to the list of areas in which locals have placed their own unique stamp.

The city features a handful of Baroque and colonial churches, a fortress where Nicaraguans fought U.S. Marines, and a museum dedicated to Camilo Ortega Saavedra, hero of the revolutionary Sandinista movement.

If shopping and historic monuments are not your thing, head up to Parque Nacional Volcán Masaya where you can walk to the edge of the active Masaya volcano. The park also has several hiking trails, including one into the Santiago pit crater.

Laguna de Apoyo, a natural volcanic lake in the area and a popular spot for Nicaraguan day-trippers, is also worth a visit. Once inside the national park, dive into the clear blue waters, paraglide through the valley or hike around the rim. The crater interior and surrounding countryside offer a particularly wide diversity of plant and animal life.

That Masaya and the neighboring towns are home to so much culture and individuality comes as little surprise. The locals still maintain strong ties to their roots in the indigenous Chorotega tribes, who inhabited the area long before the Spanish arrived. The Spanish left their own mark, most prominently in the form of soaring Catholic churches where elaborate murals hang over stern saints. The natural offerings around Masaya aren't shabby either: Laguna Apoyo's tranquil, sulfur-infused waters and the smoking wonder of Volcán Masaya are short bus rides away. Around Masaya, locals are just starting to discover how to capitalize on the many charms of their area; the infrastructure is improving drastically, new

Support VIVA! Reserve your hotels or hostels at vivatravelguides.com/hotels/

… Masaya and Los Pueblos …

Highlights

Whether you want to stick to the most popular stops in the Masaya area or head off the beaten trail to explore the less visited wonders (such as the walls of petroglyphs above Laguna de Masaya), the only hard decision you'll have is to pick out what sounds the most interesting. Here are a few suggestions:

Hike by lava light: Head to the **Parque Nacional Volcán Masaya (p. 107)** in the evening for a tour when parakeets are returning to their roosts and, against the darkness, the molten rock far inside the crater becomes visible.

Ask a witch: **Diriomo (p. 114)** is known for a tradition of brujería (witchcraft), which residents trace back to their indigenous ancestors. The current practitioners of all things magical and medicinal are easy to find, just ask a local mototaxi driver to take you there. However, bring your wallet; the cures don't come cheap and even a consult can cost around $1.85.

Befriend a potter: The most vivid pottery displays might be right at the entrance to **San Juan de Oriente (p. 113)**, but it's down the town's side streets where you'll find the true artisans. Stop in one of their houses, usually marked by small displays, and you'll not only find more elaborate ceramics, you'll have a chance to see how the locals turn a lump of clay into art.

Dance in the market: Masaya's **Mercado Nacional de Artesanías (p. 105)** in the original 19th century building is worth a visit, especially during the weekly "Jueves de Verbena" when, for a small fee, you get to watch groups perform national dances and try them yourself on the open dance floor. Updated: Jul 10, 2009.

peoples, who came to be known as the Dirianes, were creative artists and productive farmers. The Spanish arrived in the 15th and 16th centuries to find a populated land with thriving settlements, which they promptly conquered and built on. Residents still celebrate their native history with various statues of the local chief Diriangén, who fought against the Spanish. Diría, Diriomo and Diriamba are all said to be named after the prominent Cacique.

Masaya became a department in March 1883. That the residents had retained much of their individual identity and independence—particularly in the Monimbó area of Masaya—ecame apparent during the 1970s when the region was one of the foremost in the fight against Somoza's National Guard. (Check out the Museo Galería Héroes y Martires to see how they donned Güegüence masks during their street battles.)

In the 1990s, following the war, Masaya and the surrounding areas began a period of reconstruction and rehabilitation. The Mercado Nacional de Artesanías was restored and locals began to resurrect traditional art forms, most prominently the pottery of San Juan del Oriente. Today, Masaya and the surrounding areas are establishing themselves as tourist-friendly spots with plenty of opportunities for visitors. Updated: Jul 10, 2009.

When to Go

Since Masaya and Los Pueblos are best known for their artesian works (ceramic, wood, leather and wicker goods) and for their unique foods, the area can be visited at any time of year or in any weather. The rainy season might send you scurrying for cover or hopping across flooded streets, but unlike more rural areas, the wet has little effect on travel conditions, beyond limiting jaunts in the soggy countryside.

hotels and restaurants are opening and artisans are becoming increasingly savvy when it comes to marketing their product. With past traditions and culture finally catching up to modern standards, now is a great time to visit the Masaya area. Updated: Jul 10, 2009.

History

Masaya was originally inhabited by Mexican immigrants, the Chorotegano, who first arrived around 2500 B.C. The indigenous

While there are no bad times to visit, you would do well to try to stop in the area during one of the numerous festivals patronales, when towns celebrate the celestial figures that watch over them. A few of the many festivals are listed here: Catarina celebrates San Silvestre Papa between Dec. 31 and Jan. 1; Diriomo sees the Virgin de la Candelaria off on her trip to Los Jirones between Feb. 2 and 8; Masatepe has the biggest horse parade (and with several hundred hipicas, that's saying quite a bit) forty days after Semana Santa in honor of Domingo de Trinidad; Diria fetes San Pedro starting on June 17; Niquinohomo dances and parades for Santa Ana on July 26.

Some important dates in Masaya are: March 16 when La Virgen de la Asuncion blesses the waters of the lake; August 15, the day Maria Magdelena goes on tour in Monimbo; September 30, which kicks off eight days of festivities in honor of San Jeronimo; and the dance of the little devils on the last Sunday of November. Updated: Sep 30, 2009.

Safety

The area around Masaya has experienced a significant increase in tourism in the past few years, yet violence against visitors is still a rarity. In 2009, the Nicaraguan government declared Masaya to be the safest city in the country. Still, Masaya and Los Pueblos have their share of crime, and you should avoid hitchhiking or wandering into unfamiliar places late at night. As with all places you visit, stay vigilant for pickpockets, petty criminals and scam artists. Updated: Jun 26, 2009.

Things to See and Do

For those interested in the great outdoors of Masaya, Parque Nacional Volcán Masaya is a must see. The park has a wide variety of hiking trails to choose from. Masaya volcano is currently active, and if you hike the volcano in the evening you can even see the lava inside the crater. Another beautiful natural attraction in Masaya is the Laguna de Apoyo, where you can swim, hike and enjoy other adventurous activities. Be sure to keep your eyes open for the local wildlife.

Along with the naturally-made beauty, you will find plenty of locally-made artistry at the local markets and shops. You can't visit Masaya without checking out the Mercado de Artesanías and purchasing some handmade treasures. On Thursdays you can watch local dance groups perform at the market and even take to the floor yourself for a lesson. If you venture outside the market and wander side streets, you can find private homes where artisans will display their art and even demonstrate their work for you.

Tours

While it may seem that every town in the Masaya area is working on a tourism-related project, the related tour guide industry has yet to catch up. In these areas, local guides are still your best bet. Mototaxi drivers can often serve as the best informal guides; not only do they have a form of transportation, they also usually know their local area well. However, they probably won't know a lot in the way of historical context. In Los Pueblos Blancos, the mayor's office and town library can also provide information. In Masaya and Jinotepe, check in with the local INTUR office for advice on where to go and how to get there. At Laguna de Apoyo ask at Eco Hotel Apoyo, Crater's Edge or Monkey Hut about hiring a guide for a day trip. Park rangers at Parque Nacional Volcán Masaya are usually friendly and willing to provide either basic information or specific tours. Updated: Jun 26, 2009.

Lodging

Masaya and the surrounding areas do not have as many accommodation options as in cities with an established history of tourism (Leon, Granada and San Juan del Sur, for example). Smaller towns have only one or two hotels, if they have any at all. Since the demand is relatively low, the area hotels and hospedajes have very reasonable rates. In Masaya, you can find a private room with a shared bathroom for $5 or less. Try basing yourself in a city that has a solid transportation system and exploring the surrounding towns from there. Updated: Jun 30, 2009.

Restaurants

Tweaking the traditional is something of an art form in Masaya and the surrounding areas and the food is no exception. Los Pueblos Blancos are especially known for their cuisine—this is where residents perfected cow stomach soup (mondongo), marzipan-like milk sweets (cajetas) and a filling, nacatamale alternative (tamungas), after all. For a hearty meal, Nicaraguan-style, stop in at any of the local restaurants or fritanga stands and grab a plate of gallo pinto with fried chicken and plantains. Updated: Jun 26, 2009.

MASAYA

242 m | 130,113 | 52

With a nickname like "The City of Flowers," you'd expect Masaya to be a pleasant place. Generally, it doesn't disappoint. The place has a small-town friendliness about it, although with 150,000 people it's hardly a puebla.

Masaya is probably most famous for its Mercado de Artesanías, one of the largest and best

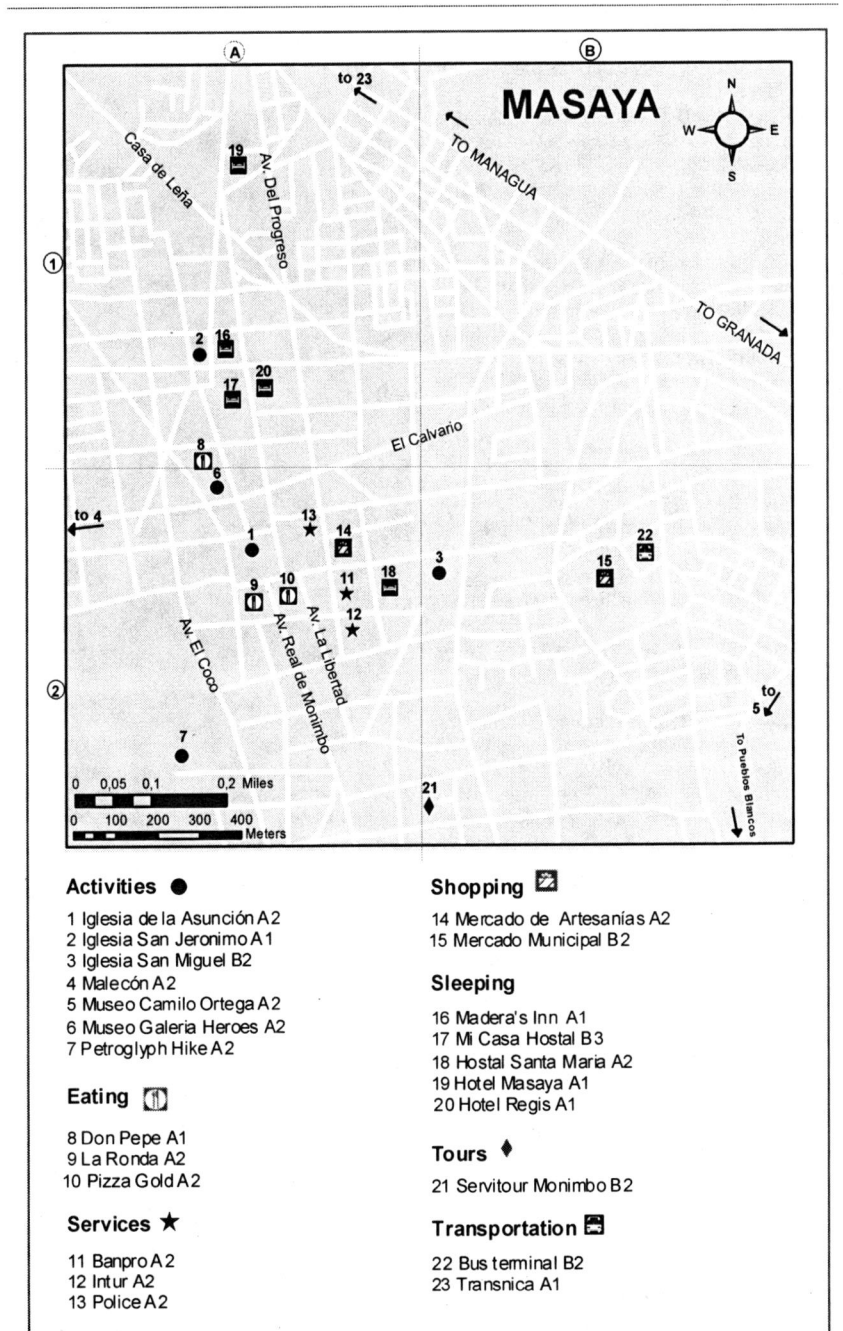

Activities ●
1 Iglesia de la Asunción A2
2 Iglesia San Jeronimo A1
3 Iglesia San Miguel B2
4 Malecón A2
5 Museo Camilo Ortega A2
6 Museo Galeria Heroes A2
7 Petroglyph Hike A2

Eating
8 Don Pepe A1
9 La Ronda A2
10 Pizza Gold A2

Services ★
11 Banpro A2
12 Intur A2
13 Police A2

Shopping
14 Mercado de Artesanías A2
15 Mercado Municipal B2

Sleeping
16 Madera's Inn A1
17 Mi Casa Hostal B3
18 Hostal Santa Maria A2
19 Hotel Masaya A1
20 Hotel Regis A1

Tours ♦
21 Servitour Monimbo B2

Transportation
22 Bus terminal B2
23 Transnica A1

handicraft markets in Central America. Many of the goods are produced locally. Beautifully painted pots and ceramics are likely to have come from Pueblos Blancos. Many of the smaller nearby communities are known for producing fine hardwood and wicker products, and you'll see several stalls devoted to these. Masaya itself is famous for producing excellent woven hammocks. If you've got the space to carry it, V!VA heartily recommends picking one up.

If you're visiting between September and December, be sure to drop in on the San Jeronimo Festival. This colossal fiesta goes on for about three months, with parades, cultural expositions, and massive street parties.

The city is also a convenient launching point for trips to Volcán Masaya. Be sure to check on the volcano's status, as it remains very active. If things are quiet, you can actually descend into the cone to see lava bubbling down below. Try for a twilight tour, when the red-glowing magma is most impressive.

Many people choose to visit Masaya as a day trip from Granada and, practically speaking, its attractions can be taken in with a full-day's sightseeing. Volcán Masaya and Laguna de Apoyo each require separate trips, but these can also be done from Granada just as easily. Ultimately, it's up to you. Masaya is a pleasant place to spend a day or two, but if you're too comfortable in your Granada digs to want to move, you can just see the city on the run.

This is not a must but is another decent half-day side-trip. It is not as beautiful as Granada but it offers two markets, the Mercado Municipal by the bus stop and the Mercado Viejo, next to the town park in an impressive castle-like building, where you can buy artesania goodies, if they take your fancy. There is also a nice malécon if you carry on from the central park away from the bus stop, with views over Lake Masaya and out to the volcano. Take Bus 9 from Granada for Cordobas / $0.50. Updated: Nov 22, 2006.

When to Go

In terms of climate, the weather here generally echoes the rest of the region. High season runs from September to May, but the city is busiest during the autumn festivals. March probably has the most pleasant weather, particularly for visiting Laguna de Apoyo. The worst weather runs from May to mid-August, when the city gets heavy rain. Updated: Jun 21, 2008.

Holidays and Fiestas

Masaya is famous for its festivals, and the grand-daddy of them all is in honor of San Jeronimo, the city's patron saint. This celebration goes on for a whopping three months, starting in mid-September and continuing, in various forms, until early December.

The biggest days of the festival are from September 27 – October 8. September 30 is the actual saint's day, when the bearded icon is taken from the Iglesia de San Jeronimo and carried around town in a flower-strewn, riotous procession. For good measure, the saint does a victory lap on October 7, accompanied by another huge parade. Of course, the party doesn't end there. The festival continues throughout the following months, waxing and waning in intensity. Celebrations are biggest on Sundays. They generally include music, street dancing, expositions, parades, and a seemingly endless amount of fireworks.

The whole spectacle finally wraps up on the first Sunday of December, just in time for the city to mark the Celebration of the Purisima, a massive Nicaragua-wide religious festival, on December 7.

Masaya also has major celebrations to mark the Día de San Lazaro on the Sunday before Palm Sunday. Masayans commemorate this feast by dressing-up dogs and bringing them into church. Updated: Jun 01, 2009.

Getting To and Away from Masaya

Because it is right on the road between Granada and Managua, Masaya gets a fair amount

Markets of Masaya

Visitors to Masaya are often surprised by what appears to be a medieval castle in the heart of a bustling city neighborhood. They're usually delighted to find that the rough, towering rocks of an old Spanish fort now house the Nicaraguan National Artisan Market. Inside the fort self-contained booths offer shoppers colorful locally made pottery, musical instruments—enough for a whole Marimba band—and all the usual souvenirs.

The laid-back atmosphere is conducive to meandering through the market and browsing its wares. Negotiating is a must, and a slight amount of back and forth is expected at any sale.

On Thursday nights, a fee of a couple dollars is charged to enter El Mercado Viejo because it also serves as a venue for cultural events, often featuring folkloric dancing. Brightly dressed performers and well-choreographed dances provide a glimpse into the history and pride of Nicaragua. During September, when the city of Masaya hosts Fiesta Patronal, the market features live music and hip-jiving Latin dancing.

The smells, sounds, and movement of Masaya's main city market are in marked contrast to the tranquility and open space of El Mercado Viejo. Located on the outskirts of town and next to the bus terminal, the city market has an abundance of artisan crafts as well as everyday merchandise. Navigating through the maze of booths and stalls is an adventure in itself. The sing-song call of vendors announcing deals-of-a-lifetime accompany the smell of fritanga (street-food) lingering in the warm, dusty air.

Both markets are intriguing and worth the trip. Prices are pretty comparable at both places, but if time permits, try and head to both for a real opportunity to compare prices and products.

Masaya prides itself on its sense of cultural heritage, so it is worth asking around about ongoing events. The city is easily accessible from both Granada and Managua. There are also many side trips to the nearby Laguna de Apoyo, Volcano Masaya National Park and the artisan towns of San Juan de Oriente and Catarina. Updated: Dec 15, 2008.

of traffic from both cities. Buses going in either direction will drop you off here for about half the normal fare. Be warned that they often won't enter the city proper, and you'll likely get dropped on the side of the highway. It's about a 30-minute walk to the center of town, or a $0.10 per person taxi ride.

The city's main bus station is located next to the Mercado Municipal, with frequent direct service to Managua and Granada. Buses to a number of other small towns in the region also leave from here. There's also a bus to Matagalpa that leaves every morning at 5:30 a.m.

TransNica has an office on Avenida Antiguo Teatro Gonzales, two blocks south of the train station, with daily service to San Jose (5 a.m., 7 a.m., and 10 a.m., $23) and Tegucigalpa (2 p.m., $28.75). The buses don't originate here, so you're best off booking the day before. Updated: Jun 01, 2009.

Getting Around

Masaya's intra-city buses are centered at the main bus terminal next to the municipal markets. If you want to get to the bus station, hop on any of these and you'll find yourself there eventually. If you want to get to Fortaleza de Coyotepe, get on any Managua or Tipitapa bound bus. Sit near the front and ask to be let off at Coyotepe, it's just outside of the city.

Taxis are found throughout the city. They will take you most places for $0.10 per person. Updated: Jun 01, 2009.

Safety

Masaya is a very safe city. Violent crime is not a serious threat. Use common sense—don't brandish valuables if you're strolling through the poorer districts. Viva's reviewer was warned that the path up to Coyotepe could be dangerous, but didn't see anything to validate that claim. Updated: Jun 01, 2009.

Services

Internet cafés are sprinkled liberally throughout the city. There are a couple of excellent ones on Avenida Antiguo Teatro Gonzales, 3 ½ blocks north of Parque Central. There are also a couple on the park itself.

Masaya

There's an INTUR office on Ave el Progreso, half a block south of the Mercado de Artesanías. Staff are predictably apathetic government workers, but they do know their stuff.

The main police station is located on Ave el Progreso, one block north of the Mercado de Artesanías. Updated: Jan 09, 2009.

SHOPPING

Most of the visitors to Masaya come to shop. The city has a range of excellent goods, from the beautiful ceramics of Pueblos Blancos to the famous locally-made hammocks. But if you're looking to buy, think twice before going to the Mercado de Artesanías. Although this is Masaya's most famous market, its status as a tourist attraction means prices will be very steep and vendors less likely to bargain. Instead, head to the Mercado Municipal a few blocks to the east. They have a large handicrafts section with all the same goods as the historic market, at a much cheaper price. For bargains on hammocks, consider heading to the manufacturers themselves. They live in the streets around the Malécon and most have set up little shops of their own. Shop around here for the best prices. Updated: Jun 23, 2008.

Things to See and Do

Most of Masaya's attractions are conveniently located within a few blocks of Parque Central. This makes visiting them easy. An energetic visitor can get to just about all of them in a single day, although it would be a busy day.

In the countryside surrounding Masaya, Laguna de Apoyo and Volcan Masaya are both outstanding and should not be missed. These two natural attractions are easily accessible and make perfect day-trips from Masaya. Updated: Jan 08, 2009.

Malécon

The Malécon is a pleasant walkway, overlooking the lush green slopes of the Laguna de Masaya. It's a nice place to hang out and enjoy a beautiful view. There are playgrounds and basketball courts in the area, as well as several lively discos. In the streets behind this lookout you'll find a clutch of hammock shops—the cheapest place to buy Masaya's most famous product. Updated: Jun 23, 2008.

Forteleza Coyotepe

Although the historical ambience of this old fortress is largely ruined by the prodigious graffiti covering its walls, it's still an interesting place to visit. For one thing, it offers a beautiful view of the region. The dark, labyrinthine corridors are also fun to explore. Coyotepe was the site of a fierce battle between Nicaraguan troops and US Marines in 1912, where resistance hero Benjamin Zeledon made his last stand. General Somoza turned the fortress into an infamous prison, and his son used it as a base to launch mortar attacks on Masaya during the 1979 revolution.

To get to Coyotepe, take a taxi or catch a Managua-bound bus from the Mercado Municipal and ask them to let you off here. From the highway, it's about a kilometer's walk uphill. It is well worth the climb. Updated: Jun 23, 2008.

Museo Galería Héroes y Martires

The Museo Galería Héroes y Martires, located just inside one of the main entrances to the Alcaldia de Masaya, is an unabashed tribute to the Sandinistas and their fight against Somoza's national guard. The 400 photographs and personal objects on display make the exhibits some of the most poignant and memorable in Nicaragua. Glass cases of rifles, mock bombs and a gas can used in an attack are interspersed with rebels' personal items: a watch, a social security card, a beret with Enrique written on the brim in magic marker.

In the back, partitions have been labeled with the date and place of important battles and then covered with photos of the Sandinistas who died. Most of the fallen look to be in their teens, and some of the portraits are obviously school photos. The museum also has various newspaper articles and several copies of professional photos. The Museo Galería Héroes y Martires provides an intimate glimpse into Nicaragua's past that you shouldn't miss. Visitors are asked for a voluntary contribution. Open 8 a.m. – Noon, 1 – 5 p.m. Closed weekends. Alcaldia de Masaya. Tel: 505-2-522-4317, ext. 123, URL: www.alcaldiademasaya.gob.ni. Updated: Jun 26, 2009.

Museo Camilo Ortega

Camilo (Mundo or Ramiro) Ortega Saavedra was a Sandinista leader, revolutionary and a brother of Nicaraguan president José Daniel

Support VIVA! Reserve your hotels or hostels at vivatravelguides.com/hotels/

Ortega Saavedra. A small museum dedicated to him is located on the Masaya city limits.

The museum mainly consists of old newspaper clippings and flags, although there are also displays of Camilo Ortega's clothing and personal items. All of the descriptions are in Spanish.

Camilo Ortega was born on Dec. 13, 1950 in Managua. As a student, Ortega became involved in politics and was particularly outspoken in denouncing poor prison conditions under the Somoza dictatorship. He also became involved in the underground military movement called Frente Sandinista de Liberación Nacional (Sandinista National Liberation Front) or FSLN, helping to train and arm young Sandinista commandos.

After graduating from college, Ortega worked with FSLN Commander José Benito Escobar and created a magazine that promoted the cause. He was arrested for his work and held for several days. Despite the arrest, Ortega continued his revolutionary efforts and fell in with similarly-minded intellectuals and artists.

In 1972, Ortega traveled to Cuba for military and political training. He returned to Masaya in 1975 and started working on a comprehensive review of the FSLN operations. As a commander of the Sandinista organization, Ortega established contacts and helped grow support for FSLN throughout the country.

Ortega led the FSLN in an attack on the city of Granada in 1977. He died in February 1978 during a raid by Somoza forces on a FSLN safe house in the town of Las Sabogal. His body, along with those of two other commanders, was transported to Managua for burial.

To get to the museum follow the main road to Rivas south for about a kilometer past the city limits. Tel: 505-475-8237. Updated: Feb 07, 2009.

Mercado de Artesanías

Nicaragua's most famous market, this market is located in an elegant century-old structure. Every Thursday, the "Night of Revelry" features folkloric dancing and music, as well as local food. It's a major tourist draw, and as such you can expect prices to be quite highly inflated (though just as highly negotiable).

It's an interesting place to see and shouldn't be missed. However, if you actually want to pick up some souvenirs, you can find much better prices at the Mercado Municipal down the street. 2 blocks east of Parque Central. Updated: Jun 23, 2008.

Churches

Masaya has several attractive churches. Probably the nicest is the Iglesia de la Asuncion, a towering Baroque building located in Parque Central. The Iglesia de San Jeronimo and Iglesia de San Sebastien are also worth a look. Iglesia San Miguel is also well-known, but the least impressive of the four. All of these buildings are far more impressive from the outside than within. If you show up to one and it's closed, don't worry about coming back later. Updated: Jun 21, 2008.

Petroglyph Hike

A long time ago, ancient residents of the Masaya region carved swirling figures of birds, snakes and suns into the limestone around Laguna Masaya. You can find what remains of their largely neglected artwork just above Cascadas Cailagua, a pretty name for a place where the city sewer empties into the lake.

To get there, walk behind Masaya's Iglesia Magdalena to the Campo Santo del Pueblo graveyard, where the street paving stones stop. Continue down the dirt road. The road will narrow into a path that winds past three blue crosses in honor of San Pablo, San Pedro and San Juan Bautista. Follow the increasingly steep path down the hill toward Laguna Masaya. You will eventually come to a series of a dozen or so very worn, colonial stairs. Immediately after the stairs, turn right (don't continue to the lake) and follow the branching path straight to Cascadas Cailagua. The petroglyphs start a few hundred feet up the gully. Locals have filled in the less eroded examples with white paint.

A few words of caution: do not attempt the petroglyph hike in the rain, when both the gully and the lake paths become extremely treacherous; wear good hiking shoes that will cover your toes; be aware that you will be walking around a dangerous neighborhood. Go in a group, not alone. Updated: Jun 24, 2009.

Tours

The city's main tour operator is called **Servitour Monimbo** (Tel: 522-7404, E-mail: servitour_monimbo@hotmail.com) and is located half a block east of Iglesia San Sebastien. They offer city tours, volcano tours, and trips to many smaller towns in the region such as Pueblos Blancos and Laguna de Apoyo. Trips are cheaper if you can find yourself a group. Open 8 a.m. – 5 p.m. No English spoken. **Madera's Inn** also offers volcano tours among other trips. See hotel listing for contact info. Updated: Jun 23, 2008.

Lodging

Masaya doesn't have a lot to offer in terms of luxury accommodations. If you're looking for five-stars, you're better off staying in Granada or Managua.

There are however quite a few sound budget options, with private rooms for as little as $4.50 – 5.50. Most of these are on Avenida Antiguo Teatro Gonzales, clustered around four blocks north of Parque Central. If one is full just check around, there are plenty in the area. Updated: Jun 21, 2008.

Hotel Regis

(ROOMS: $4 and up) The safe and relatively clean Hotel Regis is another good budget option if you find Hostal Mi Casa full. This hotel is one of the cheapest around and is actually slightly less expensive than Mi Casa. However the rooms are smaller and the place has much more of a run-down vibe. Due to the fact that this hotel is listed in a prominent guidebook it is usually busy, so it is a good idea to book in advance if possible. Av. Antiguo Teatro Gonzales, four blocks north of Parque Central. Tel: 505-522-2300, E-mail: hotelregismasaya@hotmail.com. Updated: May 12, 2009.

Mi Casa Hostal

(ROOMS: $5.50 and up) Conveniently located inside the Fruti Fruti restaurant (see p. 107), Mi Casa Hostal is a good value budget option. A relatively safe place to stay with friendly service, this hostel has a range of rooms with prices starting from as little as five dollars. All the large clean rooms have comfortable double beds and are equipped with electric fans, which are especially necessary during the hot dry season. Mi Casa also has hot showers and provides towels and soap free of charge. Av. Antiguo Teatro Gonzales, four blocks north of Parque Central. Tel: 505-522-2500. Updated: May 12, 2009.

Madera's Inn

(ROOMS: $5 – 45) The family-run Madera's Inn is a pleasant hotel with 14 spotlessly clean and very well-maintained rooms. The homey common area is fitted out with a TV, chairs, hammocks and some basic exercise equipment. Madera's has a range of rooms catering for people on a range of different budgets. The cheaper rooms have fans and shared bathrooms, whilst the pricier rooms come with air-conditioning and private bathrooms. This hotel also has an Internet service with WiFi, as well as facilities to make long-distance calls and an excellent on-site tour operator. Av. Antiguo Teatro Gonzales, 5 blocks north of Parque Central. Tel: 505-522-5825, E-mail: maderasinn@yahoo.com, URL: www.hotelmaderasinn.com. Updated: May 12, 2009.

Hostal Santa Maria

(ROOMS: $15 – 30) The owners of Santa Maria seem to think that by adding lace curtains and a few dried flowers, they can magically turn a budget hostel into a mid-range hotel. They can't. Despite the higher prices, this place remains of budget quality in terms of cleanliness, room-size, and amenities. There is no reason why anyone would pay $15 for these rooms, rather than $8 for the nearly identical ones on Avenida Antiguo Teatro Gonzales. On an apparently nameless street, half a block south of the east corner of the Mercado de Artesanías. Tel: 505-522-2411, E-mail: info@hostalsantamarianic.com, URL: www.hostalsantamarianic.com. Updated: May 13, 2009.

Hotel Masaya

(ROOMS: $15 – 35) Hotel Masaya is interestingly designed following a Harley-Davidson theme. The friendly staff are obviously biker fans and are welcoming to all, including, of course, biker groups. This nice hotel's eleven comfortable rooms are bright and freshly painted, with TVs, fans (air conditioning is available in the more expensive rooms), rocking chairs, and artistically laid-out towels. There is also an internal garden with hammocks, which is a perfect place to relax. Breakfast is on offer, and there is a kitchen for your own use. Special prices are offered for groups and students. Ent. Principal Av. los Leones, across from Parque Ruben Dario. Tel: 505-522-1030, E-mail: gerencia@hotelmasaya.com, URL: www.hotelmasaya.com. Updated: May 12, 2009.

Restaurants

Although Masaya does not have anywhere near the culinary diversity of Granada, it is possible to find some good food. There are quite a few small restaurants along Avenida

Support VIVA! Reserve your hotels or hostels at vivatravelguides.com/hotels/

Antiguo Teatro Gonzales, in the blocks south of the fire station, around Madera's Inn. However, most of these restaurants only serve basic typical food, and finding quality and variety can be tricky. The Mercado de Artesanías is another place where you can find good food as it has a few decent restaurants. Updated: Jan 08, 2009.

La Jarochita

La Jarochita is a well-known Mexican restaurant with a great reputation. There is no doubt that the food lives up to this reputation, as the enormous portions are extremely delicious. A highlight on the menu is the tasty fajitas which are served with sides of spicy salsa and fresh guacamole. Make sure that you bring an healthy appetite as you will want to finish every last piece of food on your plate. Av. Antiguo Teatro Gonzales, half a block north of Parque Central. E-mail: rest_lajarochita@yahoo.com. Updated: Jan 08, 2009.

Fruti Fruti

Fruti Fruti is primarily known for their range of fruit smoothies, which are excellent. To accompany your smoothie this restaurant also serves food and is a great place to grab either breakfast or lunch. Their omelettes are delicious, served promptly and with a smile. They offer a large range of other breakfast options as well, including pancakes, waffles, cereal and fruit salad, all of which are excellent. At lunch burgers and sandwiches are available to compliment your smoothie. Av. Antiguo Teatro Gonzales, four blocks north of Parque Central. Tel: 505-522-2500. Updated: Jan 08, 2009.

Pizza Gold

Pizza Gold is a convenient place to grab a quick bite and an extremely cheap way to satisfy your hunger. The individual slices of pepperoni pizza are great value as they are sold for just $0.15. Of course for this price the pizza is not outstanding; however, it is tasty enough. It is also possible to purchase full pizzas, although these are slightly more expensive. This pizzeria also has a delivery service. Av. Real de Monimbo, half a block south of Parque Central. Tel: 505-522-4601.Updated: Jan 08, 2009.

La Ronda

Although this place does not look like much, the food is actually quite excellent. At $1.30, the filet mignon can only be described as phenomenal. The filet is an absolutely outstanding cut of meat grilled to tender perfection and smothered in a rich and delicious mushroom sauce. Portions are very generous. The place is also has a popular bar that fills up on weekends. Parque Central, south side. Tel: 505-522-3310. Updated: Mar 11, 2009.

> **V!VA ONLINE REVIEW**
> LA RONDA
>
> *"Cold beer and hot food, great price!"*
>
> September 20, 2008

Don Pepe

Don Pepe is a wonderfully ambient Italian restaurant. The tables are well arranged around a very handsome garden. The impeccably dressed waiters also add to the atmosphere. Unfortunately the unexciting menu does not match the atmosphere, for it contains little more than standard meat-rice-and-salad dishes. Still as the prices are reasonable Don Pepe is probably worth a visit, if only to enjoy dining in such pleasant surroundings. Av. Real San Jeronimo, 2 ½ blocks south of Iglesia San Jeronimo. Tel: 505-614-4119. Updated: Jan 08, 2009.

> **V!VA ONLINE REVIEW**
> DON PEPE
>
> *"A different experience. Very cosy place with wonderful attention from the owners...The environment is colonial with a fresh garden. Food and wine are very good."*
>
> September 20, 2008

PARQUE NACIONAL VOLCÁN MASAYA

Founded in 1979, the Parque Nacional Volcán Masaya is Nicaragua's oldest national park. Its 54 sq km (34 sq mi) contain the famous Masaya volcano with the Masaya and Nidiri cones (the latter also has pit craters called Santiago, Masaya, Nidiri and San Pedro).

Volcán Masaya is still active and, through the Santiago crater in particular, spews a near continuous stream of sulfur dioxide gas into the park. Because of the emissions, the volcano has been dubbed one of the largest natural polluters in the world.

Despite occasional eruptions and frequent activity, visitors can still drive up the side of the volcano to peer into the craters. If you plan to visit the park in your car, make sure to keep a close eye on your valuables. Thieves have been known to ransack vehicles while their owners were exploring the volcano craters.

The best hiking trail is through the Santiago crater between Masaya and Nidirí. Lake Masaya features ancient petroglyphs and some unique flora and fauna. Camping is also possible in the park and you can arrange to visit some local caves where bats nest. As with all such expeditions, it's best if you arrange to have a guide take you around.

Just outside of the Parque Nacional Volcán Masaya is the town of Masaya, Nicaragua's crafts and folklore capital. Updated: Feb 06, 2009.

Getting To and Away From PN Volcán Masaya

If you want to poke your head over the edge of an active volcano, but don't have much time, then Volcán Masaya is the perfect place for you. It's hard to think of a national park that's easier to reach than the Volcán Masaya. To get there, jump on any bus between Managua and Masaya (or Granada) and ask the driver to let you off at the park's entrance at km 23. The park offers a transportation service (in addition to the $4.50 entrance fee) that costs $2.80 each way to the top of the crater in a park truck. Nationals pay $1.70.

From the entrance, it's 1 km to the visitor's center and 5 km (3.1 mi) to the top of the Volcán Nindirí crater. The road is very hot with almost no shade, so if you plan to walk, start early in the day and bring a lot of water.

If you are driving, park officials ask that you limit your speed to 40 km/h (25 mi/h) and park your car facing the exit at Oviedo's Plaza (for a quick getaway in case the volcano decides to be more active than normal). Due to the volcanic emissions, limit your visit to the Santiago Crater to 20 minutes. The park is open 9 a.m. – 4:45 p.m. daily. Tel: 522-5415, E-mail: pvmasaya@ideay.net.ni. Updated: Sep 30, 2009.

Santiago Crater

From the park entrance at the side of the main road, transport ($3 one-way) can take you up the hilly road to the edge of the active Santiago crater. It last erupted in 2000, toppling one of the previous viewpoints into the crater, but the park is otherwise well organized and safe. Views of this massive hole in the ground are impressive; there are also paths that lead to views of a large crater lake, a guided walk to a cave, and a good information centre. Volcán Masaya National Park, Near Masaya. Updated: Jan 28, 2009.

NINDIRÍ

▲ 220 m   👤 3,147

Nindirí is a small city that makes up in charm what it lacks in size. A series of dedicated municipal governments have ensured that Nindirí roads are in good order, the sidewalks are clean and the buildings brightly painted. Nindirí has two sources of pride: a lively central square, where families stroll and students play basketball in the afternoons, and a history that can be traced back to early Chorotega settlements. The statue in the central plaza is of Cacique Tenderí who had the misfortune to be the local leader when the Spanish arrived.

Museo Tenderí (Tel: 505-8-954-0570, open 8 a.m. – noon and 2 – 5 p.m., weekdays) has an extensive, if not particularly well ordered, collection of pre-Hispanic pottery, including a large display of incense burners that date as far back as 1500 B.C. The museum has over 1,500 items, including funeral pots, ceramic jaguars and even colonial era cavalry equipment.

La Iglesia Parroquial Santa Ana (1529) is home to the Cristo del Volcán (whose reputed powers kept Nindirí from harm during the massive 1772 volcanic eruption), but the lady of the house and city's patron saint is still the most celebrated. During the July Fiestas Patronales, locals culminate a week of festivities with parades, traditional dances and food. Eunice Poveda López (Tel: 505-8-969-0517) at Nindirí's city hall, can give you details of the festivities and also works as a local guide. Her day-long tours include trips to Volcán Masaya, visits to area furniture and shoe makers and stops at Iglesia Santa Ana, which was renovated in 2003.

Restaurant La Llamarada, one of the few formal eateries in Nindirí, suffered a setback in 2009 when the grandmotherly owner broke her arm. The location (one block north of Iglesia Santa Ana, Tel: 505-2-522-4110) was closed in April. Locals highly recommend the restaurant, which serves dishes such as chicken in wine sauce, beef tongue and fritanga, so stop by and see if La Llamarada has reopened while you're in the area.

Restaurant Rincon Tipico (Mains: $4.00 – 6.00; Tel: 505-2-522-2988, Carr. Masaya, km 25) is a popular local hangout for Nindirí residents (especially now that La Llamarada is closed). The eatery has a fairly standard, open plan dining area, filled with white plastic furniture. You'll never be able to accuse Rincon Tipico of haute cuisine, but the establishment does have a solid selection of bar food, from tacos and wings to ribs and pork skin crunchies.

Their main dishes are the normal beef, pork and chicken selections and the beers are cold. The restaurant is open weekdays from 10 a.m. to midnight and weekends from 10 a.m. to 2 a.m.

You won't find any guesthouses within the center of Nindirí, since the municipality is too small to draw many overnight visitors. If you're intent on staying nearby (and don't want to make the short hop to Masaya), you can find a few hotels along Carr. Masaya. Las Cabanas Encantadas de Nindirí has rustic hillside cabins and great views (Tel: 505-2-949-1363; double $60, triple $70, quadruple $80, with breakfast included. Cash only). The cabanas have cable TV and air conditioning, as well as well-equipped kitchenettes, private bathrooms and small sitting areas. (Each cabin is designed to comfortably accommodate two guests, with room for two more on a foldout bed.) Tiny porches open onto a gorgeous view of Lago Masaya and the distant volcanoes; the hotel's hammock-strung mirador is on the edge of the ancient Volcán Masaya lava field. While there is also a hot tub at the mirador, the dusty cover suggested that it isn't often in use. If you're a light sleeper, be aware that the cabins are not too far from the busy highway. Updated: Jun 09, 2009.

RESERVA NACIONAL LAGUNA DE APOYO

Said to have the clearest, cleanest water in the country, Laguna de Apoyo (Amictlan to the indigenous people) is a wonderful place to take a break from southern Nicaragua's scorching heat. Swimming, kayaking, tubing and paragliding are all popular activities for visitors, but many others come here just to kick-back, relax and enjoy the placid atmosphere.

The lake sits atop the now dormant Volcán Apoyo. Some 23,000 years ago the volcano underwent a massive eruption, leaving behind a seven kilometer-wide crater that slowly filled with water. Although there have been no more eruptions since, the area still has a great deal of seismic activity, including underwater thermal vents. In 2000 a major earthquake rocked the area, centered under the town of Catarina on the crater's western edge. The movements caused the lake to slosh back and forth, leading to rumors that its waters were boiling.

Today, the area is a national park, protecting a variety of birds, monkeys, and some unique species of fish. A non-profit organization called Proyecto Ecologico (URL: www.gaianicaragua.org/) is working in the area to chart undiscovered species. They also offer Spanish lessons, as well as overnight stays.

Many people choose to visit the Laguna as part of a day or overnight trip from Granada. Hostal Oasis (URL: www.nicaraguahostel.com/) and The Bearded Monkey (URL: www.thebeardedmonkey.com/monkeyhut.htm) both have affiliated hostels on the lake, with reasonably priced rooms. These resorts also offer tubing and kayak rentals. Snorkeling and diving in the lake are also possible.

There are some restaurants in the area, but most visitors choose to prepare their own meals. Most resorts around the lake offer guests the use of their kitchen, but if you're not sure it's best to call or e-mail ahead.

The 48 square-kilometre (30 square miles) lake is surrounded by the lush Apoyo Lagoon Reserve, a protected ecosystem for tropical wildlife like toucans, monkeys and unique varieties of butterflies. The reserve includes places where not many human beings have been. You should definitely not leave this surreal, gorgeous paradise out of your Nicaraguan places to go.

Even though Nicaragua has other volcanic lagoons, like Tiscapa in downtown Managua and Cosigüina in the north-western department of Chinandega, Apoyo is usually the best option. Located about 30 minutes from Managua, 15 minutes from Granada and right next to Masaya, buses from any of these cities will drop you off at the entrance; travelers can easily take a taxi or hike for about an hour and a half, through the countryside and down the volcanic cone. Updated: Jan 22, 2009.

Getting To and Away From RN Laguna de Apoyo

Buses from Masaya go all the way to the lagoon twice a day, at 10:30 in the morning and an afternoon bus at 3:30. The ride lasts about an hour, and then the buses turn around for the return trip. If you miss these, the "El Valle" bus will take you to the crater's rim. From there it's a 45 minute walk to the waterfront. From Granada you can catch one of Crater's Edge shuttles at Hostal Oasis, at 10:30 a.m. and 4:30 p.m. for $4 round trip; be sure to put your name on the list at the Oasis. The Monkey Hut has a transport that leaves from its sister hostal the Bearded Monkey in Granada, on Monday, Wednesday and Friday mornings and afternoons.

Taxis direct from Granada should cost $12 – 15, taxis from Masaya will be $8 – 10, and taxis from Managua are about $30 – 40. Catching a taxi from Apoyo is not impossible but not very reliable. Updated: Jan 22, 2009.

LODGING

Fundeci/gaia Escuela de Español and Estacion Biológica

(ROOMS: $8 – 10) Despite the name Fundeci/gaia Escuela de Español and Estacion Biológica doesn't offer Spanish classes at the moment, although the establishment does have scuba lessons and gear ($40 per immersion or $60 for two). Fundeci/gaia also has a handful of cramped rooms with smudged walls. The rooms cost $8 per person or $10 per person with breakfast included. Guests can use the small kitchen for an extra $1 per day fee. At least three very large dogs roam freely through the common spaces, so this is not the place to drop your pack if you have any canine phobias. Laguna de Apoyo. Tel: 505-8-882-3992 / 505-8-810-4670, URL: www.gaianicaragua.org. Updated: Jun 24, 2009.

Monkey Hut

(ROOMS: $8 – 75) Slightly cheaper and a lot less formal than neighboring Crater's Edge, the Monkey Hut draws more of a backpacker crowd. The stacked bunks of the six-bed dorm ($12) are located to the rear of the main building, with a clean-ish tiled bathroom across the hall. Private rooms (single $18 to $20; double $25 to $28) and a cabin ($45 for two; $60 for three; $75 for four) are also available, although if everything is full, the staff will throw a mattress on the floor or let you sleep in a hammock for $8.

The $6 visitor's day pass gives you access to the hotel's kayaks, inner tubes and docks (one floating, one high above the water line). The Monkey Hut has no Internet or TV, but they do have a brick oven to turn out a steady stream of pizzas. Other food can be ordered from the pulpería down the street; snacks are on the honor system. The hotel was once operated by the Bearded Monkey hostel in Granada but has since changed hands.

Support VIVA! Reserve your hotels or hostels at vivatravelguides.com/hotels/

Laguna de Apoyo. Tel: 505-8-887-3546. Updated: Jul 10, 2009.

Eco Hostal Apoyo

(ROOMS: $15 – 25) Eco Hostal Apoyo was once a lakeside residence and still has the slightly informal feel of a vacation home. The hotel has a large porch and an open-air kitchen. In the back there is a communal room with a TV and DVD player as well as a small book exchange. Set across the road from the lakefront, the hotel has no immediate access to the water, although several small paths do lead down to the shore. The double rooms ($15 per room; an extra bed is $5) are dim, but clean, with fans and insect netting. They share narrow bathrooms with pebbled walls. The hotel rents one large room with a private bathroom and refrigerator for $25. (Large groups or families can also rent the entire house, which has space for 25 people.) The hotel recycles, composts and sends whatever garbage is left to a municipal dump away from the lakeshore. Guests can also sign up for several Eco Hostal Apoyo tours to visit local hot springs, go birdwatching or tour San Juan del Oriente and Volcán Masaya, for between $5 and $8 per hour. Laguna de Apoyo. Updated: Jun 30, 2009.

Crater's Edge

(ROOMS: $15 – 44) Once a private residence (like most buildings along the lakefront), Hospedaje Crater's Edge is hushed and lovely, with wide tiled porches overlooking the lake – although rather strict with the guest dos and don'ts. Outside food and drink is not permitted, which means either a trip up the street to one of the local restaurants or the hotel's plate-of-the-day for $4. Crater's Edge is socially conscious: the owner maintains a strip of beach, employs a blind masseuse from Seeing Hands ($8 for 30 minutes, $15 per hour) and sells a range of items whose proceeds go to local projects.

The hotel has six private rooms ($22 – 44) and a 12-bed, screened dorm ($15 per person with breakfast included; towels are $1 extra) that was originally a boathouse. The $7 visitor's day pass includes access to a ranchero-style patio with hammocks and lounge chairs, as well as use of the kayaks, inner tubes and floating dock. The hotel has Internet access, including WiFi on the upper porch. Accomodations include $4 breakfast. Crater's Edge also has a shuttle service to Oasis Hostel in Granada ($4 round trip) that leaves at 10:30 a.m. and 4:30 p.m. Reservations at Crater's Edge are recommended.

Tel: 505-8-895-3202, E-mail: cratersedge@gmail.com, URL: www.craters-edge.com. Updated: Jun 24, 2009.

La Posada Ecológica La Abuela

(ROOMS: $30 – 50) La Posada Ecológica la Abuela has comfortable and bright wooden cabins with A/C, internet, kitchenette and hot water. There is also a restaurant with Nicaraguan and international food and an incredible view of the lagoon with three platforms ideal for diving off from different heights. Hanging out near the bar, Doña Iskra (La Abuela) oversees the hotel and restaurant's day-to-day business while greeting visitors and making sure you're well taken care of.

San Simian Eco Lodge

(ROOMS: $45 – 60) The San Simian Eco Lodge is in a secluded spot on the edge of Laguna de Apoyo. The lodge has five private bungalows, each with private bathrooms and their own interior design. Four of the bungalows have Balinese-type outdoor showers in rock wall enclosures that are open to the sky and one, the most expensive, has a tub. You can enjoy the included breakfast at either the on-site restaurant or bar. Other activities available at the lodge include swimming, sailing, kayaking, hiking or just relaxing in the hammocks. Shuttles leave at 11 a.m. daily in front of Kathy's waffle house or contact Casa San Francisco hotel in Granada. Off of Carretera Masaya.Tel: 552 813-6866, E-mail: sansimianresort1@yahoo.com, URL: www.sansimian.com. Updated: Aug 24, 2009.

> **VIVA ONLINE REVIEW**
> SAN SIMIAN ECO LODGE
>
> "There are 5 beautiful cabins on a crater lake, it is quiet, except for the exotic birds and howler monkeys in the morning. The restaurant is great..."
>
> *September 20, 2008*

RESTAURANTS

Bar Maria

(ENTREES: $4 – 6, LUNCH: $3) Bar Maria is one of the cheapest of the thatched restaurants that line Apoyo's shore. The upper level of the restaurant is dirty and unappealing, but the lower levels are much nicer and a strip of space near the water is particularly popular. Main dishes include beef, pork, chicken and fish. Tel: 505-8-955-7627. Updated: Jun 24, 2009.

Restaurant Apoyo Beach

(ENTREES: $4 – 15) Restaurant Apoyo Beach is one of the many eateries that line the lake shore and offers the typical options (beef, pork, chicken, fish). The top of the restaurant is dirt floored and slightly grimy although, as with all of the locations in the area, the patio near the waterfront is a lot nicer. The restaurant is open weekdays from 7 a.m. to 9 p.m. and to midnight on weekends. Laguna de Apoyo. Tel: 505-8-866-0980. Updated: Jun 23, 2009.

Montes Verdes

(Mains: $4.20 – 12) Montes Verdes is the most highly recommended restaurant in the area, possibly because the location is one of the few to use filtered water in their food preparation. The menu is largely the same as other establishments (beef, chicken, seafood and a couple breakfast options) though some visitors might be put off when they notice that turtle eggs are also listed. Montes Verdes has a series of tiled terraces with plastic tables and hammocks. The restaurant accepts credit cards, but adds a 15 percent surcharge. Laguna de Apoyo. Tel: 505-8-848-3705. Updated: Jun 23, 2009.

Los Pueblos Blancos

The names are easy to confuse (Diria, Diriomo and Diriamba anyone?) and most claim indigenous ancestry of some kind, but the personalities of the small towns in the 'Meseta de los Pueblos' are as distinctive as they are colorful. Long past the time when the houses were uniformly white, the Pueblos Blancos now sport official signage that confirms their status as the garden central (Catarina), furniture market (Masatepe) or hometown of General Agusto Cesar Sandino (Niquinohomo). These towns are easy to visit and don't require much time to thoroughly explore—a perfect combination if you want to buy spectacular San Juan de Oriente pottery on your way to Granada or Rivas. Updated: Sep 30, 2009.

CATARINA

520 m | 7,524

The first signs that you're almost to Catarina are the road stands—crude stalls filled with flowers, potted plants and cement sculptures. The city might be named after Saint Catarina de Siena, but the title "the city that lives" is a more apt description of a place where an estimated 62 percent of the residents grow ornamental plants in backyard greenhouses and then sell them in their front yards.

The windy Mirador de Catarina, with views of the deep blue Laguna de Apoyo and the wilds beyond, is the perfect feather in Catarina's green cap. On a clear day, the vista can extend as far as Granada, Volcán Mombacho and the Isla de Ometepe. The mirador is popular enough that it has also become a revenue stream for the city. Last year, the alcaldía added a new charge to access the view. Foreigners now pay $1, a flat fee that's the same if you're alone, on foot, or have squished into a car with eight buddies to split the cost.

The lookout point, aptly dubbed "Centro Turistico 'El Mirador,'" has a dozen craft stands and about 15 restaurants serving up typical Nicaraguan dishes. Whether you decide to eat on a porch with a view, or at a table in the back of the parking lot, the cost ranges from $3.40 to $12.

For a more up close view of the lake, you can either hike the steep 500 meters down to the shore or hire a horse to carry you there. The descent by horseback takes about an hour (at $6 per hour), but a shorter ride around the crater rim costs between $0.50 and $3, depending on how far you want to go. Laguna Apoyo is one of the few crater lakes in the area that is both easily accessible and free of the pollutants that have kept other spots like Laguna Masaya off limits.

If you decide not to make the trek back, there are a couple of places to rest next to the lake, such as Hotel **"El Paso del Tren"** (Tel: 505-2-888-2686/ 505-2-474-6121, Cell: 505-8-441-9371).

Right in town, and just a few blocks from the mirador, is the spacious and comfortable **Hotel Casa Catarina** (Tel: 505-2-538-0261/ 505-8-408-3482; E-mail: hotelcasacatarina@gmail.com, URL: www.hotelcasacatarina.com). The rooms open onto a courtyard of hanging ferns and lush plants which add the feeling of escaping to your private garden. The hotel also has a bar and private restaurant. The 15 rooms (single $63.25; double $97.75;

triple $103.25; suite $109.25) come with air conditioning, hot water, a continental breakfast and WiFi.

Don't have your own computer? **Cyber Catarina** (Tel: 505-8-989-7161/ 505-2-558-0270; 9 a.m. to 10 p.m. daily) is located to the north side of the health center. Internet access there costs $0.60 per hour. Updated: Jun 02, 2009.

SAN JUAN DE ORIENTE

🔺 500 m 👤 5,325

San Juan de Oriente is a city so small that it has no central square—or guesthouses or proper restaurant, for that matter. But, as the common expression goes, size can be deceiving, and the tiny city makes up for any deficiencies with an inordinately large number of pottery makers. The bright wares—wind chimes, vases, pots in animal shapes, decorative pieces—are as colorful and inexpensive as they are plentiful.

Locals celebrate their storied history of ceramics (and their ongoing love affair with the art form) in the shape of a giant vase mounted just up the street from the cream-colored Iglesia de San Juan.

A vast majority of workshops are clustered on the main entrance into the city, with the Cooperativa Quesacual being the most well-known. Venture further into San Juan de Oriente and you'll discover that almost every home has their own display. Stop inside and ask if you can see the pottery production at work; the artists are usually willing to show off their techniques as they shape the wet clay and then fire it in their kilns. (Most of the area kilns were rebuilt after a crushing 2000 earthquake). They might also tell you about how San Juan de Oriente's history of pottery making traces back to before the Spanish conquest.

City officials have recently tried to unite the disparate workshops in a new Mercado Artesanía (9 a.m. to 4:30 p.m., daily), which opened in 2008 at the edge of San Juan de Oriente. So far, the market seems to attract more goats than visitors, but the dozen small stands do sell souvenirs that are much more portable than the platter-sized wall hangings or three-foot pigs closer to the highway.

On your way back out, you can stop at San Juan de Oriente's only attempt at a restaurant, the extremely limited **Bar El Quelite** (open from noon to 10 p.m.) where the owners can fix you a plate of chicken or beef, but where you might want to stick to soda and beer. Updated: Jun 02, 2009.

DIRIA

🔺 634 m 👤 11,000

Diría was once where the Chorotega council of elders met and, like the city of Diriamba across the street, widely celebrates Chorotega chief and Spanish bane Diriangen (who both claim as a founder, along with Diriamba). Cacique Diriangén is said to have met with his foes on the site where La Parroquia de San Pedro was erected in 1650. Perhaps the chief's spirit came back to haunt the location; the church had to be rebuilt after being damaged by an earthquake in the 1700s and the congregation decided to put the bells in a separate tower. A modern renovation was completed in 2008; San Pedro, in a cowboy hat, presides over the congregation.

San Pedro may be the patron saint, but Cacique Diriangén is the obvious favorite. There is a statue of the spear-wielding warrior at one of the city's five entrances and the Chorotega chief can also be found striking a pose in the central square and about to hurl his spear over the gorgeous view at Mirador el Boquete, the low-key (and payment free) counterpart to the lookout at Catarina. The few restaurants here have been set back from the rim of the crater. A cobbled road at the far end leads the 1.5 km down to the shores of Laguna de Apoyo. Follow the road as it curves left and you'll find yourself on a steep, unpaved trail to a small green pool (the local pilar) with paths that continue to the lake.

The Perez Arevalo family has recently turned their home into Diria's only guesthouse. The hotel (Tel: 505-2-557-0221/ 505-8-485-0363) is charming, if not particularly formal, with family photos on the walls and clothing in the unused rooms. The seven rooms ($10 per person) have air conditioning, fans and shared bathrooms, with a billiard table and TV downstairs. The family also rents out their finca, under the shadow of Volcán Mombacho. Donald Felix Pérez Miranda (Tel: 505-8-485-0363)

Have a great travel story? Share it at vivatravelguides.com

provides tours of the area in either his motortaxi or, if you call ahead, a van.

The people of Diría are not shy about erecting statues to commemorate, well, anything. In 2007, they capped the new Avenida Central with a monument to the local game of la astilla where locals try and smack each other with wooden swords. Down the street is another monument: a volcanic rock dragged from the lake topped with a statue of San Pedro. The plaque below explains that Diría native and Miami transplant Alberto Sándigo and his wife, Clara, donated the road.

If you're looking for a bite to eat, you'll probably be heading out on the Avenida Central. Not too far along the highway is **Bar y Restaurante El Aguacate** (Mains: $4.30 to $8.60, Tel: 505-2-557-0072/ 505-8-849-9241, open from 11 a.m. to 9 p.m. daily), a simple restaurant with a menu of exotic meats including rabbit, venison and, sometimes, baked armadillo. Of course, they also serve the more traditional beef, chicken and seafood. Updated: Jun 23, 2009.

DIRIOMO

345 m   28,596

Sweet and witchy are the two flavors of Diriomo, a city known in equal parts for cajeta candy and for a history of brujería (Witchcraft). Locals say they can trace the roots of the "pueblo de los brujos" to the time when indigenous tribes ruled the area and herbs, lemon, garlic were part of botanic medicine. The secrets of the ancient medicinal cures have been passed down through the ages and current practitioners (some of the more famous names include: Andrea Peña, Antonio Castellón, Ismael Vargas and Miguel Gómez) welcome those who are looking for help for health, emotional and love problems. To find the proper practitioner, visitors go to the municipal park and talk to the assistants who wait there. Depending on the problem (and the medicine needed to solve it) visits to a Diriomo brujo/a can cost anywhere from $5 to $100. If you need a shot of courage before your consultation, the local fermented corn drinks are called chicha bruja and calavera de gato (cat's skull).

While you're waiting to see a brujo, stop in Iglesia Santuario Nuestra Señora de la Candelaria (constructed between 1795 and 1900), where the stone and brick walls and the cedar pillars are presided over by the Virgin Mary. During the February celebrations in her honor, residents present each other with food such as nacatamales, sweet cajetas, buñuelos and rosquillas before performing traditional dances such as las inditas, los diablitos, las negras and toro venado.

Sweet milk candy, called cajetas, is a tradition in Diriomo. The best place to try some is at **La Casa de Las Cajetas** (Tel: 505-2-557-0015, Fax: 505-2-289-7726, E-mail: Barauz848@hotmail.com, in front of the park), a family-run enterprise that has been producing cajeta for over 90 years. The sweets are now packaged in bright orange boxes with the ingredients, and even calorie information, printed on the side. Cajetas can be rather gooey, so make sure you plan to either eat what you buy or can keep the box in a cool place. The store offers a range of box sizes and cajeta flavors, including orange, milk, grapefruit and spicy butter.

Doña Marca rents three clean rooms within the court yard of her restaurant, **Los Rincones de Candelaria** (Tel: 505-8-423-0920). The single room ($10), matrimonial room ($20) and triple room ($30) have small bathrooms and TVs. The restaurant itself is open from 11 a.m. to 10 p.m. with à la carte options that range from $2 to $4.30. Updated: Jun 09, 2009.

NIQUINOHOMO

440 m   23,010

From the place the Náhuatl dubbed "valley of warriors" arose the nation's most famous fighter, General Agusto César Sandino, and the city celebrates it's favorite son with a giant statue near the highway. The only other Sandino tribute is a small museum space in the back of the local library with old newspaper articles and old photos reproduced poster-sized. A picture of Sandino's parents holding hands is heartbreaking once you read the caption; it was taken in 1934, shortly after their sons were killed.

Stepping out of the library, you may notice that Niquinohomo is built on a series of levels, like a city-wide wedding cake. A climb up multi-colored stairs will bring you to the

Support VIVA! Reserve your hotels or hostels at vivatravelguides.com/hotels/

central square, with the Parroquia de Nuestra Señora Santa Anna on a tier above that. A huge cement cross was added to the church grounds in honor of the millennium and, two years later, the church was declared a national cultural site.

City officials were still working on their latest project—a local Mercado Artesanía—in spring 2009, with a grand opening planned for the summer. The two story market, located on the north side of the church, will have space for 27 stalls, two restaurants, a clothing shop and a stage for events.

On the opposite side of the church, the **Estancia Bosquesillo** (Mains: $2 to $7.75, Tel: 505-2-558-0463, open 9 a.m. to 9 p.m. daily) serves up comida corriente on a pleasant, vine-hung patio.

There are no guesthouses in town, but there is a local Internet spot, **Cyber Cristina**, which is strangly combined with the local pharmacy. You'll have to walk past counters stocked with baby wipes, pulmo grip and Pepto-Bismol, to get to the large room of new computers. Access costs $0.60 per hour and the cyber (Tel: 505-8-498-8320) is open from Monday to Saturday, 8 a.m. to noon and 2:30 to 9 p.m., or Sunday, 9 to noon and 4 to 9 p.m. Updated: Jun 05, 2009.

MASATEPE

455 m   34,580

Upon first arriving at Masatepe, you might be tempted to venture no further than the entrance. Nicaragua's furniture capital puts on a magnificent highway display, with almost every home displaying some new way to twist wicker, wood, rattan and bamboo into furniture. The smaller displays culminate at the **Mercado de Artesanía** (URL: www.masatepecity.com, open 8 a.m. to 6 p.m. daily), where 15 vendors offer every kind of locally made sofa, table, chair, lamp and hamper (as well as some decorative wooden fruits). On summer weekends, the market hosts singers and other acts.

Across from the market, you might spot one of the numerous stands selling samplers of sweet cajetas, a catchall term for a soft candy that resembles marzipan in form (if not in taste). While the famous shops in Diriomo are more likely to sell packages of cajetas (the word literally means "small box"), Masatepe vendors mold their sweets into animal and fruit shapes.

Masatepe has as much going on around the center of town as it does on the outskirts. The wide, colonial streets will lead you to the baby blue Iglesia San Juan Bautista de Masatepe where you will find the city's patron saint, El Cristo Negro de La Santísima Trinidad. The Fiestas Patronales in honor of the Black Christ are celebrated 40 days after Semana Santa, starting with a *desfile hípico* (equestrian parade) and featuring a range of traditional dances, such as el Baile de los Indios or el Toro Venado, and local foods like *masa de cazuela*. You don't have to wait until after Semana Santa to celebrate though, as on Holy Thursday over 700 Masatepino dress up in masks and costumes to reenact the Passion of Christ as Jews and Romans.

From December 16 to December 24, young Masatepinos also flood the streets at 1 a.m. to rouse residents from their beds for 4 a.m. mass in honor of el Niño Dios. To make sure everyone is up in time, the teenagers blow whistles, bang tin cans, and shake rattles in a tradition known as latas.

Masatepe is known for the quality of its *mondongo*, or tripe soup, a regional dish that was brought to savory perfection by the culinary genius of resident Doña Néstor. The enterprising cook turned what had been a hearty stew for workers into a soup that drew hungry customers from all the surrounding cities. Doña Néstor passed away over two decades ago, but you can still taste her savory combination of cow stomach, fresh herbs and vegetables at the restaurants of her two daughters. **Doña Néstor** (open 11 a.m. – 5 p.m. daily; three blocks north of Iglesia San Juan) is low-roofed and basic, with huge, black cauldrons bubbling in the back, while around the corner, **Mondongo de Veracruz** (Tel: 505-2-486-3145, open weekdays 10 a.m. – 6 p.m. and weekends until 7 p.m.) has an open, more modern space and plenty of chicken, beef and fish on the menu if you decide that cow stomach is just not your thing. A bowl of soup in either restaurant costs around $3.25.

The owners of **Centro Ecoturistico Flor de Pochote** (Tel: 505-8-885-7576 / 505-8-617-2894, URL: www.flordepochote.com, rosario@flordepochote.com) closed their restaurant almost a year ago, due to a lack of customers, but the $1 mototaxi ride out to this working farm is still worthwhile, if only for the magnificent views of Laguna de Masaya and Volcán Masaya or a glass of sweet, homemade fruit wine. **Flor de Pachote** has three wooden cabins (singles and doubles $25; triples $30) and two dormitories ($5 per person) dotted among the finca's rolling hills. The owners can also arrange guided trips to the lake, to local communities or to the volcano. With plenty of trails cut into the hills, you're also welcome to take a stroll on your own.

Please note: although the local alcaldía still touts el Mirador Puerta del Cielo as a tourism attraction, the location is in private hands and is no longer open to the public.

Right by the highway, you'll find **Hotel Faleiros**, which owner Luis Faleiros opened in April 2008 with the hope of eventually turning his enterprise into the local equivalent of a Days Inn. Mr. Faleiros plans to eventually add a pool, Internet and 15 more rooms. The handful of existing rooms are cheerful (singles and doubles $25) and the hotel is convenient to the Pueblos Blancos, particularly Masatepe.

From the center of Masatepe, you can catch minibuses to Jinotepe ($0.40), San Marcos ($0.30) or Managua. Ordinarios also to these and other destinations regularly pass the Masatepe highway entrance. Updated: Jun 09, 2009

SAN MARCOS

510   23,347

A small city with an ancient heritage, San Marcos has a lively and vibrant spirit that is almost entirely due to the student population at **Ave Maria College of the Americas** (URL: www.avemaria.edu.ni, Tel: 505-2-535-2339), where courses are taught in English.

With over 1000 students, Ave Maria has had trouble keeping up with on-campus housing, but city residents have absorbed the overflow by taking students into their homes. Walk around the city and you'll see hand-lettered signs offering long-term rentals.

The student population means that San Marcos is sprinkled with restaurants, from thatched dives to gourmet coffee shops.

Around the central park, vendors also sell fresh fruit and bread from wicker baskets.

To help newcomers get around, the alcaldía has a large and very tourist-friendly map. They don't keep many copies on hand, but several copy shops are located around the park.

In 1995, archaeologists found evidence that indigenous tribes were living in the San Marcos area 2000 to 3000 BC, well before the Spanish invaded in 1520 AD. Locals know the overgrown locations where petroglyphs can be found, but there are no guides to the sites as yet.

Locals also recognize San Marcos as the birthplace of General Anastasio Somoza Garcia. There are no monuments to the Nicaraguan dictator, but his hometown is the first stop on the Route of Generals, a string of cities associated with Geneneral José Maria Moncada (born in Masatepe), Benjamin Zeledón (buried in Catarina) and Somoza's foe General Agusto César Sandino (born in Niquinohomo), who the eventual dictator killed in an ambush in 1934.

At the end of April 24, San Marcos explodes with fireworks, music and dancing in honor of the city's patron saint. San Marcos gets the chance to sally out from the flowery murals of Iglesia de San Marcos Agradece on April 24, when the icon famously meets with the patron saints of Diriamba, Jinotepe and La Concepción. Updated: May 04, 2009

Services

MONEY

Thanks to the student population, San Marcos has all of the services of a much larger city, including branches of **BAC** (Tel: 505-2-535-2339, www.bac.net), **Bancentro** (Tel: 2-535-2511/ 2-535-2821, Fax: 505-2-535-2551, E-mail: info@bancentro.net, URL: www.bancentro.net) and **Western Union** (Telefax: 505-2-535-2581). Both banks have 24-hour ATMs, but, while BAC accepts all major credit cards, Bancentro accepts only Visa. BAC is open between 8:30 a.m. and 4:30 p.m. weekdays and between 8:30 a.m. and noon on Saturdays. The other two facilities keep the same hours, although Bancentro opens at 8 a.m. daily and Western Union is closed on Saturdays. BAC is located next to the main gate of Ave Maria College, and Bancentro is located on the northwest corner of the central park. Western Union is one block

Support VIVA! Reserve your hotels or hostels at vivatravelguides.com/hotels/

south of Bancentro and half a block down. Updated: May 04, 2009.

Things to See and Do
Iglesia de San Marcos Agradece
When you enter Iglesia de San Marcos Agradece, look up. Above the baby blue walls are colorful murals of religious symbols. San Marcos stands on an arch before the altar, amid waterfalls, volcanoes and fields of flowers. Several years ago, the church expanded, adding two warehouse-like wings with concrete arches which add little to the overall ambiance, but do create more space for parishioners. One front arch has been painted with the likeness of San Marcos, standing among flowers, waterfalls and volcanoes. Updated: May 02, 2009.

Oldest Houses in San Marcos
Follow the street from southwest corner of the park, two blocks down and you'll come across what are known as the oldest houses in San Marcos. Although not markedly different from their neighbors, with sunken foundations, tile roofs and unadorned façades, the residents claim that these buildings are roughly 200 years old. Built with a mixture of adobe, pottery and wood known as "taquezal," the homes were once filled with gilt lamps, thick drapes and plush rugs—all the trimmings of their aristocratic owners. From their homes, the owners would ride out to check on their coffee fincas or would sell water in great wooden barrels to city residents. In 1936, General José Maria Moncada, then President of Nicaragua, stopped by for a visit. Stop in at the tiny pulpería in the front of one of the houses and you can catch a glimpse of the original wood beam roof. From the southwest corner of the park, two blocks down. Updated: May 04, 2009.

Restaurants
El Portón
One of the most popular of San Marcos' small comedors is the tiny El Portón, just outside the main gate of the college. At El Portón, the daily specials include spaghetti primavera and baked chicken, and a full plate costs between $1.70 to $2.70. Don't feel like fighting the students for a bench? Head through the spotless kitchen to the handful of tables on the back patio. El Portón also serves a good selection of breakfast dishes (6 – 10 a.m.), such as pancakes, French toast and omelets. The restaurant is open 6 a.m. – 2 p.m. daily.

Half a block from the Ave Maria gate. Tel: 505-8-901-6073, E-mail: Omarhannon@yahoo.com. Updated: May 02, 2009.

Bar and Restaurant Sagitario
Bar and Restaurant Sagitario is one of the numerous student dives around San Marcos. The front area features a low, sloping roof and green walls. Walk through to the back and you'll find "Patio Sagitario," a bamboo-lined space lit strangely with mini-traffic lights and a tiny disco ball. Sagitario serves comida typica for between $2.65 and $6.00, but the real attraction is the live band on weekends from 6 to 10 p.m. Texaco one block north, ½ block down, San Marcos. Tel: 505-8-638-3850. Updated: May 04, 2009.

La Casona Coffee Shop
Gourmet coffee is the specialty at La Casona Coffee Shop and the java options include cappuccinos, frappuccinos, cafés with kalúa and café espresso with cognac. Behind swinging doors, the restaurant has an open and surprisingly Western-style space, complete with WiFi (customers can ask for the access code), flat screen TVs and walls decorated with iron lamps and musical instruments. For lunch, La Casona serves a wide range of sandwiches ($2.65 – $3.90), giant hamburgers ($2.90 – $4.60) and "chilly dogs." A small selection of salads, tacos, main dishes ($1.95 – $7.75) and anytime breakfast ($1.85 – $3.30), mean that La Casona can satisfy almost any craving. The restaurant is open from Monday to Saturday, 11 a.m. – 11 p.m. and Sunday, from 11 a.m. – 10 p.m. From Enitel, one block north. Tel: 505-2-533-2798, E-mail: fmlacasona@yahoo.com, URL: www.lacasonasasanmarcos.com. Updated: May 04, 2009.

DIRIAMBA

580 m   57,512

A wealthy city before the Nicaraguan revolution, the Diriamba of today still bears marks of the former prosperity. Basilica Menor de San Sebastian, the public clock, and streets are lined with the swirls of 19th century architecture (featured in both well-kept homes and the shells of decaying buildings).

Diriambians claim indigenous chief Diriangen as the city's ancient founder and honor him with a brightly painted (if slightly tacky) statue. Both the local stadium and baseball team are named after the famously courageous warrior, who long resisted Spanish conquest and, according to some accounts, also founded Diriá and Diriomo.

In the Chorotengana tongue, the city's name means "grandes cerros o colinas" (large hills or heights), although, despite the hype, you'll find few hills in the city.

Diriamba is known for hosting one of the most authentic fiestas patronales, with distinctly pre-Columbian overtones. San Sebastian, who is said to have once appeared on the Pacific Coast, is carried through the city streets every year during the celebrations between January 20 and 27. Amid fireworks and drinking, locals also perform traditional dances such as the Toro Huaco, el Gigante (based on David and Goliath), las Inditas and el Güegüense o Macho Ratón.

During the rest of the year, you can find statues of poor Saint Sebastian, stuck full of arrows like a pin cushion, in the marketplace rotunda, on top of the basilica and to the right of the church's altar. Take a moment to walk inside the Basilica Menor de San Sebastian. Among the stunning biblical murals on the ceiling, you'll find works by Rodrigo Peñalba, recently restored after decades of being hidden away (church officials weren't huge fans of the Nicaraguan painter's figurative style). Also worth noting are the elaborate wood carvings (check out the lectern) that date from the 1950s.

Diriamba still lags far behind the art-filled Pueblos Blancos, but you can find a solid, if small, collection of local artwork for sale at **Artesanías Ixchell** (Tel: 505-2-534-3023 / 505-2-532-1194 / 505-8-837-8383, E-mail: ixchellartesaniasnica@hotmail.com). The famous El Güegüese is well represented in everything from key chains to wall hangings and wooden statues.

Diriamba's family-friendly ecological museum is also worth a visit. **Museo Ecológico de Trópico Seco** (Tel: 505-2-534-2129, E-mail: museoeco@ideay.net.ni, URL: www.adea.org.ni/museo_eco) has informative plaques in Spanish, a small collection of butterflies, and glass cases full of stuffed critters. The museum was founded in 1996 to teach Nicaraguans about protecting the environment, such as conserving endangered sea turtles. Tours are only available for groups, but most of the exhibits (except for a few random science experiments) are fairly self-explanatory. A visit can make for an informative half hour. The museum is open Monday to Friday, 8 a.m. – noon, 2 – 5 p.m. and Saturday, 8 a.m. to noon. The entry fee is $0.75 for nationals, $1.00 for foreigners and $0.50 for children under 12.

Diagonally opposite from the museum is **Mi Bohio** (Tel: 505-2-534-2437, E-mail: mibohio@cablenet.com.ni). The restaurant portion of the enterprise (Mains: $3.40 – 5.80, open 11:30 a.m. to 9 p.m.) has an impressive local reputation, as much for an atmosphere of upscale dining as for the huge plates of meat, chicken or seafood. Waiters speak English and are prompt, although bamboo strips woven over the walls and ceilings can make you feel like you're eating inside a wicker basket. At the front of the restaurant, Mi Bohio sells local peanut butter and other goodies.

The owners of Mi Bohio recently expanded into the building next door. Hotel Mi Bohio, while still under construction in May 2009, was shaping up to be Diriamba's answer to luxury accommodations. The seven initial rooms (seven more are planned), will have WiFi, cable TV, phones and private bathroom. Also under construction were the hotel's gym and spa; wrought iron rails outside all featured an MB logo.

Across town, **Hotel La Viña** (Tel: 505-2-534-2162 / 505-8-478-6941, matrimonial $14.50, double $19.50, triple $22) is a decent alternative. The rooms are something along the lines of a Motel 6, but cleaner, even if the mirrored headboards, flowered bedspreads and tasseled curtains are a bit much.

Jardín y Vivera Tortuga Verde (Tel: 505-2-534-2948 / 505-8-905-0313, URL: www.eco-lodgecarazo.com), located just outside of the city, is Diriamba's best hidden secret. Owner Roberto Rappacccioli has cultivated a jungle of gardens, where small paths can lead you to a tropical flower the size of a cabbage, an iron statue hefting a spear, a stand of giant bamboo or goldfish swimming around inside a bathtub. The five rooms, tucked among the green, are just as full of unexpected surprises: vivid paintings, stained glass in the windows and twisting wood balconies. Rooms start at $25 for a single (there's space for up to 22 people), but Roberto Rappacccioli is always willing to negotiate prices. Ask him to tell you about his experience in Managua, where he

Support VIVA! Reserve your hotels or hostels at vivatravelguides.com/hotels/

started one of the city's first discothèques, La Tortuga Morada, in the late 1960s.

Cyber cafes are sprinkled throughout Diriamba. On average, access costs $0.75 per hour ($0.40 per half hour), which are slightly more expensive than surrounding towns, where an hour of computer time costs between $0.50 (Masaya) and $0.60 (Jinotepe). One of the easiest to find is **Café Internet Roma**, on the south side of the Diriamba basilica. The café has a large bank of computers and also offers national ($0.20 per minute) and international ($0.07 per minute to the US and Canada) calls. The café is open from 8 a.m. to 9:30 p.m. daily.

Diramba is not a major hub, like Jinotepe, but still offers transportation to major locations. Microbuses leave from the central park to Jinotepe from 6 a.m. to 6 p.m. every 10 minutes for $0.20. You can find buses to other major locations, including La Boquita/ Casares, Managua and Masaya, leaving from near the public clock (the clock is also where groups of mototaxis park). Buses depart both from the local gas station and from the municipal terminal across the street. Updated: Jun 23, 2009.

JINOTEPE

510 m　42,109

As comfortably worn as an old sneaker, Jinotepe hides a surprising number of services behind its dingy façade. Unabashedly dedicated to the day-to-day needs of the working man (or woman), the city packs all things utilitarian into a relatively small area. In the streets around Parque Los Chocoyitos, you'll find an open-air, everything market (selling clothes, pans, vegetables, balls of string and the like), a Palí supermarket, a small artisan market, the city's lone hotel, a handful of banks, Jinotepe's post office and a small library/museum.

Jinotepe (whose rather utilitarian indigenous name means "windy hill where people live") has a history of being knocked down and getting back up again, like a scrappy fighter. Jinotepe, once burned to the ground by pirate William Dampier and later destroyed during an attack by General Mateo Espinoza, managed to maintain much of the colonial character it had as a center for coffee production.

The most impressive city landmark is La Iglesia Parroquial de Santiago (1878) with high vaulted ceilings, massive wooden doors and beautiful stained glass windows, including one pane of broom-wielding priest with a dog at his feet. Outside is a giant statue of Pope John Paul II, erected in honor of his visit.

The city's former central train station has not fared as well as the church and has fallen into a form of working disuse.The buildings, which can be found beyond the canary yellow UNAN offices, still bear the marks of their former life. The train station sign for Jinotepe is still there, under the roofline, but most of the offices are abandoned. The local **INTUR** office (Tel: 505-8-920-4236, E-mail: Jinote1@turbonett.com.ni, URL: www.visitanicaragua.com) has started talking with the university about rehabilitating the old building, but it's unlikely that the buildings will be used for storage any time soon.

In honor of his visit 100 years before, the Jinotepe alcaldía erected a monument to Ruben Dario on Dec. 7, 2007. You can see the plaque in honor of Dario's brief 1907 disembarkation at the far end of the old train station. Look for a pedestal in aquamarine tile.

Jinotepe's largest, and arguably strangest, attraction is the Hertylandia amusement park, located on the edge of the city and reachable by taxi ($0.50). Behind white turrets, reminiscent of a medieval fortress, Hertylandia has both swimming pools and carnival rides. The entrance fee of $4.40 grants you access to the water park, but rides in the dry park (which is geared toward children) cost an additional $1 to 1.45. **Hertylandia** (Tel: 505-2-532-2156/ 3081/ 3082/ 3083) is open 8:30 a.m. – 5:30 p.m., Wednesday to Sunday.

As with the rest of Jinotepe, **Hotel Casa Mateo** (Tel: 505-2-532-3284, intl. 410-878-2252, E-mail: Casamateo2000@yahoo.com, URL: www.hotelcasamateo.com) is well-worn and practical, but not particularly beautiful. The hotel, a block-and-a-half west of BDF, was previously known as Hotel Casa Grande before new owners took over four years ago. As the only hotel of any size in town (aside from a few scattered love motels that charge by the hour), Casa Mateo is the best bet for accommodations in Jinotepe. The bathrooms are a bit dingy, with shower handles that appear still under construction. However, the hotel has pleasantly tiled walkways and WiFi in the lobby. Jardin de los Olivos is conveniently located in the front. There is also hot water, laundry service and air conditioning in seven of the 37 rooms, though sadly no water in the swimming-pool-sized fountain.

Across the street from the hotel is the city's municipal library and **Central Escuela Regional de Bellas Artes de Jinotepe** where you can see small student exhibits or take a class. Contact founder César Octavio Delgado (Tel: 505-8-416-8229, E-mail: cesaroctavio66@yahoo.es) for information.

Jinotepe makes up for the disappointing accommodations market with a solid selection of restaurants, all located just north of BDF. **Tele Café Xilotepelt** (Mains: $1.20 to $2.15, Tel: 505-2-532-1305, open 6 a.m. to 7 p.m. daily and until 9 p.m. on Sundays) has pretty flower-painted tables, a faux Mexican colonial theme and a breakfast/lunch menu that includes delicious corn pancakes or juicy hamburgers.

Long known as the place to go for Mexican, **Taco a Taco** (Mains: $2 to $2.90, Tel: 505-8-474-7540, E-mail: mariorstat@hotmail.com, open 5 to 10 p.m.) has been branching out into Middle Eastern food and now has shwarma as well. The hip little hangout is one of the few places that encourages customers to write on the walls and is extremely popular with the local college crowd.

The hole-in-the-wall **Quesos La Granja** (Tel: 505-8-603-2952, E-mail: Quesos.lagranja@gmail.com, open 7 a.m. to 6 p.m.) can hardly be called a store, but is still a great stop if you want to try a hunk of delicious local cheese. La Granja also offers a small selection of organic products from Finca Santa Clara in Chontales (E-mail: fincasantaclara@gmail.com) and bottles of honey or jam.

Pizzeria Colisseo, the creation of Italian owner Faustino Delpanno, is known locally as the posh place for a night out. The savory, thin crust creations are arguably the most authentic (and some say best) pizzas in Nicaragua, although you might find yourself digging through your wallet to try one. Mr. Delpanno is so dedicated to his craft that he has no delivery service (the theory being that pizza quality declines if the pies are not served within the first 20 minutes). You may have to hock your knapsack to pay for the evening, but Colisseo's pizzas are worth the sacrifice. The restaurant (Tel: 505-2-532-2150/ 505-2-532-2646; from Bancentro 1 block north) is closed Monday, but otherwise open noon – 2:30 p.m. and 6 – 10 p.m.

Around the corner from Colisseo (and half a block east of BDF) is another solid entry in the pizza category. **Pizza To Go** (Tel: 505-2-532-0754) has mechanical rides for kids, plastic tables and, as the name suggests, no qualms about sending their pies out of the building. While the restaurant is more Pizza Hut than piece of Italy, the Pizza To Go is more economical than Pizzeria Colisseo (though the prices increased recently if the neon menu stickers are anything to go by) with options that include slices ($0.80), medium ($3.40 – 4.40) and large ($5 – 6.80). The restaurant also has hot dogs, chicken wings and a salad bar. The Jinotepe location is one of two, with the other being in Diriamba, and is open 11 a.m. – 10 p.m. daily, except Tuesday.

Non-meat eaters get a welcome break from the usual struggle to find food they can eat at **Tien Lan Zu Shi**, an vegetarian restaurant located a block-and-a-half south of the UNAN turret (Tel: 505-2-532-0102; 505-8-914-5270). Updated: Jun 23, 2009.

Getting To and Away From Jinotepe

As a transportation hub, Jinotepe is easy to reach and to leave. Minibuses from Diriamba cost $0.20 and leave at short intervals during the day, usually whenever they're full. Once you're in Jinotepe, head to the central marketplace and follow the line of vendors across the Interamericana to the main terminal. Jinotepe has abundant taxis and minibuses to all local locations (minibuses leave most regularly to Managua's UCA: $1.30, 50 minutes, every 10 to 15 minutes from 5:30 a.m. – 10 p.m.; to Diriamba: $0.20, 7 minutes, every 15 to 20 minutes from 6 am – 7 pm; and to Masaya: $0.75, 50 minutes, every 15 minutes from 5 am to 6 pm). Large, slow buses known as "locales" leave the dusty terminal for destinations such as Managua ($1, 1 hour 20, every 15 to 20 minutes from 5 am – 9 pm), Granada ($0.80, 50 minutes, every 40 minutes from 6:30 am – 4:30 pm), Masaya ($0.75, 1 hour 20, every 10 minutes from 5 am to 6 pm), and Diriamba/Nandime ($0.20 / $0.50, 35 minutes, every 25 minutes from 5 am – 6 pm). Updated: Sep 30, 2009.

LA MÁQUINA

You may notice a road sign for Centro Ecoturistico La Máquina (also spelled La Mákina) as you're barreling down the new highway between La Boquita/Casares and Diriamba. The main draw of the private reserve is access to the tiny Río La Trinidad with its series of lovely little waterfalls. Above the water tiers of balconies, mini-rancheros provide plenty of shady spots for picnickers. **La Máquina** (Tel: 505-8-901-1989, $1.45, open from 8 a.m. to 5 p.m.) is designed on levels so that you can take a dip in the deep green pool of water created by small dam, hop in one of the waterfall pools or make your way down slippery stone stairs to the shallow stream below the cascades.

There are a few short trails scattered around the 154-hectare reserve and, as of spring 2009, workers were clearing out strips of dry tropical forest to provide more space for wandering. The river bank provides a nice place for an easy hike; plenty of tadpoles, dragonflies and schools of fish make the Rio La Trinidad their home.

La Máquina has two eateries (a small grill beside the river and a large patio at the top of the embankment) although the riverside half only opens on weekends and holidays. The patio restaurant is open 11 a.m. – 5 p.m. and serves consumes, seafood and meat dishes for between $2.90 and $12.

The private reserve charges $5 per night for camping (including breakfast), though make sure to call two days ahead of time to let them know you're coming.

Buses pass every 50 minutes between 6 a.m. and 5:40 p.m. on their way between Diriamba and La Boquita/Casares. Updated: Jun 04, 2009.

LA BOQUITA

A 13 m

Centro Turistico La Boquita, a lovely beachside complex, features rows of thatched restaurants, a kiddie park and a few hotels. Like many government-run projects, La Boquita suffers from a depressing lack of custom during weekdays (if you're on foot and no one is around, the guard might even waive the $0.20 entry fee). That said, a visit during the week is perfect if you want the beach to yourself but not if you're interested in any sort of nightlife. La Boquita picks up on weekends, with families who come to escape the city heat and gets most lively during holidays such as Semana Santa and Christmas. The beach is also has a growing reputation as a solid spot for surfing. At the 13 La Boquita restaurants, you can eat with your feet in the sand and watch pelicans skim the muddy colored waves. Among the best is **Bar y Rest. Los Jicaritos** (Tel: 505-8-618-0209); ask Susy to serve you his specialty of camarón del río a la plancha, a truly enormous platter of grilled river shrimp. Daytrippers please note, the last bus leaves for Diriamba at 6 p.m., but you should leave earlier if you plan to continue on to another city. Updated: May 04, 2009.

Lodging

Hospedaje El Pelicano

(ROOMS: $10 – 15.50) El Pelicano, the cheapest hospedaje on the beach, is one of two places where the locals will regularly direct tourists, although apparently for lack of competition more than anything else. For $10 (or $15 during Semana Santa), you get a large, grimy room where the only piece of furniture is a dingy bed. The ceilings are in the midstages of collapse, the ocean-view porches have dirty dishes on them and the manager might ask you if you want the 24-hour rate. All seven rooms share two bathrooms where the light is better left off. Not even a position right on the beach is enough to redeem the Pelican, save yourself a night of tossing and pay a little more for one of the other area hotels. El Pelicano has no telephone or e-mail address. Centro Turistico La Boquita. Updated: May 04, 2009.

Olas Escondidas

(ROOMS: $10 – 80) Steven Brodie once dreamed of owning a surfer-friendly hotel in Costa Rica, until he discovered the empty beaches and cheap land in Nicaragua. Brodie's new venture, Olas Escondidas, can be found on a rise above the La Boquita complex. More guesthouse than hotel, Olas is clean and spacious; the large kitchen leads to a terrace with sweeping Pacific views. There is only one room for rent, which can accommodate four and has a very reasonable rate of $10 per person, if you're using fans. For air conditioning, the rate jumps to $80 per night, a price that doesn't vary whether there are four guests or one. For those that book ahead of time, Brodie offers a selection of packages including airport pickup

($50 each way), boat rentals ($200 per day) and meals. Centro Turistico La Boquita. Tel: 505-8-603-0571, E-mail: olasescondidas@yahoo.com, URL: www.olasescondidas.com. Updated: May 04, 2009.

Villas del Mar

(ROOMS: $40 and up) If you go to La Boquita/Casares during a high holiday and find that every other hotel is fully booked, you might turn to Villas del Mar. The hotel, built in Motel 6 style and painted bright yellow, appears clean, but is in a terrible location right between Casares and La Boquita, but near neither one, on a high bluff with no access to (and few views of) the ocean. The hotel also has a truly bizarre policy of completely shutting down when the owner is away. If you're unfortunate enough to miss her, you won't be allowed to stay or even see a room. Still, for a night or two, Villas del Mar is not a bad option and buses pass on the way to either Casares or La Boquita about every half hour. Take a right at the La Boquita/Casares roundabout, Villas del Mar is on the right about a half a mile down. Tel: 505-2-665-2850. Updated: May 04, 2009.

Hotel Bar y Restaurante Suleyka

(ROOMS: $15.50 – 100) You might find a huge bucket of water in your shower at Suleyka, as the tank-run system doesn't always work when guests arrive and the staff turns it on. Although not a standout in the hotel department, Suleyka has the greatest range of room options in Las Boquitas, with spaces that can accommodate up to a dozen people. The rooms are musty and bare but serviceable. Ask to stay on the second floor where the rooms are newer and the shared porch has a sweeping view of the ocean. Beyond the thatched restaurants, the Suleyka-run disco is located adjacent to the rooms, but what is a thumping space on holidays is mostly quiet during weekdays.Single $14.50 with fan, $24.20 with air conditioning; double $21.80 with fan, $29 with air conditioning; multiple dorm for 12, $100. Centro Turistico La Boquita, beside La Bocana. Tel: 505-8-698-3355/ 505-8-692-2777/ 505-8-904-4502. Updated: May 04, 2009.

CASARES

A 13 m

Casares is a traditional fishing village where the pace of life moves to the rhythm of the sea. The shore is lined with colorful pangas named Escarlet, Nancy Maria or Tu Loquita while locals push carts filled with ice and fish or boat motors along the streets. Diramba vendors know Casares as the place to go for the freshest seafood for their stalls.

The newly paved highway between Casares and Diramba (completed in late 2008) has started to bring some changes to what was once a relatively isolated village; however, one obvious indication is a mammoth white mansion in mid-construction along the shore. At the moment though, Casares still has the best of both worlds: the tranquility of a fishing village but the luxurious accommodation of hotels such as **Hotel Lupita** and **Hotel El Casino**. While still heavily focused on fresh seafood, the dining options in Casares have also started to expand. Try one of the upscale hotels for fine dining, a local restaurant for Nicaraguan-style fish and, for fritanga, one of the informal grills at the top of the hill where the highway meets the village.

One of the best places to rest your head or grab a meal is **Hotel and Restaurant Antiguo Casino** (also known as **Hotel El Casino and Restaurant Marcelo**; Tel: 505-8-551-6589). The hotel is a beautifully modern reconstruction of a former Casares establishment which had been destroyed in a devastating 1993 tidal wave. Rather than revert to the thatched, ranchero style, the new owners have created a space with star-spangled vaulted ceilings, stone sculptures and overstuffed leather furniture. They have been so successful at creating a feeling of comfortable, upscale living that you might start wondering if you've wandered into a private beach home by mistake.

The rooms are just as swank; on the ocean side, the gauzy curtains and colorful paintings evoke more Italian villa than a Nicaraguan fishing village. All eight rooms (single and matrimonial, $30; double $35; third bed, $10; breakfast and IVA not included.) have private bathrooms and fans; only one has a TV. Ask for one of the six rooms with beach-view balconies.

Hotel Lupita (Tel: 505-8-856-8207 / 505-8-847-1805; E-mail: hotellupita@yahoo.com), is a short walk from town, has decorations that tend toward more seashells and fishing nets than sculptures and fine art. It has two unbeatable lures: a swimming pool on the top of a cliff and another built into the base. Concrete stairs, leading from one to the other, also provide access to a trip of wave-washed rock and beaches at either end.

The rooms at Hotel Lupita (up to four people, including tax, $50; Semana Santa, $60) are arranged along several levels and connected to the main building by wide stairs (this is not the place for handicapped visitors).

The rooms are clean and spare, with TVs and private bathrooms. You might find that services such as a pool side bar and grill close down completely during the off seasons, although the restaurant is open from 6 to 10 p.m. daily. Credit cards are accepted but include a five percent fee.

Hotel Lupita is relatively isolated at the moment, but locals have plans to develop the neighboring land, where the lingering ruins of houses (also destroyed in 1993) have been removed in anticipation of new construction. Updated: Jun 19, 2009.

GRANADA AND AROUND

Map showing Rio Tipitapa, Lake Nicaragua (Cocicolba), To Masaya and Managua, Apoyo Lagoon, Granada, Las Isletas, Reserva Natural Volcan Mombacho, Isla Zapatera, Parque Nacional Archipielago Zapatera.

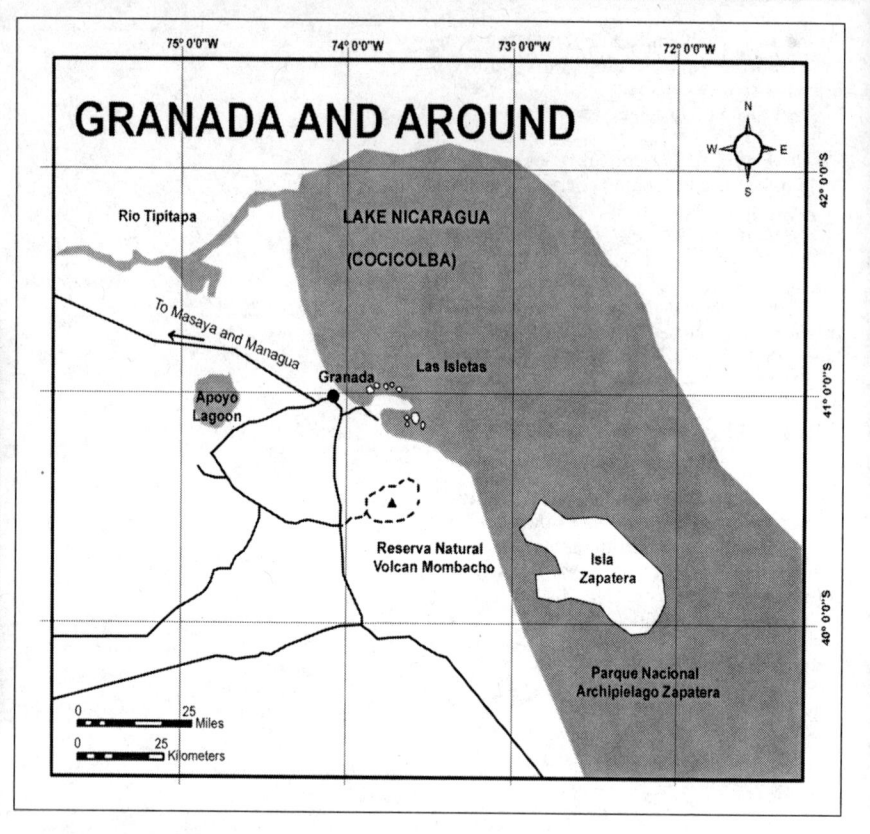

Granada and Around

Granada is Nicaragua's most popular tourist destination, and the area offers everything a traveler could want. Seeking beautiful architecture? Granada is said to be the oldest colonial city in the Americas, with an unmatched architectural heritage. Craving volcanoes? Hike up Volcan Masaya for a chance to stare into the bubbling lava that once swallowed human sacrifices. Searching for tranquil waters? Las Isletas provides cool and clean swimming opportunities, and if you head a bit further out, the crystal clear waters of Laguna de Apoyo are sure to beckon.

With so much to see and do around Granada, it's no wonder that many travelers get stuck here. Whether it's volunteering, studying Spanish or simply traveling for the fun of it, the city has a way of keeping you around. Granada has great restaurants and some of the nicest hotels and best-equipped hostels in Nicaragua. With the country being as small as it is, it's easy to use the city as a base to explore the surrounding region. Pueblos Blancas, Mombacho, and Masaya are all easy day trips from the city.

Granada is the highlight of a trip to Nicaragua. No matter your time frame or budget, you should try to spend at least a few days here. Updated: Jun 25, 2008.

History

Granada was founded in 1524 by the conquistador Francisco Hernández de Córdoba, making it the oldest colonial city in the Americas. The city was marked by conflict from the start, as the Spanish fought among themselves for control of the region's gold. Córdoba himself was ultimately beheaded by his rival Pedrarias Dávila.

Once these internal struggles had died down with the establishment of the Viceroyalty of

Enter VIVA Photo Contests: vivatravelguides.com/photography-contests/

New Spain, Granada began to grow rich as a trading center, thus becoming a tempting target for pirates, who sacked the city repeatedly during the 17th and 18th centuries.

After Nicaragua's independence in 1821, politically conservative Granada began feuding with liberal Leon for control of the country. Leon contracted an American adventurer named William Walker to help them in this struggle. The filibuster conquered Granada, but rather than turning control over to the leonese, Walker promptly declared himself president of the country. A true believer in manifest destiny, Walker reintroduced slavery and publicly announced his intention to conquer all of Latin America. Naturally, this kind of rhetoric did not endear him to the neighboring Costa Ricans, who sent him packing with an invasion the following year. Ever spiteful, Walker had the historic city torched before he left, destroying much of the beautiful architecture. He left behind a now infamous placard saying "Here was Granada." The troublesome Mr. Walker finally met his end at the hands of a Honduran firing squad after attempting to invade that country as well.

After this episode, the city of Granada devoted itself to rebuilding its heritage and largely abstaining from the violent civil wars that followed in the 20th century. Today the city is proud of its colonial legacy and architecture. The leonese have been forgiven, though the name of William Walker still provokes anger. Updated: Jun 23, 2008.

Things to See and Do

With so many things to see and do in the region that appeal to a variety of interests and budgets, the only challenge in Granada will be deciding what to do.

For the physically active there are hiking tours to Vocán Mombacho, kayaking tours around Las Isletas or visits to Laguna de Apoyo (activities at the lake range from swimming to paragliding).

There are also ample opportunities for nature lovers to see many different species of wildlife and animals that are unique to Nicaragua. Archaeology buffs can visit the statuary and petroglyph sites on the islands of Zapatera and Ometepe (which will also appeal to the amateur geologist).

Many tour companies located in and around Granada's Parque Central can arrange the transportation and accommodations for day or overnight trips to these regions, and most offer English-speaking guides. Be sure to check for student and group discounts. Updated: Jan 27, 2009.

GRANADA

A 46 m 116,000 552

Standing in the main plaza at the center of town, it's easy to imagine that Granada was once the jewel in Spain's New World crown. Everything from the immense stone Cathedral to the gorgeous colonial homes to the very name of this Central American city have been influenced with Spanish (and indirectly, Moorish) touches.

Founded in 1524, Granada dominates the strip of land between enormous Lake Nicaragua and the Pacific Ocean. The city is a hub for travelers taking day trips in the area or for those who just want to relax in this peaceful town loaded with international restaurants and inexpensive lodging. Most attractions are within a six-block radius of the Parque Central. Lago de Nicaragua is a 15-minute walk from the center of town. Just a few blocks south of the main pier on Lago de Nicaragua is a lovely stretch of restaurants, bars and picnic spots along the lakeshore.

Despite the city's birth nearly 500 years ago, most of the original buildings are no longer around. A fire in 1856 destroyed most of the city, and earthquakes, volcanoes and a 13-year civil war did the rest of the damage. Parts of the Cathedral are original, as well a handful of family homes and the gorgeous blue and white San Francisco Convent (Iglesia y Convento San Francisco). While not nearly the size of the main Cathedral, the San Francisco Convent is one of the most striking sites in Granada. The traditional brightly colored façade favored by the colonists opens into an enormous welcoming area, from which there is a nearly perfect view of the city. Tiled rooftops give way to swaying palm trees and finally to the distant volcanoes. Situated on top of the hill, it is said that in less stable times it was used as a fortress, having the distinct advantage of being able to see foes coming from either direction. Just outside you can hear the city continuing on its languid pace—old men rocking listlessly on verandas around the plaza while children play hopscotch.

Don't leave home without travel insurance: vivatravelguides.com/insurance/

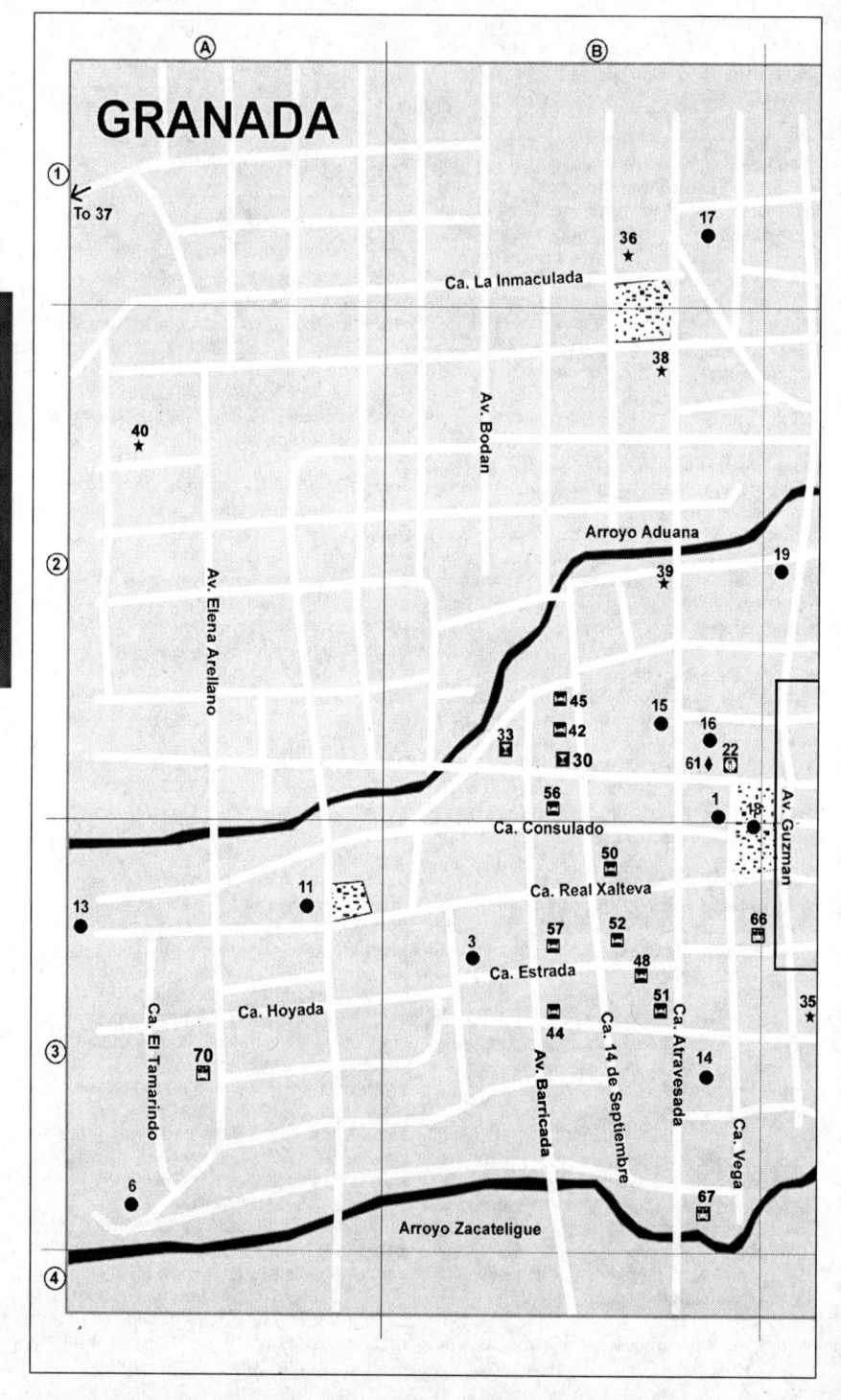

GRANADA

To 37

Ca. La Inmaculada

Av. Bodan

Av. Elena Arellano

Arroyo Aduana

Ca. Consulado

Ca. Real Xalteva

Ca. Estrada

Ca. Hoyada

Ca. El Tamarindo

Av. Barricada

Ca. 14 de Septiembre

Ca. Atravesada

Ca. Vega

Av. Guzman

Arroyo Zacateligue

Granada 127

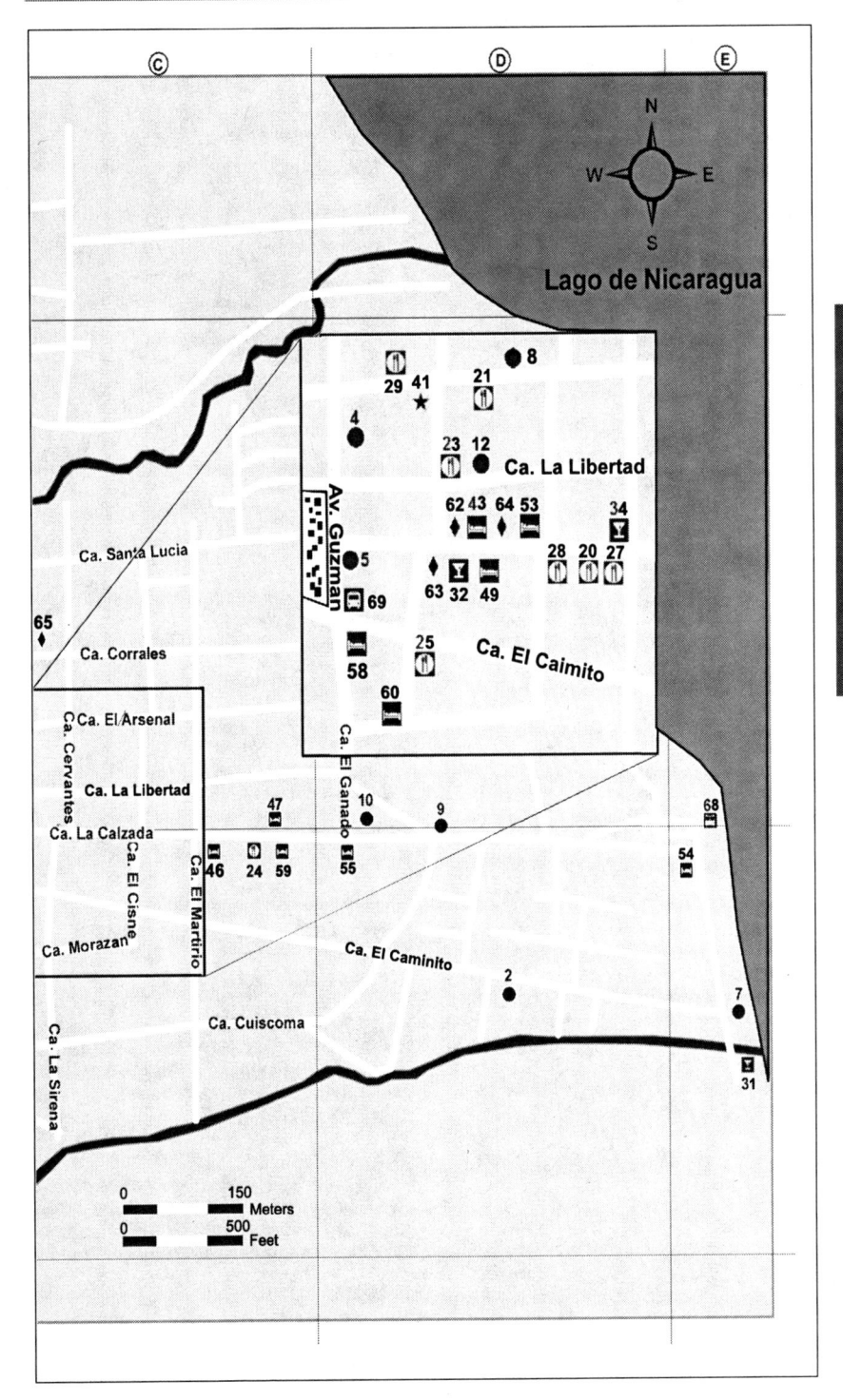

Lago de Nicaragua

Ca. Santa Lucia
Av. Guzman
Ca. La Libertad
Ca. Corrales
Ca. El Arsenal
Ca. Cervantes
Ca. La Libertad
Ca. La Calzada
Ca. El Cisne
Ca. Morazan
Ca. El Martirio
Ca. El Ganado
Ca. El Caimito
Ca. El Caminito
Ca. Cuiscoma
Ca. La Sirena

0 150 Meters
0 500 Feet

Don't leave home without travel insurance: vivatravelguides.com/insurance/

Activities

1 APC Spanish School B2
2 Carita Feliz D3
3 Casa Maria Sol Romero B3
4 Casa Tres Mundos (See inset map)
5 Cathedral (See inset map)
6 Cemetery A3
7 Centro Turistico E3
8 Convento San Francisco (See inset map)
9 Granada Spanish Lingua D2
10 Iglesia Guadalupe D2
11 Iglesia Xalteva A3
12 La Esperanza (See inset map)
13 La Pólvora Fort A3
14 Mercado Central B3
15 Mi Museo B2
16 Nicaragua Mia B2
17 Old Train Station B1
18 Plaza de la Independencia B3
19 Spanish School Xpress C2

Eating

20 Centralito C3 (See inset map)
21 El Tercer Ojo C3 (See inset map)
22 Euro Café B2
23 Garden Café C3
24 Hospedaje Ruiz C3
25 Jardin de Orion C3
26 Jimmy Alabama (See 56)
27 Pizza Don Luca C3 (See inset map)
28 Roadhouse Grill C3 (See inset map)
29 Tele Pizza C2 (See inset map)

Nightlife

30 Café Nuit B2
31 El Kayac E3
32 Tequila Vallarta C3 (See inset map)
33 The Club B2
34 Zoom Bar C3 (See inset map)

Services

35 Cairo Cybercafé C3

36 Centro de Salud B1
37 Cocibolca Hospital A1
38 Clínica Piedra Boconas B2
39 Dr Iglesias B2
40 Japan Amistad Hospital A2
41 Intur (See inset map)

Sleeping

42 Bearded Monkey B2
43 Casa San Martin (See inset map)
44 Casa Silas B3
45 Kalala Lodge B2
46 Hospedaje Cocibolca C3
47 Hospedaje La Calzada C2
48 Hostal Amigo B3
49 Hostal Central (See inset map)
50 Hostal Dorado B3
51 Hostal El Tiangue B3
52 Hostal Oasis B3
53 Hotel Dario C3
54 Hotel El Maltese E3
55 Hotel Granada D3
56 Hotel Nuestra Casa B2
57 Hotel Terrasol B3
58 La Gran Francia (See inset map)
59 Posada las Brisas C3
60 Posada San Jose (See inset map)

Tours

61 Amigo Tours B2
62 Cast C3
63 Leo Tours C3
64 Nicaragua Adventures C3
65 Oro Travel C2

Transportation

66 Buses to Managua B3
67 Buses to Rivas B3
68 Ferry Terminal E2
69 Paxeos C3
70 Transnica A3

However, not all the charm of Granada is in its history. There is a burgeoning artist community that is gaining international attention, and the city's proximity to both the lake and the ocean (not to mention jungles and volcanoes) has also been drawing outdoor enthusiasts and tourism. But above all else, it is the people of Granada that really showcase its charm. Updated: Nov 23, 2006.

Getting To and Away From Granada

BY BUS

Several stations around the city offer bus service to Managua, the most convenient of which is located half a block south of Parque Central on Calle Vega. The trip should cost $0.20 and take about an hour. This same bus can drop you off on the outskirts of Masaya for just half the price. Departures are every half hour between 4:20 a.m. and 6 p.m.

Buses to Rivas, a transport hub that serves San Juan del Sur, leave from a station 3½ blocks south and one block west. There are frequent departures between 5:45 a.m. and 3:10 p.m.

BY SHUTTLE

A company called **Paxeos** offers private shuttle buses to destinations around Nicaragua. Prices are steep; see their listing in the Tours section (p.135) for more details.

BY TRAIN

TransNica has a station on Calle Tamarindo with departures to San Jose (Costa Rica) at 6 a.m., 8 a.m. and 11 a.m.

Enter VIVA Photo Contests: vivatravelguides.com/photography-contests/

Granada

Highlights

Those with limited time in Granada should definitely explore the **historic center** of the city. **La Catedral (p.131), Parque Central (p.133),** the **Convento de San Francisco (p.131),** and the **Xalteva (p.131)**and **La Merced (p.132)** churches can easily be visited in a half-day, with a trip around to **Fortaleza la Pólvora** (p.132)and the cemetery if you have time.

For a bit of fresh air, head out on a three-hour excursion to **Las Isletas (p.143)**, a group of over 350 little islands scattered within the Lago de Nicaragua, formed by the last eruption of Volcán Mombacho, over 10,000 years ago. The islands are rich in birdlife and some have a few restaurants.

And for nature lovers, **Reserva Natural Volcán Mombacho (p.143)** is an excellent area to explore. There are excellent hiking paths that wind through a cloud forest within the volcano's national park. Other activities available in the park include canopy tours on the eastern slope of Mombacho, crater diving, and visits to the butterfly reserve.

All of these sites are well worth worth seeing, depending on personal interests. Updated: Jun 25, 2008.

BY BOAT

Granada is also served by a ferry that departs every Monday and Thursday at 2 p.m. It's a three-and-a-half hour trip to Isla Ometepe, or a 14-hour trip to San Carlos on the far side of the lake, near the Costa Rican border. Tickets should be bought in advance from the ferry office at the end of Calle la Calzada. Updated: Jun 23, 2008.

Getting Around

Taxis in Granada are relatively inexpensive, but they go by the Nicaraguan custom of charging per person. Expect to pay $0.48 – 0.96 each to get across town.

If you're looking for a more romantic form of transport, horse-drawn carriages can be hired on the west side of Parque Central. Touts will often quote a ludicrous first price in the range of $10 – $15; just start walking away and wait for the price to plummet. This VIVA correspondent ended up paying only $2.42 for a one-way, fifteen-minute ride. Updated: Jun 23, 2008.

Safety

Generally speaking, Granada is a pretty safe town, provided you stick to the tourist areas. The city's historic center is well-enough policed at night. Leave this island of security; however, and things get more dangerous rather quickly. It's definitely not wise to wander around the lakeside area at night. You'd also be wise to take a taxi back from Parque Sandino or the Forteleza la Pólrora if it's getting dark. Updated: Jun 16, 2008.

Services

TOURISM OFFICE

Granada has an INTUR office (open 8 a.m. to 1 p.m.) to provide you with all the pamphlets you desire. It's located on Calle el Arsenal, one block east of Plaza de la Independencia.

MONEY

As expected for a city of this size and touristic importance, Granada has several banks and ATMs. **Banco America Central (BAC)** is on the corner of Calle Altravesada and La Libertad and has a 24-hour ATM that gives both U.S. dollars and Nicaragua córdobas. Another bank called **BanPro** is on Calle Atravesada. There's an ATM at the Esso Gas Station, located along the main highway at the entrance into town. Inside the city itself, you can head to the ATM inside the Lacayo Supermarket on Calle Real Xalteva.

There are also money changers on the street, called *coyotes*, that exchange U.S. dollars and córdobas. You'll find them near banks, plazas and markets. Most are honest and use the same exchange rate as banks, but be cautious and calculate the conversion before you make the exchange to ensure you're getting a fair rate.

KEEPING IN TOUCH

Nearly all of the city's hostels and hotels provide free WiFi. Additionally, there are many Internet cafés in Granada, especially around the Parque Central, that charge $0.50 – $1 an hour. Some cafés have booths and headsets where you can use the Internet to make phone calls. There are also several Internet cafés in the downtown area, including one on Calle Estrada across from Hostal Oasis and another on Calle la Calzada three blocks down from Parque Central.

Don't leave home without travel insurance: vivatravelguides.com/insurance/

You can make phone calls at a pulperia; look for the word *llamadas* outside the store where you can use a payphone. Cell phones are very cheap to purchase, starting at $15 with pay-as-you-go options. The two main cell phone companies are Enitel (look for the Claro signs) and Movistar.

The post office is on Calle el Arsenal, two blocks east of Plaza de la Independencia. Updated: Jun 23, 2008.

MEDICAL

There are three English-speaking doctors in Granada: **Dr. Martinez-Blanco**, a GP at the Piedra Boconas Clinic (on Parque Sandino across from the Taxi Cooperative), and **Dr. Iglesias**, whose office is at 10a Calle Atravesada (one and a half blocks north of Karawala Cinema). Dr. Iglesias is more of an internal medicine specialist, but both doctors are good for emergencies of the walk-in kind. A consultation will cost around $7–15. There is also an English speaking doctor at Medilab - a few doors up from Dr. Iglesias at 10b Calle Atravesada.

There is also the public **Japan-Amistad Hospital**, which offers free and prompt emergency services to both nationals and foreigners, but don't be alarmed if a family of cats or dogs walk by in the examination rooms.

You will need a doctor's referral for **Colcibolca Private Hospital**. While all medical services are free, you are expected to pay for your supplies at the pharmacy. On the positive side, you don't need a formal prescription for medicine and many pharmacists are doctors themselves.

There is also the **Centro de Salud** (health center) where consultations and medicine is free, but the medication is donated, so be sure to check the expiration dates. Updated: Jan 23, 2009.

LAUNDRY

There's a speedy and cheap laundromat called Mapache Laundry located two streets east of Parque Central, half a block up from Calle la Calzada.

SHOPPING

Most travelers who have serious shopping to do head to Masaya. The city's just a half-hour away by bus and is home to the best markets in Nicaragua. If you're hoping to buy souvenirs in Granada, you can expect a hefty markup over the Masaya prices. Vendors gather daily in Parque Central to sell hammocks, ceramics, etc. If you're looking for jewelry, an Argentinine-run shop on Calle la Calzada sells beautifully made and reasonably priced earrings, necklaces and rings. It's located inside Hostal Central, two blocks down from Parque Central.

The municipal market is located two blocks south of Parque Central. Its stalls sell the usual shoes, cheap clothes and household knick-knacks. Updated: Jan 23, 2009.

Things to See and Do

Nearly all of Granada's attractions are located within a small area near Parque Central; at a brisk pace you could cover them all in one day. If you're pressed for time, visit the Cathedral and watch the sunset atop Iglesia la Merced. Granada is a very pleasant city to stroll, and covering the attractions on foot is a great way to enjoy the historic center.

Granada has several tour operators clustered around Parque Central. The trips they offer are generally quite uniform—volcano tours, city tours, trips to Las Isletas—but their prices are not, so be sure to shop around. Some sell airline tickets and offer car rentals, but these services can be tough to find. Try and avoid paying for trips in advance if you can— many operators in Granada (as well as elsewhere) stop caring about you once they've got your money. Updated: Jan 27, 2009.

Nicaragua Butterfly Reserve

Located just four kilometers (2.48 miles) outside of Granada, the Nicaragua Butterfly Reserve is a convenient day trip for travelers itching to get out of the city and back into nature. The 40,000 cubic-foot reserve used to be a farm, but was purchased by a North American couple who then cultivated the land and planted a variety of plants to attract (and feed) the butterflies. The population has since expanded to over 200 butterflies from 20 different species. Visitors can tour the flight house, learn about the various species and, if inclined, even purchase butterfly pupae (contact reserve for species, prices and permit requirements).

The Nicaragua Butterfly Reserve also has five kilometers (3 mi) of nature trails and offers both guided and self-guided walking tours. Birdwatchers will be able to spot motmots (the national bird), parakeets and the golden oriole, among others. Finally, you can take the tour a step further by staying overnight in one of the reserve's rustic cabins (prices vary; contact the reserve for details). Open 8 a.m. – 4 p.m. Closed Sundays. Right before you hit the cemetary in Granada, take a right and follow the dirt path. Tel: 505-2-895-3012 (English) / 863-2943 (Spanish), URL: www.backyardnature.net. Updated: Sep 09, 2009.

Convento y Iglesia de San Francisco

(ADMISSION: $2) This fascinating place keeps even the non-museum person interested and is certainly worth an hour's visit. The complex dates back to the 16th century and is a pleasant place planted with tall palms in the central courtyard. The rooms offer rudimentary displays about the indigenous traditions (some lack explanations, though) and temporary art exhibits, as well as a collection of photos of the city between 1890 and 1940, which accompany a diorama and maps charting the growth of Granada. The most impressive part of San Francisco is the row of 30-meter (98 ft) high carved figures that were found on nearby Isla Zapatera. Open Monday – Friday, 8 a.m. – 4 p.m., Saturday and Sunday, 9 a.m. – 4 p.m. Calle el Arsenal, one block from Plaza Independencia. Updated: Jan 29, 2009.

Kayaking Las Isletas

Kayaking around Las Islaetas is a truly fantastic experience for adventure travelers. Las Isletas is an archipiélago of 365 tree-covered islands, some inhabited and some natural, all in close proximity to the shores of Lake Nicaragua. A good kayak tour takes you first to El Castillo, an old fort with good views of the islands, then through the narrow channels to a forested area where in the late afternoon you can spot some nice wildlife before heading back for a sunset drink on the shore. You can also tour by motorboat and cover a greater area of islands, but active travelers should opt for the kayak experience. For tour operators, take a cab to Centro Turistico (p.132). Tel: 505-2-608-3646 / 614-0813. Updated: Nov 22, 2006.

Pueblos Blancos

Although probably not the highlight of a trip to Granada, Pueblos Blancos (white houses) can be a nice side trip for a few hours. The bus takes around one hour to reach Catarina, where it is difficult to spot the famed white houses, but it is interesting to see this childhood home of revolutionary hero Augusto C. Sandino. Continue on from there and you will find the mirador, a lookout point with a great view over the expansive crater of Lake Apoyo, across to Volcan Mombacho and out to Granada in the distance. The surrounding area also sells pottery and crafts. To get here, take a local bus to Catarina for $1. Updated: Jan 21, 2009.

Iglesia de Guadalupe

The crumbling façade on this ancient building gives way to a beautifully maintained interior. Decked out in Granada's traditional yellow and white with Corinthian columns, the church features an exquisite stained-glass portrait of the Virgin of Guadalupe behind the altar. One of Granada's most beautiful buildings, Iglesia de Guadalupe is definitely worth a visit. Calle la Calzada, four blocks east of Parque Central. Updated: Jun 15 ,2008.

La Catedral

This magnificent Neoclassical cathedral is the jewel in the crown of Granada's architectural beauty. Unfortunately, like most of Granada's great buildings, it had to be rebuilt after William Walker torched the city in 1856, but this does not diminish the magic of the site. The well-kept interior and beautiful stained-glass windows should not be missed, and the building's bright yellow façade is absolutely glorious when viewed at sunset. Try to be respectful and quiet when visiting—it is still used as a place of worship. Parque Central. Updated: Jan 29, 2009.

Antigua Estación de Ferrocaril

Granada's historic train station has now been restored and converted into a carpentry and metal-working school. Although this station is not a major tourist draw, as trains no longer operate here, it is housed in an attractive Neoclassical late 19th-century building. Although interesting in its own way, this place is not an essential part of the Granada itinerary unless you are particularly keen on seeing old trains (there is a restored antique specimen parked out front) or old stations. Calle Atrevesada, seven blocks north of Parque Central across from Parque Sandino. Updated: Jan 20, 2009.

Iglesia Xalteva

This elegant old church follows the usual Granada pattern: a decaying original exterior with a gleaming renovated interior. The frescoes and beautifully carved altar are worth checking out, and the visit goes well with a trip to Iglesia la Merced and the forteleza. The church, along with the adjoining park, are both named after the indigenous tribe that originally inhabited the area. Calle la Xalteva, five blocks west of Parque Central. Updated: Jun 17, 2008.

Iglesia la Merced
Described by some as the most beautiful church in Granada, Iglesia la Merced is best visited at sunset. For just $1 you can ascend to the top of the belltower and watch the sun go down over Granada's spectacular beauty. The view of this magnificent city at sunset is truly unforgettable. Calle Real Xalteva, two blocks west of Parque Central. Updated: Jun 17, 2008.

Mercado Central
Granada's main market is located on Calle Vega two blocks south of Parque Central. Although the building itself is quite attractive, the interior is mainly a collection of ramshackle stalls selling clothes, shoes and other knick-knacks. You're better off viewing the market from a distance, such as from the tower of Iglesia la Merced. Located just to the southwest of the market, Supermercado Pali is a good place to stock up on groceries. Updated: Jun 19, 2008.

Mi Museo
(ENTRANCE: FREE) Mi Museo is a small museum containing an interesting collection of pre-Columbian ceramic artefacts. Some of the paintings and patterns are quite intriguing, and if you are interested in ceramics then this is definitely the place for you. The exhibits can easily be seen in under an hour, so it's worth a visit unless you find yourself really pressed for time. Open 8 a.m. – 5 p.m. Calle Atravesada 505, in front of Bancentro. Tel: 505-2-552-7614, E-mail: mimuseo@hotmail.com, URL: www.granadacollection.org. Updated: Jan 19, 2009.

La Capilla María Romero Meneses
This tiny chapel honors the Granada-born nun María Romero Meneses who dedicated her life to helping the poor of Costa Rica. For her work, she was beatified in April 2002. The chapel is nothing special—small and newly constructed—but those who are interested in spirituality or catholicism might find the visit interesting since it's a good place to learn about the saint herself. The chapel is open for prayer 8 a.m. – 12 p.m. and 2 p.m. – 5 p.m. The house where Meneses was born, also located in Granada, has been turned into a museum and has more information (in Spanish) on her life and work (p.133). Calle Estrada, one block east and one block south of Iglesia Xalteva. Updated: Jan 27, 2009.

Centro Turistico
A long park that stretches along the lakeside, Centro Turistico features swings, picnic areas and shady paths. That park also has some nice beaches, but locals say the water is too dirty for swimming. The park is a nice place to hang out, particularly if you're traveling with youngsters. However, make sure you clear out before nightfall, as it tends to get more dangerous after dark. Updated: Jun 23, 2008.

Casa de los Tres Mundos
Housed in a beautiful early 19th-century colonial building, this international cultural center is often known by its former name, the Casa de los Leones. It aims to promote the culture of Nicaragua and hosts a variety of exhibitions and events. It's worth checking out if you're interested in seeing some local art or listening to some local music. The center is open daily 7 a.m. – 6 p.m. Visit the website for a list of up coming events. Plaza de la Independencia. Tel: 505-2-552-4176, URL: www.c3mundos.org. Updated: Jan 19, 2009.

Cemetery
This cemetery holds the remains of Granada's rich and powerful; six presidents are among those interred here. Students of Nicaraguan history will also recognize the recurring names of Chamorro and Sandino among the large, stately tombs. The eerie mausoleums of this necropolis provide interesting insight into Granadan culture and spirituality.

The complex is dominated by the Capilla de Animas, a one-third replica of a church in France. Walk about 100 meters (328 ft) behind the chapel and you'll see a large, marble tomb reminiscent of the Notre Dame cathedral. Whoever lies beneath had a lot of money—and enemies: The tomb's identifying markings have been chiseled off, adding to the cemetery's mysterious feel. Calle la Ceiba and Calle el Tamarindo. Follow Calle Real Xalteva a block past Iglesia Xalteva. Turn left onto Calle el Tamarindo. Follow the street as it curves to the southwest and it will take you to the graveyard's entrance. Updated: Jun 23, 2008.

Forteleza la Pólvora
This 250-year-old fort was built by the Spanish and later used as a torture and interrogation center during the Somoza dictatorship. The fort was rebuilt in the 1990s, and now houses a small museum and art gallery. You can also

Enter VIVA Photo Contests: vivatravelguides.com/photography-contests/

climb up the fort's turrets for a nice view of the city. Admission is by donation. Open 7 a.m. – 5 p.m. Calle Real Xalteva, two blocks west of Iglesia Xalteva. Updated: Jun 23, 2008.

Plaza de la Independencia and Parque Central

These adjoining parks are a pleasant place to hang out and are at the center of Granada's cultural and social scene. Parque Central is host to souvenir vendors, food and ice-cream stands, and artists by day, while groups of canoodling lovers move in at night. Both places are relaxing spots to people-watch, though Parque Central's shady benches offer better seating. Updated: Jun 23, 2008.

Casa Natal Sor Maria Romero Meneses

Maria Romero Meneses (1902 – 1977) is known as Central America's first official saint for her humanitarian work and miracles. At the age of 12 she suffered from a form of rheumatic fever which left her paralyzed for six months. She attributed her full recovery to the intercession and apparition of Our Lady Help of Christians. After her recovery María decided her calling was to be a Salesian sister.

The Granada native was sent to San Jose in 1931 and dedicated her life to helping the poor of Costa Rica. She taught, created food distribution centers, and opened both a medical clinic and a school for poor girls. An excellent fundraiser who was able to unite wealthy patrons with poor causes, María was able to organize the construction of new homes for poverty stricken families. María died in 1977 at a Salesian house in León and was buried in a chapel in San José. Pope John Paul II authorized her beatification on April 14, 2002. Her canonization is still pending. She has been called both the female John Bosco and the Social Apostle of Costa Rica.

The colonial house where María was born is now a small museum and sanctuary dedicated to her. The building is located one block southeast of Xalteva church and Parque Xalteva. The room where she was born has been converted into a chapel and Mass is held there twice a week. In an adjacent room are family pictures, quotations, original writings and other objects of the famous Nicaraguan nun. There is also a small shop that sells religious items and souvenirs. Note: all the information is in Spanish. Updated: Jan 27, 2009.

Studying Spanish

Granada's charm and superbly equipped hostels have made it a popular place to stick around and study Spanish. There are several excellent schools that offer a uniform weeklong package of 20 hours of private classes, textbooks, and regular excursions for $150. If you're looking to save money, try APC's no-frills package of 20 hours for just $100, or hire a private tutor for a fraction of that cost. Most Spanish schools are open to discounted group classes, as long as you take the intiative to find your own classmates. Updated: Jun 21, 2008.

School Xpress

Although the name is a bit cheesy, School Xpress offers an interesting and challenging curriculum for students, including an option of vocation-based activities. The price for 20 hours of private classes is the standard $150, but they also offer a special of $50 for 10 hours, provided that these classes are held in the afternoon when teachers are the least busy. Group discounts are possible, but you'll have to find your own classmates. Most teachers speak some English, but immersion is the general policy. Guzmán Avenue 2.5 blocks north from the Central Park. Tel: 505-2-552-8577 / 8-450-1722. E-mail: nicaspanishschool@yahoo.com, URL: www.nicaspanishschool.com. Updated: Nov 23, 2009.

Nicaragua Mia Spanish School

Nicaragua Mia offers a fairly standard Spanish study program: 20 hours of classes, including excursions, will cost you $150. The school also offers typical Nicaraguan cooking classes. The school is run as a women's cooperative and offers volunteer opportunities as well. Discounts are offered to students who volunteer, making this a good place for a combined volunteer-study package. Homestays are also available. On Caimito Street: From Central Park, 3.5 blocks West toward the lake. Also located at 104 Calle Arsenal, directly behind Hotel Colonial. Tel: 505-2-552-8193 / 552-2755. URL: http://nicaraguamiaspanish.com. Updated: Nov 26, 2009.

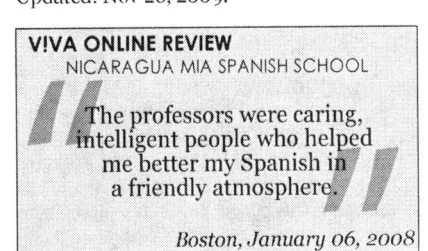

> **V!VA ONLINE REVIEW**
> NICARAGUA MIA SPANISH SCHOOL
>
> *"The professors were caring, intelligent people who helped me better my Spanish in a friendly atmosphere."*
>
> Boston, January 06, 2008

Don't leave home without travel insurance: vivatravelguides.com/insurance/

Granada Spanish Lingua
Offering small classes, homestays, cultural activities and volunteer opportunities, this Spanish school can do most of your trip planning for you. They even offer a free bicycle and personal cell phone to all students. The school also offers airport pickup. Calle la Calzada, one block east of Iglesia Guadalupe inside the Red Cross building. Tel: 505-2-522-8538, URL: www.granadanicaraguaspanish.com. Updated: Jul 16, 2009.

Carolina
Carolina is actually a private Spanish teacher who has received excellent reviews from former students. Her lessons don't include textbooks or any of the frills that come with the bigger schools. However, at just $3 per hour, private lessons with Carolina are well under half the price of what you'd pay elsewhere. Tel: 505-2-953-8670, E-mail: karolinacortes@hotmail.com. Updated: Jun 17, 2008.

APC Spanish Schools
Located in a charming building on Parque Central, APC offers a basic 20-hour Spanish course for just $100. You don't get excursions or special services, and you work with photocopies rather than textbooks, but its package is one of the cheapest week-long options available. Classes are private and all teachers can speak some English (though this is discouraged). Volunteering and homestays can also be arranged. Parque Central, westside. Tel: 505-2-552-4203, E-mail: info@spanishgranada.com, URL: www.spanishgranada.com. Updated: Nov 26, 2009.

Volunteering
Numerous hostels and Spanish schools around Granada offer volunteer options, but nearly all are affiliated with one of two institutions: Carita Feliz and La Esperanza. The former is a Spanish-based NGO, while the latter is Nicaraguan-run. Although there's good and bad about both institutions, there's no doubting the benefits they provide to the local communities. Check both to see which program fits better with your plans and schedule. Updated: Jun 23, 2008.

La Esperanza Granada
La Esperanza is possibly Granada's most popular volunteering outfit. They specialize in rural education, setting up international volunteers with teaching and tutoring positions. This requires a commitment of at least two or three months. If you aren't planning to stay that long, you can find short-term work providing help for agriculture or farming. La Esperanza also accepts donations of clothing and school supplies. Ca. La Libertad #307, 1/2 block from the lake. Tel: 505-8432-5420, E-mail: la_esperanza_granada@yahoo.com, URL: www.la-esperanza-granada.org. Updated: Nov 23, 2009.

Carita Feliz
Tranlsating to the "Spanish Happy Face Foundation" in English, this privately-financed company mainly works to feed and educate impoverished children. They also organize adoptions and work with a range of other development programs. It's a good choice if you want to work with kids. Walk down Calle Caimito which becomes Calle San Juan del Sur. It's the fifth street on the right, opposite Panaderia San Juan del Sur. Tel: 505-2-552-7979, E-mail: info@fundacioncaritafeliz.org, URL: www.fundacioncaritafeliz.org. Updated: Nov 26, 2009.

Tours
Granada has no shortage of tour operators, many of whom have international connections. As a result, it's easy to find all-inclusive packages to the area, most of which include at least one day of exploring the city before moving on to see either La Isletas, Laguna de Apoyo or, if you have a little more time, the Isla de Ometepe.

From Granada, it's easy to book tours to the surrounding region. Volcano trips, particularly to Mombacho or Masaya, are also quite popular, though most of Nicaragua's volcanoes are within day-trip distance.

If you're in Granada and heading abroad, CAST (p.135) has connections in Costa Rica and Panama for booking international tours. A few other agencies have offices in Costa Rica as well. Updated: Jun 25, 2008.

Nicaragua Adventures
From kayaking on Lake Nicaragua to all-inclusive tours of Isla de Ometepe, this French tour agency offers a wide range of services. They do trips to just about every volcano in the region, with excellent knowledge of the requirements and rewards of each ascent. Plane tickets are also sold here (but can be found for much cheaper down the street at CAST). Calle la Calzada, two blocks down from Parque Central. Tel: 505-8-988-8127, Fax: 505-2-552-8461, E-mail: info@nica-

adventures.com / travelnicacr@yahoo.com, URL: www.nica-adventures.com. Updated: Nov 26, 2009.

CAST

An international tour operator with connections in Costa Rica and Panamá, CAST is an excellent resource for booking tours or accommodations in these countries. They also book international and domestic flights at reasonable prices. CAST also offers local services, including car rentals, island tours and city tours. Overall, they're an excellent resource for travelers who like to plan ahead. Staff in the office speak English. Open 7 a.m. – 5 p.m. Calle la Calzada, two blocks down from Parque Central. Tel: 505-2-552-8302, E-mail: nicaragua@castcr.com, URL: www.castcr.com. Updated: Nov 26, 2009.

Va Pues / Paxeos

In a small blue house next to Granada's cathedral is an office that houses three separate tour agents. **Va Pues** offers volcano and nature expeditions around the country; **Isletas Express** offers moderately priced excursions to the islands around Granada; and **Paxeos** is a luxury bus company offering comfortable, air-conditioned (and expensive) transportation between Nicaraguan cities and airport transport. With all three operating under the same roof, this office is an excellent source of information and options. Parque Central, next to the cathedral. Tel: 505-2-552-8291 / 8-465-1090, E-mail: info@paxeos.com, URL: www.paxeos.com. Updated: Nov 26, 2009.

Amigo Tours

Centrally located within the Hotel Colonial, Amigo Tours offers a wide range of services. They can organize popular trips and tours, including visits to local volcanoes. They can also arrange purchasing domestic air tickets, hotel bookings, car rentals and DHL package delivery. The professional staff speak both Spanish and English and are usually helpful and informative. However, the prices can be a little steep, so it may be worth comparing the prices offered with other local tour companies before making a final decision. The office is located inside Hotel Colonial, just north of Parque Central. Tel: 505-2-552-4080, E-mail: bernal@amigotours.net, URL: www.amigotours.net. Updated: Jan 09, 2009.

Leo's Tours

Leo's Tours is a locally owned and operated organization. They offer trips to volcanoes throughout the region, as well as city tours of Granada. Although Leo's Tours is definitely one of the cheapest operators in the city, they have been known to use deceit in order to get and keep their clients. It is always best to double-check any information that you receive from this tour operator. Calle la Calzada, two blocks down from Parque Central. Tel: 505-2-829-4372, URL: www.leotours.blogspot.com. Updated: Jan 13, 2009.

NicarAgua Dulce SA

NicarAgua Dulce SA a major aquatic tour operator in Central America that specializes in sightseeing the wetlands, islands, rivers and birds, all with its own electric boat fleet. They also offer specialized photo tours. Based in las Isletas de Granada in the Marina Cocibolca in Bahia de Asese, it claims to be "Isletas de Granada best kept secret". Tel: 505-2-552-6351 / 802-0285, E-mail: nicaraguadulce@gmail.com, URL: nicaraguadulce.com. Updated: Nov 26, 2009.

ORO Travel

A well-established international travel agency and a pioneer for tour operators in Nicaragua, ORO Travel provides high quality services such as day tours, packages, circuits, self-drive tours, adventure activities, hotel reservation, car rental, private transportation, cruise ship offers and Spanish schools arrangements. Their office is located in a beautiful colonial house in the historical center of Granada, where their staff can help organize trips within Nicaragua, as well as to Honduras or El Salvador. Their team of highly trained and professional guides are fluent in English, German, French, Russian and Spanish.

ORO has a strong commitment to the local community, employs Nicaraguan people and has been involved in several conservation projects and education. They are a member of the umbrella brand Latincoming, which was founded in 1999 in order to professionally meet the trend towards cross-national tourism in Central America, Mexico, Cuba and the Dominican Republic. All partners are incoming agencies under European management. Calle Corral #205. Tel: 505-2-552-4568, Fax: 505-2-552-6512, E-mail: information@orotravel.com, URL: www.orotravel.com. Updated: Jun 03, 2009.

Lodging

Granada is a major tourist city and has accommodations to suit every taste and budget. In fact, Granada has some of the best accommodations options in Nicaragua. The cheapest places in town offer dorm beds for as little as $4 a night, but most hostels charge around $6.70 – 9 for a bed. Services and amenities obviously vary with price, but nearly all hostels are equipped with free WiFi.

The most popular spots—such as Hotel Oasis and The Bearded Monkey—tend to fill up quickly, so book ahead if your heart is set on staying there. Both are spectacularly equipped, though relatively expensive, budget options. There's also a popular hostel located atop Volcan Mombacho.

At the other end of the spectrum, hotels like Hotel Dario and Hotel Alhambra offer five-star comfort amid beautiful settings for the higher-end traveler. There are also quite a few good mid-range options along Calle la Calzada. Updated: Jan 13, 2009.

BUDGET
Hostal Central
(DORMS: $3, ROOMS: $10 and up) Hostal Central is a good place for those on a low budget. It offers a variety of accommodations, all of which are clean, though perhaps a bit scruffy (concrete is falling off some room walls). However, what you do get is a friendly hostel with two big communal areas, the front one housing a pleasant seating area with a bar and restaurant. There is also free tea and coffee, a kitchen (a rarity in Granada's most popular hostels), free Internet and tour advice. Ca. la Calzada, 1.5 blocks from Central Park/Cathedral toward the lake. Tel: 505-552-7630, E-mail: info@centralhostal.com, URL: www.centralhostal.com. Updated: Nov 22, 2006.

Hostal El Tiangue
(ROOMS: $5 and up) A new offering right in the heart of town, El Tiangue is wrapped around local shops and located near the bustling town market. Smart wooden floors on a first floor veranda lead to a small but very clean and tidy rooms, all of which have twin beds with no bath. The place lacks a communal area, apart from its dining room and public courtyard below, but overall it is a good value. Ca. Palmira, 50 meters (164 ft) from bus stop/petrol station. Tel: 552-7161, E-mail: hostaltiangue@cablenet.com.ni, URL: www.hostaleltiangue.com. Updated: Nov 22, 2006.

Kalala Lodge
(ROOMS: $6 – 10) Since the neighboring 'The Bearded Monkey' is often booked up, Kalala Lodge makes an equally economical alternative for the backpacker: its dorms and doubles all come with shared bathroom and access to secure lockers. With time, Kalala might even surpass its neighbor. Kalala Lodge also has a well-equipped kitchen that guests can use and fresh coffee and tea is complimentary throughout the day for guests. The bar is well-stocked with Nicaraguan and imported beers, as well as spirits, juices and cocktails. Although there is no Internet access in the hostel, guests are entitled to 10 free minutes per day at an Internet café across the road. Laundry service is also available at $3 per load. Ca. 14 de Septiembre. Tel: 505-440-9589, E-mail: kalalalodge@gmail.com, URL: www.kalalalodgegranadanic.blogspot.com. Updated: Feb 20, 2009.

Hostal Dorado
(DORMS: $6, DOUBLES: $35) Charming and centrally located, Hostal Dorado offers clean and new dorms as well as cozy private rooms. Comfy hammocks are set around a charming little garden. Guests are offered free WiFi as well as coffee and tea, but, unlike similarly priced area accommodations, there is a lack of common area facilities. The hostel has a book exchange, DVDs and laundry service. Private rooms are available for $12 – $25, but you can find nicer rooms for cheaper across the park. Calle Real Xalteva, 1.5 blocks west of Parque Central. Tel: 505-848-2491, URL: www.hostaldorado.com. Updated: Jun 03, 2009.

> **V!VA ONLINE REVIEW**
> HOSTAL DORADO
> "Awesome hostel for an awesome cause. The proceeds of Dorado go to a program that supports the educational and emotional needs of street kids in Nicaragua."
> USA, November 13, 2008

Bearded Monkey
(ROOMS: $8 – 10) This is one of the most popular hostels in town. It has big dorms and slightly scruffy but adequate rooms around two main courtyards, one of which houses a busy bar and the other a TV for evening movies. There are free international phone calls and Internet, as well as plenty of travel information. However, there is no kitchen and you have to pay for movies. It remains a fun and popular place to stay,

but Oasis Hostel may be better value, since it has a pool. Ca. 14 de Septembre between Ca. Coral and Ca. El Arsenal. Tel: 552-4028, E-mail: thebeardedmonkey@yahoo.com, URL: www.thebeardedmonkey.com. Updated: Nov 26, 2009.

Hostal Amigo

(ROOMS: $8 – 20) Some of the dorms at Hostal Amigo are a little shabby, but the rest of the place is quite clean. Although the rooms are relatively expensive for a budget traveler, the price does include a free breakfast, which makes the Hostal Amigo a decent value. Also included in the price are a couple of other extras including free coffee and WiFi. The hostal also has a fully equipped guest kitchen and a lavanderia on-site. The private rooms are clean and all have TVs. Ca. Estrada and Ca. Atravesada. Updated: Jan 09, 2009.

Hospedaje la Calzada

(ROOMS: $8.50 – 14) The Hospedaje la Calzada might not win any awards for cleanliness, but the 10 large rooms with private bathrooms offer excellent value. The staff at this family-run hospedaje are friendly and welcoming and succeed in creating a homey atmosphere. Guests also have access to a well-equipped kitchen, which is perfect for those on a budget. The excellent location, cheap prices and family atmosphere make the Hospedaje la Calzada an extremely sound budget option. Ca. la Calzada, four blocks down from Parque Central. Tel: 505-475-9229. Updated: Apr 21, 2009.

Hospedaje Cocibolca

(ROOMS: $15) This pleasant place is relatively cheap considering its upmarket style. A nice, open communal area with wooden chairs and clean tile floor feed through to rooms that are comfortable, well-appointed and clean. The pricier rooms come with air conditiong and TV. There is a communal kitchen for guests and Internet is available. Calle la Calzada. Tel: 505-2-552-7223/8-600-9695, E-mail: hospedaje_cocibolca@yahoo.com / reservaciones@hospedajecocibolca.com, URL: www.hospedajecocibolca.com. Updated: Nov 26, 2009.

Hostel Oasis

(DORM: $8, ROOMS: $19 – 28) Located two blocks from the center of the city, the Hostel Oasis is aptly named. The establishment is a backpacker's paradise or for those seeking refuge from the hustle and bustle (and heat) of Granada's streets.

Offering both private and shared and accommodation, the rooms are all comfortable and clean. Past the reception area is an open-air courtyard filled with trees and fenced by hammocks, where you can have an afternoon siesta or some quiet time with a good book. A row of 10 computers, complete with free Internet access, lead to a clean and cool swimming pool. Breakfast is available for purchase daily from 7:30 – 10:30 a.m.; complimentary tea and coffee are offered all day.

Free entertainment services include an extensive DVD collection and a large book exchange. Also included in the price for a night is one 10-minute international phone call per guest. Ca. Estrada 109.Tel: 505-552-8006, URL: www.nicaraguahostel.com. Updated: Mar 18, 2009.

Posada las Brisas !

(ROOMS: $15 – 30) Posada las Brisas is a family-owned and operated guest house located on the unique Calle La Calzada in Granada. The brand new rooms all have a private shower and toilet, and you can choose between a room with two beds or one with a queen-sized bed. You can feel the fresh breeze of the lake in your room, especially if you're on the second floor. Ask for Roberto and Maria Cristina; they will make you feel at home.

The guest house is located two blocks from the Central Park and the Cathedral, and is very close to Guadalupe Church and other historic sites. Even though the nightlife is very intense on La Calzada, the rooms are located in such a way that you should have a pleasant (and quiet) night.

Optional breakfast is available, as is lunch and dinner. However, if you want to enjoy the diverse and good food of Granada, just walk outside: right in front is Pizza Mona Lisa, a wood oven cooked pizza shop with good wine. Also nearby is Macondo, a bar with arguably the best atmosphere in Granada, which serves real Spanish food, tapas, sangria and many other dishes.

Optional Spanish classes are available with professional Spanish teacher Bayardo Corea, Christina's brother. All classes include private tutoring and flexible schedules so you can enjoy your experience in Granada. Ca. La Calzada, house 440, in front of Pizza Mona Lisa. Tel: 505-552-3984, E-mail: ccallejas01@gmail.com. Updated: Jan 13, 2009.

MID-RANGE

The Monkey Hut

(DORM: $10, ROOMS: $22 – 24, CABANAS: $45 – 70) Located on Laguna de Apoyo, a picturesque crater lake just 20 minutes from Granada, this is a great place to go to for a bit of peace and quiet. A variety of rooms are available and there is a kitchen, gardens and a dock leading out to the lake. Kayaks and inner tubes are available, as are other games to help keep you occupied. If you don't want to stay overnight, a day trip fee is $5 plus transport from the Bearded Monkey hostel. To get there, take a truck from the Bearded Monkey in Granada ($1) or grab a cab ($6 – 10). Laguna de Apoyo. Tel: 505-8-887-3546, URL: www.thebeardedmonkey.com/monkeyhut.htm. Updated: Nov 26, 2009.

Hotel Nuestra Casa

(ROOMS: $15 – 58) Run by the same friendly Floridian who's behind the Alabama Rib Shack, this hotel is particularly popular among Peace Corps visitors. Rooms are clean (though not immaculate). Their honeymoon suite would be a good value were it not for its location alongside their noisy terrace-bar. (It's hard to imagine a romantic getaway amid all the ruckus outside, although the party only goes until ten-thirty.) Generally speaking, the rooms with the best value are their mid-range ($25) rooms, which can sleep three and are well-suited for families traveling on a budget. 206 Calle Consulado, 2.5 blocks west of Parque Central. Tel: 505-2-552-8115, E-mail: exoticwood@hotmail.com, URL: www.jimmythreefingers.com. Updated: Nov 26, 2009.

Posada San Jose

(ROOMS: $25 – 40, DOUBLES: $30) Opened in early November 2008, Posada San Jose is a new hotel in Granada. It has seven neat and clean rooms, all with private bath, cable TV (with U.S. channels), free coffee and free WiFi throughout hotel (including the rooms). If you lack a laptop, there is also free use of the hotel computer. It's in an extremely good location, just steps off Calle Calzada. From the cathedral, take a right on Calle El Cisne. From the plaza, take a right at Tierra Tours onto Calle El Cisne; the hotel is on the right. Tel: 505-552-2270, E-mail: edgarmonterrey@hotmail.com, URL: www.laposadasanjose.com. Updated: Dec 24, 2008.

Hotel Terrasol

(ROOMS: $30 – 46) Hotel Terrasol is a small B&B with a lot of character. The 10 double rooms are fresh and immaculate. Everything is new and spotless, and the upper level rooms have a small window offering good views over the city. Rooms come with air conditioning, cable TV, hair dryers, and WiFi. There is also a restaurant on-site and continental breakfast is included in the price. During the low season the price for a room is highly negotiable, making the place a great value. Av. Barricada, 1/2 block south of Ca. Xalteva. Tel: 505-2-552-8825, Fax: 505-2-552-8683, E-mail: info@hotelterrasol.net, URL: www.hotelterrasol.com. Updated: Nov 26, 2009.

> **V!VA ONLINE REVIEW**
> HOTEL TERRASOL
>
> "This hotel is a good bargain and a real hidden gem—a great place to stay while exploring Granada and the surrounding area."
>
> Costa Rica, May 09, 2009

Hotel El Maltese

(ROOMS: $24 – 50) El Maltese is the only hotel in Granada built along the lake shore. It has ten large, bright, and well-ventilated rooms furnished with simple but good taste. All rooms have a private bathroom, air conditioning and TV. The hotel also has a two-bedroom suite with a breathtaking view of the lake. Prices do not include taxes. Fifty meters (164 ft) south of the plaza. Tel: 505-2-552-7641 / 8-893-4243, Fax: 505-2-552-7641, E-mail: elmaltese@nicatour.net, URL: www.nicatour.net/en/elmaltese. Updated: Nov 26, 2009.

Dolphin Guest House

(ROOMS: $30 – 50) The Dolphin Guest House is located in a private and safe community, with a nice breeze that comes from the lake. It's just seven minutes away from the main square of Granada. Buses go by the entrance every 10 minutes and they only charge $0.40. If you need a taxi, the hotel can call one for you at affordable prices. This comfortable and nice place was built with the intention of making you feel like home. Guests can enjoy a nice view of the Mombacho volcano, the lake, the Cathedral and the stadium. You can also swim in the fresh water pool while enjoying a a juice, cocktail or beer. Reparto san juan lote #5. Tel: 505-8-896-7514, Fax: 505-2-552-3138, E-mail: info@vacationinnicaragua.com, URL: www.vacationinnicaragua.com. Updated: Sep 01, 2009.

Casa San Francisco Hotel

(ROOMS: $45 – 60) Located in the heart of the city, Casa San Francisco Hotel is a charming colonia hotel. Each room has air conditioning, cable TV and private bathroom. Continental breakfast is included. Guests can enjoy a refreshing dip in the pool after a day of sightseeing. The hotel's staff are bilingual and friendly; they greet every guest by name to help make it a comfortable stay. Airport pickups can be arranged. 207 Calle Corral. Tel: 505-552-8235, E-mail: csfgranada@yahoo.com, URL: www.csf-hotel-granada.com. Updated: Jun 15, 2009.

V!VA ONLINE REVIEW
CASA SAN FRANCISCO HOTEL

"We loved the atmosphere, the staff, the GREAT food, the friendly owners, our room—there was nothing to dislike."

Washington DC, May 19, 2008

Casa San Martin

(ROOMS: $45 – 65) A beautifully restored colonial building, Casa San Martin has eight private rooms, each with a bathroom, cable TV, high ceiling and paintings by local Granada artists. There are many areas to sit—the upper balcony, the main dining room, or the garden courtyard—and you can start your day with the complimentary continental breakfast. Tours in and around Granada can be arranged by Eco-expeditions, conveniently located in the lobby. This two-story elegant mansion is just one minute from the central park and an eight-minute walk to Lake Nicaragua. Ca. la Calzada Catedral 1c. al lago. Tel: 505-552-6185, E-mail: javier_sanchez_a@yahoo.com, URL: www.hcasasanmartin.com. Updated: Jan 23, 2009.

Casa Silas B and B

(ROOMS: $45 – 65) Casa Silas offers very comfortable queen-sized beds and bathrooms with hot showers. The rooms are equipped with air conditioning and ceiling fans; they also have skylights through which you can see the Nicaraguan sunrise and parrots outside. The rooms look out upon the courtyard garden and swimming pool. The hotel offers a selection of fresh, local fruits, jams, pastries and heartier breakfast fare to start your morning. Casa Silas also offers nightly turn down service, mini-bar, complimentary high speed Internet, and free telephone calls to the United States, Canada and Mexico. Laundry service is available.

Full concierge services are also available, including airport shuttle, car rentals, and Spanish lessons. The staff can help arrange walking tours of the city, a boat cruise of Las Isletas, or, if you prefer to explore on your own, transport to Volcano Mombacho, Volcano Masaya, the artisan markets of Masaya, or the pottery cooperatives of San Juan de Oriente. 206 Calle La Concepcion. Tel: 505-940-1883, E-mail: mail@casasilas.com, URL: www.casasilas.com. Updated: Mar 09, 2009.

HIGH-END
Hotel Granada

(ROOMS: $46 – 110) The Hotel Granada is located between the central park and the lake, right in front of the Guadalupe church. The hotel's historical architecture recreates colonial Granada with a touch of modernity and typical details. The well-furnished rooms are equipped with air conditioning, cable TV, telephone, safety box (small local charge), king-size beds and free WiFi. The hotel also has a total of 25 apartments currently available for rent. Breakfast and evening meals are served in the friendly on-site restaurant. You can also enjoy a drink at the hotel's bar. Tel: 505-552-2178, Fax: 505-552-4128, E-mail: info@hotelgranadanicaragua.com / reservations@hotelgranadanicaragua.com. Updated: Dec 29, 2008.

Hotel Dario

(ROOMS: $85 – 125) Located in a charming 19th century Neoclassical building, the Hotel Dario seamlessly blends into the beautiful architecture of Granada's downtown. The swimming pool and flowing fountains make for an extremely pleasant and tranquil atmosphere. Hotel Dario also has a gym, restaurant and coffee shop, and can arrange pickups from Managua's airport. Since the hotel has only 22 rooms, reservations are a good idea (even during low season). The place also has conference facilities for up to 120 people. Ca. la Calzada, 1.5 blocks down from Parque Central. Tel: 505-2-552-3400, Fax: 505-552-3690, E-mail: info@hoteldario.com, URL: www.hoteldario.com. Updated: Nov 26, 2009.

Don't leave home without travel insurance: vivatravelguides.com/insurance/

La Gran Francia

(ROOMS: $90 – 160) La Gran Francia is located just steps away from Granada's central square in a renovated colonial building which some historians have dated as far back as 1524. La Gran Francia strives to be the best hotel and restaurant in the country and the quality of the rooms and food are stellar. The hotel also offers a variety of packages catering to honeymooners, business travelers and couples wanting a romantic night or two. Any of these options will cost you though, as this is one of the most expensive hotels Granada. Located on the southeast corner of Parque Central. Tel: 505-2-552-6002 / 6007, E-mail: marketing@lagranfrancia.com, URL: www.lagranfrancia.com. Updated: Nov 26, 2009.

Restaurants

Thanks to the boom of tourists (and corresponding influx of expats), Granada offers an incredible range of dining styles, from Italian to Asian fusion to the ubiquitous gallo pinto. With so many options, you're sure to find the cuisine you're craving. Street meat in the city is generally not recommended, but if you see a vendor selling *nicotamales*, a regional specialty, go ahead and give it a try—they're phenomenal. Updated: Jun 25, 2008.

NICARAGUAN / TRADITIONAL
Hospedaje Ruiz

Although not generally known as a restaurant, Hospedaje Ruiz offers mouthwatering asado at rock-bottom prices. Expect to pay only $.55 – .75 for a generous helping of grilled meat served with plátanos, salad, and chopped avocado (upon request). As far as budget eating options go, this place is tough to beat. However, the menu is somewhat limited, and this is not a place for vegetarians. Ca. la Calzada, half a block up from Iglesia Guadalupe. Tel: 505-552-2346. Updated: Dec 29, 2008.

Street Vendors in Parque Central

If the bar is closed and you're still hungry, stumble on over to Parque Central. You'll usually find the asado lady is still on duty, right across from the cathedral. The *completo* is a full-sized meal with grilled meat, cheese, vegetables and gallo pinto served in a banana leaf. The meal should cost $.40, though she's been known to charge $.50 on occasion, so be sure to ask the price first. Parque Central. Updated: Jun 16, 2008.

Centralito

Centralito is a popular, centrally located restaurant and late-night bar. During the day the lunch specials are well within the budget price range. The cheap and tasty burgers are an especially great way to fill up. Be sure to ask for their daily specials. Ca. la Calzada, two blocks east of Parque Central. Tel: 505-552-5900. Updated: Jan 20, 2009.

PIZZA / ITALIAN
Tele Pizza

(PIZZAS: $3 – 4) Any traveler will be hard pressed to find a better pizza shop in Central America (if anyone finds one please write in!) than Tele Pizza. This busy, pleasant restaurant (a bit too busy on a Saturday) offers thin and thick crust pizzas with a whole range of toppings. You will enter with a grin of anticipation and leave with a smile of satisfaction—and you will go back again. Calle El Arsenal (east of the Central Park). Tel: 505-2-552-4219. Updated: Nov 26, 2009.

Pizzeria Don Luca

Pizza is generally a luxury food in Latin America, but the pies here are a reasonable deal if split between two or three people. With crispy crusts and generous helpings of toppings, this is probably the best pizza in the city. Ca. la Calzada and Calle el Martirio. Tel: 505-2-552-7822, E-mail: acul_ilrac@hotmail.com. Updated: Nov 26, 2009.

CAFES
Garden Café

Set around a delightful garden, this open air restaurant offers a wide range of tasty sandwiches and salads. Perfect for breakfast or a light lunch, the restaurant also features fresh juices, a book exchange, and complimentary WiFi. The place comes strongly recommended. Open daily 7 a.m. – 3 p.m. Prices are between budget and mid-range. Ca. la Libertad and Av. Miguel de Cervantes. Tel: 505-552-8582. Updated: Jan 29, 2009.

Euro Café !

(DESSERTS: $1 – 3.50) This little laid-back café is situated right next to the Hotel Colonial, on the northeast corner of Granada's Parque Central. You can either sit looking out onto the square or head to the airy courtyard at the back with its fountain and quieter atmosphere.

A selection of light breakfasts, salads, bagels and paninis is available, along with ice

The Vigorón

Vigorón could be described as the fast food of colonial Nicaraguas. Over the years, this quick dish meat and vegetables, all rolled into a banana leaf, has developed into a local favorite. If you arrive unexpectedly at someone's home, vigorón is the dish you're likely to be served.

Vegetarians beware: although vigorón contains boiled yucca and a pickled cabbage salad, it can also contain either fried pork or pork rinds toasted until they're crunchy.

Each region has it's own version of vigorón: in Bluefields' Barrio Central the dish is made with salad that has been pickled with chile de cabro and mustard; in Chinandega it includes chile congo and plenty of pickled onions and carrots; a famous version from Granada, where vigorón originated, uses mimbros, a tiny, crunchy and extremely sour tropical fruit that gives the salad a unique tang.

To make vigorón yourself, first select fresh yucca (if it has blue tips, it's not fresh), peel it and cut it into three to five-inch pieces. Boil the yucca until it bursts. Add finely diced cabbage, tomatoes and onions. Mix the vegetables up with vinegar, oil, lime and chile peppers (such as chile congo from the Pacific coast). Finally, season with rosemary or cilantro and wrap in a clean banana leaf. Updated: Mar 09, 2009.

---

cream and enticing cakes and pastries. A variety of coffees (including iced) are on the drink menu, as are juices, wines, beers, sodas and spirits ($0.90 – 1.50). Euro Café is a WiFi zone so lots of people bring their laptops here. Others prefer to just sit and read, since the café is situated right next to a used bookstore. Northeast corner of Parque Central, next to Hotel Colonial. Updated: Jan 21, 2009.

MEXICAN
Tequila Vallarta
(ENTREES: $3.90 – 5.30) Top Mexican dishes are served up in plentiful portions at this pleasant restaurant just down from the main square. Big burritos, enchiladas, nachos, spicy sauces (they will burn your mouth!) and their specialty chocolate and chili sauce are all on offer. Grab some of the fliers for 2-for-1 frozen margaritas that the restaurant staff has distributed around town and settle in for the night at Tequilla Vallarta. De la Alcaldia Municipal, 1.5 blocks al Lago. Tel: 505-552-8488, E-mail: rosarionunez_31@hotmail.com. Updated: Feb 19, 2009.

EUROPEAN
El Tercer Ojo
(TAPAS: $3.15 – 4.60, ENTREES: $3.15 – 11.65, DESSERTS: $3.15) El Tercer Ojo's darkly bohemian lounge and bar, decorated in Asiatic style, leads out to an attractive patio dining area that seems to be popular in the evening. (Note: reservations are welcomed and recommended—there wasn't a spare table available on one Monday night in January.)

You can start your meal with tempting tapas-style appetizers such as black-olive cream or smoked salmon on toasted bread. For mains, the menu then focuses on a variety of pastas, grills, seafood plates, salads and crepes. There are internationally inspired meals, with plenty of options available for vegetarians. Appealing desserts are also on offer for those who have room after the generous mains. Happy hour runs from 4 to 7 pm daily and includes 2-for-1 glasses of fruity and strong sangria, wine (by the bottle and glass), beer, spirits, juices and coffee.

El Tercer Ojo offers free WiFi access to customers and an interesting selection of books to browse through. Artwork and furniture can also be purchased there. It's definitely an interesting and agreeable place to spend an afternoon, or enjoy an evening drink, as well as to dine on attractively presented and good quality food. Ca. El Arsenal, opposite San Fransisco Convent. Tel: 505-552-6451, E-mail: eltercerojo_granada@yahoo.com. Updated: Jan 16, 2009.

El Jardin de Orion
Located on the terraces of the oldest house in Granada, this restaurant serves up great cuisine in a lush, natural environment. They offer great French food, original

---

Don't leave home without travel insurance: vivatravelguides.com/insurance/

cocktails and an extensive wine list. This is an excellent place to share the day's happenings or reminisce about the past. Calle El Caimito, one block away from the central park. Tel: 505-8-429-6494. Updated: Nov 26, 2009.

> **V!VA ONLINE REVIEW**
> EL JARDIN DE ORION
>
> "The food and coktails are excellent and the atmosphere is warm and friendly. Moreover, the place is really beautiful."
>
> Netherlands, January 31, 2008

Charly's Bar and Restaurant
Charly's Bar and Restaurant is a little place that was opened by a German man in 1995. In addition to traditional Nicaraguan fare, the place serves several varieties of German sausages and brochettes. The walls are also adorned with German trinkets to satisfy any cravings for something more German than sausages. The atmosphere is quiet, the prices are reasonable and the owner is friendly, making this place a great choice for something different from the usual gallo pinto. Four blocks west and 25 meters (82 ft) south of Petronic. Tel: 505-2-552-2942, Fax: 505-2-552-4452 E-mail: charly.steinmaier@ffm-granada.org. URL: www.charlys-bar.com. Updated: Nov 23, 2009.

STEAK / RIBS
Roadhouse Grill
Roadhouse Grill offers a range of fine dining options from filet mignon to cordon bleu. The atmosphere is more bar and grill than candlelight and romance, but their patio seating provides a more scenic dining experience if that's what you're after. Service is speedy, efficient and friendly, and their food is definitely worth the price. Overall, Roadhouse Grill is a very pleasant dining experience. Ca. la Calzada, two blocks down from Parque Central. Tel: 505-552-8469, E-mail: alvarourbina24@hotmail.com. Updated: Jun 16, 2008.

Jimmy "Three FIngers" Alabama Rib Shack Bar and Grill
It's a bold statement to lay claim to the world's finest ribs, but Jimmy's backs it up: dishes here are absolutely mouthwatering. The ribs, along with other grilled options, are heartily recommended. Eating here isn't cheap, but in our opinion it's worth every penny (or Cordoba). There's a lively bar upstairs that draws a mostly local crowd. 206 Ca. Consulado, 2.5 blocks west of Parque Central. Tel: 505-552-8115, URL: www.jimmythreefingers.com. Updated: Jun 17, 2008.

Nightlife
Café Nuit
This VIVA reviewer visited Café Nuit on a Monday night and still found live music with salsa dancing until the wee hours—this place is a guaranteed party. The house band plays every night, but the music isn't overpoweringly loud. The crowd is a healthy mix of locals, expats and travelers, and the drink prices are reasonable. Ca. la Libertad, 2.5 blocks west of Parque Central. Updated: Jun 19, 2008.

Zoom Bar
Your friendly neighborhood sports bar, this place fills up whenever there's a big event, but it almost always draws a reasonable crowd of tourists, expats and locals. They claim to have the "best hamburgers in Granada"—you can decide, but they certainly are the heartiest. Ca. la Calzada and Calle el Martirio. Tel: 505-643-5655, E-mail: info@zoombar.biz, URL: www.zoombar.biz. Updated: Nov 26, 2009.

El Kayak
Granada's after-hours clubs are mainly located on a strip down by the waterfront, and El Kayak is arguably the best of them. The place gets going at around 1 a.m. and tends stay hopping until 8 or 9 a.m. The club features a dance floor and fully stocked bar. It's a great place to party and watch the sun come up. Getting there on foot requires a long walk through some sketchy neighborhoods; you're better off taking a taxi. Updated: Jun 19, 2008.

El Club
El Club has established itself as one of Granada's most happening clubs. The live DJs and great atmosphere attracts a stylish young crowd. If you enter before 10p.m. you can enjoy the happy hour; however, if you do so you will be very early, as the dancing doesn't start up until very late at night. Ca. la Libertad and Av. Barricada. Updated: Jan 20, 2009.

El Quijote
El Quijote is a popular karaoke bar that attracts a mix of locals and foreigners. The

Enter VIVA Photo Contests: vivatravelguides.com/photography-contests/

atmosphere is always friendly and the place is a sure-fire recipe for a fun night out. The only thing that might stop you from having fun is the fact that the bar is only open on Wednesdays, Saturdays and Sundays. Ca. el Caimito, one block east of Parque Central. Updated: Jan 20, 2009.

> **VIVA ONLINE REVIEW**
> **EL QUIJOTE**
> I spent six weeks in Granada and this was my favorite place by far. Especially great are karaoke nights... a total blast for all types of travelers and locals.
> Canada, August 13, 2008

AROUND GRANADA

LAS ISLETAS

With Granada's scorching summer heat, it can be a bit frustrating that the waters of nearby Lake Nicaragua are too polluted to swim in. However, if you're desperate for a dip, salvation is near in the form of Las Isletas, a chain of nearby islands where the water is just peachy.

The 365 islands that make up Las Isletas were originally formed when Volcan Mombacho blew its top some 20,000 years ago. The volcano's massive cone was scattered into the lake, forming the rocky outposts you see today.

Of the hundreds of islands, the most visited are the Castillo San Pablo and the Isla de los Monos (Monkey Island). The former is an 18th century Spanish fortress, built to defend Granada from pirate attacks (which, incidentally, it failed to do). Monkey Island, as the name suggests, is an island that hosts a family of monkeys. These creatures are relatively friendly but have come to see tourists as a food source, so think twice before disembarking—they can get nasty once you run out of goodies to hand out. You're allowed to bring along fruit for the monkeys, which you can distribute from the safety of your boat. Across from Monkey Island is a popular bar and restaurant, complete with a sun deck and diving board. Many people use this as a base for swimming.

Most tour agencies in town offer trips to the islands, but if you're traveling in a group it will be much cheaper to arrange yourself—just take a taxi to the *embarcadero* (dock) for boats to Las Isletas. It should cost around $.75 per person, depending on your negotiating skills, which will be further tested once you embark because you'll almost certainly be met by a tout offering three-hour island tours for $30. This price is already a steep discount on what the agencies in Granada offer, but you can negotiate it further (this VIVA reviewer got them down to $23).

Standard trips include visits to the two main islands listed above, with a one-hour break at the restaurant eat (and swim, if you're so inclined). If you're not interested in the sightseeing, you can just ask them to drop you off at an uninhabited island and return for you in a few hours. Bring food, water, and any other provisions you need and prepare for a relaxing day.

Another tour option is to navigate through the islands by kayak. Most tour operators in town offer kayaking trips, or you can rent one yourself from Puerto Asese, near the docks. Updated: Jun 23, 2008.

Getting To and Away From Las Isletas

Taxis in Granada will know where boats leave for La Isletas; simply tell them you want to go there and they'll drop you off at the dock located on the lakefront, past the Centro Turistico. The price to get there should be less than a dollar, but getting back to town can get significantly more expensive; taxis are few and far between and you don't have as much bargaining power. Updated: Jun 23, 2008.

RESERVA NATURAL VOLCÁN MOMBACHO

Towering over the city of Granada, the jagged crater of Volcan Mombacho is an unmistakable sight and a popular spot to visit. Rather than the typical smoke and lava, this volcano offers a rich diversity of plant and animal life, as well as pleasant trekking opportunities. The park is home to 50 species of mammals, including monkeys and big cats, and 174 species of birds. If you're lucky you can also find the rare Mombacho salamander, as well as the red-eyed tree frog that features so prominently on Central American postcards.

Mombacho is located about 10 kilometers (6.2 miles) from Granada inside the Reserva

Natural Volcán Mombacho. Most tour operators in Granada offer organized, half-day tours for around $30 per person. If you're making your own way there, the bus will drop you off at the volcano's base. From there you have a 2 km (1.2 mi) uphill walk to park entrance. Inside the entrance there's a reception area where you can wait for a ride up to the cloud forest. The park has a truck which makes the trip at 8:30 a.m., 10 a.m., 1 p.m., and 3 p.m. You can try to walk the way yourself, but it's a long, exhausting hike. If you're interested in seeing an organic coffee farm, the truck can make a stop at Hacienda el Progreso. Otherwise it will continue on to the research station. The whole trip should take about an hour and a half.

Once you reach the top you can decide whether or not you want to have a guide accompany you on your hike. It's strongly recommended that you take one, since they'll be able to point out interesting flora and fauna that you probably wouldn't notice on your own. The guides are full of interesting information and have received rave reviews.

Your hike will probably start along the 1.5 km (.93 mi) crater path. This takes you around one of the smaller, secondary craters of Mombacho. There are several excellent lookout points, and you'll see a range of beautiful butterflies and birdlife. The Crater Path hike should take about an hour and a half, and is relatively easy to hike.

About two thirds of the way around the Crater Path you'll see that the trail branches to the left. Follow it to see the fumaroles, where steam and sulfuric gases come out of the ground. On your way back down, you'll see the path branches again to the left. This will take you to the Puma Path, which leads you around the edge of Mombacho's main crater. This trail is much more difficult, and much longer (about four hours). This is where you can expect to see monkeys, and if you're lucky, sloths. Guides are strongly recommended if you're planning on hiking the Puma Path. If you're only interested in hiking the Puma Path, you can skip the bulk of the Crater Path by heading to the right, rather than to the left, when you leave the research station.

Entrance to the park costs $10 per person. It's recommended that you go during the dry season, as rain can impede the spectacular views. It's also recommended you go during the afternoon—the 1 p.m. truck is the best to catch. Guides charge a $5 flat fee to take you around the crater path, $15 to take you around the Puma Path, and $20 for both.

If you feel like spending a night in the cloud forest, there is a hostel and restaurant in the research station, or a spot where you can pitch your own tent. As of June 2008 they were offering a $35 special which included entrance to the park, a night's accommodation, a guided night-walk, and breakfast. Updated: Jan 22, 2009.

Getting To and Away from RN Volcán Mombacho

To get here from Granada, get on any Nandaime or Rivas-bound bus and ask the driver to let you off at Guanacaste. From there it's a two kilometer (1.2 mi) walk to the park entrance. Try to time your arrival just before the park jeep's departure at 8:30 a.m., 10 a.m., 1 p.m. or 3 p.m. Updated: Jan 22, 2009.

Things to See and Do

Aguas Termales La Caldera

These picturesque hot springs lie on the other side of Volcan Mombacho, but are inaccessible from the main park. If you want to visit you will need to take a taxi to Puerto Asese and hire a *lancha* (motorboat) to take you there. It'll be pricey, but the springs are quite beautiful and attract very few visitors. Updated: Jun 24, 2008.

Reserva Silvestre Privada Domitila

This is a popular ecotourism destination bordering the southwest corner of Lake Cocibalca. They offer horseback riding and trekking and specialize in all-inclusive trips. Calle Amelia Benard #107. Tel: 505-8-881-1786, E-mail: info@domitila.org, URL: www.domitila.org. Updated: Nov 26, 2009.

PARQUE NACIONAL ARCHIPIÉLAGO ZAPATERA

Established as a national park in 1983, the Zapatera Archipiélago consists of a series of islands in Lake Nicaragua. The park gets its name from the largest island, Zapatera, which makes up over half the total landmass of the park. The island is also home to the Zapatera volcano. The park has a little bit of everything, including interesting geology, birds, animals and plants, as well as pre-Columbian archaeological sites.

Enter VIVA Photo Contests: vivatravelguides.com/photography-contests/

Despite its proximity to Granada, Zapatera Island and the rest of the park are surprisingly tourist-free. There are a couple of small communities on Zapatera Island who make a living fishing, tending cattle, farming and guiding visitors, but on the whole the islands that make up the park are pristine and quiet.

However, just because tourists haven't found the park yet doesn't mean that there's nothing to do there. Zapatera Island has a number of good hiking trails, some of which go up the dormant volcano. There is excellent fishing in the waters near the island and the lake is good for swimming. Although the archaeological sites have been plundered many times, there are still some relics and ruins to be seen.

There are basically two options for those who wish to stay overnight in the park. The first is Santa Maria, a converted hacienda popular with the all-inclusive tour group set. Prices are high, but for those who demand comfort, it's the only place in the area for higher end travelers. Those on a budget can stay in a bare-bones rural lodge in the Sonsapote community. Both places can arrange transportation to the island. (At the time of this visit, there is no public transportation to get there.) Hikes and fishing can be arranged from either location. Updated: Sep 30, 2009.

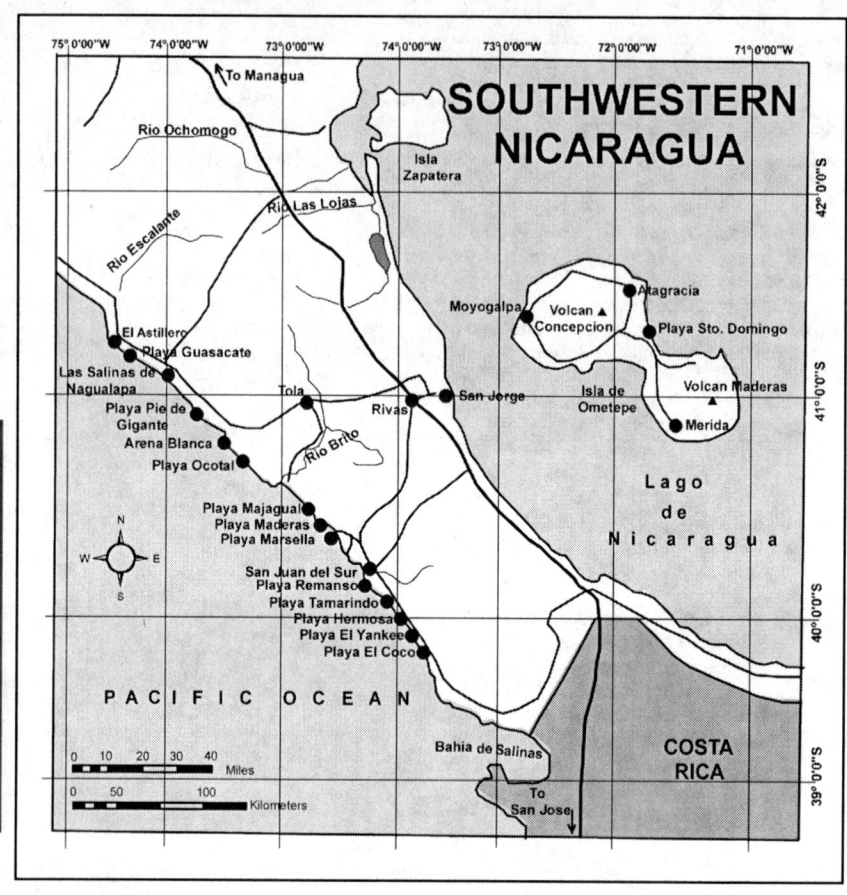

Southwestern Nicaragua

This thin spit of land, sandwiched between the Pacific Ocean and Lago de Nicaragua, has some of the best surfing beaches in the country on one side and, on the other, volcanic islands full of archaeological treasures, hikes and adventures.

Southwestern Nicaragua may be as skinny as a runway model, but head there and you discover that the area actually has a hefty number of things to do. You might find yourself in the swirling markets of Rivas, climbing one of Ometepe's volcanoes, or catching one of the country's best surf breaks.

The Southwest is rimmed with long, sandy beaches that, unlike similar places along the popular Caribbean coast or neighboring Costa Rica, have only just started to draw tourists. Take San Juan del Sur–nestled in a crescent bay, the little town is the perfect antidote to the over-hyped sands across the border. San Juan del Sur has maintained its fishing village charm while still providing all of the services travelers require, including a wide range of restaurants, hotels and Spanish schools.

When you decide to venture further afield, San Juan del Sur also makes a perfect jumping-off point for an incredible number of beaches, such as Playa Maderas, Playa Majagual and Playa Marsella, to name a few to the north. There are also enchantingly named spots like Playa Hermosa (Beautiful Beach), Playa El Coco (Coconut Beach) and Arena Blanca (White Sand).

Before you leave the area, make sure to set aside some time for the boat ride to Isla Ometepe, with Nicaragua's famous twin volcanoes. The island, which has been inhabited for some 4,000 years, has loomed large in the country's mythology, serving as a pirate base, a refuge from Nicaragua's civil wars, and as a time capsule for indigenous artifacts. The island is still half lava threat (Volcán Concepción) and half peaceful lagoon (Volcán Maderas) with land that's sprinkled with petroglyphs, hiking trails and coffee plantations. Updated: Feb 08,2009

History

Nicaragua's Pacific Southwest, a strip of land between the ocean and the country's great lake, has been both a bridge and highway since humans first wandered through Central America. Archaeologists have found evidence of the passage of peoples on Isla Ometepe and on the mainland. Rivas, for example, has been inhabited since at least 606 AD. As long as the Southwest has been a highway, it has also been desirable for its strategic location. After the Spanish claimed the land and began to settle the area, starting with Granada, English pirates regularly crossed the Pacific Ocean and Lake Nicaragua to stage attacks. Isla Ometepe served as a pirate base, with Volcán Concepción smoking ominously overhead, and Granada was attacked by William Walker in the early 19th century. The cities of the Pacific once used horses and carriages (and you can still find a few examples rolling along the streets). Aside from the major cities, though, the region remained relatively undeveloped through Nicaragua's wars and only recently started to be recognized for its gorgeous beaches, stunning wildlife and incredible watersports opportunities. Updated: Oct 14, 2009.

When to Go

The Pacific Southwest has a pleasant, tropical climate which, unlike the northern reaches of the country, doesn't become unbearably hot during the dry months (November through April). Though surfers tend to avoid the beaches during the rainiest months of September and October, the effects of the rainy season are muted by the highlands, which block the Caribbean trade winds before they reach the coast. If your plans include heading to some of those remote, untouched beaches, be aware that many roads are unpaved and can become heavy with clay mud. Plan on either renting a 4X4 or visiting in the drier months. Updated: Oct 14, 2009.

Safety

The Southwest is typically safe and peaceful. More than other parts of Nicaragua, though, this strip of country has seen a great influx of tourism, and both petty crime and scams have increased as a result. Be aware that, as a visitor, you're more likely to be overcharged for goods and services. Taxi drivers, especially around Rivas, will tell you that buses are unsafe or not in operation in order to get you to hire them for long trips; bus drivers will tell you how unsafe taxi drivers are. To avoid scams, obey the rule of threes: if three people in three different places tell you the same thing, then the information is usually fairly reliable. Be on the lookout for pickpockets, especially in crowded places such as buses and markets. The same rules of travel apply in the Pacific Soutwest as with anywhere else: be aware of your surroundings, keep an eye on your belongings, don't be obvious about valuables, always check your bills, secure items when you leave your room, and don't go strolling down dark alleyways at night. Updated: Oct 14, 2009.

Tours

Since the Pacific coast is known mainly for surfing, it's not surprising that there are so many surfing tours and lessons on offer. The best place to find a surfing instructor (or a van to a remote spot) is the popular San Juan del Sur. Within the town center, you'll find surfing-related shops on almost every corner. Ask around; there are regular shuttles to the area beaches.

If you arrive between July and December, you can also arrange for a tour to see Olive Ridley turtles nesting. Be aware that the females usually drag themselves up the beaches to lay eggs in the dead of night, so grab that cup of coffee. San Juan del Sur guides can also take you on hiking, diving, biking and fishing tours, but ask around before you settle on a price.

The best place to arrange for a tour on Ometepe is when you step off the boat, though you'll be tempted to brush right by the crowd of eager guides vying for your attention. If their group excursions and custom trips can't tempt you, ask at your hotel. Hotels often rent bicycles or smaller vehicles and can arrange horseback riding excursions. Updated: Oct 14, 2009.

Lodging

You won't be lacking for accommodation in the Southwest, though there is a significantly wider range of options in the more popular areas (San Juan del Sur and Isla de Ometepe,

Learn how to become a travel writer at vivatravelguides.com/bootcamp/

Highlights

The most popular spot on Nicaragua's coast, **San Juan del Sur (p.167)**, is the perfect place to relax in a hammock, chill on the beach, meet fellow travelers and try your hand at adventure sports. The coastline north and south of town is dotted with forgotten, deserted beaches.

Isla Ometepe (p.156) has surprises at every turn: a lake in a volcano, rocks scrawled with ancient symbols and a small island dedicated to monkeys. Instead of wondering what now, you'll be asking, what's next?

Even in a country famous for its surfing spots, the **Popoyo break (p. 153)**, near Salinas, stands out. It has won international acclaim for its consistently excellent waves. If you don't surf, this stretch of coastline is still a beautiful area to explore. Updated: Oct 14, 2009.

particularly). The swankiest places are the beach resorts spreading north and south from San Juan del Sur, but, of course, there are also plenty of places to rest your head if your wallet isn't quite so expansive. Ask around before you settle on a place, as there are some charming treasures just off the beaten path (and they're usually less costly than those on the main drag). Updated: Oct 14, 2009.

RIVAS

70 m   30,295

Most tourists headed south from Managua or Granada to the Costa Rican border make a pit stop in Rivas. Many people also use it as a transfer point to the more popular beach locations of San Juan del Sur and Ometepe Island. Although few travelers stick around long enough to explore Rivas, the small city has a unique identity and history. It also serves as an important hub for market goods. Its location—on the Pan-American Highway, between Lake Cocibolca and the Pacific Ocean, just north of the Costa Rican border—contributes to its importance as a center of trade and commerce.

Rivas is also known for its abundance of mango trees, parakeets who feast on them, and rich, concentrated sunsets.

The city of Rivas was not officially recognized until 1835, though indigenous tribes inhabited it as early as 606 AD. William Walker attacked the town—and its neighbor, Granada—in the early 19th century. Rivas also shares the tumultuous history of Nicaragua, having gone through the same battles, wars, and leaders. A visit to the Museum of History and Anthropology, which contains several pre-Columbian artifacts and Nicaraguan paintings, provides insight into much of Rivas' cultural past. There are also two historic churches and an old library.

Rivas has all the basic essentials, including a large market, bus station, hospital, 24-hour gas station and small number of hostels, hotels and scattered restaurants. There are also Internet cafés, although you will be hard-pressed to find WiFi. The supermarket has a wide variety of food. Many tourists stop to take advantage of these features before heading to more remote locations. Updated: Oct 26, 2008.

When to Go

When visiting Rivas it is important to take into account the rainy season, which typically runs from May to October. Rivas receives less rain during this period than surrounding beach towns, and temperatures are more tolerable in the city.

Temperatures are hot during the dry season, but not unbearable. Rivas' low altitude can make it hotter and more humid than nearby Granada and Managua, but the neighboring lake sends the occasional breeze its way, offering a brief respite. The heat peaks during March and April.

If you do decide to endure the heat, try to pass through Rivas during the Semana de Dolores, which is the week before Semana Santa (Easter Week). Go see the annual Peregrinación de las Carreteras, when people come in carriages from all over Nicaragua to celebrate Jesús del Rescate (the image of Jesus in the Iglesia de San Francisco). Be sure to reserve a place to stay in advance of the week-long festivities. Updated: Oct 29, 2008.

Getting To and Away From Rivas

Located on the Pan-American highway, Rivas is easily accessible by car. If your eventual destination is a more remote beach location, renting your own transportation is highly

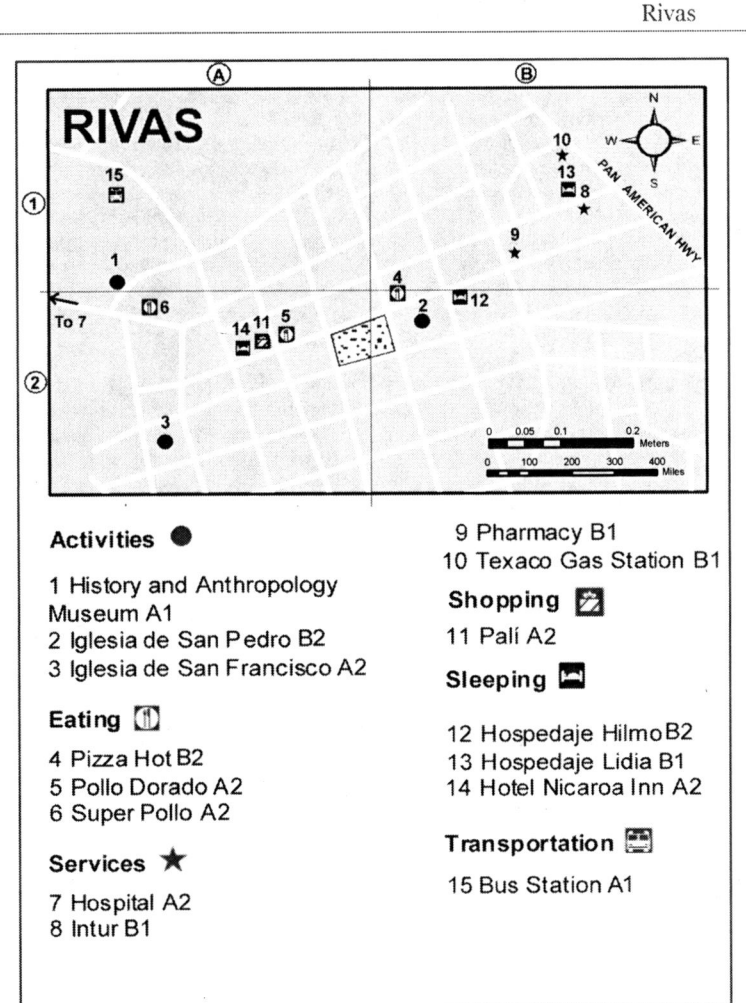

RIVAS

Activities ●
1 History and Anthropology Museum A1
2 Iglesia de San Pedro B2
3 Iglesia de San Francisco A2

Eating
4 Pizza Hot B2
5 Pollo Dorado A2
6 Super Pollo A2

Services ★
7 Hospital A2
8 Intur B1

9 Pharmacy B1
10 Texaco Gas Station B1

Shopping
11 Palí A2

Sleeping
12 Hospedaje Hilmo B2
13 Hospedaje Lidia B1
14 Hotel Nicaroa Inn A2

Transportation
15 Bus Station A1

recommended. There are a couple options: a regular car, which goes for $25 a day, and a van for up to 13 people ($60 a day). It's advisable to rent a 4X4 during the rainy season.

There are also several buses constantly coming through from Granada and Managua. They depart every 30 minutes, between 5 a.m. and 3 p.m., and cost about $2. Both trips take 1.5 to two hours. Nandaime is a common transfer point between Granada and Rivas. In Rivas, you can connect with buses to San Juan del Sur, San Jorge, Las Peñas Blancas and other bordering towns for an additional dollar. It is important to note that these buses are often very hot and crowded, and it is essential to tell the driver or his assistant your destination. Cabs are always waiting at the station to transport travelers to the Ometepe ferry and all other beach destinations for between $10-20. Updated: Nov 04, 2008.

Getting Around

Walking around Rivas, you will inevitably be confronted by several taxi drivers. Because it is a small city, most know where all the hostels, hotels and attractions are located. A taxi ride to anywhere in the city will generally cost about $0.50. There are very few buses within the city, and most run on irregular, unreliable schedules. Once in the central park, almost everything is within walking distance. There are also numerous bicycle carriages, which offer a more casual cruise through the city. Updated: Nov 07, 2008.

Learn how to become a travel writer at vivatravelguides.com/bootcamp/

Safety

Since Rivas is not a common tourist destination, visitors are very high-profile and can be easily targeted. As in many places in Nicaragua, walking around alone at night is not recommended, especially for women. During the day, the streets are crowded with people and relatively safe; just make sure to exercise caution, keep all valuables out of plain sight and be wary of pickpockets, especially in crowded areas. Updated: Nov 04, 2008.

Services

INTUR (8 a.m. – 1 p.m., Tel: 505-2-563 4914) has a tourist information office across from Hospedje Lidia, west of the main highway. There are a few banks with ATMs in town, mostly concentrated around the central park. The majority of restaurants take credit cards, but it is still advisable to withdraw money when you have the chance. Laundry services are hard to track down within Rivas, so make sure to check with your hotel or hostel if your clothes are getting a little funky. There are several clinics and pharmacies around the city that are open to foreigners, and the hospital on La Carretera Gaspar García la Vlana is open 24 hours. The main grocery store, **Pali**, is located a block west of the central park. The Texaco gas station is also open 24 hours and has a well-stocked convenience store. Updated: Jan 08, 2009.

Things to See and Do

Rivas is a bit thin on attractions, but there are enough things to do to keep you occupied for a day. Of the main attractions, there are two 18th-century churches: the Iglesia de San Pedro and the Iglesia de San Francisco. There is also a small museum of history and anthropology and a library that dates back to the early 17th century. Many war heroes and local townspeople are buried in the cemetery, which is several blocks south of the Iglesia de San Francisco. Updated: Jan 08, 2009.

Iglesia de San Francisco

The more popular of Rivas's two colonial churches, the Iglesia de San Francisco, is an elevated, beige, well-worn building. Built in 1776, the cathedral also has a large statue of a cross, erected on August 30, 1997 out front. Several steps lead up to the large archway that serves as the entrance. Unlike the Iglesia de San Pedro, the church is open all day. Four blocks west, one block south of the central park. Updated: Nov 07, 2008

Iglesia de San Pedro

Across the street from Rivas' Central Square, the Iglesia de San Pedro is a beautiful, pale blue building, decorated with small statues of religious figures. When mapping out your exploration, it is important to note that the church is only open early in the morning, from 6-8a.m., and in the evenings, from 5-7 p.m. It should take no longer than 15 minutes to look around inside, unless you decide to stay and experience mass, which is held at 6 p.m. Updated: Nov 07, 2008.

Museo de Antropología e Historia

(ADMISSION: $1.00) One block west and two blocks north of the Iglesia de San Francisco, is Rivas' very own History and Anthropology Museum. Make sure to look carefully for the museum; it is located inside on a hillside in an old Mediterranean-style farmhouse that used to be a plantation. Inside, there are three small, connected rooms. The first contains a collection of pre-Columbian pottery and artifacts. The second is filled with a compilation of taxidermy, reflecting the native wildlife. The third room contains various paintings. Very few of the displays have English captions. Open Monday through Friday 8 a.m. – 12 p.m. and 2 – 5 p.m., Saturdays 8 a.m. – 12 p.m. Closed Sundays. One block west and two blocks north of the Iglesia de San Francisco. Updated: Nov 07, 2008.

Lodging

The entrance to Rivas, along the Pan-American Highway, is lined with many hostels and hotels. There are few distinctions between them: most cost about $8 a night, are fairly clean, offer private rooms, and in some cases, private bathrooms. The establishments along the entrance to Rivas are a good choice if you are only using the town as a transfer point. However, if you do intend on exploring Rivas for a couple days, it may be worth your while to head past the Texaco and even up to the central park for something more conveniently located. Updated: Nov 20, 2008.

BUDGET

Hospedaje Lidia

(BEDS: $7.50) Located just around the corner from the local Texaco, and right off of the highway, Hospedaje Lidia is a popular place to stay in Rivas. Don't be surprised to find old women in rocking chairs watching telenovelas, or a family at the kitchen table, playing cards. Even if you don't speak the language, feel free to make yourself at home.

Hospedaje Lidia's mascot, who you might see running around the place, is a tiny white lapdog. There are clean bathrooms. A short taxi ride from all bus stops; drivers will know where it is. Updated: Jul 28, 2009.

Hospedaje Hilmor

(ROOMS: $6 – 20) A block from the central park and the Iglesia San Pedro, Hospedaje Hilmor is a good choice for those looking to explore Rivas' tourist attractions. Upon arrival, you may have to rattle the gate and yell to get the attention of the owner. Hospedaje Hilmor's rooms are spacious and all have private bathrooms. TVs are available in the $20 rooms. If you're looking to cut costs by cooking for yourself, the kitchen is also open to guests. Two blocks west of the Banpro. Cel: 505-8-830-8175. Updated: Nov 20, 2008.

MID-RANGE
Hotel Nicaroa Inn

(ROOMS: $45 – 55) This polished white, modern building with red lining is hard to miss. Hotel Nicaroa is a block from the park and is located halfway between Rivas' two famous churches. Amenities include private parking, Internet, hot water, laundry service, cable TV and air conditioning. The hotel has a well-appointed bar and restaurant downstairs. There are also catering services and business conference facilities. Forty-five dollars for a single room and $55 for a double is expensive for Rivas, but the hotel delivers good value for the money. One block west of the park. Tel: 505-2-563-3234/ 3836. URL: www.hotelnicaraoinn.com.ni. Updated: Aug 03, 2009.

Restaurants

There are not a lot of restaurants in Rivas, but most places have an adequate menu. Entrées mostly consist of pizza, chicken, pasta and seafood. Your selection may be limited by the language barrier, as you will be hard-pressed to find an English menu anywhere in town. Restaurants are spacious and relaxed, with outdoor seating available at most places. Meals generally range from $3-10. Fast food is available in the form of fried chicken or nachos. Street food (typical Nicaraguan fare, such as fritangas and gallo pinto) is available in the evenings. Updated: Jan 08, 2009.

Pizza Hot

(ENTREES: $3.25 – 7.50) Directly across the street from La Iglesia de San Pedro, Pizza Hot has a wide variety of slices, from classic pepperoni to Hawaiian. A personal pizza is about $3.25 and a pizza for four costs $7.50. There is also roasted chicken, hot wings, hamburgers and pasta. Indoor seating is available, or you can sit at the outdoor café, which is diagonal to the central park, and a good place to people watch. All credit cards are accepted and there is no minimum. Two blocks west of the park. Tel: 505-2-563-4662. Updated: Nov 06, 2008.

Pollo Dorado

(ENTREES: $3 – 11) With lots of space, several wooden tables and scattered aquatic paintings, Pollo Dorado tries to capture the atmosphere of the surrounding beach towns. The menu has a wide selection of soups, salads, sandwiches, seafood, pork, rice dishes and typical Nicaraguan food. True to its name, Pollo Dorado also offers many different portions and types of chicken. Prices range from $3 for a ¼ of a roasted chicken and fries to $11 for a Pollo Dorado Typico (a combo of almost everything on the menu). One block west of the park, across from Palí. Tel. 563-4148. Updated: Nov 06, 2008.

Super Pollo

(ENTREES: $3 – 11.50) Super Pollo is a nice place to stop for lunch or dinner after a day of exploring the town. The attractive, clean restaurant has brightly colored tablecloths covering its outdoor seating and a small, polished interior. The staff is friendly and there are several types of chicken and combination platters on the menu. A halfblock south and one block east of the History and Anthropology Museum. Tel: 505-2-563-0109. Updated: Nov 06, 2008.

TOLA

The first people to settle in Tola were the Toltecs, an indigenous Mexican tribe for whom the city is named. With the arrival of Francisco Hernandez in 1524, the town came under Spanish rule and the Toltecs were run out of the city until the rebellions of 1811, when they were able to reclaim their land.

If passing through Tola, you can check out the statue of *La Novia de Tola* (the Bride of Tola), who stands alone in the central square in front of the church. Legend has it that the bride was left waiting at the altar in 1876. Her groom never showed up, having run away with another woman.

Learn how to become a travel writer at vivatravelguides.com/bootcamp

Tola is not so much a tourist destination, but a crossroads to other locations. However, spending a couple hours to wander around town and stop in at a local restaurant, you can get to know small town Nicaraguan life. The economy in Tola is based on agriculture and cattle. It has a population of approximately 9,900 and an altitude of 38 meters (127 ft).

Getting To and Away From Tola

Only a 15-minute drive from Rivas, Tola can be reached by taxi for $10, and buses depart throughout the day. Updated: Dec 03, 2008.

Lodging

There are just a couple of accommodation options in Tola—one being in the house of a lady named Lourdes, who rents out her rooms for $7. To get to her house, head one block left of the Alcaldía and one block to the right, the house is on left hand side. It's best to call first (Tel: 505-2-563-6573).

Julisa's is a little hotel with simple accommodations and private bathrooms. It's the only actual hotel in Tola (Cel: 505-8-917-7394 or 505-8-933-4690; $7 a room). The hotel is located one block to the right, on the street before the church.

Restaurants

If you're thinking of grabbing some food in town, check out Bar La Ronda (two bocks left of the Alcaldía). Enjoy some chicken with rice for $3.50, while watching the little TV in the corner of the patio.

Another option is Bar Naranjito. There is a small inner courtyard where you can dine on rice, beans, salad and meat for $2.50. The bar is located on the left side of the central park. Updated: Dec 03, 2008.

PLAYA PIE DE GIGANTE

The golden cove of Playa Pie de Gigante, with calm spots for swimming, breaks for surfing and, further out, deep water fishing, has been cocooned from an influx of tourists by its location. The dirt track to the beach is passable most of the year (except in October when rains swamp the area), but a lack of public transportation makes the spot that locals call simply "Gigante" less accessible than the remote northern beaches of El Tránsito or Miramar.

Taxis charge at least $30 for the hour-long, one-way trip from Rivas; a bus between Rivas and Las Salinas (or Tola and Salinas) stops at the entrance to the beach road, but from there it's a hot four-kilometer (2.5 mi)walk to the shore. If you're on foot, you'll likely walk the whole way as pickups are few and far between at Gigante.

All of which is not to say that you shouldn't make the effort to reach the gorgeous strip of beach, but you might want to make reservations with one of the surf camps that line the shore. Dale Dagger Surf Tours (505-8-921-8694, dale@nicasurf.com, www.nicasurf.com) and Giant's Foot Surf Camp (505-8-924-7301, www.giantsfoot.com, giantsfoot@gmail.com, reservations@giantsfoot.com) both offer week-long packages ($1500 per person and $1299 per person, respectively) that include transfers to Managua's international airport, meals, accommodation and trips.

Dagger Surf is a bright and cheery house with the relaxed feel of a friend's beach pad; the shady Giant's Foot complex is equally chill, with porch swings made out of skateboards and an enormous library of beach novels. Despite the name, the surf camps have all the amenities: hot water, air conditioning and TVs. Dagger Surf also has WiFi and rents surfboards for $50 per week; packages from Giant's Foot include alcohol.

Between September 15th and March 15th, Giant's Foot operates as a hostel (the rest of the year is by reservation only) and rents double rooms with private bathrooms for $25 or dorm rooms for $10. The kitchen remains off-limits. Dagger Surf only rents rooms to walk-ins when there is space (in other words, call ahead).

Hotel Brio (505-8-433-9737, info@costanica.com, www.hotelbrio.com) is another solid option, set on a hill a short walk from the beach. The modern-style main building has a porch with a view and a bright restaurant/ bar. The rooms come either with ($35 per person) or without air conditioning ($30 per person) and the hotel offers Spanish lessons (as Escuela Bigfoot), surfing lessons and a long list of boat charters.

Restaurants

For such a remote location, Gigante has several surprisingly tasty restaurants right on the beach.

Get free stuff when you reserve your hotel at vivatravelguides.com/hotels/

Bar y Comedor La Gaviota
(ENTREES: $3 – 6) This little restaurant recently redid their ranchero-style roof and serves beef, pork, chicken and seafood for $3-6. In the spirit of diversification, the owners of La Gaviota also provide surfing trips ($15 per person), fishing trips ($15 per hour), surf board rentals ($5), and hope to rent five rooms with private bathrooms by December, 2009. Cel: 505-8-643-2844.

Restaurant de Gigante
(ENTREES: $7 – 18;) This spot along the crescent shore will satisfy your craving for gourmet international food. Run by Maria Esperanza and Keith Griffith (she's Nicaraguan, he's North American), the restaurant specializes in (surprise!) fresh seafood, but there is also grilled chicken, beef, pasta and vegetarian dishes on the menu. The restaurant has a pleasant, tiled patio and a policy of using hairnets and plastic gloves during food preparation. Cel: 505-8-828-4373/ 432-9740. E-mail: piedegigante@gmail.com. URL:www.piedegigante.net. Updated: Jun 09, 2009.

LAS SALINAS Y PLAYA GUASACATE

The Las Salinas economy relies on agriculture, fishing, cattle and tourism. The town has a population of approximately 3,568 people. Be advised that there are no banks in the area of Las Salinas, the closest being in Rivas. The nearest police station is in Tola, but rest assured that there is little crime in the area. Few places here accept credit cards, so make sure you have U.S. dollars or Cordobas.

Playa Guasacate, just a mile across the salt flats from the village of Las Salinas, may not be well known to most people, but with world-class waves and more than half a dozen breaks, it is a bona fide surfing destination. While the whole area is commonly referred to as Popoyo, that name actually refers to one specific beach, with an inner and outer reef break. Compared to popular surf spots in places like California, Playa Guasacate is still relatively uncrowded, but on the good days there are still 15-20 surfers in the lineup. Other surf beaches around here include: to the north, Astillero, and to the south, Playa Rancho Santana, Playa Rosada, Colorado and Panga Drops.

If you're looking for good waves, the best time to go is from May to September, when there are the most swells. However, this also happens to be during the rainy season, when driving the unpaved roads can be difficult. Avoid visiting in September and October, the wettest months of the year.

If surfing is not your thing or you're tired of the waves, there are some other ways to spend your time around town. Things to do include: visiting the hot springs (aguas termales), horseback riding, turtle watching, fishing and mountain biking. Larger hotels such as El Toro can provide information on activities and tour providers. Updated: Dec 02, 2008.

Getting to and Away From Las Salinas y Playa Guasacate

From Rivas, it costs about $50 to take a taxi to Las Salinas or to your hotel in the Popoyo area. Times vary throughout the year depending on the condition of the road, but the trip is usually 45 minutes to one hour. Additionally, buses depart from Rivas and Las Salinas throughout the day. Buses leave from Rivas at 9 a.m., 11 a.m., 12:45 p.m. 2:40 p.m. and 4 p.m., and the journey takes one and a half to two hours. Buses turn around and head back to Rivas after arriving at the last stop in Las Salinas. Updated: Dec 02, 2008.

Lodging
The typical options for beach accomodations seesaw from luxury resort to barebones backpacker lodge, with not much in the middle ground. Playa Guasacate is no exception. You can choose either expensive cottages on a bluff, complete with kitchens, or basic rooms with ocean views and shared bathrooms, where you can share a beer with surfers. Like them, most beach accomodations assume that most of your time will be spent out riding the waves and relaxing in the sand. Updated: Feb 09, 2009.

La Tica 2
(ROOMS: $6) The sister hotel of La Tica (located in Las Salinas village), La Tica 2 is a backpacker/surfer's hostel at the end of the road on Playa Guasacate. It's a two-story lodge that is always filled with

surfers and has a patio by the river where you can get some food or a beer. La Tica 2 has private rooms and shared bathrooms. It's a better value than La Bocana, across the street, but be prepared for some noisy nights. Once over the bridge in Las Salinas, take the first left when you get to a fork in the road. Cel: 505-8-456-2205. Updated: Dec 02, 2008.

La Bocana

(ROOMS: $6) Located right in front of the beach, La Bocana is a bare basics hostel that has views of the ocean from the balcony. Private rooms are available and come with shared washrooms. There is a restaurant on the main floor that serves meals which usually cost less than $5. Cel: 505-8-478-6706. Updated: Dec 02, 2008.

Las Tortugas

(ROOMS: $10) On the road to Playa Santana, you'll find this small, eight-room hotel with an outdoor patio restaurant. The restaurant has typical fried foods and cheap eats like hotdogs. Rooms are clean and simple with a private bathroom. The restaurant is closed mid-September to November. Before arriving in Las Salinas there will be a green sign on the right hand side that says "Las Tortugas". Turn left here and it is about 400 meters (1,312 ft) down the road. Cel: 505-8-478-9066. Updated: Dec 02, 2008.

El Toro

(ROOMS: $15 – 40) Set back from the road at Playa Guasacate, El Toro is a clean and comfortable hotel with a garden at the rear, and a pool. There are both shared and private rooms, all of which fill up quickly with surfers during the rainy season when the waves are optimal. The restaurant has good food and is stocked with local beer. Boat trips and other excursions can also be arranged. This hotel is one of the most expensive on this stretch of beach, but is of higher quality than most of the cheaper offerings. Cel: 505-8-885-3334 / 863-8882. URL: www.torosurfnicaragua.com. Updated: Dec 02, 2008.

Hotel Casa Maur

(ROOMS: $10 – 80) Hotel Casa Maur, located right in front of the Guasacaste beach, is a 10-minute walk to the waves at Popoyo. The hostel has a large, central common area with ping-pong table, TV, surfboard racks and dining table. Simple meals can be ordered from the kitchen. The hostel has four rooms with four beds in each, at $10 per person or $40 for a room. There is also a private upstairs room with air conditioning and a balcony with a gorgeous view of the ocean for $80. Cel: 505-8-887-3393 / 883-5057. Updated: Dec 02, 2008.

Two Brothers

(HOUSE: $100 – 225) Two Brothers occupies an ideal location, on the highest hill overlooking Guasacate, Popoyo and the surrounding farmland. There are creatively designed houses with colored glass pillars for rent, all with spectacular views. The homes vary in price according to size, but all have complete kitchens and outdoor barbeques. Families are welcome, and there is a swimming pool on the property. Boat excursions are available for an extra cost. There is a two -night minimum stay. After the bridge in Las Salinas continue along the road until you see a sign for the resort on your right hand side. There is a road leading up a hill to Two Brothers. Cel: 5055-8-877-7501, E-mail: info@twobrotherssurf.com, URL: www.twobrotherssurf.com. Updated: Dec 02, 2008.

The Surf Sanctuary

(ROOMS: $60) For the surfer seeking an all-inclusive package, the Surf Sanctuary provides accommodation, meals and transportation by truck or boat to the waves. The resort is comprised of cabañas, a swimming pool, a dining area, and a recreation room. All-inclusive package prices are available through the hotel's website, but they start at around $1,250 for a week. Additionally, you can stay at one of their cabañas for $60 a night, meals not included. Located on the road to Playa Santana, past the Hotel Las Tortugas. E-mail: info@thesurfsanctuary.com, URL: www.thesurfsanctuary.com. Updated: Dec 02, 2008.

Restaurants

Rana Roja

An Argentine-Italian couple own this pizza restaurant. Its thatched roof, bamboo walls and bar make for a modern, tropical atmosphere. The regular hours are 6–10 p.m., but it is closed for business mid-September to November when the flooded roads keep people away. Prices are more expensive than other restaurants nearby, but the authentic Italian pizza with fresh ingredients is well worth the cost. Playa Gausacate. Cel: 505-8-478-8893. Dec 02, 2008.

EL ASTILLERO

The next public beach north of Guasacate, El Astillero is still a fishing village set on a little bay. For surfing, there's a beach break that's surfable at low tide, but it is not the nicest beach for swimming as the waters are a little muddy. Vultures are a presence on the beach throughout the day, picking apart fish carcasses left by the fishermen. There is a boat launch on the southern end of the bay. Updated: Feb 08, 2009.

Hotel Casa Verde, Restaurante Bahia Paraiso

(ROOMS: $10) Hotel Casa Verde offers basic accommodations close to the sea. The rooms have cement walls, tin roofs and outdoor washrooms. The hotel can provide boats for surfing or fishing but be prepared to smell a lot of fish during your stay—fishermen's boats are located right outside the hotel. At least you'll have first pick of the catch of the day. The restaurant serves typical fried food and seafood at average prices. The hotel is located in front of the water. Cel: 505-8-407-1254. Updated: Dec 04, 2008.

Las Hamacas

(ROOMS: $25 – 50) Las Hamacas, a hotel right on the seashore, offers a better value than many other options in El Astillero. The hotel has nine rooms on a small grassy property; all rooms have private washrooms. Singles go for $25 and doubles for $30, and rooms with air conditioning are $10 more. There is also an apartment with a kitchen, a pricy but attractive option for those wishing to stay in El Astillero longer. There is no restaurant at the hotel, but several mini-supermarkets and restaurants are located nearby. The hotel can be contacted on Skype at the account: hotel.hamacas. Cel: 505-8-810-4144. E-mail: info@hostalhamacas.com. Updated: Oct 28, 2008.

Punta Teonoste

(ROOMS: $119 – 299) This resort has luxury two-story bungalows furnished with local wood and other materials. There is a turtle nesting sanctuary on the hotel's private beach and Punta Teonoste can arrange for you to help at the sanctuary or with other community projects. There is also a gym and spa on the property, as well as a variety of surfing opportunities and other activities. Punta Teonoste hotel and restaurant is the most pricy in the area, but it is a worthwhile splurge for those who appreciate natural elegance. Six kilometers (3.7 mi) towards El Astillero after the Las Salinas bridge. Tel: 505-2-563-9001, E-mail: info@puntateonoste.com, URL: www.puntateonoste.com. Updated: Dec 02, 2008.

SAN JORGE

San Jorge is where the popular ferry to Isla Ometepe docks and most visitors hurry by the center of town on their way to either the port or the beaches–with good reason. All of the best hotels and restaurants are ranged along the well trafficked ferry road. Sleepy during the rest of the year, San Jorge really gets going during Semana Santa when colorful umbrella stands cover the lakeside beach and locals settle in for a week-long party in the sun and surf. Should you visit during high season, you'll find that hotels have raised their prices (if there are any vacancies left at all), bathers choke the waterfront and the ferries are so full they seem to wallow.

Getting To and Away From San Jorge

There is a small bus ($0.50) that runs on an irregular schedule between Rivas and San Jorge, but the easiest way to get there is by taxi. Fares to the ferry start at $2, but can drop below a dollar if you're willing to share a cab. The trip back should cost $1, whether you share or not. Updated: Oct 14, 2009.

Safety

San Jorge's tiny city center is tranquil and sleepy. You shouldn't encounter any problems as you're walking around. Be more wary along the beachfront, which is where tourists (and the accompanying petty thieves) usually head first. Don't leave valuables unattended on the sand. Make sure you're clear on what you're paying for a taxi or you may find that the rate has doubled by the time you get out. Just before and during the very popular Semana Santa holiday is one of the worst times to visit beachfront locations as the celebration draws massive crowds and the bad elements that follow them in hopes of easy pickings. Updated: Oct 14, 2009.

Services
INTERNET
There is one Internet café in town, Cybercafé San Jorge, located 1.5 blocks north of the alcaldia. Cybercafé (505-2-563-4228) is open from 6 a.m. to 10 p.m. daily and charges around $0.60 per hour. Most of the area

San Jorge

hotels provide WiFi to their clients, with the only exception being Hotel and Restaurant Azteca. Updated: Oct 14, 2009.

Things to See and Do

On your way into San Jorge, you may notice a curious half arch above the road topped by a cross. This is La Cruz de España, supposedly the spot where Spanish and indigenous Nicaraguans first met in 1523. The leaders of that initial meeting, Spanish conquistador Gil González Dávila and Cacique Niqueragua are immortalized as colorful statues on either side of the road (with Dávila looking curiously like San Jorge).

If you decide to stop in San Jorge proper, you'll find a sleepy central park (most food kiosks don't open until 5 p.m.) with the alcaldia on one end and Nuestra Señor de Rescate on the other. Various images of St. George (said to have appeared on the shores of Lago Nicaragua) and his dragon appear throughout the church. In 2009, the church was in the process of having its roof retiled, which caused quite a racket among the resident parrots.

A short walk down the road from Nuestra Señor will bring you to Iglesia de las Mercedes, which likely dates from the 1500s and is said to be one of the oldest churches in Nicaragua. Las Mercedes certainly looks its age–other than a row of cracked bells, it's hard to tell from the outside that the rough wooden building is a church. Iglesia de las Mercedes is closed most of the time, but ask around and you can usually find a caretaker to let you inside to see the doll-like saints and carved altar pieces.

Lodging

Hotel Azteca

(DORMS: $5; ROOMS: $15 – 50) Located near the city center, the Azteca has eight rooms (singles $15 with fan/ $30 with air conditioning and breakfast; doubles $30/$50) and a huge pool. An extremely basic 24-bed dormitory is being renovated and should reopen by the end of the summer 2009. Azteca employees have a lackadaisical approach to guests, preferring to concentrate on the restaurant side of the business, and you might find yourself asking for a towel, soap or the TV remote. Should you decide not to stay, Azteca is still a nice spot for a quiet, poolside meal. Tel: 505-2-563-1088. Updated: Oct 14, 2009.

Hotel California

(ROOM $25 – 35) The California, down the road from Azteca but still a few blocks from the beach, has a strip of lush garden and a row of rooms. The hotel offers the full menu of services: cable TV, air conditioning, WiFi, hot water and wooden furniture. The rooms are a bit musty, but clean, and the California is a good choice if you want to escape swarms of beachside mayflies. The hotel accepts all credit cards. E-mail: myhotelcalifornia@yahoo.com. Updated: Oct 14, 2009.

Hotel Hamacas

(ROOM: $25 – 50) This extremely pleasant hotel, located near the ferry dock, is chock full of antique accents and strung with a rainbow of hammocks. There is a pool and some of the rooms have air conditioning and stocked mini-fridges. The hotel, like all the others near the water, can attract sayule flies, though the critters are very short-lived and totally harmless. Located a half-block up from the waterfront. Tel: 505-2-563-1709/ 0048/ 8-839-9735. Updated: Oct 14, 2009.

Hotel Dalinky

(ROOMS: $25 – 35) Hotel Dalinky, also located near the ferry dock, has slightly larger rooms with wardrobes and rocking chairs. The Dalinky also tends to get swarmed by sayule flies. Tel: 505-2-563-4990/ 8-912-1205. E-mail: dalinkybeach@yahoo.es, URL: www.ometepegatewayhotel.com. Updated: Oct 14, 2009.

Restaurants

Restaurants along the beach also have trouble keeping their open patios sayule-free. Try to choose a table slightly inside and not directly under a light. Bar y Restaurant El Nuevo Oasis (505-2-563-0789) has all the Nicaraguan favorites (beef, pork, chicken and seafood) for between $7.50 and $10, plus vegetable and chicken salads. Restaurant El Refugio (505-2-563-4631/ 8-851-0267) has savory skewers, among other options.

ISLA DE OMETEPE

Travel on the highway running along the western shore of Lake Nicaragua and you'll inevitably spot the majestic twin peaks of the island emerging from the slate-blue waters. This is Ometepe, composed of two volcanoes: Concepción (1,610 m / 5,282 ft), a perfect

Get free stuff when you reserve your hotel at vivatravelguides.com/hotels/

ISLA OMETEPE

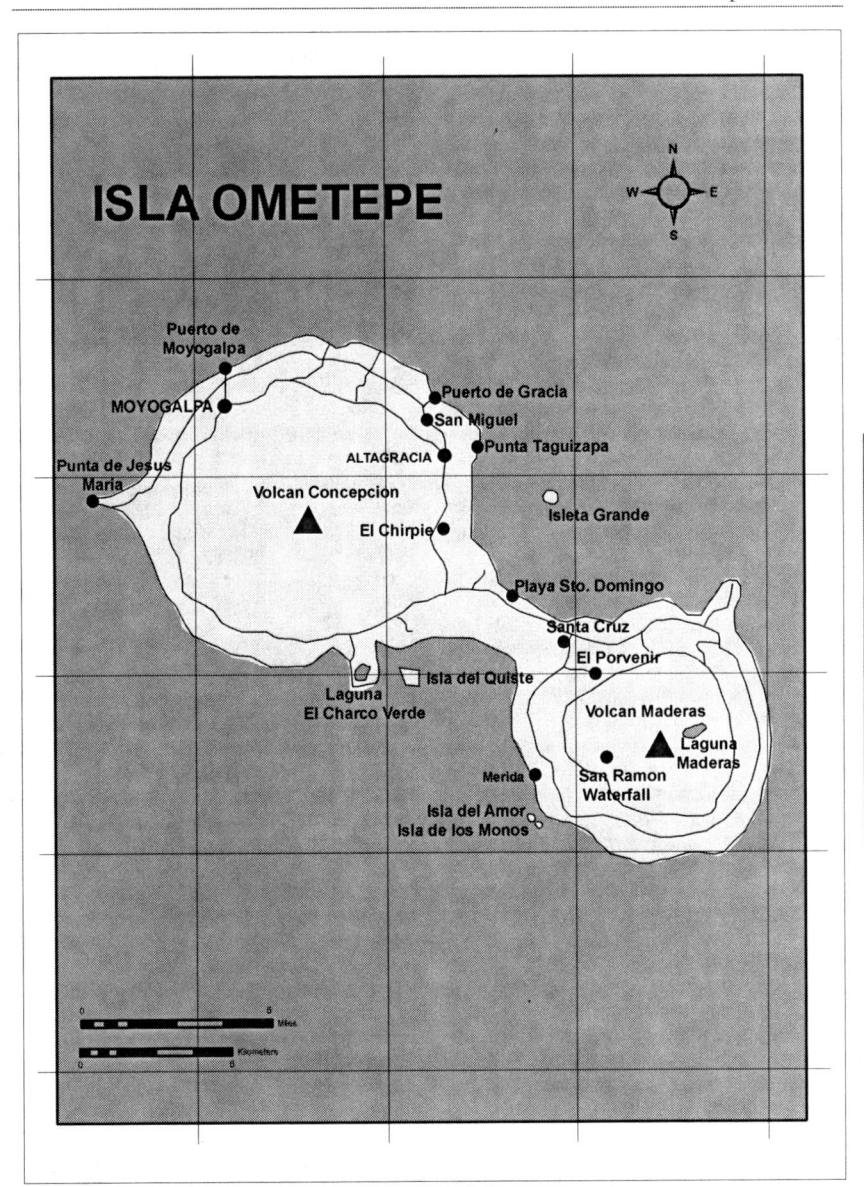

[Map of Isla Ometepe showing locations including Puerto de Moyogalpa, Moyogalpa, Punta de Jesús María, Altagracia, Volcan Concepción, El Chirpie, Puerto de Gracia, San Miguel, Punta Taguizapa, Isleta Grande, Playa Sto. Domingo, Santa Cruz, El Porvenir, Laguna El Charco Verde, Isla del Quiste, Volcan Maderas, Laguna Maderas, Merida, San Ramon Waterfall, Isla del Amor, Isla de los Monos]

cone, which often has a plume of smoke wafting from its mouth, and Maderas (1,394 m /4,573 ft). Maderas is the calm, lake-filled partner to Concepción, whose increased activity forced Ometepe to be evacuated in 2000. As this book was going to press in March, 2010, Concepción was again becoming active, spitting out gasses and ash. Travelers to Ometepe are urged to ask about the safety situation before heading to the island. Updated: March 15, 2010.

History

Unquestionably one of Nicaragua's natural wonders, the double volcano-island of Ometepe offers visitors a wealth of spectacular natural beauty. It's a place that evokes a sense of wonder and magic, and has been mythologized from time immemorial.

The evidence is scant, but experts believe that Ometepe's first inhabitants were native Nahuas who migrated from Mexico around

4,000 years ago. The area has rich volcanic soil that allowed the settlers to thrive since the land can support continuous planting without the need to let fields lie fallow. Successive waves of migration left Ometepe with a diverse archaeological record, best exemplified by the numerous petroglyphs found around the island. The twin volcanoes featured heavily in pre-Columbian mythology, and were a place of great spiritual importante for the region's early inhabitants.

The Spanish annexed the island around the end of the 16th century, but its inhabitants had more contact with the Dutch, English and French privateers who used Ometepe as a base for their attacks. The island's isolation meant that it was spared from most of Nicaragua's 20th-century upheavals, though locals experienced periodic scares from the rumbling Volcán Concepción.

Today the island supports a population of around 35,000. Many people still live off the land, though tourism is playing an increasingly important role in the local economy. Geographically, the island has an hourglass shape, with a low isthmus connecting the two volcanoes. Volcán Concepción, the taller of the two, is one of the most perfectly shaped cones in Central America. First appearing during the Holocene Epoch, Concepción lay dormant for a long period before literally exploding back to life in 1880. The volcano remains active and, although you can hire guides to take you up the sides, Concepción is far too dangerous to summit.

Concepción's sister, Volcán Maderas, is dormant and has a gorgeous lagoon within its crater. The area around this volcano is home to several farms that cultivate coffee and tobacco on the volcanic soil. Many of the farms also serve as hotels: Finca Magdalena and Hacienda Merinda are the most popular.

Ometepe offers an amazing range of activities, like biking, kayaking and hikes up the volcanoes. If you just want to relax, the beaches of Playa Santo Domingo are a perfect place to work on your tan. Either way, Isla Ometepe is one of Nicaragua's premiere attractions. Don't miss it. Updated: Jun 11, 2009.

When To Go

Ometepe puts on a pretty good show for Nicaragua's Independence Day on September 15th, but the best festivals to catch occur when the towns celebrate their patron saints. In Altagracia, stop by from November 12-17 to see the festival celebrated in honor of San Diego de Alcala. Expect bull runs and fights, sompopo dancing, and a heck of a lot of drinking. Check to see if your trip intersects with any of the local festivals around the island. They're worth checking out. Updated: Jul 11, 2008.

Getting To and Away From Isla de Ometepe

The easiest way to get to Ometepe is to catch a boat from San Jorge, a small town just outside of Rivas. The journey takes about an hour, and there are ferry departures at 7:45 a.m., 10:30 a.m., 2:30 p.m. and 5:30 p.m. Ferries return to the mainland from Moyogalpa at 6 a.m., 9 a.m., 12:30 p.m. and 4:30 p.m. The trip should cost $1.60.

There are also smaller boats that ply the same route, with far more frequent departures. These leave from the same spot, and cost $2.10 per person. Be warned; however, that the trip can be a rough one. If you're prone to seasickness, you're better off sticking with the larger, more stable ferries.

There is also a ferry that leaves Granada for Altagracia on Monday and Thursday afternoons. The trip takes around three hours and is notoriously unsteady. If you really love boats, you can hop on at Altagracia for the 14-hour trip to San Carlos, near the Costa Rican border. You'll be much more comfortable if you bring a hammock, as well as some seasickness pills. It's not a fun trip, and it's not recommended unless you want to head up the river into the Rio San Juan region and Nicaragua's rugged Southeast. If you're planning on crossing the border directly into Costa Rica it's advisable to do it by bus instead–it will be cheaper, faster and a damn bit more comfortable. Crossing into Costa Rica from San Carlos requires waiting around for a boat (just what you need after 14 hours on a boat) and then probably spending the rest of the day waiting for a bus down to San Jose. Updated: Jul 11, 2008.

Getting Around

The paved road on Ometepe only extends between Altagracia, Moyagalpa, Playa Santo Domingo and Merida. If you're biking or driving, other roads can degenerate fast. The worst roads on the island are probably those on the north side of Volcán Concepción.

Buses leave Moyogalpa for Altagracia from a station by the docks about every hour between 5:30 a.m. and 7 p.m. From there, some continue on to other destinations via Playa Santo Domingo. A bus to Merida leaves at 2:30 p.m. and 4:30 p.m. There's a bus to Bague at 10:30 a.m. and 3:30 p.m. There's also a bus that goes all the way to the San Ramon waterfalls at 8:30 a.m. and takes about three hours.

Schedules can change, and buses are frequently canceled or delayed, so don't take this timetable as gospel. Double-check before you risk missing your ferry. Updated: Jul 11, 2008.

Safety

Ometepe's generally a safe island as far as crime is concerned. The main thing to remember in terms of safety is not to attempt to climb either volcano by yourself—several tourists have died because they didn't think they needed a guide. There are also a few species of poisonous snakes, as well as scorpions, so proper shoes are important if you plan on heading into the bush. Updated: Jul 11, 2008.

Moyogalpa

As the main port of call on the island, Moyogalpa has grown into a prosperous town with a range of tourist-friendly services, hotels and restaurants. Altagracia may be closer to Volcán Concepción, but Moyogalpa is where you'll find a handful of tour operators competing to offer you experienced, bilingual guides. Moyogalpa, with a solid range of hotels, is a good place to stop for a night, catch your breath and plan out the rest of your Ometepe visit. While you're doing that, you might want to stop in quaint Parroquia Santa Ana, the bright yellow church at the end of Main Street, or Sala Arqueológica Ometepe, a combination of a souvenir store, museum and cyber café. Updated: Jun 10, 2008.

Altagracia

Altagracia is both the second largest town and second largest port on Ometepe–it has fallen behind Moyagalpa in prominence, though it was the island's former indigenous capital. The ferry from Granada usually stops by on Mondays and Thursdays (although the Monday service was briefly discontinued in the Spring of 2009), carrying passengers who chose three hours on the water over the shorter ferry ride from San Jorge to Moyogalpa. At Altagracia, you can also catch a ferry to San Carlos (a 14-hour trip) or arrange hikes to Volcán Concepción through one of the area hotels.

Altagracia is a sleepy little town with a quiet central square (where you can buy snacks during the day and fritanga in the evening) and a smattering of mid-range hotels. Set a few kilometers inland, Altagracia does not have ready access to beaches that you would find at Playa Santo Domingo, or the quality of services available in Moyogalpa. Altagracia only really gets going during Fiestas Patronales from November 12 – 17. The town celebrates San Diego de Alcala with bull fights, sompopo dancing, and a hell of a lot of drinking. During the rest of the year, Altagracia is the place where most vistors spend a day or night before moving on to hotels along the beach or closer to the volcanoes. Updated: Jun 10, 2008.

Playa Santo Domingo

Most would say that this little strip of land between Ometepe's two volcanoes is the island's best beach. It certainly is the most developed. This is where you'll find the swankiest resort hotels, as well as the only beach umbrellas and volleyball nets to be found on the island. The strip of hotels is accompanied by a few tour operators and several horse-rental shops. Updated: Jul 14, 2008.

Merida

Located on the slopes of Volcán Maderas, this community contains Ometepe's most rural and idyllic hotels. Don't expect

Learn how to become a travel writer at vivatravelguides.com/bootcamp/

conveniences—the town itself is basically non-existent. But if you're looking for quiet, peaceful isolation, this is the place for you. Updated: Jul 14, 2008.

Services

If you're staying in Moyogalpa, you'll find Internet cafés aplenty. Altagracia also has one or two. As for everywhere else on the island, you have to either connect through your hotel or learn to live without. The Moyogalpa post office is located four blocks up from the dock and a half block to the left. There's only one bank on the island, on Moyogalpa's main street. It has a Western Union and an ATM, but it's only compatible with Visa/Plus, so plan accordingly. A few places on the island take credit cards, but they pass on a whopping 10 percent service charge.

The main hospital is in Moyogalpa, four blocks up from dock and 3.5 blocks to the right. Updated: Jul 14, 2008.

Things to See and Do

Most of Ometepe's activities revolve around the area's stunning natural beauty and ecological diversity. Don't miss Charco Verde, Ojo de Agua or one of the many organized treks up the volcanoes. Some people come to Ometepe just to relax, and the island has some great beaches. Playa Santo Domingo is a prime spot with a row of hotels and restaurants. There's enough here to occupy any traveler for several days. Updated: Jun 11, 2009.

MOYOGALPA
Sala Arqueológica Ometepe

This private, family-run museum holds more than 300 pre-Columbian artifacts. The collection includes funeral urns, giant stone water filters, jewelry and a few Spanish pieces. All of the pottery, stone work and statues were unearthed on the island. The items are not well labeled, but if you understand Spanish, ask for a guided tour when you pay the small entry fee. 8 a.m. - 9 p.m. Tel: 505-2-569-4225. E-mail: susita44@hotmail.com, ligiamariagg@hotmail.com. Updated: Jun 10, 2009.

Punto Jesus María

This lookout near Moyogalpa extends to the island's west and is known as the best place on Ometepe to watch the sunset. The beach isn't spectacular, but it's the most convenient place to swim if you're staying in Moyogalpa. It's located less than 10 minutes by bus, or about 20 minutes by bicycle, from Moyogalpa. Updated: Jul 14, 2008.

ALTAGRACIA
Museo Ometepe

This small, three-room museum houses a collection of petroglyphs and ancient ceramic pots excavated on Ometepe. It's not

Photo by prizz22

Get free stuff when you reserve your hotel at vivatravelguides.com/hotels/

Isla de Ometepe

particularly stunning (how impressive can a museum in Altagracia be?), but worth a look around if you're interested in history. Monday – Saturday 8 a.m. – 12 p.m. and 1– 5 p.m., Sunday 8 a.m. – 12 p.m. One block west of the park. Updated: Jul 14, 2008.

Altragracia Beaches

The most popular beach near Altagracia is called Punta Taguizapa, and it's located just to the east of the city. If you head north towards the ferry about two kilometers (1.2 mi) out of town you'll pass a billboard with a large and conspicuous Canadian flag. After saluting proudly, follow the little path down to Playa San Miguel. It's not as picturesque as some of the other swimming spots on the island, but we can nearly guarantee you'll have this brown-sand beach to yourself. Updated: Jul 14, 2008.

PLAYA SANTO DOMINGO
Ojo del Agua Thermal Spring

(ADMISSION: $1.10) Just up from the beach on the road to Altagracia you'll see signs for this place. The Eye of the Water, as its name translates to, is confusingly described as a cold-water thermal spring. The point is, it's natural, mineral-rich water. Bathing here is supposed to be very good for your skin. The setting feels a little artificial, with concrete walls surrounding the pool, but it's still a pretty place and well worth the entrance fee. Playa Santo Domingo. Updated: Jul 14, 2008.

ELSEWHERE ON OMETEPE
Charco Verde National Park

(ADMISSION: $0.55) Charco Verde is considered one of the island's greatest treasures. Hike through the area and you're likely to see howler monkeys, egrets, ducks, owls and freshwater turtles. It's also the best place on the island to kayak. It is worthwhile to go with a guide. Located south of Volcán Concepción. Updated: Jul 22, 2008.

Isla de Quiste

The tiny, forested Isla de Quiste is a sacred place for locals, since it was on this uninhabited dot of land (the name means "cyst") that the famous chief Nicarao chose to rest forever (although you'll find his ornate tomb on the Ometepe mainland). Most tourists visit the island, on the south side of Ometepe, to see the wealth of birds that nest there. You can rent a kayak from Hotel Charco Verde or even swim there—but watch out for those freshwater sharks! Updated: Oct 14, 2009.

Museo Numismatico (El Ceibo)

This is one of Ometepe's newest museums, and it is rapidly expanding. The Museo Numismatico traces the history and evolution of money in the Americas, charting the transition from the earliest use of cocoa beans as currency to modern coinage. It's an interesting place to spend an hour or two. Located along the road from Altagracia to Moyogalpa in Charco Verde. Open 8 a.m. – 12 p.m., 1 – 5 p.m. Cel: 505-8-874-8076. Updated: Jul 14, 2008.

Petroglyphs

These ancient petroglyphs are some of Ometepe's most famous attractions. The earliest of the stone carvings date back over 4,000 years—some of the oldest art you can find in the Americas. They're scattered all over the island, but some of the best concentrations are found on Magdalena Farms and El Porvenir, both of which are on the north side of Volcán Maderas. Updated: Jul 14, 2008.

San Ramón Waterfall

The San Ramón Waterfall is a spectacular natural wonder, and one of the highlights of a trip to Ometepe. The waterfall is located about four kilometers (2.4 mi) from the village of San Ramon, on the southwestern slope of Volcán Maderas. The hike is a spectacular one, and the path that leads to the waterfalls is also one of the most popular trails for ascending the volcano, so combining the two makes a great all-day trip. Check local tour operators for the path's status and the possibility of a guided tour of them both. Located on the southern tip of the island (see Getting Around p.159 for more info). Updated: Jul 14, 2008.

Volcán Concepción

At a towering 1,610 meters (5,282 ft), Volcán Concepción is the taller of Ometepe's twin volcanoes. It's also highly active, making it the more dangerous of the two. In fact, going all the way to the top is impossible, due to the plumes of poisonous gas that emanate from its cone. But since the peak is nearly always shrouded with clouds, you're not missing much anyway. Most tours will only take you up to 1,200 meters (3,937 ft), where cloud cover usually starts.

The hike up and down is a difficult, six-hour trek. You should only attempt it if you're in good physical condition. One of the toughest parts about ascending a volcano is that there are no breaks. Unlike most hikes that have ups and downs, climbing either of Ometepe's volcanoes is a nonstop, uphill slog. Expect to be drenched by the end of it, regardless of whether or not it rains.

That said, you are better off attempting the climb during the dry season (December – May). The rain makes the way up slippery and more difficult. Expect to be hiking through plantain and banana plantations for the first part of the hike. If you're lucky, you can spot monkeys, parrots and a large, squirrel-like animal called a paca. Around halfway up, the trees will thin out and you'll get a glimpse of the fantastic view. Be sure to bring good shoes (there are poisonous snakes slithering around), repellent and two liters of water. All this should be explained to you by your guide—it's extremely dangerous (not to mention illegal) to ascend without one. Updated: Jul 14, 2008.

Volcán Maderas Climb

Volcán Maderas is Ometepe's junior volcano. rising up just 1394 meters (4,574 ft), but can offer climbs that are just as challenging as Volcán Concepción. Since Maderas is dormant, most visitors head for the summit.

A guide is absolutely essential in order to scale Madera. The climb is steep and difficult, and you need someone familiar in the area and versed in first aid in the event of an accident. When you hike, remember to wear proper shoes and bring insect repellent, plenty of water and a snack for the summit. The guided hikes take eight to 10 hours; most groups leave early in the morning to escape the worst of the tropical heat.

A hike into the crater will give you a glimpse of the magical Laguna de Volcán Maderas (you'll have to hike in to see the lake, since there are few views from the trail.) The lagoon's shores are thick with mud and you may find yourself wading for a short distance befote you can swim in the clear waters. Once inside the crater, you may be able to spot monkeys, snakes and several species of birds. Some locals claim that the area is also inhabited by fairies and supernatural spirits. This trip can be organized at Hacienda Merida. Updated: Jun 11, 2009.

Circumnavigate Maderas

One fun day trip is to circumnavigate Volcán Maderas. The path around is rough, but it can be traveled easily by motorcycle, bicycle or even a low-clearance vehicle. If you've got a lot of energy you can try and hike it, but expect to be gone all day (it's about four to five hours by bike). Along the way you'll pass gorgeous beaches, as well as lots of small farming villages. This is a great way to get a feel for what life on the island is like for the locals. The worst part of the road extends from the top of the island to Bague, and you may be asked to pay a maintenance toll as you go. Updated: Jul 14, 2008.

Motorbiking

Motorbikes can be rented from most hotels, and they are an excellent way to explore the island. Early risers can cover nearly all of Ometepe's top attractions in a day. Be warned though that some of Ometepe's roads are ghastly, and pavement can turn into a muddy quagmire very quickly. The roads between Moyogalpa and Altagracia, and down through Playa Santo Domingo and Merida are all quite good, especially if you're planning a daytrip. Rentals cost between $25 and $35 a day. Updated: Jul 14, 2008.

Kayaking

One of Ometepe's most popular activities is kayaking, particularly around the area of Charco Verde. Isla el Quiste, located just offshore, is one excellent destination. It will take you about 30 minutes to kayak there, where you can enjoy beautiful beaches and look for birds and monkeys. Another great trip is down to Rio Istiam, one of the island's top bird watching sites. Expect to pay around $5.30 per hour for a kayak. Guided tours are also available; while they're not necessary if you're an experienced kayaker, a guide will be able to spot many birds and animals you'd probably miss. Updated: Jul 14, 2008.

Horseback Riding

Horseback riding is a wonderful pastime on the island. You can rent horses for between $5-7 an hour, which should come with a guide. Where you go depends on the area you rent from. The beaches around Santo Domingo are one nice place to ride. Updated: Jul 14, 2008.

Biking

Ometepe is quite a big island, and it's unreasonable to expect to conquer the whole thing by bike. It's also important to remember that many of Ometepe's roads are brutally rough. That said, the island still has some attractive opportunities for cyclists. The trip between Moyogalpa and

Get free stuff when you reserve your hotel at vivatravelguides.com/hotels/

Charco Verde is paved, and only around 15 kilometers (9.3 mi) long. This area can be easily explored by bicycle, provided you've got a lot of energy. Bikes can be rented for a few dollars a day from all tour operators and most hotels.

One particularly rewarding bike trip is to go see the petroglyphs. The ride begins hilly but becomes flat and takes around 45 minutes to reach an isolated house, where there is a sign to the petroglyphs. There are two sites with ancient carvings on boulders, but the real treat is the unique Gator figure statue on the beach. Unfortunately this is only visible in April, otherwise it is underwater and the petroglyphs are not hugely worthwhile. The trip should be organized through Hacienda Merida. Updated: Jul 14, 2008.

Isla de Ometepe Tours

Ometepe has several excellent independent tour operators, but nearly all are located in Moyogalpa. However, most of the island's hotels either feature their own tour agency, or are affiliated with one, so you shouldn't have difficulty arranging a tour wherever you are. It's absolutely essential to have a guide if you plan on ascending either volcano. Updated: Jul 14, 2008.

MOYOGALPA
Exploring Ometepe

An excellent tour center and good information resource. They're particularly well-known for their volcano guides and offer bilingual service. Just up from the ferry. Cel: 505-8-895-5521. E-mail: exploringometepe@hotmail.com. Updated: Jul 14, 2008.

Servicios Turisticos Ibesa

One of the first agencies you'll see as you get off the ferry, Ibesa offers the usual range of island and volcano tours, as well as motorcycle and bicycle rentals. They also post bus schedules and have general tourist information. Open 9 a.m. – 5 p.m. Located on the main street just up from the dock. E-mail: ibesatourservice@yahoo.es. Updated: Jul 14, 2008.

Safari Ometepe

This is an outstanding resource, and a great place to book trips. Robinson speaks excellent English and is a fountain of information about the island. There are a full-range of services including volcano guides, motorcycle and scooter rental, and other island trips. Open from 8 a.m. to 12 p.m. and from 1 p.m. to 5 p.m. Moyogalpa, just across from the dock. Updated: Jul 14, 2008.

> **VIVA ONLINE REVIEW**
> SAFARI OMETEPE
>
> "The service indeed was very good... The thing that makes this place special compared to other shops renting motorcycles is that these guys actually take care of their bikes."
>
> -Holland, May 2009

ALTAGRACIA
Hotel Kencho

This hotel offers tours, motorbike rentals and horseback riding, but you may have to shout a bit to get service. This, along with Hotel Central and Hotal Posada Cabrera, are the only places to arrange tours in Altagracia. Half a block south of Parque Central. Updated: Jul 14, 2008.

PLAYA SANTO DOMINGO
Sendero Pena Incult

You'll see this little tourist information stand by the side of the road on the way from Altagracia down to Playa Santa

Learn how to become a travel writer at vivatravelguides.com/bootcamp

Domingo. Although their "information" on other subjects is quite limited, they do offer sound birdwatching tours. With a guide, the cost is $7 per person. Expect to observe many of the island's 63 species of birds, including the gorgeous Yellow-naped amazon. Located at Playa Santa Domingo, just north of the hotels. Updated: Jul 14, 2008.

ELSEWHERE ON OMETEPE
El Tesoro del Pirata

El Tesoro del Pirata is a pirate-themed guesthouse, restaurant and tour operator that's a good place to rent kayaks and canoes. The cost is $3 per hour, or $10 for the day. Guides can be provided for those who want to try their luck at sailing. Fishing trips are also offered. The building is located just before Charco Verde on the road from Moyogalpa to Altagracia. Updated: Jul 14, 2008.

Lodging

Looking through the entries for Ometepe, one cannot help but notice there seem to be an awful lot of rather tepid hotel reviews. Indeed, there are a lot of dodgy places in the budget category. And when it comes to midrange and high-end accommodation, the adage that "you get what you pay for" simply does not apply. Read through this section carefully before you make your choice. Updated: Feb 19, 2009.

MOYOGALPA
Hospedaje Sinai

(ROOMS: $3) The Hospedaje Sinai is the cheapest place in town to get a single room. Unfortunately, in this case you do get what you pay for. Chickens live in the courtyard, and the place has no amenities to speak of. Shared toilets lack toilet seats. Located on the island's main highway, just south of Moyogalpa's main street. Tel: 505-2-569-4215. Updated: Jul 22, 2008.

Hostel Ibesa

(ROOMS: $3 – 4) At only $4, these are some of the cheapest private rooms to be found in town, but we would hesitate to recommend Hostel Ibesa. The walls don't touch the ceiling here, meaning you're basically sleeping outside. Expect to have plenty of six-legged company at night, especially if you keep the light on after dark. Two blocks east and one block south of the port. Tel: 505-2-614-1499. E-mail: hostelibesa@yahoo.es. Updated: Jul 14, 2008.

Hospedaje Central

(ROOMS: $2 – 15) What's not to love about a hostel that has a pet deer? Minta, as the fawn is known, can be seen strolling imperially about the grounds and has developed a taste for pizza. At Moyogalpa's "backpacker hostel," the dormitories are dark and abysmal, but the private rooms are quite nice. The bar is popular on weekends, and their restaurant has received good reviews as well. Three blocks east and one block south of the port. Cel: 505-8-459-4262, E-mail: Ometepehc@yahoo.com, URL: www.freewebs.com/ometepe. Updated: Nov 25, 2009.

Hotelito Aly

(ROOM: $6) If you wanted to put a positive spin on this place, you'd call it rustic. Or, you could just be honest and say it's run-down. Rooms are open to the outside, and the whole place has a dark and depressing vibe (though the bathrooms are surprisingly clean). The service was also rather curt. One hundred and thirty-seven meters (450 ft) east of the port. Tel: 505-2-569-4196. E-mail: hotelitoaly@yahoo.com. Updated: Nov 25, 2009.

Arenas Negras

(ROOM: $7.50 – 12) This hotel is a clean, comfortable, reasonably priced place to stay. The extra few bucks buy you a room with a TV. The building also features a restaurant. Located just up from the dock. Cel: 505-8-634-6719. Updated: Nov 25, 2009.

Flor de Angel

(ROOMS: $10+) Rooms here are basically the same as those in Arenas Negras, but at a higher price. There's a disco under construction in front of the reception, so it may not be the quietest place in town once that's completed. Also, it will remain a complete mystery why the bathroom light fixture was tinted a deep, emerald green. Well – it certainly gives the toilet an ambiance. Rooms start at $10, but the price goes up with more people. Cel: 505-8-853-8953. Updated: Jul 18, 2008.

Hotel Escuela Teosintal

(ROOMS: $10 – 24) This hotel has very clean, pleasant rooms coming off of a lovely backyard garden. It's quite a nice place to stay all-around. Rooms are fairly standard. The hotel features a common room with a TV and a cafeteria, as well as a tour agency. 75

Get free stuff when you reserve your hotel at vivatravelguides.com/hotels/

Isla de Ometepe

meters north of Enitel. Tel: 505-2-569-4105. Updated: Nov 25, 2009.

Casa Familiar
(ROOMS: $10 – 25) The corridors of this place are dark and dank, but rooms are clean...extremely clean. But despite the management's enthusiasm for sanitation, you can't help but question how they justify charging $10 for the same standard, fan-rooms that are found across town for half the price. Two blocks east of the port. Tel: 505-2-569-4240. Updated: Nov 25, 2008.

Hotel Ometepetl
(ROOMS: $15 – 25) Once billed as Moyogalpa's finest hotel, the glory has faded and now only the high prices remain. The staff makes an effort, but they can't make up for the fact that the windows don't close and the pool has run dry. The ambiance is still pleasant; however, helped by the hotel's hammocks and a quiet courtyard. On the main street, just up from the port. Tel: 505-2-569-4276. E-mail: ometepetlng@hotmail.com. Updated: Nov 25, 2009.

The American Hotel
(ROOMS: $15 – 30) Newly opened, The American now wears the crown for the nicest hotel in Moyogalpa. Rooms are spotless and well-furnished, with an appealing atmosphere. The whole place shines with freshness. The hotel features hot water, screened rooms, and stored water—making the place immune to Ometepe's periodic shortages. The place is scheduled to have air conditioning by the end of 2008. Run by an elderly American couple, the hotel will particularly appeal to that demographic. Just up from the dock. Cel: 505-8-645-7193. Updated: May 12, 2009.

ALTAGRACIA
Hotel Posada Cabrera
(ROOMS: $4+) This is an old hotel, but a well-kept one and a pleasant enough place for the price. Staff are friendly and washrooms are clean. It's conspicuously family run–there are kids all over the place. Located across from the park, on the south side. Cel: 505-8-664-2788, E-mail: Anamariacabrera@yahoo.com / info@posadacabrera.com, URL: www.posadacabrera.com. Updated: Nov 25, 2009.

Hotel Central
(ROOMS: $7.50 – 30) This is one of the top choices for accommodations in Altagracia. The $4 rooms are a bit grimy, but $6 buys you an excellent place: spotlessly clean and with a pleasant little balcony outside. For $16, you can rent your own *cabañita*. The hotel also offers island and volcano tours, as well as horseback riding. Major credit cards accepted. Two blocks south of the park. Cel: 505-8-552-8770. Updated: Jul 22, 2008.

Hotel Castillo
(ROOMS: $7.50 – 30) This place is quite friendly and well-kept, although the rooms at Hotel Central are significantly nicer. The Hotel Castillo is; however, one of the only places on the island where credit cards are accepted. Altagracia. Cel: 505-8-552-8744. Updated: Jun 10, 2009.

PLAYA SANTO DOMINGO
Hospedaje Buena Vista
(ROOMS: $10 – 12) This is the budget option on Playa Santo Domingo. There is an even cheaper place next door, but it is not recommended. Rates are per person, so if you're a couple it's a great deal. Rooms are a bit faded and not as flashy as the pricier places in the area, but reliable and clean, and the staff is friendly. An excellent choice if you're looking to stay on the beach for a reasonable price. No reservations accepted. Updated: Jul 22, 2008.

Hotel Finca Santo Domingo
(ROOMS: $23 – 35) Rooms here are breezy and offer a lovely view out on the lake, although the building itself isn't as new or as attractive as Villa Paraiso. The place seemed clean, but there was an abundance of geckos in the rooms, which suggests that their six-legged prey was around as well. Still, it's a good value. Make sure to look at different rooms—the most expensive ones aren't the best. Cel: 505-8-485-6177. E-mail: santo_domingo@yahoo.com. Updated: Jul 22, 2008.

Villa Paraiso
(ROOMS: $29 – 65) Villa Paraiso is the priciest option on Playa Santo Domingo, and it definitely has a more resort-type feel. The cabins are pleasant, with a quiet atmosphere and a nice view. The cheaper offerings and the restaurant; however, are far from impressive. Villa Paraiso also offers a range of tours. Tel: 505-2-563-4765. URL: www.villaparaiso.com.ni. Updated: Mar 13, 2009.

SW NICARAGUA

ELSEWHERE ON OMETEPE

Hacienda Merida
(HAMMOCK: $2; BED: $4; ROOMS: $8)
It is a bit of a trek to get out to this place—the bus takes three hours or a cab is one-and-a-half—but it really, really is worth it. Nestled by the water on the south part of the island, this purpose-built hostel offers a range of accommodation, from a place for a hammock to nice rooms with a private bathroom. Some beds are outside in the open on the top floor with great views of the lake. There is a restaurant on-site and a pontoon where you can swim from and watch the sun go down over the lake—all with Volcán Conception looming in the distance. Volcán Maderas. Cel: 505-8-868-8973 / 8-894-2551. E-mail: haciendamerida@gmail.com, URL: www.hmerida.com. Updated: Nov 25, 2009.

Finca Magdalena
(CAMPING and DORM: $3 – 3.50; ROOMS: $10 – 55). This hotel is located on a working coffee cooperative operated by over 20 families from the Isla de Ometepe on Lago Nicaragua. Accommodation options include camping/hammocks, dorm beds, private rooms and private cabanas. Take a bus from either Puerto de Gracias or Moyogalpa (depending on which ferry you arrive on) and tell the bus driver you are going to Finca Magdalena. You may need to switch buses in Santa Cruz. Cel: 505-8-880-2041, E-mail: E-mail@fincamagdalena.com, URL: www.fincamagdalena.com. Updated: Mar 20, 2009.

> **V!VA ONLINE REVIEW**
> FINCA MAGDALENA
>
> *"This coffee plantation is the ideal place to relax whilst surrounded by countryside"*
>
> -UK, October 2008

Hotel La Omaja
(ROOM: $5 – 40) This could be the most gorgeous place on the island, perched on a spectacular hilltop lookout over the lake. The location is very isolated and rustic, rich in bird life. The wilderness ends at your doorstep; however, rooms are spotlessly clean. Dorms in particular are an excellent value, and the suites are wonderfully romantic. About the only drawback is it's quite a long distance to the beach. If you want to explore the island from here you'd need to rent a vehicle. Three hundred meters (984 ft) up the road from Merida. Cel: 505-8-885-1124. E-mail: laomaja@hotmail.com, URL: www.laomaja.com. Updated: Jul 22, 2008.

Restaurants

Nearly all of the restaurants on Ometepe are connected to hotels. Seafood is quite good, though the introduction of tilapia has robbed Lake Nicaragua of much of the diversity it once had. With a few exceptions (such as Yogi's and The American Cafe) food is generally quite standard. Unless you're staying in Moyogalpa, expect to have most of your meals in your hotel. Updated: Jul 22, 2008.

MOYOGALPA

Yogi's Cafe and Bar
Named after the lovable black dog that greets arrivals, Yogi's is a friendly expat-run bar that serves breakfast and other tasty offerings. Their hamburgers are outstanding. The bar also makes for a nice place to hang out, especially if there's a game on. They also theoretically have WiFi, though at the time of this review it was out of service. Jerry, the owner, is very affable and happy to provide information about the island. A half-block south of Hospedaje Central. Cel: 505-8-403-6961. E-mail: yogisbar@gmail.com. Updated: Jul 22, 2008.

Los Ranchitos
A popular restaurant serving the standard variety of local dishes at reasonable prices. Fish filets are heartily recommended, freshly caught on the lake and grilled, fried or steamed to perfection. Expect to do a double-take when you first walk in—no, it's not a real tree. One block south of the dock street, across from the police station. Tel: 505-2-569-4112. E-mail: djromeen@yahoo.com.ni, URL: www.losranchitos.ni. Updated: Nov 25, 2009.

Del Timbo al Tambo
Mostly a bar, this place also serves typical Nicaraguan fare. It's quite a popular place for locals to drink, though. On the main street, one block up from gas station. Updated: Jul 23, 2008.

The American Cafe
Connected with The American Hotel, this charming little eatery offers a range of tasty breakfast and lunch specials. The

western omelet and star fruit juice were thoroughly enjoyable. The owners are pleasant, welcoming, and full of information about the island. The restaurant is only open till 4 p.m., but this is definitely Moyogalpa's best breakfast spot. Located just up from the dock. Cel: 505-8-645-7193.
Updated: Jul 23, 2008.

Chido's Pizza

Pizza here is delicious, well-priced and the portions are big. It doesn't skimp on the toppings either. Service was a bit lackluster but, to be fair, the waiter was quite engrossed in the televised soccer game.
Updated: Jul 23, 2008.

Restaurante Bahia

Connected to the Hotel Bahía, this restaurant offers a range of soups, pastas and sandwiches, along with comida típica. A very budget place to grab a bite. If you want to go even cheaper, they have a fast-food stand around the corner. On the main street, just up from the gas station. Cel: 505-8-823-5743.
Updated: Jul 23, 2008.

Linda Vista

This restaurant offers wonderful meals at a great value. The menu is not particularly creative, just your typical choice of meat, fish or chicken, but it's prepared with great gusto and served in hearty portions. A plate costs around $3. The picnic tables along the beach are a wonderful place to enjoy your meal, but bring bug repellent if you're planning on watching the sunset. Punto Jesus Maria, near Moyogalpa.
Updated: Nov 25, 2009.

PLAYA SANTO DOMINGO

Comedor Gloriana

A budget, comida típica establishment. The place to go for the cheap eats on the beach. The usual plates of chicken, rice and salad as well as hamburgers and sandwiches are served here. Cel: 505-8-479-7436.
Updated: Jul 23, 2008.

SAN JUAN DEL SUR

0 m   18,500

This small town has a beautiful, crescent-shaped bay, lined with palm trees and sailboats and surrounded by mountains and volcanoes. San Juan's location in the southwest coast of Nicaragua, just north of the Costa Rican border, makes it geographically ideal. It specifically appeals to surfers, Spanish students and tourists who want a quainter atmosphere than that which is offered in the more resort-filled parts of Costa Rica. These details make it surprising that—until just recently—it was a small, untouched fishing village.

Now; however, San Juan has a healthy mix of Nicaraguans and tourists (mostly surfers), who you will often see interacting in groups, speaking Spanglish, or dancing together at the local disco. Due to this influx in tourism, most foreign needs, such as familiar products and comfort foods, can be found at numerous different stores and restaurants. There are many things offered in English, but knowing a little Spanish is very useful in getting around.

San Juan del Sur is scattered with hotels in all price ranges and of all varieties. The majority of tourists are budget travelers, but there are also a number higher-end hotels as well, which cater to well-heeled travelers.

Food options include dining on grilled fish at one of the many beachside restaurants to grabbing a late-night hot dog from a street vendor. In between, there are plenty of typical Nicaraguan, American and other options. There are also several small shops that sell beach clothes, surf gear and souvenirs. Real Estate agencies are scattered around, for those looking to invest in property.

Although San Juan del Sur has many shops and restaurants, most of the more adventurous activity can be found in the easily accessible beaches that border the town. Many surfers hop on a shuttle to a nearby beach to catch a good wave. There are also turtle tours, which will bring you around to see turtles laying eggs, and if you're lucky, you'll catch them hatching. Hiking, diving, biking, fishing and boat tours are among the other activities offered in San Juan del Sur.

If you decide to relax, spending a day in San Juan is a good way to go. Take a walk around the town and browse the shops, take a swim in the bay, or grab some lunch at one of the local restaurants. Once you get accustomed to the relaxing, friendly and fun atmosphere of San Juan, you may not be surprised to find out just how many people came here several years ago and never left.
Updated: Nov 11, 2008.

Learn how to become a travel writer at vivatravelguides.com/bootcamp/

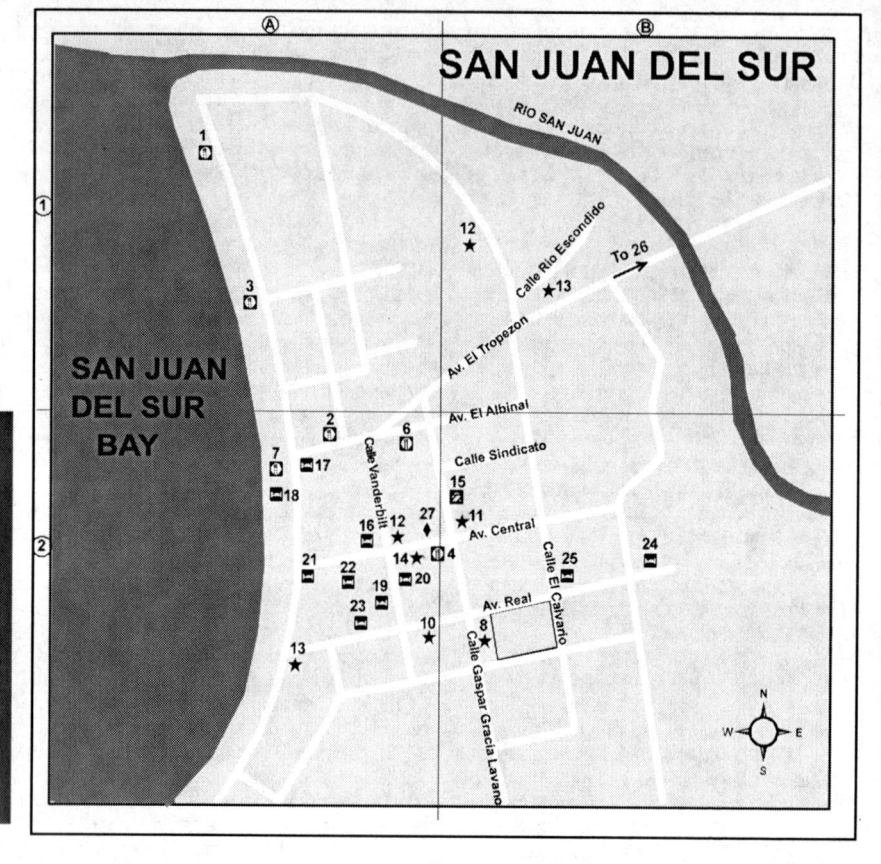

When to Go

For surfers, any time of year is a good time to visit San Juan del Sur. Most prefer the rainy season, because temperatures are cooler and the beaches are less crowded. Rainy season is usually from May to November, but hurricanes are more common during the months of September, October and November. Because of this, February to August is the preferred time for those interested in sailing or any activity involving boats.

Turtles lay eggs from July to February, and many people come to see them hatch. During Christmas and Semana Santa (Easter Week), the beaches are very crowded and reservations need to be made in advance. September 14th and 15th is Independence Day in Nicaragua and San Juan del Sur is a popular destination. While less crowded than during Semana Santa, it is still advisable to make a reservation if you're traveling around this time. Updated: Nov 11, 2008.

Getting To and Away From San Juan del Sur

Rivas is the main transfer point from Granada, Managua, and other beach locations to San Juan del Sur. Buses run from 5 a.m. to 5 p.m. from San Juan to Rivas, every 30 minutes or hour. There are express buses from San Juan to Managua that depart San Juan at 5 a.m., 5:45 a.m., 7 a.m., and 3:20 p.m. The trip takes two to three hours. Most bus rides cost $1 – 3. Big Wave Dave's also offers shuttles for $25 to Managua and Granada at 7:30 a.m. every morning. Private shuttles to and from the airport can be arranged with most hotels or through Paxeos. Look for more information at www.paxeos.com. Taxis pick up at the corner of the market entrance in San Juan. If you're looking to save some money, ask for a "colectivo" which means you will share with strangers along the way; this works out cheaply, but there is an increased risk of getting robbed. This should cost about $1.50 to Rivas. Private taxis cost about $7 to

Get free stuff when you reserve your hotel at vivatravelguides.com/hotels/

Eating

1 Bambu Beach Club A1
2 Big Wave Dave's A2
3 Coquito Bar Restaurant A1
4 El Pozo Restaurant A2
5 La Cascada Bar & Restaurant (see 24)
6 Las Flores (Mache's Bar) A2
7 Terraza Casa Blanca A2

Services

8 Casa de Promoción Municipal B2
9 Dollar Rent-Car (see 23)
10 Latin American Spanish School A2
11 Municipal Market B2
12 Papagayo – Artesanías A2
13 Post Office A2
14 Rosa Silva Spanish School A2

Shopping

15 Arena Caliente Surf Shop B2

Sleeping

16 Hotel Azul Pitahaya A2
17 Hotel Casa Blanca A2
18 Hotel Casa Feliz A2
19 Hotel Casa Oro A2
20 Hotel Colonial A2
21 Hotel Estrella A2
22 Hotel Joxi A2
23 Hotel Gran Océano A2
24 Pelican Eyes / Piedras y Olas B2
25 Villa Isabella B2

Tours

26 Da Flying Frog B1
27 San Juan Surf and Sport A2

Rivas, but can cost up to $60 to Managua. Updated: Nov 10, 2008.

Getting Around

The actual town of San Juan del Sur is small, and most tourists have no trouble walking around from place to place. Bike rentals are also available at many hostels and hotels, for usually about $6 a day. Taxis are parked across the street from the municipal market. Rental cars are also available. The most commonly used company is Dollar Rent-a-Car. Rentals can reserved online, or by visiting their station at the hotel, Pelican Eyes, located 1.5 blocks east of the central park. Updated: Nov 08, 2008.

Safety

San Juan del Sur is a small town with a tight-knit community. Because of this, it is safer than a lot of places in Nicaragua. However, it attracts a lot of tourists and those who prey on them, so it is still necessary to exercise caution. At night, it is best not to walk around alone. While most travelers don't hesitate to carry around laptops and cameras, it is still important to keep your eyes peeled for petty thieves and not leave your valuables unattended. Updated: Nov 11, 2008.

Services

The official tourist information office in San Juan del Sur is the Casa de Promocion Municipal (Tel: 505-2-568-3022, E-mail: secretariaturismosjs@gmail.com). It is located on the west side of the Parque Central, and is open from 8 a.m. – 12 p.m. and 1– 5 p.m. There are three main banks in town, all within four blocks of each other. All of the banks have 24-hour ATMs, although some are picky about which type of cards they take.

Internet cafés are plentiful, and most offer international calls and fax services. Free WiFi access is also common and is available at several bars and restaurants.

On the same block as the Municipal Market, there are a number of laundry services, which charge approximately $3 – 5 per bag.

If you need to mail a letter, the post office is located near the port, at the south end of the beach. To fill up your car, there is a 24-hour Texaco gas station on the east side of town. There are a couple small pharmacies in town, and a health center as well. However, if you get very injured or sick, the nearest hospital is in Rivas.

For entertainment, look to one of the many shops in San Juan Del Sur that offer surf equipment, diving gear, boat or bicycle rentals. The area also has a variety of tour operators and Spanish schools. Updated: Dec 26, 2008.

SHOPPING

San Juan del Sur is an excellent place to get souvenir or clothes shopping done, as there

Learn how to become a travel writer at vivatravelguides.com/bootcamp/

are many stores, most of which are well-organized and accept credit cards. However, as a prime tourist destination, prices tend to be a tad more expensive than in many other places in Nicaragua. Stores generally are open from 9 a.m. to 9 p.m. Strolling around town, you will encounter several convenience stores that also sell swimsuits and summer clothing. These are less expensive, and are generally cash-only.

Specialty stores include Artesanías Sammigo, which carries cigars, ceramics, paintings, textiles and other handcrafted art. Their most popular items; however, are their hammocks, which range from $15 – 60. Also, Papagayo Artesania Joyeria sells beautiful and decorative jewelry imported from France. Prices range from $5 – 100. Items include authentic silver rings, colorful, dangly necklaces, bracelets and handbags. Updated: Nov 11, 2008.

Things to See and Do

While many come to San Juan del Sur to take advantage of the great surfing wave breaks and beautiful beaches, there are other activities to choose from as well. You can hike up one of the surrounding mountains to catch the view of the crescent beach from above, and watch one of the breathtaking sunsets. Depending on the time of year, you may also be able to visit to the turtle sanctuary to see the turtles lay eggs or watch the hatchlings emerge. Other activities include biking around town, taking the canopy tour, going fishing, swimming, sailing or diving. Updated: Dec 26, 2008.

Refugio de Vida Silvestre La Flor

El Refugio de Vida Silvestre, located 21 kilometers (13 mi) south of San Juan del Sur, is one of few in the world where you can witness massive congregations of endangered Olive Ridley turtles (called *tortuga golfina* in Spanish). Starting each July, female turtle begin arriving at the local beaches in the thousands. They dig holes in the sand, lay up to 100 glistening white eggs and then cover their nests before making their ponderous way back into the ocean. After incubating for 50 to 60 days, the first eggs begin to hatch and the baby turtles claw their way through the sand to the surface. (The hatching process will continue until January or February). The hatching mostly occurs at night between 7:30 p.m. and 1:30 a.m.

In the past, the turtle nests have been subject to wide-spread poaching (restaurants along the coast used to offer turtle egg specials) and predation. The refuge was formed as a way to help protect the endangered marine animals and keep the Olive Ridleys that nested in Nicaragua from being completely wiped out.

Photo by prizz22

Get free stuff when you reserve your hotel at vivatravelguides.com/hotels/

Many Nicaraguan tour operators offer trips to see the turtles with guided tours costing between $25 and $35, on average. The wildlife reserve, which is open 24 hours a day, seven days a week, also permits visitors to camp in the park for a $15 fee. Seeing the endangered turtles' eggs hatch and watching thousands of baby turtles crawl into the water is an incredible experience and is highly recommended.
Updated: Dec 26, 2008.

El Ostional

If you're in the mood for a tranquil experience away from all the tourists, take a trip to El Ostional. Staying at this quiet indigenous fishing village is like taking a peek into San Juan del Sur's past. For surfers, the break here is fairly inconsistent, but the swell is best in the southwest. When the tide is high, it can be very challenging. It is just south of the turtle nesting sanctuary, toward Costa Rica.
Updated: Nov 08, 2008.

HIKING

The main hiking option in San Juan del Sur is the trail on La Questa Hill. Either rent a car or take a taxi to the northeast side of town, past the Texaco and about 6 kilometers (3.7 mi) up the road, where it ends. From there, the hiking trail begins. It takes about three and a half hours total. Some people choose to hire a guide; others go solo. Make sure to bring a lot of water, snacks and, during the rainy season, a poncho or rain jacket.
Updated: Nov 08, 2008.

BIKING

Whether you are interested in just biking around or going on an expedition, several hostels, hotels and surf shops offer bike rentals for about $5 – 6 a day. Signs are posted all around town. For those interested in a guided tour, Outer Reef offers one for $20. This involves mountain biking, with spectacular views, a break for lunch, and a swim in a waterfall. Don't forget to bring a lot of water and your bathing suit.
Updated: Nov 12, 2008.

CANOPY TOUR

For more adventurous types eager to explore the nature and wildlife of San Juan del Sur, a canopy tour is a great option. The leading canopy tour in the area is called Da Flying Frog and is located about five minutes from town. It is one of the longest canopy tours in the country, with a zip line of 2.5 kilometers (1.5 mi). The area that you fly over has abundant vegetation filled with birds and monkeys. The zip line takes about 45 minutes to complete and costs $30 per person. Cel: 505-8-613-4460/ 611-6214 / 465-6781. Da Flying Frog is located 500 meters (1,640 ft) from the entrance of Carretera a Marsella.
Updated: Dec 26, 2008.

SURFING

There are three major surf shops in San Juan del Sur, all of which are located within a four-block radius of each other in the center of town. All of them offer surf lessons for different levels, board rentals and bicycle rentals. Arena Caliente is the oldest surf shop in Sand Juan del Sur. It is owned and operated by Nicaraguans, and was started by Byron Lopez. They offer trips by car to all neighboring beaches and even have a hostel. Sol Caliente offers boat tours to private beaches for $25 per person, with no time limit. They also have the best board selection for rentals in all of town, and rent weekly and daily. They may be changing their name soon, but just send an E-mail to SolCaliente.sjdj@gmail. com, or ask around for 'Dave's Surf Shop.' Surf and Sport, owned by a man named Eu (pronounced Ay-you) also has rentals and does boat tours. For info and guides, seek out his shop. For independent surfers, transportation to nearby beaches is easily available. Head to one of the surf shops for conditions and transportation information.
Updated: Mar 11, 2009.

Schools

The two most common things to do in San Juan del Sur are surfing and studying Spanish. San Juan del Sur is the perfect place for beginners to go, as there are plenty of opportunities to speak and practice Spanish and there are also plenty of English speakers around, so the experience is not too drastic or isolating. Most schools offer homestay programs and the Spanish pupil decides how many hours to invest per week.
Updated: Dec 26, 2008.

Spanish School Casa Rosa Silva

Just west of the Municipal Market is the small, yellow schoolhouse that houses Rosa Silva's Spanish School. All lessons are one-on-one with experienced teachers who are native Spanish speakers. Each week consists of 20 hours of lessons and costs from $110 – $120, depending on the length of your commitment. Homestays cost

$200 per week, including the classes. The homestay price includes seven days' worth of accommodation in a private room with a bathroom and three meals a day. There is also an option to stay at the schoolhouse, with the same amenities as the homestay, except the bathroom is shared. Located 30 meters (98.5 ft) west of the market. Cel: 505-8-682-2938. E-mail: www.spanishsilva.com, URL: Spanish_Silva@yahoo.com. Updated: Dec 26, 2008.

Spanish Ya

Spanish Ya offers year-round programs in a San Juan Del Sur schoolhouse. The program features experienced native teachers and WiFi access, class materials, and even airport pick-up and transportation services are all included in the price. The Spanish Ya courses also include beach trips, volunteer opportunities, museum trips and other adventures. Prices vary depending on number of students and length of stay. Generally, the costs range from $100 for 15 hours a week of basic classes to $220 for 20 hours a week, including homestay. Surfing lessons, and "homestay only" options are also available. 100 meters (328 ft) north of the Texaco. Tel: 505-2-568-3010. Cel: 505-8-898-5036. E-mail: info@learnspanishya.com, URL: www.learnspanishya.com. Updated: Dec 26,2008

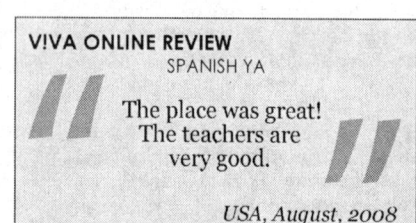

> **V!VA ONLINE REVIEW**
> SPANISH YA
>
> "The place was great! The teachers are very good."
>
> USA, August, 2008

Latin American Spanish School

This Spanish school is extremely organized, with several course levels, volunteer opportunities and a wide variety of cultural activities and excursions. Classes, which are one-on-one with native speakers, cater to individual needs and the school offers specialized classes for medical Spanish, Spanish teachers, Christian missionaries and several others. Prices vary from $175 a week to $195 a week, including the $60 cost of a homestay. You can also arrange for lessons without a homestay. A half-block west of the central park. Cel: 505-8-820-2202. E-mail: info@latinamericanspanishschool.com, URL: www.latinamericanspanishschool.com Updated: Dec 26, 2008.

Tours

Due to the large, and growing, number of tourist activities in San Juan del Sur, there are several tour operators that pretty much do it all. This includes boat tours, nature walks, canopy tours, turtle tours, etc... Most of these companies are organized, connected and can set up anything excursion you want. This is an advisable route to take if your Spanish skills are less than perfect. Most hostels and hotels are also tour operators and there are several tour companies with noticeable signs posted all around town. Updated: Dec 30, 2008.

Berman Gomez
(Independent Tour Guide)

Born in Ometepe, Berman Gomez knows a great deal about San Juan del Sur and the surrounding area. He speaks fluent English and is a certified tour guide. Gomez can be found at Pelican Eyes Hotel and Resort, where he works; he specializes in full-day tours of Granada and Masaya, excursions to Ometepe and turtle-watching expeditions. Gomez can also arrange several different types of tours upon request. As a guide, Gomez is well-informed, educated and comes highly recommended. Cel: 505-8-647-5179. E-mail: ometepeisland@hotmail.com. Updated: Feb 22, 2009.

Piedras y Olas

This hotel and resort, also called Pelican Eyes, is another option for booking tours. It offers several types of tours, such as sailing tours and turtle watching excursions. However, the most interesting option it has is its unique wildlife center and veterinary clinic, Stones and Waves. Here, you can see three different species of monkeys, tropical birds, raccoons and several other forms of wildlife native to the area. Guided tours are available to see these rescued animals. Cel: 505- 8-812-0511. E-mail: veterinarian@piedrasyolas.com. URL: www.stonesandwaves.org. Updated: Dec 30, 2008.

Lodging

San Juan del Sur is the third largest tourist destination in Nicaragua and—especially for such a small town—has an amazing number of accommodation options. So many, in fact, that any survey of the town can only include a very limited number of the actual hotels, hostels and hospedajes. New locations are opening at a furious rate as residents look for ways to capitalize on the tourist boom. Before you decide where you want to stay, walk around and see what your options are. Even during peak seasons, San Juan del Sur usually has plenty of available rooms. Updated: Aug 24, 2009.

Hotel Joxi

(ROOMS: $10 – 12) Hotel Joxi, located one and a half blocks west of the Municipal Market, is the place for travelers in need of space and comfort on a tight budget. Rooms come with an air conditioning, TV and private bathroom. There are hammocks, tables and a deck for lounging upstairs and a restaurant downstairs that serves food for $2 – 6. Credit cards are accepted. Cleaning service is free and available upon request. Tel: 505-2-568-2483. E-mail: casajoxi@ibw.com.ni. Updated: Dec 30, 2008.

Hotel Estrella

(ROOMS: $5 – 10) This beachfront hotel has several rooms with shared bathrooms on the second floor. Ask for one with a private balcony. Otherwise, the shared balcony looking out over the beach is great to relax on as the sun sets on San Juan del Sur. The real beauty of this hotel is the location. Numerous restaurants and bars are within a block or two of Estrella and the beach is right across the road. Meals are available in the restaurant/bar located on the main floor. All rooms have fans but guests are advised to bring their own towels, mosquito nets and patience as there have been mixed reviews of the service. Cel: 505-8-458-3310. Updated: Nov 25, 2009.

Casa Feliz

(ROOMS: $6 – $12) At Casa Feliz, you will find a fooseball table in the entryway, a living room with a couch and a TV, a communal kitchen open to all, and an occasional "party hostel" atmosphere. A backyard with hammocks confirms the sign in the hallway that proclaims it "The Hostel that Feels like a Home." The rooms and bathrooms are shared, creating a convivial environment. There are bike rentals, as well as surfboard and fishing gear available. There are also organized boat and surf tours, in addition to beach transportation provided. One block east of the Mercado. Cel: 505-8-689-7906 E-mail: LaHappyHouse gmail.com, URL: www.lacasafeliz.com. Updated: Aug 25, 2009.

Casa Oro

(DORM: $5; ROOMS: $16) Casa Oro is one of the most popular hostels in San Jaun del Sur, and it also has dormitory-style rooms. Lockers are free, but small. There is a communal kitchen, a big screen TV and a book exchange. The youth hostel also offers several tours, surf lessons, a Spanish school and daily beach shuttles. One block west and one block south of the bus stop. Tel: 505-2-568-2415 (Nicaragua)/ 308-210-9220 (U.S.), E-mail: information@ casaeloro.com, URL: www.casaeloro.com. Updated: Dec 26, 2008.

Hotel Azul Pitahaya

(ROOMS: $35 – 65) Hotel Azul Pitahaya is located a block from the beach, away from the shore-front noise, and is a solid option for visitors who can afford to pay a bit more for spotless rooms with the usual amenities, plus air conditioning, cable TV, hot water, WiFi and a delicious breakfast at the attached Café Espresso. If you're mainly interested in socializing with other guests, though, Azul Pitahaya is not the best choice–all of the common areas are part of the café. The eatery is open from 7:30 a.m. to 10:30 p.m. The hotel reception (walk through the dining area and turn right) is open from 7 a.m. to 9 p.m. Tel: 505-2-568-2294. E-mail: scarflor2@ yahoo.com. Updated: Jun 25, 2009.

Hotel Gran Océano

(ROOMS: $42 – 85) This newer hotel is situated less than 100 meters from the beach. They have private rooms for all group sizes —from singles to familes. The view is great, and so is the Jacuzzi! Two blocks from the central plaza. Tel/Fax: 505-2-568-2219. E-mail: hgoceano@idw.com.ni, URL: http://www.hotelgranoceano.com.ni/index.html. Updated: Nov 25, 2009.

Hotel Colonial

(ROOMS: $48 – 54) If you want luxury feel at a reasonable price, head to Hotel Colonial. There is a full bar and the backyard has a patio filled with palm trees. Each sparkling-clean room has air conditioning, cable TV, and a private bathroom. Triples are available, and breakfast is included. The hotel also offers airport transfers, private parking and 24-hour security. Located half a block south of the beach and one block west of the market. Cel: 505-8-850-6205, Tel/Fax: 505-568-2539. E-mail: hotel.colonial@ibw.com.ni, URL: www.hotel-nicaragua.com. Updated: Dec 30, 2008.

Villa Isabella

(ROOMS: $50 – 85) Villa Isabella is a stately wooden house that has been renovated into a series of private rooms and mini-suites, some containing private baths. Catering to a more upscale crowd, Villa Isabella features a courtyard swimming pool, a business center, WiFi, air-conditioned rooms, hot-water showers, free breakfast and cable TV. The hotel also offers information regarding recreational activities and investment opportunities. There is a secure parking lot, and the hotel is is one of only a few in the country that is fully-accessible for disabled travelers. English is spoken at the 24-hour reception desk. Located diagonally across from the Catholic church. Tel: 505-2-568-2568, Cel: 505-8-877-7791, Fax: 505-2-568-2549. E-mail: isabella@ibw.com.ni / villaisabella@aol.com, URL: http://www.sanjuandelsur.org.ni/isabella/. Updated: Nov 25, 2009.

Piedras y Olas

(ROOMS: $130 – 290) This socially-conscious, upscale hotel is largely built out of straw bales and other environmentally-friendly materials. Overlooking the ocean, the hotel and adjoining residential development offer the facilities of a world-class resort. The hotel is often called Pelican Eyes, as well. On Parroquia, 1.5 blocks to the east. Tel: 1-866-350-0555/505-2-563-7000, Fax: 505-2-568-2592, E-mail:reservations@piedrasyolas.com.URL:www.piedrasyolas.com. Updated: Nov 25, 2009.

> **V!VA ONLINE REVIEW**
> PIEDRAS Y OLAS
>
> *Staff was darling! Food was delicious! Rooms were beautiful and huge!*
>
> Oregon, USA, November 2008

Restaurants

Terraza Casa Blanca

More of a bar than a restaurant, this is a nice place to go for sunset cocktails. The deckchair seats are comfortable, the views are perfect, and the drinks are cheap. If you are so chilled out you don't want to move, then you could do worse than ordering a plate of their hearty fare. Middle of the seafront. Cel: 505-8-654-6801 / 568-2718. Updated: Nov 22, 2006.

El Pozo

Located in the heart of San Juan del Sur, El Pozo is a contemporary restaurant that offers a change from the traditional Nicaraguan fare. The chefs use fresh, local ingredients and offer creative dishes such as watermelon salad with goat cheese and basil. Daily fish, pasta and salad specials compliment the tasty menu options. The interior design of the restaurant features an open concept kitchen, bamboo celing and stone slab floors. Dress is classy casual. You can sit at the bar and choose a martini from their extensive list or take a seat at a table to enjoy a great meal. El Pozo is open Wednesday – Monday, 6 – 11 p.m. On the third main street off the beach, one block south of the town's central park, near the market. Updated: Aug 25, 2008.

Coquito Bar Restaurant

SNACKS: ($0.50 – 4) Not only does Coquito Bar Restaurant have the cheapest beer on the beach, they also have tasty food for a relatively low price, which is great for the budget traveler. The bar's á la carte menu allows you to mix and match whatever meats, vegetables and sides you're in the mood for. The selection changes often, and always includes at least one beef, one chicken and one fish option. They have open-mic nights every Thursday at 8 p.m., and live music on Saturday nights. North end of the beach. Cash Only. Open noon. to midnight. Located on the north end of the beach.

Café Macuas

(SNACKS: $1.25 – 4.50) This quiet coffee shop is a great place to start the day. Café Macuas is filled with small wooden tables and chairs and offers a relaxing atmosphere, as well as free WiFi. Their breakfast selection has several classics, including French toast, pancakes and omelets. For lunch, they offer tacos and burritos, but are better known for their panini selection: turkey pesto, ham and artichoke, and chicken and ranch—to name a few. Cash only. Open 7:30 a.m. to 3:30 p.m. Across from San Juan Surf and Sport and the Municipal Market. Updated: Nov 08, 2008.

Big Wave Dave's

(ENTREES: $2.50 – 7.50) Half a block from the beach, Big Wave Dave's has a spacious, tropical interior with a wide, rectangular bar. The restaurant also has one of the widest menu selections in town. Options range from classic breakfast food (served all day) to large dinners of meat, chicken or fish. There is also an assortment of pastas, chili, soups and salads. The burgers and sandwiches are served on fresh-baked bread, and vegetarian options are available. Lunch specials vary daily and run for about $2. WiFi is free. Cash only. Twenty-five meters (82 ft) east of El Timon. Updated: Aug 24, 2009.

Las Flores (Mache's Bar)

(ENTREES: $3 – 6) This bar is officially called Las Flores, but everyone in town knows it as "Mache's." It is typically open later than all the bars and clubs in town, sometimes until sunrise. It is the only bar that serves food all night. Options include sandwiches and beef, chicken and pork entrées. Opens at 10 p.m. Cash only. It is one block north of the Municipal Market, and marked with an arch that says "Sport Bar." Updated: Nov 08, 2008.

Bambu Beach

(ENTREES: $4.25 – 10.50) For gourmet food in a chic, comfortable environment at mid-range prices, head to Bambu Beach. The chef cooks up everything from organic salads with sautéed chicken and mango dressing to spicy, sesame-crusted tuna. His specials vary, and often include sushi when the fish is the freshest. While most seating is inside, there is a lounging area, a splash pool and a garden outside. Various events take place there, such as fashion shows and concerts. Movie nights are every Monday and Thursday at 8 p.m. The restaurant also offers free WiFi. All credit cards are accepted, with no minimum. Located at the north end of the beach. Open from 11-1 a.m. Closed Tuesdays. North end of the beach. Tel: 505-2-568-2101. E-mail: laidback@thebambubeachclub.com, URL: www.thebambubeachclub.com. Updated: Nov 08, 2008.

La Cascada Bar and Restaurant

(ENTREES: $6 – 20) Although it belongs to the Pelican Eyes Hotel/Piedras y Olas, this restaurant is open to the public. The stone bar is lit with candles and framed with upholstered red chairs, and the outdoor seating has a fantastic view of the mountainside. Entrées start with lobster bisque and feature specialties such as filet mignon stuffed with gorgonzola, spinach and caramelized onion. Specials change daily. All drinks are two for the price of one during happy hour, which is Wednesdays and Fridays from 5-8 p.m. All credit cards are accepted. Located 1.5 blocks east of the central park. Open 7 a.m. – 10 p.m. One and a half blocks east of the central park. Tel: 505-2-568-2110, Fax: 505-568-2511. E-mail: reservations@piedrasyolas.com, URL: www.piedrasyolas.com/dining_eng.htm. Updated: Nov 08, 2008.

Volunteering

Depending on your interests and area of expertise, there are various volunteering opportunities in San Juan del Sur. The wildlife reserve at Pelican Eyes, which is called "Stones and Waves," is dedicated to rescuing and preserving animals that are unable to survive in the wild. It is funded by donations and most of the staff is made up of volunteer nurses. If you are not medically trained, other volunteering opportunities are available. Tel: 505-2-563-700. E-mail: veterinarian@piedrasyolas.com.

If you are in San Juan del Sur learning Spanish, many of the schools also offer volunteer opportunities. The Latin American Spanish School has a variety of opportunities to choose from, including assistant teaching and working in hospitals and orphanages. They require at least one week of classes, a four-week commitment and an intermediate level of Spanish or higher (Tel: 505-820-2202, E-mail: info@latinamericanspanishschool.com). There are also opportunities to volunteer in the library (which is right behind the gas station) or teach English at the local school next to the central park. Updated: Nov 11, 2008.

AROUND SAN JUAN DEL SUR

San Juan del Sur is home to several beautiful beaches with great surf breaks. If you don't have a car, one of the best ways to get to the various beaches is by making arrangements through the Cooperativo de Turismo. There is an office next to Hotel Joxi, 1.5 blocks west of the Municipal Market. This service will find you a taxi for the best price and can also find other people to split the cost of the ride with you. There are also shuttle services that run from Casa Oro, with three departures daily to Playa Maderas, Playa Majagual, Playa Matilda and Playa Marsella. Updated: Feb 02, 2009.

Getting to the Beaches Near San Juan del Sur

If you're taking a taxi to the beaches north of San Juan del Sur, the ride is about 20 minutes and will cost you $20 round-trip. Alternatively, there are a number of surf shops in town that can provide transportation to Playa Maderas, or boat trips that drop you off on different beaches with no road access. As well, the infamous truck known as the "Indian Face" picks up people near the Centro in the morning, then passes by the beach again at about 4 or 4:30 p.m. Check with the surf shops or the hostel Casa Feliz to find out where to grab the truck each morning.

Don't be deterred by the lack of signs if you are trying to navigate in your own vehicle. Politely ask for directions from locals if you get lost. To get out of town head out to the main road, then take the first left after the Palí supermarket. Here, the road is unpaved and can be quite bumpy and muddy during rainy season. Continue straight until the signs that say "Marsella" and take a left to get to all the beaches. For Marsella, continue following the roads to the left. Take the first right for Playa Majagual, Ocotal, Arena Blanca and the north end of Maderas. For the main beach of Playa Maderas, take the right at the fork in the road.

The beaches south of San Juan del Sur can be reached along the road running south from the bridge at the entrance to town. A few buses run along this stretch of road, but the easiest way to access the beaches is by water taxi from San Juan del Sur. Updated: Feb 02, 2009.

Playa Marsella

Calm waters and a quiet beach are the star attractions at Playa Marsella. The beach is an ideal place for swimming, snorkeling, kayaking or just spending the afternoon. There is a restaurant on the beach, Restaurante Rancho Marsella, which is open from 9 a.m. to 5 p.m. You can get a fish plate for $10 and a beer for $1. Updated: Dec 15, 2008.

Playa Marsella Lodging

Hotel Villa Mar

(ROOMS: $50) This four-room hotel has basic accommodations and would be cheaper just about anywhere else, but the prime location, a stone's throw from the beach, dictates the price. There's not much to do in more than a day at Playa Marsella, but at the hotel you can enjoy some local cuisine with prices comparable to other local, mid-range restaurants. Fifty meters (164 ft) before arriving at Marsella beach, on the right hand side. Cel: 505-8-667-2954 / 663-0666. E-mail: villamar_hotel@yahoo.com. Updated: Dec 30, 2008.

Mango Rosa

(ROOMS: $80 – 120) This hotel is comfortable and stylish, arguably the most relaxed high-end place around San Juan del Sur. In addition to the lodging, Mango Rosa has a pool, music, Internet, great food and friendly folks. Five hundred meters (1,640 ft) past the bridge, on the turnoff to Playa Marsella. Cel: 505-8-477-3692 / 403-5326. E-mail: greg@mangorosanicaragua.com / chadunser@gmail.com, URL: www.mangorosaresort.com. Updated: Nov 25, 2009.

Hotel Marsella Conference and Beach Retreat

(ROOMS: $85 – 150) Resembling a fortress on a hill, the Hotel Marsella has a beautiful pool area and classy rooms. The restaurant is a bit pricey for what is offered, but consider the awesome view of Marsella Bay as part of the cost. This place is recommended for business travelers as it has Internet, phone service and conference rooms. The hotel will help organize tours and activities, as well. Located 150 meters (492 ft) before arriving at Marsella beach. Cel: 505-8-887-4836. E-mail: reservations@marsellabeach.com / info@marsellabeach.com. URL: www.marsellabeach.com. Updated: Dec 15, 2008.

Playa Maderas

Being the most popular surf beach in the San Juan del Sur area, Playa Maderas also happens to be the most crowded. Surfers head here throughout the day because of the consistent break, and the regular offshore breeze. If you're looking to avoid the masses, the best time to go is in the morning, when many are still in bed from the night before. Although most people come here for day trips, there

---

Get free stuff when you reserve your hotel at vivatravelguides.com/hotels/

are a few accommodation options close by. Surfboard rentals are available at the beach for $10 per day (you pay the ding repairs), and lessons are available ($10 per hour). Updated: Sep 10, 2008.

Lodging

The Surf Shack
(ROOMS: $2 – 5) This is a no-frills, no bathrooms (outhouses only), surfer's compound known more commonly as "the chicken shack," which is steps away from the most popular surf beach. Pitch a tent for $2 per person, or grab a dorm bed for $5. The place fills up with backpackers and surfers, but try your luck finding a room. Two small restaurants here sell light meals; breakfast costs $3, hamburgers $2.50, and a beer $1.25. On the beach. Updated: Jul 10, 2009.

Matilda's
(ROOMS: $4 – 25) On the northern, quieter end of Playa Maderas you'll find Matilda's. Matilda, the owner, has rooms that range from private, with an en-suite bathroom, to small casitas, which resemble large doghouses. Matilda's is an affordable way to stay right on the beach. Camping sites are also available, as well as dorm-style rooms. The hostel has beer and other refreshments that you can buy; there is also an outdoor kitchen for guests to use. North end of Playa Maderas. Take the road towards Playa Majagual. Cel: 505-8-456-3461 / 865-9324. Updated: Jul 10, 2009.

Lazy Jakes
(ROOMS: $20 – 50) Lazy Jakes has two types of accommodation: a bungalow that provides luxury-dorm style space for up to four people, and private double suites, some with air-conditioning. On the second floor, the Canopy Lounge is great communal area to relax in, with views and sounds of the jungle. One kilometer (.62 mi) from Playa Maderas, which can easily be reached on foot by going up and back down a hill. Cel: 505-8-462-1069. E-mail: lazyjakes@gmail.com, URL: www.lazyjakes.com. Updated: Sep 03, 2009.

Buena Vista Surf Club
(ROOMS: $90 – 100) This lodge is owned and operated by a Dutch couple, who built the hotel in a secluded spot with a view of the ocean and within a 10-minute walk of the beach. The two deluxe treehouses feature rooms complete with bathrooms, and there is a master bedroom in the main building that sleeps up to four. Buena Vista has surfboards and lessons available to guests at an extra cost, as well as yoga, massages and tours. The lodge also has a restaurant, bar, lounge and sundeck. You have to stay a minimum of two nights and breakfast is included in the cost. All-in-all, this is a worthwhile place to enjoy the Pacific coast. Playa Maderas. Cel: 505-8-863-4180. E-mail: info@buenavistasurfclub.com, URL: www.buenavistasurfclub.com. Updated: Jul 16, 2009.

The Surf Retreat
(ROOMS: $125) The Surf Retreat offers rental homes in a gated community. The homes have a bird's-eye view of Maderas beach, a view so clear that you can see the waves breaking. The houses for rent are two story, two bedroom affairs, with full kitchens and barbecues. The rentals share a tiny pool and come equipped with internet. The walk downhill to the beach takes 15 minutes. Unless you are up for hiking long distances, you'll want a car to get around. Call ahead for reservations. Playa Maderas. Tel: 505-2-568-2037. Cel: 505-8-871-7951. E-mail: info@thesurfretreat.com / office@cornerstonenicaragua.com. URL: www.thesurfretreat.com. Updated: Jul 10, 2009.

Villas Playa Madera
(ROOMS: $150 – 175) Located to the right of the entrance of the main beach, there are 10 hectares of land where Villas Playa Madera rents two- to three-bedroom oceanfront houses. The property is surrounded by tropical forests, so check out the hiking trails to possibly see, and definitely hear, howler monkeys. Located on the waterfront. Once at the main beach, take a right. Cel: 505-8-267-0675 / 877-0200. E-mail: yolanda.amaya@gmail.com. URL: www.maderabeachnicaragua.com. Updated: Jul 10, 2009.

Playa Majagual

A beautiful stretch of beach and green-covered cliffs surround the lovely Playa Majagual. Visitors to Majagual can escape the crowds and, more than likely, have a private day at the beach.

Playa Majagual Lodging

Don Martin's House (Casa Don Martin)
(ROOMS: $8 – 20) Casa Don Martin adequately provides the bare necesities: basic rooms and a

restaurant open at mealtimes. There are private rooms with bathrooms, as well as dormitories. The hotel is set back about 30 meters (100 ft) from both Playa Maderas and Playa Majagual. Meals feature burgers, sandwiches and fish entrées. The food is decent and a good value, considering you won't find many other places around to eat. Located at the north end of Playa Maderas near the entrance to the beach. Cel: 505-8-881-4727. E-mail: talaquir@gmail.com. Updated: Sep 12, 2008.

Balcones de Majagual

(HOUSE: $180) There are a number of eco-homes, called Balcones de Majagual, available for rent along Playa Majagual's bay. House rentals cost $180 per night, less for longer stays. The homes were designed by the same people behind Morgan's Rock Resort in Playa Ocotal. Tel: 505-2-568-2498 or U.S. 323-908-6730. E-mail: info@balconesdemajagual.com, URL: www.balconesdemajagual.com. Updated: Dec 30, 2008.

Playa Ocotal

Set between the beaches of Playa Majagual and Arena Blanca, Playa Ocotal is a private enclave accessible to the guests at Morgan's Rock Hacienda and Ecolodge and to others who are willing to hoof it or travel by boat. There are no other restaurants or accommodations here, so visitors may only trek to this picturesque beach by day. Updated: Sep 11, 2008.

Morgan's Rock Hacienda and Eco-Lodge

(ROOM: $177 – 352) Morgan's Rock is a resort built on 1,800 hectares of a private reserve, and is a wealthy conservationist's dream combination of environmental concern and luxury. The beautiful bungalows are made of local, sustainable wood, and the whole place was designed with understated elegance. Activities such as fishing and hiking can be arranged during your stay, as can agro-tourism ventures like reforestation projects. All food and drinks are included in the daily rates Follow the roads to Playa Majagual, and the yellow signs painted on rocks that say "M.R." Tel: 505-2-254-7989. E-mail: info@morgansrock.com / reservations@morgansrock.com, URL: www.morgansrock.com. Updated: Nov 25, 2009.

Arena Blanca

Arena Blanca is a small bay to the north of Playa Ocotal. As the name suggests, a white sand beach hugs the shore, and is backed by a lush tropical forest. Varieties of birds can be seen and heard, as well as howling monkeys. Currently there is no development here, but there is a project in the works. It's about a 15-minute walk from Playa Majagual, over the rocks to Ocotal, and across to the other side of the bay. Updated: Sep 11, 2008.

Playa Remanso

Misleadingly, Playa Remanso was formerly referred to as "Playa Sucio," despite its beauty and cleanliness. Later, it was re-named Playa Remanso. The beach is about 5 kilometers (3 mi) south of San Juan del Sur and lined with white sand and tide pools. For surfers, the breaks are relatively mild, making this is the perfect beach for beginners. Updated: Dec 30, 2008.

Playa Tamarindo and Playa Hermoso

Both of these beaches are just south of Playa Remanso, but are more difficult to access. The only way to get to the beaches is by boat or by hiking through the woods. If you choose the latter option, make sure to hire a local guide, and don't bring any valuables with you. Updated: Dec 30, 2008.

Playa El Yankee

El Yankee is a bit farther from the other beaches, but definitely worth the trip. The water is clear and the sand is white. The waves usually have heavy, difficult breaks, which will appeal to surfers looking for a challenge. Whether you surf or not, you will likely find the beach gorgeous, despite recent hillside development. There is also a beach guard so there are fewer robberies than neighboring beaches. Updated: Nov 08, 2008.

Playa El Coco

Approximately 20 minutes south of San Juan del Sur, Playa el Coco is a relaxing and beautiful beach, framed with rocky cliffs. The waves are smoother here, making it less surfer friendly, but more suitable for children or people wanting to take a mellow swim. The vibe is peaceful, and the beach has a tourist center, Parque Marítimo. Updated: Dec 26, 2008.

Parque Marítimo

(HOUSE: $80 – 220) Parque Marítimo is a small tourist center at Playa El Coco that organizes nature trips such as daily boat rides to the Costa Rican boarder to see nesting sea birds or jaunts to a nearby wildlife refuge, where turtles lay their eggs. The center offers horseback rides and bicycle rentals as well as Frisbees, volleyballs, footballs, surfboards and boogie boards. There are also a number of houses, apartments and bungalows available to rent for a night or longer, and there is a restaurant specializing in Nicaraguan and various international dishes. Tel: 1-786-623-0608 (U.S). Cel: 505-8-999-8069. E-mail: reservaciones@playaelcoco.com.ni., URL: www.playaelcoco.com.ni. Updated: Dec 26, 2008.

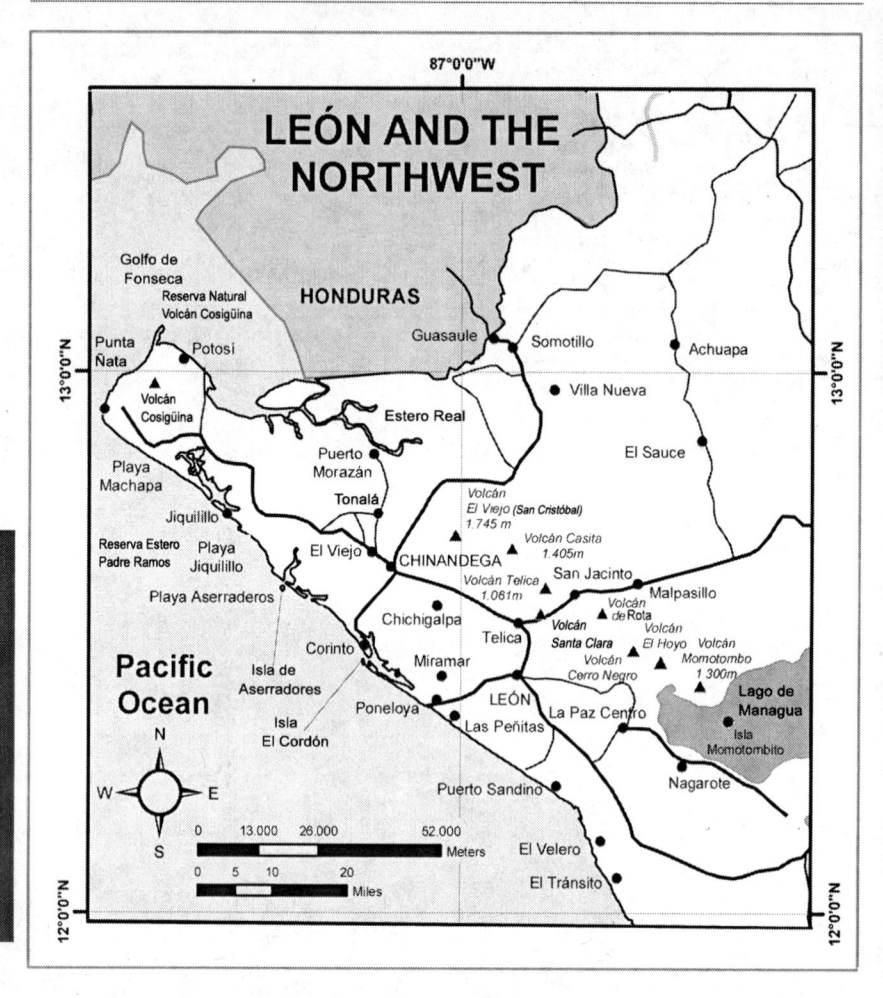

Leon and the Northwest

The northwest corner of Nicaragua is home to the highest volcano, the hottest city and the oldest Spanish ruins. While almost anywhere in the country can claim to have "a little something for everyone," the northwest is one of the few places that delivers on that promise. There are monuments aplenty, cathedrals galore, old forts, prisons with grim histories, ceramic workshops, museums, fertile agricultural fields and deep blue crater lakes—and that's just the landward side.

This region of Nicaragua is tucked between the Pacific Ocean to the west, El Salvador and Honduras to the north, and Lake Managua to the east. Characterized by both flat agricultural lands and steep volcanic peaks, the northwest has managed to earn the title of Nicaragua's bread basket while still being home to the mighty Ring of Fire. The two major cities in this area are the ever-popular intellectual center of Leon and the less-popular, but more pleasantly local, Chinandega.

Today, tourists take minibuses up from Managua to experience the colonial grandeur of the cities themselves and to relax on some of the country's most beautiful beaches. Pick your destination carefully if you plan to swim; riptides and volcanic outcroppings make the northwest the land of big waves, which attracts surfers to these waters.

Support VIVA! Reserve your hotels or hostels at www.vivatravelguides.com/hotels/

Leon and the North West

Although more likely to be overlooked in the rush—to climb Volcan Cosiguina, kayak through a mangrove swamp or hitch a ride to El Salvador—the food in the northwest region is both unique and delightful. Among the stops you shouldn't miss are: the cowboy town of El Sauce for homemade honey, Corinto for fresh seafood and Naragote, where you can get local cheese wrapped in a tortilla. Of course, if you're passing through the northwest, don't forget to grab a fragrant, meat-filled roll in Chinandega; the bread this far north is definitely worth the trip. Updated: Oct 08, 2009.

History

Nicaragua was long inhabited by indigenous peoples, and the northwest sector was no exception. When the Spanish arrived in the 1500s, they found thriving communities of Chorotegas and other local peoples. El Viejo, near Chinandega, was once an indigenous capital called Tezoatega, and Leon Viejo, the country's first Spanish capital, was founded next to the existing town of Imabite. The original Leon was founded in 1524 by Francisco Hernandez de Cordoba and had a Royal Foundry House, a blood-soaked square and a cathedral. The city was doomed to succumb to first the greed of local officials and, between 1580 and 1610, devastating volcanic eruptions. Frightened citizens fled the area and founded the new Leon in 1610. (The ruins of the original site were discovered in 1967).

Over the course of the 16th century, Spanish conquistadors spent their time riding out from the Leon capital to establish trade routes and vanquish the locals. One of the most infamous of their raids involved hanging a local chief from the branches of a tree in Naragote. The ancient tree, now a national monument, is a celebrated local feature. By 1796, they had also found time to settle Chinandega and the surrounding fertile lands.

Along with the Spanish came Christianity and every town, it seems, has an important relic with a dramatic story. Among the most important is Nicaragua's patron saint, La Virgen del Trono, which was carried to El Viejo in the 1570s by the brother of Saint Teresa of Spain. Guatemalan priests brought el Santo Christo a Esquipulas (Black Christ) to El Sauce in 1723. The Iglesia de San Nicólas in La Paz Centro was elevated to a national heritage site in 1972.

Following the country's independence from Spain, Leon and Granada fought bitterly for the title of Nicaragua's capital city. Leon finally hired William Walker, a former newspaper editor and the man who would become Nicaragua's historical villain. Walker captured Granada, but made himself president instead of turning over control to Leon. Forced out of the country, Walker set Granada alight. In 1852, the rival cities decided on Managua as the compromise in the capital fight.

The northwestern waterways have had an equally troubled history. The port of El Realajo was so often attacked by pirates that the Nicaraguan government finally moved the majority of the shipping trade to Corinto in 1858. The deep water port became an important railway stop and shipping center. But nature hasn't always been kind to such stops along the Pacific coast. A 1992 tsunami and Hurricane Mitch in 1998 hit the coast hard. Some places, such as the village of Jiquilillo, still haven't recovered from the devastation wrecked by the wind and water. Other points, such as El Transito, have not only rebuilt, but are looking at ways to become more tourist friendly. Updated: Oct 08, 2009.

When to Go

Prepare for heat when you head to the northwest corner of Nicaragua; there is a

Highlights

Leon's cathedral, **the Basílica de la Asunción (p.187)**, across from the Monument to the Martyrs of the Revolution, is the largest in Central America. Inside, find the tomb of Rubén Darío, a 19th century Nicaraguan poet, at the foot of one of the 12 apostle's statues.

Leon (p.182) features more than a dozen of the finest examples of colonial churches in Nicaragua.

Visit **Rubén Darío's house (p.188)**, now a museum, with its collection of personal photographs, portraits and a library of books and poetry in Spanish, English and French.

The Casa de Cultura (p.188) is the only place to see live folk concerts in Leon and always has rotating exhibits and events. Updated: Aug 03, 2009.

Join VIVA on Facebook. Fan "VIVA Travel Guides Nicaragua."

reason Chinandega was named the country's "hottest city" (and Leon is a close second). Temperatures usually hover between 26-30°C (79-86°F), but can climb to 38° C (100°F) in the dry season. The best time to go is at the end of the rainy period, around December to January. Surfers generally avoid the beaches during the heaviest of the rains, from late August to November. The curls may be just as good, but the downpours and thick, clay mud are enough to dampen the lightest spirits. Updated: Oct 08, 2009.

Safety
Leon and the surrounding areas have a higher amount of tourism than other parts of Nicaragua, with a corresponding level of petty crime. As in all areas, make sure to keep a close eye on your belongings. Ask in your hotel or hostel about the going rates for services such as tours, taxi rides and artesan goods. Even if the staff can't tell you the exact prices, they can usually provide a good ballpark figure. Remember—the time to ask about pricing is before you start on a trip or get into a cab, not when you arrive at your destination. Updated: Oct 08, 2009.

Things to See and Do
You won't find yourself twiddling your thumbs in Nicaragua's northwest, where attractions range from smoking volcanoes to ancient ruins. Are old churches your thing? Chinandega and Leon have them in plenty, colorful and grandiose. The beaches out in this section of the country are spectacular, although they have been battered by hurricanes. There can also never be enough said about the volcanoes around the Ring of Fire (especially not when you can head down Cerro Negro on a board—ask at BigFoot Hostel in Leon). Updated: Oct 08, 2009.

Tours
Intur, the national tourism agency, and Marea, the Ministry of the Environment and Natural Resources, have offices in both Leon and Chinandega. These official bureaus are a good place to start when it comes to locating the best tours and most reputable tour agencies. Even far from the cities, though, it's not difficult to find a local guide to take you up a volcano or across the country on horseback. Make sure to ask in Leon for cathedral tours, volcano boarding trips, hikes and adventures in area reserves. Other popular excursions include tours to Cerrania Ecologico Municipal Los Limones (ask at the Tonela city hall), the brick factories in La Paz Centro (ask at the Casa de Cultura) and Chichigalpa's Flor de Caña distillery (call the city hall two weeks in advance of your visit). Updated: Oct 08, 2009.

Lodging
Leon, as one of the most popular cities in Nicaragua, has the greatest variety of accommodation options—although the prices tend to be slightly higher than elsewhere in the country. Outside of Leon, prices drop, but so do accommodation options (in the smaller beach towns you may find there are only one or two choices). The coast has hidden gems, just make sure you have an idea of where you plan to stay so you don't get stranded sleeping on the sand. Chinandega also has plenty of hotels, but the heat is intense enough that you should probably consider paying more for air conditioning. To get the most out of isolated beaches and cliff-side views, try the Ocean Hotel in El Transito, once the getaway of a Samosa general. Updated: Oct 08, 2009.

LEON

🅰 86 m	👤 175,000	☎ 3

The second-oldest Nicaraguan town, Leon was the capital of Nicaragua until 1857 and is today considered its intellectual capital due to its large university-student population. The Monument to the Martyrs of the Revolution and other memorials indicate the liberal-leaning political opinions of the city, which is still a Sandinista stronghold. Other colorful murals and pro-Sandanista graffiti further illustrate this point. Mariachi bands and marimba players are a staple to the city and constantly stroll the streets.

One fun way to explore this quaint colonial city is a 'topless bus' night tour for around $0.25.

When to Go
Like many Central American cities, Leon puts on a blockbuster show for Semana Santa including sawdust street-paintings and re-entactments of the Passion in Barrio Subtiava.

However, our choice for the best time to visit Leon has to be during the Festival Viva, put on by the Viva Leon Jodido Youth Group to celebrate the city's cultural traditions by building enormous folkloric puppets. It's usually held in late April.

Support VIVA! Reserve your hotels or hostels at www.vivatravelguides.com/hotels/

Leon, along with other Nicaraguan cities, also has huge celebrations for La Purisima between Nov. 28 and Dec. 7. Updated: Jun 14, 2008.

Getting to and Away From Leon

Most regional transportation goes from Leon's main bus terminal, a few blocks east of San Juan park. A taxi from downtown should cost $0.75 - 1. Frequent departures for Managua and Chinandega between 4:30 a.m. and 7 p.m. The same station has buses to Matagalpa (4:40 a.m., 7:30 a.m., and 2:45 p.m. as of June 2008) and Esteli (5:20 a.m., 12:45 p.m., 2:15 p.m. and 3:30 p.m.).

For travelers who want to skip Managua entirely, Tierra Tour offers a direct shuttle from Leon to Granada. The minibus leaves Leon at 4 p.m. and arrives in Granada at 8:30 a.m. the next morning. Best to book tickets for this the day before.

If traveling by bus, it is also possible to skip traveling through Managua by going way of Tipitapa (just east of Managua)-Masaya-Granada. This works if you are taking the north-south corridor between Peñas Blancas / Rivas & Esteli - Ocotal / Somota. While it's a bit out of the way to get to León & the northwest, it's possible to take this route as far as San Isidro (part of the way to Esteli) where the highway to León comes in. This San Isidro-León is also the way to reach El Sauce & Achuapa.

International buses can be booked through Benitours (see p. 192), near the Iglesia San Juan. They offer direct buses to San Salvador, San Jose, and Guatemala City, as well as Choluteca (Honduras). Updated: Jun 14, 2008.

Getting Around

Most of the attractions in Leon will be located within walking distance of your accommodations, as long as you don't mind the heat. A taxi just about anywhere shouldn't cost more than $1.50-2 anyway. If you're going from downtown to Barrio Subtiava (or vice-versa), it's just a straight-shot down Calle Ruben Dario. Incidentally, while this street is quite safe, others running parallel are definitely not, some of which pass through barrios which are less tourist-friendly. Regular camionetas and buses also ply the route for about $0.15. Updated: Jun 19, 2009.

Safety

Generally speaking, Leon is quite safe for such a large city. The downtown area is heavily policed during the daytime. At night it's generally safe to walk, though women might not want to do this alone. It gets a bit sketchier once you leave centro. Barrio Subtiava is secure during the day, but definitely not so at night, so if you're exploring the area make sure to head home well before sunset. The area around the bus station can also get dodgy in the evening. Updated: Jun 11, 2008.

Services

Leon has a bank corner (*esquina de bancos*) where all the major bank branches are clustered (BDF, Citi, and Banexpo, among others). The banks are usually open from 8 a.m. to 4 p.m. daily and until noon on Saturdays. Most have 24-hour ATMs that accept Visa; the BAC machine accepts other major cards as well. Bancentro can cash traveler's checks. The bank corner is a convenient cash point as well as a city landmark; you can find *coyotes* (licensed money changers) outside of each bank branch. Make sure you check for identification before agreeing to any transaction. Western Union (505-2-311-2426) is open from 8 a.m. to 5:15 p.m. weekdays and until 1:15 p.m. on Saturdays.

Internet cafés are plentiful and widespread, although some are more comfortable than others, and rates range between $0.50-0.75. Many hotels also include WiFi as part of their services. Many cyber cafés have booths in the back where you can make national ($0.025 per minute) and international ($0.05 per minute to the US) calls.

Correos de Nicaragua (505-2-311-2102/ 6655, cnleon@correosdenicaragua.com.ni) can be found 8.4 meters (27.5 ft) north of the Facultad de Derecho in Barrio San Felipe. Fedex Leon (505-2-311-2426/ 7203) is 42 meters (138 ft) east of Union Fenosa.

Join VIVA on Facebook. Fan "VIVA Travel Guides Nicaragua."

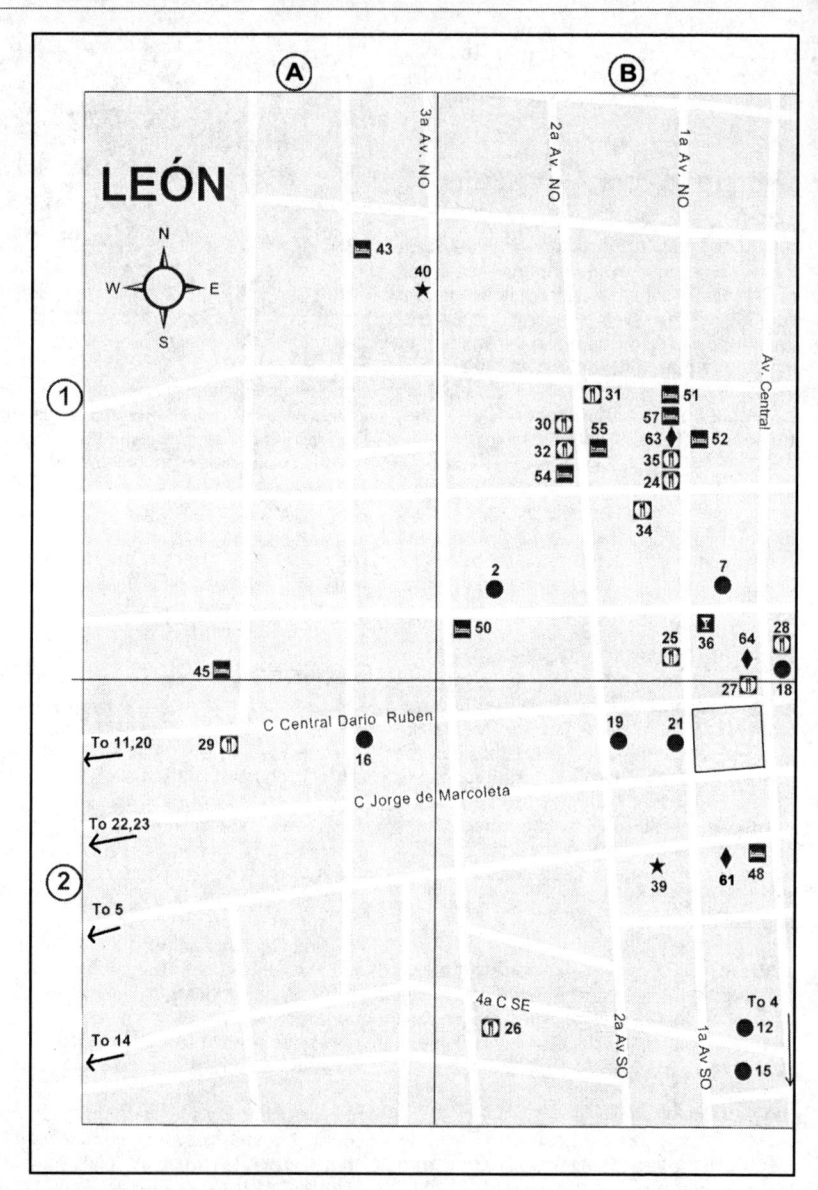

You can find the city's public laundry service, Lavamatic Express (505-2-315-2396), half a block east of the Teatro Municipal. Most hostels and hotels are also able to clean your clothes for you. Ask whether they charge by the piece or the pound.

Leon's main medical center, Hospital Esc. Oscar Danilo Rosales (505-2-311-0936), accepts tourists for treatment and is located in Barrio El Sagrario. There are also private medical practices sprinkled throughout the city where you can find doctors who speak English. You might also ask for a recommendation from one of Leon's many pharmacies, if it's only a minor health concern. Farmacia La Confianza (505-2-315-1490) is right at the bus terminal. Updated: Jun 23, 2009.

Shopping

Centro Commerical sells bags, shoes and clothes between 8 a.m. and 6 p.m. daily, but it's along Calle 2 Norte where you can find rows of bathing suit stores (as well as dentists and opticians, oddly enough). Mercado Central (open from 8 a.m. to 5 p.m. daily) is where you can find pyramids of fresh fruit, vegetables and local arts and crafts. Religious statues and crosses made out of wood and iron are Leon specialties. Leon has several supermarkets, but La Union (505-2-311-5913, open from 7:30 a.m. to 10 p.m., Monday to Saturday and until 8 p.m. Sundays) has a wide range of fresh foods and individual portions. Updated: Jun 23, 2009.

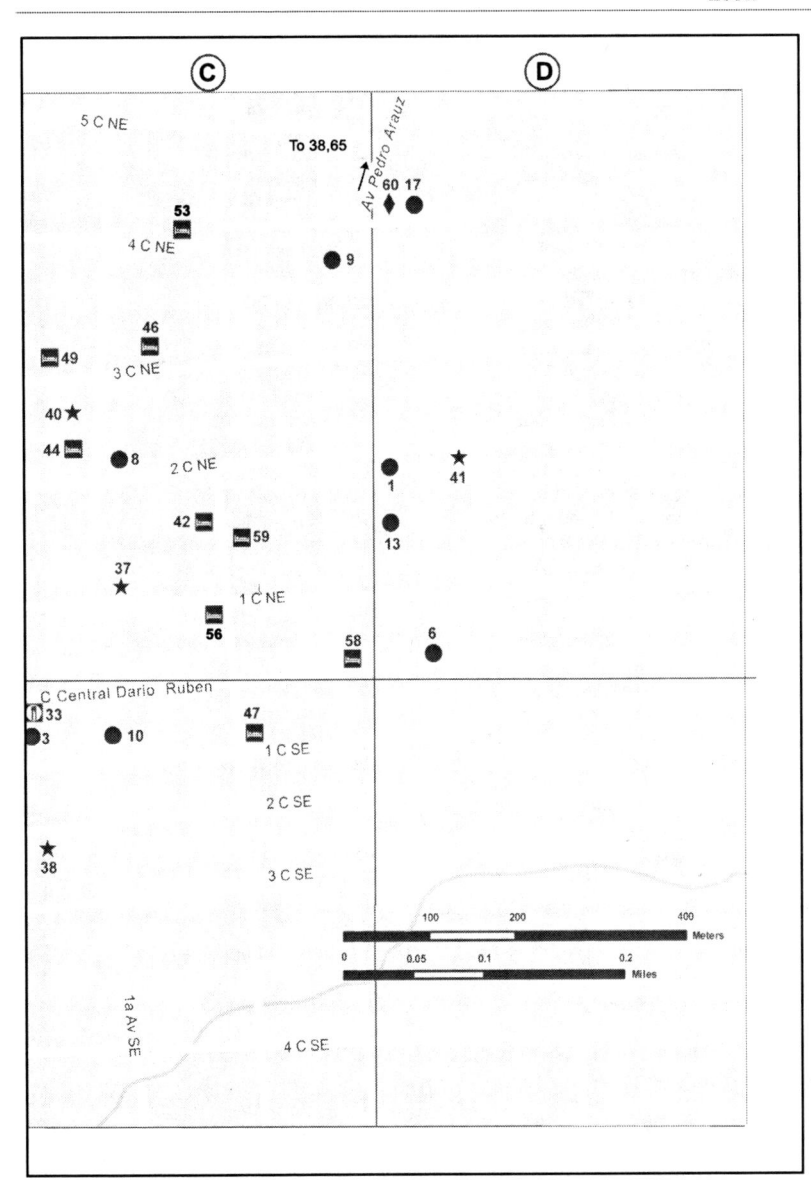

Things to See and Do

Leon could well be called the city of a thousand murals, and these colorful and invariably political expressions are a good thing to look out for while you wander the city. Some of the best ones are located around the Park of Heroes and Martyrs, and along

Activities ●

1 Academia Europea D1
2 Casa De La Cultura B1
3 Cathedral C2
4 Cementerio Guadalupe B2
5 El Tamarindo Tree A2
6 Iglesia El Calvario D1
7 Iglesia La Merced B1
8 Iglesia La Recolección C1
9 Iglesia San Juan de Dios C1
10 Mercado Central C2
11 Museo Adiact A2
12 Museo De La Revolución B2
13 Museo Entomológico D1
14 Museo Insurreccional In Casa El Buzon A2
15 Museum Of Legends B2
16 Museo Ruben Dario A2
17 Old Train Station D1
18 Park of Heroes and Martyrs B1
19 Parque Darío B2
20 Ruinas Santiago A2
21 Ruins San Sebastian B2
22 Ruinas Veracruz A2
23 Sutiava Church A2

Eating

24 Benjamín Linder Café B1
25 Bohemias B1
26 Cocinarte B2
27 El Seseto B2
28 Italian Pizza/Lebanese Food B1
29 La Olla Quemada A2
30 La Terraza M B1
31 Malibu B1
32 Mediterraneo B1
33 Mercado C2
34 Restaurant Sacuanjoche B1
35 Shark Pit B1

Nightlife

36 Don Señor B1

Services ★

37 Bank Corner C1
38 Hospital D1
39 Lavamatic Xpress B2
40 Post Office C1
41 Western Union D1

Sleeping

42 Bigfoot Hostel C1
43 El Sueño De Meme A1
44 Hostal El Colibrí C1
45 Hostal Marian A1
46 Hostel Sonati C1
47 Hotel América C2
48 Hotel Austria B2
49 Hotel Casa Leonsa C1
50 Hotel El Convento B1
51 Hotel Enrique III B1
52 Hotel La Perla B1
53 Hotel La Posada C1
54 La Tortuga Booluda B1
55 Lazy Bones B1
56 Los Balcones C1
57 Posada Doña Blanca B1
58 Parador Oviedo C1
59 Via Via Hostel C1

Tours ◆

60 Benitours D1
61 Julio Tours B2
62 NicAsí (see 59)
63 Tierra Tour B1
64 Tourist Info B1

Transportation

65 Bus Terminal D1

---

the basketball courts between Parque Central and Iglesia la Merced, but the city is covered with them.

Church Tour

Starting at the central park, check out the biggest Cathedral in Central America then climb its roof for good views of the city. From the northern corner, head five blocks east to the Iglesia de El Calvario, which is brightly painted, then three blocks west and two blocks north to the Iglesia de la Recoleccion, a bright yellow building with ornate pillars. Head two blocks west and go south to the Iglesia de la Merced, beside a pleasant little park. Then head west two blocks and south one for Iglesia de San Fransisco before going east to end up back at the central park. Updated: Nov 22, 2006.

Support VIVA! Reserve your hotels or hostels at www.vivatravelguides.com/hotels/

Basílica de la Asunción

This massive edifice is Central America's biggest cathedral, and one of the highlights of a visit to Leon. From the outside it appears as just another large church, but the towering marble columns of the interior are enough to leave a visitor breathless. A stunning display of grand neo-classical architecture, the place is beautifully maintained, and the walls are decorated with exquisite frescoes.

Perhaps the best way to fully take in this magnificent building is by climbing to the roof where you can walk right up to the edge and enjoy some amazing views. Tickets for the roof must be bought from little crypt hidden at south-east corner of cathedral, then you ascend by stairs on the left of the main entrance. Updated: July 10, 2007.

Tomb of Ruben Dario

Inside the Catedral de Leon and just to the right of the altar, look for a life-sized statue of a depressed-looking lion. Here, at the base of a massive column, lies Ruben Dario, Leon's favorite son. The monument bears his name, as well as a collection of beautiful neo-classical sculptures. Other tombs to look out for in the cathedral include Alfonso Cortes and independence fighter Miguel de Larreynaga. Updated: Jun 11, 2008.

Iglesia Calvario

With its colorful, sculptured facade and immaculately painted interior, this church is second only to Leon's cathedral in terms of beauty and should not be missed. Unfortunately, like many of Leon's churches, it seems to be closed more than it's open (it generally shuts after 10 a.m.). However, if visitors walk through the adjoining park to the back, the administrative office is often open. This connects to the church, and if you smile and ask politely they should let you in for a peek. Updated: Jun 11, 2008.

Iglesia de la Recolección

Yet another beautiful church, Iglesia de la Recolección is worth a look if you're still hungry for more religious imagery after seeing the Cathedral and Iglesia Calvario. The church was subject to an expensive restoration courtesy of the Italian and Spanish governments, and it shows. An impressive yellow facade gives way to a richly decorated interior, with elegant carvings and expressive statues of the stations of the cross. The sculpture of Jesus and God at the front, just to the left of the altar, is particularly intriguing. The church is generally open early in the morning, or after 4:30 p.m. Updated: Jan 29, 2009.

Iglesia San Juan de Dios

The façade of Iglesia San Juan de Dios, which overlooks a park of the same name, is a mottled grey and not exactly what you would call pretty. The exterior, reconstructed by Mons. Santiago Abarca in the 1850s, conceals a lovely white interior with glass cases of saints and delicate ceiling murals. The church itself was originally constructed in 1739. Be aware during your visit that the nearby park is dirty and dodgy and that, while the church itself is on the edge of Leon's relatively safe downtown, the more dangerous bus depot area is also nearby. Updated: Jun 19, 2009.

Museo de la Revolucion

Staffed by veterans of Nicaragua's numerous wars, the Museo de la Revolucion is a good place to visit if you're interested in the conflicts that wracked this nation. The museum mostly contains photos, but you can spend an interesting afternoon chatting to the soldiers about their experiences. As you might guess from the name, their allegiances swing heavily towards the Sandinistas. They also offer city tours for $10. Open from 8:30 a.m.-5:30 p.m., the museum is located in Parque Central on the eastside. Updated: Jun 11, 2008.

Join VIVA on Facebook. Fan "VIVA Travel Guides Nicaragua."

Iglesia de la Merced
The beautiful, traditional wood paneling of this sweeping church almost suggests a European style, but the massive icons betray its Latin identity. Worth checking out for its intricately carved altar, as well as statues depicting the stations of the cross. Located on Av 1 Nor-Oeste.

Casa de Cultura
With its highly political murals and bohemian layout, the Casa de Cultura represents part of Leon's rich cultural legacy. The place offers dance, guitar and sculpture classes, as well as hosts a range of performances and special events. Drop in to see what's playing, or sign up for a course if you're interested in broadening your cultural horizons. Located one block north of the Iglesia San Francisco. Tel: 505-2-311-2116, E-mail: casadeculturaleonnicaragua@yahoo.com. Updated: Nov 26, 2009.

Parque los Poetas
(aka Parque Ruben Dario)
Dominated by a statue of Leon's favorite son, the park honors other local poets as well. It's a popular spot to sit, chat, and people-watch, but doesn't offer much else to the visitor. Ave 2a West, Calle Ruben Dario.

Park of Heroes and Martyrs
Located across the street and to the north of the main cathedral, the small, modest mausoleum honors some of Leon's revolutionary fighters. Several high-ranking soldiers as well as non-military figures are buried here. While the monument is not particularly impressive, the mural surrounding it is one of the city's best, chronicling the history of Nicaragua from the Spanish conquest through the civil wars, and ending with a pair of children breaking through the barriers of the past and emerging into the bright vision of tomorrow. Updated: Jun 11, 2008.

Centro de Arte Fundacion Ortiz-Gurdian
This small art gallery features the private collection of the foundation, including paintings and sculptures by local and international artists. Entrance is $0.60, plus about $1 more if you want a guided tour. Ave 4a West, just south of Calle Ruben Dario. Open from 10:30 a.m. - 6:30 p.m. Closed Mondays. Updated: Jun 11, 2008.

Museum of Traditions and Legends
Founded by Dona Carmen Toruno, who created many of the exhibits, the Museum of Traditions and Legends celebrates the region's favorite folk tales and heroes with paper-mache figures. The museum has five rooms, four of which are filled with fables such as La Carreta Nagua, Las Ceguas, La Chancha Bruja, La Llorona and La Gigantona (the famous dancing giant). Small placards explain the legends in Spanish; you can usually get the bored curator to walk you through the rooms, if you ask. The building was once the infamous XXI Prison and, painted in the final room and on the front of the museum, there are images of men undergoing the types of tortures the National Guard once inflicted. The exhibitions themselves aren't very impressive—imagine a very extensive high school project—but the prison's bullet-scarred walls hold a lot of history. There are also some interesting political and historical murals painted on the outside. Open from 8 a.m. - 12 p.m., and 2- 5 p.m. Closed Mondays and half-days Sundays. Calle 4a South, across from the church of San Sebastien, Tel: 505-912-7246. Updated: Oct 07, 2009.

Museo Ruben Dario
Considering about half of Leon is named after him, it's perhaps not surprising that the former home of Ruben Dario is now a museum. Exhibits chronicle his life and work, including numerous photographs, letters and even a death-mask. Many rooms in the house, such as the bedroom, remain as he left them, giving an interesting insight into Nicaraguan life in the 19th century. Calle Ruben Dario O and Ave 4, Tel: 505-311-2388. Updated: Jun 14, 2008.

Museo Entomologico
For the past two decades, Jean-Michel Maes and his wife, Juana Téllez R. have been collecting all the many forms of Nicaraguan insects (beautiful blue morphos, armored rhinoceros beetles, scorpions big and small) and inviting visitors to see them. Three years ago, they opened the long-planed Museo Entomológico de Leon, the country's most extensive insect collection. The museum is a surprisingly small space, considering it contains 725,000 specimens and 10,000 species (including exotic examples from other countries). Even if the idea of creepy crawlies makes you shudder, you won't want to miss a peek into the carefully labeled cases of jewel-like bugs and glowing butterflies. The place is also a research center, so those with a serious interest in entomology will enjoy

bug-chats with the curator. The museum is open from 9 a.m. to noon and 2-4 p.m. daily and costs $0.05. Calle 2a, Ave 3 NE, Tel: 505-311-6586, URL: www.bio-nica.info. Updated: Jun 19, 2009.

Volcanoes

Nicaragua is famous for its volcanoes, and Leon is an excellent base from which to explore some of the best. Of course, Nicaragua's small size means the same volcanoes are accessible from just about anywhere in the country, and tour operators in Granada (among other cities) offer many of the same trips. It's really a question of where you want to hang your hat at the end of the day.

Although these volcanoes don't offer lava flows like Pacaya, they're by no means inactive. If you decide to climb up Volcán El Viejo, the country's most difficult, expect to be hit by periodic showers of dirt and ash from the burbling cone. Generally speaking; however, the real challenge is posed by the heat and steep nature of the ascent. You should be in excellent physical shape if you want to conquer El Viejo or Momotombo. Essential items to bring include sunscreen, insect repellent and lots of water.

Finally, no matter how experienced a climber you are, you shouldn't attempt to conquer any of these volcanoes without a guide. Nicaragua's park service actually requires guides for most ascents, and their local knowledge of the labyrinthine trails will come in handy should anything unexpected happen. Tierra Tours, located in Granada and Leon, offer the widest variety of trip options. As with most trips, it's cheaper if you book with a large group. Updated: Jan 28, 2009.

Volcán El Viejo

This grueling four hour climb is said to be the hardest in Nicaragua, as well as the most dangerous. The volcano is extremely active, but the chief difficulty is the cone's massive size, a towering 1745 meters (5,725 ft. Expect to leave at 5:30 a.m. and be back by 4:30 p.m. Bring your own lunch, as well as long sleeves, a cap, sunscreen, repellent, and at least two liters of water. A tour costs between $40-55, depending on the size of your group. Updated: Jan 28, 2009.

Volcán Momotombo

Leon is one of several cities from which tours can be booked to Volcán Momotombo, though Managua is closer to the actual volcano. Tierra Tour (see p. 192) is one of a few operators in the city that books day-trips there. Departure is at 5:30 a.m. for the two-hour drive to base camp. You should reach the top just before noon for a stunning view of Lake Momotombo and the surrounding area (including a few other active volcanoes), before heading back down to beat the scorching heat. It's Nicaragua's second hardest climb after El Viejo, with steep hills of ash and loose sand that will test your endurance. Tierra Tour will take you up for between $40-60, depending on group sizes. For those who want to go at a more leisurely pace or enjoy other attractions in the area, overnight stays are also possible. Updated: Jun 15, 2008.

Volcán el Hoyo

Volcán el Hoyo offers a much easier climb than others in the area, and is popular chiefly for the outstanding view from the 1000 meter (3,280 ft) summit. Tours depart around 6 a.m. and should have you back in Leon by 3 p.m. The trip should cost between $30-60 per person, depending on the size of your group and your negotiating skills. The trip can be extended into a two-day tour that also takes in the crystal waters of the nearby Laguna El Tigre. Contact Tierra Tour for more details. Updated: Jan 28, 2009.

Volcán Cerro Negro

At a mere 150 years old, Cerro Negro is the youngest volcano in Central America. It's also one of the most popular climbs—travelers never forget their first sight of it's cinder-black cone against the rich green of the surrounding hillsides. The Cerro Negro is one of the region's most active volcanoes, erupting about every five years. But this generally does not pose a danger to climbers, and you shouldn't expect to see any lava.

In fact, Cerro Negro is the cheapest, easiest and most popular volcano to explore in the area. The climb is often done as a half-day trip from 8 a.m to 12:30 p.m. The cone is just 673 meters (2,208 ft) high, but offers a spectacular view of the other active volcanoes in the area.

It is possible to climb Cerro Negro by yourself, with the detailed directions found here: http://www.rci.rutgers.edu/~carr/fieldtrip/fieldtext/cerro_negro_fldtxt.htm.

Still, it is recommended to go with a guide, as the path is a difficult one to negotiate if you're

Join VIVA on Facebook. Fan "VIVA Travel Guides Nicaragua."

not familiar with the area. Tierra Tour offers a trip up Cerro Negro, as does Julio tours (see p. 192. This latter combines the trip with a visit to a local farm, where visitors have the option of milking cows. There are also local establishments that offer volcano boarding trips up the sides of Volcán Cerro Negro. Updated: Jan 28,2009

Volcano Boarding

One of the best ways to see Volcán Cerro Negro is by going down the volcano's side on a board. While there are other tours, the Bigfoot Hostel version (see p. 193) starts in the late afternoon: you head out to the volcano base then climb to a viewpoint over a steaming crater. From there you continue to the top for a view over the entire volcano chain, including San Cristobal, Casita and the smoking Telca. After a look into the second crater, where you can feel hot rocks and see rising steam and sulfur deposits, you can watch the sunset then jump on a wooden board to enjoy a fun, but slightly scary, 600 meter (1,968 ft) ride to the bottom. The volcano is expected to explode soon, but the tour operator is keeping tabs. The $23 cost to board does not include the $4.50 national park entrance fee. Updated: Jan 28, 2009.

Isla Momotombito

In theory, there is a port where you can catch a boat from the mainland to Isla Momotombito (if you're desperate to see a handful of petroglyphs and statues left over from ancient ceremonies). In reality, you have to make your way to the edge of the lake from Leon Viejo and then find a fisherman willing to take you the nine kilometers (5.6 mi)to the island. Be prepared to pay over $97 for the privilege. The small volcanic cone, a baby compared to the giant Momotombo, is easily visible from the ruins of the old Leon. Updated: Oct 08, 2009.

Ruins of Saint Sebastien

This once-beautiful church was destroyed by the government's bombing of the city in 1979. A new building was hastily constructed next-door to house the church's icons, but it remains half-finished and open to the elements. The ruins themselves are rather unimpressive and derelict, only a few arches remain, and it's not particularly pleasant to walk through. Calle 4a south. Updated: Jun 15, 2008.

Cementerio Guadalupe de Leon

To visit the final resting place of many Nicaraguan dignitaries, poets, musicians, presidents and military figures, head to Cementerio Guadalupe de Leon, a sprawling site of almost 25 city blocks that was constructed in 1831 (it opened in 1834). The Nicaraguan government declared Cementerio de Guadalupe a national historical and artistic site in 1983.

The cemetery holds the remains of, among others: José Zepeda, the first head of state and a brilliant military colonel; Patricio Rivas, who was provisional president of Nicaragua from October 1855 to June 1857; José Madriz Rodriguez, president of Nicaragua from 1909 to 1910 before being forced into exile in Mexico (the Leon native's remains were brought to Nicaragua in 1965). You might also find the tomb of General Máximo Jerez Tellería, considered to be the father of Nicaraguan liberalism, who died during a diplomatic mission to Washington D.C. Or, you might stumble across the grave of General Carlos A. Castro Wassmer, who rivaled Anastasio Somoza García for head of the National Guard before being murdered in prison.

The cemetery still has an old entrance and an original wall, both dating back to around the time of construction. The wall was built with niches, but most of them are empty. A small mausoleum across from the old section of the cemetery is dedicated to Don Simon Echeverría, the cemetery's designer and master builder. Unfortunately, much of the cemetery has now fallen into ruin and is covered with weeds. If you're searching out famous tombs, be prepared to wander—there is little to mark your way. Updated: Jan 22, 2009.

Ruins of Leon Viejo

A visit to the ruins of Nicaragua's first capital, Leon Viejo, is a trip in time—back to the early years of the Spanish conquest when beheadings, slavery and native uprisings were common.

Located right outside Puerto Momotombo, Sitio Histórico Colonial Ruinas de Leon Viejo is an easily accessible park. Tours of the site include visits to merchant houses with their discreet alleyway exit routes (used during native uprisings); the crypt of Iglesia de Nuestra Señora de Merced; and the Royal Foundry House, where gold was processed and slaves were marked, giving the location the cheerful nickname "house of the howls."

Until the site was rediscovered and excavated in 1967, Leon Viejo was a Nicaraguan legend that mixed the immorality of Sodom and Gomorah with the destruction of Poneloya and the sinking of Atlantis.

Spanish captain Francisco Hernández de Córdoba founded the city in 1524—right where indigenous Chorotegas had a town called Imabite. In the same year, the busy captain had a fortress built for the new city, and also found time to settle Granada.

Two years later, Córdoba would be beheaded in Leon's central square on a charge of treason by the country's brutal ruler Pedrarias Dávila. Córdoba's head was then buried in the square while his body went into the church crypt.

Dávila, the governor of the Dárien-Panama region, had a well-deserved reputation for being bloodthirsty and corrupt. In 1528, he capped a notoriously ruthless reign with the execution of 18 Chorotega warriors—payback for the murder of half a dozen Spaniards. Dávila had the warriors dragged one by one to the plaza, where they were ripped apart by his dogs. In the park, a white and yellow statue of Dávila, with a dog at his heel, holds gourds in memory of the dead.

Dávila's daughter and grandsons would go on to murder Fray Antonio de Valdivieso, Bishop of Nicaragua and champion of indigenous rights, before also killing local Spanish officials and sacking the treasury.

It was a series of earthquakes and volcanic eruptions between 1580 and 1610 that would finally put an end to the city (some would say as divine retribution). Locals took what they could and, in 1610, fled from Momotombo's ashy fury to settle at the site of the current Leon.

Over the following centuries, Nicaraguans told tall tales of how the old city had been swallowed by fire or had plunged into Lago Nicaragua. The old city was declared a national historical site in 1994 and, in 2000, UNESCO added the ruins to its World Heritage list. Located near Puerto Momotombo, most tour operators in Leon offer packages that include visits to the old city. To get there on your own, take the bus from the Leon terminal to the terminal at La Paz Centro. Buses from La Paz Centro to Puerto Momotombo ($0.50) run hourly from 6:30 a.m. Open from Mon. — Fri. 9 a.m. — 5 p.m., and Sat. 9 a.m. — 4 p.m. Closed Sundays. Updated: Jun 22, 2009.

El Fortín de Acosasco

El Fortin is a striking symbol of the Sandinista's triumph over Somoza and his national guard. Unfortuately, this striking piece of history sits on a hill by the city's former garbage dump, where the city's poorest to scrabble for anything salvageable. This is definitely not a safe place to walk, but taxis will take you to the fort for about $5.

Built in 1889 on a hill near Sutiava, El Fortin has a gorgeous view of the city below. The building is clean, although somewhat overgrown, with a sunken building of cells and gun turrets around the edges. The fort held Somoza's political prisoners for decades, right up until July 7, 1979 when El Fortin was overrun and the Sandinista captives liberated. July, when they hold annual celebrations of the Sandinista victory, is the best time to visit the prison. The July 7 festivities include historical reenactments, a visit by Nicaragua's president and, of course, fireworks. Updated: Jul 07, 2009.

Old Train Station

Leon's Old Train Station is still intact, but is difficult to locate since all but the roofline has been obscured by the ever expanding Mercado Santo Barsesna (open 7 a.m. to 6 p.m. daily). The train station has crumbling adobe walls, a rickety wooden roof and swooping iron girders. To find the building, walk behind Iglesia San Juan, through the market and cross the other side of the street. When you come to the section where vendors sell bags of grain and feed, look up and you should be able to spot the narrow roof. Inside, you'll find barber shops and used clothing stores. Updated: Jun 23, 2009.

Academia Europea

The Leon branch (505-2-311-1813/ 8-988-4482, www.academia-europea.com) of Academia Europea offers both private and group classes in Spanish. Private classes start at $18 per hour ($540 for 30 hours), while group classes start at $20 per hour ($600 for 30 hours). The group classes are held at the academy's pleasant, adobe walled school, 1.5 blocks south of Iglesia San Juan. Tel: 505-2-311-1813/ 988-4482. URL: www.academia-europea.com. Updated: Jun 19, 2009.

Tours

Leon's downtown area has quite a few tour operators, most of which are attached to the major hostels. Via Via and Bigfoot both have in-house agencies to plan your trips around the region. The most popular trips to book are volcano-related expeditions, since these generally require a guide. Prices vary, and some agencies are more open to negotiation than others, so shop around. Leon also has two government-run tourist information offices, which don't handle booking, but are useful resources. Updated: Jun 11, 2008.

NicAsí Tours

Designed to give visitors an authentic taste of life as a Nicaraguan, Nicaragua-Así Tours takes you to places you wouldn't think of visiting. The company motto is: no secrets, no exaggerations, no covering up the truth. If you are really curious about real life in Leon, try one of these tours. NicAsí Tours was set up by travelers who were curious about the people and their lives. Among the options available: cocktails and a pedicure from a local beauty specialist; a visit on Sunday afternoon with Don Pedro and Doña Ana, who organize the traditional rooster fights; experiencing the life of a cowboy for a day; a history tour designed to take you back to the time of conquistadores and the revolution; and a cooking workshop run by a local family. NicAsí Tours also offers several different excursions around Leon and nature tours of Isla Juan Venado and Concha Negra. Del banco Procredit, 75 vrs al sur, #210. Office located inside ViaVia Hotel. Tel: 505-414-1192/8999-4754, E-mail: info@nicasitours.com/harrie@nicasitours.com, URL: www.nicasitours.com. Updated: Jul 08, 2009.

Julio Tours

Locally owned and operated, Julio Tours specializes in tours of the city but also takes groups up Volcán Cerro Negro, as well as a few other regional destinations. Julio, the owner, speaks fluent English and is an excellent resource for information about the area. If you're looking for a full-service option, Julio offers airport pickups as well. Located one block north of the Cathedral. Tel: 505-625-4467, E-mail: juliotours2000@yahoo.com. Updated: Nov 20, 2008.

> **V!VA ONLINE REVIEW**
> JULIO TOURS
>
> *It was exceptional to have the care and personalized experience provided by such knowledgeable, fun, compassionate, understanding and PUNCTUAL experts!*
>
> June 8, 2008

Tierra Tour

Tierra Tour offers just about everything, including trips up every volcano in the area, city tours, flight bookings and bus tickets. The staff are friendly, helpful and speak English. Some trips offered are unique to Tierra Tour, so definitely check out their options. Open 8 a.m. to 12 p.m. and 2- 7 p.m., seven days a week. Located 1.5 blocks north of Iglesia La Merced. Tel: 505-2-315-4278 / 552-8723, E-mail: tierratour@dds.nl, URL: www.tierratour.com. Updated: Jul 08, 2009.

Benitours

Benitours is the place to go for long-haul bus tickets. A direct bus to Guatemala City via Choluteca (Honduras) and San Salvador (El Salvador) leaves every day at 6 a.m. They also have daily departures for San Jose, Costa Rica. Both of these should be reserved at least a day in advance. Flight tickets can also be purchased here. Benitours is open from 8 a.m. to 5 p.m. Located ½ block north of Iglesia San Juan. Tel: 505-315-2349, E-mail: benitoursagency@yahoo.es. Updated: Nov 20, 2008.

Support VIVA! Reserve your hotels or hostels at www.vivatravelguides.com/hotels/

Tourist Information Office

The office staff is helpful and friendly, though their English is limited. They offer bus schedules, tour and hotel information, as well as historical information about the city and its attractions. Getting this more detailed info might take a bit of prodding however, as well as a good knowledge of Spanish. Still, they're an excellent resource. Open Mon.-Sat. from 8:30 a.m. - 12 p.m., 2 - 5:30 p.m., and Sun. from 9 a.m. - 12 p.m. Ave Central, 1/2 block north of the Cathedral. Updated: Jun 15, 2008.

Intur

Nicaragua's national tourism center has a branch in Leon, but they do little more than hand out brochures. While they do have some useful info on bus schedules, generally speaking the tourism office next to the Parque Central is more helpful. Across from Casa del Obrero, the center is at Ave 2a NO, between Calle 1 and Calle 2. Updated: Jun 15, 2008.

Lodging

As a popular tourism destination, Leon has no shortage of excellent accommodations to suit all prices ranges. For the budget backpacker, Via Via, Bigfoot and Lazybones are the best and most popular options. The last one is slightly expensive for a hostel, but take a peek inside and you'll realize why. Midrange options are mostly bed-and-breakfasts, while the glorious Hotel la Perla is probably the nicest high-end place in Centro.

BUDGET

Parador Oviedo

(DORMS: $3, ROOMS: $7.50) If cutting costs is your goal, then Parador Oviedo is the place for you. Conveniently located just a few blocks outside of Leon's city center, this hostel has few amenities aside from a common kitchen and patio that all the rooms face onto. This is a good place to meet backpackers who are bent on stretching their budget. Also, you can probably find out a few informative tidbits and tips about travel in Nicaragua and Central America from other travelers staying there. Located in front of Calvario Leon Church. Tel: 505-2-311-6750. Updated: Nov 26, 2009.

Hostel Sonati !

Just opened in August 2009, the friendly little Hostel Sonati (for Sociedad y Naturaleza Internacional) puts all its profits into environmental education and nature conservation programmes in order to ensure their sustainability. Yet the hostel owners take their business seriously and offer impeccably clean, neat rooms and dorms at reasonable prices. There are three dorms of four, six and eight beds (prices range from $5-7.50 per person), set around a small patio with hammocks, as well as a couple of private rooms which share a bathroom ($11 single occupancy, $20 double occupancy). There a computer with free Internet, a book exchange and a laundry service, plus a kitchen for guests and a water refill service. Located one block north and half a block east from iglesia la recoleccion. Tel: 505-2-311-4251, e-mail: sonati.leon@gmail.com, URL: www.sonati.org

Bigfoot Hostel

(DORMS: $6, ROOMS: $13) Bigfoot Hostel is a new place, run by an enthusiastic and ultra-friendly Aussie, Darryn, and his local staff. It's a treat to stay at Bigfoot. A popular bar in front leads to large dorm rooms. The rooms are located around a grassy, green courtyard with hammocks and wicker rocking chairs. The dorms and the four private rooms are simply decorated, with emphasis on being clean and cheap, and there is a kitchen with free coffee. There is a good vibe and it is a nice place to meet other travelers, providing it is not already full. The tours run from the hostel include trips up Volcán Cerro Negro to go volcano boarding. The boarding trips cost $23 plus park entrance fees. Av. Santiago Arguello between Ca. NE and 2a Ca. NE (opposite Via Via), URL: www.bigfootnicaragua.com. Updated: Apr 13, 2009.

Lazy Bones

(DORMS: $8, ROOMS: $15-22) Lazy Bones in Leon is a classy, modern hostel offering dorm beds and private rooms with and without on-suite bathrooms. It is a great value, especially for the dorm rooms. The hostel as a whole is clean and aesthetically pleasing, much like its sister hostel in Granada, Hostel Oasis. If you are looking for a rowdy party scene found at some hostels this is not the place, as it tends to cater to older, slightly upscale backpackers. Lazy Bones is still a good time though, with a swimming pool and inviting common areas. The 15 percent tax is included in the price. Parque de los Poetas, 2 1/2 North, Tel: 505-311-3472, E-mail: enquiries@lazybonesleon.com, URL: www.lazybonesleon.com. Updated: Nov 23, 2009.

Hostal Marian

(ROOMS: $10-30) Hostal Marian has a great location in the center of town. The rates are low and the rooms are very clean. If you have your car, you can park it in the garage at night. From the Ruben Dario Museum one block west and 1/2 block north. Directly behind the school - La Salle. Tel: 505-311-0870, E-mail: marianhostal@gmail.com. Updated: Jan 29, 2009.

> **V!VA ONLINE REVIEW**
> HOSTAL MARIAN
>
> "The hostal is in a great location, very close to museums and restaurants. The rooms were nice and clean."
>
> *July 15, 2008*

La Tortuga Booluda

(ROOMS: $10-35) La Tortuga Booluda is a clean and pleasant hostel with a wide kitchen, murals on the wall and a small book exchange. Located four blocks from the central park, La Tortuga is close enough to most attractions to make them accessible. The hostel has a small courtyard, but seemed to have less of a social atmosphere than competitors on the east side of the city. The rooms vary in price but range from $10 per person to $35 for a room with air conditioning. Tel: 505-2-311-4653, E-mail: totugabooluda@yahoo.com, URL: www.tortugabooluda.com. Updated: Jun 19, 2009.

Hotel America

(ROOMS: $12 – 22) The America has nice rooms, all of which feature a private bathroom. The place is reasonably clean and well-kept, with Internet for a fee. 2 Ave SE, Between Calle 1a SE and Ave Ruben Dario, two blocks behind the Cathedral. Tel: 505-311-5533, E-mail: rgalloa@yahoo.com. URL: www.vianica.com/hoteles/leon/hotelamerica. Updated: May 13, 2009.

El Sueño de Meme

(ROOMS: $12 single / $70 quintuple) El Sueño de Meme specializes in long-term stays and offers discounts for those sticking around for extended periods of time. All of their rooms are private with bathrooms, TVs and either a fan or air-conditioning. There is also a small, 20 person conference center. While there is nothing particularly special about the place, the single rooms are a fair price, especially those with a fan.

If you plan on staying here for more than a few days try to negotiate a deal because the hotel is used to bargaining. Three blocks West and 75 meters (246 ft) North of Colegio Mercantil, Tel: 505-2-311-5365, E-mail: hotelmeme@alfanumeric.com.ni. Updated: Nov 26, 2009.

Hostal Colibri

(ROOMS: $13 – 15) A budget option for those seeking private rooms, the Colibri's rooms are dark and rather unimpressive, partly because the windows all face into the hallway, making the place devoid of natural light. Still, it's safe and friendly, with an outstanding common kitchen and free WiFi. Located a half block north of Iglesia la Recollecion. Tel: 505-656-7730, E-mail: iguana.colibri@yahoo.com. Updated: Jun 09, 2009.

Via Via

This has been a popular hostel for a long time. There is a very lively bar/cafe out front, so lively that it shakes the front dorm room at times, which leads through to a grassy rear courtyard with hammocks and chairs. Rooms are okay and it is a toss-up between here and Bigfoot, both of which often are full by midday. Price includes breakfast, taxes and service. Del Servicio Agricola Gurdian, 75 Varas al Sur (210), E-mail: leon.nicaragua@viaviacafe.com, URL: http://www.viaviacafe.com/. Updated: Oct 12, 2009.

> **V!VA ONLINE REVIEW**
> VIA VIA
>
> "Nice cheap restaurant, with good night life. Rooms were clean, modern, and nice. Great location! The dorms looked really nice too."
>
> *November 19, 2008*

MID-RANGE
Posada Dona Blanca

(ROOMS: $32 – 70) This is one of several bed and breakfasts in the area that offers television, hot water, and air conditioning. Other places have a nicer atmosphere, but Dona Blanca's offers free WiFi. Their suites, at the high end of the price spectrum, are much larger and more impressive. There's also a small gift shop in the front. Breakfast is included. Located one block north of the Iglesia La Merced. Tel: 505-311-2521, E-mail: recepcion@posadadonablanca.com, URL: www.posadadonablanca.com. Updated: Nov 23, 2009.

Hotel Enrique 3
(ROOMS: $35 – 50) Set around a pleasant, quiet courtyard, Enrique 3 offers clean rooms with air conditioning, TVs, hot water and big comfortable beds. Enrique 3 is a new, and reasonably clean bed and breakfast. It's cozy and romantic and is a good place for couples. Price includes breakfast. Located two streets north of Iglesia la Merced. Tel: 505-311-4015, E-mail: hotelenrique3@cablenet.com.ni, URL: www.enrique3.com. Updated: Mar 13, 2009.

Los Balcones
(ROOMS: $43 – 77) This hotel is great for upscale travelers looking for comfort and amenities. They also have a conference center capable of accommodating 100 people, which makes it a great place for business retreats or excursions as well. Located in the charming colonial downtown area of Leon, Los Balcones is within easy walking distance of restaurants, movie theaters, banks and bars. They can also provide you with information regarding tours from Leon and other relevant tourist information. Tel: 1-888-535-8382 / 1-800-948-3770, E-mail: LosBalcones@centralamerica.com, URL: http://centralamerica.com/nicaragua/hotels/balcones.htm. Updated: Nov 26, 2009.

Hotel Austria
(ROOMS: $39 – 90) The low price is for a one-person standard room and the high price is for a family suite. An additional person in a standard room is $10, $12 for a mini-suite and $15 in a family suite. From the Cathedral, the hotel is one block south. Tel: 505-311-1206/ 7158 / 7179, Fax: 505-311-1368, E-mail: haustria@ibw.com.ni, URL: www.hotelaustria.com.ni. Updated: Jun 19, 2009.

Hotel La Posada del Doctor
(ROOMS: $40 – 80) Charmingly laid-out and sparklingly clean, La Posada del Doctor is a comfortable way to explore Leon's colonial past. The hotel also has an excellent restaurant and tour agency. Located 25 meters (82 ft) west of San Juan Park. Tel: 505-311-4343, E-mail: posadadr@ibw.com.ni, URL: www.laposadadeldoctor.com. Updated: Nov 23, 2009.

Hotel Casa Leonesa
(ROOMS: $45-65) Casa Leonesa is located in an old, but well-maintained building. Of the three bed and breakfasts in the area, Leonesa probably has the best atmosphere. Their suites in particular are large, impressive, and are an excellent value. Breakfast is included as is free WiFi, though their "pool" is rather unimpressive. Located three blocks north, 1.5 blocks east of the Cathedral. Tel: 505-311-0551, E-mail: lacasaleonesa@gmail.com, URL: www.casaleonesa.com. Updated: Nov 14, 2008.

HIGH-END
Hotel El Convento
(ROOMS: $70-111) This classy hotel is located in the former San Francisco convent, the oldest in Leon. There are two on-site restaurants: one offering international and national cuisine, the other is a cafeteria. It's the location in the former convent though, that gives Hotel El Convento its charm. Tel: 505-311-7053, E-mail: reservaciones@hotelelconvento.com.ni, URL: www.otelelconvento.com.ni. Updated: Jan 14, 2009.

Hotel La Perla
(ROOMS: $80-178) Who would have expected a place of such opulence in the heart of Sandinista territory? From the Italian marble staircases to the canopied showers, everything about La Perla screams luxury. The elegant building was designed by Jose Maria Ibarra, one of the nation's foremost architects. Different rooms have different features and advantages—from pool access to street side balconies, so be sure to be specific about what you want when you're making your reservation. Located 1.5 blocks north of Iglesia La Merced. Tel: 505-311-3125, E-mail: info@laperlaleon.com, URL: www.laperlaleon.com. Updated: Mar 11, 2009.

Restaurants
Leon's downtown core offers a wide range of restaurants to fit any budget and taste—from street-meat to five-star restaurants and from *comida tipica* to Italian cuisine. With the exception of a few outstanding street stands, you generally get what you pay for from eating here. If you decide to splurge on a nice meal at Mediterraneo or La Perla, you won't be disappointed. Updated: Jun 14, 2008.

El Sesteo
(ENTREES: $6-7) The setting is what makes this place, and it is the only restaurant that offers a view over to the cathedral from its outdoor patio dining area. Food is good with reasonably sized plates, but prices are very expensive for what is effectively meat, rice and beans. There are Mexican dishes

available for less money, but it may be better just to get a drink and enjoy the view. Located on the corner of Park Central. Tel: 505-2-311-5327. Updated: Nov 26, 2009.

CocinArte

(ENTREES: $8-10) CocinArte is a restaurant specializing in vegetarian and fruit plates and should not be missed by vegetarians visiting Leon. They serve both national and international cuisine so if you want something a little different from the *gallo pinto* you've probably become accustomed to, then you can find it here. There are home-made pastries as well as hot, fresh coffee and tea always available. This café should also be able to satisfy any cultural cravings you may be having as its walls are adorned with painting from local artisans. El Laborío, in front of Casa Cural. Tel: 505-2-315-4099, E-mail: cocinarte@vapues.com. Updated: Nov 26, 2009.

Mediterraneo

Just across the street from Lazybones, this Italian restaurant is between a high-end and a mid-range place, and offers excellent values. Pizzas and pastas are very highly recommended. Service is prompt and elegant, particularly for the price, making this an excellent place for budget travelers to enjoy a fine meal. Ave 2 NO, 2.5 blocks north of Parque Ruben Dario, across from Lazybones Hostel. Tel:505-8-895-9392, E-mail: xalolo@yahoo.fr. Updated: Nov 26, 2009.

La Terraza M

Next to Mediterraneo, this place offers shakes and a few cheap meal options. Their sandwiches are large, but not particularly good—they're really all bread. But it's worth it to stop by for the fruit shakes. Ave 2, 2.5 blocks north of Parque Ruben Dario, across from Lazybones Hostel. Updated: Jun 14, 2008.

Mercado

Leon's main market is located behind the cathedral, and is host to a range of food stalls offering everything from hot dishes to pastries at rock-bottom prices. The place doesn't look particularly clean, but its popularity with locals ensures its safe. Located behind the Cathedral. Updated: Jun 14, 2008.

Benjamin Linder Cafe

This breezy, streetside cafe is popular for their all-day breakfast. Food is fairly typical Western-fare: eggs, sandwiches, oatmeal etc. It's also a nice place to stop off for a *licuado* or a coffee—just sit down and watch the crowds stroll past. Open Monday – Friday, 8:30 a.m. – 5:30 p.m., Saturday 8:30 a.m.-12 p.m. Av. 1 and Ca. 2 NO. Tel: 505-2-311-0548. Updated: Nov 26, 2009.

Restaurante Sacuanjoche

Sacuanjoche is an excellent vegetarian option, specializing in soy-based meals of all stripes. However meat-lovers need not be disappointed, their 85 C pork ribs are a fantastic deal. Food is excellent, and service is friendly and prompt. All credit cards accepted. Calle 2, between Ave 2 and Ave 1 NO. Tel: 505-2-311-1121. Updated: Nov 26, 2009.

Malibu

Malibu is a restaurant and bar which offers your standard meat, rice and salad dishes. The menu might be a bit unimaginative, but the food is excellent and prices are very reasonable considering what you get. It's also a popular drinking establishment. Located 2.5 blocks north of Parque Ruben Dario, one block north from Lazybones Hostel. Updated: Jun 14, 2008.

Shark Pit

This restaurant offers a range of styles, from Western to Nicaraguan to Chinese, at cheap prices. Portions are absolutely gigantic, so bring an appetite, or consider sharing a dish between two. Either way it's an excellent value. Ave 1 NO, one block north of Igl. la Merced. Tel: 505-311-4643. Updated: Jun 15, 2008.

Italian Pizza / Lebanese Food

This is the place to go to satisfy your cravings for hummus and baba ghanouj, though we're not sure that their steep prices are entirely justified. They also serve very expensive pizzas, but these can be had for cheaper all over Leon. Calle Central, ½ block north of the cathedral, Tel: 505-311-0857, E-mail: ezaklit@hotmail.com. Updated: Jun 15, 2008.

La Perla

Attached to the hotel of the same name, the La Perla is an excellent fine dining option. With an atmosphere of extravagance, they offer a wide selection of dishes from pastas to pastries to pork. Entrees generally run around $10-15. Open 6:30 a.m. - 10 p.m. Dressing well is recommended. Ave 1 NO, 1.5 blocks north of Iglesia la Merced, Tel: 505-2-311-3125, Fax: 505-2-311-2279 E-mail: info@laperlaleon.com, URL: www.laperlaleon.com. Updated: Nov 26, 2009.

La Olla Quemada
This bar is the place to go on Wednesdays, when their karaoke night always draws a crowd. The cover charge is $1.50. Calle Ruben Dario and 6 Ave O. Updated: Feb 19, 2009.

Bohemias
Another disco that lights up on the weekends, Bohemias is popular with a younger student crowd. Food is also offered. Ave 1 NO between Calle 1 and Calle Ruben Dario. Updated: Jun 15, 2008.

Don Señor
With a restaurant-pub, bar and disco as part of the same establishment, Don Señor's can cater to any mood. It gets busy Thursday through Saturday. Calle 1a NO, between Ave 1 and Ave Central. Updated: Jun 15, 2008.

Barrio Sutiava
Barrio Sutiava, an indigenous stronghold, predates the rest of Leon. Members of the Chorotega tribe founded the original town and lived beside the Spanish Leon until their new neighbors forced them to become part of the developing city. A Chorotega revolt in 1725 was put down, but the area known as "Subtiava" was able to retain a relative independence from the growing metropolis until 1902.

The neighborhood's heavily indigenous population recently decided to change the name from the former Subtiava, since they felt the former spelling was derogatory, according to the tourism office in Leon.

The neighborhood has attractions such as San Juan Bautista Sutiava, the oldest church in Leon, and Museo Adiact, a museum that opened in 1979 and features pieces that track the history of the neighborhood, including ceramics and stonework.

During the Good Friday of Semana Santa, residents of the neighborhood make religious murals out of colored sawdust. The designs are created freehand and range in crude Jesus portraits to sweeping, sunset-colored images of angels in flight. A procession carrying religious statues eventually walks across these carpets of sawdust and wipes them out. The tradition is ancient, and may have originated with laying carpets of flowers before local kings, although modern themes are Biblically inspired. Updated: Oct 08, 2009.

Museo Insurreccional Luis Manuel Toruño
The Casa El Buzon in Sutiava just barely contains this hurly burly of memorabilia from the Sandinista revolution. Once a storehouse for weapons, the building is now where you can find the collection of newspapers and communist momentos that were gathered by owner Luis Manuel Toruno. The museum is generally open in daylight hours. Updated: Oct 08, 2009.

El Tamarindon
This ancient tamarind tree, located in the winding sidestreets of Barrio Sutiava, is said to be over 600 years old. Its most famous moment came in the late 18th century, when Chief Adiact, leader of the Sutiava tribe, was hanged by the Spanish from its branches. The tree is difficult to find and its location is nearly impossible to describe, but every local in the area knows it, so just ask around. Updated: Jun 11, 2008.

Iglesia San Juan Bautista de Sutiava
In many ways, this is a typical Central American cathedral. It's spacious, elegant, beautifully designed and badly in need of restoration. The wooden altar-piece is probably the church's most impressive aspect aesthetically, though at time of review the rich carvings were rather tackily decorated with plastic flowers and florescent lights. Look up at the ceiling and you'll see a prominent sun icon, said to have been added in an attempt to cajole the indigenous into worshiping here. Updated: Oct 09, 2008.

Ruinas Veracruz
Another casualty of the 1979 bombardment, these are probably the most impressive, intact ruins in Leon. The most likely reason for this is that they have been fenced-off, preventing people from committing the kind of sacrilegious acts that apparently take place in the Ruinas de San Sebastien. However, the only entrance is located through the front-yard of a family that's taken up residence on the grounds. They don't seem to mind you trundling through, and you don't need to pay them anything, just smile and say "Buenas" as you go. Updated: Oct 11, 2008.

Ruinas de Santiago
These are the least impressive of Leon's ruins. Only a single bell tower and a pockmarked wall remain of the original church.

Enter through an unlocked gate about halfway between Calle Ruben Dario and Calle 1a. Updated: Oct 11, 2008.

Museo Adiact

Part archaeological museum and part indigenous art gallery, the Museo Adiact is easily spotted by the ornate murals adorning its walls. It features contemporary primitivist art, as well as a few relics from excavations in the area. The place isn't too busy and Justo, the friendly director, will gladly show you around provided you're not in a rush. About $1 to enter, open from 10 a.m.-4:30 p.m. Calle Ruben Dario, two blocks north of the Iglesia San Juan Bautista de Sutiava. Tel: 505-821-8327. Updated: Jun 11, 2008.

PONELOYA

Poneloya's sweeping crescent of black and gold sand, ample fish and rolling breakers seem destined to turn this tiny town into a hotspot. Since Poneloya is located only a 40 minute bus ride from Leon, the town's single street has already filled up with vacation homes. Unless you visit during Semana Santa or other big holidays, though, you're likely to find that you have the wide beach to yourself. Accommodations and eateries are also scarce; Hotel La Casa Blanca and Hotel and Restaurante Posada del Poneloya are your only choices for sleeping. More options can be found down the beach (or about 3 km / 1.8 mi along the road) in Las Penitas. Updated: Apr 21, 2009.

Hotel Lacayo

(ROOMS: $5-10) In April 2009, Hotel Lacayo closed for much needed renovations. The hotel had offered the cheapest rooms on the beach, that is if you were willing to risk sleeping in a sagging wooden structure that appeared in worse shape (missing roof tiles, a bulging ceilings and shaky pillars) than abandoned homes along the same stretch. Hopefully, the hotel will have edged away from wrecking ball status by the time it reopens in late 2009. The room prices ($5-10 during Semana Santa) are also expected to increase after the building's rejuvenation. Tel: Cel: 505-946-0418. Updated: Apr 21, 2009.

Hotel and Restaurante Posada del Poneloya

(ROOMS: $20-35) Posada del Poneloya has long been the place to stay in Poneloya (for those not willing to risk the rickety Hotel Lacayo). The hotel has all of the amenities available in the small beach town: private bathrooms, air conditioning, TV with national channels and breakfast (included in the room rate). The open-plan hotel is a bit shabby and overgrown outside, but the 15 rooms are spacious, clean and reasonably priced. While Posada is not directly on the beach, the sand is just a short walk away. The hotel offers group discounts, tours to La Isla and transportation to Leon, Chinandega, Corinto and Cerro Negro. Posada accepts all credit cards. Del Empalme 2 c. abajo. Cel: 505-895-1513; Tel: 505-317-0378, E-mail: poasadaponeloya@yahoo.com, URL: Posadaponeloyo.blogspot.com. Updated: Apr 21, 2009.

Hotel La Casa Blanca

(ROOMS: $20-60) Hotel La Casa Blanca became the third Poneloya hotel when it opened in late 2008. Casa Blanca is just getting started (out of seven rooms, five are ready for customers), but already offers a pleasantly clean, safe and economical spot within spitting distance of the sea. All of the rooms have private bathrooms; two have air conditioning and three have TVs. (The plan is to have air conditioning and TVs in all rooms eventually). The hotel began offering a limited menu with traditional dishes in the spring of 2009 with mains (fish, meat, chicken) that range in price from $7-11. With many amenities in the works, La Casa Blanca has already become the place to stay in tiny Poneloya. Breakfast is included. Tel: 505-317-0382. Updated: Apr 21, 2009.

Getting To and Away From Poneloya

Buses to Poneloya and Las Penitas leave Mercado Felix Pedro C. in Leon every hour between 5 a.m. and 6 p.m. The trip costs $0.50 per person and is roughly 40 minutes long, due to road work. (Construction on the road between the beaches and the city started in the spring and is expected to continue throughout 2009.) When the road is not under construction, the trip takes 25 minutes. Buses stop in Poneloya first and then head back to Las Penitas. On the return trip, buses pass the Poneloya entrance.

From Poneloya, buses to Leon leave once every hour from a stop in front of Barco de Oro. (You can also catch them en route.) Make sure that, if you only plan to spend the day at the beach, you catch the last bus at 6:40 p.m. The schedule of Las Penitas departures is as follows: 5:40 a.m., 6:35 a.m., 7:30 a.m., 8:25 a.m., 9:20 a.m., 10:15 a.m., 11:10 a.m., 12:05 p.m., 1 p.m., 1:55 p.m., 2:50 p.m., 3:45 p.m., 4:40 p.m., 5:50 p.m., and 6:40 p.m. (at the corner). Updated: Apr 21, 2009.

LAS PEÑITAS

Las Peñitas might have a rockier shore than its Poneloya neighbor, but a position on the edge of Isla Juan Venado, plus a greater range of hotels, restaurants and tour guides means that Las Penitas attracts the majority of the area's tourists. Indeed, Las Peñitas is the place to go if you want a couple of days of uninterrupted loafing on the sloped and largely empty beach. While the local tourist trade has been increasing, Las Peñitas is still very much a working fishing village. Nets hang in yards, the tidal bay is full of boats, and locals clean catches of tuna, manta ray and red snapper on the sand. Shortages of water and electricity are not uncommon (particularly with the nearby road construction) and you shouldn't rely on hotels having everything they advertise. In April, only one working bicycle could be found among all the establishments that offered rentals, for example. Still, you'll find plenty to do in Las Peñitas, from surfing lessons to birdwatching trips, and the extensive variety of seafood offered at the local eateries and hotels (try the spiny lobsters, which are small but extremely savory) won't disappoint either. Updated: Jun 19, 2009.

Olazul

Since Olazul (a combination of the Spanish words "blue" and "wave") is located almost exactly halfway between the two towns (although formally in Las Peñitas), you're most likely to find the restaurant/hotel while strolling the beach. The long, thatched patio is the perfect place to grab a drink and watch the sun go down over the sea. Beside the bar, Olazul has a kidney-shaped pool (complete with sunken tables) and public restrooms. If you enjoy the relatively isolated beach location, you can stay at one of the Olazul's three cabañas. All of the rooms have private bathrooms; two have air conditioning. The clean, comfortable cabins theoretically hold three people, although king-sized beds take up the majority of space inside.

Camanica, 300 vrs. al este. Tel: 505-435-7936/910-2303. E-mail: info@hotelolazul.com, URL: www.hotelolazul.com. Updated: Apr 21, 2009.

Coco Surf School

Coco Surf School opened in April 2009 along the beach in Las Peñitas. At the thatched cabaña you can rent surfboards ($10 per day or $3 per hour) or take classes from the laidback owners Rafael and Carlos. There are already plans in the works to add a bar and other facilities. Tel: 505-8-958-7443, URL: cocosurfschool@gmail.com. Updated: Jun 19, 2009.

PUERTO SANDINO

Puerto Sandino is an end-of-the-line port town with warehouses left to rust, a seaside power plant and acres of salt evaporation ponds.

If you've made the long haul to this tiny destination, though, it's not for the scenery —at least, not on land. Puerto Sandino might have rough roads and small beaches, but the harbor reef also kicks up the hollow curls that are a surfer's dream.

Hotel Yeland (505-2-312-2256; fax 505-2-312-2288; puertosandino@hotmail.com; singles, $35; doubles, $50; triples, $60) is the only lodging in town and the only one within easy reach of major breaks at Miramar and El Velero. That the comfortable rooms are mostly rented to surfers is apparent from the board racks lining the hallway.

The hotel, located in an area with frequent water outages and potholed, manages to be surprisingly plush: cable TV, WiFi and hot water in the private bathrooms. There is a small bar/restaurant and a large pool, which was (rather typically) empty in spring 2009, due to maintenance issues. Hotel Yeland rents surfboards for $15 per day and can arrange for boats to take visitors to the reef at the harbor's mouth or other surfing spots.

Bar-Restaurant Chango (Mains: about $4.50-10; 8 a.m. to 10 p.m. weekdays, 8-2 a.m., weekends; 505-2-312-2297) is a short walk across the street from Hotel Yeland. The menu is, unsurprisingly, seafood heavy, and the restaurant is outfitted with giant TVs. If you're tired of the heat, you can eat in an air conditioned dining area for an extra 10 percent charge on your bill.

The only cyber café in town is really two computers at the back of a small store. Ciber Angy (505-2-312-2231) is open from 6 a.m. to 9 p.m. weekdays or 6 a.m. to 7 p.m. Sundays and charges about $0.70 per hour.

The best way to get around Puerto Sandino is, of course, to have your own vehicle. Beach access is a hot hike from town and public transportation (other than buses to Managua and Leon) is non-existent.

The one daily bus to Managua departs at 7 a.m. Buses on the bumpy, two hour trip to Leon (about a dollar) six times a day: 5 a.m., 7 a.m., 9:30 a.m., 11:30 a.m., 1:30 p.m. and 5 p.m. The bus makes a lot of noise as it passes through town, but doesn't actually stop longer than it takes to make a quick U-turn near the port warehouses, so jump on board. Updated: May 25, 2009.

EL VELERO

South of both Puerto Sandino and Miramar is tiny El Velero and, a kilometer beyond the town, you'll find another stretch of lovely beach.

El Centro Turistico El Velero (505-2-311-1191, open 5 a.m. to 5 p.m.) used to charge visitors a fee at the gate. You can now get in for free, but it's not because the social security administration that runs the place suddenly felt more altruistic.

In May 2008, Hurricane Alma swept through and decimated this stretch of beach. Some of the neighboring vacation homes are being rebuilt, but the center is still in limbo. The former rental cabins and seaside restaurant are decaying wrecks. You can't stay at the center any longer, but you can enjoy the gorgeous view.

As long as there is a low tide, you might consider walking back to Miramar along the beach (about 30 minutes to an hour). The shoreline stroll will save you a considerable amount of backtracking to El Velero and you won't have to worry about catching one of the private trucks that shuttle residents between the two towns.

Buses depart from Miramar to Leon roughly every two hours between 5 a.m. and 4:30 p.m. The last bus of the day also stops in El Velero before making the trip back to Leon. Updated: May 28, 2009.

EL TRANSITO

El Tránsito has a reputation of being a very isolated fishing village, but the seaside spot can actually be easier to reach than El Velero and offers more services than Miramar. A riptide current and lava seawalls also create nice swells close to shore (sometimes a little too close—this can be board breaking territory).

The rough dirt road between the old Leon-Managua highway and El Tránsito can be the most daunting transportation challenge, until you realize that pickup trucks run frequently between the highway and town. The trips cost between $0.70-1; if you're lucky enough to flag down a private vehicle you may even be able to get there for free.

El Tránsito, like many coastal areas, was destroyed by a tsunami in 1992. The Spanish government helped rebuild much of what was lost, with most residents moving up a hill and away from the sea.

The town center is paved, but there is not a whole lot of interest (other than a park in homage to the Spanish), so head down the increasingly rough streets to the seaside, where you'll find local hangouts like Bar Primavera (Mains: $10-17; 505-8-603-1013; open 10 a.m. to 10 p.m. daily; from the high school, two blocks south). Owner Jenny Castro-Ordeñana serves up *nacatamales* and a mouth-watering daily fish plate. She can also help you find a boat to rent or a room in town, although you're better off walking along the beach to the stunning Ocean Hotel, located at the same site where one of Samosa's generals once had his extravagant vacation home.

Owner Roger Wittenmyer has revived the general's amazing swimming pool (built behind a lava rock wall and fed by waves lapping over the top) and has completely rebuilt the upper complex.

The hotel's five rooms (three in the main building and two cabins) are as clean and elegantly simple as the breeze off the sea. The rooms ($65-75 or double during high holidays) have air conditioning, queen beds and, even in remote El Tránsito, WiFi. Ask for Room 3, which also has a private balcony.

The hotel has several terraces where you can jump in a hammock and take in the sweeping views of the beaches below. Ocean Hotel's remote location also means that you'll probably have the entire complex to yourself.

Support VIVA! Reserve your hotels or hostels at www.vivatravelguides.com/hotels/

Wittenmyer can arrange for airport transfers, boat rentals and special meals, if you call him in advance (505-8-431-2191 / 505-2-645-4568; oceanhoteltransito@hotmail.com). Advance reservations are recommended.

To get to El Tránsito, hop on any of the regular buses that travel between Leon and Managua along the old highway (express and micro buses use the new Leon-Managua highway) and ask to be let off at the entrance to town. Pickup trucks make regular stops to take passengers the rest of the way to El Tránsito. Updated: May 26, 2009.

SAN JACINTO

San Jacinto's bright prospects as the gateway to the Ring of Fire dimmed significantly with the closure of the Hostel La Ceiba, which had offered the town's only accommodation and rentals.

The town still has amazing views of Volcán Telica (an eight hour climb with an overnight on the mountain), Volcán Rota and Volcán Santa Clara (both three to five hours), but you should be prepared to bring all of your supplies (and a guide) if you plan to use the tiny location as a launching point for volcanic excursions. San Jacinto can offer little in terms of support.

Locals are hopeful that La Ceiba (or a different hostel) will eventually reopen. Until that happens, the town's main attraction, and source of income, is Hervideros de San Jacinto (open 7 a.m. to 5 p.m. daily, $2 for foreigners; $0.50 for nationals), a small wasteland of sulfur, sinkholes and microcraters.

A young guide (recommended donation $0.50 to $1) will run down from the town to lead you around the constantly changing volcanic minefield. The guides can offer basic information about what they call "the breath of Santa Clara," gleefully pointing out the hole that claimed the lives of three piglets or a bubbling mud cauldron that opened up the week before.

From the hervideros, you might also catch a glimpse of steam rising from the San Jacinto-Tizate Proyecto de Energia Geotermica plant.

The tour ends at stands where you can buy "ancient indigenous calendars" and other clay objects of dubious authenticity.

A hot, 15-minute walk from town will bring you to the Ojo de Agua El Chorro, where water pipes empty into the river below, creating a few muddy swimming holes. Since the neighborhood runoff also empties here, walk slightly upstream if you're in the mood for a swim.

Rancho San Jacinto (Mains, $4.80 to 8.20; 7 a.m. to 10 p.m., daily; 505-8-351-1439), near the highway, provides the town's one food and drink outlet. The tidy bar-restaurant has typical fare and cold drinks, although the low thatched roof blocks out views of the volcanoes.

Buses to Leon pass San Jacinto every half hour and cost $0.60. Updated: May 25, 2009.

VOLCÁN TELICA AND VOLCÁN SAN CRISTOBAL

Two volcanoes in the Ring of Fire are worth investigating if you want to test your mettle on a climb. Volcán Telica takes between two to three hours to summit (1060 m / 3477 ft). The two Telica craters produce gassy eruptions every five years, but hasn't had a big eruption since 1765. There is a small, overgrown campsite at the top of the volcano within walking distance of the crater. From the edge, beyond a 183-213 meter (600- 700-ft) drop, you can see lava. Volcán San Cristóbal is the highest, youngest, and one of the most active volcanoes in the Ring of Fire. The hike up 1,745 meters (5,725 ft) to the smoking top of the stratovolcano takes between six to 16 hours (depending on where you start), requires the assistance of a guide and meanders over privately owned fields. San Cristobal erupts regularly, including producing ash and gas in 1997, 1999 and 2008. Area towns were dusted with ash as recently as September 2009. Neighboring Volcán Casita is also active, enough to bury a small village in 1998. Updated: Oct 08, 2009.

EL SAUCE

Nestled among bright rivers and hills, sleepy El Sauce is the perfect escape from the crush and grind of city life. Once a stop on the Nicaragua railway system, the traces of which have since disappeared, the contemporary El Sauce is now full of *triciclos*, mototaxis, and cowboys who park their horses along the wide boulevards.

El Sauce

For pilgrims, El Sauce is best known as the home of the stubborn Santo Cristo de Esquipulas, or the Black Christ. The tiny Guatemalan figure arrived in 1723 during a Central American tour. The next stop was supposed to be Honduras, but each priest who tried to remove the figure sickened and died. The bishop of Guatemala, realizing the Santo Cristo liked the mountains, eventually agreed to leave the figure in El Sauce's care. The largest celebration of El Señor de los Milagros takes place on the third week of January when the city fills with the faithful.

El Señor experienced his own miracle in 1997 when the figure was saved from a fire that burned the Templo de El Sauce (1828) to the ground. The church was reconstructed in 1999 and has undergone several renovations, including work in 2009 to restore the roof above the high altar.

The church is regularly closed for construction, but La Capilla de Nuestro Señor de Milagros is open from 8:30 a.m. to 4:30 p.m. daily (from 7 a.m. to 5 p.m. in January). At the chapel's souvenir booth, you can buy one of several $0.25 lead charms. Pilgrims deposit the miniature cows, people, eyes, arms, hearts and houses in a box under the Black Christ in thanks or as a petition.

The El Sauce alcaldia has a very thorough, if not widely available, tourist map with icons for major attractions (including the four churches), hotels and bars. The numerous pulperias are marked as yellow dots. Some sell delicious local honey, just look for the signs. Jars range from $0.25-4.80, depending on the size.

When you start craving something more substantial, there are several local eateries. Cafetin El Sauceño serves burgers and tacos ($0.60-4.80) between 9 a.m. and 10:30 p.m., but cowboys seem to prefer the full *comida corriente* lunches at Comedor Falkis (505-2-319-2642; open 10 a.m. to 10 p.m.) for $2.40-3.60. The *fritangas* around El Sauce's bus terminal can also provide a cheap grab-and-go meal.

El Sauce's green hills can provide a great opportunity for hiking. Contact the alcaldia (505-2-319-2259, alsauce2004@yahoo.com, www.alcaldiamunipalelsauce.com) to arrange for a guide and ask them about Parque Ecológico El Sauce, a pine forest reserve proposed for the Ocotal region.

Although still in the planning stages in spring 2009, city officials were already talking about turning the park into a full-service retreat, complete with lodging. Until that dream is realized, only one truck makes the daily trip, leaving for the El Sauce terminal at 8 a.m. and returning to the Ocotal at 1 p.m. ($1.25). Contact city officials ahead of time to arrange an overnight stay with a local community member.

For closer activities, head three kilometers (1.8 mi) out of town to La Piedra de San Ramón or catch a bus bound for Achuapa and asked to be dropped off at Rio Grande (mototaxis are roughly $10). The river is full of popular swimming holes and is cleaner than the local Río El Sauce. Just make sure to jump on the last bus (passing the river around 3:20 p.m.) if you want to make it back to town.

The two hotels in El Sauce both offer rooms with air conditioning, cable TV and private bathrooms. Hotel Blanco (also known as Casa Blanca) has comfortable quarters—with tiny, oddly placed sinks—arranged around a shady courtyard (505-2-319-2403; singles with fan $9.70 / air-conditioning $19.50; doubles $14.50 / $24, triples $19 / $29). The economical Bar-Hotel El Viajero has sagging charm: an adobe roof full of parrots, a shrine in the lobby and bathroom cisterns. Since the showers may or may not have running water, plan on a cistern-inspired bucket bath (505-2-319-2325; singles $4, matrimonial bed with fan for $7, matrimonial with air-con for $14.50). Meals at the hotel range from $4-6.

Finca Campestre Cárdenas (505-2-319-2329), just outside the southwestern limits of town, has a few private rooms with air conditioning, but has an unfortunate tendency to be closed on weekdays. Ring the doorbell on the gate to rouse the watchman.

There are various Internet cafés around town, but the easiest by far to locate is the Instituto de Investigaciones y Gestion Social (INGES), behind the church (505-2-319-2401/ 2321, open from 8 a.m. to noon and 1-8 p.m. daily).

Regular buses leave for Leon ($1.50) hourly between 4-9 a.m. and between noon and 4 p.m. Microbuses ($2) also leave sporadically between 6:30 a.m. and 4 p.m. Updated: Jun 03, 2009.

NAGAROTE

Nagarote is a tidy (literally, they've won awards for it) little town whose violent past is still a point of some pride.

In the 16th century, the Spanish were still sweeping through Nicaragua, subduing the natives and establishing trade routes to their newly formed capital Leon (now Leon Viejo). Upon arriving in Nagarote, the new conquerors decided on the not-so-subtle gesture of hanging the local leader Cacique Nagrandano from a huge genízaro tree in the indigenous marketplace.

The Chorotega chief died, but the tree survived and, in 1964, was declared a national monument. El Genízaro is now estimated to be over 1,000 years old.

The tree is so well loved that, after a giant limb crashed down a decade ago, residents carved the wood into faces, bowls, signs and Nargrandano sculptures. The largest of these works, Indito de Nagarote, was installed in a pavilion near the tree. You can find the other pieces scattered chaotically around the Casa Cultura y Sala Museo El Genízaro (505-2-313-0991, open from 8 to noon and from 2-5 p.m., weekdays), which claims to be the country's only wood museum.

Two more branches have fallen from El Genízaro in recent years, but the others were considered too rotted to carve and have been left in the park. After a millennium, you might find the massive trunk looking a bit worse for wear, but the resilient tree has already started sprouting thin green limbs to replace the ones that fell.

Located on the edge of town, Mirador La Concordia is another not-to-be-missed stop, especially now that the local government has opened the tower walkway to foreign visitors (but not, disturbingly, to Nicaraguans).

Visit during working hours (weekdays from 6-11 a.m. and 2-5 p.m.; Satudays from 6-11 a.m.) and park manager Alvaro José Espinoza Perez (505-8-867-0374) will unlock the tower. A circular stairwell brings you to breathtaking views of Nagarote and the distant volcanoes. Momotombo and Momotombito are particularly clear on the horizon. Mototaxis can take you up to the mirador and back for $0.50. For a small additional fee, you can hire a mototaxi to take you on a tour around the city. Sights are sure to include the refurbished old train station with a 1887 bell, and El Templo Parroquial Santiago, whose construction in the 1600s makes it one of the oldest churches in Nicaragua.

Your guide might also tell you about how Nagarote was named "Cleanest City in Nicaragua" for four years straight (they placed second in 2002) until the national government finally declared the city to be exemplary and stopped awarding the title.

Naragote is one of two (the other being La Paz Centro) that has staked a claim as the birthplace of the *quesillo*, a corn tortilla filled with cheese, cream and onion chutney. There are small, white quesillo stands parked around the city. You can buy either the $0.50 *sencillo* (simple) version, with a flat slice of cheese, or $0.60 *trensas*, with the cheese molded into a braid.

For an upscale version, and a peek into how the cheese wraps are created, head to Quesillos Gourmet "Mi Finca," (505-2-313-0431, open from 6:30 a.m. to 9:30 p.m.), located in a cement pavilion along the highway. Quesillos Gourmet (which has a logo strangely reminiscent of Quizno's), processes their cheese right on the premises every morning. Ask for a tour if you're there between 7 a.m. and noon.

Cheese not your thing? Grab lunch at the homey Comedor Nimia (Mains: $1.70-2; 505-2-313-2642; open 9 a.m. to 2 p.m.) or head to Bar-Comedor Larry (Mains: $2-7; 505-2-313-0354; Monday to Thursday, 11 a.m. to 3 p.m. and Friday to Sunday, 11 a.m. to midnight) for a larger meal. Locals say Comedor Larry serves up some of the best food around, but even if you're not hungry, the vine-shaded courtyard is a pleasant place to sip a cool drink.

Closer to the city center is where you'll find Hotel Jerusalem, the city's first and only guesthouse. The rusty car parts outside can be a little off-putting, but the hotel is actually spacious and clean, if a little stark. You have the choice of either a fan (single $16) or air conditioning (single $32), with prices increasing roughly $5 for every additional person, up to four. The 10 rooms have WiFi, cable TV and private bathrooms. Hotel Jerusalem (505-2-313-2318) accepts credit cards and, as a strange bonus, has a *lavanderia* (about $0.30 per pound) amid the junk outside.
Updated: May 28, 2009.

Join VIVA on Facebook. Fan "VIVA Travel Guides Nicaragua."

Getting To and Away From Naragote

Buses leave the central park between every half hour to an hour for Leon (45 minutes, $0.70) and Managua (hour, $1.50). Mototaxis can take you around Naragote for about $0.25 and to the mirador and back for $0.50. For a small additional fee, you can hire a mototaxi to take you on a tour around the city. Updated: Oct 08, 2009.

LA PAZ CENTRO

La Paz Centro could justifiably lay claim to the title of Nicaragua's tile center. The city center features quesillo stands, the dilapidated old train station, and the simple Iglesia de San Nicólas, declared a national heritage site in 1972. But it is along the Leon-Managua highway where you can find the city's true claims to fame.

The most visible of these are the *tejares*, small scale operations that produce the brick red tiles and curved roof shingles that are widely used across the country. The alcaldia's Casa de Cultura (505-2-314-2295, danilomartinez@yahoo.com.ni) can arrange tours of the local factories, but you can also visit on your own.

One of the largest and most famous tejas-production centers is Tajer San Pablo (505-8-639-5100), where the giant kilns are large enough to walk through. Between their working hours of 3-10 a.m., an average worker can produce 300 raw bricks with teams of four men shaping 1,000 shingles in the same time. The shaped clay is then left to dry for several days before being baked into a hard red brick. The best time to visit is between the heavy production times of 7-10 a.m.; call ahead of time or check in at the front office before touring the grounds. To get there, either hire a mototaxi for a dollar or ask a Managua-bound bus to let you off at the San Pablo bus stop. Production stops any time there is heavy rain.

For a more refined (and colorful) version of the tejas ceramics, look no further than the Mercado de Artesanías (8 a.m. to 5:30 p.m. daily) where locals sell heavy vases, piggy banks, kissing geese, chickens and other brightly-painted creatures. The Casa de Cultura (7:30 a.m. to noon, 1:30-5:30 p.m., weekdays) has a variety of local ceramics on display, as well as an exhibit of baseball trophies and uniforms.

The tourist information booth, though, closed for lack of funding.

La Paz Centro prides itself on being the place where quesillos were invented. You can find the delicious combination of corn tortilla, local cheese, cooked onions and cream at any number of eateries along the city's entrance. The most famous is the original Quesillos Guiligüiste (505-2-314-2205, 6:30 a.m. to 7 p.m. daily) where fresh, pure ingredients are a point of no small amount of pride. Quesillos cost $1.30 and are served either with flat rounds or *trenzas* (braids) of the mozzarella-like cheese.

A few blocks up the street, you'll find Bar-Restaurant El Asador (Mains: $3-5, 505-8-898-5552, 11 a.m. to 9 p.m., Tuesday to Sunday). Locals claim the restaurant has the best food around. The menu doesn't vary from the usual beef/pork/chicken offerings but the dishes are prepared as they're ordered, to retain as much flavor as possible.

La Paz Centro has two places to stay: the small and slightly grubby rooms at Hospedaje Fonseca (previously Hospedaje Familiar), which are popular with itinerant workers and baseball players, who share a bathroom and pay $3.50 per person. Hotelito Corazón has private bathrooms (minus the toilet seats), clean tile floors and thicker mattresses, but also doubles as a love hotel. The two hour rate per room is $5-10, if you want the whole 24. Updated: Jun 19, 2009.

Getting To and Away From La Paz Centro

Buses leave from the city's terminal to Leon ($0.70) every half hour between 4 a.m. and 4:30 p.m. and to Managua ($0.90) until 6 p.m. The last bus departs for Puerto Momotombo ($0.50) at 4 p.m. Within the city limits, mototaxis charge around $0.25 per ride. Updated: Jun 19, 2009.

CHINANDEGA

70 m   122,000

The City of Chinandega, at an altitude of 60 meters (197 ft), is perhaps Nicaragua's hottest city, with average temperatures reaching above 30°C (86°F). The city was first settled in 1796 and has since become home to some 122,000 people, thanks in great part to the surrounding flat, fertile lands. Optimal for farming and other commercial businesses, these lands currently produce a wealth of crops such as peanuts, cashews, bananas, and sugar cane. Since Chinandega is the hub of agricultural productivity, many grain mills have set up shop there to process rice and other foods. Updated: Jan 12, 2009.

Getting to and Away From Chinandega

The bus schedule from the Santa Ana Market is as follows:
To Jiquilillo and Padre Ramos: every 40 minutes, from 4:30 a.m., to 3 p.m.
To Cosigüina and Potosi area: four times daily from 5 a.m. to 3 p.m.
To Aserradores: twice daily, at 7:30 a.m. and noon.
To Mechapa: twice daily, at 7:30 a.m. and noon.
To El Viejo: every 15 minutes, from 4:30 a.m. to 6 p.m.

The bus schedule from El Bisne Market is as follows:
To Managua: every hour, from 4 a.m. to 5:20 p.m.
To Leon: every 15 minutes, from 4:30 a.m. to 6 p.m.
To Matagalpa: three times daily, at 4:20 a.m., 7:30 a.m. and 2:45 p.m.
To Ciudad Darío: twice daily 5:20 a.m. and 2:45 p.m.
To Corinto: every 45 minutes, from 4:30 a.m. to 6 p.m.
To Guasaule: every hour, from 4 a.m. to 5 p.m.

Minibuses to Managua, Leon, Guasule and Corinto leave between 4:30 a.m. and 7 p.m.

The Santa Ana Market is located on Ruben Dario Avenue and is two blocks north of the Central Park. The El Bisne Market is located two blocks south of City Hall. Updated: Jan 13, 2009.

Getting Around

The downtown area of Chinandega is fairly small, and probably the best way to get around is on foot. For slightly longer distances, or to rest your tired feet, flag down one of the numerous bicycle taxis in town. The bicycle taxis can usually take you across the city for under $2. Regular taxis are also available, but ask your hotel to call one to ensure it is reputable. You can catch a bus by one of Chinandega's markets. Updated: Jan 12, 2009.

Safety

Chinandega is a fairly safe city, but as with other places in the country, common sense should prevail. Avoid carrying large amounts of money and valuables, especially when you visit crowded markets or ride local buses. Take taxis recommended by the hostels and hotels, and don't let taxis pick up other passengers during your trip. Updated: Jan 13, 2009.

Services

The tourism office (INTUR) is located in front of the BAC, hours are 8 a.m. to 5:30 p.m., Monday to Friday; Saturday from 9 a.m. to 3 p.m. The phone number is (505-341-1935).

There are three banks in the city, BAC, Credomatic and BDF (all three are open Monday to Friday, 8 a.m. to 4 p.m.; Saturday, 8 a.m. to 12 p.m.) The banks are located on Esquina de los Bancos.

There is a Western Union located across the street from Hotel El Chinandego (Monday to Saturday, 8 a.m. to 5 p.m.; Sunday, 9 a.m. to 12 p.m.).

National calls can be made at the phone booth kiosks found throughout the town. These wooden booths have a telephone sign on the front and a service person sitting inside. Calls are $0.25.

For Internet options, Cyber Explorer (505-340-1994) is one block east of Hotel El Chinandego.

There is a laundromat called Lavamatic Express (505-341-3319), which is open Monday to Saturday, 7 a.m to 9 p.m. and on Sunday from 8 a.m. to 5 p.m. It is located on the street of the banks, 68 meters (223 ft) to the north of the Guadalupe church.

The post office is located three blocks east of the San Antonio church (open Monday to Friday, 8 a.m. to 5 p.m; Saturday, 8 a.m. to 12 p.m.). Updated: Jan 13, 2009.

Things to See and Do

If you're interested in churches you're in luck, as Chinandega is full of 17th and 19th century religious architecture such as the the Santuario de Nuestra Señora Guadalupe, the Parroquia Santa Ana, with its gold altar, or the Iglesia El Calvario. The churches are open to be explored when masses or other services are not being held.

Join VIVA on Facebook. Fan "VIVA Travel Guides Nicaragua."

Activities ●

1 El Calvario Church B1
2 Guadalupe Church A2
3 Parroquia Santa Ana A1

Eating

4 Antigua Restaurant B2

Nightlife

5 La Bohemia B2

Services ★

6 Banco A2
7 Cyber Explorer B2

8 Lavamatic Express A2
9 Post Office B2
10 Western Union B2

Sleeping

11 Hotel Cosigüina A2
12 Hotel El Chinandegano B2
13 Hotel del Pacifico A2

Tours ♦

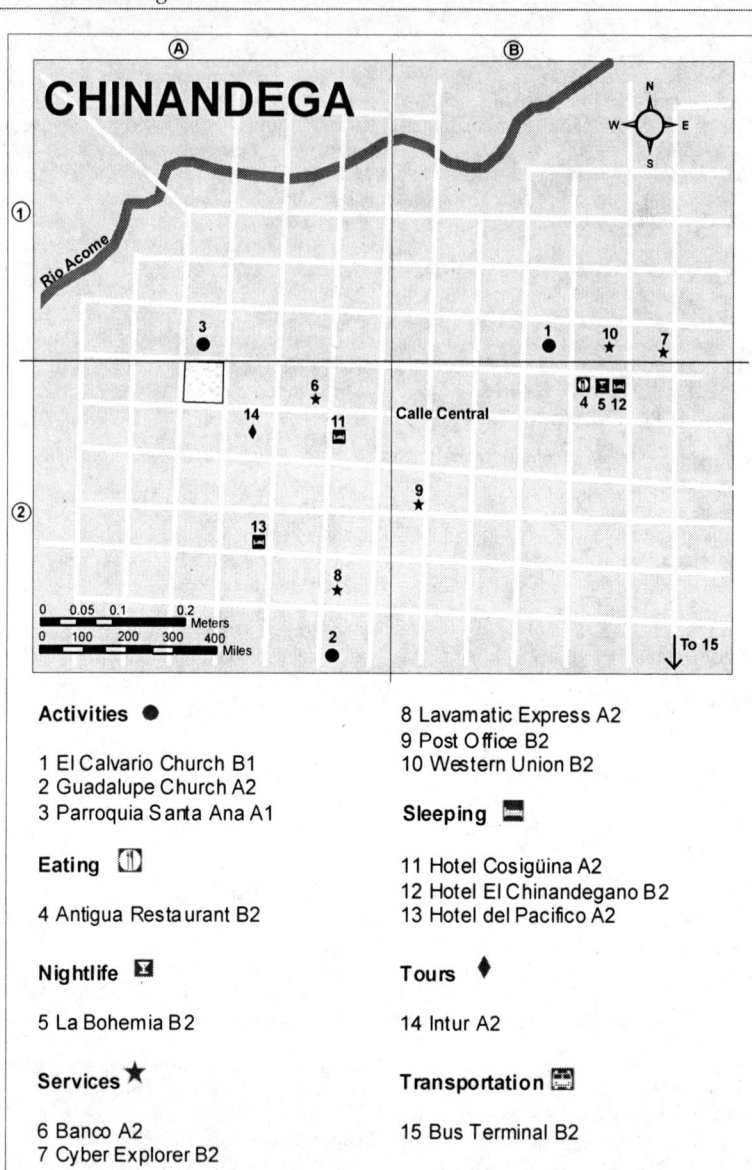

14 Intur A2

Transportation

15 Bus Terminal B2

The city is a good stopping point on the way to other nearby destinations; it's a place to explore for a day or two and maybe pick up some needed items at the market. Updated: Jan 13, 2009.

Santuario de Nuestra Señora Guadalupe

A charming bright blue church that is one of Chinandega's prettiest sights, the Santuario de Nuestra Señora Guadalupe was originally built in 1855 as an offering to its namesake during a cholera epidemic. Since then, the church has been rebuilt and restored due to natural disasters and age. It was the first iglesia in Central America to be named a sanctuary, an honor bestowed upon the church by Pope Pius IX. It is located in the Barrio Guadalupe, four blocks south of the Hotel Cosiguina. Updated: Jan 13, 2009.

Support VIVA! Reserve your hotels or hostels at www.vivatravelguides.com/hotels/

Parroquia Santa Ana

Parroquia Santa Ana is the church which Chinandega was built around and currently can be found in the middle of town, surrounded by the local park. First constructed in the 17th century, the church was damaged by an earthquake in 1885, but was later restored to its present condition. The interior features a stunning gold and blue altar with figures of Santa Ana, La Virgen and Jesus. The church is located to the north of the Central Park. Updated: Jan 13, 2009.

Iglesia El Calvario

Rebuilt by Bishop Monsignor Manual Ulloa y Calvo in 1874, this church was also destroyed in the earthquake of 1885 due to its weak adobe structure. The church's patron saint is celebrated on the last Sunday in January, in honor of the Holy Name of Jesus. Located in the Barrio El Calvario, the church is one block north of the fire station. Updated: Jan 13, 2009.

San Cristobal Volcano

In the 19th century, tropical dry forests were much more common in Nicaragua. As the local population expanded, such forests were razed and the land was used for farming. Now, 46 percent of the San Cristobal-Casitas Volcano Reserve is devoted to preserving what remains of the tropical dry forest. The San Cristobal itself is a volcanic crater that even impresses the experts.

The reserve has some 64 different tree species, 23 types of mammals, 41 birds and 79 butterfly varieties. Most common, and often on hand for visitors to see, are armadillos, deer, leopards and white-faced monkeys.

The San Cristobal Volcano Adventure tour takes you up 1,783 meters (5,850 ft) back along a trail in a Nicaraguan natural reserve. This tour is not for late risers. Visitors meet with their guides at 5:30 a.m. in Leon, to arrive at La Finca del Cerro by 7:30 a.m. The trip from Leon takes visitors along a dirt road and through Comarca La Bolsa, a tiny village whose inhabitants still rely on crops like cotton, beans and coffee for a living.

The 7 kilometer (4.3 mile) walk up the volcano takes about five hours. The trail crosses igneous rocks and through three types of natural ecosystems: tropical dry forest, pine forests, and savannahs with natural grasslands. Though it's a long way up, the summit provides a breathtaking view of the Maribios Cordillera and the Cosigüina Volcano. On a clear day, visitors can see as far as Honduras and El Salvador. Tel: 505-819-2449 / 927 -7060, E-mail: AlvaroTigerino@gmail.com. Updated: Jan 22, 2009.

Lodging

In recent years, newer and bigger hotels have been constructed for the business clientele in the areas outside the city center. There are still varied options for accommodations within the few blocks of Chinandega's core, but if you're looking for luxury accommodations, you're better off heading outside of the center. Updated: Jan 13, 2009.

Hotel El Chinandegano

(ROOMS: $35-40) Located on a street close to services and restaurants, Hotel Chinandegano has clean, simple rooms and a friendly staff. A café is located in a small courtyard to the back of the hotel, and caged budgies sing throughout the hallways. The hotel is a good value and is in a safe area of the city. Located 1.5 blocks east of Parroquia El Calvario. Tel: 505-341-4800, E-mail: elchinandego@cablenet.com.ni. Updated: Jan 13, 2009.

Hotel Cosigüina

(ROOMS: $35-45) While the exterior of the hotel leaves much to be desired, the inside of Hotel Cosigüina is actually quite pleasant. The hotel is spacious and comfortable, with 21 rooms and and lounges both indoors and outdoors. There is a Budget Car Rental service located at the front desk, and a restaurant called Fumarolas inside the hotel, which is open for breakfast, lunch and dinner. Rooms are equipped with cable TV and air conditioning. Laundry services are available as well. Located a half block south from the *esquina de los bancos*. Tel: 505-341-3560, E-mail: reservations@hotelcosiguina.com, URL: www.hotelcosiguina.com. Updated: Jan 13, 2009.

Hotel del Pacífico

(ROOMS: $36-48) Set in Chinandega's downtown, the Hotel del Pacifico provides guests with an outdoor patio garden in which to relax during the afternoon heat. The hotel has 11 rooms in total, all with air conditioning and hot water. Breakfasts are included in the cost of the room and prices are mid- to high-range for the area. Front desk service is very friendly and the hotel maintains a comfortable atmosphere. Price includes tax and breakfast.

Located one block south from the San Antonio church. Tel: 505-341-3827/3891. Updated: Jan 14, 2009.

Chinandega Restaurants

Chinandega specializes in inexpensive meals for the working masses, so don't go looking for five-star restaurants. But that being said, Chinandega is a good place to go for a taste of true Nicaraguan fare. Given the city's proximity to the ocean, seafood options are usually a good bet for fresh, tasty dishes. If you're just passing through, many restaurants also serve quick meals on the go. Updated: Jan 13, 2009.

Antigua Restaurante

Set in a colonial style building with a charming inner courtyard, the Antigua Restaurant (previously called Lagos) provides some fine dining in the city. This restaurant serves typical Nicaraguan dishes of fish, beef and chicken, along with a wide variety of *boquitas* (appetizers). Antigua is more expensive than the average restaurant in Chinandega, but prices are still very reasonable. Open 11 a.m. to 10 p.m. From the ESSO in barrio El Calvario, the restaurant is 119 meters (390 ft) to the east. Tel: 505-341-0262. Updated: Jan 13, 2009.

La Bohemia

Located right next door to Hotel El Chinandego, La Bohemia is a restaurant/bar open noon to midnight. Its interior is dimly lit, with the only natural light coming in through tinted windows near the ceiling. The resulting effect is slightly depressing, but La Bohemia is a good spot to go if you have decided to drink away the day. The menu features a selection of sandwiches and other snack foods with most everything under $5. From the ESSO in barrio El Calvario, the restaurant is 1.5 blocks to the east. Tel: 505-341-4800. Updated: Jan 14, 2009.

EL VIEJO

43 m | 45,594 | 344

El Viejo, once an indigenous capital called Tezoatega, is arguably best known as the home of Nicaraguan's patron saint, La Virgen del Trono. According to dueling legends, the name of the city was either changed to honor the powerful indigenous chieftain Agteyte or in adoration of Pedro de Zepeda, whose sister, Saint Teresa of Spain, gave him the virgin icon to bring to the New World.

La Basílica de la Inmaculada Concepción de la Virgen María now stands where both Agteyte once had his plaza and where La Virgen del Trono is said to have repeatedly reappeared after vanishing from the pack of confused Pedro de Zepeda worshippers.

The doll-like virgin was elevated to national Patron Saint status in 2000, over 430 years after she arrived in El Realejo. Pilgrims come every winter to shine up the filigree altar, located in front of the virgin's alcove, during the Lavada de la Plata (polishing the silver) on December 5 and 6. The cotton they use to clean both the altar and other offerings to the relic are saved as good luck.

While it is mostly overshadowed by the more famous fellow relic, the Basilica is also home to the ebony *Cristo del buen viaje* (Christ of the good journey), which arrived in El Realjo from Peru in 1626.

Strong indigenous and Catholic ties can't stop El Viejo from feeling more like a suburb of Chinandega than an entirely separate city, though. Ask about lodging in El Viejo and locals will suggest you make the five kilometer (3 mi) trip to more plentiful options in the bigger city.

Hostel San Marino (505-2-344-1664) offers the only accommodations in the heart of El Viejo. The hostel, which doubles as a *comida corriente* restaurant from 11 a.m. to midnight, has a brightly colored and pleasant courtyard, with a small pool, that is only sometimes filled. Take a look at the rooms, though, and you'll realize what most locals already know—"hostel" in this case stands for "love motel." Grimy sheets, giant wall mirrors and bathrooms without doors or toilet seats suggest that most clients pay the $6 per hour rate rather than $12 (with fan) or $20 (with air conditioning) to stay the night.

The area around the Basilica is where you'll find the majority of local eateries and, if you walk two blocks south, a Palí supermarket. For a quick bite, head to the *fritanga* stands that line the far side of the central park. On your way, check out the spiky sculpture in honor of FSLN founder German Pomares Ordoñez.

There are several decent restaurants to the north of the Basilica whose business picks up at night and on weekends. Restaurant Tezoatega (505-2-344-2436, Mains $4-9, open 10 a.m. to midnight) has an open courtyard and a lively dance floor: Thursdays have a "night of guitars" theme, Fridays are for karaoke, and Saturdays and Sundays are all about disco.

The namesake of Restaurant "Piscina Olímpica" looks like it hasn't been used since the revolution, even though the owners say they fill the jumbo pool every Sunday—and then charge people $1.50 to use it. On non-swimsuit days, you can get a plate of typical Nicaraguan dishes (beef, pork, chicken and seafood) for between $3.50-10. Piscina Olímpica is open from noon to midnight on weekdays and until 2 a.m. on weekends.

There is a Banco ProCredit (505-2-344-1710) to the south side of the central park and next to the El Viejo fire station. The bank is open weekdays from 8:30 a.m. to 5:30 p.m. and on Saturdays until 1 p.m.; the neighboring ATM is open 24 hours, but only accepts VISA credit cards. Updated: May 12, 2009.

CHICHIGALPA

🅰 85.45 m   👤 62,670

Chichigalpa is a colorful and charming city where the residents take as much pride in their parks as they do in their two famous factories, one for sugar and one for rum; their smoking volcanoes; and their over 500-year-old church.

Leading the Chichigalpa cheerleading squad is the city's alcaldia, one of the most helpful in the country. Give community relations manager Maria José Santana-Vegas (505-2-343-2718) a week's notice and she can arrange tours at both Ingenerio San Antonio, Nicaragua's oldest sugar mill, and the Flor de Caña distillery. (The distillery's two-hour tour ends with a taste of one of their 15 kinds of world-famous rum.)

The alcaldia can also arrange for guided tours to Parque Ecológico Municipal, where you can rent a horse for the trip up Volcán San Cristobál.

Four blocks from the alcaldia (which is used as a local landmark), you'll find Iglesia Nuestra Señora de Guadalupe. The church is still referred to as a "ruin" although walls were built between the two ancient, crumbling sections in 1984. The church is open for mass on Thursdays at 4:30 p.m. and all day Sunday, but if you arrive on an off day, don't fret. Staff in the tiny office to the left of the main building will let you in and show you around. The office was built in the tower that is said to once have contained indigenous prisoners. It now contains a 1856 painting of the Virgin de Guadalupe. The church holds a gastronomic fair on November 11, followed a month later by a celebration of the virgin and a procession on December 11 and 12.

Chichigalpa has a couple of beautiful, surprisingly well-maintained parks. Parque Central Rubén Darío features a rainbow-colored acoustic shell, put to use during city festivals, and the baby blue Iglesia de San Bias.

On the road between the alcaldia and the Ingenio San Antonio is the Parque San Antonio, donated by the local refinery in 2006. The park's highlights are its enclosures: one with geese and ducks and the other where Juancho, the alligator, presides over 100 turtles. The park, including a food kiosk, opens between 5-9 p.m. (10 p.m. weekends).

Su Internet, located across the street from the alcaldia, has telephones, basic computers and fast internet for $0.50 per hour. The café is open Monday to Saturday from 8:30 a.m. to 8:45 p.m. or on Sundays until 5:30 p.m. Tel: 505-8-445-0697.

Hotel La Vista, one block east and 75 meters (246 ft) north of the alcaldia, has a monopoly on Chichigalpa lodgings. Luckily, the hotel is pleasant, clean, and has all of the preferred amenities: hot water, cable TV, air conditioning, a parking garage and five breakfasts to choose from in the morning. Friendly staff can point you towards rooms one, five or six, if you want a view of the volcano. (505-2-343-2035. Single $35; double $45; triple $50, not including IVA).

Comedor Popular El Doctor (505-2-343-1052, Mains: $1.50 to $4.50) may look like a hole in the wall—because, well, it is a hole in the wall, complete with a line of laundry on the back patio. But the eatery, run by Dr. Juan Emulio Morales, has daily specials that are as tasty as they are economical, which is why the comedor is a favorite Chichigalpa lunch spot. The comedor, one block west of the police station, is open from Monday to Thursday from 11 a.m. to 2 p.m.; call ahead if you want dinner. On the weekends, the good doctor and his family play live music until 1 a.m.

Restaurant Rancho Tipico "Rincón Criollo" is a laid-back, local hangout with cow hide chairs and a strong smell of French fries. The menu offers beef, pork, chicken, and fish for $3-9.50. On weekends, the dance floor comes alive with disco music. Open from 2 p.m. to 2 a.m. daily. Owner José Alfredo also arranges guided hikes up the volcano and trips to the Flor de Caña plant through his organization, ChiTours. Call or stop by the restaurant to reach Alfredo. Tel: 505-2-343-3406/ 505-8-627-7231.

Don't be put off by the parked cars you find when you first open the door to El Almendro. Locals know the tiny, family run restaurant (eight tables in a living room) is their own home-grown version of gourmet food. Owner Xavier Somarriba Garcia won't give away the secret of his *pollo deshuesado* but he somehow manages to take all the bones out of an entire chicken, without cutting the meat or skin, before covering the dish with a pineapple cream sauce. Main dishes run from $7-12.50. Open from 10:30 a.m. to 9 p.m. daily. Tel: 505-2-343-2237 / 343-1071. Updated: May 20, 2009.

Getting To and Away From Chichigalpa

Buses between Chinandega and El Viejo leave from Mercado Santa Ana and the north side of the central park, respectively. Both regular buses ($0.20, every 7 minutes, 5 a.m. to 6:30 p.m.) and microbuses ($0.25, when half full, 5:30 a.m. to 10 p.m.) make the five minute trip between the two cities. At one p.m., daily, a single bus leaves from the north side of the central park in El Viejo for the two hour, $0.90 trip to Punta Ñata. Updated: May 18, 2009.

CORINTO

2.44 m   17,499

As the country's deep water port, Corinto is a city whose fortunes ebb and flow on the tide. Cruise ships and freighters bring seasonal traffic, but only irregularly; between the October to May cruise season, about one ship stops a month.

Old wooden houses and crate-filled docks can make Corinto feel industrial and a bit shabby, but the city has the benefit of being surrounded by natural jewels: emerald estuaries, surfing breaks, rocky points and a series of islands so stunning that they once inspired Rubén Darío's poetry.

City officials have recognized the value of Corinto's location and are currently working on a series of projects to promote the area, such as a pamphlet of local attractions and boat tours. Fishermen offer sightseeing tours of the major islands: Castañones, El Cordón, Aserradores, Guerrero and Encantada, which range in price from $24-45 per hour. Local guides such as Kenneth Altanirano (505-8-417-5060; tours in English and Spanish) can arrange trips and hire boats, with at least a day's advance notice.

After El Cordón, the island where Darío wrote "A Margarita Debayle," was declared a national monument, city officials developed a plan to reconstruct the house where the poet once stayed. So far, the island remains house-less, but now has a large sculpture of Rubén Darío. Boat tours can take you to visit the island. The sculpture, beside the island's lighthouse, is also visible from Corinto's rocky espigon.

Corinto celebrates a *fiesta patronal* in honor of Santa Cruz, but is better known for the annual Feria Gastronómica del Mar, a culinary celebration of seafood dishes in all their variety, that takes place during the first weekend in May. The celebration ends with a fishing contest.

Corinto was not always Nicaragua's main waterway—the peninsula inherited the job from the pirate-ravaged El Realajo, whose marauding visitors (men such as Edgard Davis, Pirate Towby, Swan Knite and William Damper) meant that the former deep water port was neglected and filled with silt. In 1858, the Nicaraguan government decided enough was enough and moved the Maritime Customs office to the tiny Punta Icaco, whose name was changed three years later to the more official "Corinto".

A railway was constructed in 1881, so trains could carry shipments of sugar, cotton, coffee and other goods from Chinandega to Corinto's Spain-bound ships. You can still find one of the old train engines off to one side of the former train station.

Support VIVA! Reserve your hotels or hostels at www.vivatravelguides.com/hotels/

The station itself has long since been converted into the bright blue Alfonso Cortes-Corinto History Museum, Library and Auditorium. The small museum has glass cases of train era artifacts and a model of the city, but is only open during the high tourist season (or if you can find someone with the keys). The library is open from 8 to 11:30 a.m. and from 2-3 p.m. daily.

Across from the old train station is Corinto's Parque Los Fundadores and the catholic church, rebuilt in 1967 as Iglesia Santo Tomas Apóstal. But it's Corinto's central park that wins the award for strange monuments. The park's various concrete sculptures include: a pink centennial clock tower from 1958; a sculpture of Padre José Schendel with an expression that says he's about to deliver a stern lecture to naughty children, and what looks like a fountain but is actually the living quarters of a monster alligator and his turtle friends. Updated: May 20, 2009.

Getting To and Away From Corinto

Regular buses leave for Corinto every 15 minutes between 5 a.m. and 6 p.m. and cost $0.40. Microbuses leave each time they fill up with 10 people between 6 a.m. and 8 p.m. and $0.40. Microbuses also continue on to Leon. Updated: May 18, 2009.

Hospedaje Luvy

(ROOMS: $7-10) The clean and simple Hospedaje Luvy is Corinto's answer to economical lodging. The super simple rooms are located along a small, plant-filled courtyard. The mattresses are thin but clean and each room comes with a pile of soap and toilet paper (for the shared bathrooms). There are also two matrimonial rooms with private bathrooms. The hospedaje accepts cash only. Tel: 505-2-342-2637. Updated: May 18, 2009.

Hollywood Street Hotel

(ROOMS: $25-50) Hollywood Street Hotel is the newest and brightest addition to the Corinto accommodation scene. The canary yellow lobby leads to rooms with an eclectic collection of furniture. You might get a single with an overstuffed chair or one with a gilt mirror and mini-armoire. The arrangement of the private bathrooms is also slightly odd, since you open a door to the shower and have to step through to the toilet. The sink, of course, is located outside the bathroom. Besides the bizarre styling, the hotel is cheerful, air conditioned, and close to the shore. Guests can also use the kitchen in front. From the central park, the hotel is 2.5 blocks south. Tel: 505-2-340-6058. Updated: May 18, 2009.

Hotel Central

(ROOMS: $30-40) Hotel Central has cable TV and private bathrooms, but has a dispirited, transitory air that perhaps comes from being across from Corinto's deep water port. The prints of flamingos and plastic flowers don't do much to cheer up the windowless rooms (for some reason, the hotel doesn't rent out its second floor). Still, Hotel Central has been the Corinto standard for guests who are looking for air conditioning and can pay in cash. Located in front of the Ministerio Portuana. Tel: 505-2-342-2380. Updated: May 18, 2009.

From Costa Azul to Espigon

Along Corinto's rocky breakwater are a series of restaurants with excellent views of the water. Restaurant Costa Azul (505-2-342-2888, mains: $8-19) and neighboring Restaurant Rancho Peruano (505-2-340-5832, Mains: $8-17.50) both have verandas that overlook Corinto's shipping channel and outlying islands. Costa Azul, a favorite of the cruise ship set, specializes in sizzling seafood dishes, served up on an iron hot plate, while more low key Peruano has fish filets and occasional mariachi music. Head north out of town and you'll find El Espigón (Mains: $9-20), named after the rocky breakwater nearby. The restaurant, located at one end of Corinto's gorgeous and largely empty beach, is more expensive than those closer to town, but makes up for the price with cocktails and the view. You can either sit at a thatched-covered table, inside the restaurant's chain link enclosure, or you can rent one of El Espigón's beach chairs and put your feet in the sand. There is also a small playground for kids. The restaurant is open from 9 a.m. to 9 p.m. Updated: May 20, 2009.

PUERTO MORAZAN

Puerto Morazán would make the perfect launching point into Reserva Natural Delta del Estero Real—if the town had any tourist infrastructure whatsoever. This end-point of the Chinandega-Morazán bus route is still a desperately poor fishing village, where outhouses have been built right over the river waters.

Just a two-hour bus ride from Chinandega, the town has been left untouched by Nicaragua's recent tourist boom and has no hotels or restaurants. You can always hire a local fisherman to take you on a tour of the delta, but if you end up here, you're far better off catching one of the hourly buses back to Tonalá.

Puerto Morazán's neighbor, Tonalá, is slightly more developed (it had a hospedaje, but it closed in April). At the moment, Tonalá's alcaldia (505-2-346-9030) does double duty as the local INTUR office and can arrange various tours to Cerrania Ecologico Municipal Los Limones, Estero Real, and to the Centro Ecotouristico Tempisque if you call a day ahead. The city hall can also arrange for boat tours of the river delta.

Regular buses stop at the Tonalá bridge on their way between Puerto Morazán and Chinandega. You can catch one every hour between 4 a.m. and 4 p.m. for $0.65 or wait for a minibus at the same corner. The minibuses cost $0.90 and depart when full.
Updated: May 18, 2009.

PLAYA ASERRADORES

Aserradores is a small fishing town that features a popular surfing beach. There is a point break just north of the marina, and a big bay with a beach break. Waves here can be pretty powerful, and it is not uncommon for people to break their boards (or their faces), so this is not a good spot for beginning surfers. Water currents can be pretty strong here as well, so take precautions even if you're a strong swimmer.
Updated: Jan 15, 2009.

Joe's Place
(ROOMS: $6-7) Joe's Place is located off the beaten track in Aserradores, a small fishing village just 30 kilometers (98 ft) from Chinandega, which hosts world class surfing breaks, great fishing, beautiful beaches and stunning scenery. There are plenty of activities to enjoy here. Aleda is an excellent cook and Joe has a wealth of fishing and boating experience to help you haul in a huge fish. The place is located a stone's throw away from the estuary and close to two excellent surf breaks. For surfers on a tight budget, there is a cabin for rent. Drive into the village of Aserradores, turn left at the small gas station before the Marina, go around the school, and look for the sign. Aserradores Village. Tel: 505-8-469-5687, E-mail: portunica@gmail.com, URL: http://portunica.freehostia.com.
Updated: Sep 17, 2009.

> **V!VA ONLINE REVIEW**
> JOE'S PLACE
>
> "At Joe's Place I had my own room for less than a dorm, the food was amazing and super cheap."
>
> September 2, 2009

Las Chancletas
(DORMS: $15-35, ROOMS: $85) Las Chancletas, on a hill overlooking the beach in Aserradores, is a hotel for surfers who like to be close to the waves. Dorm rooms and private rooms are available, as well as air conditioned rooms with ensuite bathrooms. There is a restaurant and bar that is open all day and, in addition to serving the regular fare, has fresh fruit smoothies on the menu too. Massages are offered by the trained staff at $25 an hour, and taxi and boat services to different surfing points can be arranged through the hotel also. Playa Aserradores is a half an hour from Chinandega. Tel: 505-868-5036, E-mail: surfingnorthernnicaragua@msn.com, URL: www.hotelchancletas.com.
Updated: Jan 15, 2009.

Marina Puesta del Sol Resort
(SUITES: $184-624) As stop on the Pacific for yachtsmen and fishing enthusiasts, Marina Puesta del Sol is a resort offering boat dockage. The marina also has hotel rooms with views of the ocean, an infinity pool, and a restaurant and bar next to the docks that overlook the sailboats in the harbor. Tennis courts, kayaks, horseback riding and sport fishing excursions are also available at the resort. Rooms vary from junior suites to presidential. Tel: 505-880-0013 / 883-0781, E-mail: mpuestadelsol@yahoo.com, URL: www.marinapuestadelsol.com.
Updated: Jan 16, 2009.

RESERVA NATURAL PADRE RAMOS

Long known as the most wild and pristine of Nicaragua's Pacific Estuaries, Reserva Natural Padre Ramos is just starting to come into its own as a tourist destination. Most of the reserve's 8,800 hectares are only accessible by boat, and local efforts have concentrated on establishing tours from some of the towns around the costal estuary. The reserve's various islands (including Isleta Champerico, where Padre Francisco Ramos was once exiled) contain habitat for a number of alligators, some 150 species of birds and three species of sea turtles.

Reserva Padre Ramos is accessible in a number of ways: you can find boats and information at the Padre Ramos ranger station or contact local guides such as Eddy Maradiaga (505-8-371-6761), who charges between $60-250 for boat tours through the mangroves and out into the neighboring gulf. He also speaks a bit of English. Contact Selva (505-8-884-9156, selvanic@hotmail.com) to arrange a visit or to volunteer during the sea turtles' July to December egg laying season.

PLAYA JIQUILILLO

Just south of Padre Ramos is the tiny fishing community of Jiquilillo, where the beaches are lined with vacation houses and rancheros. This town that has seen its share of natural disasters. Once, the Jiquilillo shore was lined with hotels and restaurants, but the area was hit by both a tsunami (September, 1992) and Hurricane Mitch (October, 1998). The two disasters wiped out many of the structures that previously existed and Jiquilillo has never fully recovered. Nowadays three surfer-friendly lodgings and some beach homes exist alongside remnants of abandoned thatched roof buildings. Updated: Mar 13, 2009.

Lodging

There are three accommodation options in Jiquilillo. The hostels can provide their guests with boat tours through the estuary, kayak tours with a local wildlife biologist, surfing lessons and trips to either area volcanoes or the Golfo de Fonseca. Monty's also offers horseback riding ($5 per hour) and fishing ($35 per person for 6 hours) while you can get Spanish lessons for $5 per hour at Rancho Tranquilo. However, frequent electricity and water shortages occur, so be prepared with your own flashlights and bottled water. Updated: May 18, 2009.

Rancho Esperanza

(CAMPING/HAMMOCK: $3, ROOMS: $6-10) The most well-established of the three options is Hostel Rancho Esperanza, a welcoming backpacker hostel with sandy floored cabins, an extensive library and a lofty dorm space. The prices range from $3 for a hammock, to $6 for a space in the dorm and $10 for a cabin. Owner Nathan Yue can arrange volunteer or work opportunities for guests who want to stay longer term and are looking for a room-discount. Rancho Esperanza provides three meals a day to guests, has a selection of books to borrow and has surfboards for rent. Tours to nearby destinations are provided for additional costs. Tel: 505-879-1795, E-mail: rancho.esperanza@yahoo.com, URL: www.rancho.esperanza.bvg3.com. Updated: Jan 15, 2009.

Rancho Tranquilo

(SHARED ROOM: $5, CABINS: $8) Rancho Tranquilo has better beach access, but is less developed than Rancho Esperanza. As part of an ongoing development process, in spring 2009 owner Tina Morris was building two new cement-walled cabins and a bar with a view of the sea. Currently, guests eat meals family-style in the main barn building. Tel: 505-8-968-2290, Email: tina_sungoddess@hotmail.com. Updated: Jan 15, 2009.

Monty's Jiquilillo Surf Camp

(ROOMS: $35-60) Opened in 2007, the Canadian- and Nicaraguan-owned Monty's Surf Camp is the newest and most developed of the Jiquilillo trio. Less a camp than an all-inclusive getaway, Monty's has a range of package deals (including surf packages and the very handy transport from Managua's airport) and typically operates through advance reservations. Unlike the others, Monty's has a few cabins with private bathrooms. Such convenience comes with its own price tag. Guests can rest in shaded hammocks, below a two-story wooden structure on the property, or sip local beer while eyeing the ocean from the upper deck. Guests can enjoy breakfast, lunch and dinner together, dining on homemade Nicaraguan fare in the outdoor dining area. Tel: 505-884-4461 /2-341-8721, Cell: 505-473-3255, E-mail: monty@nicaraguasurfbeach / hotel_sanjuan18@hotmail.com, URL: http://nicaraguasurfbeach.com/. Updated: Jan 15, 2009.

POTOSI

The tiny town of Potosí, located between the Golfo de Fonseca and Volcán Cosigüina, has remained a largely undeveloped end point on Chinandega's northern bus route, despite a number of natural attractions.

Potosí marks the start of the Sendero El Jovo trail, an easy (but scorching) five-hour climb to the volcano's rim and back. Ask in town about local guides and horseback riding trips.

Potosí features a long stretch of black-sand beach, marked at one end by the old ferry docks, and hills that bubble with hot springs. The local favorite feeds into an outdoor swimming pool on the edge of town. Although the springs flow from the nearby volcano, their waters are actually fairly cool, making the shaded pool the perfect end to a long Cosigüina hike.

Buses from Potosí run south to Chinandega eight times a day, starting at 3 a.m. and petering out in the afternoon. The last bus departs at 3 p.m.; if you miss it, there are several local places where you can stay.

Hotel Bar y Comedor Brisas del Golfo has single rooms for $7, double rooms with private bathrooms for $14.50 and also rents hammocks or camping space for $2.50. The restaurant portion has daily specials of *comida corriente* for between $3-7. Owner Rosalpina Cruz can also arrange for sightseeing boat tours of the rocky islands in the gulf for between $4-5.

Doña Rosa Digna Rivas has seven rooms available in her breezy home, located near the *sendero* trailhead. The rooms cost $7 (or $10 if you want the room with four beds) and have shared bathrooms.

Although still a work in progress in May, Amanecer Fonseca was set to become the newest Potosí hotel by the end of 2009. The beach-front location was expected to feature a pool, cable TV, air conditioning and, when a Potosí communications tower is completed, internet. Updated: May 18, 2009.

Getting To and Away From Potosi

There is a persistent rumor that a ferry between Potosí and La Union in El Salvador will finally resume after years of inactivity. Fanning the rumors are government plans to build two new docks at Potosí, with the materials lined up on shore, suggesting that the docks might appear sooner rather than later. Whether the ferries will head to Potosí again (rather than larger Corinto) is unknown. In the meantime, you can hire a local to make the crossing in a fishing boat; ask for Tomas Gonzales, who makes the trip to Potosí on Fridays and returns to El Salvador on Mondays. Updated: May 18, 2009.

Reserva Natural Volcán Cosigüina

At Nicaragua's northwestern tip is a reserve full of tropical dry forest with spider monkey's and scarlet macaws. The crown of the natural reserve is the massive Cosigüina crater, once Nicaragua's tallest volcano. Cosigüina's height was spectacularly reduced during a series of eruptions in January of 1835. The eruptions were so intense that fierce Cosigüina lost over 2,000 meters (6,562 ft) of altitude, from nearly 3,000 meters (9,842 ft) to the current 872 meters (2,861 ft). Central America fell under a cloud of darkness, with ashes falling in Mexico, Colombia and Jamaica. The ash fall was so thick that many terrified Nicaraguans believed it heralded the Apocalypse.

Cosigüina erupted again in 1852 and 1859 but, by the middle of the next century, appeared mostly spent. You can climb to the rim of the volcano to see the 1.5 kilometer (.93 mi) lagoon created by the eruptions. The 700-meter (2,296 ft) decent is only possible with the proper climbing gear and experience.

The volcano's sides are laced with unmarked hiking trails which can be traversed by foot, horseback or 4WD vehicles. The best known and most easily accessible routes are to the Sendero La Guacamaya, which begins at the ranger station just south of El Rosario, and to the Sendero El Jovo, with a trailhead at Potosí.

The Cosigüina trails are relatively easy and mostly shaded, but you should still pack sufficient water for what can be a three to five -hour hike.

As a reward for an incredibly hot uphill climb, you'll have a view of the Golfo de Fonseca, El Salvador's Volcán Conchagua and Volcán Amapala in Honduras.

Since the trails are largely unmarked and occasionally overgrown, the best idea is to hire a guide. In Potosí, Tomas Reyes takes groups to the crater and back for $20. Trips on horseback cost an extra $5 per person.

Fundación Lider (505-2-344-2381, funcaionlider@yahoo.es) can also arrange

tours and lodging. Check with them to see if the temporarily closed Centro Turísticos Aguas Termales is back in business.
Updated: May 18, 2009.

Border Crossing to Honduras at Guasaule and Potosí

Plans to reinstate the ferry between Potosí and El Salvador have been on the table for years, but little progress is visible. Locals are hopeful that the federal government will eventually improve the road to their town, add faster bus services, and send boats scuttling between Potosí and El Salvador. But don't expect an official service any time soon. If you're desperate to get to El Salvador from Potosí, fisherman can take you there, but will charge up to $100. Make sure you're headed for a valid border crossing, to avoid any immigration issues. Tomas Gonzales makes a weekly run in his boat, ferrying workers to El Salvador on Monday and back to Nicaragua on Friday.
Updated: Oct 08, 2009.

MIRAMAR

Bus routes between Leon and Puerto Sandino make regular stops at Miramar, a tiny seaside spot with fewer services but better beach access than its port neighbor.

Like the neighboring spots of El Velero, El Tránsito and Puerto Sandino, Miramar has a growing reputation as a surf spot. Tour companies (such as www.surftoursnicaragua.com) offer transportation so clients can take advantage of the breaks at either end of the shore.

Miramar's lovely crescent beach is lined with vacation retreat homes, ranging from shacks to extravagant mansions. Other than Semana Santa, Christmas week and other high holidays, few owners make regular trips out to the isolated village, which means that you'll likely have the entire stretch of sun, sand and clear water to yourself. There is no official accommodation in town, but you can usually find a place to string a hammock if you ask around. Mari Gonzalez (cell: 505-8-665-3482) rents out rooms with the very basics (think plank beds, well water and latrines) at Casa Adilia Telles.

Miramar also lacks restaurants of any kind, although one or two informal *fritangas*

open during lunch and dinner time. Just follow your nose to the greasy food.
Updated: May 26, 2009.

!!!!!

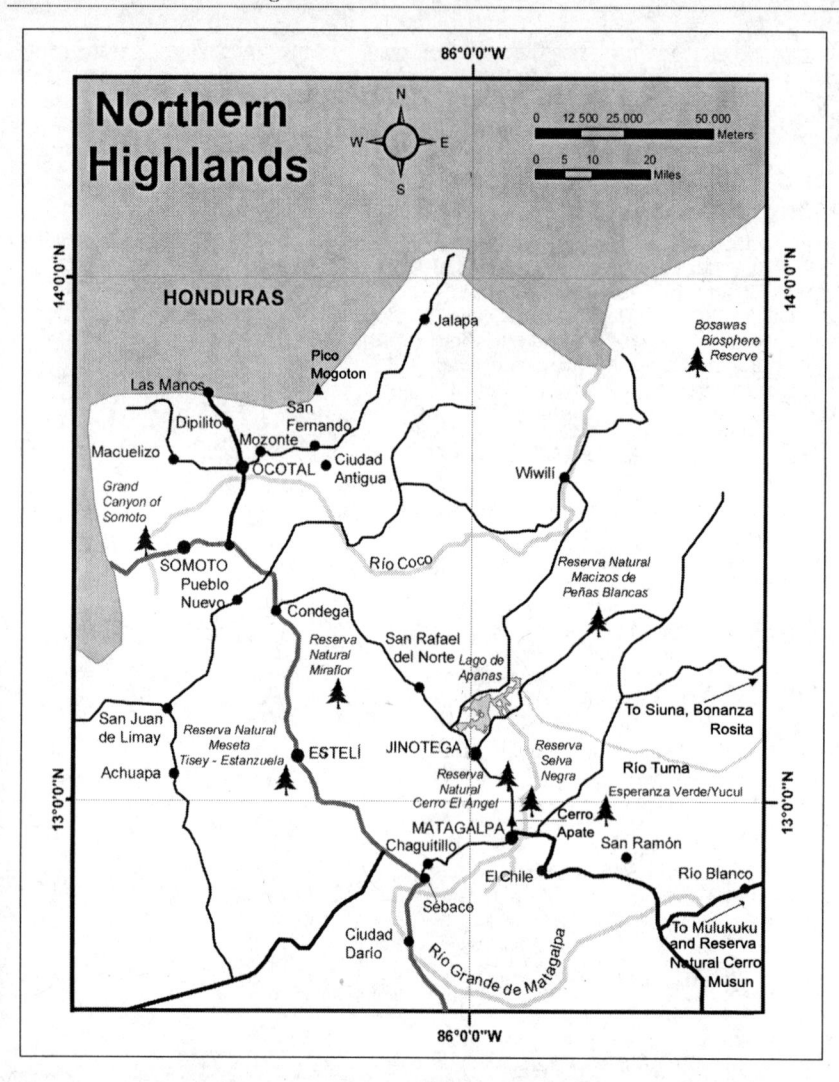

The Northern Highlands

Nicaragua's lush Northern Highlands, full of blue mountains, historical murals and coffee tours, provides the perfect antidote to the heat and crowds of the major cities. That said, the cities of the Northern Highlands—namely Matagalpa and Jinotega—are definitely worth a visit. The region has also produced some pretty famous figures, including Rubén Darío, whose birthplace adopted the name Ciudad Darío, and Carlos Fonseca, a Sandinista hero who was born in Matagalpa. Both men have museums dedicated to them in their hometowns.

The Northern Highlands also contains a number of ecological reserves, including the **Reserva Natural Miraflor** or **Tisey Estanzuela**. Visit such reserves and find yourself in a land of quiet cloud forests and sparkling waterfalls. A hike along local trails will give you the chance to see toucans, howler monkeys or a small wild cat known as a *jaguarundi*.

VIVA recommends travel insurance. Get it at vivatravelguides.com/insurance/

La Ruta del Cafe

While exploring any of the five departments of the Northern Highlands, observant travelers may notice posters and brochures around town promoting *La Ruta del Café*. Despite how it may sound, *La Ruta del Café* is not a specific route on a map, nor is it an organized coffee-hopping tour, exactly.

Working in collaboration with a Luxembourgian development agency, Nicaragua's tourism institute (INTUR) has been hard at work on *La Ruta Del Café*, a broad-based project whose objective is to strengthen the economic development of the region through tourism to both traditional and non-traditional attractions, of which coffee farms are a part. *La Ruta del Café* is one of eight development projects run by INTUR all over the country, collectively called the *Rutas Turísticas de Nicaragua*. Through funding, training and promotion, each *Ruta* slowly enables different regions in the country to capitalize on the natural and cultural resources they already have in order to build the infrastructure necessary to become tourist destinations—albeit rustic ones.

Evidence of this investment can be seen in Jinotega, whose residents have long been growing some of the world's best coffee, but who have only recently begun to open up their coffee farms to tourists, a move that can sustain them in the typically lean period after the harvest is over. See Jinotega's coffee co-op section (p.259) for more about these farms and how to visit them. Religious tourism to San Rafael del Norte and opportunities to visit historical sites relating to iconic revolutionary Agusto Sandino are similarly being developed and promoted in the area.

With marked hiking trails being cleared and homestay and camping opportunities created, the four natural reserves within Matagalpa's borders are also being developed. As in Jinotega, there are plenty of coffee farms to visit here. Heavily involved in the area's tourism development is Norlan Albuquerque, INTUR employee and passionate owner of Madretierra restaurant in Matagalpa. If you're really interested, stop by his joint to hear the inside scoop on projects in the department's future that are bursting with potential.

Initiatives in Esteli are also being strengthened, with well-run community tourism projects in the Miraflor and Tisey Reserves, and soap-stone production in nearby San Juan de Limay. Further north are the less-developed Ocotal and Somoto, both of which are surrounded by pristine natural spots, some ripe for exploration and others not quite ready for foreign footprints. Travelers looking to get a glimpse of the real northern Nicaragua—the majority of whose residents work the land—will find plenty of rural tourism opportunities in this region, as long as work-in-progress tours, lodging and other amenities are taken in stride. Updated: May 05, 2009.

Butterflies and birds can also be spotted flitting through the foliage.

For a cup of world-famous local coffee, head to one of the plantations that dot the northern countryside. **Selva Negra Mountain Resort**, in particular, is renowned for both its coffee and the owners' sustainable agriculture projects. Encouraged by the local government, other small plantations (particularly around Miraflor and Estelí), have begun welcoming visitors. Updated: Jun 24, 2009.

History

Most notably, the Northern Highlands was the birthplace of Nicaragua's left-wing nationalist movement, which was first conceived by icon Augusto Cesar Sandino in the 1920s and 1930s. Armed with machetes and rifles manufactured in the 19th century, Sandino and his militia declared war on the United States. In 1927 they attacked an American marine base in the city of Ocotal, provoking the United States to carry out the world's first ever air raid. Foreshadowing the revolutionary spirit that was to take hold there in the

Highlights

Gallery of Heroes and Martyrs (p.223) — This small but powerful museum in Estelí is a must for anyone desiring insight into the Sandinista Revolution and Contra War of the 1980s, the wounds from which are still very fresh in this region.

Miraflor and Tisey (p.228) — Arrange for an overnight homestay at a community in the well-run Reserva Miraflor, and don't miss the chance to bath in the deliciously frigid waters of Salta Estanzuela in Reserva Tisey.

Custom Cowboy Boots in Estelí (p.222) — Picky shoppers will have a ball dictating every aspect of their custom-made dream boots in the cowboy heartland of Estelí.

Jinotega (p.256) — Fall in love with tiny, peaceful Jinotega and the myriad of ecological *fincas* (farms) in the surrounding area, including the highly-regarded Selva Negra Mountain Resort.

Volunteering in Matagalpa (p.247) — Do-gooders should make a beeline for Matagalpa, home to feminist powerhouse *Grupo Venancia* and the multifaceted center for disabled children, *Centro Girasol*, among many other impressive organizations.

Somoto Canyon (p.241) — Not fully on the gringo radar yet, untouched Somoto Canyon offers a vigorous rock scramble to cool, emerald-green waters, perfect for swimming and even cliff diving. Updated: May 06, 2009.

1970s, Sandino's little army carried out raids in Estelí and the coffee-growing regions of Matagalpa and Jinotega.

Following the inauguration of Juan Bautista Sacasa, Sandino's followers who pledged loyalty to the new president were offered amnesty and given land in Jinotega on which to settle with their families. These good relations ended; however, when Anastasio Somoza Garcia ousted Sacasa and took over the presidency. The start of this four decade dictatorship was what would eventually lead to the Sandinista National Liberation Front (FSLN), founded by Carlos Fonseca and named in honor of the failed revolutionary.

Matagalpa was later to become the first city to be taken over by the *Terceristas*, an anti-Somoza movement led by current president Daniel Ortega, which later joined forces with the FSLN. This was in September of 1978, and was followed by attacks on Managua, Chinandega, Masaya, Leon and Estelí. Estelí saw much violence during the overthrow of the Somoza regime and to this day, the city continues to be the most pro-Sandinista town in northern Nicaragua. Updated: May 06, 2009.

When to Go

The weather in the Northern Highlands is temperamental, with bouts of rain and bursts of sunshine occurring all year round. The region is generally cooler than the rest of Nicaragua, with temperatures ranging from the high-20s °C to the low-30s °C (80s °F) during the rainy season (May – October). In the dry season (November – April), the temperatures rise to the mid-30s °C (mid-90s °F). In the mountains of the coffee growing regions of Matagalpa and Jinotega it is significantly cooler. Travelers hoping to catch the harvest should arrange to visit in December and January.

Major festivals in the Northern Highlands include Matagalpa's anniversary party on February 14th, Jalapa's corn festival in September and Somoto's carnival on November 11th and 12th. Updated: May 06, 2009.

Safety

Because there aren't as many tourists in this region as there are in other places in the country, there simply isn't as much petty crime here. Still, it's a good idea to be aware of your belongings, especially during rowdy outdoor festivities. Both small towns and larger ones are safe to walk around, but it's always a good idea to stay away from the outskirts, particularly at night. Matagalpa, in particular, seems to get a little seedy after dark. Updated: May 06, 2009.

Things To See and Do

Most people come to the Northern Highlands not to see monumental sights, but to get a sense of the culture. More than any other region, tourism in the highlands goes hand in hand with local industry. More and more farms are opening up to

---

VIVA recommends travel insurance. Get it at vivatravelguides.com/insurance/

Nicaraguan Cigars

HISTORY
Archaeological evidence suggests that the indigenous people of Mesoamerica and the Caribbean have been smoking cigars since the 10th century. Five decades later Christopher Columbus encountered cigars in the Bahamas and brought the trend back to Europe. The cigars the natives smoked were different from modern cigars in that the tobacco was wrapped in corn husks or palm leaves. Cigars as we know them were likely developed by the Spanish in Cuba during the 18th century, and while Cuba continues to be the world's most famous cigar manufacturer, premium cigars are also produced in Central America and the Dominican Republic.

TODAY'S CIGARS
While most cigars today are machine manufactured, those that are rolled by hand are considered to be of much higher quality. These are the types that are rolled in Nicaragua's many factories, some of which produce cigars that rival those of Cuba. However, decades of political instability have taken a toll on the country's tobacco crops and cigar manufacturers. Following the revolution, most of Nicaragua's leading cigar families lost their land to redistribution. Crops that were once used as the raw material for premium cigars began being manufactured into cheap Soviet cigarettes. Although many cigar manufacturers have since regained their land, their wills were once again tested when in 1998 Hurricane Mitch ravaged their fields. The industry is proving its resiliency; however, and in recent years Nicaragua has been making a name for itself on the international cigar scene. Today, 11 percent of premium cigars imported to the United States come from Nicaragua, and the Nicaraguan industry is growing faster than that of any other country.

HOW THEY'RE MADE
The tobacco leaves used in the cigars are cured and fermented after they are harvested, during a process in which humidity and temperature are carefully controlled. Next, leaves are sorted based on appearance and quality, to be used as either wrappers or fillers, with the wrappers coming from the widest part of the tobacco plant. Long fillers are made of the entire leaf and tend to be better quality than short fillers, which are comprised of chopped up bits. Once the cigars are rolled they are put into wooden molds and placed in a vice to hold the shape. Finished cigars are then stored in a humidor—a wooden box designed to retain the correct humidity. Tobaccos from different regions possess different tastes and aromas, and as such, different blends will suit people with different preferences. Quality is also determined by the harshness of the smoke, the ease with which smoke is drawn and the consistency of the rate at which the cigar burns. Updated: Apr 27, 2009.

---

agro-tourism, and hiking trails are slowly becoming more accessible. As this is the premier coffee-growing region of the country, many coffee plantations offer tours, and as Estelí is known for its cigars, many factories now offer tours. Overall, the Northern Highlands is a work in progress, with great potential for tourism. Updated: May 06, 2009.

Tours
With the exceptions of **Matagalpa Tours** and **Casa Estelí**, there are no official tour operators in the region. Still, some upscale hotels can arrange tours, and independent guides can also often be procured through INTUR. Tourism here is really just beginning to blossom, and as infrastructure continues to develope, more tour outfitters will surely crop up. Nonetheless, many hiking excursions in the region can be done solo, and most places of interest are not impossible to get to on your own. Though not necessarily tour guides, there are knowledgeable people involved in tourism in each city, and they are generally easy to get in touch with. Updated: May 06, 2009.

Get free e-books when you reserve your hotel or hostel at vivatravelguides.com/hotels/

Lodging

There is only one true backpackers hostel in the region, along with several upscale hotels and many, many, simple, family-run budget ones. Those watching their wallets will get much more bang for their buck here than in more popular destinations, like Granada or Leon. Although there are occasional water and electricity glitches at hotels, this is not something to worry too much about, though hot water is a real rarity. The only time hotel reservations are necessary is during a festival, when locals and tourists pour in from all over the country. Updated: May 06, 2009.

Restaurants

Most towns serve typical Nicaraguan food at extremely reasonable prices. Larger cities like Matagalpa and Estelí offer a little more variation, with a couple of finer dining options. Nonetheless, authentic-tasting international cuisine is somewhat of a rarity in the north. Updated: May 06, 2009.

ESTELÍ

844m | 112,084 | 2

Declared *The City of Murals* in 2003, Estelí is decorated with over 150 murals depicting a variety of subject matter. A lush jungle, dense with vegetation and animals, wraps around the public library, while on the next corner, ancient to modern-day Nicaraguans confront an eagle clawing Planet Earth. In the hospital, the popular history of this country is proudly on display, and just a few blocks away is a depiction of author Antoine de Saint-Exupéry's, Little Prince. These are just a few examples of the many beautiful street paintings found throughout the city.

During the Sandinista Revolution (1979 – 1990), mural workshops flourished throughout this country. Today, only in Estelí do they survive, striving to preserve the originals, while also painting new images. Two *talleres*, or workshops, are still active: one is at the **Casa de Cultura** and the other can be found at **Funarte**, where hundreds of women and children are involved with the projects.

Founded at the end of the 16th century, Estelí was a key location during the Insurrection (1978 – 1979), and was heavily bombed by then-dictator Anastasio Somoza Debayle. Throughout the 1980s, the Estelí region furthermore witnessed extensive damage from the U.S.-backed Contras. To learn more about these events, and others from the tumultuous history of Estelí, visit the **Galería de Héroes y Mártires** (run by the mothers of the victims), and **El Café del Poeta**, (operated by María de los Ángeles Rugama, sister of the poet Leonel Rugama).

But a fascinating political history isn't all this city has to offer, as the hills surrounding Estelí provide a number of attractions for the visitor. To the south, the Estanzuela waterfall cascades into a refreshing pool, while in the north there are several artisan villages, such as San Juan de Limay (p.230), where the locals carve marble, and Ducuale GrandeJ where pottery is skillfully crafted. And be sure to head to the northeast, where you'll find organic coffee farms and the cloud forest reserve of Miraflor, whose main offices are in Estelí. All these wonders of nature, as well as the history and dreams of Nicaragua, come to life in the discussions of the people of Estelí, and in the dozens of murals that decorate this northern Nicaraguan city. Updated: May 08, 2009.

When to Go

The temperature in Esetli usually falls around 27°C (80°F), but during the rainy season (June – November), temperatures tend to drop. The dry season lasts from December to May.

Most celebrations occur in December, when street fairs are held every weekend, with special cultural activities on the 8th—the anniversary of the city's founding. Estelí also celebrates its *fiestas patronales* in honor of the Virgen del Carmen on July 16th. Festivals honoring the Virgen de Rosario and the Virgen of Guadalupe fall on October 7th and December 12th respectively. The patron saint days are June 24 – 26, and the important nine-day *La Purísima* festival, culminates on December 7th. Updated: Apr 13, 2009.

Getting To and Away From Estelí

Buses to Matagalpa run from 5:15 a.m. to 4:50 p.m., while those to Managua's Mayoreo terminal run from 3:30 a.m. to 6 p.m. To get to Ocotal, Somoto and other points north of Estelí take buses from the Cotran Norte (north station). To get to Matagalpa, Managua and towns south of Estelí, take buses from the Cotran Sur (south station). Although their names imply that these

VIVA recommends travel insurance. Get it at vivatravelguides.com/insurance/

stations are located at opposite ends of the city, they are actually only three blocks apart on the Pan-American highway. Given its proximity to the Honduran border, Estelí is an easy place to arrange journeys to both Honduras and El Salvador. The luxury bus company, **King Quality**, goes to San Salvador and Tegucigalpa for roughly $30. Updated: Apr 13, 2009.

Getting Around

With a few exceptions (notably **Hotel Cualitlan**, **La Casita**, and several cigar factories) most hotels, restaurants and sites in Estelí are within walking distance of the central park. Establishments located on the eastside of the Pan-American highway (including both bus stations) are probably best reached via taxi. Taxis cost roughly $0.40 per person to travel within the city, $0.45 to go from one end to the other, and $0.50 to go out of town. Updated: Apr 13, 2009.

Safety

Estelí is a fairly safe city, and travelers should have no problem walking around at night, provided that they stick to the central areas of the city. Updated: Apr 13, 2009.

Services

TOURISM

The best resource for tourism information in Estelí is Janie "Juanita" Boyd, owner of **Café Luz** and **Hospedaje Luna**. Leaflets, fliers and maps are available at either venue and at the time of writing an official tourism office was in the works. Native Brit Janie is a wealth of knowledge on the area and is happy to assist travelers (Tel: 505-8-441-8466, E-mail: info@cafeluzyluna.com). Another good source of information is **Casa Estelí**, an operation that also runs tours. Non-Spanish speakers should note that the staff, though friendly, does not speak English (Tel: 505-2-713-4432, E-mail: CasaEstelí@asdenic.org, URL: www.asdenic.org).

Tours to cigar factories are available through Casa Estelí and Café Luz, though many of the smaller shops around town will be happy to let you poke your head in to see how the cigars are rolled. To arrange visits to **Empresa Nicaranguese** call owner Armando at 505-8-693-8053. For tours of the **Estelí Cigar Factory** call 505-2-713-5688 or e-mail etelici@ibw.com.ni. If you're just looking to buy, locally rolled cigars are widely available in stores around town.

MONEY

BDF, **BAC** and **Banpro** are all located at the intersection known as *la esquina de los bancos* (the bank corner). All have ATM machines and can exchange currency. The **Western Union** is one block south of the Supermercado Las Segovias.

KEEPING IN TOUCH

The **post office** (Tel: 505-2-713-2609) changes location frequently, as it is not always able to meet its rent. For other shipping needs, there is a **DHL** located seven blocks south of the central park, though expect to pay top dollar.

Across the street from the DHL is **Internet Conectate** and four blocks east of that is **Cybernica**. Most internet cafés also offer international calls, and are easily found around town. Internet in the region costs roughly $0.60.

MEDICAL

Hospital Regional San Juan de Dios, located south of the city, is not terribly pleasant and should only be visited in dire emergencies (Tel: 505-2-713-6300). For major health problems it is best to relocate to Managua as soon as possible. For minor ailments, visit the clean, well-equipped **Pro-Familia**, located between the north and south bus terminals on the Pan-American highway. There you can expect to pay around $5 to see a general practitioner and $10 to see a specialist.

LAUNDRY

The only place to machine wash your clothes is at **Ray Lun**, located in a convenience store between the Toyota dealership and club Axsis on the Pan-American Highway. One load costs $5 – 6, depending on how big it is.

SHOPPING

Estelí offers more shopping opportunities than any other town in the Northern Highlands, and items crafted in outlying communities can all be found at several well-stocked shops around town. These include **Artesanías La Esquina** and the slightly more expensive **Artesanía Sorpresa**, formerly known as Artesanía Nicaraguense, both of which carry pottery, soapstone sculptures, leather goods and wooden carvings. Crafts can also be found at **Casa Estelí** (tours can also be arranged), and at **Café Arte Tipiscayan**, owned by sculptor Freddy Moreno. The slightly upscale café offers typical Nica

Estelí

ESTELI

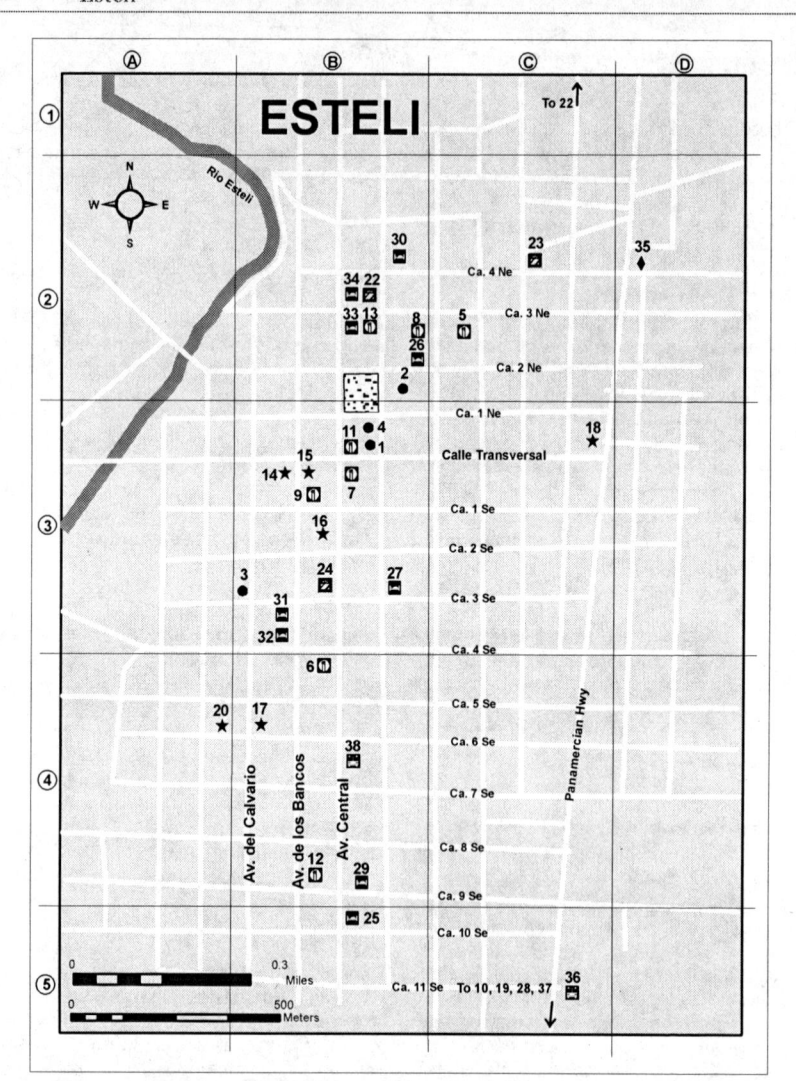

food and good coffee. Look for Freddy in the café and ask him to show you his nearby workshop. Arte Tipiscayan is located three blocks north and two blocks west of the Shell station (Tel: 505-2-713-7303 / 8-664-2942, E-mail: café_arte_tipiscayan@yahoo.com).

A plethora of leather workshops can be found along the southern half of Avenida 1. Embossed belts, saddles and of course, cowboy boots can all be made to order along this street. **Casa Fegueroa** seems to offer the lowest prices, with custom made boots going for $55. Control freaks and fashionistas will delight in choosing the exact color, texture, height and heel and toe shapes of their footwear. Feet can be measured in the store, though molds of standard sizes are used. While already-made boots can be bought on the spot, special orders take about a week to produce. Updated: Apr 13, 2009.

Things to See and Do

As one of the most developed cities in northern Nicaragua, Estelí offers the tourist a fair number of attractions. Having been the stronghold of the Sandinista movement, Estelí is home to the poignant Gallery of Heroes and Martyrs, as well as

VIVA recommends travel insurance. Get it at vivatravelguides.com/insurance/

Activities ●

1. Casa de Cultura B3
2. Catedral de Nuestra Senora del Rosario B3
3. Funarte B3
4. Gallery of Heroes and Martyrs and Museum of History and Archaeology B3

Eatings

5. Café Luz C2
6. Café Repostería Mamilou B4
7. Comedor Pinareño B3
8. Don Pollo #2 B2
9. Gran Via B3
10. La Casita C5
11. Licuados Ananda B3
12. Rincon Legal B4
13. Vuela Vuela B2

Services ★

14. BAC B3
15. Banpro B3
16. BDF B3
17. DHL B4
18. Gas Station C3
19. Hospital Regional San Juan de Dios C5
20. Internet Conectate A4
21. UCA Miraflor C1

Shoping

22. Artesanías La Esquina B2
23. Café Arte Tipiscayán C2
24. Pali B3

Sleeping

25. Hospedaje Chepito B5
26. Hospedaje Luna B2
27. Hospedaje Sacuanjoche B3
28. Hotel Cualitlan C5
29. Hotel Don Vito B4
30. Hotel El Mesón B2
31. Hotel Estli B3
32. Hotel Familiar B3
33. Hotel Los Arcos B2
34. Hotel Miraflor B2

Tours ♦

35. Casa Esteli D2

Transportation

36. Cortan Norte C5
37. Cortan Sur C5
38. King Quality B3

---

a multitude of murals depicting scenes encouraging social action and equality. On May 27, 2005 Estelí even entered the Guinness Book of World Records for having the largest mural in the world, painted by more than 2,000 children.

Gallery of Heroes and Martyrs

This moving tribute is run by the mothers and widows of soldiers killed in the Sandinista Revolution. Although the displays are a bit makeshift, the murals, photos, articles of clothing and collected stories show how deeply personal the war was to the people of this region. Walk through the gallery to learn how the people of Estelí and the surrounding countryside united and organized a highly efficient system for passing information from the Sandinistas to the populace. Also displayed are brief biographies of Augusto Sandino, FSLN founder, Carlos Fonseca and the lesser known, but emblematic Lionel Rugama Rugama, who upon being ordered to surrender, famously cried "Surrender your mother! Free country or death!" before being shot. Poetry by leaders such Rigoberto Lopez Perez is also on display, as are journal entries by an unknown soldier. Open Monday – Friday, 8 a.m. – 5 p.m. Half a block south of the central park. URL: www.galleryofheroesandmartyrs.blogspot.com. Updated: Apr 13, 2009.

Museum of History and Archeology

Adjacent to the Gallery of Heroes and Martyrs, this tiny, slightly dilapidated museum houses an eclectic collection of artifacts, from antique phones and typewriters to archaeological finds. Perhaps the most interesting feature is a diorama of the sites where pre-Columbian artifacts were originally discovered. Non-Spanish speakers beware: the docent does not speak English and the faded captions (which only occasionally accompany exhibits) are only in Spanish. Open Monday – Friday, 9 a.m. – noon and 2–5 p.m. Half a block south of the central park. Updated: Apr 13, 2009.

Catedral de Nuestra Senora del Rosario

Originally constructed in 1823, Catedral de Nuestra Senora del Rosario was remodeled in 1889 and then again in 1929, when it acquired its modern neo-classical façade. Designated a cathedral with the creation of the diocese of Estelí in 1962, the cathedral's austere, towering exterior belies the traditional interior featuring depictions of the stations of the cross and a well-kept wooden alter. With grounds covering two acres, this cathedral is the most impressive structure in Estelí. Across the street from the central park. Updated: Apr 13, 2009.

Cigar Factory

Upon entering Nick's Cigar Company in Estelí, guests are immediately greeted by the overpowering scent of tobacco. While the factory is heaven for hardcore aficionados, it should be noted that tobacco novices may feel some irritation in their eyes and throat several minutes into the tour. Once escorted inside the production rooms, visitors have a chance to see the entire cigar manufacturing process, from drying to packaging. Each roller at Nick's Cigars produces between 300 and 500 cigars a day, for a total factory output of roughly 60,000 cigars a day. Named in honor of Nicks Perdomo Jr.'s late grandfather, the *Edición de Silvio* is the highest quality cigar manufactured at the factory. Straight from the factory, a box of 20 cigars goes for $200. In the Perdomo Cigar Shop in Miami, however, a box costs $500. If you want a small souvenir but can't afford a box of Silvios, individual cigars can also be bought. And if you're really lucky, you might even be given a freebie at the end of the tour.

Km 150 on the Pan-American highway. A taxi will cost roughly $0.50 per person. If walking from town, head past the Texaco until you cross a bridge. There you'll see the kilometer sign. Turn left and walk 200 meters west. Updated: Apr 20, 2009.

Tours

The only place to arrange professional tours of the Estelí area is at **Casa Estelí**, a big yellow house on the eastfside of the Pan-American highway, four blocks north of the gas station. Apart from organized tours, Casa Estelí also sells local crafts and provides rental cars (working in partnership with Budget). All guides are trained by Intur.

Trips range from hour-long cigar tours ($7) to four-day packages to Reserva Tisey, Reserva Miraflor, Cantagallo and Somoto. Transport, lodging, food and entrance fees are all included. Also offered is a one-day artisan tour through Ducuali, Mozonte, San Juan de Limay, Pueblo Nuevo and Somoto— famous for ceramics, soapstone sculptures and rosquillas. Keep in mind that tour prices depend on the number of participants. While a solo traveler will pay $180 for the four-day tour, for example, four people will only be charged $60 per person. Those with flexible schedules can call Casa Estelí and arrange to tag along with a larger group. There is also an evening city tour that guides tourists through the city's discoteques, casinos and restaurants. The tour lasts from 7 p.m. to 4 a.m. and costs $60. Make sure to wear appropriate footware and stay caffeinated. Open 8 a.m. – 6 p.m., Monday – Friday. Tel: 505-2-713-4432, E-mail: CasaEsteli@asdenic.org, URL: www.asdenic.org. Updated: Apr 13, 2009.

Lodging

Perhaps the best equipped city for tourists in the Northern Highlands, Estelí offers sleeping options for all tastes and budgets. Travelers can choose from luxury hotels, divey flop-houses and even one real backpacker's hostel. Many lodgings are located right near shopping, restaurants and attractions, but there are a few outliers, most notably the tranquil Hotel Cualitlan.

BUDGET
Hospedaje Chepito

(ROOMS: $5) Hospedaje Chepito should be called Cheap-ito, as it is one of the most affordable lodgings in town. Tried and true backpackers won't mind that only two bathrooms are shared by all the guests, and that those with rooms on the second floor have to walk downstairs and across an open area in order to access them. Obviously rooms are spare, but they're clean enough. Ten blocks

south of the central park. Tel: 505-2-713-3784.
Updated: Apr 14, 2009.

Hotel Sacuanjoche
(ROOMS: $10) Party animals will not like the 10 p.m. curfew at Sacuanjoche, but others will enjoy the peace and quiet it affords. The owner is getting on in years and during the evenings can often be found in the front area with his feet propped up watching CNN Español. It is much harder to find him during the the day, when most of the doors are locked. Nonetheless, Hotel Sacuanjoche is cheap and clean, and is a great budget option. One block east from the Pali supermarket. Tel: 505-2- 713-2482.
Updated: Apr 14, 2009.

Hospedaje Luna !
(DORM: $7, ROOMS: $13 per person) Hospedaje Luna is the only real backpacker's hostel in Estelí. As such it features a book-swap, lots of tourist info, a common room with a TV, and friendly and knowledgeable British owner, Janie, who also runs Café Luz across the street. The décor is funky and the rooms are spotless. Also offered are free organic coffees and teas, free WiFi, bike rentals, laundry facilities and hot water. There are no private bathrooms. One block north of the cathedral. Tel: 505-8-441-8466.
Updated: Apr 14, 2009.

> **V!VA ONLINE REVIEW**
> HOSPEDAJE LUNA
>
> "Hospedaje Luna is run by someone who does so much to support the locals and the Miraflor cooperative. It's really different from anywhere else in Estelí!"
>
> *May 30, 2008*

Hospedaje Familiar
(ROOMS: $10) Doña Edith runs a tight ship, zipping between her hotel and adjoining eatery. Travelers looking for extended stays in Estelí will appreciate discounts, though Familiar is still a budget option for those only staying a night or two. Long-term guests are given use of the kitchen. Laundry services can also be arranged. Three blocks south of the esquina Los Bancos. Tel: 505-2-713-3666.
Updated: May 13, 2009.

MID-RANGE
Hotel Estelí
(ROOMS: $10 – 17.50) Don't be deterred by the bleak reception area. Upstairs, Hotel Estelí is actually quite nice, with clean, basic rooms, some of which come equipped with private bathrooms. Electric showers provide hot water. Three blocks south of the esquina Los Bancos. Tel: 505-2-713-2902.
Updated: Apr 14, 2009.

Hotel El Meson
(ROOMS: $14.50 – 27) Rooms at El Meson are homey, featuring colorful curtains, TVs, and a few personal touches. Also available are fans and air conditioners—though use of the latter will double the price of the room. There is also a copying machine on-site and WiFi in the reception area out front. Most notable is the attached Tisey Travel Agency which many may find useful. One block north of the central park, across the street from Hotel Miraflor. Tel: 505-2-713-2655.
Updated: Apr 14, 2009.

Hotel Miraflor
(ROOMS: $15) Conveniently located near Artesanías La Esquina, Restaurante Vuela Vuela and Café Luz, Hotel Miraflor is a basic option in the heart of town. The hotel provides electric shower heads with hot water, simple rooms and an on-site restaurant serving standard, budget meals. Two blocks north of the central park on Avenida Central. Tel: **505-2-713-2003**.
Updated: Apr 14, 2009.

HIGH-END
Hotel Cualitlan !
(CABINS: $20 – 50 per person) Located on a secluded side street near the bus terminal, Hotel Cualitlan is far enough outside of town to offer guests private cabins amid lush gardens with brightly colored birds. Friendly, English-speaking owner Marisela Rodriguez can cook up meals at the hotel restaurant or pack them up for day trips outside of town. Breakfast is included and rooms come equipped with hot water showers, cable TVs and ceiling fans. Private parking and WiFi are also available. It is best to make reservations, especially if coming with a large group. Km 146.5 on the Pan-American highway. Tel: 505-2-714-1075 / 8-632-5628, U.S. Tel: 1-786-664-5628, E-mail: mariselaycuallitan@hotmail.com.
Updated: Apr 14, 2009.

Hotel Don Vito
(ROOMS: $30 – 40) Brand spanking new at the time of writing, Don Vito is squeaky clean, with a strong scent of air freshener. The hotel features nice, modern décor, a sitting area with TV and a common eating

area. Despite these amenities, the staff is less than accomodating. Nine blocks south of the central park, and one north of Hospedaje Chepito. Tel: 505-2-713-4318 / 714-1420. Updated: Apr 14, 2009.

Hotel Los Arcos !

(ROOMS: $40 – 85) If you didn't notice the stunning garden, spotless rooms, amazing customer service, and high-end on-site restaurant, certainly the towels folded into swans would give away the fact that Los Arcos is Estelí's premier hotel. Do your sun salutations on the pleasant terrace or have your coffee on the patio surrounded by bright, colorful murals. Amenities include free Internet, cable TV, air conditioning, private parking and a conference room. A breakfast buffet is included. One block north of the cathedral. Tel: 505-2-713-3830, E-mail: Hotelosarcos@hotmail.com, URL: www.familiasunidas.org/hotelosarcos.htm. Updated: Apr 14, 2009.

Restaurants

Estelí is one of the few cities in the north that can be said to have a restaurant scene. Although the food is not exactly authentic, many restaurants make solid attempts at international cuisine, including Italian, Chinese and even hints of Indian. Vegetarians also have plenty of options, as soy burgers, fresh yogurt and other healthy eats can easily be found. Of course, Estelí is also home to its fair share of cheap, standard Nicaraguan restaurants.

You will also find that Estelí has a rather lively nightlife scene. Plastered with Sandinista paraphernalia, **Rincon Legal** is a happening hotspot with an fun schedule of live music. **Ixcotelli** is the place to go for a drink and a bite, while **Los Semáforos**, frequented by patrons of all ages, is a great night out. **Shami** panders to the young and beautiful crowd.

Yusvar

British-owned Yusvar is a new addition to Estelí's gringo scene. The tiny nook has a concise (English) menu of healthy smoothies, from lighter water-based mixtures to hearty yogurt drinks. Backpackers might appreciate the Anti-Parasite smoothie, which blends apple, carrot, ginger and orange juice ($1.50). For the more adventurous, papaya seeds and garlic can be added to any drink free of charge. Still hungry? Waffles with a variety of toppings are also available. Across the street and half a block west from the park. Updated: Aug 24, 2009.

La Casita

Owned by a Scottish expat, La Casita is an urban oasis located about one kilometer (.62 mi)south of the city along the Pan-American highway. The café, located amidst lush grounds, a small brook and a farm, is worth the cab fare for those who have the time and a desire to laze about in natural surroundings while drinking coffee. The menu consists of light snacks like yogurt, granola, and cheese and bread plates. Although it's easy to get a cab ride there, finding one to return to the city is sometimes a little tricky. Front desk open Tuesday – Saturday, 9 a.m. – 7 p.m.; Monday 2–7 p.m.; Sunday, 9 a.m. – 7 p.m. On Finca Las Nubes, one kilometer (.62 mi) south of Estelí along the Pan-American Highway. Tel: 505-2-713-4917, E-mail: Casita@ibw.com.ni. Updated: Apr 13, 2009.

Buffet Familiar Shalom

(ENTREES: $1 and up) With bright décor, and a clean, airy atmosphere, Buffet Familiar Shalom offers particularly well spiced typical fare at budget prices. A breakfast of gallo pinto, eggs and tortilla goes for roughly $1, while lunch and dinner options like roasted chicken, jalapeño steak and a variety of salads, average $3. One block west of the central park. Tel: 505-2-713-7243. Updated: Apr 13, 2009.

Licuados Ananda !

Known to locals as the Yoga Center, this restaurant is an offshoot of the adjacent Casa de Cultura. Here you can buy paintings by local artists or sign up for yoga, tae kwon do or dance classes. A relief for vegetarians, Licuados Ananda serves up mean soy tacos and burgers, as well as fruit juices, homemade yogurt and sandwiches. Pleasant, shaded seating is centered around an oddly empty pool. Pancakes and sandwiches average $1 while fresh juices and other drinks go for a little less. One block south of the central park. Updated: Apr 13, 2009.

Café Reposteria Mamilou

Mamilou's owner, a French-speaking Swiss national, has recently opened this adorable, European-style café. Although the entrance is off the main street, the removed setting garners a secluded, oasis-like air. The menu features different types of coffee and pastries, and the sitting area

---

VIVA recommends travel insurance. Get it at vivatravelguides.com/insurance/

offers cards and board games. And, as icing on the cake, Mamilou also boasts the nicest bathroom you're likely to come across in northern Nicaragua. Avenida 1 SO, several blocks south of Pali. Tel: 505-2-713-2878. Updated: Apr 13, 2009.

Mocha Nana

(SNACKS: $1.50 and up) Mocha Nana is a favorite among gringos, who come for the capuccinos ($1), Irish coffees ($2.75), or one of the many veggie options on the light menu. Home-made bagels with cream cheese go for $1.50 and vegetarian soup of the day goes for $3. Backpackers will also want to take advantage of the small, used English bookshop in the front. Open Monday – Friday, 9 a.m. – 7 p.m.; Saturday 10 a.m. – 7 p.m. Tel: 505-2-713-3164. E-mail: mochanana@hotmail.com. Updated: Apr 13, 2009.

Don Pollo #2

(CHICKEN PORTION: $2.25 – 10) Although it has a rather limited menu, Don Pollo #2 will definitely fill your belly and satisfy your craving for a big plateful of chicken and some starchy sides. The restaurant offers a range of portions; customers can choose to get a quarter chicken for $2.25, or a larger, shared meal with fries, rice and salad for around $10. Word on the street is that Don Pollo #2, located in the heart of town, is even better than Don Pollo #1. One block north of the cathedral. Updated: Apr 13, 2009.

Comedor Pinareno

(ENTREES: $4.175, SANDWICHES: $2.75) The Cuban-born owner of this pleasant eatery offers Nicaraguans a taste of his homeland. The menu features classic Cuban sandwiches, meaty entrees like the *Ropa Vieja* and a number of desserts—including three types of flan ($1). Top off your visit to the nearby museums and artisan shops with a hearty meal at Comedor Pinareno. Open 10 a.m. – 10 p.m., Tuesday – Sunday. One and a half block south of the central park. Tel: 505-2- 713-4369. Updated: Apr 13, 2009.

Café Luz !

(SNACKS: $2.75, ENTREES: $5 and up) Offering up dishes with an international flair such as Thai chicken, hummus, lentil dahl and lasagna, Café Luz is the only restaurant in town that caters specifically to international travelers. The best feature of this café is the owner Janie, a British transplant who's taken a keen interest in developing tourism in the area, particularly at the Miraflor Reserve. She's a great resource for all information on Estelí and is even setting up an information office at her hostel across the street. The café is also the place to arrange mural, cigar and cycling tours. Overall, Café Luz is a great place to grab your morning coffee or evening cocktail and meet other travelers. WiFi is provided and crafts are available for sale. Open 7 a.m. – 10 p.m. One block north of the cathedral. URL: www.cafeluzyluna.com. Updated: Apr 13, 2009.

Casa Vecchia

(ENTREES: $3.50 – 7.50) With mellow lighting, crisp tablecloths and real stemware, Casa Vecchia provides an elegant atmosphere for romantic dinners or special celebrations. The restaurant menu offers all the usual suspects, including a variety of pastas, chicken parmesian, lasagna and pizza. Two blocks south and one block west of the central park. Tel: 505-2-713-2569. Updated: Apr 13, 2009.

Gran Via

(ENTREES: $4.50 – 7.50) The only restaurant in town where you can drink Mexican beer and listen to mariachi music while chowing down on chop suey is Gran Via, a surprising evening hotspot. Vegetarian fried rice, lo mein and chop suey are all served, as are kung pow chicken, beef with broccoli and other entrees. While Gran Via is about as close as you'll get to Chinese food in Nicaragua, substituted ingredients limit the menu's authenticity. Take out is available. Open Monday – Saturday, 11 a.m. – 10 p.m. Tel: 505-2-713-5465. Updated: May 13, 2009.

Pullaso's Ole

(STEAKS: $6) Pullaso's Ole is Estelí's top steakhouse, and has pleasant outdoor seating as well as a colorfully decorated interior dining area. Patrons can choose from a plethora of meaty platters, with steak being the specialty. Those watching their wallet or waistline can opt for the half portions. An ample wine collection is also on offer. Open Monday – Sunday, 11 a.m. – 11 p.m. Three blocks east of the Casa de Cultura. Tel: 505-2-713-4583, E-mail: Pullasos_ole@hotmail.com. Updated: Apr 14, 2009.

Vuela Vuela

(ENTREES: $6 - 11.50) Attached to Hotel Los Arcos, this swanky restaurant offers up mainly Spanish, but also typical Nicaraguan cuisine. Entrees include steak, chicken and seafood dishes, along with several types of paella. There is also a wine list and an assortment of cocktails are available for around $2.50. Like Los Arcos, Vuela Vuela is atmospheric and airy, with views of the hotel garden. One block north of the central park. Updated: Apr 13, 2009.

RESERVA NATURAL MIRAFLOR

Situated 35 kilometers (22 mi) northeast of Estelí, this campesino-owned nature reserve became protected in 1990, and is a haven for exotic flora and fauna, including hundreds of species of birds and orchids. The best time to go is in June, as this is when the birds migrate south and the orchids bloom. A lucky visitor might also spot howler monkeys, coyotes, armadillos and other wildlife.

As all the land is privately owned, Miraflor is not easy to get to on your own. Fortunately, **UCA Miraflor**, a co-op involved in micro credit initiatives, renewable and alternative technologies and guide training, specializes in tours of the reserve. Arrangements can be made at their office in Estelí. Guides cost $15 per day. Renting a horse costs $7 per person per day, but you also have to pay $19 for the guide and his horse. This fee is paid in advance at the Estelí office where you'll receive a voucher to give to your guide.

Although it is possible to do Miraflor as a day trip, spending the night at a homestay will add a cultural dimension to your experience. These can also be arranged through UCA Miraflor. Accommodations are pretty rustic (no electricity or running water), and some houses have solar panels, but they aren't so reliable, especially in the cloud forest. It's probably a good idea to bring a flashlight. Bucket baths are the norm. Food is generally vegetarian as meat is reserved for holidays, but make sure your host family knows if you have dietary restrictions. Drinking water is provided. If you offer to help with the cooking and washing you might catch a glimpse of family life behind the scenes. Should you decide to go for several days, Café Luna can store your bags. Homestays cost $15 per person per night, 20 percent of which goes back to UCA.

Visitors can choose to stay among the five communities that spread out over the three microclimates that exist within the park, and UCA Miraflor can help you choose the one that's right for you. The dry zone community of **Coyolito** grows beans, tomatoes and other vegetables. Two families offer homestays there, one of which provides visitors with their own cabin. There

Photo by Néstor Baltodano

VIVA recommends travel insurance. Get it at vivatravelguides.com/insurance/

is a 16-meter (53 ft) waterfall nearby called Tres Cascadas. Buses go from Coyolito to La Pita twice a day.

La Pita and **Sontule** are both in the semi-humid zone just below the cloud forest, which in the 1960s and 1970s underwent major deforestation due to crop growing and cattle raising. Coffee is the primary crop in this area and there are many small producers that own between one and twenty acres of land. Sontule has two coffee co-ops and one women's co-op, and five to six families offer homestays there. The walk from La Pita to Sontule takes one and a half hours.

La Perla is the smallest community, with only one family offering a homestay. The poorest and most populated community is **Puertas Azules**, which does not currently offer homestays.

If the idea of a homestay seems a little too up close and personal for your taste, you can stay at **Finca Neblina Del Bosque**, owned by a German-Nicaraguan couple. The farm offers bamboo cabins with private baths at a rate of $25 per night. Vegetarian food made with local products and all non-alcoholic beverages are included. Neblina also offers guides for $12, a tour with a biologist specializing in birds and orchids for $20 and tours on horseback for $10. To get to the farm, ask the driver to let you off the bus at La Rampla (about an hour and a half ride) and then walk uphill for about eight minutes. Tel: 505-8-666-5245, E-mail: Isabel.zeug@web.de.

Other more upscale options include **Finca Lindas Ojos** (Tel: 505-2-713-4041) and **Posada La Sonada** (Tel: 505-2-713-6333).

When visiting the reserve, be aware that the weather is rather unpredictable and it can get quite cold, windy and rainy, so dress in layers. Cover up your feet and wear long pants to avoid ticks and black flies. Also bring insect repellent and snacks, as homestays only provide meals. Some homestays also provide mosquito nets. Beware of snakes and scorpions.

Getting To and Away From Reserva Natural Miraflor

Buses to Miraflor leave the Terminal Norte in Estelí on Monday, Tuesday, Friday and Saturday only a few times a day. Schedules are subject to change, so it's best to check with UCA before heading out. Due to the bumpy roads, the trip can last two to three hours. Updated: Jun 09, 2009.

RESERVA NATURAL MESETA TISEY-ESTANZUELA

(ENTRY: $1) Less frequented than Reserva Miraflor is Reserva Natural Meseta Tisey-Estanzuela, which is also located outside of Estelí. Trails within the expansive forest offer views of Honduras and El Salvador, as well as Leon and Chinandega's volcanoes. On a clear day, the lookout point, Mirador Segoviano, affords a panoramic view of the Valley of Estelí, the volcanoes of Los Maribios, Lake Nicaragua and all the land up until the Gulf of Fonseca.

In addition to hiking, travelers can also visit **La Ecoposada el Tisey**, a farm that has been owned and run by the Cerrato family for four generations. The farm covers 70 acres, 30 of which are maintained as a rainforest reserve. Cabins with private bathrooms can be rented for $11 per night and dorms with outhouse access for $3.50. Typical Nica food is served and there are crafts for sale. Although Ecoposada advertises guides and tours of coffee and produce farms, Tisey doesn't get a whole lot of visitors, so they aren't always prepared. For information about visting Ecoposada El Tisey, contact Liliam Cerrato Jiron (Tel: 505-2-713-6213 / 835-7044, E-mail: tisey69@latinmail.com).

Near to Ecoposada is **La Garnacha**, a community known for its goat cheese, made from an old Swiss recipe. At the entrance to the community there is a small souvenir shop and tourism office from which guides can be arranged. On the weekends, when there isn't farm work to be done, you might also be able to rent horses. Across the street is a restaurant offering cheap local fare. San Nicolas-bound buses leave at 6:30 a.m. (return at 8 a.m.) and at 1:30 p.m. (return at 3 p.m.). A 40-minute ride takes you to **Rancho San Luis**, a 5 kilometer (3 mi) walk from La Garnacha.

Perhaps one of the wackiest features of Tisey is Alberto Gutierrez, an eccentric recluse who lives in Cerro Jalacate. A self-taught sculptor, he carves animal-themed reliefs into the cliff-face overlooking his house. He's very talkative for a hermit and can tell you about his work and the area.

The main reason people usually visit Tisey, however, is to languish in **Salta Estanzuela**, a 36-meter (118 ft) waterfall that feeds into a small, refreshing (read: icy) swimming hole. Travelers can sunbathe on the pebbly shore, and if you're lucky, you may get the whole place to yourself. As it's located on the outskirts of the reserve, this is the most accessible attraction in Tisey and makes for an easy morning jaunt from Estelí.

Although it is not far from Estelí, Tisey is considerably colder, so bring extra layers. Also bring food and water, as they are not widely available and the unpredictability of transport means you can spend longer at the reserve than planned—particularly if you're dependent on hitching a ride, which is sometimes the best way to get around.

Getting To and Away From Tisey

Take the Estanzuela-bound bus from Estelí's Cotran Sur or take a cab to the hospital and walk five kilometers (3 mi) southwest to the reserve. As transport to and around Tisey is dicey, it might be a good idea to contact FIDER, an agricultural development agency, before setting out. FIDER sells maps and can help arrange tours. FIDER's Estelí office is located a half block west of the Petronic station. Tel: 505-2-713-3918, E-mail: fiderest@ibw.com.ni. Updated: Jun 09, 2009.

SAN JUAN DE LIMAY

281m 17,434

Travelers usually come to dry, isolated San Juan de Limay for just one reason: soapstone sculptures. Intricately carved and impeccably smooth, these glowing figures range from tiny nativity scenes to oversized iguanas and long-necked swans. Carving began in the early 1970s, when Father Eduardo Mejia accidentally discovered the marmolina with a group of local youth. He began to mine the soapstone from nearby Cerro Tipiscayan, and trained sculptors as a way to help them survive the poverty of this ravaged area.

In the late 1970s, Minister of Culture Ernesto Cardenal helped set up an artists' co-op in San Juan, which improved the sculptors' skills and spread their reputation across the country. The co-op has more or less collapsed since then, with many soapstone artisans moving to more developed areas to sell their work. Nonetheless, some soapstone artists still remain in San Juan de Limay, and visitors can peek into their workshops when wandering around town. Pieces here will be less expensive than in souvenir shops around the country.

The 40 kilometer (25 mi) ride from Estelí to San Juan de Limay takes two to three hours, and the road is quite bumpy. The ride costs $0.50, and leaves from Estelí's Cotran Norte several times daily. Those unwilling to brave the road twice in one day can stay at the very basic **Pension Guerrero**, located one block north of the church. El Guerrero also offers typical Nicaraguan meals. Updated: Apr 14, 2009.

PUEBLO NUEVO

606 m 4,000

The 350-year-old town of Pueblo Nuevo (not so *nuevo* anymore) is located northwest of Estelí and has a population of 24,000, only about 4,000 of whom live in the urban zone. The town itself is quite small, and the only official attraction is a tiny museum inside the Casa de Cultura featuring pottery and other miscellanea, including a human skeleton thst is roughly one thousand years old.

The real reason to come to Pueblo Nuevo is to visit its Paleolithic sites, which provide what is considered to be the oldest evidence of human existence in Central America. These are located at **El Bosque**, about 11 kilometers (7 mi) outside town. The first discoveries were made by Ruben Olivas in 1973. Finds include the preserved remains of mastodons, a ground sloth and miniature horses, among other extinct fauna, the oldest of which date to 32,000 years ago. Unfortunately, due to a lack of funds, excavations have not been terribly extensive. It is still possible to visit the sites; however, and arrangements can be made either through the mayor's office or Doña Selina, whose home is located two blocks from the central park. Doña Selina also offers the only sleeping accommodations in town, charging $3 per night.

Regular buses run from Estelí to Pueblo Nuevo. The ride costs $1.75 and takes about two hours. If you have your own vehicle you can take the highway from San Juan de

Limay. The entrance will be on the right-hand side. Updated: Apr 14, 2009.

CONDEGA

| 🅰 550m | 👤 29,000 |

Also known as the *Tierra de Alfareros* (The Land of the Potters), the city of Condega is located 185 kilometers (115 mi) north of Managua on the Pan-American highway. Declared a municipality in 1962, Condega has long been inhabited by indigenous peoples and archaeological evidence shows that these people were industrious potters. Today, ceramics continue to be an important industry.

Located 4 kilometers (2.5 mi) from Condega is **Ducuali Grande**, a community home to a women's pottery co-op (Tel: 505-2-715-2237). Travelers can visit the co-op and purchase reasonably priced pieces. For a taste of pre-Columbian pottery, visit the **Museo Arqueológico Julio Cesar Salgado** (Open Monday – Friday, 8 a.m. – 4 p.m.; Saturday, 8 a.m. – 12 p.m.; closed Sundays), which is located on the south side of the park.

Besides pottery, other products manufactured in the region include leather goods, wooden crafts and cigars. There are two cigar factories in town worth a visit, both located three blocks north of the park. The cultivation of grains, tobacco, coffee and produce, as well as cattle-raising are all central to Condega's economy. On May 15th there is a celebration honoring the town's patron saint, San Isidro Labrador. Head to the church, where a special blessing is bestowed on the town's animals and grains.

During the Contra War, Condega was a Sandinista stronghold and was the site of much violence. A testament to Condega's involvement can be found in **Airplane Park**, where one of Somoza's spy planes was shot down by revolutionaries on April 7, 1979. The aircraft has since been restored as an attraction at the top of a 100-meter (328 ft) hill. It can be reached by following the path behind the cemetery.

Getting To and Away From Condega

If traveling to Condega from Managua, take an express bus headed for Somoto or Ocotal/Jalapa from the Mayoreo terminal. The trip takes about three hours and costs $3.50. The buses leaves Mayoreo almost hourly from 5:10 a.m. to 5:15 p.m. All southbound buses from Somoto or Ocotal, and headed for Esteli or Managua, also pass through Condega. Express buses stop on the Pan-American highway in front of the cemetery. Ordinary buses (*ruteados*) pass in front of the park. The first bus to Managua passes Condega at approximately 4:30 a.m. and the last around 4 p.m. Updated: Apr 28, 2009.

Lodging

Travelers choosing to spend the night in Condega have several lodging options. **Hospedaje Framer**, on the south side of the park, offers rooms with shared bathrooms for $3.75 per person (Tel: 505-2-715-2222). For more amenities, head to **La Granja Hospedaje**, located half a block east of the southeast corner of the park (Tel: 505-2-715-2357). It features private bathrooms, TVs and fans. A double goes for $10. The hotel provides breakfast for an additional fee. Cabins can be rented at **Campestre La Granja**, located 300 meters (984 ft) east of the Marista School, right outside of Condega (Tel: 505-2-715-2521). One cabin for two to four people with a bath goes for $25. Double and single rooms are also available. There is an on-site typical restaurant as well as a pool (entrance for which costs $1.50).

Restaurants

All of Condega's restaurants serve typical Nicaraguan fare. Try some local favorites at **Pollo Express**, **El Tipico Norte**, or **Restaurante Brago**. **Las Vegas** and **El Gualca**, which also serve typical meals, turn into dancing hotspots on the weekends. Gualco also sells locally produced cheese, yogurt, wine, honey and coffee.

Tours

Outside of Condega there are several opportunities for rural tourism. Twenty-two kilometers (13 mi) northeast is Venecia, where travelers can visit local coffee farms. There is swimming and fishing at Laguna de Venecia, where boats and fishing equipment are available for rent. Two kilometers away is the **Estancia El Naranjo** (Tel: 505-2-715-2408 / 2020) which offers an on-site restaurant and bar, lodging, hiking, horseback riding and more. Rooms with a shared bath go for $5 per person; cabins for 2 – 3 people with private, hot water bathrooms cost $20; tents are also available for camping.

Tours to the area can also be arranged through Estelí-based tour operator, **Casa Estelí**. (E-mail: casaEstelí@asdenic.org, URL: www.casaEstelí.org.ni).

Twenty-one kilometers (13 mi) northeast of Condega is **Laureano Flores**, a co-op that features a hostel and on-site restaurant ($8 per night, breakfast included). Guides can be arranged at the hostel for expeditions on trails traversable on foot, horse or bicycle.

OCOTAL

500m 29,500

Most visitors swing by Ocotal on their way to the Honduran border at Las Manos, not realizing that it is a city rich with history. On July 1, 1927, Augusto Cesar Sandino gathered forces at the nearby San Albino gold mine and prepared to invade the U.S. marine garrison located where the mayor's office currently sits. Sandino warned U.S. commander Captain Gilbert D. Hatfield in his planned attack, signing his telegraph message, "I remain your most obedient servant, who ardently desires to put you in a handsome tomb with beautiful bouquets of flowers." At 1 a.m. on the 16th, the revolutionaries advanced on the town, beginning the battle by opening fire from the nearby church bell tower. With a Sandinista victory seeming imminent, U.S. planes loaded with bombs flew in from Managua, carrying out the world's first ever air raid. Sandino was defeated. The only evidence of this historic battle; however, is a plaque that can be found in the courtyard of the mayor's office.

Ocotal is named after a type of pine, as logging used to be the city's major industry. Unfortunately, years of logging eventually led to severe deforestation and Ocotal now must rely on the nearby towns of Dipilto or Jalapa for its wood supply. To get a taste of what Ocotal looked like before North American logging companies deforested the area, visit Dipilto.

While the town is pleasant enough to kick around in for a day, there is little to occupy you for too long. The impeccably groomed central park with a shady gazebo is a nice place to relax with a book. There are also a couple of churches. Should one decide to hunker down for the night in Ocotal, there are plenty of reasonably priced hotels, and even one fancy one with a pool. The food scene may not be exotic, but it is nonetheless satisfying. Updated: Apr 15, 2009.

When to Go

On August 15th the town holds a festival celebrating *La Senora de la Anuncion*, which features religious services and bullfights. On September 14th and 15th Ocotal hosts a carnival to commemorate the day of William Walker's failed conquest. Don't worry if you miss these festivals though, because Ocotal celebrates *Segovia* on night of the last Saturday of every month. Every celebration is different, but there's always a chance of catching dance performances, parades, street food and craft fairs.

The dry season in Ocotal lasts from mid-November to mid-May. The coolest months are December and January, with highs in the 80s°F (27 – 31°C) and lows in the 60s°F (16 – 20°C). April and May are the hottest months, with highs in the 90s°F (33 – 37°C). Updated: Apr 15, 2009.

Getting To and Away From Ocotal

Hop on a Managua bound bus for an express ride to Estelí, which costs $1.75. A

Ocotal 233

Activities ●
1 Central Park B1
2 Iglesia de Nuestra Señora de la Asunción B1

Eating
3 Bar Oasis B1
4 Buffet Comedor Llamarada del Bosque B1
5 La Yunta B1

Nightlife
6 Disco Sky Dancing B1

Services ★
7 Banco ProCredit A1
8 Cyber Copy Comp B1
9 Hospital A1
10 Intur (Tourism Information) B2
11 Llamadas Heladas A1
12 Police A1
13 Post Office B1
14 Profamilia Center B2
15 Shell Station A1

Sleeping
16 Hotel El Viajero A1
17 Hotel Frontera A1
18 Hospedaje Casalejos B1

Transportation
19 Bus Terminal A2

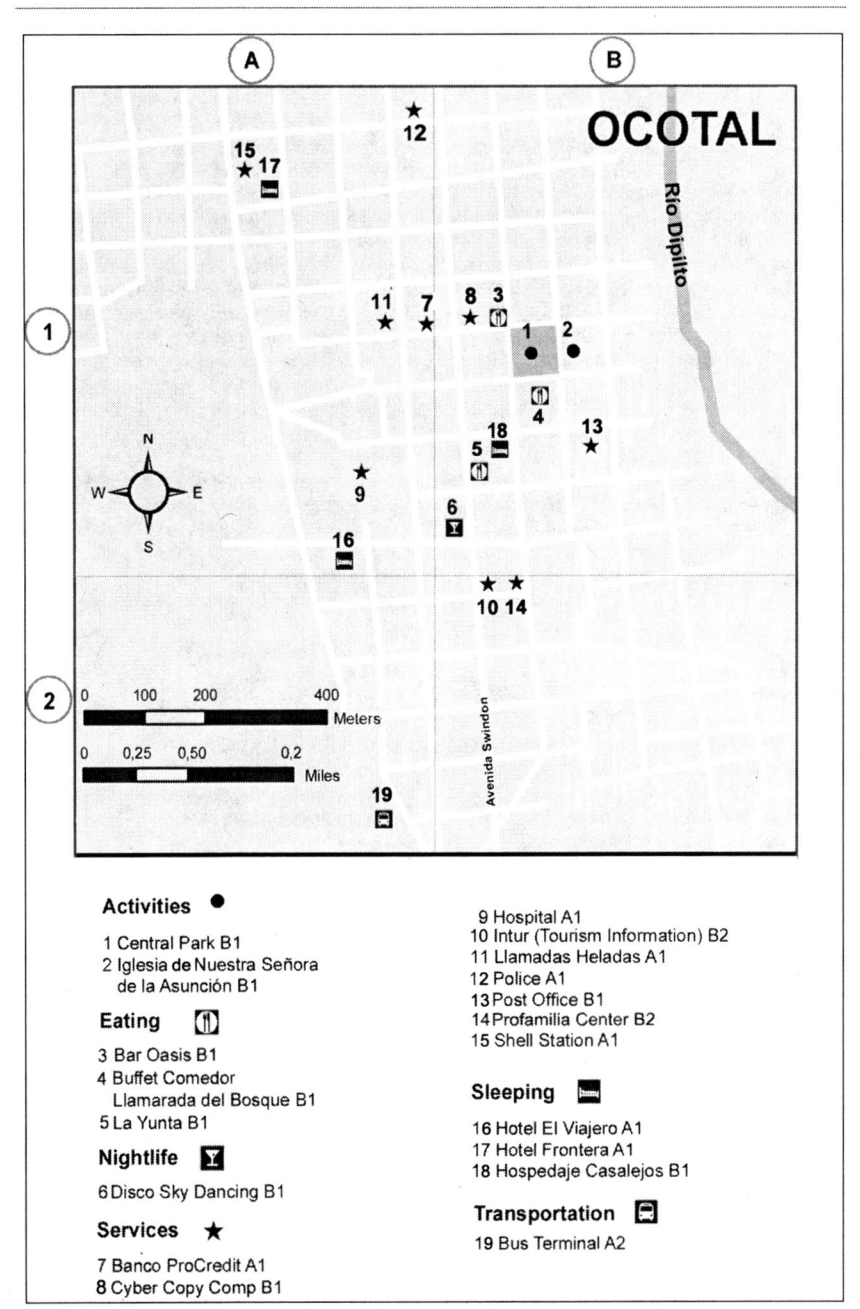

ride to Managua's Mayoreo terminal costs roughly $4, and buses run regularly from 4 a.m. to 3:30 p.m. Take a taxi to get to the border crossing at Las Manos. Updated: Apr 15, 2009.

Border Crossing at Las Manos

Located 24 kilometers (15 mi) north of Ocotal, the Las Manos border crossing to

Honduras is open 24 hours. From Ocotal take a cab or a bus, which runs from 5 a.m. to 4 p.m. At the border, there is a $3 fee to exit Nicaragua and a $7 fee to enter it, and U.S. passports are not stamped (because of the C4 agreement between four Central American countries). There is not much to be found at the border—a pulperia or two, and a money exchange office on the Honduran side. Buses to El Paraiso—from which transport to Tegucigalpa can be arranged—run every half hour. Should you desire an easier ride to Tegucigalpa, **TransNica** runs direct buses from Estelí. Updated: May 02, 2009.

Safety

It is safe to walk around in Ocotal's center at night, though visitors should be cautious entering the badly lit neighborhoods on the edges of town. The water in Ocotal is also of particularly bad quality (even for Nicaragua), so stick to bottled. Updated: Apr 15, 2009.

Services

TOURISM

The **Intur** office is located one block west and four blocks south of the park. It doesn't have a whole lot of literature, but some of the people working there are quite helpful.

KEEPING IN TOUCH

Cyber Copy-Comp is located a block west of the park and charges $0.50 for an hour of Internet. Half a block west of that is a **Llamadas Heladas** phone cabin franchise.

MEDICAL

There is a **Profamilia** clinic four blocks south of the central park, on the left side. Dr. Alberto Valle (Tel: 505-8-632-1698) works at the free clinic located in front of Banpro (2.5 blocks north of the ministry of education, on the left side). Updated: Apr 15, 2009.

Things to See and Do

Architecture buffs will enjoy Ocotal's impressive colonial structures, most of which can be seen in the town's center—namely the mayor's office, the church, La Casa de Cultura and the central park. The park itself, safe and spotless, is a true point of pride for the mayor, who keeps it locked at night to ward off potential vandals. Ocotal does not have much in the way of traditional tourist attractions, but travelers will likely only spend a night here on their way to the Honduran border at Las Manos.

Iglesia de Nuestra de la Asunción

As is the case elsewhere in Latin America, Ocotal's main church, Iglesia de Nuestra de la Asunción (or El Templo Parroquial de Ocotal) serves as the town's focal point and main hub. Blending baroque and neoclassical architecture, this church was founded two centuries ago. However, the addition of the second bell tower was completed only recently. Its newness is apparent from the glowing white paint, which stands in stark contrast with the aged and burnt appearance of the rest of the building. The cathedral has its own well tended garden and stands across the street from Ocotal's impressively manicured park. Updated: Apr 24, 2009.

Tours

Intur recommends the following tour guides for trips in and around Ocotal.

Cristhian Josue Alvarenga Lopez —
Tel: 505-8-491-0399,
E-mail: fesnuevasegovia83@hotmail.com.

Yader Ernesto Ponce Fiallos —
Tel: 505-8-694-4420.

Lenar Jimenez Zavala —
Tel: 505-8-482-1846.

Maria de los Angeles Acevedo —
Tel: 505-8-368-5259.

Nidia Damaris Molina —
Tel: 505-8-410-1547.

Scarleth Castellon — Tel: 505-8-917-1129.

Jose Fermin Torrez — Tel: 505-8-943-6166.

Dunia Moncada — Tel: 505-8-914-2351.
Updated: Apr 24, 2009.

Lodging

Accommodations in Ocotal tend to be simple, clean and budget friendly. Those in search of high class comfort will prefer the upscale Hotel Frontera. Updated: Jun 20, 2009.

Hospedaje Casalejas

(ROOMS: $4) This family-run hospedaje offers eight basic, clean rooms, all of which have shared bathrooms. The water is cold, but the price is right. Singing can often be heard from the Baptist church across the street, but those who want their beauty sleep need not worry—they always stop by 9 p.m.

VIVA recommends travel insurance. Get it at vivatravelguides.com/insurance/

One block south of the central park. Tel: 505-2-732 0554. Updated: Apr 15, 2009.

Hotel El Viajero

(ROOMS: $10) Hotel El Viajero offers big, clean rooms at an affordable price. At the time of writing, the hotel was undergoing some construction so be ready to be woken up by 7 a.m. Animal lovers will appreciate that the family who owns Viajero lives on the premises and has a number of pets, including a parrot, a macaw and a bear-like dog. There is a 10 p.m. curfew. Three blocks south and three west of the central park. Half a block off the highway. Updated: Apr 15, 2009.

Hotel Frontera

(ROOMS: $47 – 63) The premier hotel in Ocotal, Hotel Frontera provides lots of amenities, but not a lot of character. Rooms are big and clean, but have something of an institutional look. Nonetheless, guests will enjoy cable TVs, WiFi, private parking, 24-hour reception and use of the hotel pool. Those who haven't booked a room can still take a swim for a small fee: $4.25 for adults, $2.75 for children. Towels and use of shower are included.

The hotel restaurant and poolside bar are also available to non-guests, and at night the atmosphere can be described as either raucously fun or gratingly loud. The restaurant menu includes big, meaty combos, which cost about $8, and hamburgers and sandwiches for $2. Recommended are the chicken soup (which comes in enormous portions) and the garlic shrimp. Breakfast, which is not included, is either Nicaraguan (gallo pinto and eggs) or American (waffles and omelets). Hot water occasionally runs out by nightfall, so take your shower early. Three blocks north and five west of the central park. Right off the highway. Tel: 505-2-732-2669 / 2668, E-mail: hotelfronterasa@yahoo.com / Hofrosa@turbonett.com. Updated: Apr 15, 2009.

Restaurants

As in other small cities and towns in Nicaragua, Ocotal's food scene is limited to typical Nicaragua fare. Nonetheless, there are some good, inexpensive eats here—and even some relief for vegetarians. The only place in town to hear live music while enjoying a nice meal is La Yunta.

Bar Oasis

(ENTREES: $2 – 2.50) Open for breakfast, lunch and dinner, Bar Oasis serves up typical Nicaraguan fare at low prices. Gallo pinto, eggs and plantains will cost around $2. Choose chicken, beef or fish as your protein for $0.50 more. Smaller portions are available for lower prices. Across the street from the central park. Tel: 505-2-732-0987. Updated: Apr 15, 2009.

Buffet Comedor Llamarada Del Bosque

(ENTREES: $2 – 4) Those hankering for fresh fruits and veggies should make a beeline for Llamarada Del Bosque. This buffet-style restaurant has a variety salads to choose from, in addition to the usual gallo pinto, eggs, chicken and beef. There is both indoor and garden seating available. The hostel of the same name (down the block) was under construction at the time of writing. Contact them to see if it's back in business. Tel: 505-2-732-2643 / 2469, 505-8-856-0564, E-mail: Llamaradadelbosque@yahoo.com. Updated: Apr 15, 2009.

La Yunta

(ENTREES: $7.50) For good eats and live music, head to La Yunta. Every Thursday, live bands perform from 7 p.m. to 1 a.m. A wooden stage sits in the middle of an open courtyard, giving this restaurant a breezy feel. The music is eclectic and while some patrons may feel the urge to get up and dance by their tables, most are happy to sit and sip their beers. A full chicken meal with rice, fries and salad goes for $7.50. Fish, shrimp and beef are also on offer. One block west and three south of the park. Tel: 505-2-732-2180. Updated: Apr 15, 2009.

Sky Dancing

(COVER: $2) Open only on Saturdays, this is the place (literally, the only one) to get your dance on in Ocotal. The young clientele grooves to salsa, reggae, hip-hop and 1980s rock ballads. Try to get into the VIP room —it has nicer bathrooms. Occasionally Sky Dancing also has karaoke and live music. Three blocks south and one west of the park. Updated: Apr 15, 2009.

AROUND OCOTAL

COMUNIDAD INDIGENA DE MOZONTE

Five kilometers (3 mi) north of Ocotal, this small village is best known for its production of ceramics, the sort of which can be seen hanging in homes and restaurants all over Nicaragua. **Colectivo de Artesanías de Mozonte** is the largest workshop in Mozonte, and is located off the side of the highway. Other, smaller workshops can also be found all over town. Perhaps more interesting than the pottery itself is the process by which it is made. Most of the artisans dig their own clay and use manual wheels instead of electric, and many workshops are completely family run, with each member of the family manning a different stage of the production process. Those looking for unique pieces of art will likely be disappointed; pottery designs tend to be standardized and homogeneous. And although these workshops are small family businesses, the ceramics they create generally look mass-produced. Updated: Apr 27, 2009.

Getting To and Away From Mozonte

Take a Jalapa-bound bus from Ocotal and ask to be dropped off in Mozonte (roughly a ten-minute ride). You can even ask to be let off directly at the Colectivo de Artesanias de Mozonte. Alternatively, take an *interlocal* cab from the Shell Station in Ocotal (located right next to Hotel Frontera). This ride should cost roughly $0.50 per person. Inner-city taxis may also be willing to drive to Mozonte, but will likely charge more. Try to arrange for a cab to pick you up too, as transport back to Ocotal is difficult to come by. Hitchhiking back to Ocotal can also be done, though it may require long stretches of waiting and walking along the highway. Updated: Apr 27, 2009.

CIUDAD ANTIGUA

Ciudad Antigua's prosperity in colonial times was also its downfall. Frequent looting by Miskito Indians, as well as the pirates Henry Morgan, Eduardo David and Lolonnois Tampaier, forced many of Antigua's residents to flee and settle in Ocotal. This was not their first migration; however, as much of Antigua's original population came from the town now referred to as Ciudad Vieja, which happens to be the first city ever founded in the Segovias. Located at the confluence of the Jicaros and Coco rivers, Ciudad Vieja can still be visited today.

Parts of Ciudad Antigua's main church, notably the nave, can be dated to the 17th century. Next door is the **Museo de Ciudad Antigua**, home to religious artifacts as well as other ceremonial paraphernalia.

Buses to Ciudad Antigua depart from Ocotal at 7 a.m and 12 p.m. Updated: Apr 24, 2009.

MACUELIZO TERMALES

Macuelizo is best known for its hot springs along the snaking Macuelizo River; an entire kilometer of river is naturally heated. These untouched hot springs, part of private farmland, are completely undeveloped for tourism and in fact are not suitable for bathing. Nonetheless, with the help of a local guide, determined tourists can still enjoy the natural surroundings and feel the steam rising off the water. Situated 1.5 hours from Ocotal, the springs cannot be reached by bus. Updated: Apr 24, 2009.

SAN FERNANDO

Twenty-two kilometers (14 mi) from Ocotal on the road to Jalapa is San Fernando, home to over 200 coffee farms, where over two million pounds of coffee are produced each year. As of yet, no organized agrotourism exists here, but the inquisitive visitor might be able to get a glimpse into the coffee production process.

Oddly, many of San Fernando's 7,000 inhabitants have lighter skin and bright blue eyes, and there is much debate with respect to the origins of such traits. Some believe their origins can be attributed to the North American troops who occupied the area during Sandino's uprising. Older inhabitants; however, claim these features were present from the time of the Spanish conquest. Updated: Apr 24, 2009.

Pico Mogoton

Twenty kilometers (12 mi) from San Fernando and directly bordering Honduras is Pico Mogoton. At 2,107 meters (6,913 ft) above sea level, it is the highest peak in Nicaragua and is rarely traversed by tourists. This is likely due to the fact that the volcano is dotted with active landmines, the vestiges of the conflict in the 1980s. On weekdays, the military works on detonating these remaining landmines, so be ready to hear some explosions. As such, peak baggers intent on conquering Mogoton should contact local guides and finca owners Bayardo Jimenez (Tel: 505-8-833-1144 / 2-732-2267) and Roberto Castellanos (Tel:

VIVA recommends travel insurance. Get it at vivatravelguides.com/insurance/

505-8-653-3666 / 2-732-0317) for assistance. They can arrange transport directly from Ocotal, 32 kilometers (20 mi) away. The strenuous 4.2 kilometer (2.6 mi) hike passes through a thickly vegetated cloud forest and the Achuapa riverbed. Although Bayardo and Roberto charge around $60 per person, they know the area well and a cheaper deal could compromise your safety. Updated: Jun 09, 2009.

DIPILTO

1200m 3,740

Twenty kilometers (12 mi) north of Ocotal is Dipilto, a town whose claim to fame is undoubtedly its exceptional coffee. At an altitude of 1,200 meters (3,937 ft) above sea level, with average temperatures around 20°C (68°F), and consistent rainfall throughout the year, Dipilto is the perfect setting in which to grow those oh-so-fragrant beans. In 2007, one of its coffees even won the Cup of Excellence Award.

Most of Dipilto's farms are small and privately owned, and farmers generally form cooperatives. One of Nicaragua's smallest municipalities, Dipilto is overwhelmingly rural, with 90 percent of the population living in small settlements made up of adobe and tile-roofed houses. Most of the land belongs to the Jalapa Mountain Range Protected Area.

Tourists who wish to visit a coffee farm should head to **Finca San Isidro**. The farm is part of the fairly new initiative being developed by Intur called *La Ruta Del Café (p.217)*. San Isidro offers horseback riding and hiking as well as food and lodging. A bed and two meals costs $15 per person, per night.

Transport directly from Ocotal can be arranged through **Parador Turistico La Cascada Macdouglas** (Tel: 505-2-732-2620 / 8-855-0238), a restaurant that also offers cabins and a hostel. Parador Turistico is located at a waterfall just north of Santuario de la Virgen de la Piedra. There you can also pick up a guide to take you to the nearby El Volcán. Don't be fooled by the name though; El Volcán is actually a mountain and not a volcano at all. On top of the mountain is the water source for the Dipilto Rivers.

Thousands of Catholic pilgrims from Nicaragua and Honduras come to Dipilto each year to pay homage to the Virgin of Guadalupe at **Santuario de la Virgen de la Piedra** located next to a large boulder on the banks of the Dipilto River. Worshippers often take water from the river as it is considered blessed with healing properties. The statue of the virgin was erected in 1946, but was only declared holy by the Catholic Church in 1996. Updated: Apr 28, 2009.

Getting To and Away From Dipilto

From Ocotal, take a bus towards Las Manos and ask to be let off at Dipilto. Buses to Ocotal and other southern destinations leave from Dipilto about every half hour. Updated: Apr 28, 2009.

JALAPA

680m 20,000

Tiny, isolated Jalapa is home to roughly 20,000 inhabitants, many of whom work in corn, coffee and tobacco production. Until recently there were no paved roads connecting the town to the rest of Nicaragua, and its proximity to Contra bases in Honduras made it a target during the conflict in the 1980s.

Set in a mountainous wilderness, Jalapa is improving its infrastructure (including the recently paved road from Ocotal, a cell phone tower and internet access) and may become a more established destination for outdoor enthusiasts in the future. As of now, there are several undeveloped natural spots for visitors to check out, but these are not easily accessible. Updated: Apr 27, 2009.

When to Go

Jalapa's biggest party is the corn festival (*Festival de Maiz*) held each year in September. Festivities include parades, dance performances and exhibitions. Food, drinks and costumes all made of corn are also part of the program. Updated: Apr 27, 2009.

Getting To and Away From Jalapa

Buses to Jalapa leave from Managua's Mayoreo Terminal, and the ride can take 5.5 to seven hours. It is best to take a morning bus to Jalapa, as afternoon buses arrive late at night, when safety becomes a concern. To get back to Managua, there is a 9:45 a.m. bus which passes through the Mayoreo terminal, near La UCA and finally Mercado Huembes. Buses to Estelí leave at 3:45 a.m. and 10 a.m. and take four and a half hours. Buses to Ocotal leave every hour and take one and a half hours. Updated: Apr 27, 2009.

Border Crossing
Although unpaved roads lead to a border crossing at Porvenir, it is rather unregulated and not recommended. To cross into Honduras through Las Manos, travelers will have to backtrack to Ocotal. Updated: Apr 27, 2009.

Things to See and Do
Travelers with a hankering for agrotourism will likely find more to do around Estelí and Matagalpa, where the cities are better outfitted for foreigners. Nonetheless, mavericks can find some activities of interest here, including trips to hot springs and reserves. There are also workshops specializing in pine handcrafts.

Hot Springs
There are several hot springs in the Jalapa area, though none of them are developed for tourism. Still, guides procured through **Hotel El Pantano** can take you to the springs at Aranjuez and El Limon. Thirty kilometers (18.5 mi) from Jalapa, Aranjuez's lunar-like terrain features a steaming river, parts of which are safe to swim in, though difficult to access. The mineral-rich waters near the community of El Limón are the source of the multi-colored caves that surround the hotsprings. One such cave used to be former dictator Somoza's private bath. Unfortunately, the exact cave can no longer be identified due to destruction caused by Hurricane Mitch. Updated: Apr 27, 2009.

Finca La Reforma
A 45-minute walk from the community of El Limón is the pine tree farm, **Finca La Reforma**. Owner Fidel Gonzalez is currently planning to build cabins where tourists can relax and hang out on the farm. Prices will likely average around $20 a night and will include use of a pool. Electricity is still a work in process. Updated: Apr 27, 2009.

Pine crafts
Jalapa is known for its handicrafts made of pine. Bundles of needles are fashioned into sculptures, baskets and vases among other things. Doña Gloria, whose workshop can be visited in Jalapa, is a pine craft specialist. Another place to pick up samples and see the artisans at work is at **La Esperanza**, a women's cooperative with over 70 members from five different communities. Updated: Apr 27, 2009.

Lodging
El Pantano
(ROOMS: $20, CAMPING: $3.50 per person) Considered the best hotel in town, Dutch-owned El Pantano offers seven well-equipped rooms in two red-brick bungalows. Double rooms come with a hot water shower, fan and TV. Laundry services are also available. A half hour of free Internet per night comes with each reservation. Travelers on a tighter budget will appreciate that El Pantano sits on roughly six acres of land that is available for camping, with an added fee of $2.50 for use of the hot showers. An airy on-site restaurant also serves typical breakfasts for $3, while other plates can cost up to $8. Younger patrons can also amuse themselves on the playground and soccer field. Excursions to nearby natural attractions can also be arranged. Eight blocks west of the Banco Procredit. Tel: 505-2-737-2031, E-mail: info@hotelelpantano.com, URL: www.hotelelpantano.com. Updated: Apr 27, 2009.

Restaurants
Sonia's
(ENTREES: $2.50) Pork lovers will appreciate Sonia's, where the fried pig and the yucca con chancho are specialties. Especially recommended is the fresco de cacao, a milk drink made with ground cocoa beans. In front of the Casa de Poder Ciudadano, formerly (and still known as) the Casa de Cultura. Updated: Apr 27, 2009.

Las Sopas
(ENTREES: $2.50 – 4) For tasty appetizers and typical dishes, head to Las Sopas. This restaurant also serves imported liquor, so Tennesseeans who miss their Jack Daniels can get their fix. Half a block south of Parque Guadalupe. Updated: Apr 27, 2009.

Luz de Luna
(ENTREES: $2.50 – 7.50) Offering typical Nicaraguan food, hamburgers and a variety of deep fried meats, this restaurant is also one of Jalapa's nighttime hangouts. Live bands occasionally perform and the place fills with booty shakers when it turns into a disco on weekends. One block south of the main church. Updated: Apr 27, 2009.

SOMOTO

706m **35,000**

This tiny town 29 kilometers (18 mi) from Ocotal has become a hotspot for outdoor enthusiasts over the past few years. This is likely due to its proximity to the stunning geological canyon, which, thanks to a couple of Czech scientists, has garnered worldwide attention. The town itself is a comfortable base from which to visit the canyon, and features two fancy hotels as well as several lodgings offering fewer amenities. There are plenty of places to grab a bite, though most of these offer only typical fare. For cheap eats, head to the market where meaty plates with plenty of sides go for $1.90.

The university, located across the street from the central park, was originally a fort built by the U.S. marines in the 1920s. Much of the original structure remains and if you make it a point to befriend the janitor he might take you up for a look at the turrets. Although Somoto was not the site of any battles during revolution in 1970s, the Sandinistas managed to draw many of the town's citizens into its ranks. There are even rumors that the nearby caves are loaded with ammunition leftover from the war.

Like that of its neighbors, Somoto's economy is predominantly based on agriculture, cattle raising and coffee. Somoto's most famous products; however, are *rosquillas*, corn flour cookies flavored with either cheese or molasses. Many factories around town will happily give tours to inquisitive visitors. Updated: Apr 17, 2009.

When To Go

The rainy season lasts from May to October. During this time the canyon waters rise and visiting can be dangerous.

On November 11th and 12th the tiny town of Somoto plays host to 6-7,00 people when it throws a huge carnival featuring live bands, rides and bullfights. Entrance to the party is $6.50. Updated: Apr 17, 2009.

Getting To and Away from Somoto

Somoto's one bus station is located on the Pan-American highway. Buses leave for Estelí (2 hrs, $1.25), Ocotal (1 hr, $0.70) and Managua (4.5 hrs, $4). Every other Somoto-bound bus from Managua stops at Ocotal, which lengthens the trip considerably. If you happen to catch one of these, ask to be let off at the empalme and take a $0.50 cab the rest of the way. Updated: Apr 17, 2009.

Getting Around

Somoto is small enough to handle on foot, but in case you want a cab, most charge a flat rate of $0.40 per person to any location within the city. Updated: Apr 17, 2009.

Safety

Somoto's center is safe at all hours of the night, but gang violence has been known to occur in the far reaches of town. Overnight parking at the Red Cross, across the street from the hospital, is considered very safe for travelers with their own cars. Updated: Apr 17, 2009.

Services

MONEY

BDF is the only bank in town and it recently installed an ATM. Money can also be exchanged there. A **Western Union** is located four blocks south of the central park.

KEEPING IN TOUCH

Somoto has lots of places to use the Internet and make international calls, but **Café Internet** has WiFi and there's a **Fono Center** located next to Hotel Colonial.

MEDICAL

For minor ailments go to the **Profamilia** clinic near the bus station. For middle-of-the night emergencies head to the hospital on the far side of the cemetery. **Farmacia Millenio** can be found across the street from the central park on the north side.

LAUNDRY

Laundry services can be arranged through most hotels. Updated: Apr 17, 2009.

Things to See and Do

Somoto's most famous attraction is undoubtedly its canyon, 24 kilometers (15 mi) from the town itself. Since it gained distinction in 2004 it has since been designated a national monument and protected area by the Nicaraguan government, and is receiving more and more tourists each year.

The mayor's office has recently renovated the central park area and travelers

Activities ●

1 Pool/ Baseball/ Soccer/ Stadium B2

Eating

2 El Buen Pollo A2
3 El Cafecito B2
4 El Sopazo A2
5 Rosquillas A1

Services ★

6 BDF Barber Shop C2
7 Café Internet A2
8 Farmacia Milleniun A2
9 Profamilia A2
10 University B1

Sleeping

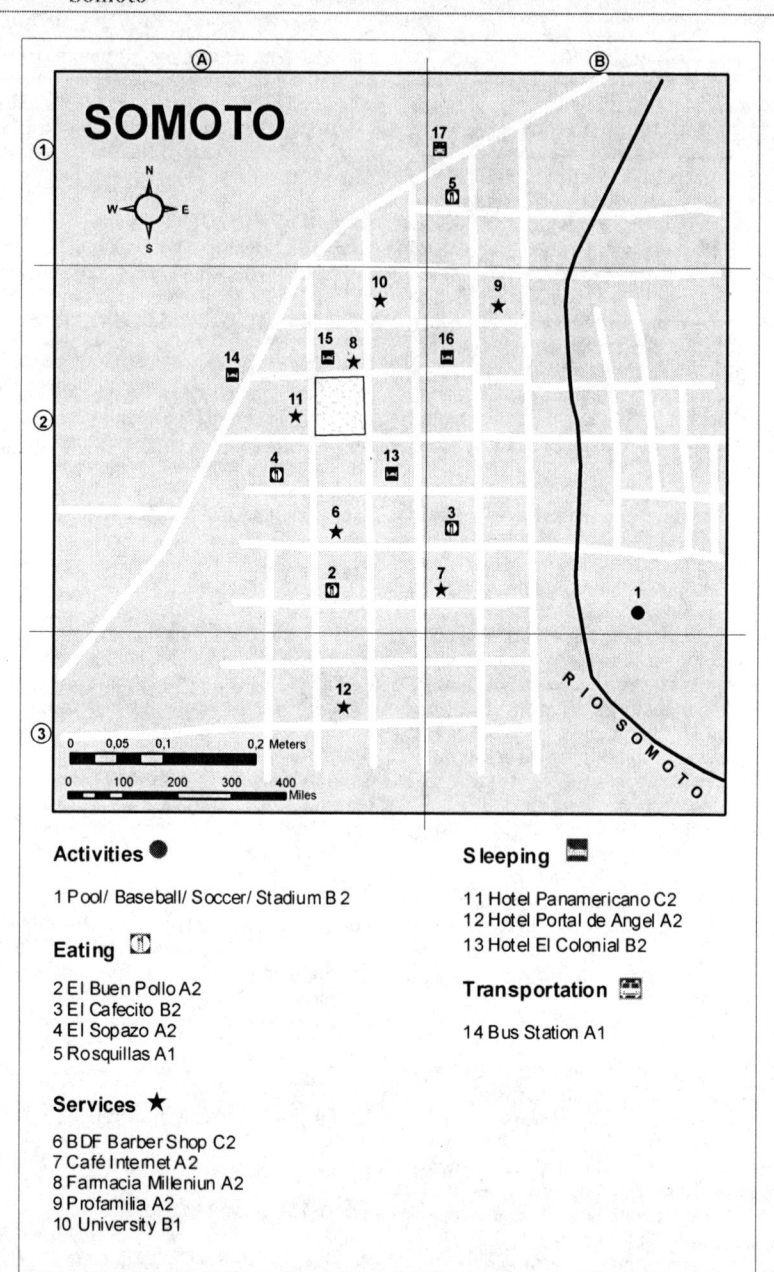

11 Hotel Panamericano C2
12 Hotel Portal de Angel A2
13 Hotel El Colonial B2

Transportation

14 Bus Station A1

wanting to spend more time there can occupy themselves by visiting rosquilla factories, the public pool ($1) or the Casa de Cultura, where concerts and other events are often held. On weekends it's possible to catch soccer and baseball games at the nearby stadium. Most locals are fervent fans, and even tickets for senior league games sell out quickly. Men staying a while might also want to indulge in a professional shave at the barbershop next to the BDF. For $2.50 a gentleman can get an hour-long facial massage. Updated: Apr 17, 2009.

VIVA recommends travel insurance. Get it at vivatravelguides.com/insurance/

Somoto

Grand Canyon of Somoto

Formed by volcanic rock, this geological marvel is between five and 13 million years old, dating back to the Miocene epoch. Eighty- to 100-meter (262-328 ft) cliffs rise sharply into the sky, walling in three kilometers (1.86 mi) of cool, clear water that is perfect for swimming. Although locals always knew about the canyon, it didn't gain fame until 2004, when a group of Czech geologists explored the area. As part of the Reserva Natural Tepesomoto-Pataste, the canyon is protected by the Ministry of the Environment and Natural Resources (MARENA).

Taxis from the Shell station leave for the canyon every fifteen minutes and usually charge between $0.75 to $1 per person. Buses to the canyon leave from the station on the Pan-American highway, but there is no set schedule. Reaching the river requires a bit of a hike, over the course of which it is necessary to pass a small stream. During the dry season, stepping stones can be used to get across, but the water here can reach a person's waist during the wet season. Visitors should bring their own food and water, and leave behind anything they would not mind getting wet. Following the river through the canyon requires scrambling over rocks or swimming, so visitors should be in fairly good physical condition.

For a more relaxed ride it's also possible to take a boat or rent an inner tube for $0.75. Guides are recommended, especially in the rainy season when they should provide ropes and life vests. Amateur guides can be found at the nearby Sonis or La Playa communities or be arranged at Hotel Panamericano. There are also a couple of professional guides who charge around $15 per person. Local guide Raemel (Tel: 505-8-817-1096) can arrange transport and has impressive knowledge of local legends concerning giant man-eating serpents and hidden treasures. Guide Edith (Tel: 505-8-667-2040) has a degree in biology and can identify much of the flora and fauna native to the canyon. She also speaks a little English and can bring along a GPS tracker if so desired. Updated: Jun 09, 2009.

Rosquilla Factory Tours

Despite its unassuming appearance, with roughly three dozen bakeries Somoto is the main producer of this most quintessential of Nicaraguan snack foods. *Rosquillas* are small, corn flour biscuits flavored with traditional cheese known as *cuajada* and molasses. Typically they are accompanied by a cup of black coffee. Although it is easy to pop your head into most of the factories, two of the most well-established are **Rosquillas Garcia** and **Rosquena**, conveniently located across the street from one another, two blocks south of the bus station. There you can observe workers forming dough into the cookie's signature medallion and doughnut-like shapes, before baking them in wood burning ovens. Updated: Apr 17, 2009.

Lodging

Hotel Panamericano

(ROOMS: $10 – 15) Somoto's best budget option has two locations. The one on the north side of the park has a bit more of an upmarket vibe and a nice souvenir shop. The annex, located a block west and across the street on the Pan-American highway, is generally reserved for the overflow, and guests still have to check in at the main site. The plus side is that rooms are about $5 cheaper than those near the park. Updated: Apr 17, 2009.

Hotel Colonial

(ROOMS: $20 – 40) In an effort to keep up with Hotel El Portal del Angel, Hotel Colonial has replaced its tacky faux-gilded furniture with more tasteful décor. One of the most striking decorative touches is a huge mural featuring voluptuous, nude indigenous women at the feet of their feather-headdress-wearing men. Rooms feature mini-fridges, fans, and TVs. Some have sofas. There's no hot water and the WiFi is bootleg and spotty, but breakfast is included and the attached bar is well stocked. Across the street from the north edge of the central park. Tel: 505-2-772-2040. Updated: Apr 17, 2009.

Hotel El Portal del Angel

(ROOMS: $35 per person) This upscale hotel is brand, spanking new and ready to compete with El Colonial—formerly the swankiest digs in town. El Portal offers guests air-conditioning, cable TV, WiFi, hot water, private parking and a complimentary breakfast. The rooms are a little on the small side, but are thoughtfully decorated, and the spiral staircase and courtyard featuring a cherub fountain will remind the visitor that they're in Somoto's most elite lodgings. Rooms on the second floor offer access to the balcony with great views of the mountains. These rooms also have air-conditioning, which, if used, adds another $10 to the price. El Portal's small bar/restaurant is open from 11 a.m. to 10 p.m. Meals there cost between $6 and $8. Two blocks east of the central park. Tel: 505-2-772-0244, Fax: 505-2-722-0310, E-mail: portalhotel@yahoo.com, URL: www.hotelportaldelangel.com. Updated: May 12, 2009.

Restaurants

Restaurante El Sopazo

(SNACKS: $1.50, ENTREES: $6 – 9.25) The big, open space at Restaurante El Sopazo becomes a dance floor on Saturday and Sunday nights, when live bands perform. Go for hot dogs and nachos or full meals featuring chicken, steak or shrimp. Half portions are also available. The bar stocks imported and domestic beers, as well as a decent array of liquors. Updated: Apr 17, 2009.

Don Chu

(ENTREES: $7) This spacious restaurant is one of Somoto's fancier haunts. The menu features steak, pork and chicken dishes and most have half portion options for around $4.50. Try the pollo vino; it's reportedly off the hook. Three blocks south of the central park. Updated: Apr 17, 2009.

MATAGALPA

700 m 109,000

Named for the Matagalpa Indians, the city of Matagalpa was founded by the Spanish in 1554, who stumbled upon the indigenous community during their quest for a route between the Atlantic and Pacific oceans. Upon hearing of discovered gold, other enterprising Europeans arrived to the area in the mid-19th century. German settlers then began to grow Matagalpa's now-famous coffee. Evidence of this European heritage is apparent in the lighter skin and green eyes of many locals. During the same period, Matagalpa became a safe haven for Nicaraguans seeking refuge from the invasion of American filibuster William Walker, who was later defeated by José Dolores Estrada, the hero for whom the main street is named. Estrada led a militia founded by Matagalpa's residents to victory against Walker.

Matagalpa's most famous citizen is without a doubt Carlos Fonseca, the founder of the Sandinista National Liberation Front (FSLN). In 1967, an FSLN-run guerilla operation, in which men and women fought side by side, took place near Matagalpa. Although the operation was unsuccessful, it created widespread enthusiasm for the Sandinista movement.

Today, along with agriculture and cattle-raising, tourism is a burgeoning industry in Matagalpa. This is largely due to a successful partnership between the government-run tourism bureau (**Intur**) and a Luxembourg-based development corporation, **Lux-Development**. Travelers will furthermore have no trouble finding food and lodging here. Hotels generally cluster around Parque Ruben Dario, and most are wallet-friendly. Matagalpa also has a veritable dining scene, though not one that can sustain real foodies for very long.

Although Matagalpa is one of the largest cities in the Northern Highlands, if you stick around town for more than a day or two, you'll start to recognize the same faces. Thankfully, there are plenty of other activities to keep the intrepid traveler busy. Within the city limits there are a couple of interesting museums, including the ramshackle **Museo de Café** (bearing a distinct lack of info about coffee) and a museum honoring Carlos Fonseca. The gleaming white church flanking Parque Morazan is one of the largest and most impressive structures in all of Nicaragua, and the block party celebrating the city's founding is one of the biggest celebrations to hit northern Nicaragua every year.

The surrounding countryside also offers an abundance of activities for outdoorsy types, including excellent hiking and coffee tours (during the season). Within walking distance from the city is **Cerro Apante**, a peak easily climbed in the morning. Farther from the city is the **Selva Negra Reserve and Coffee Estate**, which offers hiking trails as well as agro-tours. Travelers can also visit the acclaimed **Finca Esperanza Verde**, an eco-lodge with extensive grounds, a butterfly breeding center and of course, coffee.

If Matagalpa's shady parks, relaxed atmosphere and temperate climate seduce you into staying awhile, there are also plenty of volunteer opportunities (p.247) to occupy your time. Of particular note are the profusion of women's rights organizations and **Casa Girasol**, whose projects are of such broad scope as to include recycling, advocacy for the handicapped and yogurt production. Updated: May 11, 2009.

VIVA recommends travel insurance. Get it at vivatravelguides.com/insurance/

When to Go

This lush, green area enjoys plenty of rainfall and cooler temperatures, but still warms up quite a bit during the dry season. Average temperatures here are between 26 – 28°C (79 – 82° F).

February 14th is the anniversary of Matagalpa's founding, and there is a city-wide celebration, with live music, street food and much revelry. Equestrian parades, bullfights and musical performances to honor Matagalpa's patron saint take place on September 24th. Updated: Apr 28, 2009.

Getting To and Away From Matagalpa

Buses to Matagalpa leave from Managua's Mayoreo terminal roughly every thirty minutes, and the ride is two hours long. It's a three hour ride from Leon, and buses leave frequenty. To the north, the ride from Esteli lasts roughly 1.5 hours.

Once dropped off at the Cotran Sur in Matagalpa, take a 15-minute walk to the center of town, or a several-minute cab ride. At the north end of town, by the Guanuco market, is Matagalpa's other bus terminal, which facilitates travel to small towns in the area, such as San Ramon. To get to nearby Sebaco or Chaguitillo, take a Managua or Estelí-bound bus from the terminal. Updated: Apr 14, 2009.

Getting Around

Although Matagalpa is one of the larger cities in the Northern Highlands, it is best handled on foot. The walk along the main drag between the two parks is several blocks long. North of the Iglesia San Pedro and east and south of the Parque Dario the streets become rather steep. Should you decide to hop into one of the many cabs cruising the streets for customers, be sure to bargain with the driver before getting in. Note that prices are often per person. Updated: Apr 14, 2009.

Safety

Matagalapa is safe to walk around and explore during the day. At night, the bustling streets empty out and you may find yourself alone. Petty crime such as stolen wallets or ripped bags are more prevalent in the chaotic atmosphere of festivals and fiestas. Updated: Apr 14, 2009.

Services

MONEY

All the banks are clustered around the Parque Morazan. Although you can exchange money at **Citibank**, it does not have an ATM, so you're better off going to **BAC**.

KEEPING IN TOUCH

Matt's Cyber is located on Avenida Jose Dolorese Estrada (Av. Del Comercio). **Cafe Latino**, across the street from Parque Ruben Dario, has free WiFi and allows free access to their desktop computer for 30 minutes. Internet cafes are found all over town; however, and most of these also offer international calls.

MEDICAL

For middle-of-the-night emergencies, go to **Hospital Regional Cesar Amador Molina**, located at the northern edge of town between the highways to and San Ramon (Tel: 505-2-772-2059). Otherwise it's better to go to a private clinic like **Clinica Santa Fe**, three blocks east and one block north of Parque Ruben Dario. There are many pharmacies around town, but one of the most centrally located is **Farmacia Alvarado**, which is connected to the hotel of the same name.

LAUNDRY

There are no official laundry services in town. See if your hotel can arrange washing.

SHOPPING

Food and toiletries are available at the **Supermercado La Matagalpa**. The large **Pali Supermarket**, located 2.5 blocks north of Parque Morazan is slightly nicer. Produce; however, is better bought on the street, at the market by the bus stations, or at the smaller **Mercado Campesino**, where you can also grab fritangas or tortillas. Updated: Apr 14, 2009.

Things to See and Do

With stunning mountain ranges beckoning in all directions, travelers will likely want to spend more time outside of the city than in it. Still, Matagalpa is a great base for many excursions, and is also home to several attractions of its own, including parks, a couple of small museums, an array of churches.

Cemeteries

Matagalpa is home to two cemeteries. Historically, one was sanctioned for Catholics while

MATAGALPA

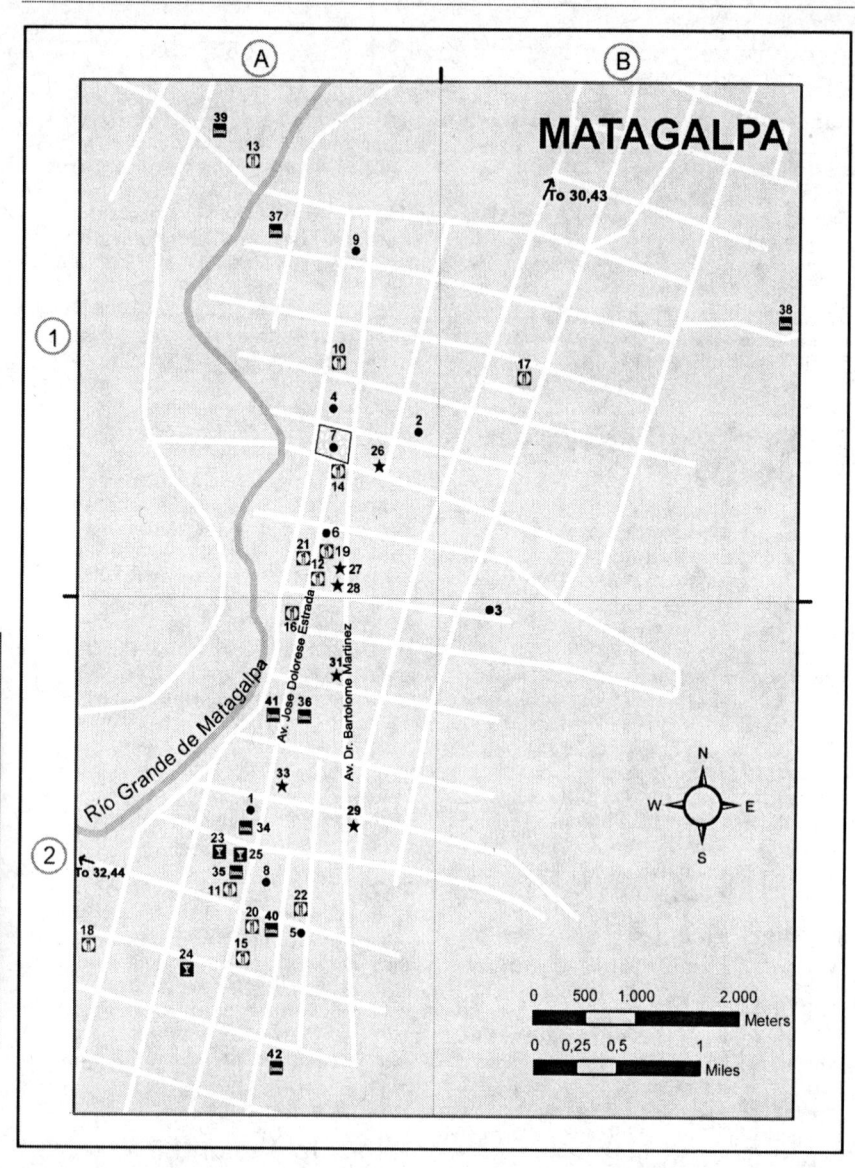

the other was for foreigners. However, today they are integrated and the former foreigner's cemetery is largely neglected. While the national cemetery is colorful and well tended (as Latin cemeteries tend to be), the foreigner's is decrepit, and somewhat creepy, but definitely intriguing. The grounds are weedy and the graves are disintegrating. Still, they represent an interesting segment of Matagalpa's population, notably the German coffee-growers and other ex-pats who for one reason or another found their last resting place in this far corner of the world. The most famous person buried in Matagalpa is actually a Jewish gringo named Benjamin Linder. Originally from California, he became inspired by the Sandinistas and moved to Nicaragua in 1986. There he used his engineering degree to bring hydroelectric power to small villages, and used his skills as a unicyclist to entertain children during a violent time. A year after his arrival he was killed by Contra forces while

VIVA recommends travel insurance. Get it at vivatravelguides.com/insurance/

Activities ●

1 Artesanías Cardoza A2
2 Cerámica Negra Tradicional A1
3 Collectivo de Mujeres Matagalpa B2
4 Iglesia Catedral San Pedro A1
5 Museo de Casa Cuna "Carlos" Fonseca Amador A2
6 Museo de Café A1
7 Parque Morazón A1
8 Parque Rubén Darío A2
9 Tablartería Santana Los Chavarría A1

Eating

10 Café Barista A1
11 Café Latino A2
12 Cafeto A1
13 Don Chaco´s A1
14 El Buen Sabor A1
15 El Sopon A2
16 La Casona A2
17 La Vita e Bella B1
18 Madretierra A2
19 Mana de Cielo A1
20 Panadería Musmanni A2
21 Picoteo Café and Pub A1
22 Pique`s

Nightlife

23 La Posada A2
24 Faraon A2
25 Rincon Paraiso A2

Services ★

26 BAC ATM A1
27 Banco Procredit A1
28 Citibank A1
29 Clínica Santa Fé A2
30 Guanuca Market B1
31 Intur A2
32 Market A2
33 Matt's Cyber Café A2

Sleeping

34 Hotel Alvarado A2
35 Hotel Apante A2
36 Hotel Central A2
37 Hotel Ideal A1
38 Hotel Lomas de San Tomas B1
39 Hotel Fountain Blue A1
40 Hotel Plaza A2
41 Hotel Soza A2
42 Hotel E & V A2

Transportation

43 Bus Terminal North B1
44 Bus Terminal South A2

---

working on a dam near San Jose de Bocay. The cemeteries are located on the southern edge of the city alongside the Rio Grande de Matagalpa and can be reached via taxi.
Updated: Apr 14, 2009.

Parque Rubén Darío

Providing leafy respite from the heat, Parque Rubén Daréo, named for the premier modernist poet in Latin America, is one of two small parks in Matagalpa. The park is a great place to grab a coffee at the snack shack, kick back and watch the *abuelitos* (grandfathers) playing poker. If you're feeling spendy, step into **La Perla** (Tel: 505-2-772-2464 / 6040), a tiny shop selling the region's characteristic black ceramics. Locals continue to chat it up, even at night, when strings of light brighten the trees, and the park takes on an enchanting air.
Updated: Apr 14, 2009.

Iglesia Catedral San Pedro

After those in Granada and Leon, Catedral San Pedro is the largest cathedral in the country. Given the fact that the city is nestled in the mountains and is far from any ports, Matagalpa was an unusual choice of location for such a monumental edifice. Construction began in 1874 and went on for twenty years —an impressive feat considering the church in Leon took a hundred years to build. San Pedro was erected in large part through volunteer labor and with donated money. The church's doorway is flanked by colorful, life-size statues of the angels Michael and Rafael, and Jesus and various saints are positioned alongside the archway columns. The interior's most notable feature is a huge, paper mache shrine to the Virgin of Lourdes. Just north of Parque Morazan.
Updated: Apr 14, 2009.

El Castillo del Cacao

Chocaholics unite! A tour through El Castillo del Cacao takes the visitor through the process of chocolate production, from the roasting of beans to the packaging of bars. The small factory, shaped like an oversized mini-golf castle, even provides fresh juice and brownies to patrons, so come with room for dessert. In the chocolate molding and packaging room, visitors will have the opportunity to taste the latest confections, all of which are made of at least 50 percent pure cocoa. On display in the reception area are global chocolate paraphernalia, including a chocolate condom—if you're into that kind of thing.

Tours to the castle can be arranged through Matagalpa Tours (Tel: 505-2-772-0108). Those who prefer to visit the castle on their own should take a cab. The ride from the center of town is roughly 15 minutes. Updated: Apr 14, 2009.

Artesanías Cardoza

Artensanías Cardoza will take care of all your mass-produced souvenir needs: cigars for the uncle you never see ($1), t-shirts for frenemies ($2.75) and CDs of traditional Nicaraguan music for coworkers ($12.50). Right next to Farmacia Alvarado, across the street from the northwest corner of Parque Ruben Dario. Updated: Apr 14, 2009.

Talabarteria Santana Los Chavarria

On a non-descript street on the north side of town is the humble workshop of a local family that has been hand-crafting saddles for generations. These intricately decorated leather pieces can take up to three days to make, and at around $75 a pop, these babies aren't cheap. By no means a souvenir shop, the best reason to stop by is to see the authentic process of making saddles for authentic cowboys. Three blocks north of Parque Morazan. Updated: Apr 14, 2009.

Ceramica Negra

While the exterior of this tiny shop is easy to miss, Dona Ernestina's pottery, ranging from tiny teapots to foot-tall Virgin Mary figures, is definitely worth examining. Using a technique developed by indigenous peoples of the region, Ernestina continues a century and a half-old family tradition. If you're lucky, and ask nicely, the artisan might let you take a peek out back where she sculpts and fires her work over an open flame to give it its characteristic black hue. Small trinkets cost about $2, while larger pieces can cost $10. Pieces here are half that of similar ones at the shop in Parque Ruben Dario. Open Monday – Friday, 9 a.m. – 5.30 p.m. One and a half blocks east of Parque Morazan. Tel: 505-2-772-2464.

Hiking Around Matagalpa

Visitors can take advanatge of several day hikes near Matagalpa. **Centro Girasol** prints maps so intrepid travelers can take on the outdoors solo. A five to seven hour hike to **Cerro El Torro**, a rock formation resembling a bull, offers picturesque views of the surrounding mountains. **Ruta de la Guerra 1978**, on which hikers will ascend and descend Cerro Apante (see below), is the same route guerillas used to flee from the national guard. This route takes four to six hours to complete and passes through coffee fields, villages and forests. **Ruta de la Guerra 1979**, a four hour hike, follows the path the national guard used when chased out of Matagalpa by guerillas. This takes the hiker through pottery workshops, valleys and mountains before culminating at a hill from which all of Matagalpa can be seen. Pass through the Centro Girasol to obtain information on other local hikes. Funds raised from map sales support the organization's initiatives involving handicapped children. Updated: Jun 09, 2009.

Hiking Cerro Apante !

This short, accessible hike is a good way to stretch your legs and get your heart rate up during your stay in Matagalpa. A guide is not necessary as the hike is a well marked loop. Starting at the traffic light on the southwest corner of Parque Dario, continue south straight up the hill for about twenty minutes. It's a steep climb out of town and past several farms. The Marena office, where you'll pay the $1.50 entrance fee, is located on your left, right before the little footbridge crossing the Rio Grande de Matagalpa. Along the way you'll encounter swarms of butterflies—most strikingly, green ones that camouflage perfectly into the foliage. At the top you'll find a lookout point from which you can see all of Matagalpa and the surrounding area. From there it's a steep walk downhill. The whole excursion, with frequent breaks for water and photos will take under two hours. **Finca San Luis**, near the Marena office, offers tours of their property, and **Finca El Socorro**, just past the entrance to the hike, is purportedly working on building tourist accommodations for those who would prefer to sleep

away from the hustle and bustle of the city.
Updated: Jun 09, 2009.

Museo de Café

Surprisingly, the Museo de Café has very little information about coffee, as most of the museum is devoted to pre-Columbian artifacts. There are stone and ceramic sculptures made by the Olmec, Toltec and Mayan, originally from Mexico and Guetmala, but found recently in nearby Sebaco. This migration of wares can be attributed to the trade route called the *Route of Good Hope* by the Spanish and the *Route of the Jaguar* by the Mayans. One artifact in particular found its way to the Rio de Matagalpa as a result of the tumultuous waters of hurricane Mitch. Also on display are funerary figurines by the Yasica culture. One wall is home to the *Gallery of Mayors*—portraits of mayors throughout Matagalpa's history. Finally, in the back of the museum you'll find antique machinery and framed copies of photographs, as well as several displays outlining the history of coffee in the region. Interestingly, the first coffee plantation in Matagalpa was established by German immigrants in 1852. Open Monday – Friday, 8 a.m. – 12:30 p.m. and 2–7 p.m. One block south of Parque Morazan on Avenida Jose Dolorese Estrada (Av. del Comercio). Updated: Apr 14, 2009.

Casa Museo Comandante Carlos Fonseca

To learn about the roots of the Nicaraguan Communist movement, you might want to visit the childhood home of FSLN founder, Carlos Fonseca. On display are photographs of Fonseca throughout his life, as a child and as the leader of the country's Sandinista uprising (look carefully to spot current president Daniel Ortega). Most interesting are photos of Fonseca in disguise. Wanted by the Samoza government, Fonseca had to go undercover to visit his mother in Matagalpa. Aside from the photographs, the museum features several of Fonseca's personal belongings, including his glasses, an AK-48, a compass and a soiled shirt. While there's a distinct lack of explanatory captions, the knowledgeable docents will be more than happy to answer your questions. Half a block south of Parque Ruben Dario. E-mail: Casacuna_carlosfonseca@gmail.com. Updated: Apr 14, 2009.

Volunteering

Matagalpa is teeming with NGOs, development organizations and young international volunteers. Some opportunities are best arranged beforehand, but all organizations will likely appreciate a helping hand if you'd prefer to just show up at their office. With high rates of domestic abuse and teen pregnancy in Nicaragua, as well as a ban on abortion, organizations focused on women's issues are particularly prevalent. Nonetheless, volunteers interested in working on practically any social issue will be able to find something to do in Matagalpa. Updated: Jun 20, 2009.

Grupo Venancia !

As of 2006, Nicaragua has become one of the only countries in the world with a complete ban on abortion. This issue, as well as those having to do with domestic violence, teen pregnancy, rape and political activism are the focus of Grupo Venancia. Through the use of educational workshops, cultural programs, popular campaigns and even a radio show, this feminist haven, made up entirely of women, seeks to combat various forms of female oppression in Nicaragua. The Grupo also hosts a variety of cultural events, including film nights and concerts. Those interested in volunteering should contact Luisa (Tel: 505-2-772-3562, E-mail: venancia9@turbonet.com). Only women fluent in Spanish are accepted as volunteers and positions are determined based on skills, experience and desired length of stay. Three and a half blocks north and five east of Parque Morazan. Updated: Apr 14, 2009.

Centro Girasol !

In all of Central America, Centro Girasol's playground is the only one that meets the needs of handicapped children. There is a physical therapist and a psychologist on the premises, and children are provided with hippotherapy off-site. In addition to the park, the organization has a number of off-shoot projects, including a recycling program that trains and employs handicapped people and their families, while also providing art and sewing classes. Particularly needed at the center are speech therapists, but anyone with a desire to help will be happily received. Contact Rebecca Trujillo, the program's founder and director, for more information (Tel: 505-2-772-6030, E-mail: Ndnica@turbonett.com.ni, URL: www.familiasespeciales.org). If you're only swinging through town, stop by the center's café, 1.5 blocks from the cemetery on Santa Julia street, and enjoy a snack. Also for sale at the café are crafts and greeting cards painted by program participants. Four blocks south and six west of Parque Ruben Dario. Updated: Apr 14, 2009.

Colectivo de Mujeres Matagalpa

Colectivo de Mujeres is the place to go for people interested in women's issues and the arts. The organization is split up into three sectors, the first dealing with education and communication, the second, health and community development and the third, human rights. As there is a particular emphasis on the arts, Colectivo de Mujeres runs several theater programs, a choir, an acrobat and art group, as well as a radio show, all aimed at spreading their message of human rights and equality for women. They also provide psychologists, legal aid, literacy classes and library access to those who need it. Two and a half blocks east of Citibank. Tel: 505-2-772-2458 / 4462, E-mail: info@cmmmatagalpaorg.net, URL: http://www.cmmmatagalpaorg.net. Updated: Apr 14, 2009.

Movimiento Comunal Nicaraguense

This group promotes the mobilization of the poor in defense of their human, economic, social and political rights. It organizes grassroots initiatives involving urban and rural populations and addresses issues of community infrastructure, food security and access to water. They also offer preventative health education to those in need. Swing by in the afternoon and if you're lucky you'll get to watch a children's karate class taking place on the premises. Next door to the mayor's brightly painted pink office building. Tel: 505-2-772-3200, E-mail: mcmt@ibw.com.ni. Updated: Apr 14, 2009.

Casa de La Mujer Nora Hawkins

Another women's rights organization, Casa de la mujer Nora Hawkins provides support and medical care for victims of domestic violence. They also run a program educating women in business. Volunteers are only needed for large projects, but if you're in town, pop your head in and see if they need help. Tel: 505-2-772-3047, E-mail: katerinebr@mixmail.com. Updated: Apr 14, 2009.

Other volunteering opportunities

Below is a short list of several more Matagalpa-based organizations that prospective volunteers can contact by phone.

Centro Las Hormiguitas works with child workers and street kids. Contact Isabel, 505-2-772-2181. Located half a block east of the Mercado Guanuca.

Centro Nutritional addresses the problem of malnutrition in this region. For more information call 505-2-772-6586.

Casa Materna focuses on combatting the high infant mortality rates in rural communities by providing healthcare to women during the critical last trimester of pregnancy. Contact English speaker Kitty Madden at 505-2-772-2102.

Secretaria Municipal Sobre Medio Ambiente is devoted to environmental issues. Those interested in volunteering should call 505-2-772-2780. Updated: Apr 14, 2009.

Tours

Northward Nicaragua Tours

The Northward Nicaragua Tours take place in Bosawás, the country's largest natural reserve with an area of 730,000 square kilometers (453,000 mi). The main tour takes 11 days and is designed to teach visitors about the history, biodiversity and culture of Nicaragua. Open daily, 7:30 a.m. – 7 p.m. From Enitel central one block east. Tel: 505-8-675-8864, E-mail: matagalpa.adventure@gmail.com, URL: northwardnicaraguatours.synthasite.com. Updated: Jun 15, 2009.

Matagalpa Tours

This well-established, highly organized tour company has options for every kind of traveler. Chocolate and coffee lovers in particular will delight in tours that shed light on how these delicious concoctions are produced. History buffs might go for the petroglyph tour in Chaguitillo, and the gold mine tour will also be of interest. Hiking enthusiasts can choose between Penas Blancas, the Reserva Natural Cerro Apante, and other treks, which can range from half- to multi-day trips. All tours include bilingual guides, entrance fees, meals and, when required, lodging. Half a block east of the Banpro. Tel: 505-2-772-0108 / 8-647-4680, E-mail: Info@matagalpa-tours.com, URL: www.matagalpatours.com. Updated: Apr 14, 2009.

Other tours

Other than Matagalpa Tours, there are no licensed tour companies in the city. However, independent guides can be contacted

Selva Negra

Cradled in the mountains of central Nicaragua is the sustainable coffee plantation, Selva Negra—and *sustainable* is the key word here. At more than 914 meters (3,000 feet), everything needed to run this little kingdom—from the food on the tables in the lakeside restaurant to the electricity in the quaint, half-timbered cabins—is produced at Selva Negra.

The Hotel Selva Negra has been in operation for 20 years. Eddy and Mausi Kühl, fourth generation descendants of the original German settlers who established the coffee industry in Nicaragua, oversee both the hotel and farm. A little taste of Germany can be found at Selva Negra when, each year, the hotel celebrates its Germanic heritage with Oktoberfest, complete with draft beer, clowns and of course, German music and food. The owners also hold a traditional Easter egg hunt on Easter Sunday.

The plantation produces a high grade of Arabica coffee produced in an "ecologically correct" manner. By employing ecologically sound processing methods the streams have remained crystal clear and the forest intact. The Kühls have thus created a prosperous coffee industry while simultaneously preserving the natural integrity of the highland forests. As protecting the environment is a main concern, they employ forest rangers to protect the flora and fauna of the area. Selva Negra also has a school for the children of its workers, a water powered generator for making electricity and a dairy farm. They are able to provide everything for their family, tourists and the 600 people who live and work on their land.

Located in the highlands of central Nicaragua, the hills of Selva Negra are draped in green year-round. Fourteen trails, six of which are designed for horses, make this beautiful and pristine cloud forest easy to explore. It's easy to spend hours wandering the trails, marveling at the twisted strangler fig, pausing to locate a singing bird or stopping to admire the beauty of a blood red flower against the deep green forest foliage. Some of the higher trails offer an impressive view of the rich green valley below.

Howler monkeys, deer, sloth, quail and guatusas all make this remarkable forest their home. Toucans, hummingbirds and gold finches make the area a bird lover's paradise, and the luckiest birdwatchers may even add a quetzal to their list. The forest is also home to an astonishing variety of flora. A visiting botanist identified more than 85 orchids. Selva Negra, in the heart of Nicaragua, is a place where the wonders of nature are just waiting to be enjoyed and appreciated. It is a place that will stay in your memory long after you have said "Auf Wiedersehen."

Km 140 Carretera Matagalpa-Jinotega. Tel: 505-2-772-3883, Fax: 505-2-772-3883, E-mail: resortinfo@selvanegra.com, URL: www.selvanegra.com (website is in Spanish). Updated: Jan 09, 2009.

and hired through the **Intur** office (Tel: 505-2-772-7060, E-mail: Matagalpa@Intur.gov.ni), located one block north of Iglesia de San Felipe de Molaguina, on the opposite side of the street (open 7 a.m. – 1 p.m., Monday – Saturday). Prices for guides are negotiated and depend on group size, destination and duration of tour. The major drawback of going with independent guides as opposed to Matagalpa Tours is that they do not provide private transport or meals. Norlan Albuquerque (E-mail: Norlan_Albuquerque@hotmail.com), who works at the Intur, is personally initiating the development of maps, hikes and other elements of tourist infrastructure the region is currently lacking. He is happy to offer assistance and is a wealth of knowledge. Updated: Apr 14, 2009.

Lodging

Most lodging in Matagalpa is scattered around Parque Dario and up the main street towards Iglesia San Pedro. Budget options abound, from spare shoebox-like rooms to better appointed quarters that are nonetheless affordable. In fact, there is only one really nice place to stay in town, and even mid-range options are hard to distinguish from their budget counterparts.

BUDGET
Hotel Ideal
(ROOMS: $5 – 12.50) Tucked away several blocks behind La Catedral San Pedro, Hotel Ideal is a quiet, secure place to spend the night. The hotel looks like it has seen better days, but it's pretty easy to negotiate a great price. Rooms come equipped with cable TVs and huge private bathrooms (with bidets!). There are several small terraces from which to take in the sight of the mountains, and there are live turtles in the lobby to keep you entertained. Two blocks north and one block west of the cathedral. Tel: 505-2-772-2483. Updated: May 12, 2009.

Hotel Alvarado
(ROOMS: $7.50 per person) Hotel Alvarado, owned by the family that runs the pharmacy next door, is one of the better deals in the area. What distinguishes this hotel from others is the quaint décor, which gives the place a homey feel. If you get locked out, just use the pharmacy entrance. Rooms include blankets, towels, TVs, fans and cold water showers. Across the street from Parque Ruben Dario. Updated: Apr 14, 2009.

Hotel Soza
(ROOMS: $10) Hotel Soza is another budget option in the heart of town. Right next door to Supermercado La Matagalpa, the hotel's front end is actually a little eatery called *Arouz*. Sleeping quarters can be accessed either through the restaurant or through the official entrance on the other side of the block. Rooms are spacious, though spartan, with semi-walled bathrooms. The shower is cold, and unlike in other budget hotels, no blankets or towels are provided. Perhaps not a first choice, Hotel Soza is nonetheless a reliable option if everything else is booked up. Across the street from Hotel Central, and 2.5 blocks north of Parque Ruben Dario. Tel: 505-2-772-3030. Updated: Apr 13, 2009.

MID-RANGE
Hotel Apante
(ROOMS: $9 – 12.50) Hotel Apante might be somewhat basic in its appearance, but the hot water coming out of your shower head will more than make up for any aesthetic shortcomings. Travelers who feel disconnected from current events will appreciate the CNN airing on the TV in the common room, where the hotel's guests like to gather to shmooze. Also included are blankets and towels. Given these amenities, plus the fact that it flanks the west side of Parque Ruben Dario, Hotel Apante is likely the most popular budget hotel in Matagalpa. Rooms all include private bathrooms. Across the street from the west side of Parque Ruben Dario. Tel: 505-2-772-6890. Updated: Apr 14, 2009.

Hotel Central
(ROOMS: $10 – 15) Travelers watching their wallets will appreciate Hotel Central, where a room with a shared bathroom goes for $10. Another five will get you your own bathroom. Hallways are narrow and rooms are pretty small, but you'll get the basics and as the name advertises, you'll be right in middle of town. Across the street is Supermercado La Matagalpa, and the main churches can be found in either direction. Av. Jose Delorese Estrada (Av. del Comercio). Tel: 505-2-712-3140. Updated: Apr 13, 2009.

Hotel Plaza
(ROOMS: $12 – 13) On the southeast corner of Parque Ruben Dario, Hotel Plaza is yet another budget crash-pad in the area. The tiny, institutional looking rooms on the second floor are not recommended. Instead, shell out the extra dollar for a double on the ground floor where you'll get your own bathroom with hot water and generally more comfortable digs. Tel: 505-2-772-2380. Updated: Apr 14, 2009.

Hotel E & V
(ROOMS: $14 – 23.50) This mid-range option is both a step and a hike (literally) up from the budget dives in the center of town. The spot on the hill affords great panoramic views of the city, which can be seen from the hotel patio. Rooms are spacious yet quaint, and private bathrooms come with hot water. Coffee's on the house. Two blocks south and one (very long and steep) block east of Parque Ruben Darío. Tel: 505-2-772-7232. Updated: Apr 14, 2009.

HIGH-END
Hotel Fountain Blue
(ROOMS: $15 – 20) Several blocks north of the teeming town center, Hotel Fountain Blue is a clean, quaint option for travelers tired of the budget scene. Practically every surface in this hotel is pleasantly peachy, down to the bedspreads and the fluffy towels. Cross the small bridge over the Rio Grande de Matagalpa, and continue straight until

you come upon the hotel on your right. Upon entering, take the garden footpath towards a slightly hidden door. Tel: 505-2-772-2733. Updated: Apr 14, 2009.

Hotel Lomas de San Tomas !
(ROOMS: $45) From its well-landscaped vantage point, Hotel Lomas de San Tomas literally and figuratively looks down at the rest of Matagalpa. With lush gardens and a stunning view, as well as spacious rooms with private balconies, this is the premiere spot in Matagalpa for a romantic weekend. Rooms come equipped with air conditioning, mini-fridges, cable TVs, and (does it even need to be said?) private bathrooms with hot water. The lobby bar stocks a variety of good liquors, and is an elegant yet comfortable place to lounge. For a good thigh workout, hike the steep but scenic path to the hotel from the city center. Otherwise, take a cab. Tel: 505-2-772-4189. Updated: Apr 14, 2009.

Restaurants
With a couple of fancier options and many smaller restaurants serving traditional fare, there is enough variety in Matagalpa to keep you satisfied for a few days, but not much longer. Despite the fact that the region is known for its produce, vegetarians will still be hard-pressed to find many vegetable dishes. Nonetheless, street vendors, particularly those bunched around the mayor's office, sell an abundance of delectable fresh fruits and humongous avocados.

BUDGET
Panaderia Musmanni
(BREADS: $0.25 – 0.75) Stroll through the Parque Dario then stop in here for fresh-baked breads and pastries. This humble looking bakery smells like heaven, so ask for something that just came out of the oven. Also on offer are strudels, cream filled confections and other goodies. Grab a loaf before heading to the hills for a day hike outside the city. On the park's southwest corner. Updated: Apr 14, 2009.

Don Chaco's !
(BREAKFAST: $2, JUICES: $1 – 1.25) Travelers who haven't seen fresh fruits and veggies in a while will be thrilled to come across Don Chaco, a great little café that offers soy options, and excellent fruit and vegetable juices and smoothies. It may sound a little wacky, but La Bomba, a terrific colon cleanser that blends broccoli, spinach, parsley and orange juice, among other things, has a surprisingly refreshing kick. Many of the smoothies are juice or milk-based, so tourists worried about tap water can rest assured. Typical Nicaraguan fare, as well as sandwiches, burgers, fajitas, and cakes are all on offer. A complete Nicaraguan breakfast here includes eggs, rice, salad, plantains and meat. Open Sunday – Thursday, 7:30 a.m. – 6 p.m. and Friday 7:30 a.m. – 5 p.m. Closed Saturday. Between Parque Ruben Dario and Parque Morazan on the east side of the street. Updated: Jun 03, 2009.

Café Barista
(CREPES: $2, COFFEE: $1.50) With so much coffee around, how could Matagalpa not have at least one gourmet java spot? Winner of the World Barista Championship 2009 (whatever that is) with a trophy to show for it, Café Barista provides a cute environment where tourists missing their Starbucks fix can feel right at home. The menu includes sweet and savory crepes and a variety of hot and cold coffee drinks. At the time of writing, the café was only seven months old, but will likely become a Matagalpa fixture. Credit cards are accepted. From Parque Morazan's northwest corner, head one block north. Updated: Apr 14, 2009.

Mana del Cielo
(ENTREES: $2.50) Another cafeteria-style option in Matagalpa, Mana del Cielo serves up local favorites like yucca, pork chops, sausage, beans and rice. Diners are welcomed by the bright yellow interior, with sunflowers on every table. When your belly is full, hit up the Intur office next door and plan your next excursion. Although there are probably set prices for each dish, you won't know your total until the lady with the calculator shows you the damage. Four blocks south of Parque Morazan, right next door to the Intur office. Updated: Apr 14, 2009.

La Casona
Average restaurant by day, live music venue by night, La Casona is sure to entertain. The place can get a little rowdy, but good cheer abounds. When the band starts to play a familiar song no one's shy about singing along or getting up to dance. There are occasional beer specials and the kitchen is open late. Across the street from the bubble-gum pink mayor's office. Updated: Apr 14, 2009.

Picoteo Café and Pub
(BREAKFAST: $2.25, TACOS: $2.50) Although it's on Matagalpa's crowded main strip between the two parks, Picoteo is an easy place to spot—just look for the bright sign with

colorful parrots. Offering up breakfast, tacos, salads, fajitas and sandwiches, as well as cold beers, this atmospheric joint is a great place to unwind in the evening. While actual tiki torches are absent, the restaurant maintains a laid-back, beachy vibe. The menu is available in both English and Spanish, and credit cards are accepted. One and half blocks south of Parque Morazan, and across the street from Don Chaco's. Updated: Apr 14, 2009.

El Buen Sabor
(PLATES: $2.50) It is easy to be seduced by the aromas wafting from this small cafeteria-style restaurant. Offering tasty renditions of simple favorites like mashed potatoes, paella, spaghetti, roasted chicken and of course, black beans and rice, patrons can pick and choose what they'd like on their plates. Although El Buen Sabor has no sign, the fact that it resembles a beach shack, complete with palm trees out front, makes it easy enough to spot. Across from Parque Morazan's south side. Updated: Apr 14, 2009.

El Sopon
(SOUPS: $3, ENTREES: $5) The loud music blasting from El Sopon might make you think you've come upon another electronics store (you'll understand this reference once you've been in Nicaragua a few days), but El Sopon is really just a restaurant specializing in soups. And once you've taken advantage of El Sopon's beer specials, the music played by local musicians starts to sound pretty good. From Parque Dario's southwest corner, head one block south. Updated: Apr 14, 2009.

Café Latino
Kind of like an upscale Dunkin' Donuts, this café is the only place in the city (and possibly all of Nicaragua) that uses styrofoam to-go cups instead of plastic baggies. Plus it's right across the street from Parque Rubin Dario. The *Mente y Chocolate* is refreshing and the *Mochaccino Supremo* tastes like liquid Oreos. Use their computer for free or bring your laptop and take advantage of the complimentary WiFi. Pastries and slushies are also available. Open daily, 7 a.m. – 9 p.m. Across the street from Parque Dario's Southwest corner. Updated: Apr 14, 2009.

MID-RANGE
Cafeto
(SANDWICHES: $3.75, COFFEE: $1.25) This clean, bright coffee shop is unique in Matagalpa for its variety of hot and cold sandwiches. Also on the menu are hot dogs, salads and fancy coffee drinks. Although it's kind of pricey, those extra Cordobas pay for the novelty of eating your food between two slices of bread. Cafeto also boasts its own Eskimo ice-cream counter serving sundaes and other creamy treats. Get a drink here (though not the sugary orange juice) if only to use the spotless bathroom. Two blocks south of Parque Morazan. Updated: Apr 14, 2009.

La Vita e Bella !
(ENTREES: $4 – 5.50) Hidden on a tiny street in the northern part of the city, this funky feminist eatery is worth going out of your way for. A large portrait of Che greets you at the entrance, and the kitchen door is plastered with lefty bumper stickers and fliers campaigning for women's reproductive rights. Whether or not you give a hoot about politics, you will certainly appreciate the shady, pleasant outdoor dining area, with plants potted in ceramic heads, and mellow music playing in the background. The owners, an Italian expat and his Matagalpan wife, serve up a menu of classic pasta dishes, as well as pizza, salads, meats and a variety of wines. Vegetarians will go for the mouthwatering penne with pesto, while meat eaters, as is always the case in Nicaragua, will have more to choose from. The place gets packed on the weekends, so be sure to make reservations. The restaurant is in a small alleyway and is easy to miss, as there is no visible sign. The alleyway is exactly one block north of the Hamburlooca, which has a big sign. From the Parque Morazan, it's 2.5 blocks north and two east. Tel: 505-2-772-5476, E-mail: Vitabell2@yahoo.es. Updated: Apr 14, 2009.

Madretierra !
(ENTREES: $3 – 8) Dark and sexy, this bohemian enclave offers great music, eclectic décor and a cozy atmosphere in which to have a drink or grab dinner. Run by the enterprising Norlan Albuquerque, who happens to be the authority on tourism in Matagalpa, Madretierra is also a great place to get the skinny on things to see and do in the area. Pastas go for $3 – 4, chicken dishes $4 – 8, and appetizers around $2.50. The wine prices here are a bit steep at $2 a glass, but your evening at Madretierra probably wouldn't be complete without it. One block south and two west of Parque Dario. Updated: Apr 14, 2009.

HIGH-END
Pique's Restaurante Antojitos Mexicano
(ENTREES: $5.50 – 8) This upscale Mexican joint serves up all the usual favorites,

---
VIVA recommends travel insurance. Get it at vivatravelguides.com/insurance/

including guacamole, tacos, chicken in mole sauce and beef with jalapeño. When it comes to beef, patrons have their choice of national meat or better quality beef for export. Smaller dishes hit the spot and are more affordable. Wash it all down with a Corona from Mexico ($2). One block east of Parque Ruben Dario. Tel: 505-2-772-2723. Updated: Apr 14, 2009.

Bar y Restaurante Pescamar
Even if you miss the sign with an image of a big fish, as soon as you set foot in Pescamar your nose will tell you're in a serious seafood restaurant. With its unassuming tile walls and cool, dim interior, it might be surprising that Pescamar is a high-end eatery. At $10, lobster is the most expensive item on the menu. Cheaper dishes include fish fillets, shellfish soups and ceviche. Open everyday. Three blocks east and one block north of Parque Morazan. Tel: 505-2-772-3548. Updated: Apr 14, 2009.

Nightlife
Faraon has karaoke and dancing and is a good place to go on Thursdays. On weekends the hot places in town are **Rincon Paraiso** (take a cab; it's on the outskirts of the city) and **La Posada**. Updated: Apr 14, 2009.

AROUND MATAGALPA
EL CHILE
To enhance your handbag collection with some truly special pieces, head to the tiny village of El Chile, located 30 kilometers (18.5 mi) from Matagalpa. Any bus heading to San Dionisio can drop you off at the base of a hill that takes roughly a half hour to climb. The community of El Chile itself consists of scattered houses along a stunningly scenic dirt road.

Eventually you will come to a brightly painted gate with a sign reading *Telares* (looms).This is the home of Marta Ruiz, an Argentine native who came to El Chile to revive indigenous weaving techniques. While the Telares group was founded in order to combat the Samoza government's attacks on indigenous culture, it has since evolved into a means by which participating women can earn a sustainable income. As such, traditional looms have since been replaced by more efficient Swedish-style models, but the textiles produced are still native in design. The seven to ten women in the cooperative create colorful purses, wallets, backpacks and wall hangings that range in price from $2 – 30, depending on the size. Independent visitors should call or e-mail ahead (Tel: 505-8-462-9210 / 416-1261, E-mail: mrtelar@yahoo.com). Organized tours can be arranged through **Matagalpa Tours**. A five-hour tour for two people costs $35 and includes lunch, transportation and guide. Arrangements can be made at Matagalpa Tours office in Matagalpa.

Those who want to support the co-op's work, but don't feel like schlepping all the way out to El Chile can buy woven pieces at the Matagalpa Tours office or look for the *Talares Nicaragua El Chile-Matagalpa* labels in other stores around town. Updated: Apr 14, 2009.

MULUKUKU
Mulukuku was originally established for refugees of the Contra War. Following the war there was a period of rebuilding aided by the establishment of several cooperatives. Unfortunately, many of these efforts were undone by the devastation caused by Hurricane Joan in 1988. The Tuma River, which divides the town, flooded and destroyed the connecting bridge. The bridge has since been rebuilt.

Mulukulu's best-known resident is the revered Dorothy Granada, an American nurse who founded a women's health clinic in 1990. During the presidency of Arnoldo Aleman, Granada was almost deported, allegedly for performing abortions and refusing to treat non-Sandinistas. Local and international outrage eventually led to the reopening of the clinic and Granada's return to Mulukuku.

The only highway that passes through Mulukuku is the one from Río Blanco to Puerto Cabezas. It isn't paved and closes during the rainy season. Updated: Apr 28, 2009.

SAN RAMON
Twelve kilometers (7.5 mi) from Matagalpa, this little town is home to the once-active La Leonesa and La Reina goldmines, which were established along with the town in the 19th century. Guided tours of the mines can be arranged at the hotel **Albergue Campestral** (Tel: 505-2-772-5003, E-mail: herma@ibw.ni). A two- to three-hour tour through the caves involves walking through waist-deep water, through which the occasional snake is known to pass. Geology buffs will appreciate the stalagmites and stalactites.

San Ramon is also the site of the **Cecocafen**, an organization made up of 11 smaller coffee co-ops. Most of the 1,900 small farmers affiliated with Cecocafen grow organic beans, and social initiatives undertaken by the organization include providing scholarships to children whose parents are in co-ops and combating soil contamination and deforestation. Interested visitors can drop by their headquarters and ask for a tour.

Direct buses frequently depart from Matagalpa, and most eastbound buses can drop you off along their route. Some Matagalpan taxi drivers might also agree to make the trip. Updated: Apr 14, 2009.

RESERVA NATURAL CERRO MUSUN

This protected national reserve, known to the Sumos people as the mountain of water, is actually an eroded volcano dating from Jurassic period. At 1,450 meters (4,757 ft)above sea level, Cerro Musun—the reserve's namesake—is the second highest peak in the country. The area possesses stunning biodiversity as well as fincas, botanical gardens, and the largest waterfalls in Nicaragua. It is also home to 84 species of birds and 51 types of mammals including giant anteaters, three toed sloths, ocelots, pumas and jaguars. Unfortunately, at the time of writing, this area was rather inhospitable to tourists and was mostly frequented by biologists and other scientists. Located in the nearby Rio Blanco; however, is an organization called **FUNDENIC** (Tel: 505-2-278-3040, E-mail: fundenic@ibw.com.ni) that can help arrange for guides if you're hell bent on experiencing this virgin forest. You can camp in Musun or you may be able to arrange accommodation at the biological station, but bring your own tent as there are no rentals. Buses from the Cotran Guanuca in Matagalapa will drop you off a 1.5 kilometers (.93 mi) from town. From there hail down a taxi or a southbound bus (towards Managua or). Updated: Apr 14, 2009.

RESERVA NATURAL MACIZOS DE PEÑAS BLANCAS

As it is 73 kilometers (45 mi) from Matagalpa, trips to Peñas Blancas usually last for about three days. Given the lack of infrastructure, the only real way to visit is to go through **Matagalpa Tours**. A two person, two day, one night tour to Peñas Blancas, La Sombra Eco-lodge and Finca La Canavalia costs $195. A two person, two day, one night tour to Peñas Blancas and the La Pavona waterfall costs $150. Both tours include meals, private transport, entrance fees and a bilingual guide.

At present, lodgings at Peñas Blancas are basic, so travelers must be willing to give up some amenities for a few days. The rustic cabins are maintained by a group called the *Guardianas Del Bosque* who can also arrange trekking tours to such waterfalls as the Cascada el Arcoiris. Rock climbers will have plenty to do here, but only if they bring their own equipment.

Hikes into Peñas Blancas can also be taken from the nearby San Rafael Private Reserve, which also offers good birdwatching. Up.dated: Jun 09, 2009.

SANTA EMELIA

For a refreshing day trip out of Matagalpa, head to the small community of Santa Emelia, which is close to waterfalls and is a popular destination for locals during the summer months. You might not want to swim there, however, as the water passes through many other villages and might be contaminated. The best sites are on private property, so make sure to stop by the first house in town and let owner Enrique Montoya (Tel: 505-8-926-8305) know that you'd like to visit his land. While there is no fee, small tips will be accepted in exchange for access to the falls. From Matagalpa take the El Tuma-La Dalia Road to Km 145. Updated: Apr 14, 2009.

Things to See and Do

Finca Esperanza Verde

Finca Esperanza Verde was founded in 1998 by **Sister Communities of San Ramón Nicaragua (SCSRN)**—a South Carolina based non-profit working to improve San Ramon—and in 2004, the 220-acre farm was named the world's best eco-lodge by *Smithsonian Magazine*. The lodge uses renewable solar energy and offers guests access to their butterfly observatory, pine tree reserve, hiking paths, campsites and organic coffee fields. During coffee season (November – February), guests can tour and take part in the entire production process—from crop to cup—by which coffee is made. Day passes to the farm cost $5 per person. Those who choose to spend the night have several sleeping options: A double with private bath costs $40 for one person and $62 for two.

Six person cabins cost between $75 and $120, depending on the size of the group. The eight person dormitory with shared bath costs $15 per person. Campsites are available for $7 per person, per night, and equipment is not included. Breakfast has a set price of $7 and lunch and dinner, $9. One of the drawbacks of Finca Esperanza Verde is that most activities come with an extra fee. The farm charges $7 for guided hikes and $6 for tortilla-making lessons, as well as tours of the coffee farm and butterfly pavilion. Even dancing with locals at a bonfire costs a group $60, while a picnic at the Wabule River Canyon costs $120.

To get to Esperanza Verde from Matagalpa take a bus towards Pancasan/ El Jobo. From San Ramon take a Rio Blanco bound bus. You will be dropped off at the town of Yucul, where signs will lead you on a 3.5 kilometer (2.17 mi) uphill walk. Tel: 505-2-772-5003, E-mail: fincaesperanzaverde@gmail.com, URL: Fincaesperanzaverde.org. Updated: May 13, 2009.

El Salto de Santa Emilia

Fifteen kilometers (9 mi) from Matagalpa, this waterfall is easily accessible by car and is a popular destination for locals during the summer months. Take the road to El Tuma-La Dalia towards the town of Santa Emilia for which the falls are named. After passing the town there are two bridges; make a right after the second. The 15-meter (49 ft) waterfall, known both as Salto de Santa Emilia and Salto el Cebollal, is surrounded by thick vegetation. Legend has it that the caves beneath the falls are home to a colony of small elves.

Many of Santa Emilia's residents work on the 12,000-acre coffee plantation creatively named Santa Emilia. Designed by an international team of architects and engineers, the farm is actually part of a project focusing on communal living and sustainability. The project was documented in a recent Dutch film called "The Hanging Gardens of Santa Emilia." Other residents work on their own small farms, which they received as part of the Sandinista's land redistribution initiative. Updated: Apr 28, 2009.

Piedra Luna

Ten kilometers (6 mi) southwest of La Dalia is Piedra Luna, a deep, refreshing natural pool where you'll find a large rock and ample cliffs for diving. Undeveloped and far off the tourist radar, plans for tourism infrastructure are currently in the works. To get there, take a bus from Matagalpa's north terminal towards Waslala or El Tuma-La Dalia. The ride to the pool is roughly one hour long. Ask the driver to let you off at Piedra Luna. It's a steep walk from the highway to the river. Updated: Apr 28, 2009.

RESERVA NATURAL CERRO EL ARENAL

Twelve kilometers (7.5 mi) from Matagalpa, this small, fertile reserve is home to organic coffee plantations, farms cultivating produce and flowers, artisan workshops producing crafts made of pine and the oldest oak trees in Central America. It is rich in animal and plant life, including quetzals, pumas and armadillos as well as a plethora of medicinal plants. The reserve's highest peak reaches 1,570 meters (5,150 ft) above sea level, high enough for it to be considered tropical cloud forest. This area gets a lot of rain, so sturdy shoes or boots and a poncho are essential for hikers. Organized tours to Cerro Arenal can be arranged through the **Matagalpa Tours** office (6 hrs, $45), or through **Selva Negra Mountain Resort**, whose property borders the reserve. Updated: Apr 28, 2009.

La Canavalia

La Canavalia is a coffee farm owned by ADDAC, a New Zealand-based Catholic agency that facilitates sustainable agriculture. Visitors to La Canavalia sleep in simple cabins, and there is hiking to nearby waterfalls and lagoons. In the evenings, music and good vibes are on offer. Visits to this truly off-the-beaten-path spot can be arranged in San Ramon. Updated: May 02, 2009.

CHAGUITILLO

A 508 m   3,500

For a half-day's excursion outside Matagalpa, consider heading to Chaguitillo. As this sleepy little town lacks restaurants and lodging, you're better off sleeping in Matagalpa and bringing your own snacks. The real reason to come to Chaguitillo is to see the 1,500 year old petroglyphs located in the outlying areas of town. These carvings depict images of crabs, deer, monkeys and other regional fauna. Chaguitillo is also now home to a well tended museum featuring pre-Columbian artifacts and colorful murals of indigenous people. From there you can arrange a hike to the petroglyphs with one of three guides (one of whom speaks a bit of English). The hike is approximately two hours and passes through a dry rocky ravine, an unshaded pasture and a shallow riverbed (so wear sturdy shoes and bring sunblock and water). Additional information about the carvings can be found at the museum. Contact Nestor Davila for more details (Tel: 505-2-775-2151, E-mail: adch@ibw.com.ni). When taking a Managua- or Estelí-bound bus from Matagalpa, inform the bus driver that you are going to Chaguitillo. The bus will let you off at the foot of the main road. Head straight for several minutes until you see a sign for the museum. From there take a left, go down one block, and then make another left. The museum will be on your right. Entrance to the museum is $1 while the fee for the guided hike is $4. Updated: Apr 14, 2009.

SEBACO

470 m — 15,000

Sebaco is the largest city in the fertile Sebaco Valley, and serves as a commercial hub where Nicaragua's farmers gather to sell their goods. The strip of highway passing through Sebaco is flanked by stands offering vibrantly colored fruits and veggies from all over the region. A recent agreement between local growers and Vidalia onion growers in Georgia now allows Sebaco's farmers exclusive export to the United States when Vidalias are not in season. McDonald's has even gotten in on the action, buying Sebaco onions for their onion rings whenever Georgia Vidalias aren't available. All this, along with a partnership with the U.S. Agency for International Development aiming to expand Sebaco's onion growing industry, has given the town the nickname, *La Ciudad de Cebollas* (The City of Onions).

After stocking up on produce, there actually isn't much left to do in town. The **Church of Immaculate Concepcion** has a small display of pre-Columbian pottery and some displays concerning the town's history. The church is located fairly far away from the main drag, so hail down a *tuk-tuk* (motorized rickshaw) if you want to see it. There are a few restaurants in town, all offering typical Nicaraguan fare, and there are also a couple of hospedajes. Visitors are better off staying in nearby Matagalpa or Estelí; however, both of which offer considerably more accommodations and attractions. Updated: Apr 14, 2009.

CIUDAD DARÍO

432m — 41,014

Turn off the Pan-American highway some 90 kilometers (56 mi) from Managua and you'll find yourself in Ciudad Darío. Formerly known as Metapa and Chocoyos, the city was renamed for native son and Nicaraguan poet, Rubén Darío. Today, the house where Darío was born has been renovated and converted into a museum; it remains one of the most popular attractions in the city. You can also head just outside Ciudad Darío to the fishing lagoons of Tecomapa, Moyúa and Playitas or to the hiking trails that lead off into the rocky terrain. Updated: Jan 09, 2009.

JINOTEGA

1,078m — 51,100

Jinotega has long been known for the battering 1980s civil war that was fought in its forested mountains. As a result, the region fell off the tourist trail for decades. In the 30 years since, Jinotega has enjoyed a highly successful postwar peace. The region features world-class coffee and the residents are very welcoming to outsiders. Jinotega's continued reputation for being off the beaten path makes it perfect for those who want to escape the crowds and spend some time in the rugged countryside. Best of all, Jinotega is just a two hour drive north of Managua.

The region has a variety of local products, including two specialties: cheese and coffee. By some estimates, the region produces 40 percent of the country's domestic products, some 30 percent of Nicaragua's exports and 25 percent of its electricity. Try eating a buttery *Manchego* (smoked Gouda) produced by *Lácteos Santa Marta*, and wash it down with the pure-filtered mountain spring water of *Naturalí*.

For the best view of the sun setting over the mountains, head to the third floor of **Tavern La Perrera** (The Doghouse), at kilometer 158.5 on the road from Matagalpa. For a bit of luxury and a hot shower, try the elegant **Hotel Café** just three kilometers (1.86 mi) away, where dinner for two with wine is under $30 and a room costs about $40. For a nominal fee, you can also go hiking or nature watching in nearby nature reserves. If you want to see horses dance to ranchera or cumbia

Activities ●

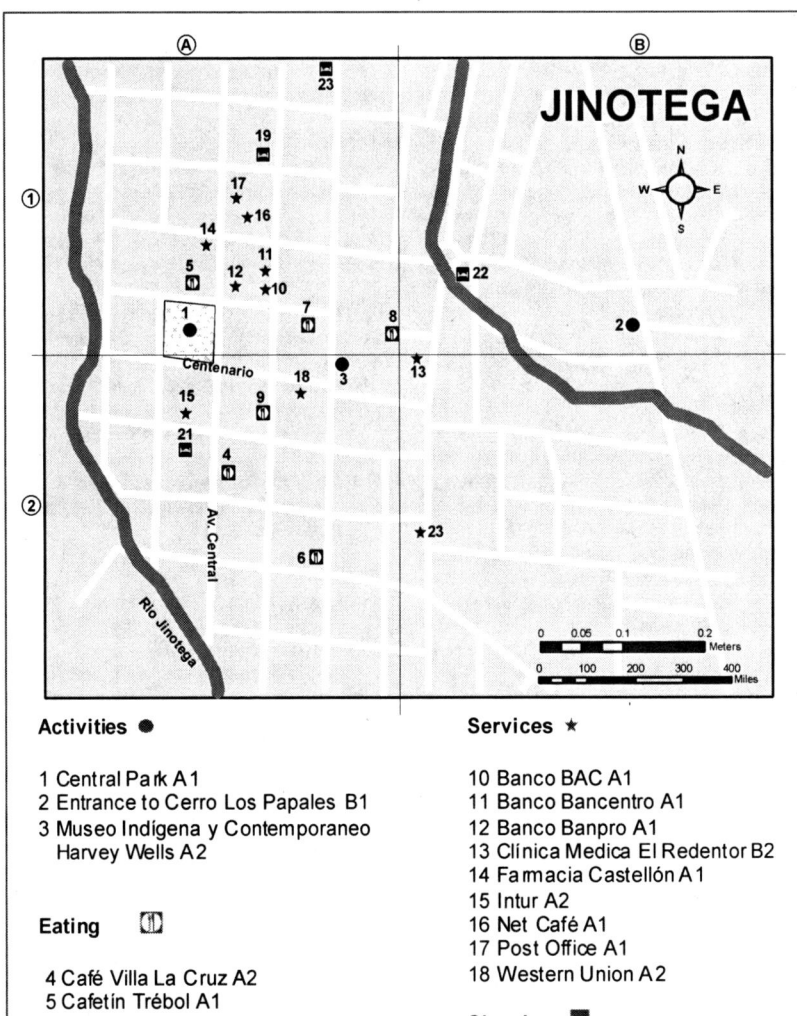

1 Central Park A1
2 Entrance to Cerro Los Papales B1
3 Museo Indígena y Contemporaneo Harvey Wells A2

Eating

4 Café Villa La Cruz A2
5 Cafetín Trébol A1
6 Restaurante Borbon A2
7 Restaurant La Colmena A1
8 Restaurante Roca Rancho A1
9 Soda Buffet El Tico A2

Services ★

10 Banco BAC A1
11 Banco Bancentro A1
12 Banco Banpro A1
13 Clínica Medica El Redentor B2
14 Farmacia Castellón A1
15 Intur A2
16 Net Café A1
17 Post Office A1
18 Western Union A2

Sleeping

19 Hotel Bosawas A1
20 Hotel Café (see 6)
21 Hotel Kiuras A2
22 Hotel La Fuente B1
23 Hotel Sollentuna Hem B2

music, be sure to schedule your adventure around one of the two annual *hipicos* (horse parades). Then grab a beer and go inspect the cattle on show, attend the rodeo or go dancing. Updated: May 11, 2009.

When to Go

The rainy season in Jinotega starts in mid-May and lasts through June, when muddy roads might inhibit visitors from climbing the surrounding mountains or visiting nearby farms. The rest of the year is considered summer, though the high altitude keeps the town from becoming too hot or humid.

Hands down, the most exciting day on Jinotega's calendar is May 3rd, when everyone in town, young and old, makes the pilgrimage

to the cross that sits atop Cerro de la Cruz. Another notable date is May 15th, when farmers from all over the province gather in the main square to display wagons of fresh fruits and vegetables. The produce is then blessed at a special mass, after which there is a contest where the best decorated wagon is chosen. Additionally, there are patron saint celebrations on June 24th in honor of Fray Juan de Albuquerque, who is not only responsible for the conversion of the indigenous Xicaques and Payas, but also for pillaging natural resources.
Updated: Apr 14, 2009.

Getting To and Away From Jinotega

Although Jinotega is only 34 kilometers (21 mi) from Matagalpa, the bumpy, windy road makes the trip 1.5 hours. Buses from Managua leave every 60 minutes. The ride lasts three to four hours and costs $5. Matagalpa and Managua bound buses both leave from the Cotran Sur (south station). All other buses leave from the Cotran Norte (north station) by the market. Every hour, from 6 a.m. to 6 p.m. buses run between Jinotega and San Rafael Del Norte, and cost $1. Regular buses also go to Estelí between 7 a.m. and 3:30 p.m. and cost $3. Buses to Wiwili costing $4 leave from 4 a.m. to 1:15 p.m.
Updated: Apr 14, 2009.

Getting Around

There is no bus system in Jinotega, but it is a fairly small town and easily traversed by foot. Taxis exist, but they are not seen as often as in larger nearby towns like Matagalpa.
Updated: Apr 14, 2009.

Safety

Compared to the somewhat seedier Matagalpa, Jinotega seems remarkably secure. All of the hotels and restaurants that travelers are likely to frequent are located around the park, so walking long distances at night is not an issue. Nonetheless, it's always a good idea for travelers to keep their wits about them.
Updated: Apr 14, 2009.

Services

TOURISM

Jinotega's **Intur** office is located one block north of the Texaco station. There you can find several people who are knowledgeable about the area and can provide contact information for a number of local tour guides. Open 7 a.m. – 1 p.m., Monday – Friday.

MONEY

Banpro, **BAC** and **Bancentro** all have ATMs, can exchange currency and are located in the same area north of the central park.

KEEPING IN TOUCH

International calls to the United States can be made at **Llamadas Heladas,** and cost $0.10 a minute. There are a handful of other internet cafes in town. Of the two on the map, **Net Café** seems to have the faster connection.

MEDICAL

For medical needs or general advice—such as where to find the best bread in the city—hit up the **Farmacia Castillon,** open from 8 a.m. to 10 p.m. and located a block and a half north of the cathedral (Tel: 505-2-782-224). Dr. Jose Miguel Altamirano can be seen at **Clinica Medica El Redentor,** which is located across from the market in a large yellow building (Tel: 505-8-632-2709).

LAUNDRY

There are no laundry services in Jinotega, but as is the case in many towns in the area, washing can possibly be arranged through your hotel. If that doesn't work, grab a bar of soap and get ready to do some scrubbing.
Updated: Apr 14, 2009.

Things to See and Do

Jinotega's mountainous terrain, ecological fincas and coffee co-ops are all good reasons to pay this provincial town a visit. However, the best reason might just be its people. Citizens of Jinotega are friendly and open, and the inquisitive traveler will have plenty of people to talk to. Of particular interest is Don Pilo, a traditional medicine man who makes the daily trek from Cerro La Cruz to sell herbs and powders at the cemetery. For sale, among other things, are cures for stomachaches and insanity, charms for warding off thieves, and herbs to summon back the one who got away. For an animated telling of Jinotega's history, visit Luis Lantaro Ruiz Mendoza. A self-described writer, documentary film-maker, journalist, musician, actor, natural medicine guru and tour guide, Luis is a wealth of knowledge and entertainment. He can be visited at the natural medicine shop he co-owns with his wife, but it'd be wise to check ahead to see if he's in town (Tel: 505-2-782-4460/ 8-858-8928, E-mail: goyomiel@yahoo.com).
Updated: Apr 14, 2009.

Cerro La Cruz

Even if you can't make it to Jinotega on May 3rd when the entire town makes a pilgrimage up to the cross on the summit, Cerro La Cruz is still worth a hike. The famous cross was planted in 1705 by Fray Antonio Margel de Jesus to ward off spells allegedly cast by the sorcerers of the Chirinagua Mountain. In fact, the offending ruckus atop the mountain was simply caused by indigenous celebratory feasts. The hike takes roughly one hour, depending on your pace, and some parts are difficult to traverse. To get there, walk from the center of town towards the cemetary, then past the wooden house just beyond it. From there it's straight a uphill hike to the top. From Cerro la Cruz, all of Jinotega and Lago Apanas will unfold. At night, the cross is lit up and the bright dot (easy to mistake for a star) can be seen all over town. Updated: Jun 09, 2009.

Central Park and Cathedral
The central park is the perfect spot for a lazy morning or afternoon. Stroll around the park and see if you can spot the mango, lemon, eucalyptus and pine trees, among many others labeled according to species and use. Set your inner child free at the colorful playground, take a seat in the gazebo, or just observe the murals and statues that adorn the square. This is also a good location for taking in Jinotega's hazy mountain sunsets. Updated: May 13, 2009.

Hiking around Jinotega
Another hike to try after mastering Cerro La Cruz is Cerro Los Papales on the mountain flanking the east side of town. This trek is a bit more challenging than La Cruz and also offers views of the whole city. From the market, head south along the highway until you reach a turquoise building on the left (roughly a five minute walk). From there, head up the dirt path past farms and wooden homes and continue to the top. Updated: Apr 14, 2009.

Lago de Apanas
The creation of Lago de Apanas is a feat of engineering that can be attributed to the bright minds of Italy, Nicaragua and the rest of the Americas. The Apanas Valley was once flooded with waters from the Tuma River, allowing for the creation of the Centroamerica Powerplant, which provides 35 percent of Nicaragua's hydroelectric power. Today, you can rent a boat at the lake from the fisherman co-op, or you might be able to pay a fisherman to take you out on the water. Bring your fishing pole and binoculars, as this is a prime spot for bird watching. Since there are no hotels or restaurants at the lake, go for the day and bring your own food. At present, property surrounding the lake is being marketed in the hopes of creating a luxury community. Buses from Jinotega leave every half hour from the north terminal and the ride costs roughly $0.25. Updated: Apr 14, 2009.

Ecological Fincas
With such fertile soil, the rolling mountains of the Jinotega province are prime territory for farming. Agro-tourism is in its infancy here, but the truly determined will enjoy getting a glimpse of these active sites which supply the country with much of its produce.

The following are farms that currently welcome visitors:

Finca San Carlos — Energetic Yvonne Castellon and her husband Manuel own a bakery (Delicias Sylvia) and pharmacy (Farmacia Castellon) in Jinotega, as well as Finca San Carlos, a family farm that specializes in blackberries, cabbage, broccoli and a variety of flowers. Finca San Carlos is slowly-but-surely being turned into an eco-tourism destination for city-weary travelers. Visitors will delight in taking walks on the farm grounds or longer hikes in the surrounding mountains.

San Carlos can house roughly six people at a time in its simple but cute rooms. At the time of writing, the owners were still in the process of making decisions regarding the menu available to guests, but veggie options using produce grown on the farm were a strong possibility. Also, prices for visiting or staying at the farm had yet to be fully established at the time of writing, but potential pricing seemed very reasonable. Plans were also in place for a tourist circuit covering not only Finca San Carlos, but also several nearby coffee farms. Finca San Carlos is located off the highway between Matagalpa and Jinotega, and can be reached from Jinotega via any Matagalpa-bound bus. Ask the driver to drop you off at kilometer 151. Tel: 505-8-853-3608, E-mail: Caballon_007@yahoo.com—att: Yvonne.

El Jaguar — El Jaguar is a well-established family-run farm that offers visitors tours of the coffee-producing process. Birders will appreciate El Jaguar's six trails devoted specifically to birdwatching; ornithologist guides are also available but must be booked a week in advance. Visitors can also visit the coffee farm, which focuses on organic growing and environmental conservation. Cabins are available for rent and come equipped with twin beds, living rooms, kitchenettes and indoor, solar heated baths. The cost per person is $60 a day and includes three meals plus entrance to the preserve. For larger groups there is a biological station equipped with bunk beds and hot outdoor showers. This costs $35 per person per day and also includes meals and entrance. Guides are provided for all overnight guests free of charge. E-mail: orion@ibw.com.ni, URL: www.jaguarreserve.org.

Finca El Gobiado — Finca El Gobiado is located 20 kilometers (12.5 mi) from Jinotega in the Datanli Reserve. Visitors can take a four hour hike over the course of which they might spot many types of fauna—most notably 75 species of land snail. Food and accommodations are also available. Tours can be arranged through the NGO, *Aldea Global*. Tel: 505-2-782-2237, E-mail: pagjino@ibw.com.ni.

Finca La Kilimanjaro — Fifty-one and a half kilometers (32 mi) from Jinotega, this farm is located in the municipality of San Rafael Del Norte. Tours of the coffee growing process, as well as horseback riding and bird watching are available. Sleeping accommodations are also offered and meals are included. Tel: 505-2-782-2113, E-mail: andres88200@hotmail.com.

Finca San Benito — Owned by Manuel Sobelvarro, Finca San Benito features waterfalls, hiking trails and the chance to see exotic birds in their natural habitat. It is located 12 kilometers (7.5 mi) east of Jinotega in the community of Esmeralda. Tel: 505-2-782-3303, E-mail manueljinotega43@hotmail.com.

Finca La Esmeralda — This farm, located in the region's sub-tropical zone, does not have food or lodgings, but is set up to host one day tours. The bus from Jinotega to La Esmeralda passes Finca La Fundador, which might be okay for a peek, though it isn't quite outfitted for tourists yet. The same is true of La Sultana and Santa Enriqueta which are in the same area south of Jinotega. Buses from the market leave at 12:45 p.m. and can stop at any of these fincas. Contact Ernesto Castillo at the *Cuculmecca*—an NGO that among other social initiatives, helps and supports coffee coops. Tel: 505-2-782-3578 / 3579. Updated: Apr 14, 2009.

Cooperative Coffee Tours

Founded in Jinotega in 1997, *Soppexcca*, a union made up of 15 small farms, supports various community initiatives, including those dealing with education, poverty, health and sustainable living. Two of the farms are open to tourism, though they have not hammered out all the kinks in their packages. The Soppexccca office is located in a cute café that sells pastries and locally grown coffee. To arrange visits, either drop by the Soppexcca office on the north side of town or contact general manager Fatima Espinoza. Angelina Mendoza can also coordinate visits (Tel: 505-8-404-4258). Private transport to both the farms can be arranged through Sopexxca for $40. Tel: 505-2-782-2617, E-mail: soppexcca@tmx.com.ni.

Finca La Estrella — La Estrella's prize-winning coffee is produced by the Montenegro family outside the tiny town of Pueblo Nuevo. Guests can take tours of the farm or stay overnight. Accommodations are $5, meals range between $2 and $4 and guided visits go for $8. From the farm, tours to Datanli can be arranged for around $20, which includes food and lodgings.

Finca El Dorado — Located in the town of El Dorado, this farm offers tourists a chance to ride horses, take boats out on the lake, and of course, to see the process by which coffee is grown and produced. Boat rental is $7, horse rental is a steep $40, lodging is $5, guides go for $8 and meals range between $2 – 4. Updated: Apr 14, 2009.

Tours

There are no traditional tour operators in Jinotega, but there are many individual guides recommended by the Intur office. Particularly recommended is Luis Lantaro Ruiz Mendoza, who owns a natural medicine shop in town, but is also a tour guide, among many other things (Tel: 505-2-782-4460 / 8-858-8928, E-mail: goyomiel@yahoo.com).

Others include:
Tania Jamileth Ballestros — 505-8-925-5066.
Edmundo Jose Fonseca — 505-2-782-2620.
Javier Ramos —`505-2-782-2352.
Nidia Francisca Soza — 505-8-698-1999.

For tours of nearby San Rafael Del Norte, contact the following:
Armando Arauz Zeledon — 505-2-782-5954 / 505-8-402-8746.
Juan Hilario Arauz — 505-2-785-5954.
Michael Tinoco — 505-8-693-2598. Updated: May 04, 2009.

Lodging

There are several places to stay in Jinotega, ranging from budget to high-end. As in most cities in Nicaragua, most hotels cluster around the central park. Visitors arriving at the south bus terminal will likely want to take a cab to the center of town, whereas those arriving at the north terminal can easily walk.

Hotel Bosawas
(ROOMS: $10) Clean and cheap Hotel Bosawas will hit the spot for budget travelers. Rooms are basic and you can get breakfast for an additional fee. Bathrooms are adequate, but the shower heaters only bring water to a tepid temperature. See if you can talk to the owner about the reserve for which the hotel is named. He's a fountain of knowledge on the subject and can show you a massive book featuring maps of the reserve. Tel: 505-2-782-3311. Three blocks north of the central park. Updated: Apr 14, 2009.

Hotel La Fuente
(ROOMS: $12.50) Some will consider Hotel La Fuente's location convenient; others will be put off by its close proximity to the crowded and noisy bus terminal and market. The décor wavers somewhere between homey and institutional, and rooms come equipped with televisions and fans. The private bathrooms come with electric heated showers. One block south of mercado municipal. Tel: 505-2-782-2966. Updated: Apr 14, 2009.

Hotel Sollentuna Hem
(ROOMS: $11 – 20) This cozy, well-decorated hotel is a nice change of pace for travelers in need of a homey touch. There's a comfortable sitting room, a cute outdoor patio and an on-site restaurant offering breakfast (not included in the room price). Rooms have blankets and bathrooms feature hot water showers, so you won't freeze your butt off in this mountain town. Three blocks north and two blocks east of the central park. Tel: 505-2-782-2334, E-mail: sollentunahem@gmail.com. Updated: Apr 14, 2009.

Hotel Kiuras Café and Restaurant
(ROOMS: $20) Only two weeks old at the time of writing, you can still smell the fresh, brightly colored paint at Hotel Kiuras. Its 20 well-decorated, comfortable rooms will no doubt make this establishment a Jinotega fixture. Downstairs, the walls are painted with funky murals, and there's a casual sitting room with a big screen TV. The well-tended garden with ornamental plants adds a touch of green to the atmosphere. Breakfast is included with your stay. At the time of writing the café was set to open soon. One and a half blocks south of the church. Tel: 505-2-782-3938 / 8-844-0026. Updated: Apr 14, 2009.

Hotel Café
(ROOMS: $45) Hotel Café offers by far the most amenities, along with the most elegant atmosphere in Jinotega. The hotel centers around a lush garden with a winding staircase leading to the upper floors. Its 25 rooms come with cable TVs, air conditioning (though you probably won't need it), WiFi and private bathrooms with hot water. If you don't have your own laptop you can use the computer in the lobby. Also available are laundry services, car rentals and private parking. There is also a classy on-site restaurant and continental breakfast is included with your stay. The hotel can furthermore arrange coffee tours. Two and a half blocks south and two east of the park. Tel: 505-2-782-2710 / 782-4308, E-mail: cafehtl@turbonett.com / reservas@cafehoteljinotega.com, URL: www.cafehoteljinotega.com. Updated: Apr 14, 2009.

Restaurants
There are many small eateries around Jinotega, though many of them lack atmosphere. A couple of nicer restaurants exist, but these don't come cheap. You can pick up fresh produce on the street or in the market, but don't expect cooking facilities at any of the hotels. Nightlife in Jinotega is not exactly swinging, but Roca Rancho occasionally has live music, and there are a few clubs where people can get their dance on. **Discoteque Jaspe** (Tel: 505-2-782-2590) is a great spot for those who enjoy dance floors that feature seizure inducing strobe lights. It also hosts live shows. It is two blocks north of the cathedral. Updated: May 11, 2009.

Café Pastelaria Villa La Cruz
(CAKES: $0.30, SANDWICHES: $0.75) Located across the street from Hotel Kiuras, this adorable brand new café offers up coffee, pastries and a variety of savory snacks. With a clean white interior and dainty pastel colored cakes, Villa La Cruz is the perfect place for afternoon tea. They also sell pizza slices. One and a half blocks south of the central park. Tel: 505-2-782-6436. Updated: Apr 14, 2009.

Cafetin Trebol
(BREAKFAST: $1.50, ENTREES: $3) Cafetin Trebol is your classic hole in the wall with plastic tables and insufficient lighting. No frills—just tasty food. The menu includes all the usual suspects: gallo pinto and egg breakfasts, meaty entrees and fried chicken plates. For $1 try the scrumptious French toast. Throw on some fruit salad and it's *perfecto*! Across the street from the north side of the central park. Updated: Apr 14, 2009.

Buffet Soda El Tico
(ENTREES: $2 – 4, BUFFET: $3.75)) Big, clean and casual, Soda El Tico features wooden furniture, local artwork and even a little jungle-gym

out back. Outdoor seating is available and patrons can choose between a cafeteria style buffet or entrees from the menu. The menu items offer more variety than the Nicaraguan buffet, and include sea bass, chicken fillets, steak and various takes on the hamburger. Try the breaded chicken or fish fillet—they're both scrumptious. Don't be surprised to find tax added onto your bill. Open Monday – Friday, 7 a.m. – 9 p.m.; weekends, 8 a.m. – 9:30 p.m. One block south of the cathedral. Tel: 505-2-782-2059, E-mail: eltico2@turbonett.com.ni. Updated: Jun 03, 2009.

Roca Rancho
(SNACKS. $2.50, BBQ MEAL: $5) Despite the fact that it's located among misty mountains, this restaurant-bar maintains a tropical vibe. The circular layout centers around a bar decorated with funky knick-knacks including maracas and figurines in sombreros. Roca Rancho is a little tricky to find, as it's on an unpaved road adjacent to an overgrown field. Still, it's centrally located—roughly three blocks east of the park. There are full meals, but if you just want a nosh to go with your beer (local brews are $1), there are greasy snacks too. Tel: 505-2-782-3730. Updated: Apr 14, 2009.

La Colmena
(SANDWICHES: $2.50, ENTREES: $7) With wood paneling, turquoise tablecloths and Chinese lanterns, this eatery is one of the most upscale places in town to grab a bite. Waiters don black and white uniforms. Open every day until 10 p.m. Located one and half blocks east of the park. Tel: 505- 2-782-2017. Updated: Apr 14, 2009.

La Perrera
At night, help yourself to the buffet and pull up a chair for a film on La Perrera's *Cena y Cine* (Dinner and a Movie) night. You'll find appetizing options, from the over-sized burger to spit-roasted chicken. Try a churrasco—a variety plate of grilled meats—fresh salads and *cuajada* (soft white cheese) on a toasted tortilla. Chef Maximo is an ace at the bar too; he stirs the martinis just right and picks mint leaves fresh from the surrounding gardens for his signature Cuban Mojitos. A *media* (a 375 milliliter bottle of *Flor de Caña*, the national rum) with a good meal will cost you around $12 for two people. Stay the night in the cozy inn over the bar and you'll pay roughly $9 extra. Kilometer 158.5 on the road from Matagalpa. Updated: Dec 16, 2008.

Restaurante Borbon
(BREAKFAST: $5, ENTREES: $9 – 12) Restaurante Borbon is easily the swankiest restaurant in Jinotega. Impress your date with a well-picked wine off the extensive list, or check out the classy on-site Hotel Café. Breakfast is included if you do happen to spend the night. Chicken dinners average around $9 and if you're feeling extravagant, get a steak for about $3 more. Three blocks south and one block east of the cathedral. Tel: 505-2-782-2710 / 4308. Updated: Apr 14, 2009.

SAN RAFAEL DEL NORTE

🏔 1,172 m   👤 5,458

Founded in 1848, San Rafael del Norte became an official city in its own right in 1962. Its temperate climate, combined with its natural beauty and historical places of interest make San Rafael Del Norte a great day excursion from Jinotega. While agriculture is still the primary industry in the municipality, tourism is fast becoming a close second.

Perhaps San Rafael Del Norte's most famous figure is Father Odorico D'Andrea, whose image can be seen in churches all over the region. Born in Italy in 1916, Father Odorico began his ministry in Nicaragua in 1953. He was an integral part of the development of an infrastructure in San Rafael Del Norte, and is credited with bringing electricity, drinking water and a health center to the town.

On March 22nd the city commemorates the anniversary of his death in 1990. His gravesite is located at the Temple Tepeyac, which was built in honor of the Virgin of Guadeloupe. The steps leading up to this chapel are extremely scenic, and religious pilgrims can occasionally be seen whispering prayers while climbing them. Father Odorico's stone coffin can be found inside the chapel. To the right is a gift shop with key chains, rosaries, and other Odorico paraphernalia. No need to feel like a silly tourist buying a T-shirt —locals wear them too. One of Father Odorico's other accomplishments was the renovation of Iglesia San Rafael Arcangel, which features a mural of the Last Temptation of Christ. Cryptically, the face of Satan looks remarkably like that of current president Daniel Ortega. Make of this what you will.

San Rafael is also the birthplace of Augusto Cesar Sandino's wife, Blanca Arauz. You can visit her family home-turned-museum, where photographs of Sandino, combat maps and newspaper articles, among other things, are all on display. Open Monday

– Sunday, 9 a.m. – 4 p.m. The entrance fee is $1. Located off the park.

While there isn't enough in San Rafael to keep you occupied for more than a day, if you do choose to spend the night, accommodations are available at **Casita San Payo** (Tel: 505-2-784-2377), a clean and quaint little hotel that also offers typical Nicaraguan food. A single room goes for $11, a double for $15, and a triple for $22.50. Across the street is the less hospitable **Hospedaje Aura** (Tel: 505-2-784-2303), which doubles as a bar. Private rooms with shared bathrooms go for $3.50 per person. Located at the entrance of town, **Hotel Rocio** is downright cute. A little tienda in the front sells snacks. Rooms go for around $11.50. Two restaurants of interest to the traveler include **Los Encuestros** and **Sabana Grande**.

Buses from Jinotega run every hour from 6 a.m. to 6 p.m. The ride takes roughly an hour and fifteen minutes. Updated: Apr 14, 2009.

BOSAWAS BIOSPHERE RESERVE

Declared a biosphere reserve by UNESCO in 1997, Bosawas is the largest protected reserve in all of Central America. At 20,000 square kilometers (12,427 mi), it's bigger than Lago Cocibolca and comprises almost 7 percent of Nicaragua. The reserve gets its name from Rio **BO**cay to the west, Cerro **SA**slaya to the south and Rio **WAS**pule to the east: BO-SA-WAS, get it?

With thousands of insect species, hundreds of bird species (including macaws and the endangered harpy eagle), as well as anteaters, crocodiles, pumas, jaguars, tapirs and howler and spider monkeys, Bosawas is a wonderland for wildlife junkies. Much of the reserve remains untouched, and it is likely that there are plenty of yet undiscovered animal and plant species here.

Thirty-five thousand people live in the reserve, 25,000 of whom are indigenous and 10,000 Mestizo. The indigenous are the Mayangna and Miskito, who mostly live by means of subsistence farming. Impoverished farmers of non-indigenous origin have been migrating in ever greater numbers to the area, causing deforestation through overgrazing and their use of slash and burn agriculture. At the moment, the reserve is mostly used for scientific studies, and ecotourism is only for the truly adventurous who are willing to undertake the journey into this difficult terrain.

As a lack of funds and resources make it difficult to protect such a massive region, conservationists have become increasingly concerned with deforestation and the extinction of wildlife. As such, in order to minimize their impact on the wilderness, tourists should get permission from the Ministry of Environment and Natural Resources before entering the reserve. Upon granting permission they will also provide information on disease carrying insects and other natural dangers of which travelers should beware. They can also suggest guides. Letters should be written well in advance to the following address:

Reserva de la Biosfera Bosawas
Apartado Postal 5123
Managua, Nicaragua
Tel: 505-2-233-1594

Most travelers enter Bosawas through Siuna, a small town in the North Atlantic Autonomous Region (RAAN). To get to Siuna you can either take a nine hour bus from Managua (which leaves daily from the Mayoreo Terminal at 5 a.m.) or fly from Managua on La Costeña airlines. The cost of the bus is $4 each way, and the flight $42.50 round trip. Guides can be arranged at the nearby community of El Hormiguero.

Groups can also arrange to take a 15-person boat up the Rio Coco from the town, of Wiwili. These trips cost about $1,000, regardless of the number of passengers, so the larger the group, the more economical it is. To go up the river to Raiti and back takes about a week. There are no accommodations along the way, so bring your own tent to use at night along the riverbank. Boats can be taken up the Rio Bocay as well, though the town of Ayapal from which the boats depart is more difficult to access than Wiwili. Both rivers end up at roughly the same point. By bus it is five hours from Jinotega to Wiwili and nine or ten hours from Jinotega to Ayapal. Wiwili has four hotels that can help arrange boat rentals. Food and water, along with your tent, are your own responsibility. Updated: Jun 03, 2009.

SIUNA

146 m   10,000

Given its location on the crossroads between several Nicaraguan regions, including the

Caribbean Coast and the cowboy inhabited highlands, Siuna encompasses a diverse mixture of cultures. Do know; however, that Siuna isn't on Nicaragua's main electricity line, so everyone's power comes from a very noisy generator. Additionally, there's only running water for a few hours each week.

While the land surrounding Siuna was once densely vegetated rainforest, much of it has since been deforested. Slash and burn agriculture has depleted Siuna's water supply, and what's left of it is contaminated by metals left over from the mining era. Water is a real problem in Siuna, seriously impacting the health of its residents. Locals hope to one day utilize a river in Bosawas in order to obtain clean drinking water, but limited resources have impeded the development of that project. Nonetheless, the conservation of Bosawas impacts not only the flora and fauna in the reserve, but also the lives of the people surrounding it.

While the town isn't especially accustomed to hositng visitors, there are a few dining and lodging options available. Serving gallo pinto and all your favorite Nicaraguan dishes, **Desnuque** is the hottest restaurant in the area. Those with more exotic tastes can grab a bite at **Hoyming**, a restaurant serving up Chinese dishes. Interestingly, during the period in which the mines were functioning, Siuna saw an influx of Chinese immigrants, most of whom left when the mines shut down in the 1980s.

Attached to Desnuque is the **Estancia del Desnuque**, which has four rooms, each with a private bathroom. These cost $5 with breakfast and $3.75 without.

Considered Siuna's top hotel, **Hospedaje Siu** offers double rooms for $6. Every two rooms share a bathroom, and visitors will be happy to hear that Hospedaje Siu has its own water tanks, providing running water 24-hours a day.

The larger **Hospedaje El Costeno** is an economical choice, with doubles going for $3.

Local couple **Pilo and Isa Padilla** also have three rooms available for sleeping in their home, located by the bank. A single costs $3 and a double $4. Meals can also be arranged. Even if you're not staying with them, you might want to get in touch, as Pilo drives to El Hormiguero—the community that is also an entrance point to the Bosawas Reserve—every morning. He leaves at 5 a.m. and charges passengers less than $1 each way. If that's too early, head to the market where buses leave for El Hormiguero at 1 p.m., 2:30 p.m. and 5 p.m. The ride lasts about an hour.

El Hormiguero (the anthill) is located 20 kilometers (12 mi) southwest of Siuna and has a population of 2,000. The town has no hotels, no restaurants, and no electricity, but it's a good place to arrange homestays and guided tours of Bosawas. Head to the **Humboldt Center** for information on and maps of Bosawas. Those looking for an extreme physical challenge can also arrange to take the three to four hour day hike up mount Saslaya. Guides in and around El Hormiguero generally cost around $5 per day, horses $2 per day, meals $1 and overnight stays $2. Updated: Jun 03, 2009.

Getting To and Away From Siuna

Daily flights from Managua to Siuna on La Costeña cost $42.50 round trip. You can also take an expresso bus at 5 a.m. from Managua's Mayoreo terminal. The ride is nine hours and costs $4. Updated: Apr 28, 2009.

BONANZA

182 m 15,000

First discovered in 1880, the gold vein in Bonanza was later taken over by a Canadian mining company, and in the 1960s and 1970s, became one of the North Atlantic Autonomous Region's most prosperous entities. The town maintains an "Old West" type of atmosphere, with cobblestone streets and horses.

Today, gold is still being mined, primarily for jewelry. There are a host of shops in town that sell inexpensive hand-crafted goods. The **Hemsa Goldmine** (Tel: 505-2-794-0066 ext.789, E-mail amilkarramos@hemconic.com) welcomes visitors for free tours of the premises, but reservations need to be made well in advance. The tour furthermore requires some agility, so travelers who aren't in tip-top condition should beware.

Hellbent on exploring the Bosawas reserve? A Bosawas information office is located two kilometers north of Bonanza. It has maps and information about visiting the reserve and getting a guide. The office also runs a farm aimed at educating local growers in organic agricultural techniques. The farm is

12 kilometers (7.5 mi) south of Bonanza, but the Bosawas office can help arrange visits.

Thirty-five kilometers (22 mi) from Bonanza is Musuwus, the largest Mayangna community, where 95 percent of the population is fluent in the native tongue. This difficult to access area doesn't have electricity or water so plan to bring supplies. There is a Mayangna organization whose office is located in Bonanza; visitors should pop in there to acquire about hiring guides.

If you're looking for a place to crash, **Hotel y Restaurante B & B** (located by the market), has singles for $4 and doubles for $5, all of which share bathrooms (Tel: 505-2-794-0017). The on-site restaurant is considered Bonanza's best, and the hotel also features a casino and pool hall, as well as a shop selling locally produced gold jewelry. Another option is **Hotel Bonanza**, located across from the mayor's office. It has clean, modern rooms and costs $11 per person per night. For dinner, head to **Restaurant El Encuentro**. A block up from B & B, it offers great views. Updated: Jun 03, 2009.

Getting To and Away From Bonanza

The 15-hour bus ride to Managua leaves twice a day at 10 a.m. and 2:30 p.m. There are also regular buses to Rosita and Siuna. The ride to Siuna is five hours and the ride to Rosita is an hour and a half. There is also an airport three kilometers (1.86 mi) from town operated by **La Costeña Airlines** (Tel: 505-2-794-0023). The Costeña Office in Bonanza, located half a block from the mayor's office, is only open two hours a day from 8 a.m. – 9 a.m., and again from 4 – 5 p.m. Updated: Apr 28, 2009.

ROSITA

58 m   450

Although Rosita offers a glimpse at an authentic "Old-West" style mining town, there really isn't much to do here. However, it's a good place from which the adventurous traveler can visit surrounding indigenous communities.

Isolated by a lack of paved roads from the Pacific Coast, the people of the North Atlantic Autonomous region don't exactly consider themselves Nicaraguan. In fact, the region was never part of the Spanish empire at all, so most Christians are Protestant and the first language of the area's inhabitants is almost always a native dialect. With that in mind, when visiting the outlying Miskito and Mayangna communities, be prepared to have communication problems. Additionally, conditions are rugged (electricity and running water are a rarity), so bring a filter or bottled water and a flashlight. Tours to nearby indigenous communities can be arranged by **The Foundation for Unity and Reconstruction of the Atlantic Coast** (FURCA). Tel: 505-2-794-1045 /249-7801 (Managua), E-mail: Furca@sdnnic.org.ni.

Laid out along one street, Rosita is a cocaine shipping hub, so it's best to stick to the main drag after dark. Hotels tend to be near the bus station, located along the middle of the main strip.

In terms of lodging, **Hospedaje El Sol** features basic rooms with shared bathrooms and a common room with a TV. Singles go for $2.50, doubles $4. Tel: 505-2-794-1129. A more upscale option, located half a block from the Mayor's office, is **Hotel Los Ensuenos**. It features amenities such as cable TV and air conditioning. There are also well-kept grounds and a parking lot. Rooms cost $10 per person, but use of the AC doubles the price. Tel: 505-2-794-1004.

To get your surf and turf fix and catch up on your TV viewing, head to **Restaurant and Video Bar Martinez**. Meals range from $3 – 7. For dinner with a view, try **Bar Campestre La Laguna Verde**, located on the hill whose path begins behind the Catholic Church. A taxi here will cost $1, or work up your appetite and take the one and a half kilometer hike up the road. Updated: Jun 03, 2009.

Getting To and Away From Rosita

La Costeña flies to the airstrip near Rosita. From there, take a $1.25 taxi ride into town. Visit the La Costeña office across the street from the Alcaldia to make return flight arrangements.

Buses to Bonanza depart at 7:30 a.m., 11:30 a.m., 1:30 p.m. and 4:30 p.m, and the ride lasts one and a half hours. Buses to Siuna leave every hour from 5:30 a.m. to 5 p.m. The ride lasts between four and five hour. Updated: Apr 29, 2009

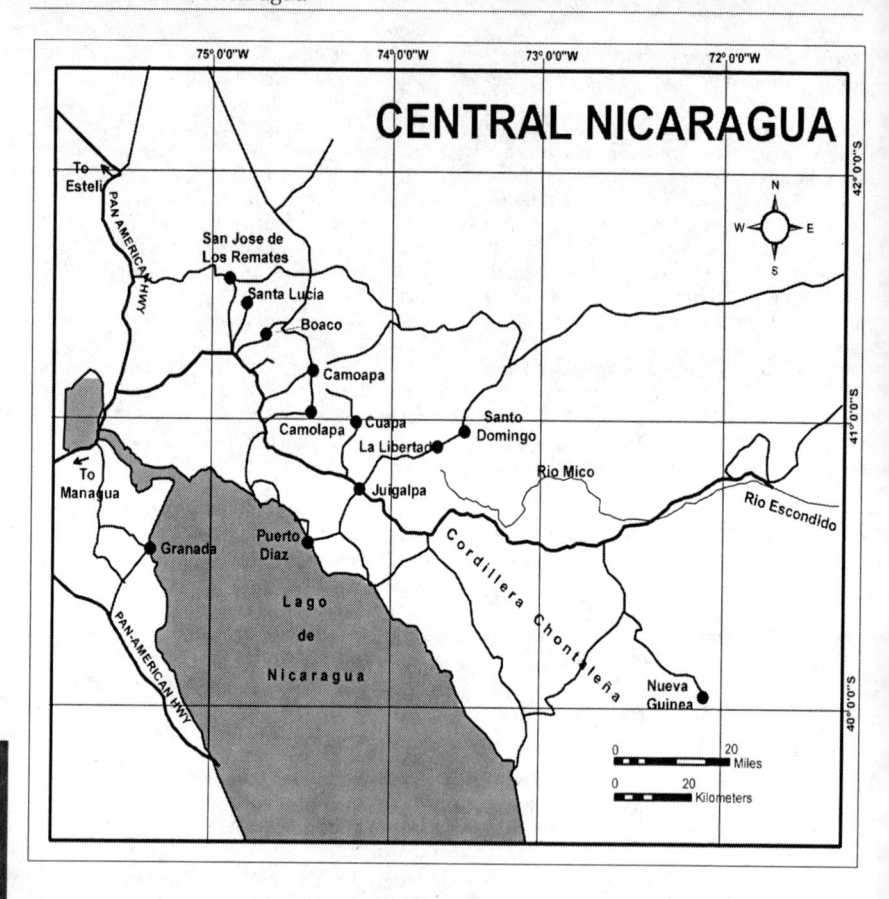

Central Nicaragua

Grazing cattle atop rolling green hills and cowboys strutting in spurred boots are common sights in the departments of Boaco and Chontales. As the primary source for most of Nicaragua's beef and dairy, cattle is very much part of the culture in these bordering departments. Rodeos and bullfights are frequent, and are probably the most exciting events a visitor can hope to attend. Juigalpa (p.273), by far the most cosmopolitan city in either Boaco or Chontales, hosts rodeos every month. You wouldn't think the bleachers at the ring would fill up every time, but Juigalpans take the sport very seriously. At their patron saint festival in August, people come from all over the world to attend the spectacular rodeos and bullfights.

If cattle isn't your thing, there are plenty of beautiful hikes to take and local farms to visit. Set among the Amerrisque mountains, Boaco and Chontales offer excellent hiking, with peaks such as Mombacho, La Cebadilla and the more challenging Quizaltepe (p.273). Bear in mind though, that since this region sees very few tourists, these places can be hard to get to.

While Boaco and Chontales haven't seen the sort of governmental investment in agro-tourism you'll find in other regions, a few entrepreneurial farmers and ranchers have opened up their properties to the public. Nueva Guinea (p.279) has La Esperanzita, a teaching farm, and San Jose de Los Remates (p.270) has plenty of coffee farms. All are good places to get a sense of the sort of development going on in this peaceful, prosperous region. Updated: May 05, 2009.

Get travel advisories and tips at blog.vivatravelguides.com

Central Nicaragua

Highlights

Museo Arqueológico Gregorio Aguilar Barea (p.275)— With an impressive collection of pre-Columbian ceramics and grimacing stone stelae, as well as taxidermied two-headed cattle and other medical oddities, this Juigalpa museum is by far the most interesting in the region.

Juigalpa Fiestas Patronales (p.274) — Starting on August 10th and continuing for two straight weeks, Juigalpa's rowdy festivities include parades, rodeos, a beauty contest and live music.

San Jose de los Remates (p.270)— Offering grassroots tourism at its best, the Mayor's office in San Jose is happy to create a personalized tour package for visitors to this tiny, undeveloped town.

The *Fritanga* Scene in Boaco (p.268)— Don't try to ask a local what is special about fritanga—they're liable to go on for hours. Although this tasty street meat is available all over Nicaragua, it is most prevalent in Boaco, and is the focal point around which the

History

As the departments of Boaco and Chontales border the Carribean region, they underwent frequent attacks by Carib Zambo and the Miskito Indians in collaboration with British colonists during the mid 18th century. Many residents were kidnapped and enslaved. In 1749, these indigenous groups attacked what is now referred to as Boaco Viejo, and burned it to the ground. The remaining population moved four times, finally settling on the fertile land where the city of Boaco currently stands. Although few native descendants remain today, Boaco retains its Mayangna and Nahuatl name, meaning "land of enchanters."

The departments of Boaco and Chontales were fairly conservative during the Sandinista Revolution. Many of their residents were cattle-raising land owners who feared the movement's aims at land redistribution. Today, the population maintains a generally libertarian attitude, and continues, for the most part, to oppose the Sandinista party in national elections. Updated: May 05, 2009.

When to Go

In the summer, temperatures range from 27°C (80°F) to 30°C (86°F), but in the winter they drop to around 18°C (60°F). If you're interested in joining the regional holidays and celebrations, visit the city of Boaco on July 25th, when it celebrates its patron saint festivals with traditional dances passed down since the 17th century. You also may want to check out Juigalpa's patron saint festival in August, which draws crowds from around the country, and is the biggest party in the region. Updated: May 5, 2009.

Things to See and Do

Most travelers won't find a burning reason to come to this area. Still, if you're in the area there are a handful of activities available—namely some pretty good hiking. With its museum, zoo and scenic park overlooking the Amerrisque mountain range, Juigalpa offers the greatest number of tourist attractions. Updated: May 5, 2009.

Safety

Towns in the departments of Boaco and Chontales are rather small and tame. There are no major safety concerns, but travelers should always keep their wits about them. Updated: Aug 12, 2009.

Tours

There are no tour operators in the region, nor is there any reason for them to exist. INTUR has not taken much of an interest in the region, and has yet to really invest in its development. Updated: May 5, 2009.

Lodging

There are plenty of clean, humble sleeping accommodations in the region, and even one or two fancy places. Don't expect any hostels or any kind of gringo "scene," though. Much of the lodging consists merely of local family homes opened up to visitors passing through. Updated: May 05, 2009.

Restaurants

Tasty local fare is in abundance, with the occasional pizza or Chinese joint thrown into the mix. Most eateries in the region are small hole-in-the-wall joints, serving primarily local and traditional dishes. Updated: May 5, 2009.

Don't want to leave? Never going back? Review it at vivatravelguides.com

BOACO

385 m | **29,500**

Boaco is situated in the central part of the country, 88 kilometers (55 mi) from Managua. In earlier times, the pre-Hispanic Ulvas who lived in the region were famed for their ability to cure illnesses by means of sorcery, though these original inhabitants did not live in the area that is the current municipality.

During the period of colonization, when most of the indigenous population was converted by the Spanish to Catholicism, the town was attacked and destroyed by neighboring Indians in alliance with English settlers. Those who survived rebuilt their town in its present location. Today, remnants of the indigenous cultures can be seen in petroglyphs throughout the area.

Oddly enough, most of Boaco's modern infrastructure can be attributed to the works of a Polish priest. Father Nieborowski, born in 1866, came to Boaco at the age of 50 after having spent many years spreading the faith in Latin America. He directed the construction of the central park and established schools, a hospital, plumbing, hydroelectric power, and even the city's first cinema. He also created a brick factory in order to build La Parroquia de Santiago Apostol (p.270), which continues to be the city's most significant edifice, and the site of his grave.

After the tumultuous 1980s, Boaco began a period of rebuilding during which many decorative monuments were created to brighten the town. This includes the Cerro El Faro (p.270), from which the verdant countryside surrounding the town can be observed. Hot and humid during the day and cool at night, with unpredictable bouts of rain, this mountainous region is a scenic respite from the urban sprawl that is the capital. Temperatures can drop to a low of 18°C (64°F) during December, the coldest month, but in the summer they can climb as high as 40°C (104°F).

As the predominant industry is cattle farming, cowboys in hats and boots are a common sight, and rodeos are a major feature of festivals and patron saint celebrations. The continued growth of the dairy industry has furthermore led to the exportation of pasteurized cheeses to the United States. Fishing as well as agriculture also play a large role in the economy, particularly the growing of coffee, corn, rice and beans.

As Boaco is a fairly small town, food and lodging are somewhat limited. Most hotels are clean and budget friendly, and all the food is typical Nicaraguan. Updated: May 5, 2009.

Photo by Enrique Padilla

Getting To and Away From Boaco

Buses heading to Boaco leave from the Mayorea Bus Terminal in Managua every half hour and cost $1.50. The ride lasts two hours and arrives at the Boaco Terminal in the lower part of the city. From there it's a ten minute walk up and down several hills to the Central Park. Buses to Managua leave every half hour from 6 a.m. to 5 p.m. There are also regular buses to Santa Lucia, Rio Blanco and Camoapa. Updated: Apr 15, 2009.

Getting Around

Boaco is not a big town and most of the hotels, restaurants and attractions are located within a small radius. However, be prepared for steep hills in every direction. Not only will a stroll about town give you buns of steel, it will also provide breathtaking views at every turn. For the less athletic traveler, cabs are readily available. Additionally there is a bus that loops around Boaco and can be picked up at the Municipal Palace, as well as from any other point along the route if you happen to catch it. Updated: Apr 15, 2009.

Safety

Though travelers are few and far between, locals are friendly and the feeling in town is one of hospitality. At night, when the central park fills and teenage boys play late night soccer in the streets, local bars are generally safe to explore. Nonetheless, as is always the case, backpackers should be alert and mindful of their belongings. Updated: Apr 15, 2009.

Get travel advisories and tips at blog.vivatravelguides.com

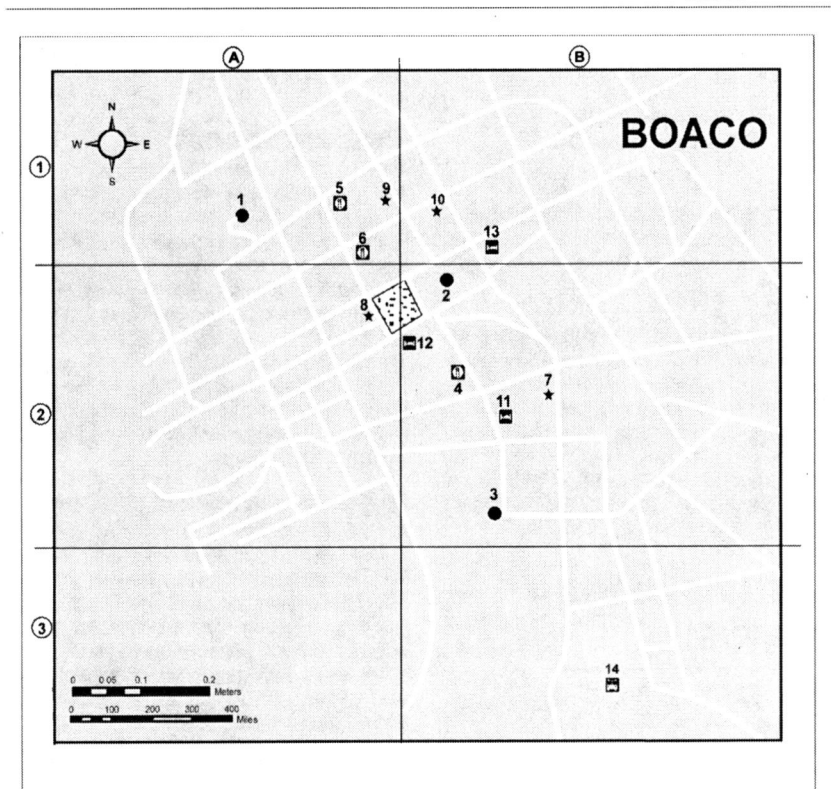

Activities ●
1 Cerro el Faro A1
2 La Parroquia de Santiago Apostol B2
3 Nuestra Señora del Perpetuo Socorro B2

Eating
4 Cafetin El Verdi B2
5 El Alpino A1
6 Marikimber A1

Services ★
7 Banpro B2
8 Cyber Space Café A2
9 Post Office A1
10 Western Union B1

Sleeping
11 Hotel Farolitos B2
12 Hotel Sobalvarro B2
13 Hotel Santiago B1

Transportation
14 Bus Terminal B3

Services

TOURIST INFORMATION
While there are several signs (which happen to point in different directions) that direct one towards the Intur Office, such a place does not actually exist. Updated: Apr 15, 2009.

MONEY
The only two banks in Boaco are located one and a half blocks away from one another, both along the route from the bus terminal to the Central Park. **Banpro** has an ATM. There is also a **Western Union** located one block north of the Santiago Apostol Church. Updated: Apr 15, 2009.

KEEPING IN TOUCH
Phones and Internet can both be found at **Cyber Olama**, conveniently located across the street from the west edge of the central park (one hour of extremely slow Internet costs $0.75). In the same area is **Cyber Space Café**, which charges $0.60

an hour for Internet, and $1.25 a minute for international phone calls. The **post office** is located one and a half blocks north of La Parroquia de Santiago Apostol. Updated: Apr 15, 2009.

LAUNDRY

There is no place to have your laundry done in Boaco, so be prepared to wash your unmentionables in a hotel sink. Updated: Apr 15, 2009.

HEALTH

Boaco is home to a newly built hospital with modern facilities. The **Regional Hospital Padre Jose Nieboroski** is located on the north edge of town and is best reached via taxi. For non-emergency situations, there is a free health center located across the street from the western edge of the park, as well as a clinic two and a half blocks south. Updated: Apr 15, 2009.

SAN JOSE DE LOS REMATES

658 m   5,000

This tiny cowboy town offers a surprising amount of activities for wilderness buffs and those interested in community development. While no traditional tourist infrastructure is in place here, the mayor's office has put together packages that include homestays, meals and guided tours of the natural surroundings. Tours include hikes to waterfalls, lookout points and canyons, petroglyph-spotting along the Malacatoya River, dips in local swimming holes, and even a visit to an organic coffee farm or local school. San Jose de los Remates also offers access to the **Reserva Natural Cerro Cumaica-Cerro Alegre**. Stay here on March 19th and whoop it up at rodeos and parades celebrating the patron Saint San Jose.

It is important to stress that this is not a town you can just show up at, ready to drop your backpack at any hostel and head for the hills. San Jose de los Remates does not have any hotels or restaurants, so all overnight visits have to be coordinated through the mayor's office. Contact **Jorge Isaacs** to arrange your stay, Tel: 505-2-542-2359, E-mail: geosanjose@yahoo.com / geosanjose@hotmail.com.

To get to San Jose del los Remates from Managua's Mayoreo terminal, there is one bus every day at 12:30 p.m. From San Jose de los Remates, one bus leaves for Boaco at 2:15 p.m. daily (1.5 hrs). Updated: Apr 28, 2009.

Things to See and Do

Travelers who come to Boaco generally seek a friendly, safe and quiet place to relax. Other than its two churches and viewing tower, there are little to no tourist attractions to speak of. However, travelers will appreciate the friendly, open nature of the locals, as well as the stunning landscapes that surround the town. Although this mountainous region seems perfect for hiking, as of yet there are no established tour guides in town. Speak to Carlos, owner of the Hotel Santiago, as he may have time to take you to the surrounding sites. Updated: Apr 15, 2009.

La Parroquia de Santiago Apostol

This cheerful, yellow church sits atop the upper part of the city and is the focal point of the town square, where people congregate at all hours to sit at the open air café and shoot the breeze. Inside, the church is decorated with paintings depicting the stations of the cross, and bright statues of Jesus, the Virgin and various saints. This includes the ubiquitous, bespectacled Maria Romero, a local nun known for her work with children, who died in 1977 and was canonized in 2002. Across the street from the central park. Updated: Apr 15, 2009.

Parroquia de Nuestra Senora del Perpetuo Socorro

Although smaller and more run down than Santiago Apostol, Nuestra Senora still retains a lot of character. The Eastern Orthodox style exterior is completely incongruous with its surroundings and can be attributed to the city's Polish founder, Father Nieborowski. The robin's egg blue painted chapel (open every day) is connected to a larger sanctuary (open only on Saturday night and Sunday) by an archway from which the curious visitor can easily peek into the priest's living room if so inclined. Alongside the north edge of the cemetery. Updated: Apr 15, 2009.

Cerro El Faro

For a panoramic view of Boaco and the Rio Mayales valley, climb the Cerro El Faro. This tower was constructed as part of Boaco's efforts to revamp the city following the destruction of the 1980s. Protruding above the city, the Cerro El Faro is meant to be a symbol of hope and encouragement. Surrounded by a beautifully landscaped garden, it is not only a great place to take in the town and its stunning surroundings, but is also a hotspot for local couples looking for a little alone time. Don't count on any star-gazing though; the gates close at 6 p.m. Updated: Apr 15, 2009.

Aguas Claras Hot Springs

(ENTRY: Children: $0.70; Adults: $1.25) If you start to miss hot water while in the Boaco area, you might want to check out the Aguas Claras hot springs, located 7 kilometers (4 miles) west of town. Budget travelers will want to get there early to avoid having to shell out for the (relatively) expensive hotel on the premises ($29 a night). These pools are filled with naturally heated bath-tub temperature water, though they are not exceptionally clean.

To get to Aguas Claras directly from Managua, take any east-bound bus from the Mayoreo terminal, but tell the driver to let you off at the springs. From Boaco, take a $4 cab ride. Tel: 505-2-244-2916, URL: www.termalesaguasclaras.com. Updated: Jun 3, 2009.

Hiking to La Cebadilla

If you're itching to strap on those hiking boots while in Boaco, head to La Cebadilla, from which there is a nice view of Boaco's rolling hills. Those with an interest in religion will also appreciate the fact that a local farmer is said to have seen visions of the Virgin Mary at Cebadilla's peak. Ruins of a shrine built by locals can still be spotted here. The six hour hike to and from La Cebadilla starts in Asedades, an impoverished community 1.6 kilometers (1 mi) east of Empalme Boaco, located 12 kilometers (8 miles) from town (take a cab). Arrange for a guide in Asedades, and be sure to bring food and water for yourself as well as the guide. To get to Asedades, take the dirt path on the south side of the highway next to Empalme Boaco. Updated: Apr 15, 2009.

Restaurants

While Boaco isn't home to exotic cuisine, it is possible to eat well on a budget here (as long as you like gallo pinto and meat). Although there are a handful of nicer eateries, small open air establishments generally dominate. You also won't want to miss the mariachis who frequent the restaurants and pubs in the evenings. Updated: Apr 15, 2009.

Cafetin el Verdi

With good food and friendly service, this hole-in-the-wall is a great stop for the budget traveler in need of a hot meal. The food is typical Nicaraguan fare—chicken, beef stew, plantains and of course, gallo pinto. The kitchen is right in the back, so you can watch all the cooking action take place, and the seating opens out to the street, providing a good view of passersby. One block south of the central park. Updated: Apr 15, 2009.

Marikimber

(PIZZAS: $5.75 – 7) If you're tired of gallo pinto and have a hankering for some pizza, head to Marikimber, where your pie comes with a side of English chit chat with the Pennsylvania-born owner, Shad, an ex-cop. This hangout, only one year old, is popular with locals and peace-corps volunteers alike. It is one block north of the central park, though be warned that there is no sign outside. If you can't find it just ask anyone where the "gringo pizza" is. Pasta, burgers and sandwiches are also offered. Pizza prices depend on toppings and size. One block northwest of the central park. Updated: Apr 15, 2009.

El Alpino

Perhaps Boaco's fanciest place to have a bite, El Alpino features steaks, seafood, chicken, and hamburgers, served in a large, spotless dining room (with tablecloths!). If you're looking for a reason to get dressed up while on the road, this is it. Have a steak with some wine and then head to the surrounding bars for a weekend night out. Two blocks northwest of the central park. Updated: Apr 15, 2009.

Lodging

Boaco offers few lodging options, all of which are are budget friendly, simple, and clean, though hot water is out of the question. Ask to see the bathrooms and check out the water situation before you commit to anything. As Boaco is a relatively small place and completely traversable on foot, there is no need to worry that your hotel is out of the way. All are located near and around the central park. Updated: Apr 15, 2009.

Hotel Santiago

(ROOMS: $10) The best reason to choose this clean, inexpensive hostel is its owner, Carlos Obando, a friendly English speaker who, if he has time off from his cattle ranch, will be happy to take you on hiking excursions in the outlying areas of town. He also has a washing machine, which he might let you use if you ask nicely. The toilets and showers are reliable, though, as is the case in most parts of town, there is no hot water. Two blocks northeast of the central park. Tel: 505-8-829-0671. Updated: Apr 15, 2009.

Hotel Sobalvarro

(ROOMS: $10 – 17.50) Flanking the central park's south side, Hotel Sobalvarro is a basic, clean, and convenient option for the adventurous ones who actually stay in Boaco long enough to sleep. Rooms congregate around a sunny courtyard, and the back patio has a stunning view of the surrounding city. Bathrooms only have running water in the evenings; in the morning you'll have to make do with a bucket shower. Sobalvarro's best feature might be its adjoining ice cream shop, where on a breezy evening you can indulge in a scoop and some people-watching from the outdoor patio. Hamburgers and hotdogs are also on the menu. South of the central park. Tel: 505-2-542-2515, E-mail: HotelSobalvarro@yahoo.com. Updated: Apr 15, 2009.

Hotel Farolitos

(ROOMS: $10 and up) For slightly more upscale lodgings in Boaco, try the Hotel Farolitos, located halfway up the hill between the central park up the Nuestra Senora church. Rooms here are a bit pricier than the other lodging options, but include TVs, fans, and private bathrooms (with real doors and tiled floors). There is a clean, pleasant balcony from which to watch the goings-on below. Entrance to the hotel is best attempted through the adjacent clothing and shoe store. Two blocks south of the central park. Tel: 505-2-542-1938. Updated: Apr 15, 2009.

SANTA LUCIA

62 m   1,869

Santa Lucia was established in 1904 to centralize scattered farming communities in the region north of Boaco. Here, travelers will delight in the petroglyphs that can be found at **Piedra de Sapo**, as well as the view from the volcanic rim. Military buffs will not want to miss **Cueva Santo Domingo**, where discarded Sandinista military equipment can be found. Be aware that this steep hike is not for the faint of heart. Like San Jose de los Remantes, Santa Lucia does not have any hotels, so contact the **mayor** to arrange your stay. Tel: 505-2-273-3600, E-mail: santaluciaalcaldia@yahoo.com). Buses leave regularly from the Boaco bus station in the market. Updated: Apr 15, 2009.

CAMOAPA

551 m   36,500

Founded August 23, 1858, this cowboy town—the second largest in the region after Boaco—is best known for its crafts made from *pita*, a leafy plant originating in Mexico. In Nicaragua it is mostly grown in the Masigue area north of Camoapa. Descendents of the indigenous community once ruled by the cacique, Taisiwa, continue to pass down artisan skills necessary to produce pita hats, ornaments and other items that make great souvenirs. Some of these are so finely crafted that they can take up to three months to manufacture.

Crafts can be found at **Artesanias La Palmate** (Tel: 505-2-549-2338), half a block east of the mayor's office. Camoapa is also a good place to pick up cowboy accessories. Leather goods are an easily found commodity; some stores where they can be purchased include **Taller Hermanos Flores** (Tel: 625-2638) and **Casa de las Monturas** (549 2381). For boots, head to **Taller Salazar** (549 2043). In addition to pita crafts and leather goods, Camoapa also produces an abundance of dairy products, much like the rest of the region.

If you're planning to sleep in Camoapa, **Hotel Las Estrellas** (Tel: 549 2240), located seven blocks east of the church's north side, features an on-site restaurant; adventurous eaters will want to try the house specialty, bull testicle soup. A double without air-conditioning goes for about $10, and with is $13. Smaller but more conveniently located is **Hotel Taisiwa** (Tel: 849 2304). Rooms are about $5 per person and include a private bath. A solid restaurant option is **El Bosquecito**, which offers soups, meat and seafood. If you prefer your food with a view, try **La Terraza** (Tel: 424 8605), located 4 and a half blocks from the Alcaldia Municipal; it has a terrace with a panoramic view of the city.

Camoapa also functions as a base from which plucky travelers can go on various hikes in the region, including to Quizaltepe, Mombacho and Pena La Jarquina.

Buses heading to Camoapa depart from the Mayoreo bus terminal in Managua Monday through Saturday, early morning to early afternoon. Buses to Managua leave all day until 5 p.m. Updated: Apr 15, 2009.

Get travel advisories and tips at blog.vivatravelguides.com

COMALAPA

277 m | **11,800**

Comalapa sits at the mouth of the Cuisala river, borders Lake Cocibolca, and is home to Piragua Hill, a forest reserve, making it a tranquil place to take in the scenery. Patron Saint celebrations take place February 2nd, and honor the Virgin of Candelaria. The feast of the apostle Saint Bartholomew is celebrated in August.

As one of the oldest municipalities in Chontales, much of Comalapa's atmospheric colonial architecture is intact, making it a good place to get a sense of Chontales's history. The construction of its main church—which has since been declared a national monument—was completed in 1816.

The only way to get to Comalapa is by taking the bus that leaves Camoapa at 6:30 a.m. and returns to Camoapa at 4 p.m. Located 129 kilometers (80 mi) from Managua and 30 kilometers (19 mi) from Juigalpa, and 20 kilometers (12 mi) from Camoapa. Updated: Apr 15, 2009.

Hiking Quizaltepe

At 300 meters (984 ft) high, this monolith (whose name in Nahautl means "place of the grinding stone") is visible from all over the Boaco province. The volcanic material from which the peak is comprised was used by indigenous peoples for manufacturing tools to grind corn. Hikers will want to be in good shape to attempt this climb, which can last up to six hours and is very steep. At the top your efforts will be rewarded with a view of the Pacific ocean. The only way to ascend is from the rock's north face, as the other sides are not traversable. The main point of access is the *Empalme de Camoapa* (also called San Francisco), a stop on the highway. A guide for this climb is imperative, and you may be able to arrange for one at Hotel Las Estrellas in Camoapa, or in Barrio Cebollin, a community slightly west of the highway. Updated: Apr 15, 2009.

Hiking Mombacho

For an easier day hike outside of Camoapa, consider heading to Mombacho, a forested peak offering beautiful views of the surrounding lowlands. With ideal soil for growing coffee, this mountain is the site of several plantations that can be seen along the hike. The point of entry is located a long the Salida de Sangre de Cristo. Starting at the ENITEL in Camoapa center, head six blocks west until you hit the school; from there make a right and head north until you arrive at the the Salida de Sangre de Cristo, which can be recognized by the church of the same name. The hike lasts three to four hours, depending on your pace. Updated: Apr 15, 2009.

JUIGALPA

122 m | **53,890**

Juigalpa was believed to have been originally inhabited by the Chontal people who, of the area's natives, were some of the most resistant to Spanish invaders. The modern city was founded in 1668 as a stopover for travelers headed from Granada to the mines of La Libertad (p.278) and Santo Domingo (p.278). It later grew, eventually becoming the department capital in 1877.

As the cowboy boots and ten gallon hats might suggest, Juigalpa's modern day economic engine is cattle ranching. Ninety-six million liters of milk and 100,000 cows are slaughtered there each year, providing 90 percent of Nicaragua's beef. An enthusiasm for rodeos and bullfights is deeply embedded in the culture and every year about five people die in bullfight related injuries. Rodeos occur about once a month at Plaza Taurina, which interestingly, was built with the financial support of the Taiwanese government.

Visitors to Juigalpa can peruse the **Museo Arqueológico Gregorio Aguilar Barea (p.275)**, which houses an impressive collection of pre-Columbian artifacts, as well as an assortment of random macabre objects. **Zoologico Thomas Belt (p.276)** displays dozens of wild animals in tiny, bare cages. If you consider your extremities dear, don't put your fingers through the bars. The verdant **Parque Palo Solo (p.276)** offers a great view of the surrounding Amerrisque Mountains and is a nice place to grab a beer and a bite in the evenings.

Juigalpa has one upscale hotel, and most others are clean, basic and cheap. And it's easy to keep your stomach full of inexpensive gallo pinto and meat. Updated: May 6, 2009.

Juigalpa

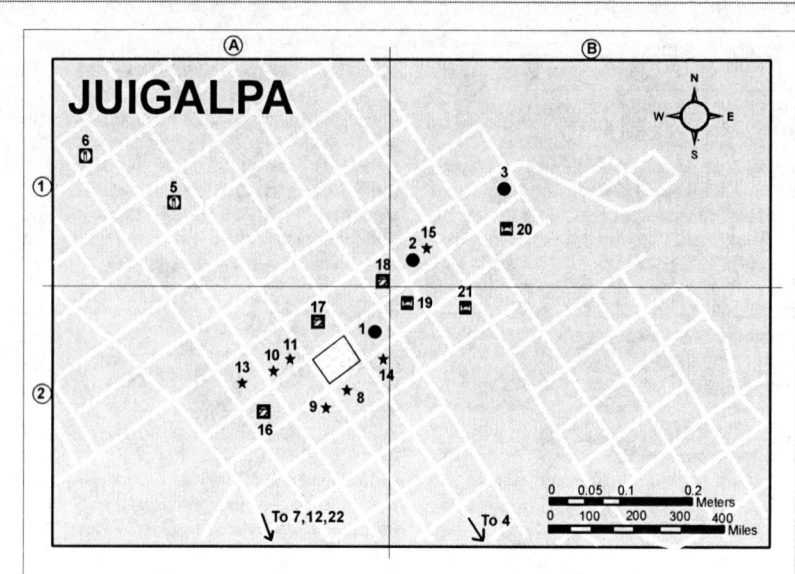

Activities ●

1 Catedral Nuestra Señora de la Asunción C3
2 Museo Arqueológico Gregorio Aguilar Barea D2
3 Parque Palo Solo E4

Eating

4 Zoológico Thomas Belt
5 Carne Asada Raquel A1
6 La Cazuelita C2

Nightlife

7 La Quinta C4

Services ★

8 Banpro C3
9 BDF C3
10 Cyber Siquiera C2
11 Farmacia La Salud C3
12 Hospital Asunción D4
13 Lab Lafayette and Salazar C3
14 Post Office C3
15 Universo Cyber D2

Shopping

16 Supermercado San Antonio C3
17 Kodak Express C2
18 Tienda Cowboy D2

Sleeping

19 Hospedaje Nuevo Milenio and Hotel El Regreso D2
20 Hotel Casa Country D2
21 Hotel Los Arcangeles D3

Transportation

22 Bus Terminal B3

When to Go

Juigalpa is warm and dry during the summer months of November – May, but wet during the winter months from June – October. The most exciting time to visit is during the *Fiestas Patronales*, which start on August 10th and continue for two weeks. Activities include parades, bullfights, rodeos, musicians, raffles and a beauty contest, all of which draw visitors from all over Nicaragua and the world. Additionally, dancers from Bluefields come in to perform the *Palo de Mayo*, also known as "the dirty dance," and who would want to miss that? Updated: Apr 15, 2009.

Getting To and Away From Juigalpa

From Managua's Mayoreo terminal the ride to Juigalpa is two and a half hours, and costs

$2.50 for the nice bus and $2 for the regular old converted school bus. Juigalpa's bus terminal is 300 meters south of the hospital. Updated: Jan 21, 2010.

Getting Around

Juigalpa is wholly manageable on foot. Nonetheless, cab rides are recommended at night, especially if you dance the night away at **La Quinta**, a discoteque located off the main highway and rather far from the main square. This ride will cost you $0.50. Updated: Apr 15, 2009.

Services

TOURIST INFORMATION

There is a tourism office in Juigalpa, but the pamphlets offered are outdated and the people working there are of little help. Updated: Apr 15, 2009.

BANKS

Money can be exchanged at either **Banpro** (which also has an ATM) or **BDF**, located across the street from one another on the south corner of the central park. Updated: Apr 15, 2009.

KEEPING IN TOUCH

The **post office** is located around the corner from the church. At $0.60 for an hour of Internet, **Universo Cyber** is a good deal. There you can also purchase various electronics including iPod shuffles and USB sticks. A slightly cheaper Internet option is **Cyber Siquiera**, which charges $0.50 an hour for Internet, and allows patrons to make international calls for a mere $0.05 a minute. It also has air conditioning. Updated: Apr 15, 2009.

HEALTH

Hospital Azunción can be found on the main highway, across the street from La Quinta Hotel and Discoteca. More conveniently located (two blocks west of the park) and perhaps better suited for travelers is **Lab Lafayette and Salazar**, a private clinic (Tel: 812-0932). There are many pharmacies around town, but one option is **Farmacia La Salud** (Tel: 812-2292) on the northwest corner of the central park. Updated: Apr 15, 2009.

LAUNDRY

There are no laundromats in Juigalpa, but you might be able to arrange some washing at your hotel. Otherwise, sink washing is your only option. Updated: Apr 15, 2009.

SHOPPING

Groceries and toiletries can be bought at **Supermercado San Antonio**, one block southwest of the park. Fresh produce, however, is better bought on the street. For minor camera repairs, batteries, film, and photo development, head to the **Kodak Express**, on the north corner of the park. Digital photos can be printed for $0.85 each. Updated: Apr 15, 2009.

Tienda Cowboy

Your one-stop shop for western apparel in Juigalpa, Tienda Cowboy has a large array of cowboy boots, hats, belt buckles, and shirts, all perfect for working on the ranch—or showing off to your friends when you get home. Tienda cowboy even sells soy products and assorted spices; reportedly, there is a demand for these items by travelers passing through. The cheapest cowboy boots here go for $100. North of the cathedral. Tel: 505-512-2314. Updated: May 12, 2009.

Things to See and Do

Juigalpa has a few traditional attractions that make it worth kicking around town for a day or two. The Museo Arqueológico and Zoológico are both noteworthy in their oddity, and both highlight the differences between Nicaraguan and American attitudes towards these type of institutions. Juigalpa also has two parks, one of which offers great views of the Amerrisque Mountains and the Mayales River. The other, the central park, is home to a statue of a shoe-shine boy honoring the late mayor Isaac Deleo, who shined shoes in his youth. A plaque below it reads, "work dignifies man." Directly across the street is Catedral Nuestra Señora de la Asunción, a spare, gymnasium-like church that is worth a peek. There is a rodeo that takes place once a month in Juigalpa, though the exact schedule changes at the whim of the city council. Updated: Apr 15, 2009.

Museo Arqueológico Gregorio Aguilar Barea

Part portrait gallery, part museum (and part old fashioned freak show), this eclectic assemblage of artifacts is the one place in town where Juigalpa's history is on display. Half the museum consists of beautiful pre-Columbian ceramics, most notable of which are the adorable shoe-shaped funerary vessels that bring Dutch clogs to mind. Spanish speakers will benefit from the poster-boards discussing the disputed origins of the Central Nicaraguan population and the Spanish explorers who later came and conquered the region.

For the macabre minded visitor there is a collection of taxidermied animals, many of whom show genetic deformities such as two heads. Most stomach-turning, perhaps, is the preserved body of a cyclops baby born to local parents in the 1980s. Additionally, the museum displays portraits of Juigalpa's citizens and manufactured objects from the 19th and early 20th century, including cash registers, typewriters and various cowboy paraphernalia. Two blocks northeast and half a block northwest of the central park. Open Monday – Friday, 9 a.m. – 12 p.m., 2 p.m. – 5 p.m. Tel: (505) 512-0784. Updated: Apr 15, 2009.

Parque Palo Solo
This clean and airy park is a great place to catch a view of Juigalpa's stunning surroundings. Around the central monument (an oversized corn-on-the-cob) groups of teenagers and couples, and the occasional guitar-playing cowboy can be observed. There is also an on-site restaurant and bar serving standard fare at reasonable prices. The park closes around 10 p.m. Updated: Apr 15, 2009.

Jardin Zoológico Thomas Belt
The largest of only two zoos in Nicaragua, Thomas Belt will come as a shock to most western travelers. Lions, jaguars and other large animals dwell lethargically in spare, cement-floored, iron-barred enclosures. The sign that warns that the zoo is not responsible for accidents that may happen to unsupervised children is necessary as most of the animals can easily stick their heads, paws and other extremities from their cages. The gorilla has been known to throw feces at camera-wielding tourists. Consider yourself warned. Open daily 8 a.m. – 5:30 p.m. It's a seven block walk from the central park to the zoo, heading southeast. Tel: 512-086. Updated: Apr 15, 2009.

Balneario Las Penitas
Las Penitas is known locally as the *balneario* (spa), but don't expect a salt scrub or massage—it's really more of a recreational pool area. Overlooking the Rio Mayales, Penitas features two pools, a restaurant and a dance floor. A local beer goes for $0.80, and meals average at $3.50. Call ahead, as it occasionally closes for private functions. To get there, hail down a Managua-bound bus on the side of the highway and ask the driver to drop you off at the balneario. While the ride is only five minutes and will set you back fifty cents, the walk along the un-shaded, winding highway is not recommended. Tel: 505-512-1292. Updated: Jun 3, 2009.

Rodeo at Plaza Taurina Alberto Homberto e Isabel Mongrio
Thanks in part to a generous donation by the government of Taiwan, the town boasts an impressive rodeo ring where the monthly rodeo is held, along with a variety of contests amid the shouts and cheers of passionate fans. Although the festivities officially begin at 6 p.m., the action doesn't start until after 7 p.m., and most people arrive fashionably dressed and fashionably late. If you do get there "on time" grab a beer and listen to the live orchestra play patriotic tunes. Once the emcee announces the national anthem, things really get rolling, with bull-riding, children racing goats and timed calf roping. Events vary each month. Take a taxi five minutes out of town; this should cost under $1. Tell the driver you're going to the rodeo. Updated: Apr 15, 2009.

Lodging
Juigalpa has many options for the budget traveler that all offer basically the same things: clean, simple rooms with TVs and, for an extra fee, air conditioners. There are also mid-range and more upscale hotels in town which offer better furnished rooms and more amenities. You don't have to go too far to find lodgings near the Central Park and Park Palo Solo, and although there are a few hostels down by the highway, they are not recommended. Updated: Apr 15, 2009.

Hotel El Regreso and Hospedaje Nuevo Milenio
(ROOMS: $12 – 12.50) The small, colorful rooms wrapping around the bright second-floor terrace at El Regreso will do the trick for most budget travelers. Rooms have TVs, fans and air conditioners, though use of the AC will cost you extra. The owners, Ronaldo and Gladys, speak English, having lived in Miami for many years. Next door is the similarly priced Hospedaje Nuevo Milenio, which offers the same amenities, but is slightly less pleasing to the eye. Both are located a block and a half northeast from the park, and one block from the museum. Tel: Hotel El Regreso: 512-2068; Hospedaje Nuevo Milenio: 512-0646. Updated: Apr 15, 2009.

Hotel Casa Country

(ROOMS: $18 – 20) Conveniently located across from Parque Palo Solo, Hotel Casa Country is a decent mid-range option for travelers looking for slightly nicer digs. Rooms have actual furniture, and the private bathrooms come with doors, a rarity in these parts. Although the attractive blue exterior indicates a quaint upscale hotel, Hotel Casa Country doesn't actually offer more amenities than its budget counterparts. Across from the southern edge of Parque Palo Solo. Tel: 505-512-2546. Updated: Apr 15, 2009.

Hotel Los Arcangeles

(ROOMS: $25 – 40) A swanky option east of the cathedral, Hotel Los Arcangeles may be the closest thing to an American-style hotel in Juigalpa. Rooms are spacious, with well-crafted wooden furniture, quilts, flat-screen TVs, air conditioning, WiFi, and spotless private bathrooms. There is also a common lounge area, with patio furniture, live parrots, and wooden chess boards. Several computers are also available for guest use. Double rooms cost $40 a night (breakfast included), but those watching their wallet can opt for the $25 room with shared bathroom, and no breakfast. Credit cards are accepted. Tel: 505-512 0847, E-mail: Losarcangeles@cablenet.com.ni, URL: www.hotellosarcangeles.com. Updated: Apr 15, 2009.

Restaurants

Juigalpa is not a tourist town, and as such, the restaurants don't cater to foreigners. Most establishments are set up in the front of people's homes and all generally offer the same food. Pizza may be the most international dish available. Like elsewhere in Nicaragua, *fritangas* are readily available on many street corners (especially in the evenings) and Eskimo ice cream shops abound. Updated: Apr 15, 2009.

Reposteria Doris

(ENTREES: $0.80 and up) For a sweet breakfast treat, hit up the Reposteria Doris, sandwiched between the Archeology museum and the Universo Cyber Internet café. The restaurant offers muffins and colorfully frosted cakes, as well as sweet or savory pastries. Doris, the owner, also has rooms available in the back comparable to the nearby hotel El Regreso, but prefers to house women travelers, as she lives alone. A double room with shared bath costs $10. Next to Museo Arqueológico Gregorio Aguilar Barea. Tel: 505-512-1004. Updated: Apr 15, 2009.

Carne Asada Raquel

(ENTREES: $1.50 and up) Carne Asada Raquel offers traditional Nicaraguan food at traditional Nicaraguan prices. While the menu is standard, the food is particularly flavorful here. The proprietess stands in the corner ladling out gallo pinto, chicken, plantain chips and cabbage salad, which can either be taken to go in plastic bags, or eaten on-site. For your daily dose of culture, there's a TV airing telenovelas. There is no sign outside, but Carne Asada Raquel can be found four and a half blocks northwest of the park. Updated: Apr 15, 2009.

La Casa de Queso

(BURGER: $4, CHINESE FOOD: $5) Casa de Queso is the only establishment in Juigalpa open round the clock, and as the name might suggest, it sells a variety of cheeses. If you're hankering for a late night bite, this is the place to get it, but during the day there are plenty of tastier and cheaper options to choose from. The menu includes pizza, wings and "Chinese food," which has an instant-soup like quality. This place is popular with locals, and hosts karaoke on Thursday, Friday and Saturday nights. Across from the cathedral. Tel: 505-512-0968, E-mail: Res7_24@yahoo.es. Updated: Apr 15, 2009.

La Cazuelita

(ENTREES: $7.59 – 20) While the food at La Cazuelita is standard and more expensive than at other establishments in the city, there are two main reasons to eat here: the air conditioning, and the English menu—perhaps the only one you'll find in Juigalpa. There are several salads offered, but vegetarians should not get too excited; fried onion rings are considered a salad. The dining area and bathrooms at this reported Peace Corps hangout are spotless, and credit cards are accepted. Seven blocks north and one west of the central park. Tel: 505-512-1986. Updated: Apr 15, 2009.

PUERTO DIAZ

🅰 31 m   👤 3,590

Once one of the most important ports in Nicaragua, Puerto Diaz, which sits on Lake Cocibolca, was the base from which gold ingots, honey, cocoa, corn and beans were shipped. Today, most locals support themselves by fishing, and seafood lovers will happily note that fresh fish dishes are in abundance. The only place to sleep in town is a single bare room for $12 found at **Mirador Vista Linda**, which has recreational pools (505-2-512-2699). During the rainy season the 28 kilmoeter (17 mi) road from Juigalpa to Puerto Diaz deteriorates so trips during this time are not recommended. Buses leave Juigalpa at 4:30 a.m., 5 a.m., 7 a.m., 3 p.m. and 4:30 p.m.

On the road between Juigalpa and Puerto Diaz there are a few farms that offer agrotourism, particularly relating to cattle-raising. At the Santa Marta farm, owned by the Meneses family, travelers can milk cows and learn how cow insemination and cattle-breeding works. This can also be combined with a visit to the Punta Mayales Biological Reserve, home to more than 200 species of migrant birds. Contact Rene or Minerva Meneses at 505-2-512-2322. At Hato Grande Farm, 8 kilometers (5 mi) from Juigalpa, cow milking and breeding tours are also available. Accommodations can be found at their turn-of-the-century ranch house. Updated: Apr 28, 2009.

LA LIBERTAD

446 m   2,191

Bordering the Amerrisque mountain chain, La Libertad is located 174 kilometers (108 mi) from Managua and 34 kilometers (21 mi) from Juigalpa. Spaniards and Mestizos originally came to La Libertad during the eighteenth and early nineteenth centuries to raise cattle and convert the natives, but quickly changed their game plan when they discovered the natives had gold. The birthplace of President Daniel Ortega and Archbishop Miguel Obando y Bravo, La Liberatad is worth a peek to get a sense of the gold rush era. There are also Patron Saint celebrations May 9 – 12 in honor of La Virgen de la Luz. Unfortunately, as of yet there are no hotels in town.

SANTO DOMINGO

867 m   7,304

Originally a miner's camp called *El Mineral de Santo Domingo*, Santo Domingo was first settled in the 19th century by indigenous miners from Las Segovias in the north. There is still an active mine here, which, second to cattle raising, is the largest source of employment in town. This mine, one kilometer outside of Santo Domingo, uses machinery from the early twentieth century, which can be heard all over town. Ask at the mayor's office about arranging a tour of the mine.

While at the mayor's, look into tours of **La Pena Blanca**, a traversable peak in the Santo Domingo Valley. This two hour trek leads to a view of Lake Nicaragua, and on a clear day, the Pacific Ocean. The one hotel in Santo Domingo is **Bar Hotelito San Jose**, which offers basic rooms and an on-site restaurant. Rooms without bath go for $4 per person per night (505-2-855-6217). The Patron Saint celebrations here take place on the third of May, and include bullfights and parties.

Buses leave for Juigalpa every hour, and the ride is two and a half hours long. Updated: May 5, 2009.

CUAPA

293 m   1,100

The cowboy town of Cuapa is located 152 kilometers (94 mi) from Managua and 25 kilometers (16 mi) from Juigalpa, at the foot of stunning Amerrisque Mountain Range.

While the Contra War wreaked havoc on cities and villages throughout Nicaragua, Cuapa was the site of a particularly bloody skirmish. In 1985, the execution of 12 Sandinista activists by contra forces led to a retaliation that ended in the deaths of nearly 40 Sandinista soldiers. However, the town is perhaps better known for a series of Virgin Mary sightings. In the early 1980s Bernardo Martinez, a local farmer, claimed to have seen her likeness on several occasions, and as such a yearly pilgrimage to the site occurs on May 8th. The shrine dedicated to the virgin is located 2 kilometers (1.5 mi) from town.

You can hike the seventy-five meter (246 ft) high Cuapa Monolith, a giant granite outcropping. Any young local might be happy to accompany you and show you the way up. The steep hike takes around two and half hours, depending on the individual's speed. Beware, however, the rock is said to be inhabited by ghosts.

Grub and a place to crash can be found at **Restaurante Hospedaje la Maravilla**. Rooms cost $4 per person per night. Updated: Apr 28, 2009.

Getting To and Away From Cuapa

Buses leave Juigalpa for Cuapa several times a day, starting early in the morning until the late afternoon. From 6 a.m. to 4:30 p.m. buses leave regularly from Cuapa's town center and head towards Juigalpa. Updated: Apr 28, 2009.

NUEVA GUINEA

184 m 53,000

Nueva Guinea was created in the 1960s as part of a federal homesteading initiative backed by the American government. During the next decade it was used as a haven for those affected by earthquakes and volcanic eruptions. These new settlers, not having the information or resources to do otherwise, turned what was a rich tropical rainforest into an infertile wasteland. Since then there have been some improvements to the region, including the establishment of **La Esperanzita**, a teaching farm intended to show locals how to better tend the land.

In recent years it has also begun offering packaged agro-tours. Visitors to La Esperanzita can learn to make tortillas, see an underground tank used to convert cow manure into natural fuel, or hike in the nearby **Indo-Maiz Biological Reserve** (the MARENA in Nueva Guinea can also arrange guides). Accommodations are available for overnight stays. Tel: 505-2-575-0174 / 505-2-843-5010, E-mail: Esperanzita84@yahoo.com.

Thirteen kilometers (8 mi) outside of town you can find the **Auxilio Mundial Farm** (Tel: 505-2-275-0066 / 505-2-275-3430), which cultivates tens of thousands of plant species from around the world. These are being investigated to see how well they grow in different climates and conditions. Both farms can be reached by taxi.

There are a couple of hotels in Nueva Guinea to choose from, the swankiest being **Hotel Nueva Guinea**. It offers amenities such as cable TV and an on-site restaurant. A double with air conditioning goes for $40 (Tel: 505-2-575-0090). A more wallet friendly option is **Hospedaje Central**, where a room with shared bath costs $2 per person per night (Tel: 505-2-620-8949).

New Guinea features two pizza joints, **El Penon** and **Pizza Hot**. For a nicer meal head to **Llamas Del Bosque**, where you can also boogie down with the locals in the evenings.
NOTE: When in the Nueva Guinea area it's best to take a poncho, as this is one of the wettest areas in Nicaragua. Updated: Apr 28, 2009.

Getting To and Away From Nueva Guinea

Buses to Juigalpa depart hourly and the ride is four hours. The 293 kilometer (182 mi) ride to Managua is roughly seven hours, and buses leave every two hours. Updated: Apr 28, 2009.

!!!!!

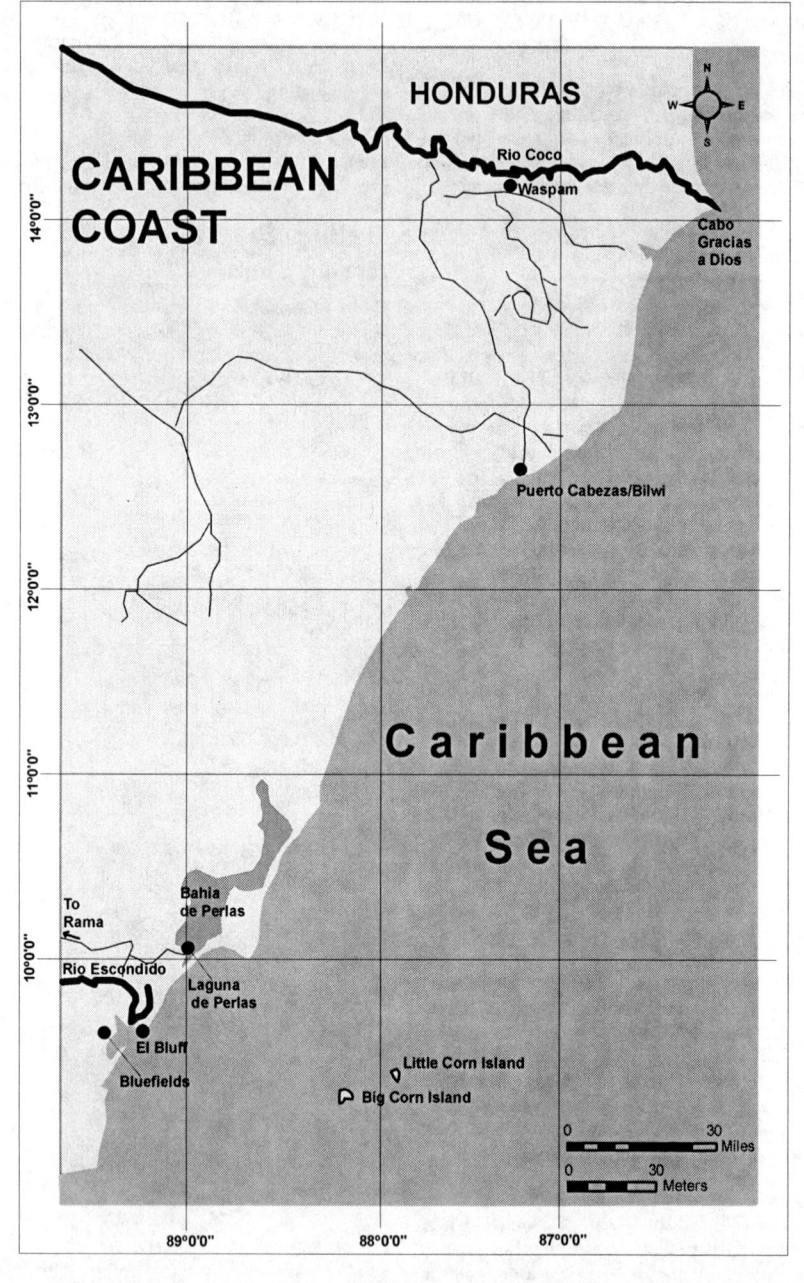

Caribbean Coast and the Islands

The Caribbean Coast of Nicaragua, also known as the *Moskito Coast* (after the Indian tribe that inhabits most of the land), is the most geographically and ethnically diverse region of Nicaragua. Uninhabited jungles, coastal rainforests and mangrove swamps

Caribbean Coast and the Islands

occupy the majority of the region, which is comprised of the South Autonomous Atlantic Region (RAAS) and the North Autonomous Atlantic region (RAAN), and occupies over 50 percent of the national territory. The coast is also the site of several wildlife reserves, such as the Wawa Sham, Indio Maize and Yolanda reserves in the South, and the Bosawas Reserve and the Cerro Cola Blanca Nature Reserve in the North.

Over 300,000 residents call the coast home, with the two biggest cities being Puerto de Cabezas in the northern region, and Bluefields in the south (both with around 35,000 people). The area itself is not only extremely different from the rest of the country, but is internally diverse as well. The northern region is almost entirely inhabited by Moskito Indians, who also speak their own language. In the south, English Creole and Caribbean cultures dominate, though there are still many Spanish-speaking Nicaraguans, as well as African tribes with their own unique languages.

The most popular destinations for tourists on the Caribbean Coast are the Corn Islands (Big Corn Island and Little Corn Island), which are two tropical islands with coral reefs, clear water and palm trees, located about 80.5 kilometers (50 mi) east of the coast. Laguna de Perlas, 40 kilometers (25 mi) north of Bluefields has a beautiful blue lagoon, great fishing and a clean and tranquil atmosphere. Updated: Sep 28, 2009.

History

As you may discover, the Atlantic Coast and Pacific side of Nicaragua tend to seem like two completely different countries. The main reason behind this is that different countries governed both bodies separately. Spain took control of the Pacific side of Nicaragua, completely integrating their blood, language and culture into the land, which had been once inhabited by native tribes. This resulted in a predominant *mestizo* population—people of mixed Spanish European and Native American descent.

In contrast, the Atlantic Coast took on a completely different fate. In order to fend off the Spanish invaders, the indigenous tribes of the Atlantic Coast formed an alliance with both pirates and the British, who formed a protectorate over the region until 1894. Another large contributing aspect to the current culture of the Atlantic, were the Africans that arrived and eventually formed a pact with the indigenous people to repel the Spaniards.

Photo by Elicia Bolton

In 1979, the Sandinistas obtained power over both of the regions and tried to merge the segregated areas under one rule. This only lasted for five years; however, when due to political choices, the Sandinista government backed an autonomy order recognizing the rights of indigenous peoples.

In 1987, the Statute of Autonomy of the Atlantic Coast was finally approved. Today, three surviving indigenous groups occupy the area, including the *Miskitu, Sumu, Rama* and a number of multi-ethnic communities, including the *Creole* and *Garifunu*. Updated: Sep 28, 2009.

The Miskito Coast: From Piracy to Independence

The Miskito coast is separated from the rest of the country by a mountainous range, from which rivers run down to the sea, spreading into lagunas and marshes. The separation is more than geographical; however, as the coast has a very strong identity of its own, stemming from a distinct history and preserved indigenous culture.

The existence of the coast and the "savage tribes" inhabiting it was first chronicled by Columbus on his fourth trip to the New World in 1502. The name Miskito itself first

Highlights

Corn Islands— The best reason to visit the coast. Hike through tropical forests, laze on the beach, and swim, snorkel and dive with rays, sharks and dolphins. **Big Corn (p.299)** is built up and bustling; **Little Corn (p.305)** is infinitely more chill.

Laguna de Perlas (p.295)— Stop in at this rustic village to fish or watch turtles nest. Snorkel in the nearby **Pearl Keys** and boat to to **Orinoco (p.297)**, where you can mingle with the friendly locals. Updated: March 23, 2010.

first appeared in English pirate William Dampier's account, *A New Voyage around the World*, published in 1697. The Miskitos, the largest ethnic group, may have taken their name from a patriarch called *Miskut*, who settled by the Río Coco, the largest river in Central America. The other groups present in the region were the *Mayangnas*, who lived as small nomad clans in the forest, and the *Ramas*, a very isolated, endogamous group that occupied that area between Punta Gorda and Río San Juan. The Ramas have since disappeared, bar a small group on Rama Cay in Bluefields lake.

The low, rainy coast, apparently devoid of gold, was not the most profitable to the Spanish colonizers. Some Franciscan missionaries tried to establish a mission in the 17th century, with little success. Meanwhile, seafarers from the Netherlands, England and France tried their luck doing commerce from Cabo Gracias a Dios (the northernmost point of 21st-century Nicaragua). Among them, Abraham Bluevelt, a Dutchman, left his name to a laguna, anglicized into Bluefields. In fact, 17th-century Nicaragua was an age of piracy, with ruthless seamen ambushing Spanish ships carrying gold from the colonies.

The English were the first to bring in African slaves to chop down trees. But racial integration truly began after the shipwreck of a Portuguese vessel in 1641, when slaves onboard escaped to the coast and eventually mixed with the natives, forming the *Sambo* people.

The 17th and 18th century saw the English and the Spanish fight for hegemony of the Caribbean coast and islands. The bellicose Miskitoes sometimes even fought alongside the pirates, serving as guides for the English buccaneers who sailed up the Río San Juan attacking Spanish cities. The English crown and its colonies in Jamaica succeeded in establishing a protectorate (mostly to shield their own commercial interests) over what is now the Nicaraguan and Honduran coast: the Miskito Kingdom. At its head was a Miskito-Sambo king.

Even though the English eventually recognised Spanish soveriegnty over Caribbean territories, the Spanish still lacked resources to control the land and subdue the locals. Nicaragua's independence from Spain in 1821 did not solve the problem. Eventually, England renounced its colonial pretensions over Nicaraguan soil in 1850, and the Nicaraguan central government integrated those territories for good in 1894.

In later years came a program of castellanization, but the Miskito managed to escape the more radical Spanish colonization, and the indigenous culture remains strong today. The Miskito language counts around 850 words of English origin (including shoe, beer, rice and beans). The native tongue is still Miskito in many parts, and in some communities, Spanish is not even spoken at all.

During the war in the 1980s, the Miskitos mostly sided with the Contras in their fight against the Sandinista government, and, largely in an attempt to mollify the Miskitos, the government passed the 1987 Autonomy Law, which granted the North and South Atlantic Autonomous Regions (RAAN and RAAS) a high degree of autonomy.

THE MISKITOS OF TODAY

The two regions presently hold their own elections, electing 90 representatives to a regional council. But the autonomous status has left some unsatisfied. The regional council is perceived by some as a political tool of the central government, and the more isolated communities hardly feel cared for—some without schools, teachers or health facilities. In particular, many voices are asking why the Miskito region remains so poor when its soil contains gold, silver and even oil. Most communities live off subsistence agriculture, depending on their cattle and the harvest of rice and beans.

Recently, a minority movement has emerged demanding full independence, with the idea that the indigenous should take control of the vast natural resources. The Council of Ancients (*consejo de ancianos*), a body formed 10 years ago by community leaders (*wihtas*) gathered in Puerto Cabezas in August of 2009. There, they declared the independence of *La Gran Nación de la Moskitia* and gave the government six months to hand over power. This did not happen.

As the three-month deadline drew near, in October of 2009, the Nicaraguan government sent in troops and set roadblocks to prevent massive demonstrations. A march took place in Puerto, but with little effect. The police threw tear gas and a few people were injured (at time of writing). It is unlikely that things will move much in the coming months or even years. The independence movement does not have a broad enough base; in fact the more isolated communities are pretty much unaware of it (or feel it is irrelevant to their lives). Many are arguing for a more progressive and cautious path to greater autonomy, fearful of another civil war. The bloodbaths of the 1980s are not far enough behind. Updated: Oct 27, 2009.

When to Go

The rainy season on Nicaragua's Caribbean coast lasts from May to September, and rains are often heavy enough to produce enough freshwater runoff to adversely effect mangrove swamps and even farmland. This area of Nicaragua receives the most rainfall in all of Central America. From October to April, it's relatively dry, but a little cooler. September, October and November, although rather dry, do occasionally see a good drenching from a passing hurricane. People on the Mosquito Coast still vividly remember Hurricane Felix, a category five monster that ripped the area apart in 2007. Fear of hurricanes should not cause you to reschedule your trip, but if you're there and hear that one is coming, you may want to head for higher ground. Updated: Oct 19, 2009.

Safety

The Caribbean Coast can be dangerous, but you should be fine if you're careful. The region is relatively remote, and armed gangs of highwaymen have been known to rob the unwary, but such occurrences are uncommon. Remember, the Caribbean Coast is the poorest part of a very poor country, and leaving valuables around may prove irresistible to locals.

Another important safety factor that is often overlooked has to do with the weather: hurricanes between July and November can hit the region hard, wiping out whole towns and roads. Be sure to keep a close eye on the weather reports and skip town if a storm appears to be on the way. Updated: Oct 19, 2009.

Things to See and Do

The Caribbean Coast and Corn Islands have much to offer, most of it what you'd expect: watersports, fishing, nightlife and more. What's occasionally overlooked is the rich cultural heritage of this area: the people are a mixture of the Miskito and other indigenous tribes, descendents of African slaves and Nicaraguans who have moved to the area from the rest of the country. The result is a rich culture with fun traditions, great food and memorable festivals. Between dives and fishing trips be sure to get a taste of the unique local culture. Updated: Oct 19, 2009

Tours

Nicaragua's Caribbean Coast and Islands are serviced by several different tour operators, and most of them are dive shops. The Corn Islands are known for good diving and snorkeling, but the same tour operators can also take visitors on cultural or fishing tours. Updated: Oct 23, 2009.

Lodging

Lodging options on the Caribbean Coast tend to be aimed towards backpackers and mid-range travelers. The area is not yet massively developed for tourism, and for that reason, many find it more pleasant than the typical touristy hotspots. This situation could change soon; however, as the region increasingly draws more visitors, so if you prefer to avoid other tourists, head there now. Updated: Oct 23, 2009.

PUERTO CABEZAS

🔺 8 m   👤 30,000   📞 279

The sweltering backwater town of Puerto Cabezas is relatively isolated and has almost no tourist attractions. In fact, it is quite possible that you will be the only foreigner in town (bar a few missionaries), which means that you will attract attention, especially if you happen to be female. Still, Puerto Cabezas is a great base from which to explore coastal communities, or, for the extremely adventurous, the Miskito Keys Reserve.

The Miskito area was originally inhabited by the Miskito and Mayangna people who called it *Bilwi*, meaning, "snake under a leaf." The place was then briefly called Bragmann's Bluff, after an English pirate who is said to have landed here some centuries before. It wasn't until 1929 that the city was officially named Puerto Cabezas, after the general who brought the English-dominated region under full control of the Nicaraguan government.

Strictly speaking; however, Bilwi is the name of the city and Puerto Cabezas is the name of the department, though locals will refer to the town with either name. Puerto Cabezas did a brisk trade in lumber culled from the forests of the hinterland through the first decades of the 20th century, but the revolutionary turmoils of the 1930s and the 1941 hurricane sent it into a relative decline. The port was still of strategic importance, though, as the invasion of the Bay of Pigs was prepared from Puerto Cabezas. In later years the city served as an arrival point for military aid to the Sandinists from Cuba and the USSR.

Today, like many points on the Caribbean Coast, Puerto Cabezas is used as a transit port for cocaine traffickers, so be mindful. That said, most puerteños make a living off of small-scale fishing and agriculture. The tourism industry is by no means a source of income, yet there is some infrastructure for those who make it here; a couple of decent hotels, a handful of budget accommodations, a few restaurants and some basic services are available. Updated: Oct 19, 2009.

When to Go

The best time to visit is during the months of March and April, when rain is less frequent. The festivals worth checking out in Puerto are the following:

King Pulanka (February) — An important Miskito celebration, where a "king" and "queen" dress up as mock royalties—originally as a satire of the English monarchy—and parade.

Maypole / Mayoya (May) — A Creole festival giving thanks for the harvest. A "Tree of Fertility" is decorated with ribbons and fruit, and people dance around it at night.

Sihkru Tara (August 9) — A shamanic Miskito ritual celebrated in honor of dead souls.

Feria de la Autonomia (October 30) — Ethnic groups showcase traditional food and artwork to celebrate the region's autonomy (granted in 1987). Updated: Oct 27, 2009.

Getting To and Away From Puerto Cabezas

BY AIR

The simplest way to get to Puerto Cabezas is by plane. **La Costeña** has three daily flights to and from Managua. Flights depart Puerto at 8 a.m., noon and 4 p.m., and Managua at 8 a.m., noon and 10 p.m. ($148.80). It is also possible to fly from Puerto to Bluefields on Mondays, Wednesdays and Fridays ($148.20). La Costeña has a desk at the airport (Tel: 505-2-792-2282), and a small shoe shop next to the Hospedaje El Viajante also serves as an agency (Tel: 505-2-792 2349, open 7:30 a.m. to 6.30 p.m.).

BY BUS

Buses to Waspám and the mining triangle (Siuna, Rosita) leave from the terminal a couple of kilometers out of town, though terminal is a bit of an overstatement—think dirt lot littered with trash. Buses to Waspám (4 – 6 hours, $6) depart daily at 6 a.m. and 7 a.m. Buses to Krukira (30 – 45 min) leave from El Cortijo in the morning. Updated: Oct 27, 2009.

Getting Around

Puerto Cabezas is manageable on foot, but you should get a ride to the beaches of Bocana. Taxis (shared) are widely available and cost $0.50 to anywhere in town. The streets are not marked, nor are the houses numbered, so indications are usually given with vague hand gestures and reference points such as the central park or the city hall. Updated: Oct 20, 2009.

Safety

While it's safe to walk alone through Puerto during the day, you really shouldn't do so after dark. Also avoid going to the beach alone, and always keep an eye on your belongings. Remember that drugs transit through the area, so beware of shady characters in bars and never accept packages from strangers; penalties for drug use and trafficking are high in Nicaragua. And don't forget your insect repellant as the region is infested with mosquitoes. You also may want to take malaria medication as a precaution. Updated: Oct 20, 2009.

Services

TOURISM

Nobody in town seems to know that an **INTUR** office exists, yet it can indeed be found in a small yellow house across from the municipal market in barrio Pedro Joaquin Chamorro. The office doesn't have any city maps, but the staff can answer specific questions and direct you to **AMICA**, an indigenous women's association that also functions as a tour operator. The manager, Janice, is the best informed of the lot. Open Monday – Friday, 8 a.m. – 1 p.m. Tel: 505-2-792-1564.

The **police station** (Tel: 505-2-792-2256) is in Barrio Filimon Rivera.

MONEY

Puerto only has two banks. **Bancentro**, on the main street near the city hall, is open Monday – Friday, 8 a.m. – 4:30 p.m.; Saturday, 8 a.m. – noon. Its ATM accepts Visa. **Banpro**, one block south of the central park, is open Monday – Friday, 8:30 a.m. – 4:30 p.m.; Saturday, 8:30 a.m. – noon. Its ATM accepts Visa, Mastercard, Cirrus and Maestro. **Western Union** (Tel: 505-2-743-2337) operates from inside a shop selling Barbie dolls and other junk, but you can't miss the huge yellow Western Union marquee. It's open 8:30 a.m. – 6 p.m.

KEEPING IN TOUCH

There are several cybercafés in town, including **Tejada Tapia (**Tel: 505-8-919-7120), beside Santagaz, 100 meters (328 ft) from the city hall in barrio Revolución, with Internet access for $0.75 an hour. It's open 8 a.m. – 7 p.m. There is also **Saralen**, next door to Casa Museo Judith Kain, and open until 6 p.m.

The **post office**, situated inside the city hall, is open Monday – Saturday, 8 a.m. – 1 p.m.

There also are a few places from which to make calls, such as **ENnitel** (right by the central park), and **La Gata Multiservicios** (in the middle of the municipal market), which offers international calls from $2.50 a minute to the USA and $3 a minute to Europe.

MEDICAL

The public hospital (Tel: 505-2-792-2243) is in barrio Nueva Jerusalem near the bus terminal, but if you have the money, you're better off calling a private clinic, such as **Cadamuc** (Tel: 505-2-792-2619).

SHOPPING

Puerto Cabezas is filled with little shops selling basic items. There are also a few slightly larger supermarkets in town, like the **Monter** by the stadium. You can also pick up some food at the municipal market, which is located along a street that runs from the north side of the central park. Updated: Oct 27, 2009.

Things to See and Do

Puerto itself offers few real attractions, but its colorful streets and the busy local market—with gnarled fruits and veggies, raw fish and maybe even a gored, chopped-up turtle—can be quite entertaining. Aside from the Museum Judith Kain, the best way to get to know the local culture is to do an excursion to a nearby indigenous community. Updated: Oct 19, 2009.

Casa Museo Judith Kain

The former home of painter Judith Kain Cunningham is a bright and spacious house. It showcases her colorful paintings, some slightly grotesque puppets showing local traditions like the Maypole, as well as some personal photos and belongings. While not all the objects on display are worthy of attention, there are some interesting pieces from the Sandinista revolution. The museum is also one of Puerto's better hotels. Open 9 a.m. – 4 p.m. Barrio Aeropuerto, by the Moravian church. Tel: 505-2-792-2225, E-mail: casamuseojudithkain@hotmail.com, URL: www.casamuseonicaragua.org. Updated: Oct 19, 2009.

The Pier

The old pier, which was built in 1924 with local hardwoods, is a testimony to Puerto's better days as an important shipping point. Visitors may have been able to stroll along it in the past, but entry is now prohibited by a high chickenwire fence, multiple red signs and security guards. You can talk your way past the first checkpoint and walk halfway out to check out the boats, but no further. Updated: Oct 26, 2009.

Indigenous Communities

An excursion to one of the Miskito communities of Tuapí, Krukira, Hanlover, Karata or Wawa Bad will certainly make your visit to Puerto Cabezas worthwhile. The residents of these communities still lead traditional lives, and you can easily spend a day or two observing them as they fish, gather fruit or cook. While some locals speak Creole English, most tend to communicate in Spanish or Miskito. If you make the trip on your own, be sure to introduce yourself to the *wihta* (chief/judge) or the pastor, as he will surely be able to set you up with a host family. Just 17 kilometers (10.5 mi) from Puerto Cabezas, Tuapí is the closest community, and is accessible via a

30- to 45-minute bus ride. To reach the other communities, head down to the little beach by the pier and negotiate transport with a boat owner, but be aware that this can be expensive. You can also get AMICA to arrange an excursion. Updated: Oct 27, 2009.

Miskito Keys Biological Reserve
The many islets that form the Miskito Keys are hard to get to, and they also lack any sort of tourism infrastructure. Only 15 to 20 families live out there, alongside a few fishing companies. If you make it out to the keys, you can rent a canoe or get a local to show you around the mangroves. Do know that you will need to find your own accommodation. A hammock should do the trick. A panga ride to the keys (3 hours) will cost at least $500 – 800, as the cost of gasoline is quite high. Alternatively, ask the Naval Force (stationed in Puerto Cabezas) which fishing boats are headed out there and try to negotiate a ride (which may cost you around $15). This is not recommended for women; however, as it would require spending hours on a boat with dozens of men and no bathroom. Also be aware that you are heading off at your own risk, with no guarantees as to when you might get a return ride. Updated: Oct 27, 2009.

Tours
AMICA, the local association of indigenous women, which develops projects for women's rights and the environment, also doubles as the only tour operator in Puerto Cabezas. Provided that you give them advance notice (1 – 2 days), these ladies can arrange visits to the communities of Wawa Bad, Karata, Hanlover (by boat, via lake or sea) and Tuapí and Krukira (by land). Such trips will cost around $100. The organization also welcomes volunteers (male and female) to work on projects such as reforestation. AMICA also runs an eatery in their office building. Open Monday – Friday, 8 a.m. – 5:30 p.m. Tel: 505-2-792 2219, E-mail: asociacionamica@yahoo.es. Updated: Oct 27, 2009.

Lodging
Puerto has a few nice hotels as well as some acceptable hostels and cabins. Wherever you go, be prepared to share the garden or yard

---

Caribbean Coast Dance
Nicaragua is a country of dances. While the Pacific Coast is salsa territory, to the north and center of the country you'll find cowboy-style *quebraditas*. But it's along the Caribbean coast where reggae is king and residents shake their hips to *calypso*, *punta* and *soca*. As with much of Central America, local music has evolved through an eclectic mix of African, European and indigenous influences.

To see local dancing at its wildest, try to visit Bluefields in the spring. During the month of May, the city celebrates with concerts, street parties, neighborhood maypoles and dance competitions in each barrio. Each neighborhood forms a group of at least 60 dancers for the competitions; in the past, top contenders for the city-wide honor have been barrio Beholdeen and Cotton Tree.

The May celebrations are also when residents prove themselves as dancers. You'll be able to find small groups performing all across Bluefields. Some of the most well-known local figures include: Wanda Lee Morgan, Merida Obando, Donald Benard, Francis Ellis and the single-named dancers Papo and Doko.

While you're visiting, you might also want to check out **Ethnic Expansion**, **Bluefields Indian**, **Caribbean University Ballet Co.** or **Erupción Caribeña**. All of the groups hold performances of regional dances, so inquire about dates.

If you're visiting the area during the fall, head north of Bluefields to Orinoco. On November 19th, indigenous residents celebrate Garifuna Day with tribal dances such as Punta, Punta Rock, Punta-Punta Palacio, Conga and Yau Kuno (the war dance).

To bust a move with the locals and practice some of the steps you've been seeing, try stopping in at one of the dimly lit but breezy clubs that line the coast. Some options include **Cima Club** and **4 Brothers** in Bluefields, **Drop Draws** in Pearl Lagoon, **Anastasia** and **Sapo** on the Corn Islands, or **Jumbo** and **Malecón** in Bilwi. Updated: Jan 23, 2009.

Did a unique trek? Got way off the beaten path? Tell other travelers at vivatravelguides.com

with chickens and dogs, beneath lines of drying laundry. Except in the higher-end places, expect bucket showers and bucket-flush toilets. Prices are higher for rooms with air conditioning. Updated: Oct 20, 2009

Hospedaje Bilwi
(ROOMS: $7.50 – 15) In a large blue house right by the sea, Hospedaje Bilwi is a decent option if you can tolerate the tattered linoleum that covers parts of the floorboards. Of the 19 rooms, the cheaper ones come with shared bathrooms and the others with TVs, air conditioning and private bathrooms. There is a balcony with a view of the sea at the far end of the building, and a bar area blasts reggae until midnight. Barrio Libertad, behind the parque infantil. Tel: 505-8-364-4163 / 2-764-7490. Updated: Oct 20, 2009.

Casa Museo Judith Kain
(ROOMS: $12 – 27) Set in the same lovely wooden-beamed building as the museum, the hotel Judith Kain offers 16 good-value rooms. The comfortable singles and doubles all come with private bathrooms (regular, not bucket shower), TVs and fans or air conditioning (more expensive). Breakfast (an additional $4) is a feast of porridge, pancakes, fruit salad, and tea or coffee, and can be taken on the garden terrace. Barrio Aeropuerto, by the Moravian church. Tel: 505-2-792-2225, E-mail: casamuseojudithkain@hotmail.com, URL: www.casamuseonicaragua.org. Updated: Oct 20, 2009.

El Cortijo 1 and El Cortijo 2
(ROOMS: $23 – 28) Guesthouse El Cortijo 1 offers ten rooms in a large house on the main street (Calle Revolución). The first-floor rooms are dank and dark, but the ones upstairs are somewhat brighter, all with private bathrooms, air conditioning and TVs. One of the hotel's nicest features is the veranda that overlooks the garden. Ca. la Revolución. Tel: 505-2-792-2223.

(ROOMS: $23 – 28) El Cortijo 2 (same owner, a block down towards the sea on calle San Pedro) only has five rooms, but they are nicer (and cost $25) than those in El Cortijo 1. This guesthouse also has a long walkway through a tranquil garden, that leads to a romantic mirador with access to the beach. Breakfast ($2.50 – 4) is not included. Ca. San Pedro, Tel: 505-2-792-2340. Updated: Oct 27, 2009.

Restaurants
The gastronomical scene in Puerto is nothing to write home about. Apart from the three better seafood restaurants in town (Kabu Payaska, Miramar and El Malecón), there are a couple of Chinese places that never seem to be open. You can also find several little eateries serving cheap lunches ($2.50). The two by the west end of the central park seem to be the most popular among locals. Updated: Oct 20, 2009.

Kabu Payaska
The most pleasant restaurant in Puerto, Kabu Payaska is set on a ridge just over the beach, with a spacious, breezy terrace. Although the place serves the usual suspects, people generally come here to enjoy the seafood. The recommended lobster a la plancha ($9) comes sizzling, with an accompaniment of rice, potatoes and cabbage salad. Staff will also watch your clothes if you want to top off your lunch with a dip in the sea. There is music and a disco area at night. Open noon – midnight. Located on Bocana beach (take a taxi to get there). Updated: Oct 27, 2009.

WASPAM AND RÍO COCO
The peaceful town of Waspám lies in the heart of the Miskito territory, pretty much as far off the beaten path as possible. Its name in the Miskito language may come from the phrase *was-pana*, meaning river with trees, or from *was-pam*, where the water is big. Life in the area revolves around the Río Coco, which flows brown during the rainy season, and forms the border with Honduras. Be warned, though, that any river trip, whether to visit an indigenous community or the Bosawás reserve, is quite expensive.

Waspám itself, though it offers no real tourist attractions, is quite pleasant, with extremely friendly people, and streets lined with hedges bursting with carmine hibiscus and raspberry-colored bougainvillea. As there are no virtually no cars here, the air is filled with the sounds of day-to-day life: chatter (in Miskito), the cries of roosters, the squawking of domesticated parrots and the clatter of carts. The town cattle, like the sacred cows of India, wander the streets freely, sometimes to be shooed away by cyclists and street vendors. At night the men play volleyball in the central park lined with a gaudily painted fence. Just across the street, horses graze by the decrepit white Moravian church.

When to Go

A good time to visit Waspám and the Río Coco—always hot and humid, with daytime temperatures in the mid-30s°C (80s°F)—is outside of the rainy season. Tropical downpours, as well as the episodic hurricane, come through between May and December. Otherwise, come for the *Sihkru Tara* dance festival, which starts on August 5 – 7, and reaches Bilwi on the 8th and 9th of August. Semana Santa is also a festive time, when the locals lounge about the sandy beaches left by the low waters of the Río Coco.

But no matter when you come, there will most certainly be malevolent mosquitoes. Take adequate precautions against malaria and dengue fever by taking a cholorquinine or doxocycline preventive treatment, and using plenty of repellent. If you are going to travel along the river and eat with indigenous communities, be aware that they cook their food with water taken directly from the river, unfiltered. It may not be a bad idea to take anti-parasite medicine in the days following such meals. For further information about Waspám, consult www.wangky.net.

Getting To and Away From Waspam and Río Coco

BY AIR

The easiest way to travel to and from Waspám is by air. **La Costeña** flies three times a week, on Tuesday, Thursday and Saturday, departing from Waspám around noon, for $160 return. La Costeña has an office by the airstrip, open mornings—until the flight leaves—and the only contact number is the manager's cell phone (Tel: 505-8-932-4416).

BY LAND

It's a bumpy ride on an unpaved road to and from Puerto Cabezas ($6 one-way), and the trip can last between four and six hours, depending on the state of the road (more potholes during rainy season), pit stops and breakdowns. Buses depart from the central park at 6 a.m. and 7 a.m. A taxi (which can only be hired in Puerto Cabezas) will cost between $100 and $150. You can also catch a bus to Managua via the Mining Triangle (Rosita, Siuna) and endure 24 hours on the road. The ride costs $25, and there are departures Monday, Tuesday, Wednesday and Saturday.

BORDER CROSSING INTO HONDURAS

There is now a Nicaraguan immigration office in Leimus, a 30-minute ride from Waspám. In Leimus itself—within walking distance—is the Honduran immigration office, from which pick-up trucks can take you to Puerto Lempira, seven or eight hours away. Updated: Oct 27, 2009.

Services

MONEY

Waspám offers very little in terms of services. There is no bank, so come with a supply of cash (preferably cordobas).

MEDICAL

There is a **public hospital** near the high school staffed with reputedly good Cuban doctors, as well as a day clinic run by English-speaking nuns (beyond the Catholic church). The **police station** is the blue building by the airstrip.

KEEPING IN TOUCH

Your only link to the outside world is the **Cybercafé Wankinet**, at La Estancia de Rose, also by the airstrip. It offers surprisingly decent Internet connection on its 10 computers for $1.50 an hour; phone calls cost $1.50 a minute.

SHOPPING

There are plenty of little shops (*pulperías*) where you can buy basic groceries and supplies. Street vendors offer fruit, coco bread, *naka tamales* (a mixture of pork, chicken and corn dough cooked in a banana leaf) and banana chips.

Things to See and Do

One block away, the Iglesia San Rafael, of Catholic denomination, is being refurbished, its twin front towers already painted with gaudy colors. The main building was destroyed during the civil war but for the bell tower, which was used as a lookout point by the Sandinistas, and until three years ago still bore bullet marks.

The only other place of mild touristic interest is the **Museo Auka Tangni**, on the ground floor of a peach-colored house on the western side of town. Owner Dionisio Melgara has dedicated his time to the preservation of Miskito culture. Give him a call (Tel: 505-8-417-8128) for a quick tour. He will show off a few artifacts that he personally gathered, including his mother's fishing

---

Did a unique trek? Got way off the beaten path? Tell other travelers at vivatravelguides.com

net, and a collection of his own works about the Miskito language and culture, including trilingual dictionaries and translations of the Bible in Miskito.

Tours

To arrange a trip downriver or into the jungle, travelers should visit the **MARENA** (the ministry of environment) office, a green house behind the municipal market. Various packages can be negotiated with Homer (Tel: 505-8-431-0943), who also belongs to **EMSERTA** (E-mail: emsertasa@hotmail.com), the boat transport cooperative. Given the high cost of gasoline, all of the packages are pricey (a panga uses $20 – 25 worth of gas for an hour trip). Two- to three-day packages visit the downriver communities all the way to Cabo de Gracias. Others bring travelers to rapids located eight hours upstream, with a 15-hour hike up to Cerro Moco and a cave along the way. Packages cost around $500, plus $250 worth of gasoline per day; you had better come as a large group and try to negotiate.

The MARENA office is also your contact to arrange excursions into the Bosawás biosphere reserve, to see parrots, monkeys and other wildlife. In all cases, plan to spend at least three or four days in the area and be prepared to negotiate on the spot rather than in advance; the people of Waspám are a laid-back bunch and electronic communication is unreliable. You had also better speak good Spanish (unless you are fluent in Miskito or Mayangna, the other indigenous language) as very few people speak English.

Lodging

La Estancia de la Rose, which belongs to the leader of the local indigenous women's movement, is the coziest lodging option in town. The 11 rooms—five with air conditioning ($20 per night) and six with fans ($12.50)—are set in large wooden houses. All have their own bathrooms (bucket showers but regular toilets) and TVs, and there are pleasant screened-off sitting rooms with rocking chairs and couches. Located across from the airstrip. Tel: 505-2-792-9112.

Hotelito Piloto has neat and clean rooms, with TVs and real showers, for $25 – 30. There is a laundry service and restaurant. Located on the main street, a couple of blocks up from the river. Tel: 505-2-792-9045 / 8-642-4405.

Restaurants

There are basic comedors all around town offering the basic fare of rice, beans and cheese, with chicken or meat for $2.50 – 3.50, and all hotels have a food service.

The one restaurant in town with a varied menu is **Papta Watla**, in barrio Emilio Amador, between the church and the docks. Besides beef, chicken and pork prepared in sauce, fried or with garlic, the restaurant offers shrimp, fish and vegetarian dishes, and on Sundays, all soups go for $3.50 – 5. Occasionally there is wilder meat such as venison or *guardatinaja* (a type of wild pig). Open Tuesday – Sunday, 11 a.m. – noon. Tel: 505-2-792-9059. Updated: Oct 27, 2009.

EL RAMA

Although you won't find many foreign travelers there, the small town of El Rama plays a significant role in Nicaragua's trade route. The town also serves as an affordable means of transport between the mainland and the Caribbean Coast.

El Rama is situated at the mouth of three rivers: the Mico, the Rama and the Escondido—the latter being the most significant of the three. Seeing as the Río Escondido empties into the Atlantic Ocean, El Rama is situated in an ideal location for both coast-to-coast and international trade. The town's international port does frequent business with Panama City, Tampa, Miami, New York and other cities.

During Hurricane Joan (1988), El Rama was completely submerged under water; there have since been warning devices installed to warn residents before hurricane surges so that they have a chance to evacuate. Before the hurricane, the town had already been in the center of an invasive and economically draining military trade during the Nicaraguan civil war. During this time, the Contras destroyed a large part of the Rama highway, but the Nicaraguan government was able to rebuild the route in 2000.

Despite a history of adversity, El Rama has recovered and is now a well-functioning town with over 5,000 people. Catholic missionaries from the United States contributed largely to the development of the town's church, which is called *La Iglesia de Dios de la Profecía*, or The Church of the Prophecy of God. They also assisted in the development of schools and several local human rights and community organizations.

Today, El Rama is a small and friendly port town with several services such as banks, tourist information centers and Internet cafés, along with a few stores and restaurants. Updated: Sep 28, 2009.

When to Go

Like most places in Nicaragua, El Rama is full of festivities and traditional celebrations during *Semana Santa* (Easter week). Also, on May 11th, there is a *Ferias* festival where people come from various parts of Nicaragua to sell and buy clothing, horses, motorcycles and an assortment of other things.

As far as weather is concerned, El Rama is most pleasant in the summer (December – March), though the area is generally quite breezy all year-round. Updated: Sep 28, 2009.

Getting To and Away From El Rama

El Rama is a pivotal point for local connections from the rest of Nicaragua to the Caribbean Coast. There are express buses that cost $8 and run from Managua to El Rama from 2 a.m. to 9 p.m. on the hour. The trip takes six hours, and you should always try to take a bus that will arrive in El Rama during daylight hours. Make sure the bus is an *expreso*, or they might leave you stranded at the midway point, Juigalpa, where some of the buses dead-end. Return buses run on about the same schedule. There are also buses to Laguna de Perlas, which cost $6 and take four hours. One leaves El Rama at 4:30 p.m. every day.

Between 5 a.m. and 4 p.m., there are six fast boats that leave for Bluefields, but the frequency of their departures depends on how quickly they fill up. These boats cost $10 and take an hour and forty-five minutes. There are also boats that leave directly from El Rama to Big Corn Island on Thursdays at 5 a.m. and 10 p.m., and on Saturdays at 7 p.m. (schedules are subject to change). These also cost $10 and can take anywhere from 12 to 20 hours. It is important to note that many of these are not passenger boats and you may wind up on a long, uncomfortable journey, sleeping on piles of cargo. Make sure to check at the port for the details before investing in a ticket. Updated: Sep 28, 2009.

Getting Around

El Rama is very small and most places are walkable, but don't be surprised if you get a little lost among the windy paths and nameless streets. There are regular taxis, but the most popular form of transportation are moto-taxis. These are similar to golf carts, with open cabs without doors and room enough for three people. During the day, there is a flat rate of $0.25 per-person, which increases to $0.50 at night. Updated: Sep 28, 2009.

Safety

Like most places in Nicaragua, El Rama is very safe. However, because not many outsiders travel there, visitors are more easily targeted by petty thieves. With this in mind, keep your belongings close to you and exercise caution when walking around after dark. Updated: Sep 28, 2009.

Services

Although not very large, El Rama has just about every service a traveler or resident could need. That said, El Rama is very small, and has very few paved streets—none of which are labeled, so expect to spend a bit of time wandering around and searching for signs. There is a **transportation office**, equipped with up-to-date bus and boat schedules in the central square where the buses depart to and arrive from Managua. For money needs, you will find quite a few banks and **Western Unions**, but no ATMs. There are phone services for both Nicaraguan companies, Enitel and Movistar, as well a couple Internet cafes (no WiFi). For medical needs, there is a doctor's office and several pharmacies as well as a health center and a Red Cross. El Rama also has its own hospital for medical emergencies. Boats at the harbor are available for rent, as are fishing equipment or services. Prices vary, especially according to the cost of gas, but can average around $20 per trip. Updated: Sep 28, 2009.

Things to See and Do

Like many other transfer points in Nicaragua, El Rama is not very touristy. Most people use it as a midway stop between Managua and Bluefields. However, taking a walk around the town can be very enlightening and informative. There are a wide variety of stores selling CDs, DVDs, electronic equipment, clothing and almost anything you can think of. Scattered around town are small casinos with slot machines, a few restaurants, bars and a discoteca—all of which are good sources of entertainment. There is also a park, with a mirador that overlooks the river, which is a nice place to go if you want to relax. Updated: Sep 28, 2009.

Did a unique trek? Got way off the beaten path? Tell other travelers at vivatravelguides.com

Lodging

Accommodation options vary from several $3 – 5 hospedajes, with small beds and fans in each room, to $35 hotel rooms with double beds, air conditioning, cable TVs and 24-hour running water.

Hospedaje Velasquez

(ROOMS: $3 and up) The cheapest hostel in town, Hospedaje Velasquez, is not for the faint-of-heart. This farm-style hostel is full of simple rooms, equipped with single beds and fans. If you need to wake up early, don't worry about setting an alarm—there are plenty of roosters. There is no running water, but the well water is fresh and clean. Located just around the corner from the bus stop, Velasquez is also a good place to store your things while you explore the area by renting a room for the day for around $1.50. Located just around the corner from the bus stop. Tel: 505-8-403-1967. Updated: Sep 28, 2009.

Hotel Costa Verde

(ROOMS: $11 – 25) If you're spending the night in El Rama and are looking for something comfortable, Hotel Costa Verde is a great find. The most inexpensive rooms cost $11 per night with single beds, TVs and a private bathrooms. The priciest rooms cost $25 a night and include air conditioning, double beds and cable TVs. All rooms can be shared at no extra cost. The hotel has 24-hour running water, with complimentary soap and towels. Costa Verde also has both a bar and restaurant downstairs. One hundred and fifty meters (492 ft) from the Red Cross. Tel: 505-2-517-0336. Updated: Sep 28, 2009.

Restaurants

Most restaurants in El Rama serve typical Nicaraguan fare, but there are a few standouts. Local specialties include anything from $1 *Nacatamal* (a potato stuffed with meat and cheese, wrapped in a banana leaf) to lobster for $15.

Roy's Café

(ENTREES: $1.50 – 5) A small, family-owned café, Roy's is the perfect place to sit outside and enjoy a cup of coffee while listening to Latin music and watching people pass by. There is also a clean, spacious indoor seating area with mahogany and red fabric chairs and polished tables. Framed pictures of inviting coffee cups line the wall. Food is mostly typical fare, including main dishes of grilled chicken and hamburgers, pork and several seafood dishes (when they have them). All of the main dishes come with sides of plantains, rice and beans. Located in front of the Municipal Gym. Tel: 505-8-635-6452 / 429-1483. Updated: Sep 28, 2009.

Hotel Costa Verde Restaurant

(ENTREES: $3 – 15) Soothing sea-green walls lined with silver-framed paintings of the sea contribute to the tranquil vibe of Hotel Costa Verde Restaurant. Although the establishment is considered one of El Rama's higher-end restaurants, the prices are very affordable. Prices average between $5 – 6 per meal, and there is a healthy selection of seafood entrees, including some rich and hearty soups. If you're on a budget, try the *Comida Corriente* for $3. The set meal gives you the choice of chicken, fish, pork or beef with plantains, rice and beans, a side salad and cheese. One hundred and fifty meters (492 ft) from the Red Cross. Tel: 505-2-517-0336. Updated: Sep 28, 2009.

BLUEFIELDS

A few years ago a European NGO decided to build Bluefields a badly-needed road connecting it to the outside world. But when they called a meeting with the city's elders to discuss the project's implementation, they were surprised at what they heard. The elders informed them that they did not want the road, out of fears that it would dilute their traditional way of life.

As a result, Bluefields has remained largely in isolation. With the town's rich culture, colorful Palo Mayo celebrations, and proximity to spectacular sights like the Corn Islands and Laguna de Perlas, it should be cashing in on Nicaragua's tourism boom. Instead, the town remains as it was 20 years ago. Their traditional way of life has indeed remained intact, along with the poverty that accompanied it.

If you do decide to visit, V!VA wholeheartedly recommends that you spring for the plane ticket. Otherwise be prepared for a wet, uncomfortable and difficult ride. Read through the Getting There and Away section (see below) very carefully, and make sure your trip is timed appropriately.

Other than the Palo Mayo celebrations and a thumping nightlife, Bluefields itself does not offer a whole lot to visitors. There are some excellent restaurants, and the Garifuna culture is something to explore, but if you're heading to the Corn Islands you'll find both of these in far richer abundance, with gorgeous

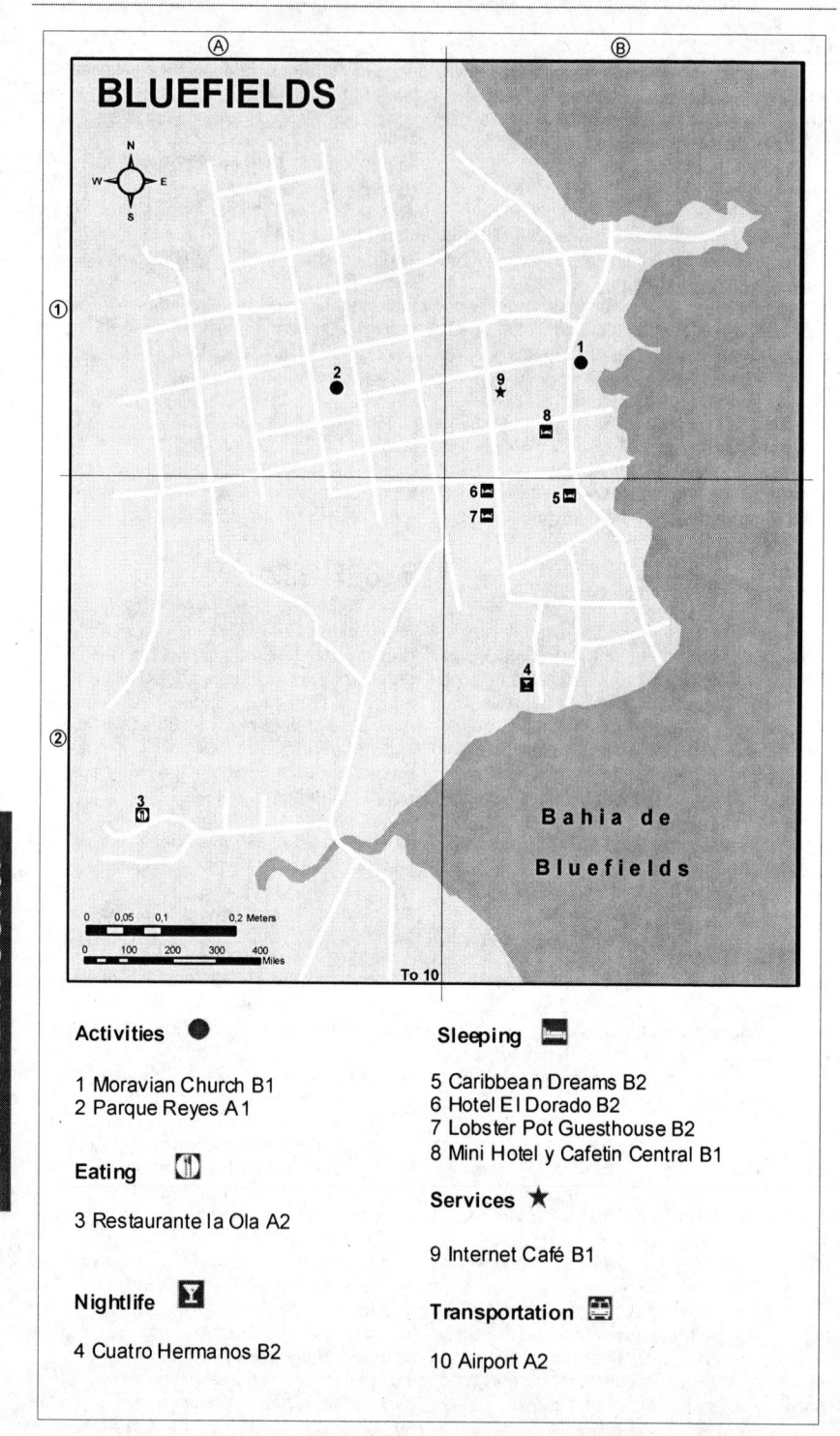

BLUEFIELDS

Activities ●

1 Moravian Church B1
2 Parque Reyes A1

Eating

3 Restaurante la Ola A2

Nightlife

4 Cuatro Hermanos B2

Sleeping

5 Caribbean Dreams B2
6 Hotel El Dorado B2
7 Lobster Pot Guesthouse B2
8 Mini Hotel y Cafetin Central B1

Services ★

9 Internet Café B1

Transportation

10 Airport A2

Did a unique trek? Got way off the beaten path? Tell other travelers at vivatravelguides.com

beaches and excellent hotels to boot. The vast bulk of visitors just use Bluefields as a base for exploring the area. Recently, there's been talk that Bluefields' intended road will instead be built to Laguna de Perlas, connecting that city to El Rama and the main road network. There's talk on the islands that once this road is completed, ferries should be re-routed to Laguna de Perlas as well. If this happens, expect Bluefields to disappear from travelers' itineraries for good. Updated: Jun 17, 2008.

When to Go

By far the best time to visit Bluefields is during the Palo Mayo celebrations. These run throughout May, but reach a stupendous climax in the last days of the month. They feature massive street parades, cultural shows, the election of the Festival Queen, and drinking parties that the whole city attends. Check local listings, as the schedule varies from year to year, but generally the biggest celebrations fall on May 28th and May 31st. Updated: Jun 17, 2008.

Getting To and Away From Bluefields

BY AIR

Bluefields' lack of a road connection makes it an infernally difficult place to visit. By far the easiest option is to fly in. **Costeña** and **Atlantic Airways** both offer daily flights to and from Managua ($82 one-way, $127 return), and to and from the Corn Islands ($65 one-way, $105 return).

BY BUS

If flying isn't in your budget, you could try the terrestrial route, but know that it's an unpleasant trip. Coming from Managua, you can take a bus as far as the port city of El Rama (6 hours, $7.25) easily enough. There is one bus company called **Empresa Vargas Peña** (Tel: 505-2-280-1812) which apparently offers Managua to Rama buses that feature a direct panga connection to Bluefields, but we were unable to independently verify this.

BY BOAT

The route from El Rama to Bluefields is served by high-speed pangas that depart from the dock whenever it fills (2 hours, $9.70). Unfortunately, the relative isolation of both Bluefields and El Rama means the trip is not a popular one, and the pangas won't leave until absolutely every seat is filled. V!VA's reviewer made the trip twice, and each time was forced to wait in excess of six hours for the boat to leave. This is the reason why few people are able to make the trip in one day.

If you do find yourself stuck in Rama for the night, make sure you wake up very early in the morning, as a panga will almost certainly leave around 6 a.m. or 7 a.m., and if you miss that you might have to wait all day. If you're hoping to continue on to the Corn Islands, the ferry schedule is even more erratic, and information is nearly impossible to find in Bluefields. Look for an Atlantic Airways sign near the dock; the woman working there seems well informed.

A boat also leaves San Juan del Norte and heads to Bluefields on Wednesdays and Saturdays at 8 a.m. Trips from Bluefields to San Juan del Norte depart Thursdays and Saturdays at 8 a.m. The trip costs $30 and lasts 2.5 hours. Plans are in line for an even faster boat, scheduled to begin running by November 2009. With the new boat, departures will also be available on Sundays (from San Juan del Norte) and Tuesdays (from Bluefields).

This new line should also go to Barra de Colorado and Tortuguero (Costa Rica) on Tuesdays, Thursdays and Sundays, allowing visitors to leave from San Juan del Norte at around 10 a.m. Updated: Oct 06, 2009.

Getting Around

Bluefields is quite a small place, and taxis shouldn't cost more than $0.95 or so. The price jumps considerably at night, when taxis are most necessary. It's about a 10 – 15 minute drive from downtown to the airport, but less than five minutes driving from downtown to the docks. Updated: Jun 17, 2008.

Safety

Bluefields is fairly safe by day, but gets quite sketchy at night. It's a poor community, so the standard precautions (such as not brandishing valuables) apply. Always take a taxi at night, even if you're only going a few blocks. Keep an eagle eye on your belongings in the area of the bus station and the dock. Updated: Jun 17, 2008.

Services

Frustratingly, Bluefields has nothing that even remotely resembles a tourist information office. If you need information about boat departures, there's an office on the south side of the pier that can help. Look for a glass window past a metal gate. This is also where pangas to local destinations, such as Laguna de Perlas, depart. There's an excellent Internet cafe across the street from the Catholic church, immediately east of Parque Reyes. Updated: Jun 17, 2008.

Things to See and Do

Bluefields does not generally have a whole lot to offer visitors. Day trips to Laguna de Perlas and Rama Key are the highlights. If you're here for a weekend, head to a club for some lively Caribbean music. And say what you will about the Garifuna, they certainly know how to have a good time. Updated: Jan 09, 2009.

Moravian Church

This handsome, stately church was rebuilt in 1992 after Hurricane Juana flattened the original, 19th-century building. It seems to be closed more than it's open, which is a shame, since the interior, viewed through the windows, looks quite nice. Updated: Jun 17, 2008.

Rama Key

Rama Key is a small island about two hours from Bluefields that is populated by small fishing villages of the indigenous Rama people. Some visitors are charmed by the simple lifestyle and traditions of the fisherman, while others find the place cramped and depressing. Either way the place lacks the charm of Laguna de Perlas, which is a far better day trip.

Pangas for Rama Keys depart from the office on the main pier and cost $9.70; they leave whenever they're full. The first one generally runs at 5:30 a.m., the last one at 3:30 p.m. Updated: Jun 17, 2008.

Parque Reyes

Bluefields' main park is called Parque Reyes, three blocks west of the sea. This is the center of the action during the Palo Mayo celebrations, but it doesn't have a whole lot to offer at other times of the year. It is quite a peaceful and pleasant spot though, a gathering place where children play and locals come to lounge about and gossip. Updated: Jun 17, 2008.

Tours

Bluefields has no tours or tour operators. There are several shops and hotels around town that sport prominent Atlantic Airlines signs, but these are apparently decoys. If you want to buy airline tickets, your best bet is to go directly to the airport, which is only a few kilometers outside of town.

Boat tickets are sold at the pier, and it's impossible to buy them in advance. Most departures leave from an enclosed area on the south side of the main dock. A woman in a small glass booth will sell you tickets to some destinations. She is the only reliable source of information about schedules and times. Updated: Jan 09, 2009.

Lodging

Bluefields' tourism sector is rather undeveloped, and hotel options are limited. There are no hostels, and your budget choices are basically just Lobster Pot and Hotel El Dorado. They're right down the street from one another, so check them both out before you pick a room. There are a few nicer hotels around as well, offering breezy terraces or air conditioning. You get what you pay for here. Updated: Jun 18, 2008.

Lobster Pot Guesthouse

(ROOMS: $5 – 6) The Lobster Pot Guesthouse is one of Bluefields' cheapest places to stay. However, most of the rooms are a bit on the small and dark side. A few rooms do have windows that open to the outside, but most of them open into the corridors, which make the rooms a little stuffy. This hotel isn't outstandingly clean, nor is it disgusting, and is an acceptable place to stay, considering the price. Two blocks inland from the market. Updated: Jan 20, 2009.

Hotel el Dorado

(ROOMS: $7.50 – 12.50) Some have rated Hotel el Dorado as Bluefields's best budget option, but during our stay there were some serious problems involving water and sanitation. Taps and toilets did not function properly, and the smell from the bathrooms was overpowering. That being said, the rooms were not a bad deal. Check the place out if you visit, and make sure to see whether the hotel has fixed their plumbing issues before you check in. Some rooms are much nicer than others, so have a look first. Two blocks west (inland) from the market. Tel: 505-8-822-1435. Updated: Jun 17, 2008.

Mini Hotel y Cafetin Central

(ROOMS: $12 – 26) Clean, with a smart and friendly staff, Mini is an excellent option for travelers on a budget looking for slightly nicer digs. All rooms come with cable TVs,

---

Did a unique trek? Got way off the beaten path? Tell other travelers at vivatravelguides.com

fans, telephones and private bathrooms. The three-person room for $26.60 is a particularly good deal if you can find people to share it with. The restaurant has received good reviews. Two blocks south of the pier, 1.5 blocks inland. Tel: 505-2-572-2362. Updated: Jun 18, 2008.

Caribbean Dreams

(ROOMS: $22 – 27) Caribbean Dreams is located in a handsome blue and white building. The hotel occupies a great location and it's best feature, a breezy common patio, has excellent views of the sea. The hotel is both extremely clean and exceptionally safe, making it a a good mid-range option. All rooms are equipped with cable TVs, air conditioning and private bathrooms. Towels are are also included, and are cleverly folded into swans. Around the corner south from the market, one block inland from the sea. Updated: Apr 17, 2009.

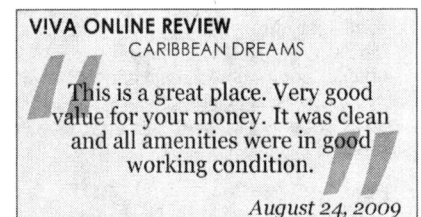

> **VIVA ONLINE REVIEW**
> CARIBBEAN DREAMS
>
> "This is a great place. Very good value for your money. It was clean and all amenities were in good working condition."
>
> August 24, 2009

Restaurants

Bluefields has excellent seafood restaurants. Show up during one of the lobster seasons when the spiny critters are sold for a song. If you get a chance, try the *rundown*, a traditional Caribbean dish made with fish or lobster. There are also several comida tipica restaurants, which are the cheapest eating options.

Comida Tipica

There are several set-piece comida tipica restaurants around Bluefields, but this one is the best. Food is very cheap, tasty and reasonably fresh. This is a good place to fill up if you're on a budget. One block north of Hotel El Dorado. Updated: Jun 18, 2008.

Restaurante la Ola

Restaurante la Ola is a bizarre cross between an ice cream parlor and a bar. Even stranger, it's also the best place to go for breakfast—few places in Bluefields seem to offer toast and eggs. La Ola also features a jukebox stocked with '80s rock. Food really does taste better while you're listening to "Paradise City." One block up from the market. Tel: 505-2-572-2779. Updated: Jun 18, 2008.

Twins Restaurant and Bar

Twins Restaurant is an excellent option for seafood in Bluefields. Prices are very reasonable, with fish dishes starting from $4.85. The *Pescado Ramakay*, a fish filet garnished with mussels, is highly recommended. Service is prompt, and the atmosphere is family friendly. Upstairs there is a lively bar, popular with locals. Just down from Hotel El Dorado. Tel: 505-2-572-0186. Updated: Jan 09, 2009.

4 Hermanos

A swinging reggae joint, 4 Hermanos is where locals comes to party. Don't show up expecting disco balls and bouncers; the building itself is pretty rundown. But the crowd is lively and there's a cool island vibe. There's often a cover ($0.96 – 2.40), but drinks are cheap. Located about two blocks south of Hotel El Dorado, it is quite difficult to find (and the surrounding streets are nameless and featureless). Ask for directions; every local and taxi driver will know the place. Updated: Jun 18, 2008.

LAGUNA DE PERLAS

Forty miles north of Bluefields, the relatively undiscovered cultural enclave of Laguna de Perlas (Pearl Lagoon) is a quiet, clean village with very friendly locals. While the entire Caribbean Coast is a unique blend of indigenous tribes, languages and cultures, Laguna de Perlas is where they all seem to come together within miles of one another. This is only fitting, considering it is the political and economic center of the region.

The town itself is small with paved sidewalks, plenty of greenery and a well-constructed Moravian church with beige walls and a burgundy roof. Several small indigenous villages (Moskito, Mayagna Awas and Garifuna) surround the area, with the English-speaking Creole population as the town's main cultural influence.

Fishing is the main source of income for the village, but tourism is gradually growing. Laguna de Perlas is the largest coastal town in Nicaragua, and is lined by the Pearl Keys (Cays), a set of 18 islands, about 145 kilometers (90 mi) offshore. The islands are inhabited by mostly fisherman, and are a great place for a day getaway to go fishing or snorkeling, or to see the endangered Hawksbill Sea Turtle.

Most people in the town are educated and passionate about the preservation of wildlife. They encourage sport fishing, turtle protection and legal lobster fishing. The owner of the local restaurant Queen Lobster, Nuria Dixon, not only encourages preservation, but also teaches tactics to local fisherman as well as tourists. Her premise is, *Give a man a fish, he eats for a day. Teach a man to fish, he eats for life.*

There are other restaurants in town as well, all of which serve seafood, along with Caribbean style *Gallo Pinto* (with coconut), and choices of chicken or meat, all for under $10. There are also a couple of quaint and affordable hotels, such as the Green Lodge Bed and Breakfast and the Casa Blanca, both with friendly owners. Updated: Sep 28, 2009.

When to Go

The best time to go to Laguna de Perlas is during the dry season (January – April). On October 30th, the *Fiesta de los Cangrejos* celebrates the liberation of slaves. There are parties, historical re-enactments and a pageant to crown *Miss Pearl Lagoon*, complete with judges, prizes and lots of food. The full week of events lasts from October 25th to the 31st. And of course, Semana Santa (Easter Week) is full of festivals and celebrations as well. Updated: Sep 28, 2009.

Getting To and Away from Laguna de Perlas

BY BUS

A bus leaves everyday at 5 a.m. for El Rama and costs around $7. The ride takes about four to five hours and can be slow and bumpy. The bus from El Rama to Laguna de Perlas returns around 4:30 p.m. There is also a bus from Laguna de Perlas to Kukra Hill that goes back and forth four times a day and costs $2.50.

BY BOAT

The first boat to Bluefields from Laguna de Perlas leaves the wharf at 6:30 a.m. every day, but it is advisable to arrive half an hour early. The second one leaves between 9 a.m. and 1 p.m., depending on when it fills up. Tickets cost $8 and should be purchased one day in advance. Three boats a day go to Laguna de Perlas from Bluefields at 9 a.m., 12 p.m. and 4 p.m. The ride takes 45 – 55 minutes. Updated: Sep 30, 2009.

Getting Around

Laguna de Perlas is small and easily navigable. Locals are friendly and eager to help you with directions. There are no buses. The main form of transportation around the town, aside from walking, is the *caponere*. These small cars without doors look like a cross between a golf cart and a turtle. The flat one-way fee is $0.50. Updated: Sep 30, 2009.

Safety

Unlike neighboring Bluefields, smaller, more peaceful Laguna de Perlas has a friendly and welcoming community. Violence is rare, as is petty theft. However, it is still wise to exercise caution, especially females and those traveling alone. Updated: Sep 30, 2009.

Services

MONEY

If you are planning on taking a trip to Laguna de Perlas, make sure to come prepared with a sufficient amount of cash as there are no banks, money wiring services or ATMs. The nearest place with these conveniences is Bluefields, a 45-minute boat ride away.

KEEPING IN TOUCH

The mail service is sent through **Enitel**, so it can be received in Laguna de Perlas, but if you need to send something, you'll have to do so from Bluefields. There are phone services for all Nicaraguan companies, including Enitel, Claro and Movistar and one Cyber Café with Internet access (but no WiFi).

MEDICAL

There is a public heath center and two pharmacies, but no hospital.

SHOPPING

Local specialties include fishing equipment rentals and guides, as well as bike rentals for $1 per hour. Updated: Sep 28, 2009.

Things to See and Do

Laguna de Perlas is a beautiful town with an incredible amount of cultural diversity and enjoyable activities. Take a walk around and see the Moravian Church, of Czechoslovakian influence. Alternatively, witness the ethnic diversity by visiting Orinoko or taking the Paisaje de Awas to hear five different languages spoken by the wide variety of natives. Or take a trip to the tranquil Pearl Keys and spend the day fishing or snorkeling. Updated: Sep 28, 2009.

Did a unique trek? Got way off the beaten path? Tell other travelers at vivatravelguides.com

Turtle Nesting

Unlike the turtles on the Pacific, the Green turtle and the Hawksbill sea turtle do not lay eggs by the thousands. In fact, since the Indians and Creoles used to eat them, they have become endangered over the past 10 years. However, recent limits have been placed on turtle consumption. The best time to see the turtles is during the full moon and the new moon, night or day. To arrange a tour, ask for Bill McCoy, across from the Green Lodge. Turtles nest at the Pearl Keys, and expeditions cost $8 a day, plus the cost of gas. Each trip requires 25 gallons and boats hold up to seven people. Updated: Sep 30, 2009.

Paisaje de Awas

This unique journey takes you from Laguna de Perlas to one of the many unique, outlying *Mayagna Awas* indigenous communities. The trail from town is a 40-minute walk along a cement path surrounded by grass and trees. Along the way, you'll pass Creole children and families swimming and biking, before entering the Moskito village. After passing thatched roofs and rowdy children, you'll cross a bridge to the more quaint village of Awas. Ask around for directions, or head to Casa Blanca for a written desciption of how to get there. Updated: Sep 30, 2009.

Sport Fishing

Due to the large depletion of fish and lobster on the Caribbean Coast, sport fishing is highly preferred. Sit in a boat on the calm lagoon all day and catch a wide range of fish, including Jack, Snook, Tarpon and Catfish, then take a picture and set them free. Head out with a local tour company (ask around) for about $1.50 a foot traveled. All fishing equipment is available. Updated: Sep 28, 2009.

Snorkeling

The clear waters of Laguna de Perlas and the surrounding Pearl Keys are a great place to snorkel. See coral reefs, sea grass, conches, hermit shells, sea cucumbers and more. **Casa Blanca** arranges whole day trips to the Pearl Keys with snorkel equipment and fishing lines: Tel: 505-2-527-0508, E-mail: casa_blanca_lp@yahoo.com. Also check with **Snorkel Jungle River Tours**: Tel: 505-8-447-9522, E-mail: camp77ss@hotmail.com. Updated: Sep 28, 2009.

Pearl Keys

The Pearl Keys, a set of 18 islands, are located about 145 kilometers (90 mi) offshore from the Laguna de Perlas. Most of the islands are uninhabited, except for a few which are occupied by fishermen. The Pearl Keys are the best place in the area to go fishing and snorkeling, and to see the nesting of the endangered Hawksbill sea turtle. There are no restaurants or hotels, so make sure to pack a lunch. Trips take about 45 minutes on a panga and cost around $90 – 350 per day, depending on the size of your party. Updated: Sep 28, 2009.

Orinoco

Orinoco, located about 24 kilometers (15 mi) north of the Laguna de Perlas basin, can be reached by a small boat from Laguna de Perlas. The village is home to one of the many unique ethnic groups in the region, the Garifuna. This African tribe originally came from Venezuela, but eventually migrated to Central America. The Garifuna of Nicaragua live in the small village of Orinoco and are comprised of the Sambola and Velasquez families, who speak English as well as their own language, Garifuna. However, because of low literacy rates, only 50 people still speak the language. The village, comprised of about 1,000 people (known for their friendliness), sits in lush green farmland. Aside from observing the diverse birds, animals and plantlife, interacting with the unique Garifuna is an unforgettable experience in and of itself. Updated: Sep 28, 2009.

Tours

Since Laguna de Perlas is new to the tourism scene, most tour guides are found through word of mouth. Tours can be arranged through the **Casa Blanca** hotel, which leads several trips for tourists. Most trips are $350 (for up to seven people) and include full-day trips to the Pearl Keys for fishing or snorkeling. Journeys up the Wawa Shang River to visit Pueblo Nuevo and Orinoco can also be arranged. Contact **Mr. Sudland** (Tel: 505-2-572-0508, E-mail: casa_blanca_lp@yahoo.com) for a boat trip to see crocodiles, birds and monkeys for $90. Another local tour operator is **Pearl of the Caribbean** (Tel: 505-8-447-9522/424-4135, E-mail: camp77ss@hotmail.com), offering opportunities for snorkeling and tours through the jungle. Updated: Sep 30, 2009.

Lodging

Green Lodge Bed and Breakfast

(ROOMS: $7.50 – 20) Located in the 'First of May' neighborhood on the north side of Enitel, the Green Lodge Bed and Breakfast has a family feel and clean rooms. The most economic option is the single bed for $7.50. A double bed is $10, and can be shared by a couple at no extra cost. Four bunk beds are either $20 per room or $5 per person. Home-cooked meals are also available from $2–3.50, but have to be ordered in advance. Tel: 505-2-572-0507. Updated: Sep 28, 2009.

Casa Blanca

(ROOMS: $15 – 35) Casa Blanca, one of the most accommodating and comfortable places in Laguna de Perlas, is located less than 100 meters (328 ft) north of the Municipal Stadium. The hotel offers Internet services and tours, as well as the option of renting bikes, canoes and diving equipment. There are seven rooms available with or without private bathrooms and TVs. They also have a restaurant—rumored to be the best in town—with comfortable outdoor seating and a menu with full meals, ranging from chicken for $4 to lobster for $15. Tel: 505-2-572-0508, E-mail: casa_blanca_lp@yahoo.com. Updated: Sep 28, 2009.

Restaurants

Fry Fish

(ENTREES: $3.50 – 4.59) For a casual, bar-like setting, head to Fry Fish, one block north of Queen Lobster. Set in a bamboo hut with red lighting at night, relaxed music and red picnic-style tablecloths, Fry Fish serves exactly what their name suggests: fried fish, fried shrimp and fried chicken. A full bar menu is available as well. Open 8 a.m. – 12 a.m., seven days a week. Tel: 505-8-410-5197. Updated: Sep 28, 2009.

Queen Lobster

(ENTREES: $5 – 10) Situated right on the lagoon, this stylish and eco-friendly lobster joint is not only unique, but also offers delicious meals. Entrees include fish and chips, lobster in coconut sauce, and a *Rundown*, a typical Caribbean dish made with seafood, coconut milk and vegetables (available on Saturdays and Sundays). Aside from the food, owner Nuria Dixon also holds cooking classes, where students not only learn how to cook typical island food, but how to fish and buy their own vegetables as well. Queen Lobster is available for special events, and is 200 meters (656 ft) north of the Municipal Wharf. Open Monday – Friday, 11 a.m. – 11 p.m., and Saturday and Sunday, 10 a.m. – midnight. Tel: 505-8-662-3393, E-mail: njdixonc@yahoo.es, URL: www.queenlobster.com. Updated: Sep 28, 2009.

The Corn Islands

The islands of Little Corn (p.305) and Big Corn (see right) are lined with picturesque palm trees and surrounded by beautiful coral reefs covered in crystal-clear water. Little Corn has no electricity or phones, so plan to spend most of your time relaxing on the beach—if you can handle that. Big Corn, an hour away by dinghy or panga, is a major Nicaraguan vacation spot. Snorkeling is excellent from both islands. Keep your eyes peeled for a Spanish galleon wreck.

Big Corn is best reached by plane from Managua, or plane or boat from Bluefields. The best time to visit is March-April. Credit cards are not accepted on the islands (with the exception of a few high priced hotels) but U.S. dollars are. The local language is English. Updated: May 07, 2009.

History

The Corn Islands were originally home to indigenous cultures such as the Sumu and Kukra Indians, who (fortunately for them) did not have the sort of wealth that attracted Spanish conquistadors during the colonial era. The natives were warlike enough to drive off most attempts to contact them. In fact, the British commonly referred to the islands as the "Skeleton Islands."

While the British, Dutch and French pirates used the islands as bases from which to attack Spanish treasure fleets, they did not leave any lasting settlements. Most notably, the infamous Henry Morgan was one of many pirates who used the islands as a base for raiding.

In the late 17th century the British became actively involved with the Miskito Indians along Nicaragua's coast, and the Indian area was later named a protectorate of the British Empire. Interestingly, Miskito kings were often educated in England and the language therefore became quite common among the islanders. In 1894, the British formally left the Miskito area and the Corn Islands, ceding the region to Nicaragua. In 1914 the islands were leased to the USA for 99 years, but the agreement was broken in 1971.

Before 1988, the islanders mostly lived off of fishing and the production of coconut oil. In 1988, the islands were devastated by Hurricane Joan and many of the coconut trees were destroyed. Since then, lobster fishing and tourism have taken over as the islands' key industries. Updated: Oct 07, 2009.

Lodging

Nicaragua's Corn Islands offer many lodging options, save for the high-rise 5-star fare of larger cities. The isolation of the islands' hotels gives them their charm, as no two are alike. Walking up and down either island provides visitors with a multitude of choices. There are choices for all budgets—especially for those not wanting to break the bank.

BIG CORN ISLAND

Eighty kilometers (50 mi) east of Bluefields, on the Atlantic Coast, Big Corn Island is one of the most popular tourist destinations in Nicaragua. Travelers come from all around to dive and snorkel in the clear waters and to lounge on the soft, white sand. Because it is on the Caribbean Coast, the culture is different from other places in Nicaragua. English is the primary language on the island, though most inhabitants speak Spanish as well. You will also find many principal Nicaraguan dishes, such as Gallo Pinto (rice and red kidney beans) laced with sweet hints of coconut. Curry is popular, as well as chop suey, left over from the large Chinese population that once inhabited the island. Fish is fresh, and the local Rundown dish—made from coconut oil, fish, meat and vegetables—should not be missed. Reggae and country music can be heard throughout the island day and night.

Big Corn Island is quickly becoming one of the most touristed destinations in Nicaragua. It is not only less expensive than its neighbor, Costa Rica, but it also has all the comforts and necessities a traveler could need or want. Simple hotels can be found for $10 per night, and more luxurious places on the beach, such as Arena Beach or Casa Canada have all the amenities you could desire for around $90 per night.

The highest point of the island is Mount Pleasant (p.302). Take a hike or horseback ride up the path for a bird's eye view of the tropical surroundings. Updated: Oct 01, 2009.

When to Go

During the dry season (from January to July), Big Corn Island is generally cooler and breezier than other parts of Nicaragua. The rainy season lasts from August until late December. During that time, the waters overtake the beach on the north side of the island, so it is best to book a place to stay on the south end. It is also important to note that rates are generally lower during this time, and although there is the occasional torrential downpour, there are also several sunny days and the weather is generally warm.

Big Corn Island shares many holidays with the rest of Nicaragua, including **Sandinista's Day** on July 19th and **Independence Day** from September 14th – 15th. It is a very popular destination during **Semana Santa** (Easter Week), as well. **Crab Fest** is celebrated from August 27th – 28th, which is unique to the Caribbean Coast and commemorates the liberation of the slaves. During this celebration there are colorful parades, activities, and an election to crown Miss Corn Islands. Updated: Oct 01, 2009.

Getting To and Away From Big Corn Island

BY AIR

The most popular way to get to Big Corn Island is by plane, from either Managua or nearby Bluefields. Planes run daily, one in the morning and one in the evening, through **La Costeña** airlines. From Managua, the flight costs $170 and takes about 1.5 hours, but it is best to get there at least half an hour

BIG CORN ISLAND

Brig Bay

Caribbean Sea

Activities ●
1 Marine Park B1
2 Mt. Pleasant B1

Eating
3 Arenas Beach Restaurant (see 14)
4 Hotel Morgan Bar and Restaurant (see 18)
5 Picnic Center: Under the Sun A2
6 Fisher's Cave A1
7 Martha's Bar and Restaurant A2
8 Nautilus Restaurant (see 22)
9 Sweet Dreams Restaurant (see 20)

Services ★
10 BanPro Bank A2

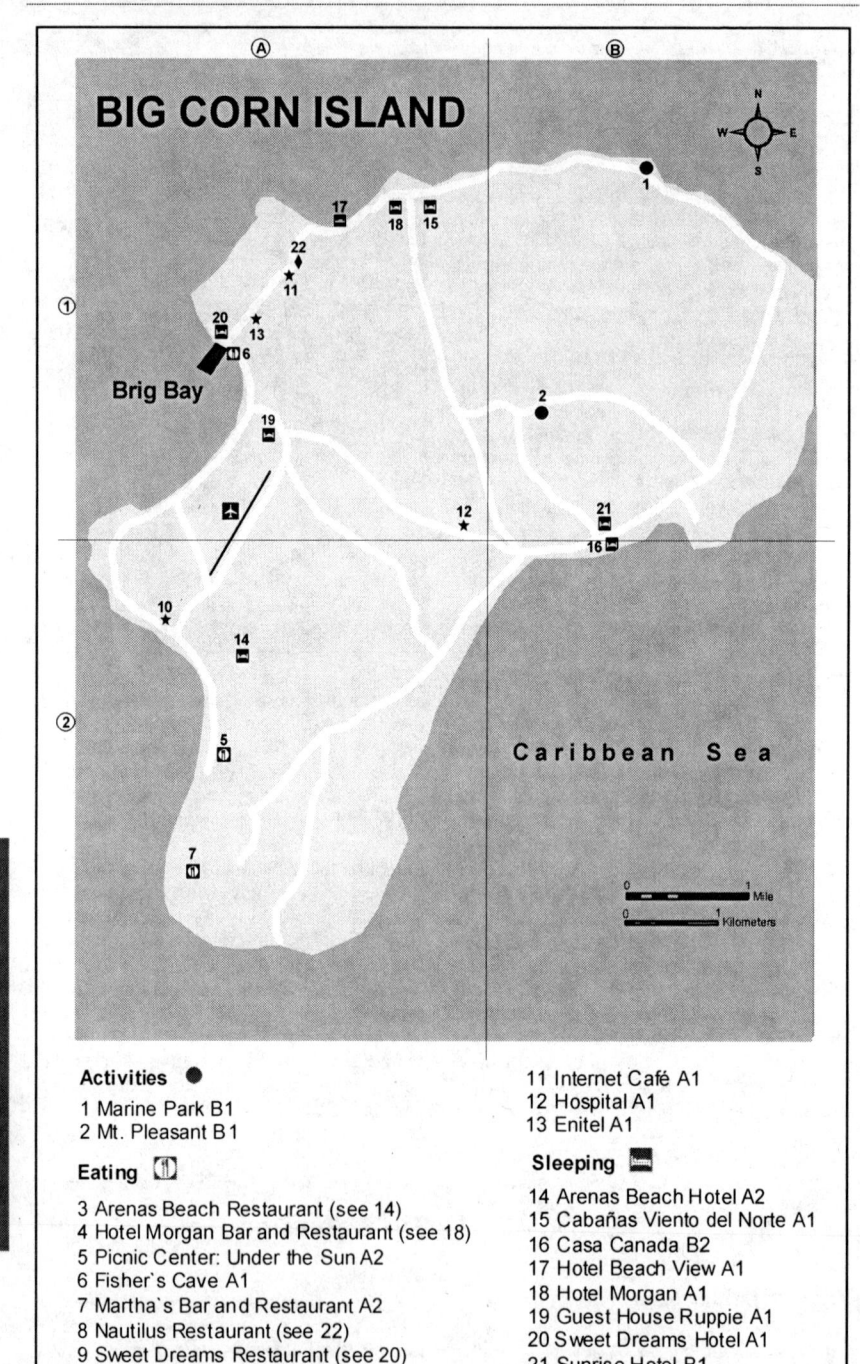

11 Internet Café A1
12 Hospital A1
13 Enitel A1

Sleeping
14 Arenas Beach Hotel A2
15 Cabañas Viento del Norte A1
16 Casa Canada B2
17 Hotel Beach View A1
18 Hotel Morgan A1
19 Guest House Ruppie A1
20 Sweet Dreams Hotel A1
21 Sunrise Hotel B1

Tours ♦
22 Nautilus Diving Center A1

Did a unique trek? Got way off the beaten path? Tell other travelers at vivatravelguides.com

early. For current schedules and price information, visit www.lacostena.com.ni or call 505-2-263-2142 for reservations.

BY BOAT

The boat from Bluefields takes about seven hours and costs $10. There are several different companies that provide this service and schedules are constantly changing. Ask around at your hotel or at the harbor for specific information. The least popular method is to take a boat directly from El Rama (p.289). Small boats run from Big Corn Island to Little Corn Island twice a day at 7 a.m. and 3 p.m. They cost $5-10 and take about a half an hour. Updated: Oct 01, 2009.

Getting Around

Big Corn Island has one 12 kilometer- (7.5 mi-) long road that circles the island. It takes three hours to walk the entire thing, or about half an hour in a golf cart. Golf cart rentals are available at the **Sunrise Hotel** (Tel: 505-8-828-7835, E-mail: southendsunrise@yahoo.com) on the south end for about $10 an hour. Taxis have a flat rate of $1 during the day and $2 at night. There is a bus for $0.25 that circles the island, but don't rely on it. Updated: Oct 01, 2009.

Safety

During the day, Big Corn Island is a relaxing tropical paradise. However, at night, there are few street lights, and the roads can be very dark and vacant; take a cab after nightfall. While there is a 24-hour police patrol, and violent crime is very rare on the island, it is still important to be cautious, and, as always, look out for pickpockets and petty thieves. Updated: Oct 01, 2009.

Services

TOURISM

Hotel Anastasia has a tourism office, located between North End and South End. It is open Monday – Saturday, 10 a.m. – 1 p.m. and 3–6 p.m.

MONEY

Because Big Corn Island is so isolated, it is important to be prepared. Bring sufficient cash with you and any products you feel you can't live without. Traveler's checks are not widely accepted. The upscale hotels and restaurants accept most credit cards, especially Visa, and many places only accept cash. There is a bank, **BanPro**, that keeps regular business hours.

KEEPING IN TOUCH

The main phone company, Enitel, is located in North End. There is also an Internet café near the Nautilus restaurant, which costs about $1.50 per hour. **Casa Canada** and **Arena Beach** hotels also have WiFi, if you have your own laptop. There is no post office on the island.

MEDICAL

As far as medical necessities go, there is a 24-hour **hospital** on the island and a **private doctor** (Tel: 505-2-575-5184/ 8-641-5803) who speaks English. Consultations cost $5 –10. There is also a **Public Health Center** and four **pharmacies** scattered around the island.

LAUNDRY

All laundry services are arranged through the hotels and cost up to $5 for a large bag of clothes. Updated: Oct 01, 2009.

SHOPPING

Most of the shopping on the island exists between North End and Brig Bay, and at the southernmost tip of the airfield. Stores carry a variety of products, including souvenirs, carvings, postcards, bags, groceries, hardware, cosmetics, baked goods and Caribbean clothing.

Eat and Art, located in North End, offers local handcrafts, hand-woven bags, souvenirs, healthy food and even homemade pizza for delivery. Open Monday – Sunday 8 a.m.– 7 p.m. Tel: 505-2-575-5077.

Rodriguez Distribution is another miscellaneous store that bears the slogan *Anything You Can Imagine*. They carry groceries, household appliances, electronics and of course a variety of unique little knickknacks. Near the airport. Tel: 505-2-575-5233. Open Monday – Saturday 6 a.m. – 6 p.m. and Sunday 6 a.m. – noon.

Susy's Southend Styles is the only boutique on the south end, and carries good-quality clothing for all ages. 505-8-644-0929. Open Monday – Sunday 9 a.m. – 6:30 p.m. Updated: Sep 28, 2009.

Things to See and Do

Big Corn Island offers a variety of activities to a wide range of travelers. For a relaxed day, lounge with a book on the white sand beaches while sipping on a cocktail at Casa Canada's breathtaking Infinity Pool. For the more adventurous traveler, hike or horseback ride to

---

Support VIVA by reserving your hotel or hostel at vivatravelguides.com/hotels/

Mount Pleasant, the highest point on the island. Take advantage of the incredible variety of marine life and clear water by snorkeling or scuba diving at the coral reefs. Sport fishing, fly-fishing and kayaking are also available, either through independent rentals or guided tours. Updated: Jun 05, 2009.

Snorkeling

The barrier reef system surrounding Big Corn Island makes for incredible views of intact coral reefs and tropical marine life. Without any previous experience, snorkelers are able to swim among the vast array of coral, rays, sponges, Nurse sharks and even dolphins. The biggest snorkeling lure on the island is the **Marine Park**, located 30 meters (98 ft) offshore from **Anastasia's on the Sea**, which rents snorkeling equipment from $2.50 per hour to $10 per day. **Nautilus Diving Tours** also provides snorkeling tours for $20, in addition to its breathtaking glass-bottom boat tour for the same price. Updated: Sep 28, 2009.

Diving

Scuba diving is one of the most popular activities on Big Corn Island. Divers exploring the sea around Big Corn will have plenty of eye candy, especially the famous "Blowing Rock." This volcanic rock formation is about a 30-minute boat ride east of the island. From 30.5 meters (100 ft) below the water the rocks rise up and break the surface of the Caribbean Sea. The formations are covered with coral that attracts a wide variety of sea life, including lobsters, turtles, barracudas and even sharks. Updated: Sep 28, 2009.

Mt. Pleasant

Big Corn Island is composed of 10 square kilometers (4 mi^2) of tropical forest and mangrove swamps, framed by a path of white sand beaches. The main road lines the ocean and beaches, encircling the mostly impassable forested interior. However, anyone who wants a 360° view of the island can horseback ride or hike a trail to the top of the 97.5-meter (320-ft) tall Mt. Pleasant, also known as *The Watch Tower*. The trail can be found through the Sunrise Hotel. 505-8-828-7835. South end, across from Casa Canada. Updated: Sep 28, 2009.

Tours

Dive tours, scuba gear and boat rentals are available throughout the island. Two-to-three day PADI scuba training and a one-day tours are available for beginners through **Nautilus Diving Center** in North End. Other hotels on the island also offer dive tours, such as **Sunrise Hotel** on the south end and **Picnic Center and Arena Beach** on the southwest beach. Check with your hotel or one of the above to arrange a dive tour. Updated: Jun 05, 2009.

Nautilus

Located in North End, Nautilus Diving Center offers dive tours for both the experienced and rookie diver. For those who have never dived before, their "Discover Scuba Diving Tour" takes you out without any training for half a day for $80. PADI dive courses are also available, from three-day open-water courses to two-day advanced courses ($230 – 280). For the more experienced, tours average around $35 – 40. Refresher courses are also offered and trips to "Blowing Rock" include two tank dives ($95). E-mail: divechema@yahoo.com, URL: www.divebigcorn.com. Updated: Sep 28, 2009.

Lodging

Because Big Corn Island is a bit pricier than most parts of Nicaragua, the budgeting traveler would be best advised to hook up with a group; most establishments charge per room, not per person, and do not increase their prices when a number of people stay in one place. There are several hotels with private cabins around the island, as well as budget hostels. **Casa Canada** and **Arena Beach** are the two luxury hotels, located on the southern part of the island. Both hotels offer amenities such as WiFi, restaurants, and outdoor bars and areas for sunbathing. Updated: Sep 29, 2009.

BUDGET
Guest House Ruppie

(ROOMS: $10) One of the cheapest deals on the island, Guest House Ruppie is perfect for budget travelers just looking for a place to crash and store their belongings. Rooms include a bed, a fan and a shared bathroom. There is also a small stand right outside the hotel that sells $1 tacos and $4 sandwiches. The stand also has coffee, juice, soda and beer. Guest House Ruppie is located a short walk from the dock in Brig Bay, next to the Reggae Palace Discothèque, across from the Western Union. Cash only. Updated: Mar 16, 2009.

Hotel Beach View

(ROOMS: $10 – 35) This popular backpacker spot sits on stilts just a 15-minute walk north of the dock. The large deck is stocked with plenty of chairs and tables and overlooks the ocean. Guests can fish right off the deck. Rooms are simple with fans and beds with mosquito nets. Owner Gaynell Campbell is a jovial woman who sits across the street in her office and is willing to negotiate prices depending on your needs. Tel: 505-2-575-5062. Updated: Mar 16, 2009.

Cabañas Viento del Norte

(ROOMS: $10 – 50) With small clusters of rooms in private cabins, Cabañas Viento del Norte is economically ideal for groups, as the price is not altered per person. The $50 rooms include air conditioning, TVs, microwaves, toasters, refrigerators and ocean views, with space for up to four people. If you are traveling solo and/or on a budget, there are rooms available for $10 per person with fans and private bathrooms. Other amenities include laundry, meals and drinks (for a small charge), and free airport transportation. Visa is the only credit card accepted. Tel: 505-2-575-5112 / 8-464-0204, Fax: 505-575-5112, E-mail: ikestanmar@yahoo.com. Updated: Mar 16, 2009.

Hotel J

(ROOMS: $12.50 – 25) Conveniently located at the north end of the island, next to Brisas Mar, Hotel J is a good deal for the budget traveler who prefers a room with air-conditioning. All rooms also include double beds, fans and private bathrooms; the rooms can be shared at no extra cost. Although the hotel is located right next to the popular North End bars, the owners tend to lock the doors around 10 or 11 p.m., so make sure to arrange a way back in if you plan on staying out later than that. Tel: 505-2-575-5175. Updated: Mar 16, 2009.

MID-RANGE
Sweet Dreams Hotel

($15 – 35) You can find the sign for Sweet Dreams Hotel perched above streetlights and rooftops, just meters north of the harbor at a bend in the road. The hotel has clean, affordable and spacious rooms at reasonable prices. Rooms with fans, TVs and shared bathrooms range from $15-25 and can be shared between two or three people. You can also upgrade to matrimonial beds, air-conditioning and a private bathroom for $35. Checkout time is at noon. The hotel only accepts Visa. Reception is open from 6:30 a.m. to 10 p.m. Tel: 505-2-575-5195 / 8-841-3216. Updated: Mar 16, 2009.

Hotel Morgan

(ROOMS: $15 – 35) In North End, a cute cluster of light pink cabins and palm trees make up Hotel Morgan. The atmosphere here is friendly and the rooms are clean and spacious. A simple, single room with a bed, fan and shared bathroom goes for $15 per night. Ten dollars more will get you air conditioning, cable TV and a private bathroom. If you're traveling with someone else, a room with two double beds, a refrigerator and all the aforementioned amenities is $35 per night for up to two people without extra charge. Each additional person pays $5 extra. The hotel has a bar and restaurant. Credit cards are accepted. Tel: 505-2-575-7052 / 8-835-5890, E-mail: kerrygean@gmail.com. Updated: Mar 13, 2009.

Anastasia Hotel

(ROOMS: $20) Framed with marine murals of bright blue seas and tropical fish, Anastasia Hotel's interior is as refreshing as the cool breezes of the north shore, where it is located. Rooms are large, with two beds, cable TVs, air conditioning and decks that overlook the turquoise waters of the Caribbean Sea. Tel: 505-8-937-0016, E-mail: contact@cornislandresort.com, URL: www.cornislandparadise.com. Updated: Mar 16, 2009.

HIGH-END
Sunrise Hotel

(ROOMS: $35 – 55) Located across from Casa Canada, Sunrise Hotel is an economical, quiet option with a family-like atmosphere and 24-hour security. Owners Lonmar and Rowena Kandler are very accommodating and down-to-earth. Rooms all come with 24-hour hot water, cable TVs, DVD players, WiFi, ceiling fans and air conditioning. The hotel also organizes outdoor activities, such as snorkeling, fishing, diving, hiking and horseback riding ($30 – 60). Golf cart rentals are available for $40 – 60 for three to 12 hours. Tel: 505-8-828-7835 / 414-1909, E-mail: rowenakandler@yahoo.com, URL: www.southendsunrise.com. Updated: Mar 16, 2009.

Casa Canada Hotel

(ROOMS: $75 – 109) Composed of 17 cabins and four rooms, Casa Canada's South End resort offers luxury with the comforts of home. Each cabin contains a king-sized bed, a private bathroom with 24-hour hot water, a sofa, a TV with cable and a DVD player, as well as a refrigerator, a patio with ocean view, a mini-bar and access to the outdoor Infinity Pool. The rooms are less expensive and

Support VIVA by reserving your hotel or hostel at vivatravelguides.com/hotels/

have everything that's in the cabins, except for a sofa. The hotel also has an outdoor bar and restaurant. Breakfast is included. Credit cards accepted. Tel: 505-8-644-0925, E-mail: casacanada@canada.com, URL: www.casa-canada.com. Updated: Mar 16, 2009.

Arenas Beach Hotel

(ROOMS: $75 – 115) If you're looking for the ultimate in comfort and convenience, head straight to Arenas Beach Hotel, located on the Southwest Bay. The hotel has its own private white sandy beach with lounge chairs, a bar and a restaurant. All rooms have one to two queen beds, air conditioning, hot water, cable TVs, free WiFi and private balconies with ocean views. You can choose between a Comfort Room ($75), Suite ($115), or a Bungalow ($105). All credit cards accepted. Tel: 505-8-851-8046 / 2-575-5223, E-mail: info@arenasbeachhotel.com, URL: www.arenasbeachhotel.com. Updated: Mar 16, 2009.

Restaurants

The restaurants on Big Corn Island are mostly clustered around North End. The majority have mid-range prices, with meals averaging around $7. The fusion of sweet and spicy Caribbean food and typical Nicaraguan fare is unique to the area. Seafood, especially lobster, is fresh, plentiful and reasonably priced. Make sure to try the coconut bread sold along the street or, if you're wary of street vendors, head to Nautilus Restaurant, where the smell of coconut fills the entire block at baking-time. Updated: Mar 16, 2009.

BUDGET
Restaurant Brisas Mar

(ENTREES: $1.25 –3.25, ICE CREAM: $0.50 – 1.50) This fast-food joint/ice cream parlor, which can be found in the midst of hectic North End, is a great place to grab a quick, cheap bite to eat. The Eskimo ice cream shop sells cones and cups of tasty classic flavors. If you're looking for food, entrées include fried chicken, pork or beef; each dish includes your choice of sides—spaghetti, rice, beans or fried plantains. You can also get Instant Chicken Noodle soup for $1.25, served directly from the cardboard cup. Located in Brig Bay, sector 2. Open Monday – Sunday, 7 a.m. – 10 p.m. Closed until 4 p.m. on Saturday. Tel: 505-8-421-7832. Updated: Mar 16, 2009.

Fisher's Cave

(ENTREES: $3.50 – 12) Located directly on the dock, Fisher's Cave has quite the view. Sitting on its large deck around mid-day or sunset, you can watch the hectic scene of boats unloading passengers and cargo while fisherman reel in their prizes for the day. The indoor seating area has a large glass window so you don't miss the display. Fisher's is also filled with both the aroma of fried fish and music to fully feed your senses. The menu has a wide selection of lobster, shrimp and fish; all of the options are freshly caught and most are offered fried. Cash only. Open 11 a.m. – 11 p.m. Tel: 505-2-575-5191. Updated: Mar 16, 2009.

Martha's Bar and Restaurant

(ENTREES: $5 – 10) Just south of the Picnic Center, Martha's Bar and Restaurant is the perfect place to have a nice, quiet dinner on the beach. Considering the quality of the entrees and the location, it is certainly one of the best deals in town. The shrimp and lobster come grilled, breaded or served in either a white or wine sauce. There is also a variety of chicken, fish, pork, beef and chop suey dishes. All entrees come with a side of vegetables, salad, rice and fries or plantains. On the Southwest Beach. Cash only. Open 7 a.m. – 9 a.m and 1 p.m.– 7 p.m. Updated: Mar 16, 2009.

MID-RANGE
Sunrise Hotel and Restaurant

(ENTREES: $4 – 17) If you're looking for a breath of fresh air, Sunrise Restaurant is the only non-smoking place on the island. There is an indoor seating area as well as an outdoor patio, where you will find a family atmosphere, country music, a friendly staff and a gated parking area. There are plenty of seafood, spaghetti and Chop Suey entrees to choose from, with your choice of three or four side dishes. If you're budgeting, or just looking for a snack, there are also appetizers, sandwiches and hamburgers for around $4. Across from Casa Canada, South End of the beach. Cash only. Open daily 7 a.m. – 10 p.m. Tel: 505-8-490-5350. Updated: Mar 16, 2009.

Picnic Center: Under the Sun

(ENTREES: $4 – 20) Next to Arena Beach, the Picnic Center is an inexpensive place to hang out for a beer or a bite to eat. The eatery's large rotunda has a full bar, several tables and an air conditioner. You'll find straw huts with picnic tables directly on the sand. The huts line the rotunda, where music can be heard all day. The menu ranges from hot dogs and hamburgers to

---

Did a unique trek? Got way off the beaten path? Tell other travelers at vivatravelguides.com

grilled lobster and filet mignon. Southwest Bay. Cash only. Open 8 a.m.–10 p.m. Updated: Mar 16, 2009.

Nautilus Restaurant

(ENTREES: $4.50 – 13.50) Big Corn Island's Caribbean fare can be appreciated in style and class at Nautilus restaurant. The interior is decorated with dangling seashells, conch-shell chandeliers and Caribbean paintings of crabs and boats, so feasting at one of their blue tables is an experience in and of itself. You can either sit indoors and scope out their art gallery or play one of their several board games on the deck. Entrees include Caribbean seafood dishes, fish filets and curry; the fresh-baked coconut bread, in particular, is not to be missed. Located a 10-minute walk north of the dock. Cash only. Open 8 a.m. – 10 p.m. Tel: 505-2-575-5077. Updated: Mar 16, 2009.

Sweet Dreams Restaurant

(ENTREES: $5 – 10) Sweet Dreams restaurant sits above the hotel of the same name. Both locations are slightly hidden, right where the road bends just north of the dock. There is a small, pillared deck that overlooks the ocean; inside, the restaurant is spacious, with tiled floors, carved wooden chairs and picnic-style tablecloths. Entrees include a variety of meat, chicken, fish, shrimp and lobster dishes and all are offered fried, boiled or in wine sauce. The prices are excellent. Open Monday – Saturday 7 a.m. – 9 p.m. Accepts Visa only. Tel: 505-2-575-5195 / 8-841-3216. Updated: Mar 16, 2009.

HIGH-END
Arena Beach

(ENTREES: $4 – 19) Head to the luxurious Arena Beach restaurant and bar, where you can lounge on a beach chair and order from the selection of cocktails, or sit at one of the shaded picnic tables and enjoy fresh lobster, shrimp or conch creations. There is also an indoor dining area with a patio and free WiFi. The menu is varied and the staff is attentive and efficient. Credit cards accepted. Open daily 7 a.m. – 10 p.m. Tel: 505-8-851-8046 / 2-575-5223. E-mail: info@arenasbeachhotel.com, URL: www.arenasbeachhotel.com. Updated: Mar 16, 2009.

Casa Canada

(ENTREES: $5 – 16) On the patio of Casa Canada you can hear waves crash, while the aromas of the sea and freshly cooked Caribbean food fill the air. Lounge by the Infinity Pool, which has the illusion of overflowing into the ocean, and enjoy a cocktail or *ceviche* (a raw fish cocktail, marinated in lime and spices). The restaurant specializes in lobster, steak, shrimp, chicken and fish; the menu also has pasta, rice, soup and sandwiches. Located in South End. Credit cards accepted. Open 7:30 a.m. – 10:30 p.m. Tel: 505-8-644-0925, E-mail: casacanada@canada.com, URL: www.casa-canada.com. Updated: Mar 16, 2009.

Hotel Morgan Bar and Restaurant

(ENTREES: $7 – 13) Hotel Morgan's red-lit, two-story bar and restaurant are hard to miss, particularly since they sit next to bright pink cabins. The quaint restaurant has a wide variety of seafood dishes, and the lobster is very reasonably priced ($11 – 13). Morgan's is also the place to find one of the best deals for a Rundown. Fifteen minutes north of the dock. Credit cards accepted. Open 8 a.m. – 10 p.m. Tel: 505-2-575-5052 / 8-835-5890, E-mail: kerrygean.morgan@gmail.com. Updated: Mar 16, 2009.

LITTLE CORN ISLAND

Little Corn Island is literally an unspoiled paradise. It's a place of phenomenal beauty, where coconut trees sway in the evening breeze and every section of beach seems cut and pasted from a postcard. With its Caribbean vibe and slow pace, Little Corn is a wonderfully easy place to get stuck. Schedules should be adjusted, vacations extended. Doing nothing has never been so satisfying.

Development here has been extremely limited. There's just one paved footpath on the island, very few motorbikes and no cars. Most places only offer electricity at night, and every restaurant or hotel is responsible for generating its own power. The island also lacks a bank or ATM, so be sure and take enough cash with you.

Although there are a few Western-owned hotels, the islanders have done a remarkable job of preventing big companies from moving in, and the vast majority of businesses are locally run. The locals themselves are generally quite a friendly bunch, in the bantering Garifuna tradition. Spanish, English and Creole are all spoken here, but English is the default language. Juggling their mixed linguistic heritage, many islanders seem to have difficulty understanding tourist

LITTLE CORN

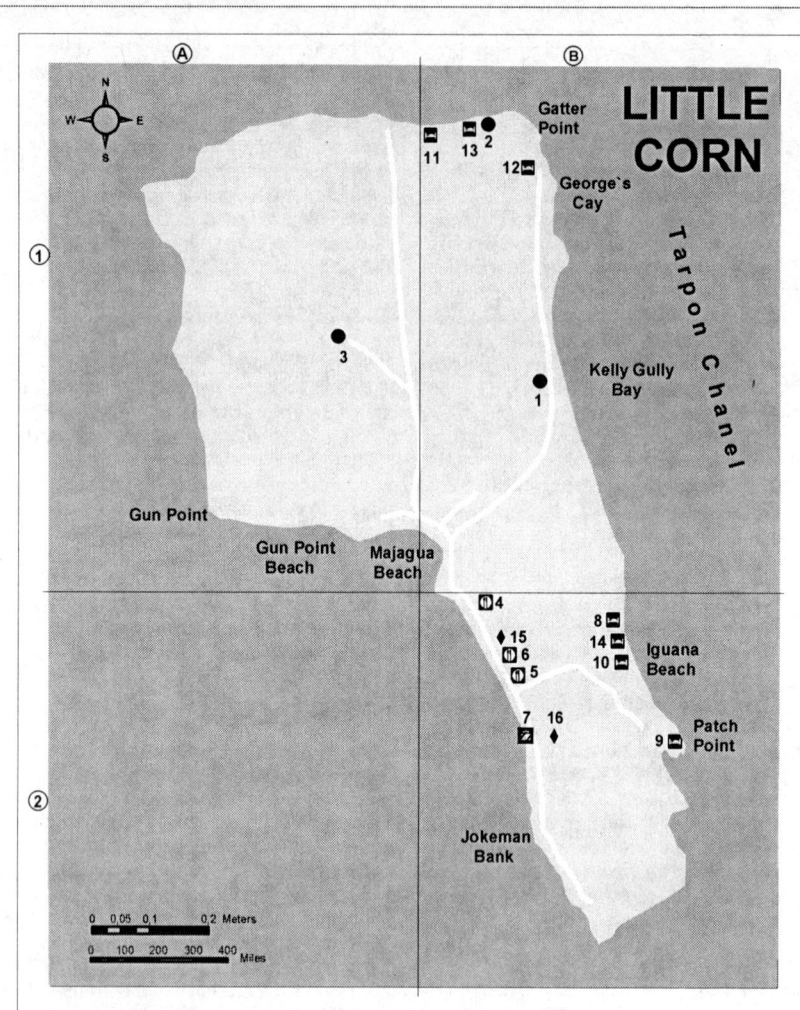

Activities ●

1 Baseball Field A2
2 Farm Peace and Love A2
3 Lighthouse A1

Eating

4 Barra Intel Habana B2
5 Lobster Inn B2
6 Sweet Oasis B2

Shopping

7 Dolphin Dive B2

Sleeping

8 Carlito's Sunrise Paradise B2
9 Casa Iguana B2
10 Derek`s Place B1
11 Ensueños B1
12 Elsa`s Sweet Breeze B1
13 Farm Peace and Love B1
14 Gracies´s Cool Spot B2

Tours ♦

15 Dive Little Corn B2
16 Dolphin Inn B2

Did a unique trek? Got way off the beaten path? Tell other travelers at vivatravelguides.com

Spanish. Try to open a conversation with the standard "Hablas Inglés?" and you'll often get a befuddled look, followed up by "Whatcha talkin?" Best to just switch over to English while you're here.

The locations that attract the most attention are the dive shops. Divers and snorkelers can find local guides running daily trips out to the reef: Little Corn's underwater wonderland includes caves, caverns and overhangs. Virtually every reef fish classified as Tropical Caribbean is present in the waters; un-chummed shark encounters are frequent. The sharks are friendly, as are Dive Little Corn's instructors.

In general, the vast majority of visitors seem to get sucked into the island lifestyle of doing nothing. Simple acts like checking your e-mail at the island's lone Internet cafe or collecting mangos make up the day's productive activities, interspersed with long periods of lounging, swimming, basking in the sun and lying around. Take advantage of the island's abundance of hammocks—a wonderful way to spend a few days...or a few months.

Photo by Elicia Bolton

To get to Little Corn, take a quick bounce across the open sea by boat from Big Corn Island. When you arrive you'll have to either jump directly into the tide or use a plastic beer crate to step ashore. The island tempo is easy to fall into: simply slip out of as many clothes as you feel comfortable with—retaining the minimum required for modesty—and wander. Updated: Jan 09, 2009.

When to Go

Little Corn used to have consistent wet and dry seasons, but recently the weather seems to have grown more unpredictable. Generally speaking, the high season runs from December to April and the place gets particularly busy during Semana Santa. The best diving is from August to early October. Updated: Jun 13, 2008.

Getting To and Away From Little Corn Island

The only transportation to or away from Little Corn is via pangas that depart twice daily from the docks headed to Big Corn. They leave Little Corn at 7 a.m. and 2 p.m. and depart from Big Corn at 10 a.m. and 4:30 p.m.

It should be noted that these boats don't run on "Caribbean time." Show up at precisely 2:02 p.m., and you'll be just in time to see the boat speeding into the horizon. If you miss it, but the boat is still in sight, then get to the edge of the dock and wave your arms and yell. If they see you, they'll come back for you. The trip costs around $5, and takes a little under half an hour. It's also very bumpy, so try to find something to sit on, if they don't give you a cushion. Updated: Jun 13, 2008.

Getting Around

Public transportation on Little Corn is nonexistent and unnecessary, as everything is within walking distance. The walk from the dock to the east or north coast takes about 15 minutes, but it can feel like much longer if it's midday and you're lugging a backpack. Sometimes locals hang out near the dock and will offer to carry your things in a wheelbarrow for a nominal fee. You might want to give this some consideration—though, a strenuous hike does make jumping into the cool sea that much more satisfying.

If you're staying at the pricier hotels on the north side of the island, some will pick you up from the dock in their own boat. E-mail ahead to find out if yours offers this service. Updated: Jun 13, 2008.

Safety

Generally speaking, Little Corn is quite safe and has almost no violent crime. Visitors to the budget hostels on the east side should beware of Dennis, a shifty character who hangs out around there and has a reputation for scamming travelers in order to feed his cocaine addiction. Any money given to him will disappear. Do not believe him if he claims to work for any of the hotels.

The absence of development means that after nightfall the island quickly turns pitch-black. If you're going somewhere after 5 p.m., be sure and bring a flashlight. You don't want to be caught in the interior of the island without one. Updated: Jan 09, 2009.

Support VIVA by reserving your hotel or hostel at vivatravelguides.com/hotels/

Services

One of the drawbacks of an "unspoiled paradise" is an almost total lack of modern amenities. Few hotels have 24-hour power and the island seems to have almost no telephones. Most hotels will only take reservations via e-mail. The island does have a radio system for internal communication, but this hardly helps you in your quest to call mom on her birthday.

MONEY
There are no ATMs or banks on the island, so make sure to bring enough cash.

KEEPING IN TOUCH
If you want to make a long distance call, your two options are the **Enitel Office** and the **Dolphin Inn**, both of which are located in the village on the main road. The latter also offers the island's only pay-Internet service, which runs relatively fast but costs $0.60 an hour.

SHOPPING
Generally speaking, shopping on Little Corn is expensive and selection is narrow. You're best off buying everything you think you'll need before you get there.

Essentials such as sunscreen and bug repellent are sold, but at vastly inflated prices. Shops are in the area of the village, along the paved road to the north of the hotels and restaurants. There is one interesting shop worth checking out just south of Dolphin Inn. Walk down the path and you'll see a building made entirely out of glass bottles. It's owned by the deputy mayor of the island and contains a range of goods, including some locally made crafts.

For groceries, head to **Oliver's Grocery** on the main path about five minutes from the dock. Supplies are still expensive here, but not outrageously so. Updated: Jun 13, 2008.

Things to See and Do

Little Corn is probably best known for its beaches and laid-back atmosphere, but there are quite a few activities if you want to keep busy. Snorkeling and diving are the most popular; marine life around the island is abundant and diverse. You can also go horseback riding or hiking. The island is a great place to explore since its small size means getting lost isn't a real issue. The northwest part of the island is largely undeveloped, if you feel like hiking through some jungle—just make sure not to head out close to sunset. Updated: Jun 13, 2008.

HIKING
A popular hike is to head up to the lighthouse, which offers spectacular views of the entire island. The trail is located off of the inland north-south path, a little south of the baseball field. It's not a particularly long or strenuous hike and the best time to do it is near the end of the day so you can watch the sunset. Don't forget to take a flashlight. Updated: Jun 13, 2008.

BASEBALL
Baseball is serious business in Nicaragua, and Little Corn is no exception. There are games every Sunday at the field located inland in the north of the island, on the main path through the interior. The men's game starts at 11 a.m., followed by women's softball at 2 p.m. There's typically a little league match between the two. Updated: Jun 13, 2008.

HORSEBACK RIDING
Farm Peace and Love offers horseback riding tours along trails in the uninhabited north end of the island. Excursions should be booked the day before in person, or via the radio in Casa Iguana. You can also E-mail, but this must be done several days in advance since the proprietress doesn't go online very regularly.

The ride is an easy one and no experience is necessary. The horses are quite docile ($25 per person for about 1.5 hours of riding). E-mail: farmpeacelove@hotmail.com, URL: www.farmpeacelove.com. Updated: Jan 09, 2009.

SNORKELING
Both dive centers and many hotels will rent out a mask and flippers, with the option of taking a boat out a little ways. On such trips you should expect to see Nurse sharks, rays and barracudas. Sea turtles sometimes make an appearance. The trips generally cost around $15 per person. A cheaper option is to rent only the equipment. If you head up to **George's Caye** on the east side of the island, a little south of Derek's Place, the coral comes right up to the beach. Updated: Jun 13, 2008.

DIVING
Many people come to Little Corn to get their PADI Open Water certification ($305) and it's hard to think of a more pleasant environment in which to do so. You'll almost certainly see Nurse sharks and barracudas, and Caribbean reef sharks and Eagle rays are also often spotted. Dolphins and Hammerhead

sharks are occasionally seen. Diving is generally quite shallow, and most of the best sites only go down to around 17 meters (55 ft). The nearest decompression chamber is 3 – 4 hours away by panga—one of the reasons why dive shops here generally only do one-tank dives, costing around $35.

August, September and early October are generally the best months to dive, when there is better visibility and a weaker current. Updated: Jun 13, 2008.

Dolphin Dive is a small, personal dive shop with a mixture of local and European staff. In this shop, guests really do come first and can even choose the dive sites. Dives go out three times a day (about a 10-minute journey) and each lasts from 50 minutes to an hour. Some sites are shallow enough for snorkeling. Dolphin Dive offers PADI courses, from Discover Scuba Diving to Divemaster, and usually has the flexibility to start whenever the customer wants. Lessons take place in the dive shop classroom and on the beach. Student numbers per instructor are kept low. Dolphin Dive also has a small shop selling insect repellent, sunscreen and a free book exchange.

From the pier (and facing inland), turn left and walk about 10 minutes to Los Delphines (Dolphin Inn). Dolphin Dive is right on the beachfront. Open 7:30 a.m.– 6 p.m. Tel: 505-8-690-0225, E-mail: info@dolphindivelittlecorn.com, URL: www.dolphindivelittlecorn.com. Updated: Jul 23, 2009.

Tours

Little Corn's dive shops offer similar services. Diving, snorkeling, and kayaking can be booked for around the same price. However, **Dive Little Corn** mainly offers certification courses, so their schedules are largely fixed. Snorkeling can also be booked at many of the hotels for around the same price ($15). Updated: Jun 13, 2008.

Dive Little Corn

The more popular and sociable of the dive shops, Dive Little Corn, is managed by an extremely friendly young English couple. Equipment is new and their safety record is excellent. The place is staffed by long-term island residents, so it's also a great source for information, and the staff will be happy to help you out even if you're not diving. The Dive Little Corn staff gives out an excellent map of the island, marked with many of the best hotels and restaurants. Located in the village, five minutes from the dock. URL: www.divelittlecorn.com. Updated: Jun 13, 2008.

Dolphin Inn

Smaller, but just as safe and professional, Dolphin Inn offers basically the same things as Dive Little Corn. Their prices are marginally lower; however, and the primary advantage of going with them is that you'll likely be given your choice of dive sites. Updated: Jun 13, 2008.

Lodging

Accommodations on Little Corn are relatively expensive, particularly if you're traveling alone. You won't find a room for less than $10 a night. On the bright side, pretty much every room is beachfront property. The village has a few higher-end hotels, and the budget places are located in a row on Iguana Beach, the island's southeast side. The most romantic and secluded hotels are located on the north coast. Updated: Jun 13, 2008.

BUDGET

Elsa's Sweet Breeze

(ROOMS: $10 – 30) Elsa's is one of three similar budget hotels along this beach, and probably the best known. Rooms are basic, but clean. Expect a mosquito net, double bed, hammock and, in most cases, a private bathroom. Prices vary depending on how many people you have. The hotel has a basic bar, and sells food as well. The fish burgers come well recommended. Electricity is cut off at 9 p.m., the earliest of the three budget hotels. Located on Iguana Beach on the east side. Updated: May 12, 2009.

Gracie's Cool Spot

(ROOMS: $10 – 30) Gracie's, the loudest and most raucous of the Iguana Beach budget hotels, is the only one that does not raise its rates based on the number of people in a room, making it the best deal if you've got a group of three or four (and don't mind sharing a double bed). Check out a few different rooms if you can; some are better, newer and cleaner than others. Also, not all have mosquito nets. Power normally cuts off at 10 p.m., but the bar is frequently the scene of loud parties lasting well into the night. Gracie's rooms don't have light switches, so your light will stay on until they turn off the power (unless you unscrew it).

Travelers beware—this hotel is the main hunting ground for Dennis, the con artist mentioned in the safety section. Updated: May 12, 2009.

Carlito's Sunrise Paradise

(ROOMS: $12 – 40) Carlito's is the most expensive of the budget places. It's definitely the nicest of the three, but for $40 you can get a far nicer room on the north of the island. All rooms have a private bathroom and some have a fan—a rarity on the island. It's also the only hotel of the three to have electrical outlets in the room—something you'll appreciate if you want to charge up something expensive. Power runs until 10:30 p.m. Carlito's sells dinner and breakfast, but has no common kitchen. Tel: 505-8-820-2923. Updated: May 12, 2009.

MID-RANGE
Ensueños

(ROOMS: $15 – 50) At Ensueños, you can relax in a hammock under swaying palm and coconut trees on a white sand beach, while looking out into aquamarine waters. The hotel also offers beautiful cabins constructed from natural materials swept in from the ocean. Ensueños serves good Hispano-French cuisine for breakfast ($4) and a three-course dinner ($10). Guests enjoy meals together in a very social atmosphere. An on-site garden provides much of the produce. Snorkeling equipment is available to rent for $5, as the coral reef is a short distance from shore. Located at the northern end of the island, Ensueños is a 20-minute walk in the forest from the village on the path bisecting the island, or a longer and much more beautiful beach walk. Boat captains, when asked, may drop you off at EnsueñnRL: www.ensuenos-littlecornisland.com. Updated: Sep 08, 2009.

Derek's Place

(ROOMS: $40 – 50) Derek's offers small rustic cabins on the island's secluded northern coast. Cabins are remarkably clean, considering they're made of palm and bamboo, and the common bathrooms are spotless. Electricity generated from solar panels and a wind turbine is available at night, and a cool, constant breeze eliminates the need for a fan. The hotel offers meals, but the prices are rather high. Since there's no common kitchen and the nearest restaurant is a good 30-minute hike away, your food bills could get quite hefty. URL: www.dereksplacelittlecorn.com. Updated: Apr 15, 2009.

HIGH-END
Casa Iguana

(ROOMS: $35 – 75) Although Casa Iguana is one of the few hotels that doesn't offer beachside rooms, it makes up by offering a phenomenal view of the sea from your private balcony. The hotel also has an excellent restaurant and offers the most friendly and convivial atmosphere of the higher-end places; all guests eat and drink together. The place is not quite as romantic as the casas on the north side of the island, but all guests who book in advance will be greeted with a bouquet of fresh flowers. Located on Patch Point, near the southeast tip of the island. URL: www.casaiguana.com. Updated: Jan 09, 2009.

Farm Peace and Love

(ROOMS: $60 – 75) Farm Peace and Love is one of the most romantic getaways on the island. Prices are high, but well worth it. From the picture-perfect private beach to the flowers that screen your outdoor shower, this is as close as you'll get to paradise. There are only two cabins, so reservations are absolutely essential. The pricier one is slightly larger, but the smaller one is far more charming. The proprietress cooks delicious Italian meals and you can prepare breakfast and lunch in your private

---

Did a unique trek? Got way off the beaten path? Tell other travelers at vivatravelguides.com

kitchen. The hotel also offers horseback riding tours. E-mail: farmpeacelove@hotmail.com, URL: www.farmpeacelove.com. Updated: Jan 09, 2009.

Restaurants

Don't expect to find budget restaurants on Little Corn. It's next to impossible to get a meal for less than $5, and a dish with meat will cost at least $7 – 10. If you're looking to keep costs down, you can gorge on the island's wild mangos, star fruits, avocados and coconuts. Also keep an eye out for Jake the Patty Man, the next cheapest way to fill up. At the other end of the spectrum, Little Corn has some absolutely excellent restaurants as well. Dining at Casa Iguana, for example, is a life-changing experience. Updated: Jan 09, 2009.

Jake the Patty Man

Jake can be found wandering the island selling his wares just about every day. At $0.05 each, his tiny meat and fruit pies are a fantastic way to fill up for cheap. Like most treats, they taste best hot. Catch Jake at home between 10:30 and 11 a.m. and you can purchase pies right out of the oven. Just follow the main path in town to the northwest along the seaside until the paved section ends. Jake's house is just 100 meters (328 ft) farther up and to the right. There's no sign, but just ask around—everybody knows Jake. Updated: Jan 09, 2009.

Dona Briggette

This is an absolute "must do" on Little Corn. Known for her prawns, Briggette accompanies two of these local delicacies with salad, rice and fried plantain for $7. Located next to the dive shop, set back a bit from the sidewalk. Updated: Sep 08, 2009.

Lobster Inn

One of several similar and rather unremarkable restaurants in the village, Lobster Inn offers basic fish, meat and chicken dishes. The chicken in wine sauce is good, but nothing to scream about. Updated: Apr 13, 2009.

Sweet Oasis

Although getting service here is like pulling teeth, the food is quite good. The icy cold, fresh-blended juices are extremely refreshing and a perfect antidote to Little Corn's stifling heat. The burgers are also tasty and relatively cheap. Breakfast is offered, but the staff stops serving it at an absurdly early hour. Located in the village, five minutes south of the dock. Updated: Jun 13, 2008.

Vista al Mar

Although it's better known for cocktails and rum-filled coconuts, this place has far and away the best breakfast on the island—offered until 11 a.m., well after most other places on Little Corn stop serving. Expect to be warmly greeted by Georgette, the delightful owner, as well as her charmingly inquisitive little daughter, Brenda. Open 6 a.m. – 11 p.m. Tel: 505-8-421-7172. Updated: Jun 13, 2008.

Barra Intel Habana Libre

Barra Intel Habana Libre is one of the best restaurants on the island, and certainly one of the best bargains. For just a couple of dollars more than the village's other restaurants, you get food that is a world apart. Portions are big and hearty, and the rich, homemade sauce is highly recommended. This restaurant also offers some of the island's best cocktails, including sensational margaritas and daiquiris. When ordering these, be sure to request it frozen, otherwise you'll just get a plain, liquid drink. Located in the village, just north of the dock. Tel: 505-2-572-9086. Updated: Jun 13, 2008.

Casa Iguana

(ENTREES: $15 and up) Casa Iguana provides some of the best food on the island, but the delicious meals don't come cheap. Set meals include a salad, a main course and a dessert. Dishes vary, but are generally Mediterranean style. Meals must be reserved earlier that day, since the food is all prepared together. Casa Iguana, which is also a hotel, is a popular spot for breakfast—famous for its pancakes. Located at Patch Point, near the southeast tip of the island. URL: www.casaiguana.com. Updated: Jan 09, 2009.

!!!!!

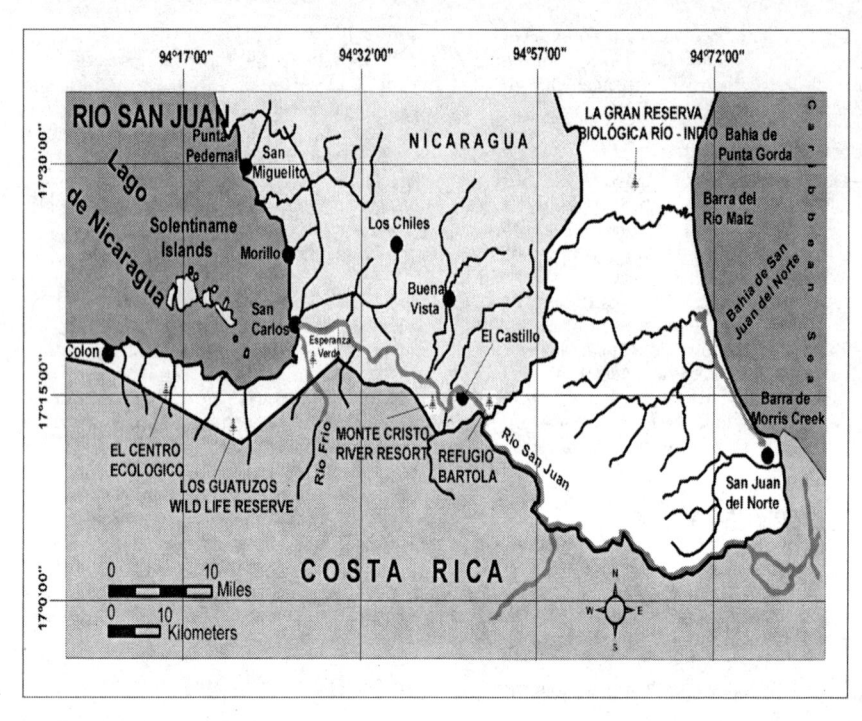

Río San Juan

The very remoteness of the Río San Juan region makes it one of the least visited regions in Nicaragua; however, this very isolation is where its wild charm lies. In the quiet islands of Solentiname you will find that the communitarian and artistic spirit inspired by revolutionary priest Ernesto Cardenal lives on. You will also find tremendous natural beauty in the wide meanders and abandoned forts of the Río San Juan and the nearby extensive reserves of protected wildlife.

On the flip side, the region's isolation makes travel a little more difficult than in more touristy parts of Nicaragua. Patience is a virtue in Río San Juan. For example, you have time on your hands to wait for those twice-weekly boats to Solentiname or to Los Guatuzos, unless you can afford to pay big bucks for private transportation. Also, as you go further downriver, the costs of food and other goods increase as everything must be brought in by boat. Everything costs a good 20 percent more than elsewhere.

Because of this, the Nicaraguan government and its European partners have made great efforts to improve transport and information. The million-dollar *Ruta del Agua* project is a much needed beefing up of the infrastructure. While it may look like a bit of an overkill to put up Intur offices everywhere (including one on Mancarrón), the effects can be positive. In particular, the new twice-weekly boat service from San Juan de Nicaragua to Bluefields may draw more visitors to the far end of the Río San Juan. There is even a possible future connection to the rest of the Caribbean coast and the Corn Islands. In the meantime, enjoy being a bit of an adventurer, follow in the footsteps of pirates and gold diggers, and be prepared for the best off-the-beaten path experience in Nicaragua. Updated: Nov 12, 2009.

History

The history of the area, unsurprisingly, was mostly shaped by the exploration, trade and battles that took place on the Río San Juan, which flows 192 kilkometers (119 mi) from Lake Nicaragua into the Caribbean.

EARLY EXPLORATION

The first Spanish explorers in the 16th century reported the existence of three main

Find the lowest prices on flights to Nicaragua at vivatravelguides.com/flights/

indigenous groups along the river. The *Guatuzos* inhabited the area between Río Frío and Solentiname. The *Ramas*, the "mother group" of southeastern Nicaragua, occupied the area north of the river all the way to Punta Gorda. Finally, the *Votos* were a smaller group who lived to the south and in present-day Costa Rica. These societies were based on simple agriculture, with corn a staple, complemented by gathering and hunting.

The Spanish conquistadors soon discovered the strategic nature of the river. As early as 1524, Hernán Cortés wrote that a passage between the two oceans would mean "dominating the world." In 1525, captains de Soto and de Benalcazar found the place where the waters of Lake Nicaragua—so vast it was called the Mar Dulce (freshwater sea)—flowed towards the Caribbean. Several expeditions were sent to explore the river throughout the next decade. In 1539, Alonso Calero reached the coast and baptized the mouth of the river San Juan del Norte, having reached it on June 24, day of Saint John. It is only two years later, in 1541, that a military garrison was installed there, effectively founding San Juan del Norte as a settlement. It is also at that time that the river started being referred to as the Río San Juan.

COLONIAL CONFLICT

Over the course of the 17th century, English pirates, the most famous of whom was Henry Morgan, got into the habit of sailing up the river to loot and burn Granada, then one of the empire's richest cities. The Spanish crown decided they could not let those buccaneers fleece them. By 1724, a dozen forts defended the river and, after a number of battles, hostilities eventually ceased between Spain and England.

PLANS FOR A CANAL

Around that time, various proposals started taking shape regarding the construction of a canal linking the Pacific and the Atlantic by way of the Río San Juan and Lake Nicaragua. A numbers of projects, were planned by the English, the French and even the Dutch, some reached the first stages of implementation, but all were abandoned one after the other. In the late 1840s, the British and the American fought a bitter turf war for control of the gateway to the proposed canal. Neither was victorious.

The river's importance came most into light when it served as an alternate route from the East Coast of the U.S.A to California and its newly discovered gold. From 1848 famed entrepreneur, Cornelius Vanderbilt, set up the American Atlantic and Pacific Steamship Company to transport gold-seekers via Nicaragua. The route originated in New Orleans, went down to San Juan del Norte, up the Río San Juan, across the lake, then by stagecoach over to San Juan del Sur and again by boat to San Francisco. It was a 36-day journey, which thousands of adventurers undertook during the decades of the "Ruta del Transito." In 1854, a peak year on the route, 13,000 passengers traveled to San Francisco and another 10,000 undertook the journey in the other direction. But with the inauguration of the Union Pacific railway through the vast American territory, the Nicaraguan route came to an end. Then in 1903, at the insistence of American President Teddy Roosevelt, Panama was chosen over Nicaragua as the place where to link the oceans. All works that had been started with earlier canal hopes were dropped, and the river never became the international shipping lane it could have been.

MODERN RÍO SAN JUAN

Today the Río San Juan still serves as an important transport route for the area. Long, narrow *lanchas* (motorboats) carry supplies to the small farming communities along its shores. Incidentally, modern-day pirates trafficking drugs are said to use the route as well. The difficulties that plagued earlier transport have not been completely sorted yet. The rapids at El Castillo are navigable, but boats sometimes still get stuck in shallow waters during dry season. Updated: Nov 12, 2009.

When to Go

No matter when you travel to the Río San Juan, be prepared to get wet. Nicaragua's rainy season runs from May to November, but around the Río San Juan locals are always prepared for a shower. But before you let the thought of so much rain keep you away from the river, know that rain does not usually last all day. Any avid fisherman should head to the Río San Juan in mid-September, during the huge annual fishing tournament. Updated: Nov 12, 2009.

Safety

PREVENTING ILLNESS

You can prevent illness or injury by taking a few precautions. Avoid drinking river or well water, and be careful where you swim. Only enter the

Highlights

Visit the conveniently located city of **San Carlos (p.315)**, and be sure to check out the views from the Spanish fortress, **Fortaleza de San Carlos (p.317)**.

The town of **San Miguelito (p.319)**, situated within expansive wetlands, is an ideal location for spotting birds and reptiles.

Go island hopping through the **Solentiname Archipelago (p.321)** where you can listen to the islanders recount the days when Father Ernesto Cardenal brought the community together to write the revolutionary Gospel of Solentiname. Watch craftsmen carve brightly colored birds, fish and turtles out of light balsa wood.

El Castillo (p.329) is a clean, colorful town in close proximity to the **Raudal El Diablo** (The Devil's Rapids). It is most famous for **El Castillo de la Inmaculada Concepción de María (p.330)**, a historic fortress built by the Spanish to defend the region from raiders and pirates in the early 1670s.

Of course, you can't miss the **Río San Juan** itself. The long ride down from San Carlos to San Juan de Nicaragua takes you through untouched tropical rainforest on one side, and tiny, isolated cattle ranching communities on the other–you are truly in the depths of Nicaragua.

Updated: Nov 12, 2009.

are in need of more intensive care, head back to Granada. Updated: Nov 12, 2009.

Things to See and Do

If you are interested in seeing exotic flora and fauna, or exploring wild forests and wetlands, then the Río San Juan region is yours to discover. A large part of the area is protected under the **Reserva Indio Maiz**. This area of the tropical rainforest is virtually untouched and is home to hundreds of species of birds, reptiles, amphibians, mammals and, of course, plants. A number of private reserves are also scattered along the shores of the river and the lake, and offer comfortable lodge stays with excursions to view wildlife. Those who like fishing should visit San Carlos in September for the annual tournament.

For a cultural experience, visit the Solentiname archipelago, where the artisans will let you watch them make colorful work, and the older islanders will recount the days of the revolution. Mancarrón, the largest of the 36 islands in the archipelago, has a prominent artisan community where locals allow visitors to watch them work. You will also find a few museums, cultural centers and churches scattered among the bigger islands.

If you want to delve into the rich history of the region, peopled by conquistadors, pirates and all types of gold seekers, you can get an excellent background in the museum and fort of El Castillo. History buffs should also visit the remains of Greytown by San Juan de Nicaragua. Updated: Nov 12, 2009.

Tours

If you're short on time, an organized tour is a good way to visit the reserves and other attractions in the area. Such tours can be organized from any town along the river, namely in San Carlos, El Castillo and all the lodges in between. You can also organize one from Managua and Granada. While you can also arrange day tours with local guides in all of these locations, be aware that some places can only be visited on an official tour. The reserve of Refugio Bartola, for instance, must be done with an official guide, and places like the ruins of Greytown are only accessible by boat, so you need to hire a local anyway. Most day tours are in the $15–30 range. They can cost much more if you are visiting a distant location like the Solentiname Islands, as the cost of gasoline consumed by motorboats is quite high. Updated: Nov 12, 2009.

water if it looks calm and has been designated as safe by a local or guide. Mosquito borne illnesses can be a problem in this area. Dengue fever in particular is quite common. Although malaria is not a huge risk, it won't hurt to defend yourself against it. You might want to consider taking anti-malaria medication as a precaution.

Your best bet is to bring plenty of insect repellent with a high percentage of DEET and use mosquito netting. Mosquitoes aren't the only creatures in the jungle that bite, so keep your feet covered in boots. Most snakes are not venomous, but you probably don't want to risk getting too close to them.

MEDICAL SERVICES

There are small *puestos de salud* in every village, but should you become severely ill and

Find the lowest prices on flights to Nicaragua at vivatravelguides.com/flights/

Lodging

When it comes to lodging in the area, you basically get what you pay for. While there are a number of cheaper options available in most towns, don't expect 24-hour electricity in the less than $10 accommodations. That said, there are some perfectly decent places, with electric fans, mosquito nets and sometimes private bathrooms, for just $10 - 20 per night. If you are willing to pay at least $40, several river lodges offer all-inclusive packages with lodging in private cabañas, three meals a day, and kayak or horseback rides, as well as tours to nearby attractions. For a more authentic taste of rural Nicaragua, you can also try a homestay on the Solentiname Islands for as low as $12 a night. Updated: Nov 10, 2009.

SAN CARLOS

The port town of San Carlos is most commonly used as a transfer point to Los Chiles, Costa Rica. There are also a few tour operators that organize private or group rides through the San Juan River to the small, but beautiful, towns of El Castillo and Boca de Sabalos. Small boats also leave twice a week to Solentiname. If you are headed to any of these destinations, it is important to do any online errands and withdraw all the funds you might need while you are in San Carlos. It is impossible to access either the Internet or your bank account in the rest of the region.

It is rare for tourists to stop for any length of time in San Carlos. One reason why San Carlos may not have taken off as a tourist hotspot is that it is literally too hot for visitors. In addition to being extremely uncomfortable, the thick humidity also attracts several species of mosquitoes; if you plan to visit, don't forget your bug spray.

Despite its lack of visitors, San Carlos actually has a very rich history. In 1300 BC many indigenous tribes settled on the southern coast of Nicaragua. When the Spanish arrived in the 16th century, the newcomers forced the original inhabitants to gradually move into the jungles of what is now San Carlos. Their descendants became known as the *Guatuzos* Indians. These indigenous people managed to contribute quite a few characteristics to current day San Carlos. Their influence can be found in the local economy, based on agriculture and corn harvests, along with hunting and fishing practices.

The geographical location of San Carlos, at the meeting point of Lake Nicaragua and the San Juan River, has also played an important role in local history. Between the years 1640 and 1780, pirates used the river and the lake to reach the Spanish cities of León and Granada. Since the pirates' actions were often subtly condoned by the English (such as Henry Morgan's trip there in 1670), the attacks on the Nicaraguan cities only increased tensions between the two great empires of Spain and England. To deter pirate activity and defend their land, the Spanish constructed a fort in San Carlos during the 17th century. This fort is the only real tourist attraction in San Carlos and has been renovated to include a library and a cultural center with informative plaques about the region. Updated: Mar 10, 2009.

When to Go

The weather in San Carlos is slightly less rainy in June, July, November and December. If you don't mind the showers, good times to visit are during **Semana Santa** (Easter week), or on November 4, when the town celebrates its patron saint, **San Carlos Boromeo**, with processions and vigils. The other big festive moment in San Carlos is the **International Fishing Tournament**, which takes place every year on September 13, 14 and 15. Updated: Oct 30, 2009.

Getting To and Away From San Carlos

BY BUS

Buses run from **Managua to San Carlos** daily from 6 a.m. to 10 p.m. and from **San Carlos to Managua** from 5 a.m. to 6:30 p.m. Trips cost around $10 and take about 10 hours. The trips on Sundays are less frequent. There are also buses **between San Carlos and Granada** that leave Granada on Mondays and Thursdays at 3 p.m. and depart from San Carlos on Tuesdays and Fridays at 3 p.m. The cost is $7 and the ride takes 11 hours.

One bus goes from **San Carlos to El Rama** at 2:30 p.m. every day except Sunday. The ride takes nine hours and costs $8. However, it is important to note that the road between the two towns is not designed for vehicles. Because of this, trips can often be uncomfortable, bumpy and even dangerous.

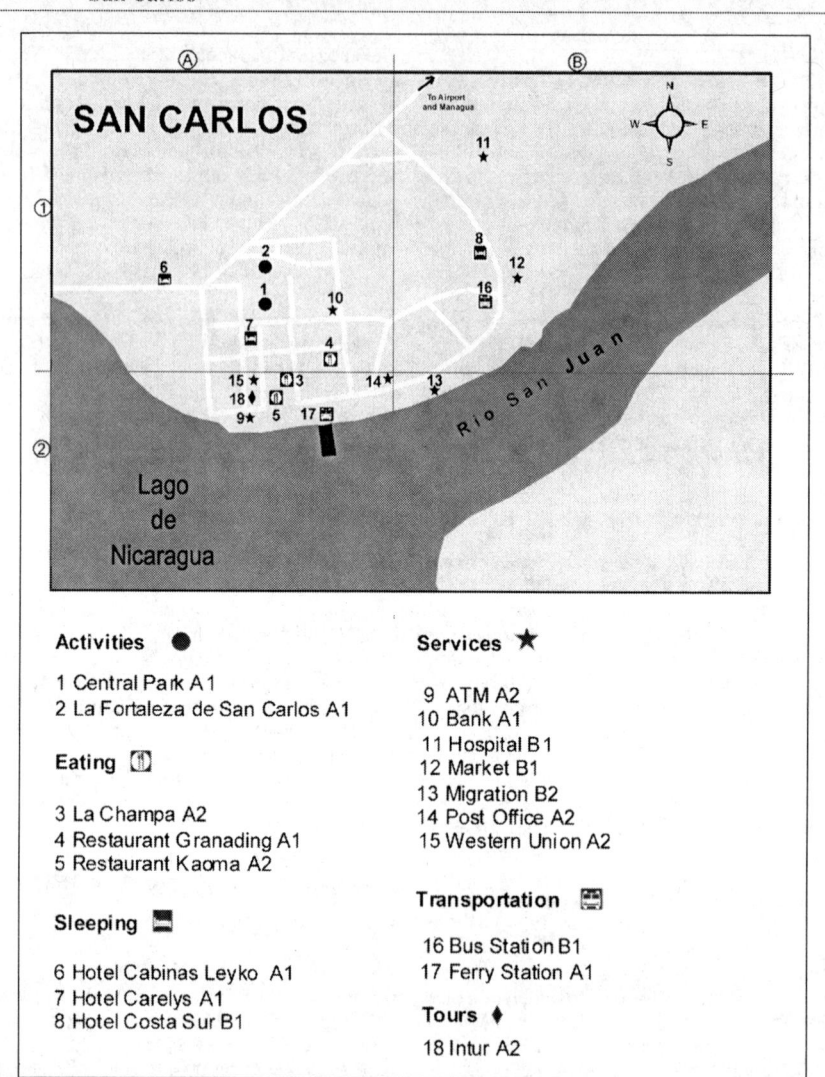

SAN CARLOS

Activities ●
1 Central Park A1
2 La Fortaleza de San Carlos A1

Eating
3 La Champa A2
4 Restaurant Granading A1
5 Restaurant Kaoma A2

Sleeping
6 Hotel Cabinas Leyko A1
7 Hotel Carelys A1
8 Hotel Costa Sur B1

Services ★
9 ATM A2
10 Bank A1
11 Hospital B1
12 Market B1
13 Migration B2
14 Post Office A2
15 Western Union A2

Transportation
16 Bus Station B1
17 Ferry Station A1

Tours ♦
18 Intur A2

BY BOAT
Ferries run between Granada and San Carlos with the same schedule, stopping in Altagracia on Ometepe Island along the way. Updated: Mar 10, 2009.

BORDER CROSSING WITH COSTA RICA
Many people use San Carlos as a passageway to Los Chiles, Costa Rica. Every day from Monday to Saturday two boats leave the harbor at 10 a.m. and 4 p.m. On Sunday there is one boat that leaves at 2:30 p.m. You should try to get to the dock half an hour early in order to secure a place on the boat. The ride takes about an hour and costs $10. The crossing takes you directly to Costa Rica customs, where there is an occasional wait and a border-crossing fee of $7. There is also the option to buy private trips to Costa Rica for $70 with local transportation companies that will get you through the border quickly and seamlessly. Ask about this option at the harbor. Updated: Sep 25, 2009.

Getting Around
San Carlos is a small town and just about any destination is within walking distance (though there are a few steep hills). Two city buses circle around San Carlos all day until 6 p.m. There is a taxi stand in front of the

Find the lowest prices on flights to Nicaragua at vivatravelguides.com/flights/

market and other taxis that drive around the city, especially during rainy season. Rides anywhere within San Carlos are about $0.50 during the day and $1 after 10 p.m. Updated: Mar 10, 2009.

Safety

San Carlos is a pretty safe town for travelers. On the weekends you may see a couple of drunks brawling in the street, but violence is not common, especially against tourists. There are also tourist and regional police that patrol the streets. Petty theft is not frequent, but has been known to occur from time to time. As always, exercise caution, keep your valuables from public view and be aware of your surroundings. Updated: Mar 09, 2009.

Services

TOURISM
The tourist office, Malecon, is near the river.

MONEY
Make sure you have plenty of cash before you head to San Carlos or any part of the Rio San Juan area. San Carlos has the only bank in the region, but there are no ATMs. If you run out of cash and need to get some from a family member, the town has a **Western Union**.

KEEPING IN TOUCH
The town has a **post office**, **public phones** and a handful of **Internet cafés** that charge about $0.75 per hour (but don't have WiFi access). Most cafés are located around the park.

MEDICAL
There is one **hospital**, two **private clinics**, one **health center** and four **pharmacies**.

LAUNDRY
Although there are no designated laundry places, most hotels and hospedajes offer some form of laundry service. Updated: Mar 09, 2009.

Things to See and Do

Although San Carlos is more commonly a transitional point than an actual tourist destination, there are still several options for daily explorations. There is a Central Park, which provides an elevated view of the town and the San Juan River. Just behind the park is a library and a historic Spanish fortress. Within the fortress is a cultural center with a small outdoor area that displays several signs detailing the history, geography, flora and fauna of the region. Updated: Mar 09, 2009.

Fishing
Due to the town's location, fishing is not only an enjoyable recreational activity for tourists, but it also helps sustain the economy through trade and tourism. The Silver King Tarpon is available year-round on the river, and the lake is known for its plenitude of sea bass. The best time for fishing is between the months of May and October. On September 14th and 15th, the San Carlos municipal government holds an international fishing competition. There are opportunites to win prizes, trophies and trips in various weight and species categories. Ask at the harbor if you'd like to rent a boat and fishing equipment. Updated: Mar 09, 2009.

La Fortaleza de San Carlos
(ENTRANCE: FREE) The main tourist attraction in San Carlos, La Fortaleza de San Carlos, is an ancient fortress that was constructed in the 1666 by the Spanish to defend their trade route from pirates. The position was also used to support and defend nearby El Castillo, which was frequently assaulted by British and Dutch pirates. In 1670, English pirates captured the San Carlos structure. The fort was then abandoned for over half a century, though it has at times been used as a prison and a police station. La Fortaleza was recently renovated and now includes a museum, library and cultural center. Today the cement walls that once saw so many battles lead to an outdoor area with plaques outlining the history of the region. The elevated position provides a pleasant view of the river. Open Monday to Saturday, 8 a.m. – 5 p.m. Closed Sundays. Updated: Mar 09, 2009.

Tours
With its central location in Nicaragua's Rio San Juan region, San Carlos is the best place to organize a guided tour for surrounding areas. Through one of the local tour guides you can plan a trip along the river to the nearby towns of Boca de Sabalos or El Castillo, or to the archipelago of Solentiname. The area is well known for its flora and fauna and contains several wildlife reserves, such as the Refugio de Vida Silvestre Los Guatuzos.

There are a variety of tour companies in San Carlos where you can arrange either a day trip or an extended journey to surrounding tourist attractions.

Ryo Big Tours
Ryo offers five different types of tours to all of the aforementioned destinations. Their guides will even take you as far as San Juan de Nicaragua, a tranquil and intimate village on the Atlantic Coast with an interesting history. Tours are all-inclusive and range from three days and two nights for $240 per person, to six days and five nights for $370. Located across from the Movistar store, near the port. Tel: 505-8-828-8558/ 644-5938, E-mail: RyoBigTours@hotmail.com.

Ortiz Tourist Services
This tour operator provides private transportation to any areas of the region. Costs vary from $20 – 70. One block south of the Cristo Rey School. Tel: 505-2-583-0039/ 839-2878.

Tropic Tours
Next to the Marena, Tropic Tours offers all-inclusive trips to Solentiname and spots along the river for around $15. Tel: 505-2-583-0010, E-mail: tropictours@tropictours.net.

Hotel Cabinas Leyko
Catered to the nature lover, Leyko offers tours that feature horseback riding, birdwatching and guided nature hikes. Tours last from one to two days and cost $20 – 30. Located two blocks west of the church. Tel: 505-2-583 0354, E-mail: leyko@ibw.com.ni. Updated: Mar 09, 2009.

Lodging
Near the harbor of San Carlos are loads of dingy, cheap hotels with rooms for around $7 per night. Don't be surprised to find unfriendly hosts, lopsided cots and the occasional cockroach. Even if you're on a budget, it may be worth spending an extra $3.50 cab ride to Hotel Costa Sur, which is clean and has private rooms. There are also a few hotels around the park in the $10 price range. If you're looking for something a little more upscale, **Hotel Cabinas Leyko** offers private rooms with air conditioning and private bathrooms for up to $50. Updated: Mar 10, 2009.

Hotel Carelys
(ROOMS: $10) This small and pleasant establishment is conveniently situated in the center of town, half a block south of the park. Hotel Carelys has clean, comfortable rooms and friendly staff. Each room comes with a fan and a private bathroom, complete with complimentary soap and towels. There is also 24-hour water, a rarity considering water in the area is known to disappear for hours at a time. Tel: 505-2-583-0389. Updated: Nov 06, 2009.

Hotel Costa Sur
(ROOMS: $10 – 30) Located along the shoreline, Hotel Costa Sur is a quiet family-owned hostel with a nice porch lined with rocking chairs. The place is clean, the service is friendly and the rooms are private. Both the dining room and kitchen are open to guests. Meals are also available from $3 – 4. Accommodation options range from a twin bed with a fan and a shared bathroom for $10, to a full-size bed with air conditioning, cable TV and a private bathroom for $30. Hotel Costa Sur accepts all major credit cards. Located 80 meters north of the harbor. Tel: 505-2-583-0224 / 505-8-853-6728, E-mail: suzam2483@hotmail.com. Updated: Mar 09, 2009.

Hotel Cabinas Leyko
(ROOMS: $13 – 50) One of the nicer options in San Carlos is Hotel Cabinas Leyko, located two blocks west of the church. The place is large, with over 20 rooms along two stories. There is a porch on the first floor and the second floor has a balcony with a view of the serene Lake Granada. Rooms range from single beds with fans and shared bathrooms for $13, to double beds with air conditioning and private bathrooms for $50. Credit cards are accepted and breakfast is included. Located two blocks west of the church. Tel: 505-2-583 0354, E-mail: leyko@ibw.com.ni. Updated: Mar 09, 2009.

Restaurants
Whether you are in San Carlos to visit, or are just passing through and looking for a bite to eat, be sure to take advantage of the town's geographical location and order some fish. Around the local Central Park there are several places to eat with outdoor decks, nice views and fresh seafood. If you are looking for a quick, cheap but filling meal, check out one of the many *comedors* scattered around town. All of these local eateries offer set meals with a main meat dish, fried plantains and *gallo pinto* (rice and beans) for around $2. Updated: Mar 09, 2009.

Friend's Bar and Restaurant
(ENTREES: $2 – 5) Also known as *Amigo's*, Friend's Bar and Restaurant has a tranquil atmosphere and features typical Nicaraguan food. The outdoor seating area is framed with greenery and topped with a tropical tiki roof. The restaurant has patio seating and hammocks for lounging. There

is also indoor seating on the second floor. Food options include chicken, pork and beef entrees, along with sandwiches, hamburgers and tacos. Ask for their specialty, a rich lamb dish called *Pelihuey*. Open every day from 10 a.m. – midnight. One hundred and twenty-five meters (410 ft) north of the Petronic gas station. Tel: 505-8-835-1343 / 485-1031, E-mail: DickGross73@hotmail.com. Updated: Mar 09, 2009.

Restaurant Granadino
(ENTREES: $3.50 – 10) The wide, spacious dining area and VIP room of El Granadino makes the establishment the perfect place for private parties or special events. Rustic, tribal artifacts and paintings line the polished wooden walls, while chandeliers hang from the ceilings. The menu includes a variety of beef, chicken, pork and seafood dishes, with rice and soup entrees and an à la carte menu as well. There is a full bar with a cocktail menu. All credit cards are accepted. Open Monday – Thursday, 8 a.m. – 10 p.m.; Friday – Sunday, 8 a.m. – 2 a.m. Located in front of the Alejandro Granja sports hall. Tel: 505-8-450-2041 / 894-3430. Updated: Mar 09, 2009.

Restaurant Kaoma
(ENTREES: $7 – 12.50) The open-air deck of Restaurant Kaoma offers a great view of the lake and the rooftops of the surrounding town. Enjoy the fresh fish and seafood as the refreshing lakeside breezes provide a much needed break from the humidity of San Carlos. In addition to seafood, the restaurant also has pork, beef and chicken entrees. Appetizers include *ceviche* (bowls of raw, marinated fish), seafood cocktails, skewers of meat, soups and salads. For those on a budget, Kaoma has fried filets and sandwiches for around $3.50. The restaurant also has a full bar. Open Monday – Friday, 8 a.m. – midnight; weekends, 9 a.m. – 2 a.m. Credit cards are accepted. Tel: 505-2-583-0293, E-mail: Hsandinorsj.com@yahoo.com. Updated: Mar 09, 2009.

Nightlife
La Champa
(COVER: FREE) Although San Carlos is not known for its nightlife, there is one lively place where every one goes on the weekends called "La Champa." Here you will find people dancing mostly to salsa and other Latin music. The vibe is friendly and intimate, and you won't have any trouble finding a partner to help you with your dance moves. Surprisingly, Sunday is when you'll find the liveliest parties. Open Thursdays – Sundays: 8 p.m. – 2 a.m. (or until the last customer leaves). Half a block south of the park. Updated: Mar 09, 2009.

SAN MIGUELITO
San Miguelito is a small lakeside town situated in wetlands that, because of the biodiversity of the area, have been declared a RAMSAR (Convention on Wetlands of International Importance) site. The wetlands are home to a vast variety of bird species and a great number of reptiles, specifically alligators. The nearby islands of Guarumito, Carrizal and El Boquete are especially good locations for spotting the wildlife. El Boquete also has nice beaches for swimming. In additino, you can go canoeing and fishing on the lake or visit the iguana farm of Los Guanabanos. If there's time, treat yourself to a bit of relaxation at the Camastro River hot springs.

Most eateries in San Miguelito serve very simple dishes of rice, beans and fish. Try **Restaurante Vega Torrez**, **Comedor La Mojarra** or **Comedor Marizam**.

Lodging in San Miguelito can be hard to come by; **Hotel Cocibolca** is the nicest and most comfortable option. Rooms ($12) come with a fan, mosquito net and offer pleasant views. Breakfast is included. El muelle de San Miguelito. Tel: 505-2-552-8803, E-mail: hotelcocibolca@yahoo.com.

Those on a budget can try **Hospedaje Fumsami** (Dorm: $ 2, Doubles: $ 4.50) or **Hospedaje Sandoval** (Doubles: $3 with shared bathroom).

Getting To and Away from San Miguelito
BY BUS
Buses leave **Managua** daily at 6.a.m. ($10, 11 hrs). You can also take a bus from **Granada** ($7, 9 hrs) or **San Carlos** ($3, 3 – 4 hrs, 1 p.m., 2:20 p.m., 4:30 p.m.). Do know, however, that the roads are bumpy and muddy, making for some pretty long and uncomfortable rides.

BY BOAT
Private *pangas* (boats) from San Carlos are pricey at $40, but they do shave

considerable time off the journey—the trip takes about an hour. Alternatively, **public ferries** leave San Carlos at 2 p.m. every Tuesday and Friday and cost only $2; the journey takes two hours.

It is also possible to take a ferry from **Granada**. The boat leaves Mondays and Thursdays at 2 p.m ($3 – 6), but it would be wise to arrive at least an hour in advance to secure a space for your hammock—the journey lasts about 10 hours! Updated: Sep 10, 2009.

REFUGIO LOS GUATUZOS

The wildlife refuge of Los Guatuzos is a 457-square kilometers (284 mi) reserve covering pretty much the entirely of the south-eastern shores of Lake Nicaragua. Specifically, the area from San Carlos, Río Medio Questo and the mouth of Río Pizote, all the way to the border with Costa Rica. The tropical forest and wetlands—among the best-preserved wetlands in Nicaragua—are home to over 400 species of birds (toucans, hummingbirds, herons, roseate spoonbills, etc.), myriads of butterflies, plenty of reptiles and amphibians, as well as mammals such as spider monkeys, sloths, armadillos and otters. The most common species is, unfortunately, the vicious mosquito, so make sure you wear long sleeves, long pants and douse yourself in repellent.

Getting To and Away From Refugio Los Guatuzos

To get to the refuge, head to the Ecological Center in Papaturro. From San Carlos there are public boats (2 hours, $4.50) running to Papaturro on Tuesdays, Wednesdays and Fridays at 9 a.m. They make the return trip to San Carlos on Mondays, Tuesdays and Thursdays at 9 a.m. You can also rent your own boat but it will cost you upwards of $200.

Tours

A variety of guided tours can be done from the Ecological Center situated at Papaturro, two hours from San Carlos by boat. Around the center are a butterfly farm (mariposario) where you can follow the creatures' life cycle, a caiman nursery and a turtle nursery, where you can observe the little critters coming and going, as well as an orchid garden and heliconia garden. A 150-meter (492 ft) suspension bridge gives you a great view over the wetlands and their wildlife.

The guided walking tours are:
• **Sendero Las Guatuzas** ($5/person, 30 minutes): to see the orchids, heliconias and caiman farm.
• **Paseo El Peresozo** ($8/person, 1 hour): takes you through the butterfly farm, the orchid garden, to the caimanero and over the bridge.

The two tours can be combined for $11 per person.

Then of course there are **birdwatching tours** to observe resident and migratory species, from cormorants to ibises and kingfishers. The first tour covers three kilometers (1.86 mi) by boat, one kilometer (.62 mi) on foot, and costs $25 per person. The second tour is a much longer outing on the lake, following the shore until Río Zapote and costs $138 per group.

One of the most spectacular tours is the **night tour** (1.5 hour, $11 a person). You will see caimans, or rather just their eyes shining at the surface of the water, and might spot owls, opossums and red-eyed frogs.

Kayaks can also be rented for $12 – 20. If you like to see humans in this area—after all, they inhabit the area, too—visit the coffee and cacao producers of the area.

Lodging

The **Ecological Center** offers accommodation in rooms with shared baths ($11 per person) or private bathrooms ($13 per person), as well as meals.

Volunteering

There may be volunteering opportunities in projects involving reforestation, cacao and coffee cultivation, or animal care. Those interested can contact the Spanish association **Amigos de la Tierra**, which administers the center. The Managua office may be contacted for further information (Tel: 505-2-270-3561, E-mail: Nicaragua@tierra.org, URL www.tierra.org), as the small office in San Carlos, up the street from the bank, is not very helpful. Additionally, the **Centro Ecologico** has its own website (URL: www.losguatuzos.com) and may be contacted via E-mail at info@losguatuzos.com.

RESERVA ESPERANZA VERDE

Also within the Guatuzos reserve is the 4,000-hectares private finca Esperanza Verde, situated along the Río Frío. Since it is just 30 minutes from San Carlos by boat, it makes for a good day trip of wildlife exploration.

There are three different paths to explore, preferably after spraying yourself with liberal amounts of mosquito repellent:

Sendero Peter (40 minutes) follows the river, with stops to get to know the tropical trees and their uses, including avocado, coffee, cinnamon and zapote trees, for those who like to know where their food comes from. There is an iguana farm along the way, as well as a pen for several couples of guarda tijanas, which resemble large agoutis.

Sendero Mirador (20 minutes) leads to a deck from which to observe the wetlands and their fauna such as waterhens, ibises and, at night, caimans. Squirrels, butterflies and a wide variety of songbirds can be spotted on the way.

Sendero Coralillo (3 hours) goes through primary rainforest, where you can observe a denser type of vegetation, blooming orchids, monkeys, and if you are lucky maybe a tigrillo (ocelot) or its pawprints.

Tours

Day tours ($25 a person, minimum 2 people) can be arranged from San Carlos; if you want to stay the night, the **Interpretation Center** offers rooms ($40 per person, including transport and three meals). To set up tours and lodging, enquire at **Fundeverde** (Tel: 505-2-583-0127, E-mail: leykou7@yahoo.es, URL: www.fundeverde.org), which operates out of **Cabañas Leyko (p.318)** in San Carlos. The Fundeverde foundation also welcomes researchers and volunteers interested in reforestation or animal conservation projects.

The reserve can be visited independently, in which case entry costs $1, plus $5–10 for the guided tour of the paths. You will need to take a Los Chiles-bound boat from Migración in San Carlos and ask to be dropped at Esperanza Verde. The boats leave daily at 10.30 a.m. and return to San Carlos around 4 p.m.

Lodging

La Esquina del Lago

(ROOMS: $30 –80) If you want the jungle experience with the comfort of a lodge, you can stay at this breezy lodge set on the lake, right across from San Carlos at the mouth of Río Frío. The lodge offers large wooden rooms (singles and doubles) with private bathrooms. You can pay for rooms or a package, which includes three meals. From the lodge you can go on kayaking tours, outings into Los Guatuzos, and try your hand at tarpon fishing. The French owner is a very serious fishing amateur and will provide tackles (and expertise). Tel: 505-8-849-0600, E-mail: riosanjuan@racsa.co.cr, URL: www.nicaraguafishing.com/www.riosanjuan.info.

ISLAS SOLENTINAME

31 – 257m   1,000

With no roads, limited electricity and running water, the 36 ancient volcanic islands of the archipelago Solentiname deliver sheer isolation and tranquility. The islands are covered with tropical rainforests and agricultural meadows, and are home to a vast variety of vibrantly colored bird species. There are only 1,000 residents who make up the artisan community for which the archipelago is famous.

Solentiname, whose name derives from "Celentinametl", or "place of many guests" in Nahuatl, is an enchanting archipelago in the southeast of Lake Nicaragua. Out of the 36 islands, only 17 are inhabited (though "inhabited" may be an overstatement, since all are covered in lush, tropical vegetation, with just a few houses sprinkled on the shore).

It's no wonder, then, that such a simple, rural corner of Nicaragua was chosen as the setting for a spiritual and artistic experiment in the 1960s. Father Ernesto Cardenal, a Nicaraguan priest, poet and strong proponent of Liberation Theology, settled in the islands and created a religious community. It was also under his guidance that a native art movement was born. The colorful crafts that flourished thereafter are a main source of income for the archipelago's inhabitants today, and have given Solentiname the nickname *Islas del Arte* (Art Islands).

The islands are part of tropical rainforest zone that form an extremely rich ecosystem, making it a paradise for birdwatchers and wildlife lovers. Over 100 species of birds are present, from waterfowl like majestic

ISLAS SOLENTINAME

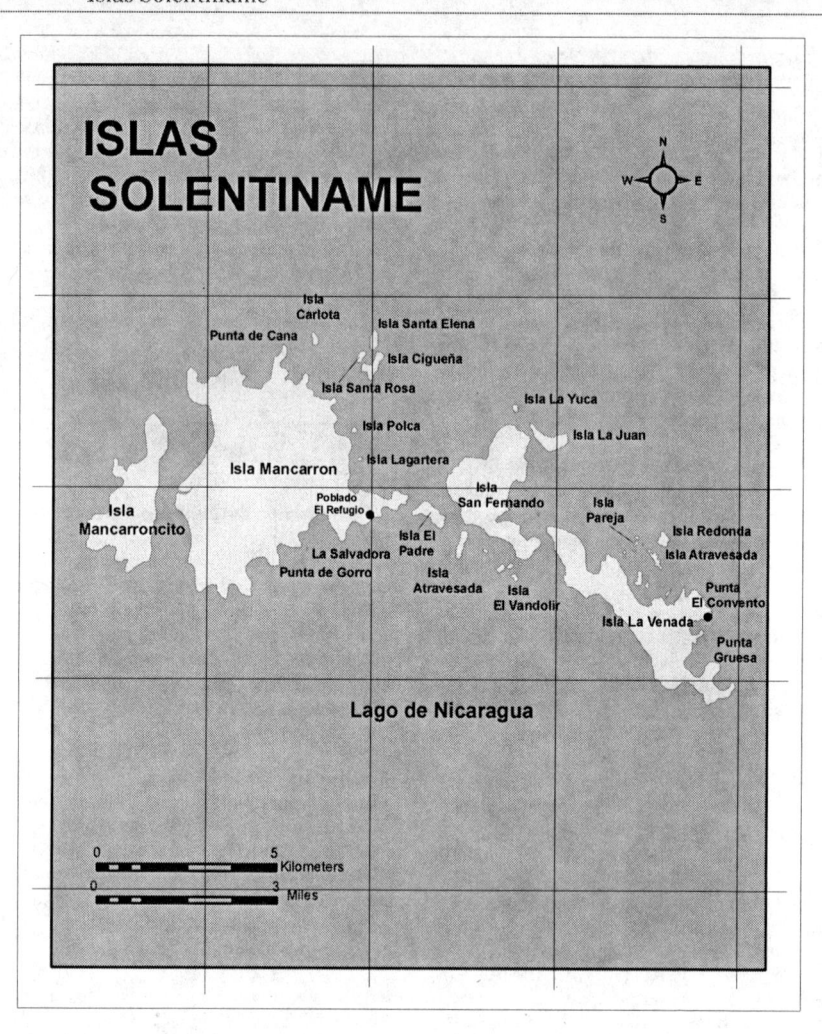

Map labels:
- Isla Carlota
- Punta de Cana
- Isla Santa Elena
- Isla Cigüeña
- Isla Santa Rosa
- Isla La Yuca
- Isla Polca
- Isla La Juan
- Isla Mancarron
- Isla Lagartera
- Isla Mancarroncito
- Poblado El Refugio
- Isla San Fernando
- Isla Pareja
- Isla Redonda
- La Salvadora
- Isla El Padre
- Isla Atravesada
- Punta de Gorro
- Isla Atravesada
- Isla El Vandolir
- Punta El Convento
- Isla La Venada
- Punta Gruesa
- Lago de Nicaragua

ibises, roseate spoonbills and common cormorants, to exotic tropical birds and golden hummingbirds. Otters, caimans, red-eared slider turtles, green iguanas, as well as (fortunately rare) coral snakes can all be spotted. The waters surrounding the islands are full of fish, in case you want to spend a while dangling a line hoping to catch dinner. The rare freshwater sharks for which the lake had become famous have been hunted to near extinction.

Tours to the nearby **Guatuzos Wildlife Refuge** may also be organized from Solentiname (at a cost, though). The earlier islanders also left some curious petroglyphs that can be visited on a day or half-day tour.

All in all, these isolated islands are a beautiful place for nature lovers and contemplative minds to relax in a hammock, to walk down the paved footpaths watching birds, to fish or to watch artisans carving balsa wood while they recount the days when the Padre, "Ernesto", had them discussing the gospel and selling their first paintings.

Enough tourism comes this way that a basic infrastructure exists, from simple *hospedajes* to nice cabins, but there are neither real restaurants nor bars nor any other forms of urban entertainment; those who like to go out on the town are better off visiting Solentiname as a day tour from San Carlos. Updated: Nov 23, 2009.

Ernesto Cardenal

It is impossible to separate the name of Solentiname from that of Ernesto Cardenal, a Nicaraguan Catholic priest and poet who transformed the life of the archipelago in the 1960s and 1970s.

Born in 1925 into an upper-class family of Granada, Ernesto Cardenal studied literature in Managua and Mexico, before traveling to the United States and Europe. Back in Nicaragua, he participated in the failed 1954 "April Revolution" against dictator Somoza and had to flee the country. He eventually entered a Trappist monastery in Kentucky, U.S.A., where he was heavily influenced by another priest-cum-poet, Thomas Merton.

Upon his return to Nicaragua in 1965, Ernesto Cardenal was ordained as a priest. The following year, 1966, he went in search of an isolated place where he could put Liberation Theology into practice, and found Solentiname. Liberation Theology, which mostly took root in Latin America, is a Christian mission to bring justice to the poor and the oppressed, specifically via political activism. And indeed, in those days the islanders were poor peasants, with no shoes on their feet, no schools, and no motorboats to reach the mainland.

When Padre Ernesto celebrated mass on Sundays, he encouraged the campesinos to comment on the Gospel, which in turn led them to reflect on the injustice of their condition. The islanders' comments were eventually recorded, transcribed and published as The Gospel of Solentiname. Meals were taken in common after mass, and little by little a true community emerged.

Also in the late 1960s, the priest noticed the traditional scenes painted on bowls of jicara and, along with his friend the painter Roger Pérez de la Rocha, encouraged the islanders to take up painting. Pretty soon whole families were rendering the natural scenes of the islands in bright hues and careful detail. This primitivist art tradition is still alive today, and the sale of canvases, as well as that of brightly colored balsawood carvings, are an important source of income.

Over the course of the 1970s, the inhabitants of Solentiname became more and more involved with the Sandinista movement. The sense of community grew as the hardships of war forced the islanders to share what little they had. In October of 1977, a group composed mainly of islanders attacked the military barracks of the Somoza Guard in San Carlos.

A few days later came a brutal retaliation: the houses and livelihoods of many on Solentiname were destroyed, and those who could, including Ernesto Cardenal, fled into exile in Costa Rica. When the Sandinista Revolution triumphed in 1979, a "beautiful moment" for those of that generation, a number returned and rebuilt their lives. Cardenal himself became minister of culture in Managua.

But when the Sandinista Front lost the elections in 1990, what was once a community in Solentiname began to slip into a regular, more individualistic society. Cardenal renounced membership of the Sandinista National Liberation Front (FSLN) in 1995 and now sits on the board of the cultural Casa de los Leones in Granada. He occasionally spends time on the island, where he owns a house, and is said to like to talk poetry with his neighbors. Sadly though, the younger islanders show little interest in the history of the spiritual and artistic community. But those who experienced it are still happy to recount the days of "the most beautiful revolution." Updated: Nov 23, 2009.

When to Go

Summer, or dry season, which runs from December to May, lowers the lake water by a couple of meters, giving you access to the petroglyphs on Isla La Venada. However, during the rainier months (June to November), the islands burst with the greenest foliage, so visits during either season has their costs and benefits. No matter when you visit, though, it is going to be hot and humid; pack and prepare accordingly. Updated: Nov 23, 2009.

Getting To and Away from Islas Solentiname

You will need either time or money in order to travel through Solentiname, as cheap public transport is infrequent and private transport is expensive. A collective boat leaves the green pier of San Carlos for the archipelago, calling in all the larger islands, every Tuesday and Friday at 1 p.m. It makes the two-hour, $3.50 trip in the opposite direction, from Solentiname to San Carlos, at 5 a.m. on the same days.

Alternatively, you can rent your own motorboat, which is only worthwhile as a group since it costs close to $70. If you are feeling lucky, you can just hang about the green pier and hope for a ride; islanders sometimes come in for groceries or to pick up the teachers who go in to teach every other weekend. Updated: Nov 23, 2009.

Getting Around

On each of the main islands, the larger settlements are criss-crossed by cement footpaths with wooden handrails, courtesy of the recent *Ruta del Agua* infrastructure improvement project. To reach more remote parts of the islands, you can try following muddy paths, but be aware that you are likely to be crossing private property; you will need to enquire whether the owners allow passersby. To travel between the islands, hitch a ride by asking around in the villages, or get your hotel to find one for hire. A boat ride will cost $10 – 25, depending on how far you are going. If you are staying on one island, your hotel will likely organize tours to sites on the other islands. Updated: Nov 23, 2009.

Safety

All the islands are extremely safe, but lock your hotel room for peace of mind. Lots of nasty critters are present on the archipelago, the most annoying being mosquitoes, so lather yourself with repellent. It is OK to swim by the piers of the larger islands, but make sure nobody has sighted any crocodiles nearby, and don't venture too far out, just in case (no fatal incidents have ever been recorded, though). Tarantulas are present, but they are not aggressive; however, be aware that the hairs they shed can cause itching. Updated: Nov 23, 2009.

Isla Mancarrón

Mancarrón is the largest and most populated island in the archipelago; it is also the place where Ernesto Cardenal established the original community. As you reach the main pier, you can already catch sight of the whitewashed church where the Padre's famous masses were celebrated. The original building was partly destroyed in 1977 but was subsequently rebuilt, and the islanders take good care of it. Inside, simple paintings of birds, boats and flowers adorn the walls lined with bold blue paint.

Nowadays, mass is held when the islanders can get a Catholic priest to come all the way to the islands, which only happens every couple of months (prompting some to turn to Protestantism). Ernesto Cardenal himself has not celebrated any ritual ever since the Pope forbade him to do so in 1982.

Between the church and the pier are red, blue and yellow swings and slides for the children. A short walk uphill, eastwards, leads you to the **local library**. Its shelves are jammed full with the works of Ernesto Cardenal (of course), lots of revolutionary literature and some general reference books for school children. It is also the only place on the island that offers **Internet**, thanks to a generator and router to which you can connect your laptop. The building opposite, still undergoing work at the time of writing, is due to open in December of 2009 as an archeological museum, showcasing ceramics, reproductions of petroglyphs and other artifacts by the pre-Columbian islanders.

Doña Esperanza Guevara, who lives just up from the library, is the president of the **APDS** (Association for the Development of Solentiname, founded by Padre Cardenal) and is an excellent source of stories about the days of the community. Going back down the hill, you can swim by the pier (if you don't mind sharing your bathing area with turtles and cormorants).

Heading up the hill in the other direction, westwards, past the football field, is **El Refugio**, the only official village in the archipelago. People here get few visits and will greet you from the comfort of their hammocks or beckon you into their crafts shops. Updated: Nov 23, 2009.

Services
MEDICAL

There is a **nurse** in Mancarrón, but if you are seriously ill, it's best to head back to San Carlos. Updated: Nov 23, 2009.

Volunteering

Those who fall in love with these magical islands and wish to stay longer can inquire about volunteering opportunities with **Alianza de Solentiname**. This organization has started classes in computer literacy and English for the brighter students of the islands, who unfortunately only get four days of formal education per month once they reach secondary school. Tel: 505-8-478-5243 / 452 1231, E-mail: esperanza@solentiname.org, URL: www.solentiname.org. Updated: Nov 23, 2009.

Tours

Tours may be organized to the archaeological sites of the different islands and to Los Guatuzos, though the cost quickly adds up as the price of gas is quite high. A tour to San Fernando will cost around $35 per person; to La Venada (4 – 5 hours) around $55; and to Los Guatuzos $80 – 100. For more information about tours, you can e-mail **Evert**, a local guide, at evert_diciembre@yahoo.es. Updated: Nov 23, 2009.

Lodging

There are two official accommodations here, both offering meals (since there are neither restaurants nor even comedores on the island). Alternately, you can arrange a homestay for around $12 with three meals. Doña Esperanza Rosales, on the western side of the village, and incidentally the president of the local NGO, Alianza de Solentiname, offers rooms equipped with mosquito nets. She cooks an excellent ceviche and rents canoes for $5 a day.

Hostal Familiar Buen Amigo

(ROOMS: $6 – 10) The more budget option of the two, this hostel is run by Reynaldo and Andrea, who also own one of the only shops in town. They offer five basic rooms with shared bath, as well as rooms with private bathrooms. Meals are $3. There is 24-hour water, but the electricity only runs for two hours a day. Reynaldo also owns a boat that he allows guests to rent. Tel: 505-8-869-6619. Updated: Nov 23, 2009.

Hotel Mancarrun

(ROOMS: $35 per person) This mid-range hotel is located just up from the church and offers 15 simple, but comfortable double, triple and twin rooms, each with private bathrooms and fans. The room price includes three meals. The hotel offers free tours to the church, and a few dollars extra will pay for trips to local attractions or other islands. The hotel also rents out two very pleasant wooden cabins with comfortable rooms, a kitchen, and 24-hour electricity (thanks to solar panels). Their spacious decks, complete with rocking chairs, overlook the lake. Cabins cost $50 per person, with three meals included. Tel: 505-2-277-3495 / 8-966-7056, E-mail: solpita@hotmail.com.

Isla San Fernando

The second largest island of the archipelago, San Fernando is a pleasant one to stay on. Although its two main attractions—the museum and the crafts gallery—will not keep you busy for long, the island is just as relaxing as Mancarrón and boasts some nice accommodations. Updated: Nov 23, 2009.

Things to See and Do

The light blue house just by the main pier is a **CANTUR** office (of the chamber of small businesses of the tourism sector) and gives out tourist information every day (except Sunday) from 8 a.m. to noon and 1-5 p.m. They can find you a guide to take you on the one-hour hike up the **Sendero to the Mirador** ($5 entrance fee; $15 with a guide), where you can observe some interesting petroglyphs.

Just above CANTUR, on the other side of the footpath, is the **John Brentlinger Memorial Library**. The small room, named after an American scholar with a passion for Nicaragua and the revolution, is stocked with left-leaning material by the likes of Che Guevara, Lenin, as well as some classics like Agatha Christie—good to know if you run out of books.

Higher up on the path is the **Casa Taller**, which showcases and sells art and crafts by the islanders. One room exhibits paintings which are known as primitivist scenes of the islands, with lots of details of the flora and fauna—picture red flowers dripping down trees with gracefully detailed leaves, canoes riding up rivers and other idyllic scenes. Most of them are in the $60 – 120 range. The other room has row upon row of black toucans, red and blue parrots, orange, blue and green striped fish, as well as butterfly mobiles, all carved out of the light balsa wood found on the island. The smaller pieces cost as little as $1 – 3, the larger ones and the mobiles $10 – 20. All of these make for good gifts.

At the far end of the path, climbing up the hill, you will find the MUSAS or **Museum of Solentiname Archipelago** ($2, open 8 a.m. – noon, 1–5 p.m.). You can breeze through pretty fast if you already know a bit about Solentiname; otherwise, you will get some eclectic information about the habits of a few common species (the turtle and the iguana) as well as the pre-Columbian inhabitants with their petroglyphs. Updated: Nov 23, 2009.

Lodging

Just as on Mancarrón, all hotels offer tours to sites on other islands along with fishing trips and walks to see the artisans carving, sanding or painting little blue parrots out of balsa.

Hospedaje Mire Estrellas

(ROOMS: $8) The only budget accommodation on the island, Don Julio's Mire Estrellas offers seven basic, small rooms (twin and triple) set right on the water. This place is really for backpackers who don't mind sacrificing a little comfort. The shared bathroom is on the other side of the path and there are no meals included. However; Elena, the owner's sister, can cook something up for you, or you can just hike up to Cabañas Paraíso's nice comedor. Updated: Nov 23, 2009.

The Albergue Celentiname !

(ROOMS: $20 – 35)This is the original guest house of Solentiname—Doña María has been running it since the first visitors came to the archipelago. It's made up of a row of neat little wooden cabins overlooking the lake house. The guest house offers double and triple rooms, all with private bathrooms and 24-hour electricity, as well as small, shady balconies. In the main house, there is a nice wooden deck with rocking chairs where the tame parrots of the house chatter as Doña María paints. Tel: 505-8-399-3764 / 893-1977, E-mail: celentiname7@yahoo.es.

Cabañas Paraíso

(ROOMS: $45 – 50 with meals) Another comfortable option on the island, Cabañas Paraíso is a series of cement cabins housing bright and airy rooms with firm beds and 24-hour electricity. Its large capacity (there even are quadruple rooms) makes it good for groups. There is also a book exchange and a little postcard stall. All major credit cards are accepted. Tel: 506-9-928-7493 (Costa Rican cell) / 505-2-278-3998, E-mail: hcpsolentiname@yahoo.com.

THE OTHER ISLANDS OF ISLAS SOLENTINAME

Isla La Venada

Most of this island is private property, but you can visit its most famous attraction, the petroglyphs, on a tour from any other island. The stone carvings are found inside a cave, known as the Cueva del Duende, which is partially submerged during the rainy season. There are 161 images of animals, human faces and fertility symbols that have been carved into the rock. It is believed that these figures were carved as a homage to the early islanders' dear departed, since most figures are facing east, where the indigenous cultures located their Gods. Also, one of the animal figures seems to represent a dog, which was meant to guide souls to the other world.

Isla Mancarroncito

The farthest of the main islands, Mancarroncito has the archipelago's best preserved tropical forest. There are also some archeological sites that can be visited on a day tour from either of the two main islands.

Isla Atravesada

This island is private property; the only way of glimpsing at its rich wildlife is by circling it in a boat. It is also host to a family of very large caimans.

Isla Zapote

This small island is home to so many birds that it is commonly referred to as *Isla de Los Pajaros* (Bird Island). You can come close to the thousands of aquatic birds on a boat trip, but these tend to be costly, so your best bet is to hire your own transport and make a little detour on your way to San Carlos.

Isla La Juana

A large avocado farm here produces the giant avocadoes that are sold in San Carlos.

Isla El Padre

This island is the only one to host a colony of howler monkeys (*monos congo*). If you ride past it by boat, you will hear their tremendous roars. Updated: Nov 23, 2009.

BOCA DE SÁBALOS

🅐 37m 👤 1,270

The village of Boca de Sábalos takes its name from the river running through it. The river, in turn, is named after the tarpon fish that inhabits its waters.

Sitting at the confluence with the Río San Juan, Boca de Sábalos (commonly called Sábalos) was born around 1940 as a large cattle estate, around which the workers eventually put up houses. In 1979, an Austrian sawmill opened in order to process the dozens of kinds of woods growing nearby (including cedar, mahogany, laurel, and almond). Today, most of the population lives off farming, growing the ever-present rice, beans, tubers, plantains and corn. Cacao is also grown for export, as is the African palm, which is used for oil.

Hoping to attract visitors, a few businesses in town offer tours and lodging. You can find some decent accommodation and food on the main road, where the few hospedajes are concentrated.

There isn't much to see or do in Sábalos, but it makes for a good day trip if you want to get off the beaten path and soak up the atmosphere of rural Nicaragua before continuing on to El Castillo. Nearby are a couple of more upscale lodges (by the standards of this remote region) from which to organize tours into the Indio Maiz reserve. They will also help you organize fishing trips. Sábalos is also a great place to cast lines for the massive tarpons that thrive in the heavy-flowing waters of the Río San Juan. Updated: Nov 04, 2009.

When to Go

The area is very rainy for most of the year. The best time to visit is probably during the local summer, when the weather is optimal (January – May). If you are interested in fishing, try visiting in the middle of September for the **Fiestas del Sábalo Real**. Updated: Nov 04, 2009.

Getting To and Away From Boca de Sábalos

BY BOAT

To El Castillo (40 min, $1 – 1.50)
• **Monday – Saturday:** 7:30 a.m., 10 a.m., 11:30 a.m. (fast) 2 p.m., 3 p.m., 4:30 p.m. and 5:30 p.m.
• **Sundays:** 7:30 a.m. (fast) 10 a.m., 11:30 a.m. (fast) and 4 p.m.

To San Carlos (1 hr 45 min, $3.30)
• **Monday – Saturday:** 5 a.m., 6 a.m., 7 a.m., 8 a.m., 11:30 a.m. (fast) and 3 p.m.
• **Sundays:** 6 a.m. and 3 p.m., 4 p.m. (fast).
Updated: Nov 04, 2009.

Getting Around

Sábalos is a small village split in two by the river of the same name. From the riverbank, by the pier, starts the one paved road (which actually peters out pretty fast into a dirt road). If you wish to reach the communities out in the forest, one of the collective **4x4 taxis** can take you. You can also get paddled across the river, from which you will find a couple of paved footpaths snaking between the simple houses. Updated: Nov 04, 2009.

Safety

Sábalos is a community with nearly no violent crime. Do however, keep your possessions safe from petty theft. It is also recommended that you take precautions against malaria and dengue, as mosquitoes are present in large (and annoying) numbers. Updated: Nov 04, 2009.

Services

There is a **police station** and a small **hospital** up the hill along the main road, as well as a **pharmacy**. You can make phone calls from several of the shops, including the *pulpería* beneath Hotel Kateana, which will also change dollars and Costa Rican colones. Updated: Nov 05, 2009.

Things to See and Do

Boca de Sábalos is a very quiet riverside community with virtually no tourist attractions. What you will get here; however, is an authentic slice of simple Nicaraguan life, especially if you take a couple of hours to visit the cacao producers or paddle up the river to observe the natural surroundings. Sábalos can also serve as a base for nature and fishing tours. Updated: Nov 11, 2009.

COSEMUCRIM Cacao Cooperative

For those who are curious to know where their sweet goodies come from, the cacao producers' cooperative in town, which provides beans for the German chocolate brand Ritter, happily gives short free tours of the installations. These tours explain the different grades of cacao beans, as well as the extraction, fermentation and drying processes. They haven't started organizing tours that go all the way to the cacao-growing *finca* yet, but it may very well happen in the near future. Located five minutes up the main road, on the right. Tel: 505-8-927-0216, E-mail: cosemucrim_organico@yahoo.es. Updated: Nov 05, 2009.

Aguas Termales Escalera

Way out in the middle of the forest is a stream with seven bubbly sources of scalding hot water. You can take a dip in the hot springs, but they extremely rustic with no showers, changing rooms or steps leading into the water. Just reaching the place is a challenge in itself, since they are a 30-minute walk from Las Maravillas, which is 25 kilometers (15.5 mi) out of Sábalos. You can go independently, hiring a taxi for around $35. There is also a $5 entrance fee, unless you decide to take tour, which will undoubtedly be more expensive. Updated: Nov 05, 2009.

Tours

Just like El Castillo, Boca de Sábalos can serve as a base for fishing or nature-watching tours on the Río San Juan and into the Indio Maíz reserve. Trips can be arranged by the three upscale lodges in the vicinity. Otherwise, you can go through one of the town guides who have set up a small tourist information point right by the pier (it is the wooden green hut behind the statue of the jumping fish). **Julio** (Tel: 505-8-431-2390) is usually the one who meets visitors as they step off the boat, since he speaks good English. Either he or Moyses can set up the following tours:

Nature walking tours passing along the river and through local farms ($80 per group); **Caiman night tours** ($50 pergroup); **Tubing** down from Santa Rosa (2 – 3 hours, $40 per group); **Fishing tours** ($200 per groups of 1 to 3 persons); **Tours to private fincas** like Quebracho ($80 pergroup, 5 to 6 hours); and **Tours to the Aguas termales** ($85 per group, 5 – 7 hours).

They also offer a six-day trip to San Juan del Norte by canoe, with a walking tour of Greytown and a motorboat trip up the Río Indio ($250 per person, 4 to 12 persons. Price includes guide, canoes, accommodation and food).

NOTE: *Rates given are quoted as a "first price" and can be bargained down.* Updated: Nov 05, 2009.

Lodging

There is a string of cheap hospedajes along the main road walking up from the pier, offering more or less equivalent basic rooms for $4 – 10. On the other side of the river you'll find the much nicer Hotel Sábalos, which overlooks the Río San Juan. If you prefer to stay out of town in a self-contained river lodge with better amenities, the more expensive Sábalos Lodge and the Montecristo, both downstream, are very good choices. Updated: Nov 11, 2009.

Hotel Kateana

(ROOMS: $5 – 10) Above the family house and shop are the nine rooms of Hotel Kateana, the most pleasant of Sábolos's budget hotels. The rooms are small but sufficient, with comfortable beds and electric fans (but no mosquito nets). If you are squeamish, shell out the extra $5 and get one with a private bathroom, as using the shared bathroom involves walking down a staircase inhabited by a family of shy but persistent bats. Doña Rosario can cook a breakfast of gallo pinto ($2.50) and offers laundry service at $0.30 per piece. She allows guests to use her kitchen—great for those on a budget. One hundred meters (328 ft) up from the pier on the right. Tel: 505-2-583 0178 /8-633-8185. Updated: Nov 11, 2009.

Hotel Sábalos

(ROOMS: $18 – 36) The most comfortable rooms in the town of Sábalos can be found in this wooden hotel sitting right at the confluence of the two rivers. The pleasant rooms come with firm mattresses, mosquito nets, fans, private bathrooms with hot water and an unparalelled view of the river from the spacious deck. There is an on-site restaurant, and the hotel can organize a variety of tours: to a cacao finca (5 hours, $80 pergroup), horseback riding ($24 per person); to the sunken steamships ($35 per person); and to see caimans (2 hours, $50 per group of 2). To get there, take a canoe from the pier, or have their motorboat pick you up. Price includes breakfast. Tel: 505-8-659 0252 / 2-271-7424, E-mail: hotelsabalos@yahoo.com, URL: www.hotelsabalos.com.ni. Updated: Nov 05, 2009.

Montecristo River Lodge

(PACKAGES: $65) If you want to enjoy river activities and walks in the forest from the comfort of an all-inclusive lodge, then the Montecristo is for you. Packages include lodging in one of the cabins with spacious private bathrooms, three full meals with drinks (including vegetarian fare upon request), use of the Jacuzzi and all other activities, including kayaking, horseback riding and walking down the paths of the 250 acres of private reserve. There is also a small library as well as a computer with Internet access. Packages cost $65 in high season, with special rates for groups. Pick-ups can be organized from Sábalos or even from San Carlos, where Montecristo has an office around the corner from the port. Ask to be dropped off by the boat that goes down to El Castillo. Tel: 505-8-649-9012 / 2-583- 0197, E-mail: montecristoriver@yahoo.com, URL: www.montecristoriverlodge.com. Updated: Nov 05, 2009.

Restaurants

As with accommodation, you have a choice between a row of cheap but decent comedors lined along the main road, or a pricier, fancier meal at one of the lodges. If you really want to rough it, you can buy street food from vendors by the pier. The bar just over the pier is a decent place to grab a beer, and opposite the comedors is another no-name establishment where the town youth shoot pool. Updated: Nov 11, 2009.

Comedor Gómez
(ENTREES: $2.25) This comedor serves basic lunches and dinners of chicken, beef or pork accompanied by the usual rice and beans and washed down with a soda. Its second-floor terrace that overlooks the main square is a good place to people watch. Updated: Nov 05, 2009.

Comedor Gladys y Elena
(ENTREES: $2.50) Comedor Gladys y Elena sits next door to Gómez (and also serves as a good observation point for town life). This eatery managed by two sisters serves surprisingly decent meals of basic Nicaraguan fare, along with fresh carrot and orange juices. Updated: Nov 05, 2009.

Hotel Sábalos Restaurant
(ENTREES: $3.50 – 14) If you want to splurge and dine on freshwater shrimps (crayfish) from a pleasant, breezy deck, cross the river to Hotel Sábalos. The on-site restaurant serves up breakfasts for $3.80, including omelettes or toast (in addition to the eternal gallo pinto), soups and ceviches ($3.50 – 4.50), as well as dishes of shrimp ($14), pasta ($5) and vegetables ($4.50). Updated: Nov 05, 2009.

EL CASTILLO !

El Castillo is an attractive riverside town whose fort—the last of the fortifications built by the Spanish to ward off pirates' attacks— was the siege of epic battles. Today roughly 3,700 people live there. A trip to see the fort is the highlight of any trip down the Río San Juan. Its shore is lined with painted wooden houses, many of which are built upon stilts over the water itself. Above them looms the dark mass of the Fortaleza de la Inmaculada Concepción.

History

The fort, which dates back to 1675, is the only remainder of a series of a dozen fortifications built by the Spanish crown in the late 17th century to repeal pirate attacks. British privateers, buccaneers and their Miskito allies regularly sailed up the Río San Juan to sack Granada and Leon until the end of the 18th century. El Castillo once again became a key point on the river during the days of the "*Ruta del Transito*", which started in 1848 with the California Gold Rush.

The thousands of adventurers who traveled up the Río San Juan on their way to California had to disembark in El Castillo, where the roaring rapids hindered passage. Passengers and freights were offloaded from the steamships and then ferried 300 meters (984 ft) up by railroad before getting on board once again. As dreams for an interocean canal waxed and waned, so did the fortunes of El Castillo. When Panama was eventually chosen for the said canal in 1903, the village stopped growing.

El Castillo is now a quiet town where people mostly work as farm laborers, often crossing into Costa Rica or commuting to the nearby sawmills. Many hopes are pinned on tourism, and a number of nice hotels and some decent restaurants have opened, like Soda and Hotel Vanessa, the Albergue El Castillo and Hotel Victoria. Every shop in town seems to offer kayak tours and boat trips to the nearby Refugio Bartola, the only part of the huge Indio Maiz Biosphere Reserve that can be visited. Updated: Nov 11, 2009.

When to Go

As with the rest of the area, it is more pleasant to visit outside of the rainy season, which lasts from June to December. The town comes alive on March 19 for the *Fiestas Patronales of San Jose*, as well as during Easter week. If you are into fishing, September is the time to come. Updated: Nov 07, 2009.

Getting To and Away From El Castillo

BY BOAT

To San Carlos
(By way of Sábalos, 2 hrs, $3.58)
• Monday – Saturday: 4 a.m., 5 a.m., 6 a.m., 7 a.m. and 2 p.m.
• Sundays: 5 a.m. and 2 p.m.

Note: There is rapid service (1.5 hours, $6) Monday – Saturday at 5:30 a.m., 11 a.m., 3:30 p.m.; Sundays 5:30 and 3:30 p.m.

To San Juan de Nicaragua (6.5 hours, $12)
• Tuesdays, Thursdays, Fridays: 9:30 a.m.

Note: There is an express service on Tuesdays and Fridays at 8 a.m. (4 hours, $20) Updated: Nov 07, 2009.

Getting Around

El Castillo has only one main "street"—if the narrow cemented footpath running by the river may be so called—plus a few other footpaths branching up and turning into staircases. Nearly all points of interest are concentrated on that street. Updated: Nov 07, 2009.

Safety

El Castillo is generally a very safe place. Although it is advisable to be careful with your belongings, you will probably find that your biggest safety concern is the pesky mosquitoes. Updated: Nov 11, 2009.

Services

TOURISM

Intur is in a little wooden hut opposite the pier and it is the place to go not only for information, but also to organize tours to nearby Refugio Bartola and other tours. Open Monday – Saturday, 8 a.m. – noon and 2–5 p.m. (except when the girl staffing it is at English class). Tel: 505- 8-902-1694.

MONEY

Most shops in town accept both U.S. dollars and córdobas, but there is neither a bank nor ATM nor Western Union, so come with enough cash.

KEEPING IN TOUCH

Three places in town offer Internet access. **Soda Vanessa** houses the only real cyber-café in town, with $1 per hour Internet, fax machines and national and international phone services ($2.50 a minute). **Border's Coffee** offers Internet on its one computer for $1 per hour, and **Albergue El Castillo** has several computers with Internet ($0.75 an hour) as well as WiFi access for guests.

MEDICAL

There is a small clinic on the path behind the fort, and a **police station** downstream from the pier. Updated: Nov 07, 2009.

Things to See and Do

The main attraction of El Castillo is the hard-to-miss fort (see Highlighted Box) with its good museum. There is also a butterfly farm, which is currently closed but should reopen at some point.

El Castillo is a good base from which to organize river tours and jungle excursions into Refugio Bartola. Updated: Nov 11, 2009.

Tours

Several hotels and restaurants in town offer tours, all more or less identical and for similar prices. Your best bet is to organize one via Intur, which has the widest range and will contact the guides and transporters directly. Few guides speak English though, so if necessary, you must specifically request one.

Intur will organize the following tours: **Hiking along Refugio Bartola's** two paths ($65 and $75 per group of 2 to 5 people); **horseback riding** along the Costa Rican border (3–4 hours, $15 per person); **fishing** ($50 per person); **Caiman night tours** ($40 per group of 4 people); and various hikes to nearby communities.

Nena Lodge and Tours is attached to the hostel of the same name (p.331). This operator offers the following tours: **canoe tours** on the Río San Juan and its tributaries ($10 to $15 per person); **caiman tours** ($40 per group of 4 persons); and **tours to the two paths of Refugio Bartola**, with adjusted prices depending on where you go and the size of the group ($64 per group of 4 to Sendero Bartola, $72 per group to Sendero Aguas Frescas). For more information, ask a lady named **Ceyla** at the Nena Lodge: she's a good source of information regarding wildlife in the reserve. Tel 505-8-821-2135 / 419-8158, E-mail: nenalodgeandtours@yahoo.es, URL: www.nenalodge.com. Updated: Nov 07, 2009

The History of Fortaleza de la Inmaculada Concepción

The squat fortress that stands on the highest point of El Castillo was completed in 1675 as part of the Spaniards' defense against British-led attacks on Granada and Leon. In 1762, the little castle was the scene of a battle worthy of a Hollywood film.

RAFAELA HARRERA'S DEFENSE
An expedition was sent by the governor of Jamaica to take the fort; the commander of the fort, Don Pedro Herrera, had just died of natural causes, so the attackers figured it would be a walkover and demanded the keys. But the plucky 19-year-old daughter of the commander, Rafaela Herrera, proclaimed herself head of the garrison and refused. She literally held the fort—she is even said to have fired the cannon which sank the main British ship—and the attackers gave up after five days.

THE ENGLISH RETURN
The English did not give up so easily, however. In April of 1780, a fleet with 2,000 men led by Horatio Nelson (of later Trafalgar fame) attacked the fort and took it after a hard battle of one week. But their victory did not last long. The rainy season brought a cohort of tropical diseases—malaria, dysentery and yellow fever—which properly decimated the conquering troops, who had to abandon the Fortaleza. Eventually, in 1783, the British and the Spanish signed a peace treaty and the Castillo, free of battles, was left to slowly fall apart.

MODERN FORTALEZA DE LA INMACULADA CONCEPCIÓN
Starting in 1990, with the help of the Spanish cooperation, heavy work was undertaken to preserve the ruins of the fortress. The fortifications, including a few intact rooms that now house the public library, are now open to the public, and are definitely worth a visit, at least for the unique view over the meandering Río San Juan.

There is also an excellent museum in a new building (opened May 2009) on the same site. You might want to skip the obligatory pre-Columbian ceramics, but take a look at the displays in Spanish and English that chronicle the life of the fort, with clear explanations and rescued objects like cannonballs. It also indicates a good chronology of the inter-oceanic canal plans for Nicaragua, with pictures of El Castillo and Greytown in better days. Open Tuesday to Friday, 8 a.m. to noon and 1-4:30 p.m.; Saturdays and Sundays 9 a.m. to noon and 1-4 p.m. Updated: Nov 11, 2009.

Lodging

There are enough nice hotels here to keep all travelers satisfied, from the mid-range visitor, who can chose from Victoria or Vanessa, to the tightest shoestringers, who can shack up at Hospedaje Universal for just $5. Most lodgings include breakfast. Updated: Nov 11, 2009.

Nena Lodge
(ROOMS: $6 – 20) This place at the far end of town (4 minutes from the pier) rents out a handful of small but clean rooms above the family's home. There is a double with a private bathroom, a double and a twin with shared bathrooms, and some single rooms with shared bathrooms. Breakfast, lunch and dinner can all be prepared on the spot for $2.50 per meal. Laundry can be done for $0.25 per piece, and the same family offers tours from the house next door. Tel: 505-8-928-2572, E-mail: nenalodgetours@yahoo.es. Updated: Nov 07, 2009.

Albergue El Castillo !
(ROOMS: $15) The Albergue, as it is known in town, comes recommended as an excellent value option. The guest house is comfortable and the service is friendly. Set in a large hardwood building overlooking the pier, Albergue has nine rooms, most with a great view from a balcony with hammocks. All rooms are equipped with mosquito nets, fans and lots of shelf space, but they do share a dorm-style bathroom. There is a book exchange and Internet ($1 per hour). The delicious breakfast is included in the price. Tel: 505-8-924-5608, E-mail: mrcrsls116@gmail.com. Updated: Nov 07, 2009.

Hotel Tropical/Restaurant Vanessa
(ROOMS: $20) Recently opened in September 2009, this small hotel above Vanessa's offers the most pleasant rooms in town, all very clean, with wood floors, private bathrooms, TV and fans or air conditioning. There is nice balcony overlooking the rapids and breakfast with coffee is included in the rate. Tel: 505-2-583-0129 / 8-447-8213. Updated: Nov 07, 2009.

Restaurants
There are only a couple of official restaurants in El Castillo (Vanessa's and Cofadito are the most patronized), offering good fish dishes and expensive but tasty crayfish. Otherwise, you can fall back on the usual comedor or get your meals from your hotel. Updated: Nov 11, 2009.

Comedor Conchita
(ENTREES: $2.50 and up) For those on a budget, there are a handful of cheap comedors offering regular Nicaraguan fare— meat, rice, beans, soft drink—for around $2.50. Conchita is one of the better ones, with a first-floor terrace. Updated: Nov 07, 2009.

Border's Coffee
(ENTREES: $3 – 10, DRINKS: $0.75 – 2) From coffee shop's first-floor terrace strategically overlooking the pier, you can sip real coffee, juice and tea while waiting for your boat. Although the decoration is definitely over the top, and the prices a bit high for El Castillo, the food is diverse and tasty, catering to multiple cravings. Fajitas, vegetarian dishes ($3–5), breakfasts ($2–3) and pasta or fish dishes ($5–10) are all on offer. There's also a computer with Internet ($1 an hour). E-mail: borderscoffee21@yahoo.com. Updated: Nov 07, 2009.

Restaurant Vanessa
(ENTREES: $6–12) Vanessa's terrace, set directly over the rapids, is a good place to knock back a couple of beers as the evening mists swirl in (along with the mosquitoes!). The fish dishes, in a sweet and sour tomato sauce, in garlic or just grilled, are excellent and come with bananas, rice and cabbage salad. Just keep an eye out for the house cat, who will sit beneath your table looking cute and waiting for a morsel to fall. Located 200 meters (656 ft) downstream from the pier. Updated: Nov 07, 2009.

REFUGIO BARTOLA
This huge swath of tropical forest covering most of the southeastern corner of Nicaragua has been declared a protected area as the Biosphere Reserve of Indio Maiz. Although most of the 3,180 square-kilometer (1,976 mi) of rainforest is basically off-limits and can only be entered for the purpose of scientific investigation (and with proper credentials from Marena in Managua), there are some parts that can be visited on guided tours, such as the Refugio Bartola.

The Refugio Bartola is situated by the Río Bartola, just six kilometers (3.7 mi) downriver from El Castillo. Within Bartola two different paths can be followed: **Sendero Bartola**, which makes for a two-hour hike, and **Sendero Aguas Frescas**, which takes closer to three hours. The paths are extremely muddy—rubber boots are indispensable! If you are leaving from El Castillo, boots can be rented for $1 from Hotel Victoria, Hospedaje Universal or Albergue El Castillo, or lent for free if you are a guest. Other recommended items include a rainproof jacket, mosquito repellent, hiking boots and binoculars.

With some luck, some of the least shy denizens of the forest can be spotted, as the reserve literally teems with wildlife. Three different types of monkeys roam the treetops: the howler monkey, spider monkey and white-headed capuchin. In addition there are sloths, toucans and all types of tropical parrots. Iguanas and the tiny venomous green and red tree frogs are also common sights, as are caimans, river otters and kingfishers. While it is very rare luck to come face to face with a jaguar, tapir or feral pig, you might come across their footprints. Your guide will also point out the hundreds of species of giant trees and plants and explain their medicinal uses. Updated: Nov 18, 2009.

Getting To and Away From Refugio Bartola
The best way to visit the reserve is on a day tour from Boca de Sábalos or, better still, El Castillo. Counting transport down the river, the hike and maybe a quick dip in the Río Bartola, a tour lasts four to five hours and will cost between $15-30 per person, depending on the size of your group. Updated: Nov 18, 2009.

Lodging
Refugio Bartola
(PACKAGES: $50) If you prefer to explore the forest in a leisurely manner, you can

stay at this rustic lodge that offers its own trails ($5 admission for non-guests) and also rents canoes. Packages include accommodation in wooden cabins and three meals per day. To get there, reserve a spot in advance and arrange for pick-up from El Castillo, or take a collective boat headed down to San Juan de Nicaragua and ask to be dropped off at the Refugio. Tel: 505-8-401-0341, E-mail: refugiobartola@yahoo.com. Updated: Nov 18, 2009.

SAN JUAN DE NICARAGUA

San Juan de Nicaragua, formerly (and illogically) known as San Juan del Norte, is a small backwater town pretty much at the end of the line on any trip down the Río San Juan. That said, there are regular boat connections to Bluefields and to Costa Rica, but the few houses scattered by the Río Indio retain little of the former strategic port's energy.

History

San Juan del Norte was christened on June 24, 1539 and a small garrison was installed in 1541 by the Spanish. However, the settlement that controlled entry to the strategic Río San Juan was captured by the British and their Miskito allies. The Spanish were able to establish a commercial presence here in 1778. However, the British once again seized San Juan in 1841, when it looked like the Río San Juan would be opening to large-scale commercial transport from the Atlantic to the Pacific ocean. In 1848, the governor of Jamaica, Charles Grey, even renamed the port Greytown, after himself.

In the following years Greytown boomed as it turned into a terminal for the newly formed American Atlantic and Pacific Ship Canal Company, which ferried thousands of gold seekers to California. Hotels, restaurants, as well as embassies, bordellos and other businesses popped up in what became a bustling Victorian town.

As plans grew hotter for an inter-ocean canal, important work was undertaken: telegraph lines went up, the lagunas were dredged, several miles of train tracks were built, and new piers stretched out. In the end, Panama won as the eventual location of the major canal link in 1903. As a result, works in Greytown came to a halt, boats stopped coming to the bay, the steel from the tracks was taken apart and sold, and the town slipped back into obscurity.

During the civil war in the 1980s, the town was razed by the Contras, and what was rebuilt was flattened by Hurricane Joan. San Juan del Norte was rebuilt in 1990. However, the new location—by the Indio River—sits a few miles away from the original site. The town has since been renamed San Juan de Nicaragua. Updated: Nov 23, 2009.

When to Go

Since this corner of Nicaragua is a very wet one, try to come during the somewhat drier summer months. During June 23–28 the town hosts a food festival and dance. Updated: Nov 12, 2009.

Getting To and Away From San Juan De Nicaragua

Most traffic to San Juan de Nicaragua comes via the collective boat from San Carlos, which makes the eight-hour journey three times a week: Tuesdays, Thursdays and Fridays. It makes the return trip to San Carlos ($20) and El Castillo ($12) on Thursdays, and Saturdays and Sundays at 5 a.m. There is now a fast boat service to Bluefields (2.5 hours, $30) departing Wednesdays and Saturdays at 8 a.m.

Coast Rica Border Crossings

Getting to Costa Rica by public transport is a little complicated: you need to get your exit stamp from Nicaragua in San Juan before going up river to the first delta, where you can catch pick-up trucks with Nicaraguan farm workers. However, a new boat service to Puerto Viejo should be starting in 2010, allowing travelers to go through immigration formalities there. Updated: Nov 23, 2009.

Getting Around

San Juan de Nicaragua is really just a scattering of houses set by the river, organized along three or four parallel footpaths. Most of the shops in town can be found on its only paved street, which is only a couple of hundred feet in length. To reach any sight outside of town, you must hire a boat. Updated: Nov 23, 2009.

Safety

San Juan de Nicaragua is a very small and safe community in terms of personal safety. However, make sure you carry a flashlight at night since not all footpaths are well lit. Also, be aware that the entire Caribbean coast is a drug-trafficking route, so watch out for shady dealings. Updated: Nov 12, 2009.

Services

TOURISM
Services are virtually nonexistent in San Juan de Nicaragua. That said, there is a small medical clinic, a police station and an immigration office that can stamp your passport if you are bound for Costa Rica. **Intur** is building an office by the pier and is scheduled to open sometime in 2010.

MONEY
There are neither banks nor ATMs in San Juan de Nicaragua, but all shops in town accept three currencies: U.S. dollars, Nicaraguan *córdobas* and Costa Rican *colones*. Some hotels will even accept euros if you have nothing else. There are plenty of tiny *pulperias* (grocery stores), but they are expensive; for example, a 1.5-liter bottle of water costs nearly $2. This is because almost everything is brought in from Costa Rica.

KEEPING IN TOUCH
The **public library** (a blue building a couple of blocks south of the pier) has a few computers on which they offer Internet access for $1 per hour (if there's electricity and if the school children are not using the equipment for their computer literacy classes). Updated: Nov 23, 2009.

Things to See and Do
Once you have walked up and down the narrow cement footpaths in town and chatted with the friendly locals and their parrots, you've pretty much covered all the excitement that San Juan has to offer. Outside of town, the one attraction worth a visit is the ruins of Greytown, which can be visited on a half-day tour, taking in a sunken steamship on the way. Otherwise, you can take a tour up the Río Indio and visit some of the most remote communities in Nicaragua or go fishing for massive tarpons. Updated: Nov 13, 2009.

Greytown !
The few remains of the once thriving port of Greytown (now buried in the jungle) lie just a 15-minute boat ride from town. All that is left standing are a couple of concrete foundations of colonial houses and the four cemeteries (one for the English, one for the Americans, one for the Catholics and another for the Freemasons). Despite the ruins' lack of size, this butterfly-filled site makes for a nice visit on a sunny day. You can see the remains of a sunken steamship and rusty dredge still standing in the middle of a laguna. To get here, hire a boat in town. Updated: Nov 12, 2009.

Laguna Azul
Just across the river from San Juan is a small and very pleasant freshwater lake surrounded by low vegetation. If you get someone to take you there for a few dollars, you can spend a couple of hours taking a refreshing swim and enjoying a picnic in the shade. Updated: Nov 12, 2009.

Río Indio
If you take a boat trip up the Río Indio, you can get a glimpse of wildlife in the eastern reaches of the Reserva Indio Maiz. A tour can take you through lagunas up the river to basaltic rock carvings. From there you can take a hike where you may spot monkeys, iguanas, snakes and tapirs. There are also small Rama communities upriver that you can visit. Updated: Nov 13, 2009.

Tours
Several people in town offer tours to Greytown, which usually culminate with a dip in Laguna Azul. There are also fishing tours and others boat tours up the Río Indio. Recommended guides: **Donald Reyes**, who lives in a two-story house right by the river (ask around); **Alfredo**, who works out of Comedor El Tucan (Tel: 505-8-419-5356); and **Enrique**, who works through Hotelito Evo.

A tour to Greytown costs about $60 for a group of four. A two-day tour up the Río Indio with overnight stay in a Rama community will be around $380 per group. A fishing tour starts at around $100 per person. Updated: Nov 12, 2009.

Lodging
There aren't many options in town, and they all seem to offer similar basic lodgings at a rate of $10. The only upscale hotel with 24-hour electricity is the fancy **Río Indio River Lodge** situated out in the lagunas. Packages (expensive) can be booked via the office in Costa Rica (URL: www.rioindiolodge.com). Updated: Nov 13, 2009.

Cabinas Urbinas
(ROOMS: $10) Right by the river is this handful of simple and somewhat darkish wooden cabins equipped with private bathrooms, mosquito nets and fans. The family who owns the place is currently building more—maybe counting on some improbable tourist boom in San Juan. To get here,

head 200 meters (656 ft) north of the pier along the river. Tel: 505-8-407-5767. Updated: Nov 13, 2009.

Hotel Disco-Bar Paraíso Virgen

(ROOMS: $10) Located in a big yellow building at the furthest end of town from the pier, this hotel/restaurant/bar, formerly known as *Melvin's*, rents out five decent rooms. Each room comes with a private bathroom, mosquito net and electric fan. Give the mattress a poke before picking a room, though, since they greatly vary in levels of firmness. The disco, slated to open in December 2009, might turn this otherwise quiet hotel into a noisy place, though. The hotel can be found at the very far end of the path by the river. Tel: 505-8-843-3074 / 498-1790. Updated: Nov 13, 2009.

Hotelito Evo

(ROOMS: $10) The rooms at this family-run hostel are not exactly spotless, but they are comfortable and the service is friendly. There are three double rooms, three twins and one single. Some rooms have private bathrooms, and all come with mosquito nets and electric fans. There's a covered area in the back with hammocks. The owner, Enrique, or his son can offer guided tours, and his wife, Emelda, can cook meals and lets guests make use of her kitchen. Hotelito Evo is located on the fourth footpath parallel to the river. Tel: 505-2-583-9019 /8-859-0275, E-mail: evohotel@yahoo.es. Updated: Nov 12, 2009.

Restaurants

You will be hard-pressed to find a proper restaurant in San Juan de Nicaragua. The only places selling meals are unmarked comedors, and they're a bit pricey since most food items are imported from Costa Rica. If you have access to your hotel's kitchen, you are almost better off buying a few supplies from one of the many little grocery shops and cooking for yourself. Updated: Nov 13, 2009.

El Tucan

(ENTREES: $4 – 5) The only eatery marked as such can be spotted by its sign adorned with the painting of a toucan. The simple eatery serves up lunches of fried chicken with bananas and cabbage, as well as dishes of fish fillet, pork and beef. Meals can be washed down with a juice or soda ($1). El Tucan is located on the main street. Updated: Nov 12, 2009.

Other comedors

Ask around for Las Brisas del Río and La Amistad; both offer set lunches for around $5. The restaurant at Paraíso Virgen might offer a better choice of dishes after it opens in December 2009. Updated: Nov 12, 2009.

!!!!!

Index

4 Hermanos, 295

A
Academia Europea, 191
Aderezo: Comida Casera, 84
Aguas Claras Hot Springs, 271
Aguas Termales Escalera, 328
Aguas Termales La Caldera, 144
Albergue El Castillo, 331
Altagracia, 159
Altragracia Beaches, 161
Amigo Tours, 135
Anastasia Hotel, 303
Angel Azul Hotel Boutique, 88-89
Antigua Estación de Ferrocaril, 131
Antigua Restaurante, 208
APC Spanish Schools, 134
Arboretum Nacional, 74
Arena Beach, 305
Arena Blanca, 178
Arenas Negras, 164
Around Managua, 92-93
Around San Juan del Sur, 175-176
Artesanias Cardoza, 246
Augusto Sandino, 16

B
Balneario Las Penitas, 276
Bambu Beach, 175
Bar and Restaurant Sagitario, 117
Bar Maria, 111
Bar Oasis, 235
Bar y Restaurant El Muellecito, 80
Bar Y Restaurante Pescamar, 253
Barra Intel Habana Libre, 311
Barrio Boloñia, 84
Barrio Martha Quezada, 81
Barrio Sutiava, 197
Baseball, 308
Bearded Monkey, 136-137
Benitours, 192
Benjamin Linder café, 196
Berman Gomez (Independent Tour Guide), 172
Best Western Hotel Las Mercedes, 79
Big Corn Island, 299-305
Bigfoot Hostel, 193
Bistro Sebastian, 91
Bluefields, 291-295
Boaco, 268-270
Boca De Sábalos, 327-329
Boheme, 92
Bohemias, 197
Bonanza, 264-265
Border Crossing, 34-35
Border Crossing at Las Manos, 233-235
Border Crossing with Costa Rica, 316
Border's Coffee, 332
Bosawas Biosphere Reserve, 263
Buena Vista Surf Club, 177
Buffet Comedor Llamarada Del Bosque, 235
Buffet Familiar Shalom, 226
Buffet Soda El Tico, 261-262

C
Cabañas Viento del Norte, 303
Cabinas Urbinas, 334-335
Café Barista, 251
Café Latino, 252
Cafe Luz, 227
Café Macuas, 174-175
Cafe Mirna, 83
Cafe Nuit, 142
Café Pastelaria Villa La Cruz, 261
Café Reposteria Mamilou, 226-227
Cafetin el Verdi, 271
Cafetin Trebol, 261
Cafeto, 252
Camoapa, 272
Camping, 52
Canopy Tour, 171
Caribbean Coast and the Islands, 280-283
Caribbean Coast Dance, 286
Caribbean Dreams, 295
Carita Feliz, 134
Carlito's Sunrise Paradise, 310
Carne Asada Raquel, 277
Carolina, 314
Casa Canada Hotel, 303-304
Casa de café, 89
Casa de Cultura, 188
Casa de La Mujer Nora Hawkins, 248
Casa de los Tres Mundos, 132
Casa Familiar, 165
Casa Feliz, 173
Casa Iguana, 310
Casa Linda, 84-85
Casa Mexico, 80
Casa Museo Comandante Carlos Fonseca, 247
Casa Museo Judith Kain, 285
Casa Natal Sor Maria Romero Meneses, 133
Casa Oro, 173

Casa Presidential, 77
Casa San Francisco Hotel, 139
Casa San Martin, 139
Casa Silas B and B, 139
Casa Vanegas, 81-82
Casa Vecchia, 227
Casares, 122-123
CAST, 135
Catarina, 112-113
Catedral de Nuestra Senora del Rosario, 224
Cementerio Guadalupe de León, 190
Cemeteries, 243-245
Central Nicaragua, 266-267
Centralito, 140
Centro Commercial and Carretera Masaya, 87-92
Centro de Arte Fundacion Ortiz-Gurdian, 188
Centro Girasol, 247-248
Centro Nicaragüense de Escritores, 78
Centro Turistico, 132
Ceramica Negra, 246
Cerro El Faro, 270-271
Cerro La Cruz, 258-259
Chaguitillo, 255-256
Chaman, 80
Charco Verde National Park, 161
Charly's Bar and Restaurant, 142
Chichigalpa, 209-210
Chido's Pizza, 167
Chinandega, 204-208
Chocoyero - El Brujo Nature Reserve, 93
Church Tour, 186
Churches, 74
Cigar Factory, 224
Circumnavigate Maderas, 162
Ciudad Antigua, 236
Ciudad Darío, 256

Climate, 13-14
Cocinarte. 87
CocinArte, 87
Coco Surf School, 199
Colectivo de Mujeres Matagalpa, 248
Comalapa, 273
Comedor Conchita, 332
Comedor Gladys y Elena, 329
Comedor Gloriana, 167
Comedor Gómez, 329
Comedor Pinareno, 227
Comida's Sara, 83
Condega, 231-232
Cooperative Coffee Tours, 260
Corinto, 210-211
COSEMUCRIM Cacao Cooperative, 327-328
Crater's Edge, 111
Cuapa, 278-279
Culinary Vocabulary, 52

D

Del Timbo al Tambo, 166
Derek's Place, 310
Dipilto, 237
Diria, 113-114
Diriamba, 117-119
Diriomo, 114
Dive Little Corn, 309
Doctors, 58
Dolphin Dive, 309
Dolphin Guest House, 138-139
Dolphin Inn, 309
Don Chaco's, 251
Don Chu, 242
Don Martin's House (Casa Don Martin), 177-178
Don Pan, 90
Don Pepe, 107
Don Pollo #2, 227
Don Senor, 197
Dona Briggette, 311

E

Eco Hostal Apoyo, 111
Ecological Fincas, 259
Economy, 18-19
El Alpino, 271
El Buen Sabor, 252
El Caramanchel, 81
El Castillo, 329-332
El Centro Cultural Managua, 78
El Chile, 253
El Club, 142
El Cortijo 1 and El Cortijo 2, 287
El Fortín de Acosasco, 191
El Garabato Cafe y Antojitos, 90
El Grillito, 86
El Jardin de Orion, 141-142
El Kayak, 142
El Ostional, 171
El Pantano, 238
El Portón, 117
El Porvenir, 78-79
El Pozo, 174
El Quijote, 142-143
El Rama, 289-291
El Salto de Santa Emilia, 255
El Sauce, 201-202
El Sesteo, 195-196
El Sopon, 252
El Sueño de Meme, 194
El Tamarindon, 197
El Tercer Ojo, 141
El Tesoro del Pirata, 164
El Timon, 175
El Toro, 154
El Transito, 200
El Tucan, 335
El Velero, 200
El Viejo, 208-209
Elsa's Sweet Breeze, 309
Embassies and Consulates, 30-32

Ensueños, 310
Estatua al Soldado, 76
Estelí, 220-228
Euro Café, 140
Exploring Ometepe, 163

F

Farm Peace and Love, 308
Festival de Maiz, 237
Finca Esperanza Verde, 254
Finca La Reforma, 238
Finca Magdalena, 166
Fincas, 50
Fisher's Cave, 304
Fishing, 46
Flor de Angel, 164
Flora and Fauna, 12-13
Flora's Buffet, 84
Fortaleza de la Inmaculada Concepción, 331
Forteleza la Pólvora, 132
Free Trade, 24
Friend's Bar and Restaurant, 318
Fruti Fruti, 107
Fry Fish, 298
Fuente Audiovisual, 77
Fundeci/gaia Escuela de Español and Estacion Biológica, 110
Fussion Chill-Out Bar Concert & Gallery, 80

G

Gallery of Heroes and Martyrs, 223
Gallo Pinto, 50
Garden Café, 140
Gay and Lesbian Travelers, 64
Geography, 12
Gracie's Cool Spot, 310
Gran Pacifica, 95
Gran Via, 227
Granada, 124-143
Granada Spanish Lingua, 134
Grand Canyon of Somoto, 241
Green Lodge Bed and Breakfast, 297
Greytown, 334
Grupo Venancia, 247
Guest House Ruppie, 302

H

Hacienda Merida, 166
Health and Safety, 55-58
Hiking and Trekking, 42
Hiking around Jinotega, 259
Hiking Cerro Apante, 246
Hiking Mombacho, 273
Hiking Quizaltepe, 273
Hiking to La Cebadilla, 271
Hippa Hippa, 92
Hippo's Grill and Tavern, 90
History, 14-17
Holidays and Fiestas, 26-27
Hollywood Street Hotel, 211
Horseback Riding, 44
Hospedaje Bilwi, 287
Hospedaje Buena Vista, 165
Hospedaje Casalejas, 234
Hospedaje Central Isla de Ometepe, 164
Nueva Guinea, 279
Hospedaje Chepito, 224
Hospedaje Cocibolca, 137
Hospedaje Dulce Sueño, 82
Hospedaje El Pelicano, 121
Hospedaje Familiar, 225
Hospedaje Hilmor, 151
Hospedaje la Calzada, 137
Hospedaje Luna, 225
Hospedaje Luvy, 211
Hospedaje Lidia, 150
Hospedaje Mesa, 81
Hospedaje Ruiz, 140
Hospedaje Velasquez, 291
Hospedaje Sinai, 164
Hospitals, 57-58
Hostal Amigo, 137
Hostal Central, 136
Hostal Colibri, 194
Hostal Dorado, 136
Hostal El Tiangue, 136
Hostal Marian, 194
Hostal Santa Maria, 106
Hostel Sonati, 193
Hostel Ibesa, 164
Hostels, 49
Hotel Alvarado, 250
Hotel America, 194
Hotel and Restaurante Posada del Poneloya, 198
Hotel Apante, 250
Hotel Austria, 195
Hotel Azul Pitahaya, 173
Hotel Beach View, 302
Hotel Bosawas, 261
Hotel Cabinas Leyko, 318
Hotel Café, 261
Hotel Carelys, 318
Hotel Casa Country, 277
Hotel Casa Leonesa, 195
Hotel Casa Maur, 154
Hotel Casa Verde, Restaurante Bahia Paraiso, 155
Hotel Castillo, 165
Hotel Central, 165, 211, 250,
Hotel Colon, 87
Hotel Colonial San Juan del Sur, 173
Somoto, 241

Join VIVA on Facebook. Fan "VIVA Travel Guides Nicaragua."

Hotel Cosigüina, 207
Hotel Costa Sur, 318
Hotel Costa Verde, 291
Hotel Costa Verde Restaurant, 291
Hotel Cualitlan, 225
Hotel Dario, 139
Hotel del Pacífico, 207
Hotel Disco-Bar Paraíso Virgen, 335
Hotel Don Vito, 225
Hotel E&V, 250
Hotel El Chinandegano, 207
Hotel El Convento, 195
Hotel el Dorado, 294
Hotel El Maltese, 138
Hotel El Meson, 225
Hotel El Portal del Angel, 241
Hotel El Regreso and Hospedaje Nuevo Milenio, 276
Hotel El Viajero, 235
Hotel Enrique 3, 195
Hotel Escuela Teosintal, 164
Hotel Estelí, 225
Hotel Estrella, 173
Hotel Europeo, 85
Hotel Farolitos, 272
Hotel Finca Santo Domingo, 165
Hotel Fountain Blue, 250
Hotel Frontera, 235
Hotel Gran Océano, 173
Hotel Granada, 139
Hotel Ideal, 250
Hotel Intercontinental Metrocentro, 89
Hotel J, 303
Hotel Joxi, 173
Hotel Kateana, 328
Hotel Kencho, 163
Hotel Kiuras Café and Restaurant, 261
Hotel La Casa Blanca, 198
Hotel La Fuente, 261
Hotel La Omaja, 166
Hotel La Perla, 195
Hotel La Posada del Doctor, 195
Hotel Lacayo, 198
Hotel Lomas de San Tomas, 251
Hotel Los Arcangeles, 277
Hotel Los Arcos, 226
Hotel Los Cisneros, 83
Hotel Los Robles, 89
Hotel Mansion Teodolinda, 85
Hotel Marsella Conference and Beach Retreat, 176
Hotel Masaya, 106
Hotel Miraflor, 225
Hotel Morgan, 303
Hotel Morgan Bar and Restaurant, 305
Hotel Nicaroa Inn, 151
Hotel Nuestra Casa, 138
Hotel Oasis, 137
Hotel Ometepetl, 165
Hotel Panamericano, 241
Hotel Plaza, 250
Hotel Posada Cabrera, 165
Hotel Regis, 106
Hotel Sábalos, 328
Hotel Sábalos Restaurant, 329
Hotel Sacuanjoche, 225
Hotel San Luis, 87
Hotel Santiago, 271
Hotel Sobalvarro, 272
Hotel Sol y Luna, 87
Hotel Sollentuna Hem, 261
Hotel Soza, 250
Hotel Summer, 95
Hotel Mansion Teodolinda, 285
Hotel Terrasol, 138
Hotel Tropical/Restaurant Vanessa, 332
Hotel Villa Mar, 176
Hotel Vista al Mar, 95
Hotel Vistamar, 95
Hotelito Aly, 164
Hotelito Evo, 335
Hotels, 49
Hot Springs, 111, 144, 153, 214, 236, 238, 271, 319, 328

I
Iglesia Calvario, 187
Iglesia Catedral San Pedro, 245
Iglesia de Guadalupe, 131
Iglesia de la Merced, 188
Iglesia de la Recolección, 187
Iglesia de Nuestra de la Asunción, 234
Iglesia de San Marcos Agradece, 117
Iglesia de San Pedro, 150
Iglesia El Calvario, 207
Iglesia la Merced, 132
Iglesia San Juan de Dios, 187
Iglesia Xalteva, 131
Indigenous Communities, 285
Intermezzo del Bosque, 80
International Boats, 34
International Buses, 33
International Flights, 33
Internet, 59
International Calls, 59
Isla de Ometepe, 156-159
Isla de Quiste, 161
Isla Mancarrón, 324-325
Isla Momotombito, 190
Isla San Fernan-

do, 325-326
Islas Solentiname, 321-326
Italian Pizza / Lebanese Food, 196

J
Jake the Patty Man, 311
Jalapa, 237-238
Jardín de Italia, 83
Jardin Zoologico Thomas Belt, 276
Jimmy "Three Fingers" Alabama Rib Shack Bar and Grill, 142
Jinotega, 256-262
Jinotepe, 119-120
Joe's Place, 212
José Daniel Ortega Saavedra, 17
Juigalpa, 273-277
Julio Tours, 192

K
Kabu Payaska, 287
Kalala Lodge, 136
Kayaking, 10, 40, 42, 44, 109, 111, 125, 131, 134, 143, 158, 162, 176, 302, 309, 321, 329,
Kayaking and Rafting, 44

L
La Bocana, 154
La Bohemia, 208
La Boquita, 121-122
La Canavalia, 255
La Capilla María Romero Meneses, 132
La Casa de Los Nogueras, 92
La Casa de Queso, 277
La Casita, 226
La Casona, 251
La Casona Coffee Shop, 117
La Catedral Nueva, 74

La Catedral Vieja, 74
La Cazuelita, 277
La Champa, 319
La Colmena, 262
La Concha Acustica, 76-77
La Esperanza Granada, 134
La Fortaleza de San Carlos, 317
La Gran Francia, 66, 140
La Jarochita, 107
La Olla Quemada, 197
La Parroquia de Santiago Apostol, 270
La Paz Centro, 204
La Perla, 196
La Perrera, 262
La Plaza de la Revolucción, 76
La Posada del Angel, 85
La Posada del Angel Restaurant, 86
La Ronda, 107
La Ruta del café, 217
La Suisse, 84
La Terraza M, 196
La Tica 2, 153-154
La Tortuga Booluda, 194
La Vita e Bella, 252
La Yunta, 235
Lago de Apanas, 259
Lago de Nicaragua, 38, 96
Laguna Azul, 334
Laguna De Apoyo, 45, 98, 100, 109-112
Laguna de Perlas, 282, 295-298
Lake Nicaragua, 12, 96
Las Cazuelas, 84
Las Chancletas, 212
Las Flores (Mache's Bar), 175
Las Hamacas, 155
Las Huellas de Acahualinca, 73-74

Las Isletas, 129, 131, 143
Las Nenas, 86
Las Peñitas, 199
Las Salinas y Playa Guasacate, 153-154
Las Sopas, 238
Las Tortugas, 154
Latin American Spanish School, 172
Lazy Bones, 193
Lazy Jakes, 177
Leo's Tours, 135
Leon, 182-197
León Viejo, 190-191, 203
Licuados Ananda, 226
Linda Vista, 167
Little Corn Island, 305-311
Living in Nicaragua, 48-49
Lobster Inn, 311
Lobster Pot Guesthouse, 294
Los Balcones, 195,
Los Cardones, 95
Los Pueblos Blancos, 100, 112-121
Los Ranchitos, 166
Los Ranchos, 86-87
Luz de Luna, 238

M
MacuelizoTermales, 236
Madera's Inn, 106
Madretierra, 252
Malécon Masaya, 104
Puerto Cabezas, 287
Malibu, 196
Mana del Cielo, 251
Managua, 10, 68-92
Mango Rosa, 176
Maracas Inn, 85
Marcelo's Sports Bar, 92
Marea Alta Seafood Bar and Grill, 90
Marikimber, 271

Marina Puesta del Sol Resort, 212
Martha's Bar and Restaurant, 304
Masatepe, 115-116
Masaya, 100-107
Masaya and Los Pueblos, 98-123
Matagalpa, 42, 54, 216, 218, 242-253
Matilda's, 177
Mediterraneo, 196
Mercado Central Granada, 132
Leon, 185
Mercado de Artesanías La Paz Centro, 204
Masaya, 98, 100, 104, 105, 107
Merida, 159-160
Meson Español, 91-92
MetroCentro, 73
Mi Casa Hostal, 106
Mi Museo, 132
Mini Hotel y Cafetin Central, 294-295
Miramar, 215
Miskito Keys Biological Reserve, 286
Mocha Nana, 227
Monkey Hut, 110-111
Montecristo River Lodge, 328-329
Montes Verdes, 112
Montibelli Reserve, 93-94
Monty's Jiquilillo Surf Camp, 213
Moravian Church, 294
Morgan's Rock Hacienda and Eco-Lodge, 178
Movimiento Comunal Nicaraguense, 248
Moyogalpa, 159
Mozonte, 235-236
Mt. Pleasant, 302
Mulukuku, 253
Museo Adiact, 198
Museo Arqueologico Gregorio Aguilar Barea, 267, 273, 275-276
Museo Camilo Ortega, 104-105
Museo de Café, 242, 247
Museo de la Revolucion, 187
Museo Entomologico, 188-189
Museo Galería Héroes y Martires, 104
Museo Insurreccional Luis Manuel Toruño, 197
Museo Numismatico (El Ceibo), 161
Museo Ometepe, 160-161
Museo Ruben Dario, 188
Museum of Traditions and Legends, 188
My Space Sports Bar, 92

N
Naragote, 203-204
Nautilus, 302
Nautilus Restaurant, 305
Nena Lodge, 331
NicarAgua Dulce SA, 135
NicAsí Tours, 192
Nindirí, 108-109
Niquinohomo, 114-115
Northern Highlands, 10-11, 216-265
Northward Nicaragua Tours, 248
Nueva Guinea, 279

O
Oasis Hostel, 111, 137
Ocotal, 232-235
Ojo del Agua Thermal Spring, 161
Olas Escondidas, 121-122
Olazul, 199
Old Train Station, 191
Orinoco, 282, 286, 297
ORO Travel, 135

P
Paisaje de Awas, 297
Palacio Nacional de la Cultura, 74
Panaderia Musmanni, 251
Parador Oviedo, 193
Park of Heroes and Martyrs, 188
Parque De La Paz, 75
Parque Historical Nacional "Loma de Tiscapa," 74-75
Parque los Poetas (AKA Parque Reuben Dario), 188
Parque Maritimo, 178-179
Parque Nacional Volcán Masaya, 10, 98, 99, 100, 107-108
Parque Palo Solo, 273, 276
Parque Reyes, 294
Parque Ruben Dario, see Parque los Poetas
Parroquia de Nuestra Senora del Perpetuo Socorro, 270
Parroquia Santa Ana, 207
Pearl Keys, 295, 297
Pelican Eyes, 172
Petroglyph Hike, 105
Petroglyphs, 161
Picnic Center: Under the Sun, 304-305
Pico Mogoton, 236-237
Picoteo Café and Pub, 251-252
Piedra Luna, 255
Piedras y Olas, 172
Pine crafts, 238
Pique's Restaurante Antojitos Mexicano, 252-253
Pizza Gold, 107
Pizza Hot, 151
Pizzeria Don Luca, 140

Playa Aserradores, 212
Playa El Coco, 178-179
Playa el Yanke, 178
Playa Guasacate, 153-154
Playa Jiquilillo, 213
Playa Maderas, 176-177
Playa Majagual177-178
Playa Marsella, 176
Playa Ocotal, 178
Playa Pie de Gigante, 152-153
Playa Remanso, 178
Playa Santo Domingo, 159, 161, 163, 165, 167
Playa Tamarindo and Playa Hermoso, 178
Plaza de la Cultura de Guatemala, 76
Plaza de la Fé Juan Pablo II, 76
Plaza de la Independencia and Parque Central, 133
Plaza de la República, 76
Plaza Inter, 73
Pochomil and Masachapa, 93, 95-96
Pollo Dorado, 151
Pollo Estrella, 86
Poneloya, 198-199
Posada Dona Blanca, 194
Posada Las Brisas, 137
Posada San Jose, 138
Potosi, 213-215
Pueblo Nuevo, 230-231
Puerto Cabezas, 283-287
Puerto Diaz, 96-97
Puerto Morazan, 211-212
Puerto Salvador Allende, 75
Puerto Sandino, 199-200
Pullaso's Ole, 227
Punta Teonoste, 155
Punto Jesus María, 160

Q
Queen Lobster, 298

R
Rama Key, 294
Rana Roja, 154
Rancho Esperanza, 213
Refugio Bartola, 332-333
Refugio de Vida Silvestre La Flor, 170-171
Reposteria Doris, 277
Reserva Natural Cerro El Arenal, 255
Reserva Natural Macizos de Peñas Blancas, 254
Reserva Natural Meseta Tisey-Estanzuela, 229-230
Reserva Natural Miraflor, 228-229
Reserva Natural Padre Ramos, 212-213
Reserva Natural Volcán Cosigüina, 214-215
Reserva Natural Volcán Mombacho, 143-144
Reserva Silvestre Privada Domitila, 144
Restaurant Apoyo Beach, 112
Restaurant Brisas Mar, 304
Restaurant Girasoles, 86
Restaurant Granadino, 319
Restaurant Kaoma, 319
Restaurant Vanessa, 332
Restaurante Bahia, 167
Restaurante Borbon, 262
Restaurante El Sopazo, 242
Restaurante la Ola, 295
Restaurante Lakun Payaska, 80
Restaurante Sacuanjoche, 196
Rincón Español, 87

Río Indio, 334
Río San Juan, 312-315
Rivas, 148-151
Roadhouse Grill, 142
Roca Rancho, 262
Rodeo at Plaza Taurina Alberto Homberto e Isabel Mongrio, 276
Rosita, 265
Rosquilla Factory Tours, 241
Roy's Café, 291
Ruben Dario, 25-26
Ruinas de Santiago, 197-198
Ruinas Veracruz, 197
Ruins of Saint Sebastien, 190

S
Safari Ometepe, 163
San Carlos, 315-319
San Cristobal Volcano, 207
San Fernando, 236-237
San Jacinto, 201
San Jorge, 155-156
San Jose De Los Remates, 270-272
San Juan De Limay, 230
San Juan De Nicaragua, 333
San Juan de Oriente, 113
San Juan Del Sur, 167-175
San Marcos, 116-117
San Miguelito, 319-320
San Rafael Del Norte, 262-263
San Ramon, 253-254
San Ramón Waterfall, 161
San Simian Eco Lodge, 111
Santa Emelia, 254-255
Santa Lucia, 272
Santiago Crater, 108
Santuario de Nuestra Señora Guadalupe, 206

Join VIVA on Facebook. Fan "VIVA Travel Guides Nicaragua."

Savor, 91
Scampi, 91
School Xpress, 133
Sebaco, 256
Selva Negra, 249
Seminole Plaza Hotel, 89
Sendero Pena Incult, 163-164
Senior Travelers, 64-65
Shark Pit, 196
Sign Language, 21
Siuna, 263-264
Sky Dancing, 235
Snorkeling, 297
Social and Environmental Issues, 27-28
Somoto, 239-242
Sonia's, 238
Spanish Ya, 172
Sport Fishing, 297
Suggested Reading, 67
Sunrise Hotel, 303
Super Pollo, 151
Sushi Itto, 91
Sweet Dreams Hotel, 303
Sweet Oasis, 311

T
Talabarteria Santana Los Chavarria, 246
Teatro Nacional Rubén Darío, 78
Tele Pizza, 140
The American Cafe, 166-167
The American Hotel, 165
The Corn Islands, 298-299
The Monkey Hut, 138
The Pier, 285
The Surf Retreat, 177
The Surf Sanctuary, 154
The Surf Shack, 177
The Vigoron, 141
Tienda Cowboy, 275
Tierra Tour, 192
Tips For Budget Travelers, 65-66

Tips For Mid-Range Travelers, 66
Tola, 151-152
Tomb of Ruben Dario, 187
Tortas Locas, 89-90
Tourist Visas, 32
Travel Tips, 63
Traveling with Kids, 65
Turtle Nesting, 297
Twins Restaurant and Bar, 295
Two Brothers, 154

U
Using Credit Cards, 61

V
Va Pues / Paxeos, 135
Valenti's Pizza, 90
Via Via, 194
Villa Isabella, 174
Villa Paraiso, 165
Villas del Mar, 122
Villas Playa Madera, 177
Visa Information, 32
Vista al Mar, 311
Volcán Cerro Negro, 189
Volcán Concepción, 161-162
Volcán el Hoyo, 189
Volcán El Viejo, 189
Volcán Momotombo, 189
Volcan Telica and Volcan San Cristobal, 201
Volcano Boarding, 190
Volunteering, 47-48
Vuela Vuela, 227-228

W
Waspám and Río Coco, 287-289
Wildlife Watching, 47
Wiring Money, 61-62
Women Travelers, 64
Woody's Pizza Pub and Grill, 91
Woody's Wings,

Pub and Grill, 91
Work Visas, 33

Y
Yogi's Cafe and Bar, 166
Yusvar, 226

Z
Zoom Bar, 142

Environmental Tips for Travelers

By Nicola Robinson, Nicola Mears and Heather Ducharme, Río Muchacho Organic Farm, Ecuador.

While traveling in a foreign country, it is important to minimize your impact. Here are some tips you should keep in mind while on your trip. Some of this advice may be more difficult to take on board while traveling than it would be to incorporate into your daily lives at home. However, even if you only put into practice three or four of the suggestions, on the road or at home, it will certainly help reduce your impact on the planet.

GARBAGE

- Carry a water bottle and always check if there is somewhere to fill it up at your hotel / restaurant—most hotels and restaurants have purified water in 20-litre bottles called *botellones*. These places usually also sell water in small bottles and might be reluctant to begin with as they think they are losing a sale. Of course you will need to pay for the refill also. If you have to buy bottles, buy the biggest you can and just refill from there, especially if you plan to be in the same place for a while.

- Purify your own water to avoid creating garbage.

- Try to avoid excessive wrapping and plastic bags which are all too readily dished out for each small purchase. If you can, explain to the shopkeeper why you want to give the bag back. If you shop in a local market, take your own bag or have them place everything in one large plastic bag instead of numerous small ones.

- Use a digital camera instead of film. The process of developing film can produce a lot of waste, and unwanted photos are non recyclable and often end up in the trash.

- Use a reusable container for soap so you can use your own instead of the small hotel soaps, which come individually wrapped. If you use hotel soap, use one and take the remainder with you—it will just be thrown out.

- Avoid using excessive cosmetic products such as hairspray, mousse, aftershave and perfume, or try to find effective environmentally-friendly alternatives such as biodegradable shampoos and crystal deodorants, which last longer (most containers for these products are non recyclable). Avoid using disposable products such as plastic razors and single-use contact lenses.

- Try to use rechargeable batteries or eliminate use of batteries entirely. For example, use a wind-up or solar torch or radio.

- Use recycled paper for letters home, trip diaries and toilet paper.

- Buy in bulk if you are traveling in a large group to reduce packaging.

- Recycle whatever you can in the country you are traveling. Some products that can not be recycled in the host country can be recycled in your home countries (such as batteries), so please take them home if possible.

FOOD AND HEALTH

- Avoid eating foods that you know are from endangered or threatened species (research these before you come to the country). Buy and eat locally grown and locally processed foods wherever possible, rather than food shipped from long distances, which use more energy and packaging.

- Consider using alternative natural medical products for common travelers' illnesses. This may be healthier for you and keeps you from leaving behind pharmaceuticals in the local water and soil (this is becoming a detectable problem in first world countries, thought to affect aquatic organisms like fish and frogs).

NATURE, FLORA AND FAUNA

- Avoid buying souvenirs of local fauna. Many stores sell cases of bright colored butterflies, spiders and insects which are caught by the hundreds in the Amazon. The sales people will tell you that they are not caught but that they raise them—it is not true!

- Avoid buying souvenirs that are made with endangered species or species that have to be killed to be made into a craft. Support crafts made from renewable resources.

- Don't collect insects, flora and fauna without a permit. Leave them for everyone to enjoy.

- When walking, stay on the trails and close gates behind you.

CAMPING AND WATER

- Use toilets where they exist. If there are no toilets, bury human waste in a hole 20 centimeters deep. Human waste should be buried at least 50 meters (164 ft) from water sources.

- Use biodegradable soaps and detergents.

- Don't wash shampoo and detergent off directly in rivers, but rather as far away as you can (4 meters (13 ft) minimum).

- Avoid making fires.

- Use a T-shirt when snorkeling as sunscreen is harmful to marine life.

TRANSPORT

- Use public transport instead of private (e.g. bus instead of rental car) when possible to reduce fossil fuel use. Share rental cars and taxis with others. If possible, walk or use a bicycle. It not only helps the planet, but it keeps you in shape as well!

ELECTRICITY

- Lights, fans, TVs, radios, or computers: If you are not using it, turn it off!

TRAVELING WITH CHILDREN AND BABIES

- Try and teach your child about the local environmental issues. Point out good and bad practices.

- Encourage your child to snack on fruit, which has a biodegradable wrapper!

- If traveling with a baby, why not use cotton diapers? Disposable diapers are becoming a major waste issue in developed countries and are becoming a desirable product in the developing world. Using cotton will set a good example to others and reduce the promotion of disposable diapers.

LOCAL ENVIRONMENTAL ISSUES

- Try to learn about the important environmental issues in the country. Good environmental practices (e.g. reduce, reuse, recycle!) are often the same in different countries, but the specific issues are often different (e.g. different recycling options, different endangered habitats and species, different laws and policies, etc.)

- Think about where you are eating and staying, and support the more environmentally friendly businesses. If you stay in an ecolodge, talk to the owners / managers, ask how they manage their garbage (including human waste), if they recycle and if they use grey water systems to reuse their water. Where do their building materials, food, and power come from? Do they practice or contribute to conservation? Do they support the local community? Be constructive rather than critical if you don't get a good response—some people truly think that it can be called an ecolodge if it is built with natural materials.

- Many countries have interesting volunteer opportunities with environmentally oriented organizations, and volunteering is an option. Research carefully—some volunteer opportunities are not what they say they are. The Web site www.volunteersouthamerica.net has links to several free and low-cost volunteer opportunities around South America.

The following is a list of helpful environmental websites for further information:

Advice and links to places you can buy environmentally friendly products:
www.ecomall.com and **www.greenhome.com**

Ministry of the Environment and Natural Resources, Nicaragua (in Spanish):
www.marena.gob.ni

A list of endangered species around the world by the International Union for Conservation of Nature and Natural Resources: **www.iucnredlist.org**

Packing lists

(* indicates something that might not be available in Nicaragua)

GENERAL PACKING LIST:
There are a number of items that every traveler should consider bringing to Nicaragua:
- [ ] Medicines and prescriptions (Very important. Bringing all relevant medical info and medicines may well save you a lot of grief in Nicaragua)
- [ ] Photocopies of passport and other relevant identity documents
- [ ] Paperback novels (sometimes you'll be sitting on buses or airports for a long time. It is possible to find and /or exchange books in several places in Nicaragua, but don't count on much selection if you don't read Spanish)
- [ ] Plug converter (many older buildings in Nicaragua have 2-prong, flat blade outlets only, although the voltage is the same)
- [ ] A good camera (see photography section)
- [ ] Water bottle (bottled water is readily available in Nicaragua, but you may want your own bottle)
- [ ] Sunglasses & sun hat
- [ ] Motion sickness medicine
- [ ] Lip balm
- [ ] *Tampons (difficult to find outside the major cities)
- [ ] Condoms and other contraceptives
- [ ] *Foot powder
- [ ] Antacid tablets, such as Rolaids
- [ ] Mild painkillers such as aspirin or ibuprofen
- [ ] *GPS device (especially for hikers)
- [ ] Watch with alarm clock
- [ ] Diarrhea medicine (i.e. Imodium)
- [ ] Warm clothes (The highlands are cooler than you think)

BACKPACKER PACKING LIST:
- [ ] Rain poncho
- [ ] Plastic bags
- [ ] *Swiss army knife/Leatherman
- [ ] Toilet paper
- [ ] *Antibacterial hand gel
- [ ] Small padlock

CARIBBEAN COAST PACKING LIST:
- [ ] Extra film/camera supplies
- [ ] Waterproof disposable camera for snorkeling
- [ ] Sunscreen
- [ ] Good, wide brimmed hat
- [ ] Long pants, lightweight
- [ ] Long-sleeved shirt, lightweight

RAINFOREST PACKING LIST:
- [ ] Rubber boots (most jungle lodges have them, call ahead)
- [ ] *Bug spray (with Deet)
- [ ] Flashlight
- [ ] Waterproof bags
- [ ] Rain poncho
- [ ] First aid kit
- [ ] *Compass
- [ ] Whistle
- [ ] Long-sleeved shirt and pants
- [ ] Malaria/yellow fever medicine
- [ ] Original passport
- [ ] Mosquito net (if your destination does not have one; call ahead)
- [ ] Biodegradable soap

Find the best price on a flight to Nicaragua: vivatravelguides.com/flights/

ADDITIONAL ITEMS TO PACK:

☐ _____
☐ _____
☐ _____
☐ _____
☐ _____
☐ _____
☐ _____
☐ _____

ANTI-PACKING LIST: THINGS NOT TO BRING TO COLOMBIA:

- Expensive jewelry. Just leave it home.
- Nice watch or sunglasses. Bring cheap ones you can afford to lose.
- Go through your wallet: what won't you need? Leave your drivers' license (unless you're planning on driving), business cards, video-club membership cards, coffee club card, social security card and anything else you won't need at home. The only thing in your wallet you'll want is a student ID, and if you lose your wallet you'll be grateful you left the rest at home.
- Illegal drugs. You didn't need us to tell you that, did you?
- Stickers and little toys for kids. Some tourists like to hand them out, which means the children pester every foreigner they see.
- Really nice clothes or shoes, unless you're planning on going to a special event or dining out a lot.

V!VA TRAVEL GUIDES BRINGS YOU A TEAR-OUT LIST OF USEFUL CONTACTS IN NICARAGUA

Feel free to tear out or photocopy this sheet for your use—stick it in your pocket or tuck it in your bag.

EMERGENCY NUMBERS

All emergencies	118	Fire	265-0162
Ambulance	265-1761		

MEDICAL

Managua:
Hospital Metropolitanio Vivian Pellas
Km. 9.8 Carr. Masaya
Tel: 505-2-255-6900

Granada:
Dr. Martinez-Blanco- Piedra Boconos Clinic
Parque Sandino, across from the Taxi Cooperative

Dentist (Managua): Dr. David Madriz- Shopping Ctr, Las Colinas, Tel: 505-2-276-1603, Cel: 088-34562, E-mail: drmadriz@cablenet.com.ni. Speaks English and Spanish.

ENGLISH-SPEAKING LAWYERS (CRIMINAL)

Luis Manuel, Perezalonso Lanzas
Las Brisas N-86,
Entrada Hospital Escuela Antonio Lenín Fonseca
1 C. Oeste y 6½ C. Norte, Managua
Tel: 505-2-266-4355
Cel: 505-8-860-8956

Aguilar Castillo Love
Km 4.5 Crtra. a Masaya
Costado Este Centro BAC, Managua,
Tel: 505-2-267-1035 / 1099
Fax: 505-2-267-0758
E-mail: tcb@aguilarcastillolove.com

TRAVELER GUIDANCE
V!VA Travel Guides: www.vivatravelguides.com

Tourist Information Office:
From the Hotel Crowne Plaza, one block
to the south, one to the west., Managua
Tel: 505-2-254-5191 ext. 237

POST OFFICE (CORREOS)
Correos de Nicaragua
Half a block south of Enitel Central, Managua
Tel: 505-2-549-2552

INT'L COUNTRY CODES
United States and Canada—1
United Kingdom—44
Australia—61

TRANSPORT
Taxis (Managua): Taxis 20 de Agosto, Tel: 505-2-264-0130, or Cooperativa de Taxis Rene Chavez Managua, Tel: 505-2-222-5700

COMPLETE THE SECTIONS BELOW FOR YOUR CONVENIENCE:

My Tour Operator:

My Hotel Address:

Taxi Directions to My Hotel:

Find the best price on a flight to Nicaragua: vivatravelguides.com/flights/

COPA Airlines (Panamanian)
Building CAR #6, Kilometer 4 ½ Masaya highway
Tel: 505-2-267-0045
Fax: 505-2-233-1680
URL: www.copaair.com

TACA (Central American)
Málaga building, Plaza España,
behind McDonald's
Tel: 505-2-266-6698
Reservations: 505-266-3136
URL: www.taca.com

Aeromexico (Mexican)
Plaza España, one block to the east
Tel: 1-800-226-0294
URL: www.aeromexico.com

Brazil
Km. 7 3/4 Carretera Sur, Quinta Los Pinos,
Tel: 505-2-65-1729 / 0035 / 1681, Fax: 505-2-65-2206
E-mail: ebrasil@ibw.com.ni

Colombia
2da. Entrada Las Colinas, 1 cuadra arriba, 1/2 cuadra al lago, Casa No. 97,
Tel: 505-2-76-2149 / 0864, Fax: 505-2-76-0644
E-mail: emanagua@cancilleria.gov.co

Costa Rica
Rpto. las Colinas, Ca. Prado Ecuestre, No. 304 primera etapa
Tel: 505-2-76-1352 / 0115, Fax: 505-2-76-0115
E-mail: infembcr@cablenet.com.ni

Honduras
Rpto. Las Colinas, Paseo Ecuestre, No. 298
Tel: 505-2-76-2406, Fax: 505-2-76-1998 / 2524
E-mail: miespino@yahoo.com/embahonduras@yahoo.es

El Salvador
Las Colinas, Av. del Campo y Pasaje, Los Cerros No. 142
Tel: 505-2-76-0712 / 0160, Fax: 505-2-76-0711
E-mail: embelsa@cablenet.com.ni

Panama
Rpto. Mántica, del Cuartel General de Bomberos 1 cuadra abajo, Casa No. 93
Tel: 505-2-66-8633, Fax: 505-2-66-8633
E-mail: embdpma@yahoo.com

AIRLINES IN MANAGUA:
American Airlines (US)
Plaza Espana,
Rotonda El Güengüense 300 meter south
Tel: 505-2-255-9090
URL: www.aa.com

Continental Airlines (US)
Ofiplaza Building, 2nd level, building 5
Tel: 505-2-278-7033
Fax: 505-2-278-2838
URL: www.continental.com

Delta Airlines (US)
Rotonda El Güengüense 100 meter east,
in front of main entrance of Price Smart
Tel: 505-2-254-8130
Fax: 505-2-233-3777
URL: www.delta.com

EMBASSIES IN MANAGUA:
United States of America
Km. 5 ½ Carretera Sur, Frente al Parque de "las Piedrecitas"
Tel: 505-2-52-7100 / 7237 / 7515, Fax: 505-2-52-7300
E-mail: EmbassyInfo@state.gov

Canada
Costado Oriental de la Casa Nazareth, Calle El Nogal, #25
Tel: 505-2-68-0433 / 2-68-3323, Fax: 505-2-68-0437
E-mail: mngua@international.gc.ca

France
Reparto El Carmen Iglesia 1 1/2c. abajo, Bolonia
Tel: 505-2-22-6210 / 6615, Fax: 505-2-68-5630 / 5475
E-mail: info@ambafrance.ni.org
URL: http://www.ambafrance-ni.org/

Germany
De la Rotonda El Güegüense 1 1/2 c. al lago, contiguo Optica Nicaragüense
Tel: 505-2-66-3917 / 3918 / 7500 / 7944 , Fax: 505-2-66-7667
E-mail: alemania@cablenet.com.ni
URL: http://www.managua.diplo.de/Vertretung/managua/es/Startseite.html

Italy
Reparto Bolonia, De la Rotonda El Güegüense 1c. al Lago 10 vrs. A bajo.
Tel: (505) 2-66-6486 / 2961 / 2918 / 4319, Fax: (505) 2-66-3987
E-mail: ambasciata.managua@esteri.it

Useful Spanish Phrases

CONVERSATIONAL

Hello	Hola
Good morning	Buenos días
Good afternoon	Buenas tardes
Good evening	Buenas noches
Yes	Sí
No	No
Please	Por favor
Thank you	Gracias
It was nothing	De nada
Excuse me	Permiso
See you later	Hasta luego
Bye	Chao
Cool	Chévere
How are you (formal)	¿Cómo está?
" " (informal)	¿Qué tal?
I don't understand	No entiendo.
Do you speak English?	¿Habla inglés?
I don't speak Spanish.	No hablo español.
I'm from England / USA	Soy de Inglaterra / los Estados Unidos

HEALTH/EMERGENCY

Call....	¡Llame a...!
an ambulance	una ambulancia
a doctor	un médico
the police	la policía
It's an emergency.	Es una emergencia.
I'm sick	Estoy enfermo/a
I need a doctor	Necesito un médico.
Where's the hospital?	¿Dónde está el hospital?
I'm allergic to...	Soy alérgico/a a
antibiotics	los antibióticos.
penicillin	penicilina
peanuts	maní
shellfish	los mariscos
milk	leche
eggs	huevos
wheat	trigo

GETTING AROUND

Where is...?	¿Dónde está...?
the bus station	la estación de bus?
a bank	un banco
an ATM	un cajero automático
the bathroom	el baño
Where does the bus leave from?	¿De dónde sale el bus?
Left, right, straight	Izquierda, derecha, directo.
One city block	Un cuadro
Ticket	Boleto

ACCOMMODATION

Where is a hotel?	¿Donde hay un hotel?
I want a room.	Quiero una habitación.
Single / Double / Marriage	Simple / Doble / Matrimonial
How much does it cost per night?	¿Cuanto cuesta por una noche?
Does that include breakfast / taxes?	¿Incluye el desayuno / los impuestos?
Is there 24-hour hot water?	¿Hay agua caliente veinticuatro horas al día?

Find the best price on a flight to Nicaragua: vivatravelguides.com/flights/

Notes...

Get these other guidebooks before your trip!

V!VA
TRAVEL GUIDES

Ecuador Climbing and Hiking Guide

Don't put on your boots without it! For over 20 years this has been the definitive guide to trekking and mountaineering Ecuador's high Andean summits, rolling paramo, rugged cloudforests and lowland rainforests. Get detailed descriptions of over 65 hikes, 27 climbs, extensive maps and color photos showing climbing routes. Buy it online or in Ecuador at Libri Mundi, South American Explorer's or Tattoo outfitters.

V!VA Peru

V!VA Travel Guides Peru is the most up-to-date guidebook available for Peru, period. Hundreds of days of on-the-road research by a team of Peru experts in addition to daily reports from travelers like you have yielded the most trustworthy guidebook on Peru to date. If you liked V!VA Ecuador, you'll love this book. It's best to buy it online, as there may not always be availability in Ecuador and Peru.

V!VA Ecuador

This book was written by journalists who have lived and traveled throughout this fascinating country for years and contains extensive coverage of all corners of Ecuador and the Galapagos. Amazingly enough, V!VA is headquartered in Quito, Ecuador. We know Ecuador like no other guidebook company can, because we have lived and traveled here for years (unlike most companies who send a newbie to a country for a few weeks or months). We invite you to experience our amazing country, and drop by the office and say hi when you're in town.

Or go to shop.vivatravelguides.com to get them direct!

Find the best price on a flight to Nicaragua: vivatravelguides.com/flights/